Knowledge Structures in Close Relationships: A Social Psychological Approach

Knowledge Structures
in Close Relationships:
A Social Psychological Approach

Edited by

Garth J. O. Fletcher
University of Canterbury

and

Julie Fitness
Macquarie University

LAWRENCE ERLBAUM ASSOCIATES, PUBLISHERS
1996   Mahwah, New Jersey

Lawrence Erlbaum Associates, Inc., Publishers
10 Industrial Avenue
Mahwah, New Jersey 07430

Library of Congress Cataloging-in-Publication Data

Knowledge structures in close relationships : a social psychological
approach / edited by Garth J. O. Fletcher and Julie Fitness.
    p. cm.
    Includes bibliographical references and index.
    ISBN 0-8058-1431-0 (cloth : alk. paper). — ISBN 0-8058-1432-9
(pbk. : alk. paper)
    1. Interpersonal relations. 2. Cognition. 3. Knowledge, Theory
of. 4. Social perception. 5. Social psychology. I. Fletcher,
Garth-J. O. II. Fitness, Julie.
HM132.K583 1995
158'.2—dc20   95-23702
                                                          CIP

Books published by Lawrence Erlbaum Associates are printed
on acid-free paper, and their bindings are chosen for strength
and durability.

Printed in the United States of America
10 9 8 7 6 5 4 3 2 1

Contents

Preface   ix

Introduction
Garth J. O. Fletcher and Julie Fitness   xi

I: KNOWLEDGE STRUCTURES AND INDIVIDUAL/COUPLE DIFFERENCES

1   Close Relationship Lay Theories: Their Structure
and Function
Garth J. O. Fletcher and Geoff Thomas   3

2   Attachment Styles and Internal Working Models
of Self and Relationship Partners
Phillip R. Shaver, Nancy Collins, and Catherine L. Clark   25

3   An Interdependence Analysis of Accommodation Processes
Caryl E. Rusbult, Nancy A. Yovetich, and Julie Verette   63

4 The Construction of Relationship Realities
    Sandra L. Murray and John G. Holmes   91

5 Sociosexuality and Relationship Initiation:
    An Ethological Perspective of Nonverbal Behavior
    Jeffrey A. Simpson, Steven W. Gangestad,
    and Christi Nations   121

6 Gender and Thought in Relationships
    Linda K. Acitelli and Amy M. Young   147

DISCUSSANT CHAPTER: PART I

    What We Know, What We Don't Know, and What We
    Need to Know About Relationship Knowledge Structures
    Harry T. Reis and C. Raymond Knee   169

II: KNOWLEDGE STRUCTURES AND EMOTIONS

7 Emotion Knowledge Structures in Close Relationships
    Julie Fitness   195

8 Prototype and Script Analyses of Laypeople's Knowledge
    of Anger
    Beverley Fehr and Mark Baldwin   219

9 Some Thoughts and Findings on Self-Presentation
    of Emotions in Relationships
    Margaret S. Clark, Sherri P. Pataki,
    and Valerie H. Carver   247

DISCUSSANT CHAPTER: PART II

    The Role of Emotion Scripts and Transient Moods
    in Relationships: Structural and Functional Perspectives
    Joseph P. Forgas   275

III: KNOWLEDGE STRUCTURES
AND RELATIONSHIP DEVELOPMENT

10 Changes in Knowledge of Personal Relationships
    Sally Planalp and Mary Rivers   299

11 Self and Self-Expansion in Relationships
    Arthur Aron and Elaine N. Aron   325

12 Rewriting Relationship Memories: The Effects of Courtship
    and Wedding Scripts
    Diane Holmberg and Joseph Veroff   345

13 The Pursuit of Knowledge in Close Relationships:
    An Informational Goals Analysis
    Jacquie D. Vorauer and Michael Ross   369

DISCUSSANT CHAPTER: PART III

    Knowledge Structures in Developing Relationships:
    Progress and Pitfalls
    Catherine A. Surra   397

    Author Index   415

    Subject Index   429

Preface

We (the editors) are writing this preface immediately after returning from the June, 1994 meeting of the *International Society for the Study of Personal Relationships* held in Groningen, Netherlands. If we had needed confirmation that the study of cognition and affect in close relationships settings was booming, then this conference provided plenty of evidence. Every second symposium or paper seemed to be concerned with some aspect of this domain. Moreover, 75% of the chapters in this book represent one or more of the authors who presented papers at the conference.

This volume, then, presents a picture of work at the cusp in social psychology that is concerned with cognition and affect in close relationship settings (especially, as the title implies, the role of knowledge structures).

In many ways this book represents a follow-up to the volume edited by Fletcher and Fincham (*Cognition in Close Relationships*), which came out in 1991 and was also published by Lawrence Erlbaum Associates. The differences in the two books indicate how this field has progressed over the last 4 years. The earlier book was short on research but long on programatic statements, had chapters written by authors whose major fields of work were not concerned with close relationships, and contained major theoretical statements that consisted mainly of the application of standard social cognitive models to close relationship processes.

In contrast, the present volume contains a wealth of research findings, is written almost entirely by authors who have both feet firmly in the close relationship arena, and contains influential theoretical accounts, which spring as much from indigenous work in the close relationship field as from purebred social cognition. In short, this field has exhibited remarkable growth over a relatively short period.

Because this book deals with a fast moving field, we felt it especially important to avoid the long delays that often occur with edited books (chapters are sometimes written years before they appear). The fact that we have done so is a testament to Lawrence Erlbaum Associates and the set of authors who willingly agreed to meet some tough deadlines. We thank all the contributors for their enthusiasm, support, and gracefulness in response to the occasional, but inevitable, editorial chivvying that occurs with books of this type.

Garth J. O. Fletcher
Julie Fitness

Introduction

Garth J. O. Fletcher
Julie Fitness

In this introduction the volume is placed in the wider historical context of close relationship work, and we briefly describe a few general themes that tie the three sections of the book together. To begin, however, the reader might be curious about the title of the book: Why "knowledge structures" and why "a social psychological approach"?

The idea that past experiences are encoded and stored in terms of dispositional cognitive constructs is a fundamental assumption in contemporary psychology. The study of close relationships is no exception. Indeed, such cognitive constructs play a central role in the development of recent close relationship theories (Berscheid, 1994; Fletcher & Fincham, 1991a). However, such unanimity dissolves when the variety of theories and concepts used by relationship scholars is examined at a more detailed level. For example, there is an abundance of dispositional cognitive constructs in common currency including scripts, schemas, prototypes, appraisal patterns, working models, mental models, and so forth.

Our mission for this book was not to gloss over such theoretical diversity, but rather to let 1,000 flowers bloom—albeit with the hope that some general principles or theoretical integration might emerge. Our reason for selecting the particular phrase *knowledge structures* was simply to choose a term that was generic enough not to close off any theoretical options that contributors might have chosen to pursue. It should be pointed out, however, that although the focus of this volume is on relationship cognitive structures stored in long-term memory, this does not mean the chapters have a narrow focus. Indeed, authors were encouraged to examine the full range of social-psychological phenomena, including on-line processing and interactive behavior.

The decision to limit this book to a "social psychological" approach is derived from two postulates. First, we believe that a social psychological approach represents an exceptionally fruitful one (naturally enough, as we are social psychologists). Second, relationship research and theorizing is spread across several academic domains, each with its own assumptions, theories, and preferred methods; such domains include sociology, communication, clinical psychology, sociobiology, and social psychology. This is both the glory and the nemesis of the close relationship area. Its glory resides in the encouragement of theoretical cross-fertilization, and the inhibiting of scientific chauvinism. Its nemesis is the difficulty in developing coherent close relationship theories from the welter of empirical findings, springing as they do from such diverse foundations.

Accordingly, there is something to be said for developing the study of close relationships within certain theoretical contexts. A social-psychological approach implies a focus on the relation between structures and processes at the individual level, with those operating at the dyadic level (including interactive behavior). This does not imply that the study of societal/structural level factors is not important, or that it is not useful to locate dyadic relationships within wider social contexts, or that the study of the neuropsychological processes underpinning relationship behavior is not a pivotal endeavor, and so forth. To gain a complete understanding of close relationships, all such approaches will probably prove necessary. However, the development of such a grand integrative theory is not the mission of this volume.

In order to appreciate or critically appraise the book, it is helpful to know something of the history of close relationship work that has adopted a social-psychological perspective. Work up to the late 1970s in social psychology read like a shopping list of variables that would lead people to be attracted to one another (propinquity, similarity, physical attractiveness, and so forth). In the 1980s, the zeitgeist shifted toward the study of the much greater complexity inherent in the development and maintenance of extant dyadic relationships, especially romantic relationships.

This paradigm shift was probably prompted by several developments. First, research by folk such as Gottman in the clinical area, which focused on dyadic interaction patterns in married couples, attracted the attention of social psychologists. Second, the work on love by Rubin and others and the related development of individual difference measures encouraged a focus on complex real-world relationship processes. Third, the bellwether book by Kelley et al. (*Close Relationships,* 1983), and an earlier book by Kelley (*Personal Relationships: Their Structures and Processes,* 1979), presented the first expansive programatic statements that attacked close relationships from a full-blooded social-psychological perspective. Finally, this shift in the zeitgeist was cemented in place by an influential review of the interpersonal attraction/close relationship work by Berscheid (1985), which appeared in the *Handbook of Social Psychology*.

Kelley has wielded substantial influence over contemporary social-psychological work in the close relationship area, generating ideas or theories that can be found throughout this volume. For example, in the first chapter of this book, "Close Relationship Lay Theories: Their Structure and Function," Fletcher and Thomas develop a key idea first formulated by Thibaut and Kelley; namely, that judgments of ongoing relationships are based on what people perceive they have against some ideal standard. The distinction between general relationship beliefs, or lay theories, and relationship-specific accounts is an important one, and can be found in several chapters. Another key insight developed by Fletcher and Thomas, also repeated in other chapters, is that not all cognition is conscious or controlled. Much of the cognitive activity in close relationships, like icebergs, resides under the surface and is automatic and/or unconscious (also see the erudite and whimsical commentary by Reis and Knee, "What We Know, What We Don't Know, and What We Need to Know About Relationship Knowledge Structures," this volume).

Kelley's overarching theory of interdependence in close relationships, with its detailed analysis of interdependence patterns, is superbly exploited in its most extensive form by Rusbult and her colleagues, who have applied it to the analysis of accommodative behavior in relationship settings (see Rusbult, Yovetich, and Verrete, "An Interdependence Analysis of Accommodation Processes," this volume).

Kelley's work in attribution theory has also had a profound influence in this area. Indeed, much of the work explicitly investigating the role of cognition in close relationships in the 1980s adopted an attributional perspective (see Fletcher & Fincham, 1991b). It is important to understand, in this regard, that although attribution theory is a cognitive theory specifically concerned with explanatory processes, it was developed prior to the emergence of modern social cognition. Social cognition, in turn, borrowed most heavily from the concepts and methodologies of cognitive psychology.

In social psychology in the 1990s, the study of attribution processes in intimate settings has faded and been overtaken by more general social cognitive/close relationship models. Such a development is clearly seen in the present volume. This does not mean that social psychologists have discarded attribution theory, or believe that attributions are not important within close relationship contexts (as is evident in several of the chapters in this volume, most notably in the compelling contribution by Planalp and Rivers, "Changes in Knowledge of Personal Relationships"). Rather, the focus has shifted towards the development of more general models in which attributions or attributional schemata may constitute one cognitive component.

The overall structure of the book encapsulates the most recent trends in the study of knowledge structures in close relationships. In the first part, various chapters lay out theories and research programs that are directly concerned with the role of individual and couple differences in knowledge structures (some of which have already been mentioned). For example, in the provocative chapter "Gender and Thought in Relationships," Acitelli and Young argue that the raft of documented gender differences in close relationships are rooted in fundamental differences in the ways that men and women view the social world. In another pioneering chapter, "Sociosexuality and Relationship Initiation: An Ethological Perspective of Nonverbal Behavior," Simpson, Gangestad, and Nations adopt an ethological perspective in analyzing the functions of procedural knowledge of nonverbal behavior in close relationship contexts.

Special mention should also be given to the impact of attachment theory in social psychology, an area that has expanded rapidly since the big bang created by the original article by Hazan and Shaver (1987). In the chapter by Shaver, Collins, and Clark, "Attachment Styles and Internal Working Models of Self and Relationship Partners," the core construct of working models is expanded and exploited in terms of contemporary social cognitive theory.

In another chapter in the first part by Murray and Holmes, "The Construction of Relationship Realities," the authors develop a theme, already gaining considerable attention, that specific relationship accounts seem to be marvellously malleable in the service of maintaining rose-colored and pollyanna-like perspectives. The general notion that people will happily rewrite their relationship memories on the basis of current motivational or other concerns, is also supported in the intriguing chapter in the third part of the book by Holmberg and Veroff, "Rewriting Relationship Memories: The Effects of Courtship and Wedding Scripts."

For the antithesis to the strong argument presented by Murray and Holmes, look no further than the persuasive chapter by Vorauer and Ross, "The Pursuit of Knowledge in Close Relationships: An Informational Goals Analysis." These authors develop a diametrically opposed theme to that of Murray and Holmes, namely, that people are motivated by the epistemic desire to make accurate judgments of their relationships. However these issues are decided, we believe that these kinds of disputes are healthy and help speed theoretical development.

The second part of this volume deals with an area of obvious and central importance to close relationship processes: the role of affect and emotions. Of course, in one way or another, affect creeps into every chapter in the volume (it being obvious that much cognition in close relationships is hot cognition). However, the detailed analysis of emotion and affect in close relationships has only just begun. The first two chapters by Fitness, "Emotion Knowledge Structures in Close Relationships," and Fehr and Baldwin, "Prototype and

Script Analyses of Laypeople's Knowledge of Anger," address this lacuna by applying or exporting a knowledge structure approach to the understanding of how specific emotions function within close relationships. The chapter by Clark, Pataki, and Carver, "Some Thoughts on Self Presentation of Emotions in Relationships," takes a different and pioneering tack in analyzing the goals and motives underlying the strategic self-presentation of emotions in relationships. The commentary by Forgas, "The Role of Emotion Scripts and Transient Moods in Relationships: Structural and Functional Perspectives," completes the picture by briefly discussing the role of mood states in relationship settings (his own special and influential area of expertise).

The final part of the book deals with the role of cognition and knowledge structures in relation to the developmental course of close relationships. Apart from the chapters already cited, it contains a review and discussion of a theory (and related elegant research) developed by Aron and Aron known as self-expansion theory ("Self and Self-Expansion in Relationships," this volume). A fitting capstone to the book is provided in a scholarly commentary by Surra, one of the leading experts in the role of relationship cognition in the development of close relationships: "Knowledge Structures in Developing Relationships: Progress and Pitfalls."

In the earlier volume on cognition in close relationships, edited by Fletcher and Fincham (1991a), it was argued that work on the interface between social cognition and close relationships holds two promises: First, that a social-cognitive framework offers a valuable resource for developing our understanding of close relationships, and second, that studying cognition within close relationships has the potential to inform our understanding of basic social cognitive processes. The evidence from the current volume is that both promises are on their way to being met.

REFERENCES

Berscheid, E. E. (1985). Interpersonal attraction. In G. Lindzey & E. Aronson (Eds.), *The handbook of social psychology* (pp. 413–484). New York: Random House.

Fletcher, G. J. O., & Fincham, F. D. (1991a). *Cognition in close relationships*. Hillsdale, NJ: Lawrence Erlbaum Associates.

Fletcher, G. J. O., & Fincham, F. D. (1991b). Attribution processes in close relationships. In G. J. O. Fletcher & F. D. Fincham (Eds.), *Cognition in close relationships* (pp. 7–35). Hillsdale, NJ: Lawrence Erlbaum Associates.

Hazan, C., & Shaver, P. (1977). Romantic love conceptualized as an attachment process. *Journal of Personality and Social Psychology*, 52, 511–524.

Kelley, H. H. (1979). *Personal relationships: Their structures and processes*. Hillsdale, NJ: Lawrence Erlbaum Associates.

Kelley, H. H., Berscheid, E., Christensen, A., Harvey, J. H., Huston, T. L., Levinger, G., McClintock, E., Peplau, L. A., & Peterson, D. (Eds.). (1984). *Close relationships*. San Francisco: Freeman.

I

KNOWLEDGE STRUCTURES AND INDIVIDUAL/COUPLE DIFFERENCES

1

Close Relationship Lay Theories: Their Structure and Function

Garth J. O. Fletcher
Geoff Thomas
University of Canterbury, New Zealand

Love sees not with the eyes, but with the mind;
and therefore is wing'd Cupid painted blind.

—William Shakespeare, Midsummer Night's Dream

One of the most well-established principles both in psychology and common sense alike is that experiences are recorded in terms of knowledge constructs that substantially influence subsequent processing and behavior. And, consistent with the Bard's musing just cited, nowhere is this proposition more strongly represented than in the study of close relationships, especially romantic relationships.

However, there is little consensus in (social) psychology on how such mental constructs should be defined or measured, or what part they should play in overarching scientific theories of close relationship processes. Moreover, there is an embarrassing abundance of concepts available including scripts, schemas, prototypes, appraisals, working models, mental models, and so forth. The purpose of this chapter, then, is to provide some theoretical organization and concision using the notion of lay relationship theories as the cornerstone on which to build a general theoretical model.

The initial part of the chapter presents an overall account in which we first discuss the functions or aims of lay relationship theories, and second explicate a general taxonomy of such theories. The second section deals with the links

3

between lay theories that apply to specific relationships and those that apply to relationships in general or hypothetical relationships. The third section describes some research that concerns the links between lay relationship theories and cognitive processing in relationship contexts. Finally, the connection between lay relationship theories and interactive behavior is discussed.

LAY THEORIES IN CLOSE RELATIONSHIPS: A CONCEPTUAL INFRASTRUCTURE

The Functions of Lay Relationship Theories

There is no difficulty in general terms in understanding why people might develop relatively elaborate theories concerning close relationships. First, for most people their personal relationships are a central and enduring theme in their lives—in other words we all have a continuing stream of relationship experiences that we need to make intelligible. Second, at least in Western society, we are bombarded with a mountain of information about close relationships in both fictional and nonfictional forms. Third, we have role models aplenty to observe (such as our own parents) to help us build relationship theories even before sexual maturity is reached and we become involved in romantic relationships.

The motivation for building and using such relationship lay theories can be split into two categories. One set of motivational goals or aims is epistemic in character, including prediction, explanation, and control, whereas an alternative set of aims are constituted in terms of relationship or self-enhancement. The epistemic aims conjure up a scientific image of people being motivated by the desire for accuracy or truth, dispassionately processing the information to hand in an objective fashion. The alternative set of aims, on the other hand, is based on the motive to maintain or enhance the positivity of attitudes or beliefs about the self or the relationship. This latter set of aims suggests an image of affectively driven cognition that is anything but dispassionate or objective.

Arguments concerning these two motivational sets have been endemic in social psychology over the last few decades. For example, there has been considerable argument whether people are primarily motivated to seek information that provides accurate information about the self, or whether people select and interpret information to maintain or boost their levels of self-esteem (Strube, Lott, Le-Xuan-Hy, Oxenberg, & Deichmann, 1986; Swann, Pelham, & Krull, 1989).

This general debate has also been played out on a much grander scale in terms of general paradigm shifts in social psychology. For example, the decline of cognitive dissonance theory in the 1960s, and its replacement by attribution theory in the 1970s, involved a move from a model of humans as rationalizing animals driven by negative affect, to the more cerebral "naive scientist" image at the heart of attribution theory.

Not surprisingly, then, the same clash between these cold and hot models of motivation can be seen in close relationship research (as evidenced in this volume). For example, the work on attribution processes in close relationships has typically used the classic attribution accounts that are based on the naive scientist model. Yet, it has often been noted that people in close relationship contexts are frequently concerned with justifying themselves and assigning blame rather than dispassionately assessing the most accurate causal explanation (Fletcher & Fincham, 1991), and often appear to inhabit a world in which relationships are seen through thoroughly rose-tinted glasses (see Murray & Holmes, this volume).

The centrality of the need to maintain a positive relationship account has been well demonstrated recently in a series of clever experiments by Murray and Holmes (1993, this volume). For example, in Study 1, these authors first induced subjects in dating relationships to perceive their partners as rarely initiating disagreement, using a set of exercises that were structured to encourage this viewpoint. Then, this apparent virtue was turned into a fault by feeding subjects a bogus article from *Psychology Today* that stressed the importance of open disagreement and conflict resolution as a key path toward a truly intimate relationship. In later questionnaires and open-ended descriptions of their relationships, subjects exhibited considerable fluency and ingenuity in reinterpreting and rewriting their relationship accounts that were clearly aimed at maintaining positive attitudes toward their relationships. For example, compared to a control group, subjects were more likely to both stress the way their partners openly engaged in conflict resolution and to construct rationalizations for their partners' failures to initiate problem-solving discussions.

However, in considering this debate it is important for relationship scholars not to reinvent the wheel. Past debates in social psychology concerning this clash between epistemic motivation and esteem maintenance, some of which were alluded to previously, have generally been resolved in the same way. First, it is notoriously difficult to ascertain whether particular processes are produced by either cold or hot motivational sets. Second, the most plausible resolution is that both motivational sets are often in play, sometimes at the same time, sometimes separately. Which motivational set is currently dominant will depend on individual/couple differences and the circumstances. In short, the question becomes not which motivational set is correct, but under what conditions does each motivational set become primary?

The same conclusions will almost certainly apply to the close relationship arena. Take, for example, the research already described by Murray and

Holmes (1993). One interpretation of their results is in terms of esteem maintenance, in which case the subjects' performance can be viewed as clever post-hoc rationalizations designed to retain positive relationship conceptions.

Conversely, it is plausible that believing their relationships were successful, subjects attempted to explain and interpret relationship events in such a way as to maintain consistent and coherent relationship accounts. Viewed in this way, subjects could be seen as motivated by a set of eminently rational and scientific values or aims of good theory construction (see Fletcher, 1993), for example, the need to explain and integrate apparently disparate pieces of evidence (providing unifying power), and the need for logical internal consistency and consistency with other accepted knowledge (providing internal and external coherence).

And, of course, it is possible to posit that both sets of aims were in train at the same time; namely, that subjects were attempting to produce coherent and plausible accounts that were accurate, but with the additional constraint that the positivity of their relationships were to be maintained (as much as possible).

Little research has been directed at the conditions under which individuals are primarily motivated by the desire to produce accurate and truthful explanations or predictions, rather than simply retain rose-tinted relationship conceptions (but see Vorauer & Ross, this volume). One set of conditions may derive from the developmental stage of the relationship. For example, it seems plausible that the need to produce accurate predictions and explanations becomes paramount when important decisions need to be made in relationships: "Do I leave him?" "Should we get engaged?" "Do I date him again?" "Should we have a baby?" "How do I handle this problem?" and so forth. At such times, the degree of commitment to relationships (and related judgments such as amount of love, relationship satisfaction, etc.) are precisely what are in question, so that the motive to retain positive relationship conceptions may loosen its shackles on the cognitive machinery.

Alternatively, for couples settled into a comfortable maintenance phase of their relationship, such epistemic aims may seldom be invoked and the esteem-maintenance aims will be dominant. There is little direct research evidence concerning these speculative ideas, although they are consistent with the evidence that attributional activity is more prominent when relationships become unstable or disruptive events occur (Fletcher, Fincham, Cramer, & Heron, 1987; Planalp & Rivers, this volume).

Having presented at least a preliminary account of the functions of lay relationship theories, we now consider their cognitive architecture.

The Structure of Lay Relationship Theories

The basic model we explicate is shown in Fig. 1.1. This model distinguishes between general lay theories that represent idealizations or models of

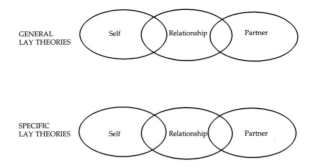

FIG. 1.1. Lay close relationship theories: A conceptual infrastructure.

hypothetical relationships, and theories of specific actual relationships that may be ongoing or in the past. This dimension is cross-cut with three kinds of overlapping targets: the self, the relationship, and the partner (see Baldwin, 1992).

To give some examples, we posit that individuals will enter new relationships with extant general representations of their own relationship-oriented self (e.g., talkative), their ideal partner (e.g., strong and silent), and some model of their ideal relationship (e.g., passionate and romantic). The relationship model might also include some sort of ideal developmental sequence (e.g., delayed sexual activity, and living together before getting married).

The specific lay theories are divided into the same overlapping cognitive categories and include self-related material (e.g., "For some reason I can't talk to this guy"), partner-related material (e.g., "He is delicate and intelligent"), and relationship-level descriptors (e.g., "The sex is boring, and he wants to get married already").

One important postulate in our account is the idea that judgments and decisions concerning particular relationships will be derived, in part, from the match between general lay relationship theories and lay theories dealing with specific relationships. To take the illustrations just cited, for example, the match between the general and the specific accounts clash alarmingly—we might predict in such a case that an individual who held such competing beliefs would not be very satisfied with, or committed to, the relationship.

This kind of theorizing is not new, being originally formulated by Thibaut and Kelley (1959) in terms of the contrast between what people believe they deserve (comparison level) and their perceived level of rewards (outcomes) derived from particular relationships (also see Rusbult, Yovetich, & Verette, this volume). However, comparison levels are defined in terms of an average level of reward value that might be obtained from relationships. We suspect, instead, that people's comparisons will operate along a more detailed content-rich set of dimensions or relationship prototypes that are embedded in relatively elaborate theories. For example, take an individual who perceives the current outcomes as exceptionally positive in a given relationship, but who also judges his partner and himself as dissimilar in basic values and beliefs. If this person strongly believes that successful relationships are built on strong similarities between partners, this may prompt him to label his feelings as infatuation and think of the relationship in terms of a short-term fling. In contrast, a person who believes strongly that differences between partners make for an exciting and successful relationship, all else being equal, may well label his feelings in terms of love and attain a good measure of commitment to the relationship.

Evidence for the Overall Structure. The general outlines of this model are, we believe, both plausible and consistent with a good deal of previous research and theorizing. For example, theorists who have applied attribution theory to close relationship contexts have often highlighted the distinction between the three targets of self, relationship, and partner in relation to specific relationships (Fletcher & Fincham, 1991). In addition, the research evidence suggests that relationship-oriented attributions (e.g., "We communicate openly," "He gets angry when I am late") are common in free-response descriptions of relationships (Fletcher et al., 1987), and explanations for relationship change (Planalp & Rivers, this volume).

With respect to general lay theories, Fletcher (1994) had 174 subjects rate the importance of 20 relationship descriptors (e.g., best friends, secure, equality, etc.), and 20 partner-based descriptions (attractive, sexy, rich, etc.), in terms of an ideal relationship. A factor analysis of the results showed a fairly clean two-factor structure differentiating between the two classes of descriptors. This result is consistent with the work of Simpson and Gangestad (1992), who found strong individual differences in terms of two classes of potential partner descriptions: a partner's physical and sexual attractiveness and social visibility, versus descriptions that were more directly relationship-oriented such as affectionate, and faithful.

The most detailed investigation of the structure of general lay relationship models has been carried out by Rusbult, Onizuka, and Lipkus (1993), using university students. In a series of studies that used a combination of free response data and multidimensional scaling, two dimensions were found to describe the derived configuration: superficial versus romantic, and practical versus nontraditional. The associated four quadrants were defined by Rusbult et al. as picturebook fantasy, marital bliss, utilitarian involvement, and companionship. The picturebook fantasy model (romantic/traditional and superficial) included a focus on partner characteristics (appearance, car, etc.), and represented a romantic, passionate, love-at-first-sight, kind of relationship. Subjects who endorsed the marital bliss model (romantic/traditional and intimate) emphasized marriage and the family, a high level of intimacy and commitment, and a de-emphasis on sex as the basis of a relationship. Utilitarian involvement was a mirror image of the marital bliss model (superficial and practical/nontraditional), and seemed to represent the desire for a wild fling, but without the sentimentality or intensity of the traditional romantic stereotype. The final quadrant (intimate and practical/nontraditional) representing companionship stressed slow development, friendship, and a practical orientation.

Rusbult et al. (1993, Study 3) also reported that this kind of structure was in evidence when another group of student subjects were asked to describe an actual, ongoing relationship—provisional evidence for the kind of linkage previously proposed between general and specific lay relationship theories.

A different, perhaps complementary approach to describing the general outlines of general lay theories was taken by Fletcher and Kininmonth (1992), in the development of the Relationships Beliefs Scale. This scale attempts to measure the beliefs that people hold concerning the importance of different factors in producing successful relationships. Initially, these authors designed a study to unearth the shared prototypical beliefs in the community. A university-based student sample and a nonuniversity sample wrote down all the factors that they believed would produce a very successful and loving heterosexual relationship (either married or unmarried). The resultant list of beliefs are shown in Table 1.1, divided into four groups according to the results of a factor analysis, and with representative examples of the three scale items subsequently developed to measure each belief. Significantly, this list of factors is similar to those reported by Rusbult et al. (1993) in the research described earlier.

An exploratory factor analysis ($n = 981$) revealed four factors that were interpretable and labeled as in Table 1.1: intimacy, external factors, passion, and individuality. The results also showed that these belief factors possessed adequate internal reliability and test–retest reliability. Moreover, this four-factor structure was remarkably stable across samples: comparing men with women, and comparing subjects who were currently involved in romantic relationships with those not in relationships. Two further studies also provided convergent and discriminant validity for the four belief factors, using a variety of other scales (Fletcher & Kininmonth, 1992).

As predicted, relationship satisfaction was largely unrelated to how strongly the beliefs were held. However, evidence was found, as predicted, that relationship beliefs moderated the relations between self-reports of behaviors in romantic relationships and relationship satisfaction. For example, a sample of subjects who had strong beliefs in the importance of intimacy had stronger links between their levels of relationship satisfaction and their self-reported levels of intimacy behavior (e.g., good communication) in their relationships ($r = .69$), than another group of subjects who had relatively weak beliefs in the importance of intimacy ($r = 32$). This pattern of correlations was

TABLE 1.1
Factor Labels, Individual Beliefs, and Example Items From the Relationship Beliefs Scale

Intimacy

Trust	There must be complete honesty between partners
Respect	Mutual respect in the foundation for the best relationships
Communication	People must always listen to their partner's underlying messages
Coping	Conflict in a relationship must be confronted directly
Support	In the best relationships partners work hard at satisfying each other's needs
Acceptance	In happy relationships partners totally accept one another
Love	Close relationships cannot work without love
Friendship	Your partner should be your best friend
Compromise	Both partners must make sacrifices in relationships
External Factors	
Personal security	If both partners come from secure and caring families the relationship is much more likely to succeed
Important others	Having friends in common cements relationships
Finance	Money is as important as love in a relationship
Commonality	Partners must share the same beliefs and values
Children	Having children brings couples together
Passion	
Sex	Without good sex, relationships do not survive
Vitality	Relationships must be exciting
Individuality	
Independence	Each partner has a right to absolute personal privacy
Equity	Men and woman must equally share household chores

repeated across the other three belief scales. These results confirm, as depicted in Fig. 1.1, that components of general lay theories (such as relationship-success beliefs) overlap with, but are distinct from, relationship-specific accounts or judgments (which include relationship satisfaction and memories of relationship behavior).

Before moving to the question of how such knowledge structures influence on-line processing in relationship settings, we briefly discuss three important questions (already touched on) in more depth: (a) How does this account accord with other relationship theories dealing with knowledge structures? (b) What is the content of relationship theories, and how can they be measured? and (c) What is the role of affect in this account?

How Does This Account Accord With Other Relationship Theories Dealing With Knowledge Structures?

Broadly speaking, alternative relationship theories that posit knowledge structures typically occupy certain subsections of the proposed typology. For example, the concept of working models proposed in attachment theory consist of expectations and beliefs that concentrate on the self vis-à-vis close relationships, and in terms of our model, occupy the general lay theories section (see Shaver, Collins, & Clark, this volume). In contrast, Aron and Aron's self-expansion theory (see this volume) specifically concerns the linkages between self, relationship, and partner at the specific lay theory level.

This is not to assert that either of these theories are wrong or underdeveloped. Indeed, both theories are informative about important aspects of the present schema, and deal at length with some critical questions not dealt with here. For example, attachment theory deals extensively with the origin and development of general lay theories, and self-expansion theory principally concerns the ways in which self-concepts (or self-theories) are influenced by specific relationships. However, one advantage of the present taxonomy is its potential to reveal lacuna that may be profitably worked on. For example, a key theme of the present account, already discussed at some length, concerns the links between general and specific lay relationship theories.

The Content and Measurement of Lay Relationship Theories

As the reader may have noted, the analysis so far presented does not offer a systematic analysis of the *contents* of close relationship lay theories. This has partly been a deliberate strategy, as we think such theoretical closure may be premature. However, a few points are made that we think deserve consideration.

Procedural Versus Declarative Memory. Baldwin (1992) argued that an important distinction is between *procedural* (knowing how) and *declarative* (knowing that) memory structures. Procedural knowledge can be conceptualized as consisting of if–then production rules (e.g., if my partner does X I do Y), that are operated automatically and unconsciously. Given the routine and often repeated nature of much close relationship interaction, we might expect such knowledge to be part and parcel of lay theories in the form of implicit expectations. Declarative knowledge, on the other hand, consists of images or verbal material that can be accessed consciously and put to a variety of uses, including the generation of explanations or predictions in relationship settings.

As suggested in this thumbnail sketch of procedural versus declarative knowledge, the two kinds of knowledge structure tend to be connected to two different kinds of cognitive processing. Declarative memory structures are more likely to produce controlled, explicit, and conscious processing, whereas procedural memory is more likely to trigger off automatic, implicit, and unconscious processing. We return later to this distinction between controlled and automatic processing, when discussing the role of knowledge constructs via-à-vis on-line processing.

Exemplar Versus Abstract Structures. A standard debate that has waxed hot in both cognitive psychology and social cognition, concerning how knowledge structures are stored, contrasts *exemplar* models with *abstract* models (e.g., see Klein, Loftus, Trafton, & Fuhrman, 1992).

Applying this distinction to general lay relationship theories, it is quite conceivable that people use exemplars that consist of specific past relationships or partners they have observed, or been involved with, to compare and contrast with their ongoing relationship experiences. For example, one's ideal partner might be a film star (e.g., Tom Cruise or Sharon Stone), and one's relationship prototype might consist of one's parents' relationship. Exemplars of relationships and partners could also be jumbled amalgams of bits and pieces derived from many sources.

Alternatively, people may store their general relationship ideals in terms of a set of abstract principles or generalizations; for example, ideal relationships being founded on open communication, strong similarity, and physical attractiveness.

Indeed, it is possible that both kinds of general relationship model are stored and used, depending on the individual and the context. This issue has not been dealt with in the close relationship arena, and thus remains an open question.

Measurement Problems. We mention one problem that has plagued the development of scales measuring general close relationship knowledge constructs; namely, such scales often include items that apply to a respondent's specific relationship, in addition to items that apply to relationships in general. Examples include well-used scales such as the Relationship Belief Inventory (Eidelson & Epstein, 1982) and the Love Attitudes scale (Hendrick & Hendrick, 1986). The problem is compounded in that such scales usually include many items that are set up along positive–negative dimensions; for example, "I cannot tolerate it when my partner disagrees with me"; "I feel that my lover and I were meant for each other." Hence, the scale items that apply to a respondent's particular relationship are similar to those included in widely used measures of relationship satisfaction.

Obviously, research that uses such scales to compare such ostensibly general lay beliefs or attitudes with judgments of a specific relationship (such as relationship satisfaction) becomes problematic because of item overlap, although in fact a good deal of such research has been published (see Fletcher & Fitness, 1993).

The Role of Affect

Finally, it is worth reminding ourselves that cognition in close relationship settings is often "hot cognition," and the content of relationship knowledge structures is no exception. It is doubtless the case, for example, that the sort of knowledge structures we have been describing will be shot through with affect and emotion. Any general theory of knowledge structures in close relationships will need, at some point, to deal with this issue. We have not attempted to do so here, possessing neither the hubris nor the space; instead we have gladly left treatments of this topic to others in this volume (especially Clark, Pataki, & Carver; Fehr & Baldwin, and Fitness).

Conclusion

To conclude, we have presented a general organizing framework that describes both the functions and structure of lay relationship theories. Although much work remains to be done, we believe this structure offers a useful beginning point. However, we have not yet explicitly dealt with the relations between such knowledge structures and on-line processing in relationship contexts—a task to which we now turn.

RELATIONSHIP LAY THEORIES AND ON-LINE PROCESSING: CONTROLLED VERSUS AUTOMATIC PROCESSING

The Role of Relationship Theories or Knowledge Structures

A critical insight from cognitive psychology over the last few decades is that on-line processing, and memorial processes in general, are inextricably intertwined with the operation of stored knowledge structures (or lay theories as we have described them here; Schank, 1982). In relationship settings, for example, we would expect relationship lay theories (both general and specific) to direct people's attention to certain categories of events, to guide the way such events are processed, to influence the way such events are both stored and recalled, and finally to influence behavior.

To give an example, we might expect an individual who strongly believes in the importance of sex or passion in close relationships, and who has an exceptionally positive view of his relationship, to (a) become concerned that his wife has recently become disinterested in sexual relations, (b) explain this behavior in terms of an attribution that avoids casting his wife or the relationship in negative terms (e.g., she is having a hard time at work), and (c) recall this behavior in terms of how his wife was going through a rough patch, rather than in terms of her insensitivity. Such processing, in turn, may influence his behavior; for example, given that he believes his wife is not a particularly good communicator, he may decide to help her more with the housework, or to buy her some treats to demonstrate his concern and love. Such an account is not fanciful—there exists a considerable body of evidence that supports most of the steps exemplified in the example described (for reviews see Fletcher & Fincham, 1991; Fletcher & Kininmonth, 1992).

An important distinction that is implicitly alluded to in this example concerns the availability versus the accessibility of knowledge structures. There are a potentially huge number of knowledge structures that are available for retrieval, but such structures will vary in terms of their accessibility. Some knowledge structures may only be retrieved on certain occasions within close relationships; for example, specific beliefs and memories concerning a partner's relationship with his father may only be retrieved when a rare visit is made to the in-laws. However, other constructs will be what is termed *chronically accessible*. Such constructs can relatively permanently prime the generation of thoughts or feelings quite unconsciously and unintentionally. For example, levels of relationship satisfaction may routinely help generate attribution processes in relationship contexts—simply being with one's partner may be a sufficient condition to elicit this knowledge construct with its powerful overlay of affect.

In addition, there is a wide array of events or conditions that will prime particular knowledge constructs, or elicit cognitive processing that, in turn, invokes such constructs. These events may occur either within or outside relationship interaction. For example, one's partner may induce some relationship processing by paying an unexpected compliment. However, watching a play, reading a book, or merely noticing a stranger who resembles one's partner may also evoke some thinking and associated affect concerning one's relationship. Alternately, thoughts and feelings of anger or love, or daydreaming about one's loved one, may also trigger off processing (see Fitness & Fletcher, 1993).

To further explicate the connection between lay relationship theories and on-line cognition, we now discuss the distinction, already alluded to, between controlled and automatic processing.

Controlled Versus Automatic Processing

It is difficult to see how ordinary dyadic interaction, with its multiplicity of cognitive processing demands, would be possible unless a large number of processes were not carried out simultaneously (i.e., in parallel). Hence, a tremendous amount of cognitive processing must occur rapidly and silently. Indeed, the distinction between automatic processing and controlled processing, or similar kinds of distinctions, are commonplace in cognitive psychology (see Fletcher & Fincham, 1991).

This distinction has been characterized in a variety of ways, with automatic processing variously described as fast, unconscious, effortless, not readily verbalizable, and carried out in parallel. In contrast, controlled processing is typically considered relatively slow, conscious, effortful, controllable, and serially produced.

Now, there is a continuing debate concerning whether, and to what extent, such features are necessary or most important in relation to definitions of the two processing modes (see Uleman & Bargh, 1989). Indeed, we agree with Bargh's (1989) argument that it remains an open question concerning the extent to which these different "defining" characteristics of the automatic/controlled processing distinction might operate independently of one another. However, certain points appear to be commonly agreed upon. First, the distinction is best represented as a continuous dimension rather than in terms of two discrete categories. Second, a key difference between clear-cut examples of the two processing modes is that controlled processing has marked attentional capacity constraints, whereas automatic processing has relatively little capacity constraints. This characteristic is related to the idea that automatic processing is carried out in parallel, whereas controlled processing is serially produced.

An important issue that arises concerns the conditions under which each processing mode may be dominant in relationship contexts. In dealing with this question, the critical function performed by lay relationship theories will again be apparent.

When Does Controlled Processing Occur? Research and theory suggest three factors that encourage controlled processing in relationship contexts. The first factor, already outlined, concerns the nature and status of the relevant knowledge structure. A chronically accessible construct, for example, will be likely to produce more processing (both controlled and automatic) than a construct that is not accessible. As we explain, in due course, chronic accessibility facilitates either controlled or automatic processing, depending on the role played by other variables.

The second factor concerns the inconsistency of information with an accessible knowledge structure. General attributional research has uncovered two key triggers of conscious, explicit, explanatory activity: negative events and unexpected outcomes (see Weiner, 1985, for a review). Indeed, the same two factors have also been identified as important factors in motivating conscious, attributional processing in close relationships (for a review see Fletcher & Fincham, 1991). However, one problem with this research is that negativity is typically confounded with the degree of expectedness. In close relationships, for example, negative events will typically also be unexpected given the Pollyannalike positive bias with which most people imbue their close relationships (see Kanazawa, 1992). We suspect that expectedness is the critical variable here; namely, that both unexpected positive events (e.g., a gift of flowers out of the blue), and unexpected negative events (e.g., not receiving a gift for one's birthday), will tend to receive conscious and explicit processing, centered around explaining the behavior.

The third category of variables includes circumstances or contingencies that influence the importance or perceived need to make certain decisions. For example, an individual who asks his partner to marry him is likely to prompt a good deal of controlled processing from his partner. Alternately, such controlled processing may occur simply because an individual's general theory of relationship development dictates that such a decision is appropriate, given the stage at which the relationship has reached (e.g., occurrences of attributions of love, staying overnight at each other's apartments). There is limited research support for such speculations. For example, Fletcher et al. (1987) found that subjects reported spending more time analyzing their relationships when they were either considering separation or increasing their levels of commitment.

When Does Automatic Processing Occur?   Utilizing the same three factors as just described, we would hypothesize that automatic processing is more likely to occur than controlled processing when (a) the constructs are highly accessible (b) the information being processed is consistent with the relevant knowledge structure or relationship theory, and (c) the circumstances do not encourage extensive or explicit analysis. For example, the act of kissing one's spouse before leaving for work will be unlikely to occasion more than automatic processing, if the marriage is happy and this is a regular and, hence, expected behavior.

Of course, it is not so easy to test such ideas with respect to automatic processing, given that the lack of evidence for controlled processing (spontaneous attributions or other cognitions) is consistent with either automatic processing or no processing occurring at all. However, ingenious methods have been developed within cognitive psychology to test for the presence of automatic processing. Indeed, one such method, termed the *concurrent memory load paradigm* (Logan, 1979), was recently used by Fletcher, Rosanowski, and Fitness (1994) to test some of the ideas already presented concerning the connection between the accessibility of general relationship beliefs and the automaticity of processing in relationship contexts.

This experiment was based on the postulate that general close relationship beliefs that were strongly held, would operate as chronically accessible constructs. Accordingly, such beliefs should tend to prime and automatically process the perception and encoding of relevant relationship behavior. As already noted, one of the key characteristics of automatic processing is that, unlike controlled processing, it is relatively free of attentional capacity constraints. Hence, strongly held beliefs should enable the simultaneous processing of belief-relevant behavior and another cognitive task that absorbs cognitive capacity in working memory, with no diminution of speed in processing the belief-relevant material. In contrast, under the same conditions, the performance of those with weak (and hence little used) relationship beliefs should suffer when they are required to process the two tasks simultaneously.

To test this hypothesis, Fletcher et al. (1994) first screened a large sample of students all currently in close relationships, using the Relationship Beliefs Scale previously described (Fletcher & Kininmonth, 1992). Based on norms from the large sample used in the development of the scale (Fletcher & Kininmonth, 1992), only those subjects who scored in the top and bottom 15% distributions, for either the intimacy or passion belief factors, were selected. Using a reaction-time paradigm, based on a study by Bargh and Tota (1988), subjects were required to judge whether a set of adjectives was descriptive of their relationships. Based on pretesting, positive and negative adjectives were selected that were semantically relevant and irrelevant to the two concepts (intimacy and passion). For example, "exciting," "passionate," "boring," and "unaffectionate" were selected as passion-related adjectives, and "warm," "accepting," "withdrawn," and "undependable" were examples of intimacy adjectives. Belief-irrelevant terms included adjectives such as "traditional," "unique," "violent," and "complicated." Filler tasks, such as deciding if an adjective included a certain letter, were also included to prevent subjects from settling into a set style of response.

There were two experimental conditions in this study. In the cognitive-loading condition, subjects were required to memorize a six-digit numeral while answering yes or no to each question. In the nonloading condition, subjects simply answered each question without completing the simultaneous digit-recall task. The predictions were that, regardless of belief strength, all subjects would take longer in the cognitive-loading condition when deciding whether the belief-irrelevant adjectives applied to their own relationships. However, for the belief-relevant adjectives we predicted an interaction such that weak belief subjects would evince the same pattern as already described (taking more time in the cognitive loading condition than the no-loading condition), whereas strong belief subjects would take a similar amount of processing time regardless of whether the tasks were completed under cognitive-loading or no-loading conditions.

As can be seen in Fig. 1.2, the results confirmed the predicted results. Moreover, the interaction in the belief-relevant condition just described remained significant when a variety of possible mediating variables was

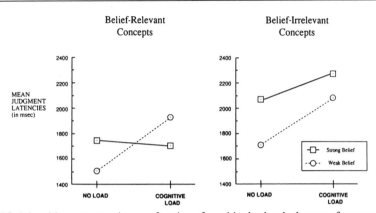

FIG. 1.2.   Mean response time as a function of cognitive load and relevance of concepts being assessed.

controlled for including relationship satisfaction, relationship length, the number of numerals correctly recalled, the proportion of yes responses, and the speed of response for the belief-irrelevant adjectives.

In summary, these results suggest that general close relationship beliefs can influence how everyday material is processed in an automatic fashion. A general related point here is that research and theorizing carried out by close relationship researchers typically equates thinking or cognition with the kind of verbally reported judgments that are most likely to be part of conscious, controlled cognitive processing (see Fletcher & Kininmonth, 1991). If, as we believe, rapid and automatic cognition is endemic in close relationships settings, then this often tacit assumption is clearly problematic (see Berscheid, 1994).

CLOSE RELATIONSHIP LAY THEORIES AND BEHAVIOR

This section discusses the role that lay relationship theories (in conjunction with on-line processing) might play with respect to behavior.

Are Relationships All in the Mind?

To begin with, we think it is important to rebut the view that the present account ineluctably leads to a radical brand of constructionism, in which relationship realities are reflections of whatever theories people happen to construct. It is certainly true that a cognitive approach, of the sort presented here, does entail that interpersonal behavior and events are interpreted, and gain meaning, in the context of the individual's lay theories. However, interpersonal events and behavior also have a raw reality that exert real consequences. Regardless of an individual's lay theorizing, if someone is physically attacked he or she is likely to get hurt, or if a person's partner breaks off the relationship he or she will be forced to face that reality.

Moreover, one of the fascinating aspects of relationships is the way in which both interpersonal behavior and the nature of the relationship lay theories themselves are, to some extent, a joint product of the couple. Accordingly, each partner has the capacity to test and stretch the relationship theories held by the other. Sometimes such meta-relationship talk can be explicit (see Acitelli, this volume). More often, such theories may be challenged by events in a more indirect fashion (e.g., "I thought she loved me, but she forgot my birthday").

Of course, as noted previously, individuals do have a remarkable talent for keeping their rose-tinted specific relationship theories insulated from bleaker and perhaps more accurate assessments of their relationships. In this respect, we are drawn to Murray and Holme's (1993) suggestion that the integrity and coherence of specific lay relationship theories will typically be maintained as long as possible, until under the weight of the evidence they cataclysmically collapse (much like popular scientific theories that suddenly go under). Such a hypothesis is certainly consistent with the accounts that people offer of relationship dissolution. For example, in Fletcher's (1983) study of accounts for marital separation, one common attribution related to sudden realizations that the marriage was over; for example, "After 4 years of marriage I woke up one morning and realized I could not conform to what I saw was the accepted norm in other marriages of the husbands' boozing and screwing around."

The upshot of this discussion is that relationship theories are certainly malleable, but on the other hand they also depend for their credibility and utility on how well they predict and explain the realities of interpersonal interaction and relationship events. If an individual's relationship theory becomes too divorced from reality, it is likely to be a poor tool for predicting, explaining, or controlling relationship interaction or events. To recapitulate an earlier theme, such epistemic aims provide a powerful motivational set that goes beyond merely maintaining a positive viewpoint.

The Links Between Knowledge Structures and Relationship Behavior

A plethora of research findings have shown that knowledge structures, such as self-reports of relationship satisfaction and depression, have strong relations to both interactional behavior and relationship outcomes (e.g., see Fincham & Bradbury, 1990). For example, relationship satisfaction has been consistently found to predict both the behavior of couples in interactional contexts (see Weiss & Heyman, 1990) and relationship dissolution (e.g., see Gottman & Levenson, 1992; Simpson, 1987).

In short, there is considerable documentation of the fact that lay theories massively influence the course and outcomes of close relationships. However, less progress has been made in understanding how such influence is wielded. A social cognitive approach, of the sort we offered in this chapter, would stress the importance of understanding the connections between relationship lay theories or knowledge constructs, on-line processing, and finally behavior. In particular, we give some examples of how the controlled–automatic processing distinction can help explain some of the puzzling findings that researchers have reported concerning the relations between knowledge structures and behavior.

Remarkably little research has examined the relations between knowledge structures, on-line processing, and behavior all in the context of particular studies (see Fletcher & Kininmonth, 1991, for a review). Doubtless, one of the main reasons for this lacuna are the severe methodological difficulties in measuring on-line cognition in the midst of couple interaction. One promising methodology is the technique initially developed by Ickes, Robertson, Tooke, and Teng (1986), in which subjects independently, and immediately, review videotapes of prior dyadic interactions in which they have participated. Subjects are instructed to stop the videotapes whenever they remember experiencing a thought or a feeling, and describe it in writing. Such protocols can then be coded in terms of the spontaneous occurrence of different kinds of cognitions and emotions.

In Icke's original research paradigm, couples were typically strangers and were surreptitiously videotaped while sitting together, ostensibly waiting for an experimenter to contact them. However, Fletcher and Fitness (1990) successfully adapted this technique to be used with couples in long-term romantic relationships. These couples had 10-minute problem-solving discussions that they knew in advance were being videotaped.[1]

Fletcher and Fitness (1990) found that couples who reported more positive on-line cognitions and emotions were substantially more positive in their verbal behavior (coded by observer raters), but did not differ from less positive couples in terms of their posture or facial expressions. Conversely, couples who had more positive attitudes toward their relationships did not differ from less positive couples in terms of their observed verbal behavior, but did exhibit more positive nonverbal behavior.

---

[1]There is a range of evidence that suggests the resultant protocols represent reasonably veridical accounts of on-line consciously experienced thoughts, provided that these videotape reviews are carried out immediately following the discussions and it is stressed to subjects that they must not manufacture their thoughts afresh (see Fletcher & Fitness, 1990; Fletcher & Kininmonth, 1991; Ickes et al., 1986).

This latter result replicated a common finding in the marital interaction literature (e.g., Gottman, 1979), and is typically explained in terms of nonverbal behavior being a more sensitive indicator of underlying affect than verbal behavior. However, this interpretation is inconsistent with the finding by Fletcher and Fitness (1990) that the positivity of on-line cognitions and emotional attributions were found to be unrelated to nonverbal behavior. The explanation offered by Fletcher and Fitness (1990) was in terms of the controlled versus automatic processing distinction; to wit, that verbal behavior is typically monitored more closely and is under tighter intentional control than nonverbal behavior in conversational contexts. In contrast, underlying accessible relationship attitudes tend to leak through into nonverbal behavior in an uncontrolled and automatic fashion (see Simpson, Gangestad, & Nations, this volume).

More recently, Thomas and Fletcher (1995) adapted the same videotape reviewing technique in order to study the correlates and sources of empathic accuracy in a large sample of married couples ($n = 74$). This was done by selecting 10 of the thoughts and feelings that each partner had written down, along with transcriptions of the number of seconds elapsed in the problem-solving discussions that were electronically embedded in each tape. These numbers indicated precisely where such spontaneous cognitions had occurred. Subjects were then required to play through each tape again, stopping the tape at the points indicated by their partners, and describe (a) what they themselves were thinking and feeling at this point, and (b) what their partners were thinking and feeling. Coders were able to reliably rate the concordance between these descriptions to obtain three ratings that were summed to give three scores for each subject: actual similarity, projection, and accuracy.

Controlling for the effects of projection, the results revealed an intriguing pattern of correlates with both accuracy and projection. Here, we focus on just a few findings, the first of which was that couples who were less accurate had been married significantly longer ($r = -.28$). Interestingly, when we controlled for the number of times that subjects stopped the tape in the first review session, the correlation between accuracy and relationship length sank close to zero. This result, along with various other analyses we have not the space to present here, suggested the following explanation. Over long periods of time relationships become more routine and stereotypical; partners make fewer efforts to actively assess their partner's feelings and thoughts, and active meta-communication diminishes. The dyadic style, in turn, becomes less engaged. In short, in comparison to relationships at earlier developmental stages, partner attributions become more automatic and less subject to effortful, controlled processing.

A second finding was that accuracy was not related to the confidence ratings that subjects provided for their attempts to assess their partners' thoughts. This result is consistent with both Ickes' own research, and the general failure of attempts, over decades, to predict accuracy in interpersonal judgment from self-report scales assessing people's estimates of their own empathic abilities (for a review see Ickes, 1993). There do appear to be reliable individual and couple differences in empathic ability, but people seem to have inaccurate understandings of how good they actually are.

As Ickes (1993) argued, it is not difficult to think of plausible explanations for this apparently poor level of meta-awareness concerning empathic accuracy; for example, lack of feedback, and lack of realization of the extent to which partners censor the expression of their private thoughts and feelings. More generally, we would expect that people's judgments in long-term relationships (such as marriage) would be substantially driven by their extant relationship theories. This reliance on relationship theories may either enhance or depress accuracy, depending on the nature of the theories. Some support was obtained for the hypothesis that empathic accuracy judgments are substantially theory-driven in the Thomas and Fletcher (1995) study. Observer raters observed each video, and assessed (on a 3-point scale) the extent to which subjects' reports of their own cognition could be easily inferred from their own accompanying behavior. The ease with which such private cognitions could be inferred was, in fact, unrelated to the levels of empathic accuracy attained.

This result does not necessarily mean that subjects would have achieved greater accuracy if they had concentrated on the surface behavior, and forgotten about their relationship theories. But, it does strongly suggest that subjects' on-line empathic judgments were, to a considerable extent, being driven by their lay relationship theories. If our previous research findings and theorizing are in the ball-park, then it also follows that such processing will often be guided automatically by relevant and accessible relationship knowledge constructs.

CONCLUSION

To conclude, the connections among lay relationship theories, on-line processing, and behavior are clearly not straightforward. Different categories of relationship knowledge structures seem to have different, and sometimes opposing, relations with both on-line cognition and relationship behavior. In this chapter we have outlined the bare outlines of a theoretical framework that attempts to explain the nature of some of these connections.

Shakespeare was right: Love is at least partly in the mind. Further research and theorizing on the structure and function of lay relationship theories promises to be a rich lode-stone in the development of more powerful scientific theories of relationship processes.

REFERENCES

Baldwin, M. W. (1992). Relational schemas and the processing of social information. *Psychological Bulletin, 112,* 461–484.

Bargh, J. A. (1989). Conditional automaticity: Varieties of automatic influence in social perception and cognition. In J. S. Uleman & J. A. Bargh (Eds.), *Unintended thought* (pp. 3–51). New York: Guilford Press.

Bargh, J. A., & Tota, M. E. (1988). Context-dependent automatic processing in depression: Accessibility of negative constructs with regard to self but not to others. *Journal of Personality and Social Psychology, 54,* 925–939.

Berscheid, E. (1994). Interpersonal relationships. *Annual Review of Psychology, 45,* 79–129.

Eidelson, R. J., & Epstein, N. (1982). Cognition and relationship maladjustment: Development of a measure of dysfunctional relationship beliefs. *Journal of Consulting and Clinical Psychology, 50,* 715–720.

Fincham F. D., & Bradbury, T. N. (Eds.). (1990). *The psychology of marriage.* New York: Guilford Press.

Fitness, J., & Fletcher, G. J. O. (1993). Love, hate, anger, and jealousy in close relationships: A prototype and cognitive appraisal analysis. *Journal of Personality and Social Psychology, 65,* 942–958.

Fletcher, G. J. O. (1983). The analysis of verbal explanations for marital separation: Implications for attribution theory. *Journal of Applied Social Psychology, 13,* 245–258.

Fletcher, G. J. O. (1993). The scientific credibility of commonsense psychology. In K. H. Craik, R. Hogan, & R. N. Wolfe (Eds.), *Fifty years of personality psychology* (pp. 251–269). New York: Plenum Press.

Fletcher, G. J. O. (1994). [Lay ideals of relationships and partners.] Unpublished raw data.

Fletcher G. J. O., & Fincham, F. D. (1991). Attribution processes in close relationships. In G. J. O. Fletcher & F. D. Fincham (Eds.), *Cognition in close relationships* (pp. 7–35). Hillsdale, NJ: Lawrence Erlbaum Associates.

Fletcher, G. J. O., Fincham, F. D., Cramer, L., & Heron, N. (1987). The role of attributions in close relationships. *Journal of Personality and Social Psychology, 53,* 481–489.

Fletcher, G. J. O., & Fitness, J. (1990). Occurrent Social cognition in close relationship interaction: The role of proximal and distal variables. *Journal of Personality and Social Psychology, 59,* 464–474.

Fletcher, G. J. O., & Fitness, J. (1993). Knowledge structures and explanations in intimate relationships. In S. Duck (Ed.), *Individuals in relationships* (pp. 121–143). Newbury Park, CA: Sage.

Fletcher, G. J. O., & Kininmonth, L. (1991). Interaction in close relationships and social cognition. In G. J. O. Fletcher & F. D. Fincham (Eds.), *Cognition in close relationships* (pp. 235–256). Hillsdale, NJ: Lawrence Erlbaum Associates.

Fletcher, G. J. O., & Kininmonth, L. (1992). Measuring relationship beliefs: An individual differences scale. *Journal of Research in Personality, 26,* 371–397.

Fletcher, G. J. O., Rosanowski, J., & Fitness, J. (1994). Automatic processing in intimate contexts: The role of relationship beliefs. *Journal of Personality and Social Psychology, 67,* 888–897.

Gottman, J. M. (1979). *Marital interaction: Experimental investigations.* New York: Academic Press.

Gottman, J. M., & Levenson, R. W. (1992). Marital processes predictive of later dissolution: Behavior, physiology, and health. *Journal of Personality and Social Psychology, 63,* 234–246.

Hendrick, C., & Hendrick, S. (1986). A theory and a method of love. *Journal of Personality and Social Psychology, 50,* 392–402.

Ickes, W. (1993). Empathic accuracy. *Journal of Personality, 61,* 587–610.

Ickes, W., Robertson, E., Tooke, W., & Teng, G. (1986). Naturalistic social cognition:

Methodology, assessment and validation. *Journal of Personality and Social Psychology, 51*, 66–82.

Kanazawa, S. (1992). Outcome of expectancy? Antecedent of spontaneous causal attribution. *Personality and Social Psychology Bulletin, 18*, 659–667.

Klein, S. B., Loftus, J., Trafton, J. G., & Fuhrman, R. W. (1992). Use of exemplars and abstractions in trait judgments: A model of trait knowledge about the self and others. *Journal of Personality and Social Psychology, 63*, 739–753.

Logan, G. D. (1979). On the use of concurrent memory load to measure attention and automaticity. *Journal of Experimental Psychology: Human Perception and Performance, 5*, 189–207.

Murray, S. L., & Holmes, J. G. (1993). Seeing virtues in faults: Negativity and the transformation of interpersonal narratives in close relationships. *Journal of Personality and Social Psychology, 65*, 707–721.

Rusbult, C. E., Onizuka, R. K., & Lipkus, I. (1993). What de we really want? Mental models of ideal romantic involvement explored through multidimensional scaling. *Journal of Experimental Social Psychology, 29*, 493–527.

Schank, R. C. (1982). *Dynamic memory.* New York: Cambridge University Press.

Simpson, J. A. (1987). The dissolution of romantic relationships: Factors involved in relationship stability and emotional distress. Journal *of Personality and Social Psychology, 53*, 683–692.

Simpson, J. A., & Gangestad, S. W. (1992). Sociosexuality and romantic partner choice. *Journal of Personality, 60*, 31–51.

Strube, M. J., Lott, C. L., Le-Xuan-Hy, G. M., Oxenberg, J., & Deichmann, A. K. (1986). Self perception of abilities: Accurate self-assessment versus biased self-enhancement. *Journal of Personality and Social Psychology, 51*, 16–25.

Swann, W. B., Pelham, B. W., & Krull, D. S. (1989). Agreeable fancy or disagreeable truth? Reconciling self-enhancement and self-verification. *Journal of Personality and Social Psychology, 57*, 782–791.

Thibaut, J. W., & Kelley, H. H. (1959). *The social psychology of groups.* New York: Wiley.

Thomas, G., & Fletcher, G. J. O. (1995). *Empathic accuracy and projection in married couples.* Unpublished manuscript, Psychology Department, University of Canterbury, Christchurch, New Zealand.

Uleman, J. S., & Bargh, J. A. (Eds.). (1989). *Unintended thought.* New York: Guilford Press.

Weiner, B. (1985). Spontaneous causal thinking. *Psychological Bulletin, 97*, 74–84.

Weiss, R., & Heyman, R. (1990). Observation of marital interaction. In F. D. Fincham & T. N. Bradbury (Eds.), *The psychology of marriage* (pp. 87–117). New York: Guilford Press.

2

Attachment Styles and Internal Working Models of Self and Relationship Partners

Phillip R. Shaver
University of California, Davis

Nancy Collins
State University of New York at Buffalo

Catherine L. Clark
University of California, Davis

Research on *attachment styles*—relatively coherent and stable patterns of emotion and behavior exhibited in close relationships—is based on the assumption that relational orientations are due to, or perhaps consist in, something called *internal working models of self and others* (Bowlby, 1969; Collins & Read, 1994; Shaver & Hazan, 1993). That is, attachment theory (Ainsworth & Bowlby, 1991), which emerged originally from psychoanalytic object relations theory, is in large part a social-cognitive theory. It explains the continuity of attachment patterns over the life span, from infant–caregiver attachment to emotional bonds between adult lovers, in terms of cognitive models, partly conscious and partly unconscious, that persist over time. This chapter examines the working-models component of attachment theory in some detail, considering what it meant to Bowlby and has meant to subsequent attachment theorists, how it is similar to and different from other conceptions of social-cognitive structures (e.g., schemas and scripts), and how it might be productively researched.

We begin with a brief overview of attachment theory, showing how it led to seminal research on individual differences in relational orientations. We then describe the role played in the theory by internal working models and explain how these models are related to discourse processes in close relationships. Next, we summarize research on infant and adult attachment, showing that it can be organized around the internal working-models construct. We then show how internal working models are similar to and different from other social-cognitive constructs, such as scripts and schemas. We use emotion regulation as an example of important psychological domains in which working models operate. Finally, we conclude with suggestions for future research on attachment and internal working models.

BRIEF OVERVIEW OF ATTACHMENT THEORY

Attachment theory began in a series of talks entitled "The Influence of Early Environment in the Development of Neurosis and Neurotic Character," given by Bowlby, a psychiatrist, to the British Psychoanalytic Society in 1939 (see Bowlby, 1940; Shaver & Clark, 1994). Over a period of years, these papers were expanded into a three-volume series, *Attachment and Loss* (1969 [revised, 1982], 1973, 1980), and two books of lectures, *The Making and Breaking of Affectional Bonds* (1979) and *The Secure Base* (1988). During most of those same years, Ainsworth helped to develop the theory and, more importantly, provided a powerful set of empirical methods for studying attachment processes in infancy (e.g., Ainsworth, 1967, 1982; Ainsworth, Blehar, Waters, & Wall, 1978). The history of attachment theory has been discussed by Ainsworth and Bowlby (1991) and by many other writers (e.g., Bretherton, 1985, 1991, 1992; Karen, 1994; Shaver & Clark, 1994). Research on attachment theory has been summarized in a host of books and articles (e.g., Bartholomew & Perlman, 1994; Belsky & Nezworski, 1988; Bretherton & Waters, 1985; M. Greenberg, Cicchetti, & Cummings, 1990; Hazan & Shaver, 1994a, 1994b; Lamb, Thompson, Gardner, & Charnov, 1985; Parkes, Stevenson-Hinde, & Marris, 1991; Paterson & Moran, 1988; Pottharst, 1990; Shaver & Clark, 1994; Shaver & Hazan, 1993; Sperling & Berman, 1994). Here, we provide a brief sketch of the theory sufficient to allow readers to understand subsequent sections of this chapter.

Bowlby acquired his psychoanalytic training in England during the years when Anna Freud, Melanie Klein, Donald Winnicott, and others were developing object-relations theory, the variant of psychoanalytic theory that emphasizes the role in personality development of close relationships and their mental representations (J. Greenberg & Mitchell, 1983). With the benefit of hindsight, it is possible to see that the early object-relations theories lay, in a sense, halfway between Sigmund Freud's drive or instinct model of psychoanalysis and Bowlby's attachment theory, which is based on ethology and cybernetic control theory. Both object-relations theory and Bowlby's attachment theory focus on early relationships, especially those between infants and their primary caregivers; but object relations theory retains much of Freud's emphasis on sexual and aggressive fantasies, whereas Bowlby's theory focuses on emotions and emotional bonds in actual close relation-ships.

Central to Bowlby's theory is the proposition that, beginning in early infancy, an innate component of the human mind—which Bowlby called the "attachment behavioral system"—in effect asks the question: Is there an attachment figure sufficiently near, attentive, and responsive? If the answer to this question is yes, certain emotions and observable behaviors are triggered. When infants notice that their attachment figure is available, interested, and responsive, they become more playful, less inhibited, visibly happier, and more interested in exploration. When an adolescent or adult falls in love, we would argue, similar positive emotional effects are seen because the same underlying system is involved (Shaver, Hazan, & Bradshaw, 1988).

If the answer to the attachment system's central question is no—that is, if an attachment figure is not sufficiently near, attentive, or responsive—fear and anxiety mount and a hierarchy of increasingly intense attachment-related behaviors is elicited. In infancy, these behaviors include visually searching for the attachment figure, calling and pleading to re-establish contact, toddling or running to the attachment figure, crying, and clinging. In the case of adult lovers, anxious vigilance seems functionally very similar, although the forms of calling and making contact are more diverse and, at least sometimes, more sophisticated.

If the hierarchically organized set of attachment behaviors repeatedly fails to reduce anxiety, the human mind seems capable of deactivating or "suppressing" its attachment behavioral system, at least to some extent, and defensively attempting to attain self-reliance. This leads eventually to the condition Bowlby called *detachment*. We know that this state is defensive, rather than reflecting a simple erosion of attachment (like a natural fading of memory), because it can be quickly transformed into a state of attachment-system activation if an infant begins to believe that his or her temporarily lost or unresponsive attachment figure is once again available.

Humans enter the world with a quickly developed capacity to monitor attachment figures, to become anxious when left alone, to protest the absence of adequate care, and to defensively suppress such protestation when it becomes evident that noisy anger is more harmful than helpful from the standpoint of safe attachment. One of the attractive features of attachment theory is the way in which it explains important individual differences in terms of this single universal behavioral system.

Individual Differences

Ainsworth's major contribution to attachment theory was to show how the attachment behavioral system interacts with different caregiving environments to produce lasting differences in personality (e.g., Ainsworth et al., 1978; see also subsequent literature reviews by Bretherton, 1985; Paterson & Moran, 1988; Rothbard & Shaver, 1994). In what Ainsworth called a *secure* infant–mother dyad, the infant seems to believe, even when mother is temporarily absent, that she will be accessible and responsive if called upon for help. Secure infants are effective explorers of a novel play environment, such as Ainsworth's well-known laboratory Strange Situation, and are easily comforted upon reunion with their mothers following short separations. *Anxious–ambivalent* dyads are marked by inconsistent and unreliable caregiving. Infants in this category are somewhat wary of unfamiliar people and new environments. Upon separation from mother, they cry intensely, and upon reunion are difficult to soothe. Anxious-ambivalent infants often throw tantrums and appear to seek contact with their mother while simultaneously rejecting her attempts to offer comfort. Infants in *avoidant* dyads appear to believe that their mothers are reliably *un*available and *non*responsive. Infants in this category appear to be prematurely independent and unconcerned about mother. They often do not cry when she departs and purposefully avoid her when she returns.

Scores of studies have confirmed Ainsworth's observations and extended her ideas to the study of later childhood. The evidence, as reviewed by Elicker, Englund, and Sroufe (1992), Rothbard and Shaver (1994), and Sroufe, Carlson, and Shulman (1993), supports the claim that these attachment patterns persist past infancy and are likely to be manifested, as Bowlby (1979) said, "from the cradle to the grave" (p. 129). This evidence for continuity across the life span is heterotypic; that is, there is "a *conceptual* rather than a literal continuity among behaviors or attributes" (Caspi & Bem, 1990, p. 554). The strategies adults employ to maintain proximity with an attachment figure are not presumed to be (nor are they) identical to the ones used by infants in the Strange Situation, but they are conceptually parallel and empirically predictable. It is this demonstrated continuity in attachment dynamics that Bowlby and other attachment researchers attribute to internal working models.

What these models are and how they function are not yet clear. Moreover, no one has clearly established whether, and if so how, internal working models differ from other hypothesized cognitive structures such as scripts and schemas. We begin our examination of these unresolved issues with a brief review of the internal working-models construct and its history.

BOWLBY'S ADOPTION OF THE WORKING
MODELS CONSTRUCT

Bowlby first used the term *working models* in 1969, in *Attachment*, the first volume of his *Attachment and Loss* series. In an extensive review of the cognitive aspects of "behavioral systems" in certain animals, he said: "Members of all but the most primitive phyla are possessed of equipment that enables them to organise such information as they have about their world into schemata or maps" (p. 74). Later, he acknowledged that the term *map* is misleading, "because [it] conjures up merely a static representation of topography. What an animal requires is something more like a working model of its environment" (p. 110). He borrowed from a psychologist, Craik (1943), and a brain scientist, Young (1964), the idea that the purpose of working models is to allow one to make predictions and create simulations of future events in a particular domain of experience. "The notion that brains do in fact provide more or less elaborate models that 'can be made to conduct, as it were, small-scale experiments within the head' is one that appeals to anyone concerned to understand the complexities of behavior and especially of human behavior" (p. 111; the phrase in single quotation marks is from Young).

Bowlby went on to distinguish between two kinds, or aspects, of working models in the attachment domain: "If an individual is to draw up a plan to achieve a set-goal not only does he have some sort of working model of his environment, but he must have also some working knowledge of his own behavioural skills and potentialities. . . . The two working models each individual must have are referred to respectively as his environmental model and his organismic model" (p. 112). Because in the study of attachment the relevant environment is mostly social and the relevant aspects of the self are more often psychological than "organismic," these two models have come to be called *model of others* (especially of attachment figures, or close relationship partners) and *model of self* (e.g., Bartholomew, 1990).

Bowlby (1969) drew explicit connections between the concept of working models and other psychoanalysts' notions about object relations, or internal representations of important relationship partners: "The environmental and organismic models described here as necessary parts of a sophisticated biological control system are, of course, none other than the 'internal worlds' of traditional psychoanalytic theory seen in a new perspective" (p. 113). Like other psychoanalysts, Bowlby attributed a great deal of psychopathology to inadequate, inaccurate, distorted, or conflicting models. He noted that working models are often used long after they become outdated; they can be partially or entirely unconscious; and conscious examination and verbal articulation of models is an essential part of psychotherapy and of the everyday equivalents of psychotherapy (self-examination and deliberate self-change):

> Many of the mental processes of which we are most keenly conscious are processes concerned with the building of models, with revising or extending them, checking them for internal consistency, or drawing on them for making a novel plan to reach a set-goal. Although it is certainly not necessary for all such processes always to be conscious, it is probably necessary that some should be so sometimes. In particular it seems likely that revising, extending, and checking

of models are ill done or done not at all unless a model is subjected from time
to time to whatever special benefits accrue from becoming conscious. (p. 113)

Thus, a major feature of healthy development in the attachment domain is
the articulation of models of self and relationship partners, and the revision
and updating of unsatisfactory, inconsistent, or antiquated models (Bretherton, 1993).

It is noteworthy that Bowlby at times considered working models to be,
like scripts or schemas, largely descriptive (i.e., they refer to what relationships are like, what happens when one takes certain actions within relationships, how much one is typically loved, etc.). A key feature of a person's
"model of the world" is the person's "notion of who his attachment figures
are, where they may be found, and how they may be expected to respond.
Similarly, in the working model of the self . . . a key feature is [the person's]
notion of how acceptable or unacceptable he himself is in the eyes of his
attachment figures" (Bowlby, 1973, p. 203). At other times, Bowlby (1988)
expressed a more complicated view of the possibilities, based largely on
clinical experience.

He suspected, for example, that "it is not uncommon for an individual to
operate, simultaneously, with two (or more) working models of his attachment figure(s) and two (or more) working models of himself" (Bowlby,
1973, p. 205). These models can easily be inconsistent with one another,
particularly when one is based on a person's own experience and another on
an attachment figure's alternative interpretation of that experience. Often the
attachment figure has given explicit instructions and warnings concerning the
examination of this kind of conflict: "[A person may find] himself unable to
review the representational model(s) he has built of his attachment figure(s)
because to do so would infringe a long-learned rule that it is against one or
both his parents' wishes that he study them, and their behavior towards him,
objectively. A psychological state of this kind in which a ban on reviewing
models and action systems is effected outside awareness is one encountered
frequently during psychotherapy" (Bowlby, 1980, p. 56). In later theoretical
writings, such as Main, Kaplan, and Cassidy (1985), internal working models
themselves were said to include such rules and taboos regarding the processing of attachment-related information, and the models thereby acquired
a degree of dynamic complexity rarely attributed to social-cognitive constructs such as scripts and schemas.

Bowlby stressed that the alteration of well-established working models is
difficult. When new information clashes with such models:

it is the models which win the day—in the short run almost always, in the long
run very often. Although in the short term an existing model, if strongly held,
tends to exclude new information incompatible with it, in the long term an old

model may become replaced by a new one. Nevertheless, much evidence exists that we undertake such replacement only very reluctantly. . . . When embarked on the task [of altering models] we proceed only in fits and starts, and revert often to the old and familiar model even though we know it to be outdated. (pp. 230–231)

Bowlby devoted most of Volume 3 (*Loss*) of the *Attachment and Loss* series to an analysis of the difficulty of accepting the death of important attachment figures. It is quite normal for people to hallucinate the presence of recently deceased attachment figures (at the door, at the dining table, in bed, etc.), to hold imaginary conversations with them, to maintain their rooms or possessions as if the deceased might continue to need them, and to imagine the lost loved one existing in an afterlife where he or she might be consulted. To a large extent, mourning processes can be judged as healthy rather than unhealthy based on the degree to which working models are reconstructed in a way that allows life to proceed in an adaptive fashion. Ordinary "non-mourning" life can be viewed similarly: Everyone is required to update and sometimes to replace antiquated working models of self and attachment figures. This is most easily done when one is not enmeshed in the past or motivated to defensively exclude all references to it.

COMMUNICATION AND ATTACHMENT

Attachment scholars, such as Main, Bretherton, and Kobak, suggested that communication and discourse processes are the mechanisms by which relatively stable patterns of attachment are formed and perpetuated. Bretherton (1990) argued, for example, that "secure relationships . . . go hand in hand with the partners' ability to engage in emotionally open, fluent, and coherent communication, both *within* attachment relationships and *about* attachment relationships. Insecure relationships, by contrast, seem to be characterized by selective ignoring of signals, as well as by certain forms of incoherence and dysfluency when discussing attachment relations" (p. 58).

In infancy, coherent communication is marked by sensitive parental caregiving in which an infant's emotional signals are accurately decoded and addressed in clear, direct ways. When communicative behavior is analyzed in the Strange Situation, secure infants are found more likely than avoidant infants to engage in "direct communication" by using obvious verbal and nonverbal signals to relay their emotional states to caregivers. In the less frequent situations in which avoidant infants use direct communication strategies, they do so only under conditions of low distress (Grossmann, Grossmann, & Schwan, 1986). In other words, it appears that it is not "safe" or wise for an avoidant infant to display (or perhaps even to feel) negative emotions. Anxious–ambivalent infants, in contrast, have no trouble experiencing and expressing emotions, but their emotions seem conflicted, incoherent, and difficult to manage. The term *ambivalent* points to the seeming illogic of crying for contact and support and then angrily flailing and twisting in the parent's arms when support is offered.

The same patterns are evident in adulthood, when research subjects are asked to recall and discuss childhood attachment relationships with parents (Main, 1991). Secure adults have little apparent difficulty in retrieving emotion-laden memories from childhood, and they present a realistic, well-integrated portrait of their parents. Secure adults recall both positive and negative experiences in childhood but, overall, seem to have a positive, understanding, forgiving, and relatively autonomous attitude toward their parents. In most cases, their childhood relationships with parents seem to have been largely warm and supportive, but in cases where abuse or neglect was involved, the secure adult seems to have moved beyond it, gained a coherent perspective on it, or come to understand it as the best his or her parent(s) could do under the circumstances. Secure adults exhibit what Main called *coherence of discourse* and *coherence of mind with respect to attachment*. They provide an interviewer with enough information, and sufficiently well-organized information, to answer the interviewer's questions without getting lost in emotional detail. Interestingly, an adult who exhibits this kind of coherence of discourse when discussing attachment is very likely to produce children who act securely in Ainsworth's Strange Situation (Fonagy, Steele, & Steele, 1991; Main et al., 1985). In other words, it seems likely that accurate, coherent communication on the part of a parent regarding attachment-related emotions is a major determinant of an infant's secure attachment to that parent.

Dismissingly avoidant adults have trouble recalling attachment-related events from childhood and tend to proffer bland, positive summary statements about relations with parents that cannot be backed up with concrete examples. There seems to be a defensive barrier between their semantic and episodic memories, at least in domains related to attachment. When questioned about possible pain and vulnerability in childhood, dismissingly avoidant adults tend to deny it; and when asked about the importance of attachment relationships, in childhood and in the present, they tend to pooh-pooh them (hence the term *dismissing*). If skin conductance is monitored during the attachment interview, avoidant adults produce spikes in conductance at exactly the points in the interview where they are inclined to deny negative experiences and emotions (Dozier & Kobak, 1992). This kind of parent has been found to have children who in turn avoid them in the Strange Situation (Fonagy et al., 1991; Main et al., 1985).

Preoccupied (anxious–ambivalent) adults tend to recall attachment-related events in incoherent emotional bursts, somewhat reminiscent of the incoherent responses of anxious–ambivalent infants in the Strange Situation. It is not uncommon for them to get so involved in a long tirade about one or both parents that it becomes necessary to ask, "What was the question again?" Unlike secure adults who may have had negative experiences with parents during childhood but now seem to have separated themselves from the pain, preoccupied adults are still enmeshed, still angry and upset. (Main called them *enmeshed and preoccupied with attachment*.) Such adults tend to produce children who are classified as anxious-ambivalent in the Strange Situation.

Main and her coworkers (1985) discovered empirically that a fourth group of infants, labeled *disorganized/disoriented*, have parents whose attachment interviews are marked by local incoherence when discussing attachment-related traumas or losses (a finding replicated by Ainsworth & Eichberg, 1990). Main and Hesse (1990) speculated that unresolved traumas and losses lead a parent to become "frightened or frightening" when a needy infant approaches, thus forcing the infant to disrupt the natural flow of attachment behavior.

These remarkable findings concerning the strong psychological and communicational links between parental and infantile attachment patterns suggest that internal working models, and their role in emotion regulation, are shaped by parent–child interactions. If a child is helped to detect feelings accurately and to act appropriately on them, he or she develops what Main and her colleagues called a more *coherent* mind, which is reflected eventually in coherent, unobstructed, effective communication about emotions and close relationships. If a child is forced to suppress and deny feelings, or encouraged to amplify them to gain attention, he or she develops one of two major kinds of incoherent mentation and discourse. Finally, if a child finds that approaching a parent for support results in extreme, if momentary, distress to the parent, the child may become disorganized and disoriented, which can lead to dissociation or passivity in the face of distress. In all cases, internal working models and externally communicated thoughts about attachment are closely related.

ATTACHMENT RESEARCH CONSIDERED FROM A WORKING-MODELS PERSPECTIVE

Since Ainsworth and her students first showed how to identify reliable individual differences in the quality or form of attachment, hundreds of individual-difference studies have been conducted. In this section, we recount some of the highlights, focusing particularly on findings related to the internal working-models construct. Within each section, studies are reviewed in age-related clusters, beginning with studies of infants and children, and ending with studies of adults.

Anxious–Ambivalents

Infants and Children. Anxious–ambivalent infants are vigilant concerning their caregiver's presence or absence, preoccupied with the caregiver's behavior, and very upset when the caregiver disappears for a few minutes. Upon reunion, these infants seem angry and difficult to soothe. Home and laboratory observations of the caregivers' actual behavior reveal that it is "inconsistent, hit-or-miss, or chaotic" (Sroufe et al., 1993, p. 320). Theoretically, anxious–ambivalent children are preoccupied with their attachment figures and are quick to cry or express anger because these reactions have been associated in the past, at times (on a partial reinforcement schedule), with success in attaining the desired attention and contact. Anxious–ambivalent children are relatively poor independent problem-solvers and, once in school, become overly dependent on teachers. In peer relations, such children are subject to victimization by other children, especially avoidant ones (Troy & Sroufe, 1987). When asked during middle childhood to draw a picture of their family, anxious–ambivalent children produce drawings characterized by vulnerability (Fury, 1993; Kaplan & Main, 1985). By age 10 or 11, anxious–ambivalent children are less skilled in peer relations than secure children and exhibit negative biases and anxieties when discussing peer relations (Elicker et al., 1992).

Adults. Anxious–ambivalent adults (also referred to as *preoccupied*, or *preoccupied with attachment*) are obsessed with romantic partners, suffer from extreme jealousy (Carnelley & Pietromonaco, 1991; Collins, 1994; Hazan & Shaver, 1987), and report a high breakup rate (especially in relationships with anxious–ambivalent partners) (Hazan & Shaver, 1987; Kirkpatrick & Hazan, 1994; Shaver & Brennan, 1992). More often than people with other attachment styles, they break up with their partner and then get back together again (Kirkpatrick & Hazan, 1994). They are excited about leaving home and going to college but become socially dissatisfied and lonely after the first semester (Hazan & Hutt, 1993). They have relatively low and perhaps unstable self-esteem (Collins & Read, 1990; Feeney & Noller, 1990), prefer to work with others but feel unappreciated and misunderstood at work, and tend to daydream about success and slack off after receiving praise (Hazan & Shaver, 1990). They become very emotional under stress and hence are forced to use emotion-focused coping techniques (Mikulincer, Florian, & Weller, 1993). They describe parents as intrusive and unfair, which is perhaps their interpretation of what infancy researchers call *inconsistent* parenting (Hazan & Shaver, 1987; Rothbard & Shaver, 1994).

Preoccupieds worry about rejection during interactions; indiscriminately self-disclose too much, too soon; and approve of others who self-disclose freely (Mikulincer & Nachshon, 1991). They tend to be argumentative, intrusive, and overcontrolling (Kunce & Shaver, 1994). They often assert their own feelings and needs without adequate regard for their romantic partner (Daniels & Shaver, 1991). Preoccupied mothers are more likely than their secure or avoidant counterparts to neglect their children (Crittenden, Partridge, & Claussen, 1991). They are both consciously and unconsciously afraid of death, which they seem to conceptualize as "the ultimate separation" (Mikulincer, Florian, & Tolmacz, 1990).

In summary, what begins with attempts to keep track of and hold onto an unreliable caregiver during infancy leads to an attempt to hold onto teachers, peers, and romantic partners, but to do so in ways that frequently backfire and produce more hurt feelings, anger, and insecurity. (This tendency toward self-fulfilling prophecy is characteristic of all of the major attachment patterns.)

Avoidants

Infants and Children. Ainsworth et al. (1978) included only one avoidant category in their typology of infant attachment patterns, but Main and Solomon (1986, 1990) later noted that many attachment researchers had left a certain proportion of infants unclassified because their behavior did not fit any of Ainsworth's three scoring prototypes. These disorganized/disoriented infants were marked by "sequential and simultaneous displays of contradictory behavior patterns," "undirected, misdirected, incomplete, and interrupted movements and expressions," "stereotypies, asymmetrical movements, mistimed movements, and anomalous postures," "freezing, stilling, and slowed movements and expressions," "apprehension regarding the parent," and "disorganization or disorientation" (Main & Solomon, 1990, pp. 136–140). Most attachment studies have not included this new category, so we generally restrict our summary of avoidance to Ainsworth's avoidant category. When there is evidence for all four categories, however, we draw a distinction between two kinds of avoidance—(a) dismissing of attachment and (b) disorganized or fearful. The four-category adult attachment typology recently proposed by Bartholomew (1990; Bartholomew & Horowitz, 1991) includes a similar distinction between dismissing and fearful adults.

Dismissingly avoidant infants seem to become prematurely independent and self-reliant after being repeatedly rebuffed in their attempts to seek contact or reassurance. (Their mothers appear to dislike close body contact and in some cases wish they had not had a child; Main, 1990.) When left alone in the Strange Situation, avoidant infants seem to suppress feelings of anxiety (while exhibiting elevated heart rate [Sroufe & Waters, 1977]—perhaps a sign of hidden anxiety) and do not seek contact with their mother upon reunion. In preschool, peer pairs containing at least one avoidant member form relationships that are less deep (less characterized by mutuality, responsiveness, and affective involvement) and more hostile than relationships involving children with other attachment styles (Pancake, 1989). Avoidant children are more often aggressive toward other children and more likely to receive angry rebukes from teachers. When asked during middle childhood to draw a picture of their family, avoidant children produce drawings characterized by stiff figures with rigid postures and missing arms or feet and a lack of individuation of and distance between family members (Fury, 1993; Kaplan & Main, 1985; Sroufe et al., 1993). By age 10 or 11, avoidant children have the worst peer relations of the original three attachment groups, exhibiting negative perceptual biases equal to those of anxious–ambivalent children and also seeming not to understand social relations very well.

Disorganized, or fearful, children lack self-confidence and have low self-worth (Cassidy, 1988; Jacobsen, Edelstein, & Hofmann, 1994). They suffer from attentional difficulties, being "restless" and "easily losing interest" (Jacobsen et al., 1994). They are not adept at perspective taking and perform more poorly on concrete operational reasoning tasks than secure and dismissingly avoidant children (Jacobsen et al., 1994). By the age of 6, some disorganized children appear controlling and parental toward their own parents (Main & Cassidy, 1988). Disorganized infants and children are more likely than members of the other attachment groups to be the offspring of emotionally disturbed parents (Cicchetti, Cummings, Greenberg, & Marvin, 1990; Cummings & Cicchetti, 1990; Main & Hesse, 1990) and to be victims of parental abuse and neglect (Carlson, Cicchetti, Barnett, & Braunwald, 1989; Crittenden, 1988; Egelund & Sroufe, 1981).

Adults. In adult studies based on a three-category typology similar to Ainsworth's, which probably involves placing a mixture of dismissing and fearful individuals into the avoidant category, avoidants have proved to be relatively uninvested in romantic relationships (Shaver & Brennan, 1992); they have a higher breakup rate than secures (Hazan & Shaver, 1987; Kirkpatrick & Davis, 1994; Shaver & Brennan, 1992) and grieve less following a breakup (Simpson, 1990), although they often feel lonely (Hazan & Shaver, 1987). They prefer to work alone and use work as an excuse for avoiding close relationships (Hazan & Shaver, 1990). Avoidants describe their parents as rejecting and somewhat cold (Hazan & Hutt, 1993; Hazan & Shaver, 1987; Rothbard & Shaver, 1994), report having poor relationships with parents while attending college (Hazan & Hutt, 1993; Rothbard & Shaver, 1994), and are more likely than secures or anxious–ambivalents to have an alcohol-abusing parent (Brennan, Shaver, & Tobey, 1991). They tend to withdraw from their romantic partners (i.e., avoid care and support) when experiencing stress (Simpson, Rholes, & Nelligan, 1992), attempt to cope with stress by ignoring or denying it (Dozier & Kobak, 1992), and later exhibit psychosomatic symptoms (Hazan & Hutt, 1993; Mikulincer et al., 1993). Avoidants tend to feel bored and distant during interactions—another sign of low involvement or denial of interest (Tidwell, Shaver, Lin, & Reis, 1991). They do not like to share intimate knowledge about themselves and do not approve of others who self-disclose freely (Mikulincer & Nachshon, 1991). Avoidants are somewhat pessimistic and, in fact, may appear cynical about long-term relationships (Carnelley & Janoff-Bulman, 1992). They claim not to be consciously afraid of death but reveal unconscious death anxiety when responding to TAT pictures (Mikulincer et al., 1990).

In studies that draw a distinction between dismissingly and fearfully avoidant adolescents and adults, dismissing avoidants have high self-esteem, are cold, competitive, and introverted (Bartholomew & Horowitz, 1991). They are notably not anxious, depressed, or dependent (Bartholomew & Horowitz, 1991). Dismissings are defensively autonomous and prefer not to rely on others for emotional support (Bartholomew, 1993). Fearful avoidants, on the other hand, are introverted and unassertive, and tend to feel exploited (Bartholomew & Horowitz, 1991). They lack self-confidence and are self-conscious (Bartholomew, 1993). On the whole, they feel more negative than positive about themselves (Clark, Shaver, & Calverley, 1994). Compared to the other three groups, fearfuls are anxious, depressed, and hostile (Bartholomew & Horowitz, 1991; Carnelley, Pietromonaco, & Jaffe, 1994; Dutton, Saunders, Starzomski, & Bartholomew, 1994; Shaver & Brennan, 1992). They are self-defeating, report a large number of physical illnesses, and (more often than other groups) exhibit indicators of borderline personality (Alexander, 1993; Dutton et al., 1994). Fearful avoidance in adults has been positively correlated with reports of severe punishment and abuse during childhood (Clark et al., 1994) and, in turn, with dominating, isolating, and emotionally abusing one's spouse during adulthood (Dutton et al., 1994).

In summary, what begins with attempts to regulate attachment behavior in relation to a primary caregiver who does not provide contact comfort or soothe distress tends to become dismissing avoidance—defensive self-reliance accompanied by somewhat cool and distant representations of close relationship partners and cool, sometimes hostile, relations with peers. In contrast, what begins as conflicted and disorganized/disoriented behavior in relation to a frightening or distressed caregiver may translate into desperate, ineffective attempts to control the behavior of romantic partners in adulthood.

Secures

Infants and Children. Secure infants appear confident both in themselves and in the availability of their caregivers (Elicker et al., 1992). When reunited with a caregiver, they readily seek contact, are easily soothed, and quickly return to exploring the environment (Ainsworth et al., 1978). Secure children are generally happy (LaFreniere & Sroufe, 1985), easy-going, cooperative (Arend, Gove, & Sroufe, 1979), empathic (Sroufe & Fleeson, 1988), and creative (Elicker et al., 1992). They seem to work well with parents and teachers, and in problem-solving situations can comfortably accept direction and guidance (Arend et al., 1979; Matas, Arend, & Sroufe, 1978; Sroufe & Fleeson, 1988). Secures tend to get along well with peers and enjoy close friendships (Elicker et al., 1992; Pancake, 1989; Sroufe et al., 1993). Family pictures drawn by secure children show individuated, complete figures that are grounded or centered on the page. The figures tend to be appropriately spaced, showing a natural proximity among family members. Secures also include other aspects of family life in their drawings, such as bicycles, pets, and trees (Fury, 1993; Kaplan & Main, 1985; Sroufe et al., 1993).

Adults. Secure adults are highly invested in relationships and tend to have long, stable ones characterized by trust and friendship (Collins & Read, 1990; Hazan & Shaver, 1987; Keelan, Dion, & Dion, 1994; Kirkpatrick & Davis, 1994; Kirkpatrick & Hazan, 1994). They describe their parents favorably (although in balanced and realistic terms) and have good relationships with them while attending college (Hazan & Hutt, 1993; Hazan & Shaver, 1987; Levy, Blatt, & Shaver, 1994; Rothbard & Shaver, 1994). Secures have relatively high self-esteem and high regard for others (Collins & Read, 1990; Feeney & Noller, 1990), and feel well liked by coworkers (Hazan & Shaver, 1990). When stressed, secures cope by seeking social support (Mikulincer et al., 1993), and they support their romantic partner when the partner is under stress (Simpson et al., 1992). They seek integrative, mutually satisfactory resolutions to conflicts (Pistole, 1989), self-disclose appropriately, and like other people who self-disclose (Mikulincer & Nachshon, 1991). They often adopt parents' religious views and imagine God to be a warm, trustworthy attachment figure (Kirkpatrick & Shaver, 1990, 1992). They are relatively unafraid of death, both consciously and unconsciously (Mikulincer et al., 1990).

Overall, it seems that secure infants, children, and adults have mastered the complexities of close relationships sufficiently well to allow them to explore and play without needing to keep vigilant watch over their attachment figures and without needing to protect themselves from their attachment figure's insensitive or rejecting behaviors.

THE CONTENT AND STRUCTURE OF
WORKING MODELS

Given the extensive evidence concerning differences between three or four major attachment styles, how can these differences be understood in terms of internal working models? In the sections that follow, we address this question by drawing on attachment theory as well as more general theoretical and empirical work in social psychology dealing with the nature of cognitive representations.

What are Working Models?

Working models are cognitive representations of self and others that evolve out of experiences with attachment figures and are concerned with the regulation and fulfillment of attachment needs. Early working models organize a child's memory about attempts to gain comfort and security, and the typical outcomes of those attempts (Main et al., 1985). Given a fairly consistent pattern of caregiving throughout childhood and adolescence, models are expected to become solidified through repeated experience and increasingly become a part of the child's developing personality. Thus, what begin as representations of specific relationships and specific partners result in the formation of more abstract, generalized representations of self and social world.

Internal working models of attachment are similar in many ways to other cognitive structures studied by social psychologists, such as schemas, scripts, and prototypes. Like all such cognitive structures, working models are not directly observable; they are hypothetical constructs presumed to be stored in long-term memory. Internal working models are organized representations of past behavior and experience that provide a framework for understanding new experiences and guiding social interaction. Like other social schemas, working models help individuals fill gaps in the information available in particular social situations (Jones, 1990).

Although working models share many features with other social-cognitive structures, they are also unusual in certain respects. First, unlike traditional approaches to schemas, which tend to focus on factual knowledge and verbal propositions, the attachment-theoretical approach to working models places greater emphasis on the representation of motivational and behavioral tendencies. Social psychologists have tended to focus on conscious cognitions that can be easily articulated, but working models of attachment contain unconscious elements that are difficult to verbalize. Thus, internal working models of attachment are not simply "cognitive," if cognitions are assumed to be "cool," verbal, and descriptive. Instead, cognitive aspects of working models are closely interwoven with wishes, goals, concerns, psychological defenses, and behavioral tendencies. This view of working models is consistent with more general theories of personality and mental representation. For instance, goals and behavioral strategies have been described as fundamental elements of the self-concept (e.g., Emmons, 1989; Markus & Ruvolo, 1989; Markus & Wurf, 1987) and are viewed as essential to understanding the cognitive basis of interpersonal interaction and self-regulation (e.g., Cantor & Kihlstrom, 1985; Miller & Read, 1991; Pervin, 1983; Trzebinski, 1989).

Working models should not be viewed simply as a set of organized beliefs or propositions about oneself and others. Collins and Read (1994) suggested that working models contain four interrelated components: (a) autobiographical memories, (b) beliefs and attitudes, (c) goals and motives, and (d) behavioral strategies. The first component, *autobiographical memories* of attachment experience, should include not only memories of specific interactions and concrete episodes, but also constructions placed on those episodes, such as appraisals of experience and explanations of one's own and others' behavior. The second component of working models is a rich set of attachment-related *beliefs, attitudes, and expectations* about self and others. This social knowledge is presumed to be fairly general, abstracted largely from concrete experiences, and organized into units or schemas. In addition, this information is thought to be independent of when and how it was acquired. A third component is *attachment-related goals and motives* (or wishes). Although the attachment system serves the universal goal of maintaining felt security, a person's history of achieving or failing to achieve this goal is expected to result in a characteristic set of social and emotional needs, motives, wishes, and defenses. For example, individuals with different attachment styles differ in their motivation to seek intimacy, avoid rejection, deny feelings of vulnerability, maintain privacy, and so on. The final component of working models is a set of *behavioral plans and strategies* aimed at the attainment of particular goals. These generalized strategies are based on repeated sequences of interaction with attachment figures and are apt to be stored in the form of "if–then" production rules (Anderson, 1982; Kihlstrom & Cantor, 1983) that are automatically evoked in response to particular situational cues or emotional experiences (Crittenden, 1990; see also Stern, 1985).

A second way in which working models of attachment differ from other social-cognitive structures is that working models are expected to be more heavily affect-laden than the schemas typically studied in social psychology. Although some social-cognition scholars are now recognizing the affective aspects of social schemas (e.g., Andersen & Cole, 1990; Clark, Pataki, & Carver, this volume; Fehr & Baldwin, this volume; Fiske & Pavelchak, 1986; Fitness, this volume; Greenwald & Pratkanis, 1984), little attention has been paid to the representation of affect beyond the assumption that schemas vary in their positive or negative valence. As noted earlier, working models are formed and elaborated through emotional communication, and much of their content concerns the regulation of emotions and the fulfillment of emotional needs. Hence, emotions are likely to be triggered automatically when models are activated (Fiske & Pavelchak, 1986), which helps to explain attachment-style differences in social perception, subjective emotional experience, and behavioral expression of emotion.

A third way in which working models differ from other social schemas is that they are explicitly interpersonal and relational in nature. Internal working models contain images of self and others, not in isolation, but in highly interdependent situations. Fortunately, there has recently been a general shift toward a more relational treatment of social schemas. For example, Baldwin (1992) advocated the notion of *relational schemas,* which he defined as cognitive structures that represent regularities in interpersonal relating. The elements of the relational schema include a self-schema representing the way in which the self is experienced in a particular relationship, a schema for the other person, and an interpersonal script that describes the typical interaction patterns between self and other. Along similar lines, Ogilvie and Ashmore (1991) emphasized the importance of understanding the self-concept, not in isolation, but in relation to particular others. They suggested that information about the self is stored in "self-with-other units" that contain personal qualities that characterize an individual when he or she interacts with a particular other person.

A final way in which working models differ from other knowledge structures is that they are likely to be broader, more multidimensional, and more complex than other social representations. Attachment working models include schematic features, scriptlike features, attitudinal features, and so on. Moreover, these various features are apt to be encoded in memory in a variety of forms, including the forms Tulving (1985) labeled *episodic* (autobiographical), *semantic* (pertaining to general knowledge), and *procedural* (referring to actions, strategies, and skills). As noted by Crittenden (1990), one implication of this complexity is that different aspects of working models may be stored separately and may contain different representations of the same experience. Some individuals will have difficulty coordinating the different memory systems and may be at risk for developing the kinds of inconsistencies noted by Bowlby between the various elements within their models. Moreover, certain aspects of memory will be more readily available than others to conscious awareness and examination. For example, one's repertoire of defensive and behavioral strategies is likely to be represented in the form of procedural knowledge that is relatively inaccessible to awareness.

Attachment Representational Networks

There is a strong tendency to discuss working models of the self and others in the singular, as if individuals could have only one model of each kind. There are good reasons to question this assumption, however. First, as documented earlier in the present chapter, individuals can maintain separate and somewhat independent models of attachment. Not only did Bowlby claim this based on his clinical experience, but developmental psychologists have shown that an infant's attachment style with one parent does not strongly predict his or her style with the other parent (Bridges, Connell, & Belsky, 1988; Lamb, 1978;

Main & Weston, 1981; see Fox, Kimmerly, & Schafer, 1991, for a review). This suggests that young children develop a separate working model for each parent. Second, because adult representations of attachment are based on a variety of relationship experiences, they should be more complex and differentiated than childhood models. For example, adults are likely to have somewhat different working models for their roles as son or daughter, spouse, and parent (Bretherton, Biringen, Ridgeway, Maslin, & Sherman, 1989; Crittenden, 1990; George & Solomon, 1989). Consistent with this line of thinking, in one study that directly compared representations of attachment to peers with representations of attachment to parents, there was significant overlap between the two but considerable distinctness as well (Bartholomew & Horowitz, 1991, Study 2). Finally, it is unreasonable to assume that a single, undifferentiated model can effectively guide the full range of attachment-related behavior in adulthood. Multiple models of attachment provide the flexibility necessary for individuals to function adaptively and to satisfy attachment needs across diverse circumstances and relationships.

One solution to the problem of multiple models is to view attachment representations as a multifaceted collection, or *network*, (Collins & Read, 1994). Based on studies of the general nature of mental representation (Cantor & Mischel, 1979; Holland, Holyoak, Nisbett, & Thagard, 1986), it is useful to think of this network as hierarchically organized. At the top of the hierarchy are the most *general* representations of self and others, abstracted from a history of relationship experiences with caregivers and other important attachment figures. These abstract, generalized models can apply to a wide range of relationships and situations, although they may not apply to any one of them very well. Further down in the hierarchy are more specific models that correspond to particular kinds of relationships (e.g., parent–child relationships, friendships, love relationships), and lowest in the hierarchy are models corresponding to particular partners (e.g., my husband John, my baby daughter Chris). Models higher in the hierarchy fit a wide range of situations but are often misleading guides to behavioral responses because they are not closely matched to the details of particular situations. In contrast, models lower in the hierarchy are apt to provide a better fit to certain relationships or situations, although at the cost of failing to generalize widely.

Working models differ in ways other than abstractness. Some are more complex and elaborated than others; some may be positive, some negative; some may be fairly clear and internally consistent, others may be relatively inconsistent and incoherent; and some may be more central or important in the network, whereas others are more peripheral. Central or core models are probably the most elaborated and densely connected to other knowledge structures. For example, given their primacy and extended history, models of parent–child relationships are likely to be central and deeply embedded in the network structure. Working models of other major attachment figures (such as a spouse) should also be highly elaborated and differentiated.

It is important to consider the dynamic and interdependent nature of the components of the attachment network. As individuals move in and out of relationships, there is a continual interchange between general and specific levels of the hierarchy. For example, in infancy and early childhood, working models begin as representations of specific relationships with primary caregivers. Over time, additional experiences result in the formation of more abstract, general models of self and others (Bowlby, 1973) that then influence the construction of more specific models in future relationships. In this way, models that develop early in one's personal history have the potential to shape the construction of all subsequent models. By the same token, new relationship-specific models provide opportunities for the continued revision and updating of more general models. Although different models may be somewhat distinct, they are probably linked through a rich set of associations and are likely to share many elements. Thus, we would expect a fair amount of overlap between various models of self and other. In fact, we might speculate that images of the self are more consistent across different models than images of others. This may be partly due to a motivation to develop a coherent self-image and partly to the greater stability in behavior and experience within an individual as opposed to between individuals.

Although the norm may be toward the development of an increasingly complex and differentiated set of attachment representations, there may be some important individual differences in the structure of people's representational networks. Crittenden (1990) distinguished among three important meta-structures. The first and most simplified structure is an internal representational model that gets applied to all relationships. This meta-structure impairs interpersonal functioning because it requires that all relationships be distorted to fit a single model. This organization may be characteristic of abusing and neglecting mothers and their children (Crittenden, 1988). The second structure is characterized by multiple, unrelated models that permit the representation of unique aspects of relationships but preclude the development of a coherent sense of self. This structure may be characteristic of the preoccupied and fearfully avoidant attachment styles. The third, most complex, and presumably most adaptive meta-structure includes an integrated generalized model along with differentiated relationship-specific submodels. This kind of structure is a hallmark of secure attachment.

Which Model Will Be Activated and Used?

The idea that individuals possess a network of attachment representations is consistent with cognitive theories of the self that view the self as a dynamic collection of self-representations. For example, Markus and Wurf (1987) argued that the self-concept is best viewed as a continually active, shifting array of accessible knowledge. At any one time, only some subset of the potentially available representations (the working self-concept) is activated and invoked to regulate or interpret an individual's behavior. This general approach provides a useful framework for conceptualizing the dynamic nature of attachment representations: Not all representations that are part of the complete attachment network will be accessible at any one time. How, then, can we predict which model, or model components, will be activated and used to guide social perception and behavior?

As summarized by Collins and Read (1994), activation is likely to depend on characteristics of the models themselves, features of the prevailing social situation, and the individual's current motives and mood. Some models will be more readily accessible than others because of their density or strength. The strength of a model will depend on variables such as the amount of experience on which it is based, the number of times it has been applied in the past, and the density of its connections to other knowledge structures. This implies that models based on major attachment figures (such as parents and spouses) will be easily activated and chronically accessible (Bargh, 1984; Higgins, King, & Mavin, 1982).

Whether or not features of the situation match features of the working model will also affect its accessibility. Among the features that should be important are characteristics of the interaction partner and the nature of the relationship. For instance, characteristics of the interaction partner such as gender and physical appearance should be important cues to model-matching. Consistent with this view, Collins and Read (1990) showed that in heterosexual romantic relationships, one's model of the opposite-sex parent is a better predictor of aspects of the relationship than is the model of the same-sex parent. Presumably, the nature of one's current relationship should also be an important cue. For example, models based on relationships with parents may be more relevant when interacting with one's children than when interacting with peers. Such models may also be more relevant in situations that bear some resemblance to parent–child interactions—for example, in situations in which one is in a position of relatively low power or status. This functional specificity of working models was illustrated in a study by Kobak and Sceery (1988) in which young adults' representations of their childhood experiences with parents (as measured by the Adult Attachment Interview; George, Kaplan, & Main, 1985) predicted the extent to which the young adults perceived that social support was currently available from their family, but did not predict their judgments about available support from friends.

An individual's currently active goals and mood states will also affect which model gets activated and used. Some models will be more or less automatically activated in response to specific situational stimuli or appraisals. Others will be recruited or invoked in response to whatever motives the individual is striving to fulfill. Some emotion-specific models are probably activated automatically in response to particular emotional appraisals. For example, in the heat of an argument with his romantic partner, a man may suddenly feel threatened or hurt in ways similar to what he felt earlier in life in interactions with his mother. These time-worn responses may trigger an angry outburst, aimed as much at the man's working model of his mother as it is at his physically present partner: "You are constantly spying on me, intruding into my personal thoughts and space; you don't give me room to breathe!" Later, in a mood of calm reflection on the partner's actual qualities, such an outburst can seem remarkably inappropriate.

As the discussion so far makes clear, attachment researchers need to be more precise in specifying which aspects of the attachment representational network are under study at a particular time. Just as it is incorrect to speak of a single model of self or others, it may be incorrect to speak of a person's single attachment style. Although this possibility has not been made explicit in the literature, it is already reflected in the various approaches used to measure adult attachment. Attachment styles have been measured with respect to memories and representations of childhood relationships with parents (Main et al., 1985), overall experiences with intimate peers (Bartholomew & Horowitz, 1991), general orientations toward romantic relationships (Collins & Read, 1990; Hazan & Shaver, 1987), and attachment quality within a single current romantic relationship (Kobak & Hazan, 1991). These approaches differ in the particular content they target (e.g., parents, peers, romantic partners), and in the general/abstract versus specific/concrete nature of that content (e.g., relationships in general versus one specific relationship). The varying methods of measuring adult attachment may activate different aspects of the attachment representational network. They also assess different aspects of particular models. For example, self-report methodologies (e.g., Hazan & Shaver, 1987) may assess surface-level beliefs and motives which individuals can consciously experience and articulate. In contrast, inferential interview methodologies (e.g., Bartholomew & Horowitz, 1991; George et al., 1985) may reveal unconscious, procedural aspects of working models, as well as their structural features such as inconsistency and incoherence. Thus, a more detailed understanding of working models will facilitate the integration of research using different methodologies and may help explain inconsistencies in attachment categorizations that occur across different measurement instruments, or even over time using the same instrument.

ATTACHMENT AND EMOTION REGULATION: WORKING MODELS IN ACTION

To this point, we have argued that internal working models are cognitive structures, some of which are likely to be automatically activated whenever attachment-related events occur. Once activated, the models shape cognitive processing of social information, the appraisal of important changes in the internal and external environments, and the selection of social behaviors. We need not assume that people are consciously directing these processes or are even aware of them; in fact, we suspect that much of this psychological system operates automatically (Bargh, 1984; Fletcher & Thomas, this volume)—that is, spontaneously, with little effort, and outside of awareness. One way to illustrate the effects of working models is to examine their role in emotion regulation.

The goal of the attachment system can be described either in terms of behavior or in terms of emotion regulation. Bowlby tended to focus on behavior, because he was primarily interested in the biological function of attachment during infancy: protection from predation and other dangers, through reliance on a concerned caregiver. When studying infants, a scientific observer necessarily has only indirect, inferential access to a research subject's feelings. Sroufe and Waters (1977) argued, however, that proximity-seeking behavior is guided by a search for a particular emotional state, felt security. Actually, the range of attachment-related emotions is quite large and includes fear of abandonment, jealousy, the joy of reunion, anger at separation, and sadness and grief following loss. What the attachment research field needs, therefore, is a cognitively oriented model of emotion and emotion regulation that overlaps with, or includes a plausible role for, internal working models.

Many contemporary emotion theorists (Ekman, Frijda, Lazarus, Roseman, and Weiner, to name a few), working partly on separate tracks and partly in response to each other, have arrived at what Fischer, Shaver, and Carnochan (1990) called the *consensus* theory of emotion (i.e., the theory that most current investigators accept, at least to a large extent). The essential features of the theory, shown in Fig. 2.1, are (a) wishes, goals, or concerns; (b) a notable change in the internal or external environment; (c) an appraisal of the change in relation to salient wishes or concerns; (d) emotion-specific action tendencies and the physiological processes that support them; (e) emotional

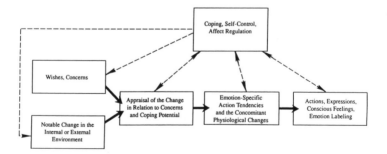

FIG. 2.1. A diagrammatic representation of the consensus theory of emotion.

behavior and self-labeling; and (f) coping, or self-control, efforts. Each component of the process can be affected by attachment history, as explained here.

Wishes, Concerns

Imagine seeing your romantic partner flirting with one of your colleagues. Would you care? What emotion would you experience—panic, amusement, jealousy, admiration? The occurrence of any emotion would indicate that you care. According to the consensus theory of emotion, if you had no wishes, no preferences, and no investments, your partner's flirtations would be just another cognitively acknowledged event.

According to attachment theory, what an infant cares about is the comfort and safety provided by a familiar caregiver (hence proximity-seeking behavior) and the pleasures of exploring and mastering novel environments. Bowlby and Ainsworth envisioned a dynamic reciprocity between these two desirable states—attachment and exploration. Interestingly, in a series of studies of adult psychotherapy sessions, Luborsky and his colleagues (see Luborsky & Crits-Christoph, 1990), working almost independently of contemporary emotion theorists, noticed that the core themes in the stories told in these therapy sessions include a wish on the part of the client, a reaction by another person, and the client's emotional reaction to that person's reaction. For example, a client, David, wishes that Helen would admire his artwork (thereby admiring him); she doesn't, so he feels angry or hopelessly disappointed. When all such wishes are coded from therapy tapes or transcripts, they fall into only two large clusters: the wish to be close and accepting and to be loved and understood (both of which Luborsky called "being close") and the wish to assert oneself and be independent ("being independent"). Of course, these themes recur throughout psychology: for example, Bakan's (1966) agency and communion, Mahler's (Mahler, Pine, & Bergman, 1975) symbiosis and separation–individuation, and Baxter's (1988) connectedness versus autonomy dialectic.

When pursuing these two universal goals, individuals with different attachment styles, as described earlier in this chapter, presumably harbor somewhat different wishes and concerns. Preoccupied people, for instance, wish to be very close to others, perhaps in some cases to merge psychologically with them. Dismissing individuals wish for independence and are concerned when relationship partners get too close. Fearful people wish they could be close but are concerned about being hurt or abandoned. Secure people wish for an intimacy that supports and leaves room for autonomy.

Notable Events or Changes in Events

A wish by itself does not cause an emotion; an emotion is caused (again, according to the consensus theory) by the appraisal of notable events or changes in events (e.g., noticing that your partner is flirting) in relation to wishes, goals, or concerns. Although most of the "action" in this part of the model is due simply to the fact that the external world and a person's internal environment (hunger, pain, unbeckoned thoughts, etc.) are constantly in flux, there are also individual differences in what is regarded as notable, what is considered most likely to be threatening, and so on. Viewed in terms of attachment dynamics, preoccupieds are highly vigilant about possible rejection, neglect, or abandonment, and so are likely to notice their partner's whereabouts and interests in other people, which primes them for frequent feelings of anxiety and jealousy. Dismissings are less likely to monitor the presence or whereabouts of their relationship partners and hence are less likely to become emotional. Less is known about fearful avoidants, but we suspect that they monitor their partners' comings and goings while attempting to suppress the resulting emotions (suppression being a form of emotion regulation; see later). Secures probably notice their partners' actions but generally appraise them in nonthreatening ways, thereby producing positive or neutral rather than negative emotional reactions. The same kind of analysis could be focused on notable changes in the self. Dismissings, for example, attempt to ignore their own emotional reactions; preoccupieds are overly sensitive to their own reactions.

Appraisal

Emotion results from an appraisal of events in relation to a wish or goal. David wants Helen to admire his work; he eagerly studies her reaction and appraises it as indicating that his wish is not fulfilled—she doesn't seem to care. Suppose David had perceived things differently: Helen's lack of interest in his work means nothing about her feelings for him. Such changes in the appraisal process make all the difference for the resulting emotion. In the study of attachment, the role of appraisals can most easily be seen in relation to anxious–ambivalent, or preoccupied, individuals. Their vigilance is an indication that they lean toward a particular interpretation: "He or she is leaving me, cares more for someone else, will lose interest if I don't make a scene." They easily become jealous because of this appraisal proclivity (Collins, 1994; Hazan & Shaver, 1987; Pietromonaco & Carnelley, 1994). Secure individuals also lean toward certain kinds of appraisals: "Other people are trustworthy, I am likeable, I don't need to be unduly vigilant" (Hazan & Shaver, 1987). Lying behind dismissing avoidance there is probably a complex network of beliefs: "If I get too close, I am bound to be hurt; life is better when one doesn't risk deep involvement; life is safest when one relies on oneself." In other words, even though the defenses (coping strategies) of dismissing individuals are perhaps their most distinctive characteristic, the defenses are closely tied to beliefs and appraisals contained in internal working models. What characterizes fearfuls is a model-based appraisal of the self as relatively helpless and hopeless, the kind of appraisal that generates sadness and depression.

Emotion-Specific Action Tendencies

According to the consensus theory (as spelled out, e.g., by Lazarus, 1991; Shaver, Schwartz, Kirson, & O'Connor, 1987), particular appraisals evoke particular emotions. For example, fear is elicited by a perceived threat to life or personal safety, including the threat of physical harm or social rejection. Sadness is caused by irrevocable loss or failure—the perception of harm already done. Anger stems from the appraisal that one's legitimate goals are being interfered with or one's legitimate status is being denied or demeaned. Joy arises from the appraisal of success or of being liked, loved, or appreciated. And so on. In other words, preceding each discrete emotion in most real-life situations is a particular, potentially identifiable constellation of appraisals that directly triggers the emotion (presumably because of innate neural circuits; Ekman, 1984; Panksepp, 1990). The emotion can be viewed as a functional, or at least generally functional, response to the events being appraised: preparation for fight or flight, abandonment of fruitless protest in the face of loss and failure, or consolidation of successful thoughts and behaviors following success.

According to the consensus theory of emotion, the link between appraisals and emotion-specific action tendencies is cross-culturally universal (Lazarus, 1991; Shaver, Wu, & Schwartz, 1992). Thus, attachment-related individual differences must be attributed to differences in wishes, appraisals, or defensive maneuvers—all aspects of internal working models—not to the link between appraisals, once made, and the consequent universal action tendencies.

Actions, Feelings, and Labels

If not interfered with by coping or defensive processes, emotional action tendencies and their physiological supports will be expressed in behavior and experienced or noticed in a variety of ways—facial expressions, vocal qualities, gestures, self-perception of autonomic changes, and self-labeling of emotional states. What Ekman (1984) called "display" rules can affect this process, as can what Hochschild (1983) called *emotion work*. These authors were thinking primarily about cultural and subcultural norms when they invented these terms (e.g., crying at funerals, smiling when one's photograph is taken, acting angry when working as a bill collector). But there are ideographic versions of these processes as well, including the suppression of feelings and expressions of vulnerability, and exaggerating one's feelings of jealousy. These personal feeling rules are, according to attachment theory, adopted in response to

certain patterns of parental behavior. If expressions of neediness and vulnerability result in rejection, as occurs in the early lives of avoidant children, a
child learns to suppress those feelings. If such expressions result in the receipt
of attention from an otherwise unreliable caregiver, an infant learns to
exaggerate them, as can be seen in the case of anxious–ambivalence. If a
caregiver seems to respond appropriately to whatever feeling is naturally
expressed, an infant has no need to learn how to distort the expression and
experience of emotion. The result is the coherent emotional discourse and
coherence of mind characteristic of securely attached children.

Coping, Affect Regulation

Emotion can be regulated by the application of defenses and coping strategies
at every point in the process diagrammed in Fig. 2.1. The "coping,
self-control" box in the figure refers to the kinds of processes that psychoanalysts since Freud have called *defenses* and that contemporary researchers,
following Folkman and Lazarus (1990), call *coping mechanisms*. These regulatory processes are indicated by dotted lines in Figure 1. Emotional outcomes
can be altered by changing one's wishes or the degree to which wishes are
allowed to become conscious, or they can be altered by failing to scan certain
aspects of the environment or by attending to certain aspects more vigilantly.
Appraisals can be altered in countless ways—by reinterpreting a partner's
intentions or reassigning blame, by deciding that something that seemed
threatening is actually benign, and so on. Emotional action tendencies and
their expression can be suppressed or countered with opposing tendencies,
and feelings can be ignored or labeled in a variety of ways. People with
different attachment styles differ systematically in all of these respects.

   An interesting example is provided by an experimental study by Lutkenhaus, Grossmann, and Grossman (1985), in which they analyzed the affective
behavior of 3-year-olds who had been assessed in the Strange Situation with
their mothers at 12 months of age. An unfamiliar adult visitor played a
competitive game with the children while the children's emotional reactions
to winning and losing were noted. The avoidant children looked sad during
the game when they were losing, but they appeared to mask their sadness
after the game, when they were talking with the experimenter. (Some even
replaced sadness with smiles.) Children who were classified as securely
attached at 12 months of age freely displayed their sadness to the experimenter after a losing effort. As stated by Cassidy (1992), "It is striking that
this masking of true feelings of sadness is evident as early as 3 years of age. It
is also striking that this pattern of masking emotions is used so readily with a
new social partner, with someone with whom the child has no history of
social interaction" (p. 17).

   In summary, when viewed from the perspective of emotion-regulation processes, internal working models of self and others can be seen to contain or play a role in all of the components in Fig. 2.1: wishes, attentional strategies, appraisal proclivities, action tendencies, distortions and mislabeling of feelings, defenses, and coping efforts. Attachment styles themselves can be viewed as organized complexes of emotion-regulation processes, observable manifestations of experience-based internal working models.

RESEARCH STRATEGIES FOR STUDYING INTERNAL WORKING MODELS

At present, there are relatively few studies that directly examine the content, structure, and functioning of working models. In this final section, we briefly review the ways in which these topics have been studied and might be productively studied in the future. Two broad areas deserve attention. The first concerns the contents and structure of working models. Like all cognitive structures, internal working models are not observable or directly measurable. The general research strategy, then, is to focus on observable responses that are presumed to be shaped by, and reflective of, mental representations.

In the developmental literature, researchers have typically drawn inferences about the content of working models from infants' responses to structured laboratory settings. In addition, a number of projective measures have been developed to examine attachment representations in school-aged children; these include story completion exercises (Bretherton et al., 1989) and family drawings (Fury, 1993; Kaplan & Main, 1985, 1989). Of course, the drawback of these procedures is the difficulty of arriving at unambiguous interpretations of responses.

In the adult literature, researchers have begun their exploration of working models by asking people to report on their attachment-relevant beliefs, attitudes, expectations, and motives (e.g., Collins & Read, 1990; Hazan & Shaver, 1987; Mongrain & Emmons, 1993; Shaver et al., in press). The self-concept literature offers additional research strategies which may be useful for exploring the structural features of working models. For example, there are techniques to measure the complexity of working models (Linville, 1985), the clarity or certainty of one's image of self and others (Campbell, 1990; Kerr & Clark, 1994), and the degree to which positive and negative images are either integrated or compartmentalized within particular models or across different models (Showers, 1992). In addition, response-time measures (Baldwin, Fehr, Keedian, Seidel, & Thomson, 1993; Fazio, 1986; Markus, 1977) may be helpful for examining the strength and accessibility of particular models or model-based appraisals.

One shortcoming of many of these techniques is that they are limited to the aspects of working models that individuals can consciously observe and articulate. Thus, additional strategies are required to uncover unconscious or nonlinguistic components of working models. Slade (1993) inferred attachment-related defensive styles from Rorschach responses. Bartholomew (Bartholomew & Horowitz, 1991) and Main and her colleagues (1985) drew inferences about the nature of working models from interview protocols that focused not only on content but also on the coherence and quality of discourse. Other strategies include the recording of behavioral observations during laboratory interactions (e.g., Kobak & Hazan, 1991; Simpson et al., 1992) and the use of psychophysiological techniques to index nonconscious emotion-regulation strategies (e.g., Dozier & Kobak, 1992; Feeney & Kirkpatrick, 1994). Reponse-time methods, just referred to, can also be used to infer unconscious and automatic processes.

A second important topic for future research is the identification of the mechanisms through which working models operate. Although such mechanisms are only beginning to be studied in the adult attachment field, empirical work in social psychology more generally demonstrates that social cognition is heavily influenced by top–down, theory-driven processes in which existing goals, schemas, expectations, and attitudes shape the way people view new information (e.g., Bargh, 1984; Brewer, 1988; Devine, 1989; Eagly & Chaiken, 1993; Higgins et al., 1982; Markus & Sentis, 1982). Although much of this research involves thinking about strangers, the processes involved are increasingly being explored in the context of close relationships (e.g., Baldwin, 1992; Fletcher & Fitness, 1993; Holmes & Rempel, 1989; Planalp, 1985).

There is good reason to believe that internal working models will shape the way people construe their social world, and recent studies support this belief. In two laboratory studies, for example, Collins (1994) demonstrated that working models of attachment shape the way individuals explain and interpret events that occur in their relationships. Anxious adults, for example, tended to explain their partner's behavior in ways that reflect low self-worth, a lack of confidence in the partner's love, and low trust. In contrast, secure adults provided more benign explanations that tended to minimize the negative impact of the partner's behavior. The influence of working models on emotional responses was examined in a recent study by Pietromonaco and Carnelley (1994). In that study, adults with different attachment styles responded differently to a set of hypothetical relationship partners. Regardless of the partner's behavioral description, for instance, preoccupied subjects reported that they would feel more anxious and jealous in the imagined relationship. In a study by Dorfman Botens and Shaver (1994), college students with different attachment styles were asked to recall childhood emotional interactions with their mothers. Dismissing individuals recalled fewer emotional memories per unit time, and the events they remembered tended to occur at much later ages than the events recalled by secure individuals. This study indicates that the defensive aspects of working models can be measured. In a study by Clark et al. (1994), college students were asked to describe the interpersonal qualities they exhibit in interactions with various relationship partners—mother, father, lover, same-sex friend, and so on. These qualities were then judged by the students to be positive, negative, or neutral, and to be central or peripheral to the self. Secure and fearfully avoidant individuals differed powerfully in the extent to which negative interpersonal qualities were portrayed as central to self-structure.

CONCLUDING COMMENTS

Reaching beyond his training in psychoanalysis and object relations theory, Bowlby incorporated seminal ideas from ethology, cybernetic control theory, and cognitive and developmental psychology. Ainsworth, working closely with Bowlby, showed that his theory could be tested—in preliterate cultures (1967), in U.S. homes, and most tellingly, in the laboratory Strange Situation. Ainsworth's characterization of stable individual differences in attachment patterns during infancy set the stage for a continually expanding body of research on attachment patterns in childhood, adolescence, and adulthood.

Both Bowlby and Ainsworth attributed the relative stability of attachment patterns to cognitive representations of self and others called internal working models. Although this concept has been stretched almost to the breaking point—incorporating not only the descriptive and evaluative aspects of ordinary scripts and schemas, but also the defensive and adaptive aspects of emotion regulation, characteristic relational behavior patterns, and patterns of exploration—it is still a mainstay of attachment theory and research. We have tried to show how the concept of internal working models can be differentiated, brought into contact with ideas and measurement techniques from experimental social psychology, and integrated with the reigning theory of emotion. Attachment theory has already inspired hundreds of interesting studies, and it will continue to inspire valuable research if its central construct, internal working models, can be clarified, rendered conceptually more sophisticated, and operationalized in some of the ways suggested by contemporary social cognition researchers. We hope this chapter points fruitfully in some of the right directions.

REFERENCES

Ainsworth, M. D. S. (1967). *Infancy in Uganda: Infant care and the growth of love*. Baltimore, MD: Johns Hopkins University Press.

Ainsworth, M. D. S. (1982). Attachment: Retrospect and prospect. In C. M. Parkes &

J. Stevenson-Hinde (Eds.), *The place of attachment in human behavior* (pp. 3–30). New York: Basic Books.

Ainsworth, M. D. S., Blehar, M. C., Waters, E., & Wall, S. (1978). *Patterns of attachment: Assessed in the strange situation and at home.* Hillsdale, NJ: Lawrence Erlbaum Associates.

Ainsworth, M. D. S., & Bowlby, J. (1991). An ethological approach to personality development. *American Psychologist, 46,* 333–341.

Ainsworth, M. D. S., & Eichberg, C. (1991). Effects on infant-mother attachment of mother's unresolved loss of an attachment figure, or other traumatic experience. In C. M. Parkes, J. Stevenson-Hinde, & P. Marris (Eds.), *Attachment across the life cycle* (pp. 160–183). London: Tavistock.

Alexander, P. C. (1993). The differential effects of abuse characteristics and attachment in the prediction of long-term effects of sexual abuse. *Journal of Interpersonal Violence, 8,* 346–362.

Anderson, J. R. (1982). Acquisition of cognitive skills. *Psychological Review, 89,* 369–406.

Andersen, S. M., & Cole, S. W. (1990). "Do I know you?": The role of significant others in general social perception. *Journal of Personality and Social Psychology, 59,* 384–399.

Arend, R., Gove, F., & Sroufe, L. A. (1979). Continuity of individual adaptation from infancy to kindergarten: A predictive study of ego-resiliency and curiosity in preschoolers. *Child Development, 50,* 950–959.

Bakan, D. (1966). *The duality of existence.* Boston: Beacon Press.

Baldwin, M. W. (1992). Relational schemas and the processing of social information. *Psychological Bulletin, 112,* 461–484.

Baldwin, M. W., Fehr, B., Keedian, E., Seidel, M., & Thomson, D. W. (1993). An exploration of the relational schemata underlying attachment styles: Self-report and lexical decision approaches. *Personality and Social Psychology Bulletin, 19,* 746–754.

Bargh, J. A. (1984). Automatic and conscious processing of social information. In R. S. Wyer & T. K. Srull (Eds.), *Handbook of social cognition* (Vol. 3, pp. 1–44). Hillsdale, NJ: Lawrence Erlbaum Associates.

Bartholomew, K. (1990). Avoidance of intimacy: An attachment perspective. *Journal of Social and Personal Relationships, 7,* 147–178.

Bartholomew, K., & Horowitz, L. M. (1991). Attachment styles among young adults: A test of a four-category model. *Journal of Personality and Social Psychology, 61,* 226–244.

Bartholomew, K. (1993). *Interpersonal dependency and attachment in adulthood.* Unpublished manuscript, Simon Fraser University, Burnaby, British Columbia, Canada.

Bartholomew, K., & Perlman, D. (Eds.). (1994). *Advances in personal relationships* (Vol. 5). London: Jessica Kingsley.

Baxter, L. A. (1988). A dialectical perspective on communication strategies in relationship development. In S. Duck (Ed.), *Handbook of personal relationships* (pp. 257–273). New York: Wiley.

Belsky, J., & Nezworski, T. (Eds.). (1988). *Clinical implications of attachment theory.* Hillsdale, NJ: Lawrence Erlbaum Associates.

Bowlby, J. (1940). The influence of early environment in the development of neurosis and neurotic character. *International Journal of Psychoanalysis, 21,* 1–25.

Bowlby, J. (1969). *Attachment and loss: Vol. I. Attachment.* Middlesex, England: Penguin Books.

Bowlby, J. (1973). *Attachment and loss: Vol. II. Separation: Anxiety and anger.* New York: Basic Books.

Bowlby, J. (1979). *The making and breaking of affectional bonds.* London: Tavistock.

Bowlby, J. (1980). *Attachment and loss: Vol. III. Loss.* New York: Basic Books.

Bowlby, J. (1988). *A secure base: Parent–child attachment and healthy human development.* New York: Basic Books.

Brennan, K. A., Shaver, P. R., & Tobey, A. E. (1991). Attachment styles, gender, and parental problem drinking. *Journal of Social and Personal Relationships, 8,* 451–466.

Bretherton, I. (1985). Attachment theory: Retrospect and prospect. *Monographs for the Society for Research in Child Development, 50* (1–2), Serial No. 209, 3–35.

Bretherton, I. (1990). Open communication and internal working models: Their role in the development of attachment relationships. In R. A. Thompson (Ed.), *Nebraska symposium on motivation, Vol. 36: Socioemotional development* (pp. 57–113). Lincoln University of Nebraska Press.

Bretherton, I. (1991). Pouring new wine into old bottles: The social self as internal working model. In M. Gunnar & L. A. Sroufe (Eds.), *Minnesota symposium on child psychology, Vol. 23: Self processes in development* (pp. 1–41). Hillsdale, NJ: Lawrence Erlbaum Associates.

Bretherton, I. (1992). The origins of attachment theory: John Bowlby and Mary Ainsworth. *Developmental Psychology, 28,* 759–775.

Bretherton, I. (1993). From dialogue to internal working models: The co-construction of self in relationships. In C. A. Nelson (Ed.), *Minnesota symposium on child psychology, Vol. 26: Memory and affect in development* (pp. 237–263). Hillsdale, NJ: Lawrence Erlbaum Associates.

Bretherton, I., Biringen, Z., Ridgeway, D., Maslin, C., & Sherman, M. (1989). Attachment: A parental perspective. *Infant Mental Health Journal, 10,* 203–221.

Bretherton, I., & Waters, E. (Eds.). (1985). *Growing points of attachment theory and research. Monographs for the Society for Research in Child Development, 50* (1–2), Serial No. 209.

Brewer, M. B. (1988). A dual process model of impression formation. In T. K. Srull & R. S. Wyer, Jr. (Eds.), *Advances in social cognition* (Vol. 1, pp. 177–183). Hillsdale, NJ: Lawrence Erlbaum Associates.

Bridges, L. J., Connell, J. P., & Belsky, J. (1988). Similarities and differences in infant-mother and infant-father interaction in the strange situation: A component process analysis. *Developmental Psychology, 24,* 92–100.

Campbell, J. (1990). Self-esteem and clarity of the self-concept. *Journal of Personality and Social Psychology, 59,* 538–549.

Cantor, N., & Kihlstrom, J. F. (1985). Social intelligence: The cognitive basis of personality. In P. Shaver (Ed.), *Review of personality and social psychology* (Vol. 6, pp. 15–33). Beverly Hills, CA: Sage.

Cantor, N., & Mischel, W. (1979). Prototypes in person perception. In L. Berkowitz (Ed.), *Advances in experimental social psychology* (Vol. 12, pp. 3–52). New York: Academic Press.

Carlson, V., Cicchetti, D., Barnett, D., & Braunwald, D. (1989). Disorganized/ disoriented attachment relationships in maltreated infants. *Developmental Psychology, 25,* 525–531.

Carnelley, K. B., & Janoff-Bulman, R. (1992). Optimism about love relationships: General vs. specific lessons from one's personal experiences. *Journal of Social and Personal Relationships, 9,* 5–20.

Carnelley, K. B., & Pietromonaco, P. R. (1991, June). *Thinking about a romantic relationship: Attachment style and gender influence emotional reactions and perceptions.* Paper presented at the annual meeting of the American Psychological Society, Washington, DC.

Carnelley, K. B., Pietromonaco, P. R., & Jaffe, K. (1994). Depression, working models of others, and relationship functioning. *Journal of Personality and Social Psychology, 66,* 127–140.

Caspi, A., & Bem, D. J. (1990). Personality continuity and change across the life course. In L. A. Pervin (Ed.), *Handbook of personality theory and research* (pp. 549–575). New York: Guilford.

Cassidy, J. (1988). Child-mother attachment and the self in six-year-olds. *Child Development, 59,* 121–134.

Cassidy, J. (1992). *Emotion-regulation: Influences of attachment relationships* .Unpublished manuscript, Pennsylvania State University, University Park.

Cicchetti, D., Cummings, E. M., Greenberg, M. T., & Marvin, R. S. (1990). An organizational perspective on attachment beyond infancy. In M. T. Greenberg, D. Cicchetti, & E. M. Cummings (Eds.), *Attachment in the preschool years* (pp. 3–50). Chicago, IL: University of Chicago Press.

Clark, C. L., Shaver, P. R., & Calverley, R. M. (1994). *Adult attachment styles, remembered childhood abuse, and self-concept structure*. Paper presented at the annual meeting of the American Psychological Association, Los Angeles, CA.

Collins, N. L. (1994). *Attachment style differences in patterns of explanation, emotion, and behavior*. Unpublished manuscript, State University of New York, Buffalo.

Collins, N. L., & Read, S. J. (1990). Adult attachment, working models, and relationship quality in dating couples. *Journal of Personality and Social Psychology, 58*, 644–663.

Collins, N. L., & Read, S. J. (1994). Cognitive representations of attachment: The content and function of working models. In K. Bartholomew & D. Perlman (Eds.), *Advances in personal relationships* (Vol. 5, pp. 53–90). London: Jessica Kingsley.

Craik, K. J. W. (1943). *The nature of explanation*. London: Cambridge University Press.

Crittenden, P. M. (1988). Relationships at risk. In J. Belsky & T. Nezworski (Eds.), *Clinical implications of attachment* (pp. 136–174). Hillsdale, NJ: Lawrence Erlbaum Associates.

Crittenden, P. M. (1990). Internal representational models of attachment relationships. *Infant Mental Health Journal, 11*, 259–277.

Crittenden, P. M., Partridge, M. F., & Claussen, A. H. (1991). Family patterns of relationship in normative and dysfunctional families. *Development and Psychopathology, 3*, 491–512.

Cummings, E. M., & Cicchetti, D. (1990). Toward a transactional model of relations between attachment and depression. In M. T. Greenberg, D. Cicchetti, & E. M. Cummings (Eds.), *Attachment in the preschool years* (pp. 339–374). Chicago, IL: University of Chicago Press.

Daniels, T., & Shaver, P. R. (1991). *Attachment styles and power strategies in romantic relationships*. Unpublished manuscript, State University of New York at Buffalo.

Devine, P. G. (1989). Stereotypes and prejudice: Their automatic and controlled components. *Journal of Personality and Social Psychology, 56*, 5–18.

Dorfman Botens, D., & Shaver, P. R. (1994). *Adult attachment: Individual differences in defensive strategies and implications for physical health*. Unpublished manuscript, University of California, Davis.

Dozier, M., & Kobak, R. R. (1992). Psychophysiology and adolescent attachment interviews: Converging evidence for repressing strategies. *Child Development, 59*, 1273–1285.

Dutton, D. G., Saunders, K., Starzomski, A., & Bartholomew, K. (1994). Intimacy-anger and insecure attachment as precursors of abuse in intimate relationships. *Journal of Applied Social Psychology, 24*, 1367–1386.

Eagly, A. H., & Chaiken, S. (1993). *The psychology at attitudes*. Fort Worth, TX: Harcourt Brace Jovanovich.

Ekman, P. (1984). Expression and the nature of emotion. In K. R. Scherer & P. Ekman (Eds.), *Approaches to emotion* (pp. 319–343). Hillsdale, NJ: Lawrence Erlbaum Associates.

Egelund, B., & Sroufe, L. A. (1981). Developmental sequelae of maltreatment in infancy. In R. Rizley & D. Cicchetti (Eds.), *Developmental perspectives in child maltreatment* (pp. 77–92). San Francisco: Jossey-Bass.

Elicker, J., Englund, M., & Sroufe, L. A. (1992). Predicting peer competence and peer relationships in childhood from early parent–child relationships. In R. Parke & G. Ladd (Eds.), *Family–peer relations: Modes of linkage* (pp. 77–106). Hillsdale, NJ: Lawrence Erlbaum Associates.

Emmons, R. A. (1989). The personal striving approach to personality. In L. A. Pervin (Ed.), *Goal concepts in personality and social psychology* (pp. 87–125). Hillsdale, NJ: Lawrence Erlbaum Associates.

Fazio, R. H. (1986). How do attitudes guide behavior? In R. M. Sorrentino & E. T. Higgins (Eds.), *Handbook of motivation and cognition: Foundations of social behavior* (pp. 204–243). New York: Guilford.

Feeney, J. A., & Kirkpatrick, L. A. (1994). *Attachment and psychophysiology*. Unpublished manuscript, College of William and Mary, Williamsburg, VA.

Feeney, J. A., & Noller, P. (1990). Attachment style as a predictor of adult romantic relationships. *Journal of Personality and Social Psychology, 58*, 281–291.

Fischer, K. W., Shaver, P. R., & Carnochan, P. (1990). How emotions develop and how they organise development. *Cognition and Emotion, 4*, 81–127.

Fiske, S. T., & Pavelchak, M. A. (1986). Category-based versus piecemeal-based affective responses: Developments in schema-triggered affect. In R. M. Sorrentino & E. T. Higgins (Eds.), *Handbook of motivation and cognition: Foundations of social behavior* (pp. 167–203). New York: Guilford.

Fletcher, G. J. O. & Fitness, J. (1993). Knowledge structures and explanations in intimate relationships. In S. Duck (Ed.), *Individuals in relationships* (pp. 121–143). Newbury Park, CA: Sage.

Folkman, S., & Lazarus, R. S. (1990). Coping and emotion. In N. Stein, B. Leventhal, & T. Trabasso (Eds.), *Psychological and biological approaches to emotion* (pp. 313–332). Hillsdale, NJ: Lawrence Erlbaum Associates.

Fonagy, P., Steele, H., & Steele, M. (1991). Maternal representations of attachment during pregnancy predict the organization of infant-mother attachment at one year of age. *Child Development, 62*, 891–905.

Fox, N. A., Kimmerly, N. L., & Schafer, W. D. (1991). Attachment to mother/attachment to father: A meta-analysis. *Child Development, 62*, 210–225.

Fury, G. S. (1993, March). *The relation between infant attachment history and representations of relationships in school-aged family drawings.* Paper presented at the biennial meeting of the Society for Research in Child Development, New Orleans, LA.

George, C., Kaplan, N., & Main, M. (1985). *The Berkeley Adult Attachment Interview.* Unpublished protocol, University of California, Berkeley.

George, C., & Solomon, J. (1989). Internal working models of parenting and security of attachment at age six. *Infant Mental Health Journal, 10*, 222–237.

Greenberg, J., & Mitchell, S. (1983). *Object relations in psychoanalytic theory.* Cambridge, MA: Harvard University Press.

Greenberg, M. T., Cicchetti, D., & Cummings, E. M. (Eds.). (1990). *Attachment in the preschool years: Theory, research, and intervention.* Chicago, IL: University of Chicago Press.

Greenwald, A., & Pratkanis, A. (1984). The self. In R. S. Wyer, Jr. & T. K. Srull (Eds.), *Handbook of social cognition* (Vol. 3, pp. 129–178). Hillsdale, NJ: Lawrence Erlbaum Associates.

Grossmann, K. E., Grossmann, K., & Schwan, A. (1986). Capturing the wider view of attachment: A reanalysis of Ainsworth's Strange Situation. In C. E. Izard & P. B. Read (Eds.), *Measuring emotions in infants and children* (pp. 124–171). New York: Cambridge University Press.

Hazan, C., & Hutt, M. (1993). *Patterns of adaptation: Attachment differences in psychosocial functioning during the first year of college.* Unpublished manuscript, Cornell University, Ithaca, New York.

Hazan, C., & Shaver, P. R. (1987). Romantic love conceptualized as an attachment process. *Journal of Personality and Social Psychology, 52*, 511–524.

Hazan, C., & Shaver, P. R. (1990). Love and work: An attachment-theoretical perspective. *Journal of Personality and Social Psychology, 59*, 270–280.

Hazan, C., & Shaver, P. R. (1994a). Attachment as an organizational framework for research on close relationships. *Psychological Inquiry, 5*, 1–22.

Hazan, C., & Shaver, P. R. (1994b). Deeper into attachment theory. *Psychological Inquiry, 5*, 68–79.

Higgins, E. T., King, G. A., & Mavin, G. H. (1982). Individual construct accessibility and subjective impressions and recall. *Journal of Personality and Social Psychology, 43*, 35–47.

Hochschild, A. (1983). *The managed heart: The commercialization of human feeling.* Berkeley: University of California Press.

Holland, J. H., Holyoak, K. J., Nisbett, R. E., & Thagard, P. R. (1986). *Induction: Processes of inference, learning, and discovery*. Cambridge, MA: MIT Press.

Holmes, J. G., & Rempel, J. K. (1989). Trust in close relationships. In C. Hendrick (Ed.), *Review of personality and social psychology: Vol. 10, Close relationships* (pp. 187–220). London: Sage.

Jacobsen, T., Edelstein, W., & Hofmann, V. (1994). A longitudinal study of the relation between representations of attachment in childhood and cognitive functioning in childhood and adolescence. *Developmental Psychology, 30,* 112–124.

Jones, E. E. (1990). *Interpersonal perception*. New York: Freeman.

Kaplan, N., & Main, M. (1985, April). *Internal representations of attachment at six years as indicated by family drawing and verbal responses to imagined separations*. Paper presented at the biennial meeting of the Society for Research in Child Devleopment, Toronto, Canada.

Kaplan, N., & Main, M. (1989). *A system for the analysis of family drawings*. Unpublished manuscript, University of California, Berkeley.

Karen, R. (1994). *Becoming attached: Unfolding the mystery of the infant's-mother bond and its impact on later life*. New York: Warner Books.

Keelan, J. P. R., Dion, K. L., & Dion, K. K. (1994). Attachment style and heterosexual relationships among young adults: A short-term panel study. *Journal of Social and Personal Relationships, 11,* 201–214.

Kerr, K. L., & Clark, C. L. (1994). *Clarity of representations of self and others: An attachment-theoretical approach*. Unpublished manuscript, State University of New York, Buffalo.

Kihlstrom, J. F., & Cantor, N. (1983). Mental representations of the self. In L. Berkowitz (Ed.), *Advances in experimental social psychology* (Vol. 17, pp. 1–47). San Diego, CA: Academic Press.

Kirkpatrick, L. A., & Davis, K. E. (1994). Attachment style, gender, and relationship stability: A longitudinal analysis. *Journal of Personality and Social Psychology, 66,* 502–512.

Kirkpatrick, L. A., & Hazan, C. (1994). Attachment styles and close relationships: A four-year prospective study. *Personal Relationships, 1,* 123–142.

Kirkpatrick, L. A., & Shaver, P. R. (1990). Attachment theory and religion: Childhood attachments, religious beliefs, and conversion. *Journal for the Scientific Study of Religion, 29,* 315–334.

Kirkpatrick, L. A., & Shaver, P. R. (1992). An attachment-theoretical approach to romantic love and religious belief. *Personality and Social Psychology Bulletin, 18,* 266–275.

Kobak, R. R., & Hazan, C. (1991). Attachment in marriage: The effects of security and accuracy of working models. *Journal of Personality and Social Psychology, 60,* 861–869.

Kobak, R., & Sceery, A. (1988). Attachment in late adolescence: Working models, affect regulation, and representations of self and others. *Child Development, 59,* 135–146.

Kunce, L. J., & Shaver, P. R. (1994). An attachment-theoretical approach to caregiving in romantic relationships. In K. Bartholomew & D. Perlman (Eds.), *Advances in personal relationships* (Vol. 5, pp. 205–237). London: Jessica Kingsley.

LaFreniere, P., & Sroufe, L. A. (1985). Profiles of peer competence in the preschool: Interrelations between measures, influence of social ecology, and relation to attachment history. *Developmental Psychology, 21,* 56–69.

Lamb, M. E. (1978). Qualitative aspects of mother–infant and father–infant attachments. *Infant Behavior and Development, 1,* 265–275.

Lamb, M. E., Thompson, R. A., Gardner, W., & Charnov, E. L. (1985). *Infant–mother attachment: The origin and developmental significance of individual differences in Strange Situation behavior*. Hillsdale, NJ: Lawrence Erlbaum Associates.

Lazarus, R. S. (1991). *Emotion and adaptation*. New York: Oxford University Press.

Levy, K. N., Blatt, S.J., & Shaver, P. R. (1994). *Attachment styles and representations in young adults*. Unpubished manuscript, Yale University, New Haven, CT.

Linville, P. W. (1985). Self-complexity and affective extremity: Don't put all of your eggs in one cognitive basket. *Social Cognition, 3,* 94–130.

Luborsky, L., & Crits-Christoph, P. (Eds.). (1990). *Understanding transference: The CCRT method.* New York: Basic Books.

Lutkenhaus, P., Grossmann, K. E., & Grossmann, K. (1985). Infant-mother attachment at 12 months and style of interaction with a stranger at the age of 3 years. *Child Development, 56,* 1538–1572.

Mahler, M., Pine, R., & Bergman, A. (1975). *The psychological birth of the human infant.* New York: Basic Books.

Main, M., (1990). Parental aversion to infant-initiated contact is correlated with the parent's own rejection during childhood: The effects of experience on signals of security with respect to attachment. In K. E. Barnard & T. B. Brazelton (Eds.), *Touch: The foundation of experience* (pp. 461–495). Madison, CT: International Universities Press.

Main, M. (1991). Metacognitive knowledge, metacognitive monitoring, and singular (coherent) vs. multiple (incoherent) model of attachment. In C. M. Parkes, J. Stevenson-Hinde, & P. Marris (Eds.), *Attachment across the life cycle* (pp. 127–159). New York: Routledge.

Main, M., & Cassidy, J. (1988). Categories of response to reunion with the parent at age six: Predictable from infant attachment classification and stable over a one-month period. *Developmental Psychology, 24,* 415–426.

Main, M., & Hesse, E. (1990). Parents' unresolved traumatic experiences are related to infant disorganized status: Is frightened and/or frightening parental behavior the linking mechanism? In M. T. Greenberg, D. Cicchetti, & E. M. Cummings (Eds.), *Attachment in the preschool years* (pp. 161–184). Chicago, IL: University of Chicago Press.

Main, M., Kaplan, N., & Cassidy, J. (1985). Security in infancy, childhood, and adulthood: A move to the level of representation. *Monographs of the Society for Research in Child Development, 50,* (1–2), Serial No. 209, 66–104.

Main, M., & Solomon, J. (1986). Discovery of a new, insecure-disorganized/disoriented attachment pattern. In M. Yogman & T. B. Brazelton (Eds.), *Affective development in infancy* (pp. 95–124). Norwood, NJ: Ablex.

Main, M., & Solomon, J. (1990). Procedures for identifying infants as disorganized/disoriented during the Ainsworth Strange Situation. In M. T. Greenberg, D. Cicchetti, & E. M. Cummings (Eds.), *Attachment in the preschool years* (pp. 121–160). Chicago, IL: University of Chicago Press.

Main, M., & Weston, D. (1981). The quality of the toddler's relationship to mother and to father: Related to conflict behavior and the readiness to establish new relationships. *Child Development, 52,* 932–940.

Markus, H. (1977). Self-schemata and processing information about the self. *Journal of Personality and Social Psychology, 35,* 63–78.

Markus, H., & Ruvolo, A. (1989). Possible selves: Personalized representations of goals. In L. A. Pervin (Ed.), *Goal concepts in personality and social psychology* (pp. 211–242). Hillsdale: Lawrence Erlbaum Associates.

Markus, H., & Sentis, K. P. (1982). The self in social information processing. In J. Suls (Ed.), *Psychological perspectives on the self* (Vol. 1, pp. 41–70). Hillsdale, NJ: Lawrence Erlbaum Associates.

Markus, H., & Wurf, E. (1987). The dynamic self-concept: A social psychological perspective. *Annual Review of Psychology, 38,* 299–337.

Matas, L., Arend, R., & Sroufe, L. A. (1978). Continuity of adaptation in the second year: The relationship between quality of attachment and later competence. *Child Development, 49,* 547–556.

Mikulincer, M., Florian, V., & Tolmacz, R. (1990). Attachment styles and fear of personal death: A case study of affect regulation. *Journal of Personality and Social Psychology, 58,* 273–280.

Mikulincer, M., Florian, V., & Weller, A. (1993). Attachment styles, coping strategies, and posttraumatic psychological distress: The impact of the Gulf War in Israel. *Journal of Personality and Social Psychology, 64,* 817–826.

Mikulincer, M., & Nachshon, O. (1991). Attachment styles and patterns of self-disclosure. *Journal of Personality and Social Psychology, 61,* 321–331.

Miller, L. C., & Read, S. J. (1991). Inter-personalism: Understanding persons in relationships. In W. Jones & D. Perlman (Eds.), *Advances in personal relationships* (Vol. 2, pp. 233–267). London: Jessica Kingsley.

Mongrain, M., & Emmons, R. A. (1993, April). *Personal strivings and attachment: A goal-based analysis of attachment styles.* Paper presented at the annual meeting of the American Psychological Society, Chicago, IL.

Ogilvie, D. M., & Ashmore, R. D. (1991). Self-with-other representation as a unit of analysis in self-concept research. In R. C. Curtis (Ed.), *The relational self: Theoretical convergences in psychoanalysis and social psychology* (pp. 282–314). New York: Guilford.

Pancake, V. R. (1989). *Quality of attachment in infancy as a predictor of hostility and emotional distance in preschool peer relationships.* Unpublished doctoral dissertation, University of Minnesota, Minneapolis.

Panksepp, J. (1990). The neurobiology of emotions: Of animal brains and human feelings. In H. Wagner & A. Manstead (Eds.), *Handbook of social psychophysiology* (pp. 5–26).New York: Wiley.

Parkes, C. M., Stevenson-Hinde, J., & Marris, P.(Eds.). (1991). *Attachment across the life cycle.* London: Tavistock.

Paterson, P. J., & Moran, G. (1988). Attachment theory, personality development, and psychotherapy. *Clinical Psychology Review, 8,* 611–636.

Pervin, L. A. (1983). The stasis and flow of behavior: Toward a theory of goals. In M. Page (Ed.), *Personality: Current theory and research* (pp. 1–53). Lincoln: University of Nebraska Press.

Pietromonaco, P. R., Carnelley, K. B. (1994). Gender and working models of attachment: Consequences for perceptions of self and romantic relationships. *Personal Relationships, 1,* 63–82.

Pistole, C. (1989). Attachment in adult romantic relationships: Style of conflict resolution and relationship satisfaction. *Journal of Social and Personal Relationships, 6,* 505–510.

Planalp, S. (1985). Relational schemata: A test of alternative forms of relational knowledge as guides to communication. *Human Communication Research, 12,* 3–29.

Pottharst, K. (Ed.). (1990). *Research explorations in adult attachment.* New York: Peter Lang.

Rothbard, J. C., & Shaver, P. R. (1994). Continuity of attachment across the lifecourse: An attachment-theoretical perspective on personality. In M. B. Sperling & W. H. Berman (Eds.), *Attachment in adults: Theory, assessment, and treatment* (pp. 31–71). New York: Guilford.

Shaver, P. R., & Brennan, K. A. (1992). Attachment styles and the "big five" personality traits: Their connections with each other and with romantic relationship outcomes. *Personality and Social Psychology Bulletin, 18,* 536–545.

Shaver, P. R., & Clark, C. L. (1994). The psychodynamics of adult romantic attachment. In J. M. Masling & R. F. Bornstein (Eds.), *Empirical perspectives on object relations theory* (pp. 105–156). Washington, DC: APA Books.

Shaver, P. R., & Hazan, C. (1993). Adult romantic attachment: Theory and evidence. In D. Perlman & W. H. Jones (Eds.), *Advances in personal relationships* (Vol. 4, pp. 29–70). London, England: Jessica Kingsley.

Shaver, P. R. Hazan, C., & Bradshaw, D. (1988). Love as attachment: The integration of three behavioral systems. In R. J. Sternberg & M. L. Barnes (Eds.), *The psychology of love* (pp. 68–99). New Haven, CT: Yale University Press.

Shaver, P. R., Papalia, D., Clark, C. L., Koski, L. R., Tidwell, M., & Nalbone, D. (in press). Androgyny and attachment security: Two models of optimal personality. *Personality and Social Psychology Bulletin.*

Shaver, P. R., Schwartz, J., Kirson, D., & O'Connor, C. (1987). Emotion knowledge: Further exploration of a prototype approach. *Journal of Personality and Social Psychology, 52,* 1061–1086.

Shaver, P. R., Wu, S., & Schwartz, J. C. (1992). Cross-cultural similarities and differences in emotion and its representation. In M. S. Clark (Ed.), *Emotion,* Vol. 4: *Review of personality and social psychology* (pp. 175–212). London: Sage.

Showers, C. (1992). Evaluatively integrative thinking about characteristics of the self. *Personality and Social Psychology Bulletin, 18,* 719–729.

Simpson, J. A. (1990). The influence of attachment style on romantic relationships. *Journal of Personality and Social Psychology, 59,* 971–980.

Simpson, J. A., Rholes, W. S., & Nelligan, J. S. (1992). Support seeking and support giving within couples in an anxiety-provoking situation: The role of attachment styles. *Journal of Personality and Social Psychology, 62,* 434–446.

Slade, A. (1993, March). *Affect-regulation and defense: Clinical and theoretical considerations.* Paper presented at the biennial meeting of the Society for Research in Child Development, New Orleans, LA.

Sperling, M. B., & Berman, E. H. (Eds.). (1994). Continuity of attachment across the lifecourse: An attachment-theoretical perspective on personality. *Attachment in adults: Theory, assessment, and treatment.* New York: Guilford.

Sroufe, L. A., Carlson, E., & Shulman, S. (1993). Individuals in relationships: Development from infancy through adolescence. In D. C. Funder, R. D. Parke, C. Tomlinson-Keasey, & K. Widman (Eds.), *Studying lives through time* (pp. 315–342). Washington, DC: American Psychological Association.

Sroufe, L. A., & Fleeson, J. (1988). The coherence of family relationships. In R. A. Hinde & J. Stevenson-Hinde (Eds.), *Relationships within families: Mutual influences* (pp. 27–47). Oxford, England: Oxford University Press.

Sroufe, L. A., & Waters, E. (1977). Heart rate as a convergent measure in clinical and developmental research. *Merrill-Palmer Quarterly, 23,* 3–27.

Stern, D. N. (1985). *The interpersonal world of the infant.* New York: Basic Books.

Tidwell, M., Shaver, P. R., Lin, Y., & Reis, H. T. (1991, April). *Attachment, attractiveness, and daily social interactions.* Paper presented at the annual meeting of the Eastern Psychological Association, New York.

Troy, M., & Sroufe, L. A. (1987). Victimization among preschoolers: The role of attachment relationship history. *Journal of the American Academy of Child and Adolescent Psychiatry, 26,* 166–172.

Trzebinski, J. (1989). The role of goal categories in the representation of social knowledge. In L. A. Pervin (Ed.), *Goal concepts in personality and social psychology* (pp. 363–411). Hillsdale, NJ: Lawrence Erlbaum Associates.

Tulving, E. (1985). How many memory systems are there? *American Psychologist, 40,* 385–398.

Young, J. Z. (1964). *A model of the brain.* London: Oxford University Press.

3

An Interdependence Analysis of Accommodation Processes

Caryl E. Rusbult
Nancy A. Yovetich
Julie Verette
University of North Carolina at Chapel Hill

Few relationships ride an ever-increasing wave of uninterrupted bliss. The health and vitality of an ongoing relationship may be challenged not only by external threats such as the presence of a tempting alternative, but also by threats internal to the relationship itself—threats such as satiation or boredom, disagreement regarding central life issues, or destructive interaction sequences initiated by the hostile acts of one or both partners. This chapter addresses one important threat to couple adjustment, reviewing research and theory regarding an interaction pattern termed *accommodation*. This interaction phenomenon involves a sequence of interdependent responding that is initiated when one interacting partner engages in a potentially destructive act—for example, when the partner is rude or thoughtless, behaves in an inconsiderate manner, belittles or humiliates the individual, or worse. Accommodation refers to the individual's willingness to inhibit the impulse to respond destructively in kind, instead reacting in a constructive manner.

Our analysis of accommodation is based on the principles and constructs of interdependence theory (H. Kelley, 1979; H. Kelley & Thibaut, 1978; Thibaut & Kelley, 1959), and rests on the assumption that although accommodative behavior promotes couple well-being, such acts frequently are personally costly and effortful. Thus, to understand how couples sustain long-term, healthy functioning, we must explain how and why partners become willing to depart from their direct, self-interested preferences, instead coming to place greater value on pro-relationship behavior—behavior that will solve the partners' interaction problem and promote couple well-being. The psychological process by which individuals come to forego self-interested behavior for the good of a relationship involves transformation of motivation. The transformation process is most directly shaped by the emotional reactions and cognitive interpretations that accompany a given interaction problem; this process is indirectly shaped by more distal determinants, including interpersonal dispositions, relationship-specific macromotives, and social norms.

The chapter begins with a brief review of the existing empirical literature on couple interaction processes—a review that serves as the springboard for introducing the exit–voice–loyalty–neglect (ELVN) typology of interaction behaviors. This is followed by a discussion of the interdependence structure of accommodative dilemmas, addressing the manner in which close partners' direct, self-interested inclinations are sometimes transformed into benevolent, pro-relationship preferences. The determinants of pro-relationship transformation are then reviewed, including (a) distal determinants that color interpersonal motivation, including three forms of interpersonal orientation—interpersonal dispositions, relationship-specific macromotives, and social norms; and (b) proximal determinants such as the emotional reactions and cognitive interpretations that accompany a given interaction. In a concluding section we consider fruitful directions for future research.

COUPLE INTERACTION PROCESSES AND THE EXIT–VOICE–LOYALTY–NEGLECT TYPOLOGY

Many social scientists have attempted to determine what distressed couples do that nondistressed couples do not do (and vice versa). The existing literature on couple functioning has emphasized the role of interaction processes in shaping couple well-being (Geiss & O'Leary, 1981; Hayes, Chavez, & Samuel, 1984; Markman, 1981; Noller, 1980). For example, in comparison to nondistressed couples, distressed couples enact a greater number of negative communicative acts (e.g., Jacobson, Follette, & McDonald, 1982; Wills, Weiss, & Patterson, 1974), exhibit poorer problem-solving abilities (e.g., Billings, 1979; Margolin & Wampold, 1981), and enjoy fewer shared interests (e.g., Argyle & Furnham, 1983; Sullaway & Christensen, 1983). In addition, researchers studying more complex interaction sequences demonstrated that distressed couples are more reactive to recent events in the relationship (e.g., Jacobson et al., 1982), display less responsiveness to their partners' attempts at persuasion (e.g., Koren, Carlton, & Shaw, 1980), and exhibit greater negative reciprocity over the course of interaction (e.g., Billings, 1979; Gottman, Markman, & Notarius, 1977; Schaap, 1984). Moreover, some researchers have implicated individual-level dispositions as contributing factors in the emergence of troubled interaction patterns, including such traits as neuroticism and weak impulse control (e.g., E. Kelley & Conley, 1987; Kurdek, 1993).

Unfortunately, the literature on interaction processes is limited in several respects. First, much of the existing research explores behavior during the course of specific conflicted interactions (e.g., a 10-minute simulated argument). However, many problems interdependent partners confront do not involve overt disagreement (e.g., "I'm afraid my partner doesn't love me enough"), and in everyday life partners often react in ways that circumvent overt conflict (e.g., quietly forgiving and forgetting). Second, the literature has tended to place inappropriate emphasis on verbal exchanges. Some interaction behaviors may not appear in a simulated conversation because they do not involve talk (e.g., ignoring the partner by watching television). And third, few researchers have studied couple processes using theoretically based taxonomies of interaction behavior. We believe that the best route to understanding the fundamental principles of interaction rests on the application of a comprehensive typology of responses that are known to differ along theoretically meaningful dimensions.

The EVLN typology was developed in response to these concerns (Rusbult, Zembrodt, & Gunn, 1982). The EVLN model serves an integrative function by identifying systematic links among the full range of available interaction behaviors, identifying four primary categories of response (Rusbult & Zembrodt, 1983):

Exit: actively harming or terminating a relationship (e.g., separating, abusing the partner physically or emotionally, screaming at the partner, threatening to leave);

Voice: actively and constructively attempting to improve conditions (e.g., discussing problems, changing oneself or urging the partner to change, seeking advice from a friend or therapist);

Loyalty: passively but optimistically waiting for conditions to improve (e.g., waiting and hoping that things will improve, supporting the partner in the face of criticism, praying for improvement); and

Neglect: passively allowing conditions to deteriorate (e.g., refusing to deal with problems, ignoring the partner or spending less time together, criticizing the partner for unrelated matters, letting things fall apart).

The EVLN response categories differ along two dimensions, as displayed in Fig. 3.1. First, the response categories differ in constructiveness versus destructiveness—voice and loyalty serve to sustain or revive a relationship, whereas exit and neglect are relatively more destructive to couple well-being. Here, we refer to the impact of a response on the relationship, not to its impact on the individual. For example, exit reactions clearly are destructive to relationships, even though this type of response might be healthy for an

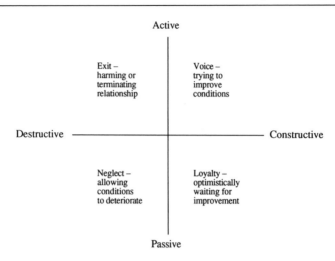

FIG. 3.1. The exit–voice–loyalty–neglect typology.

individual who is involved in deeply troubled relationship. Second, the response categories differ in activity versus passivity. Exit and voice involve direct action with respect to a problem (i.e., repairing the relationship or destroying it), whereas neglect and loyalty are relatively more passive with regard to the problem at hand. Here, we refer to the impact of a response on the couple's interaction problem, not to the overt character of the behavior itself. For example, leaving the room so as to avoid an argument involves overt action, but this response is passively neglectful with regard to the couple's problem.

Early research employing the EVLN typology sought to identify the predictors of reach response, demonstrating that response tendencies are shaped not only by broad qualities of interdependent relationships (e.g., commitment level) but also by individual-level dispositions (e.g., psychological femininity; Rusbult, Johnson, & Morrow, 1986a; Rusbult, Morrow, & Johnson, 1987; Rusbult et al., 1982; Rusbult, Zembrodt, & Iwaniszek, 1986; for reviews, see Rusbult, 1987, 1993). Early work on the EVLN model also assessed the functional value of the four responses, examining their links with healthy couple functioning (Rusbult, Johnson, & Morrow, 1986b). This research revealed two important interaction regularities, the first of which is termed the *good manners* principle: Examining absolute frequencies of behavior from the four categories (i.e., ignoring sequential patterns of interaction), it becomes apparent that whereas destructive responses (exit and neglect) are exceptionally harmful to couple functioning, constructive responses (voice and loyalty) are not commensurately promotive of healthy functioning. Thus, close partners would do well to maintain "good manners," behaving in a consistently constructive manner toward one another.

Unfortunately, close partners do not exhibit uniformly good manners. Accordingly, this research examined sequences of interdependent responding, focusing on the contingent effects of each category of response (e.g., when one partner "behaves badly," what is the impact of a voice reaction?). This analysis revealed a second important interaction principle termed *accommodation*: When a partner has behaved constructively (voice or loyalty), the individual's reaction is only weakly related to couple functioning. In contrast, when a partner has behaved destructively (exit or neglect), couple functioning is enhanced when individuals inhibit their tendencies to react destructively, instead behaving in a constructive manner. Congruent with our earlier definition, accommodation is operationally defined as the tendency— when a partner engages in a potentially destructive act (exit or neglect)—to (a) inhibit impulses to react destructively (inhibit exit and neglect) and (b) instead react in a constructive manner (engage in voice or loyalty).

Other researchers studying couple functioning have observed similar phenomena, demonstrating that in comparison to nondistressed couples, distressed partners exhibit greater levels of "negative reciprocity," or lesser tendencies to "sidetrack or diminish negative affect chains" (e.g., Billings, 1979; Gottman & Krokoff, 1989; Gottman et al., 1977; Greenshaft, 1980; Margolin & Wampold, 1981). However, previous research has tended to describe the interaction patterns associated with healthy functioning rather than attempting to understand why couples behave as they do. Thus, one important goal in our research program is to develop a theoretical understanding of the dynamics by which individuals come to accommodate rather than retaliate when a partner behaves poorly. This analysis is founded on the interdependence concept of transformation of motivation.

THE GIVEN MATRIX, THE EFFECTIVE MATRIX, AND TRANSFORMATION OF MOTIVATION

Our analysis attempts to understand and explain accommodation using the interdependence theory distinction between given matrix and effective matrix interaction preferences. The theory employs matrices as tools for representing the structure of individuals' preferences and choices in interdependent situations—situations in which each actor's behavior has relevance for the outcomes of the other. For example, Fig. 3.2 portrays a situation in which each partner can enact either a constructive or a destructive act. Partner A's feelings about each possible joint outcome are listed above the diagonal in each cell of the matrix; Partner B's feelings are listed below the diagonal. Given that the accommodative dilemma is instigated by one partner's potentially destructive act, the Fig. 3.2 matrices focus on the portion of the

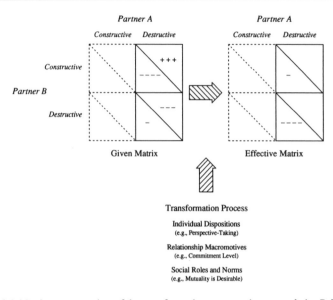

FIG. 3.2.Matrix representation of the transformation process. Accommodative Behavior: Transformation of Motivation in Reaction to Partner A's Destructive Act—Partner B's Max Joint Transformation.

response domain where Partner A has behaved destructively (i.e., the right-hand columns of the matrices).

Given Matrix Interaction Preferences

Given matrix preferences depict the structure of the interdependence situation from a self-interested perspective, representing partners' direct, self-oriented feelings about various joint outcomes. The pattern of outcomes in the given matrix portrays each partner's preferences taking into account their "gut-level" interpretations of the situation. As illustrated in the Fig. 3.2 given matrix (see matrix on left), when Partner A is upset or irritated and engages in a destructive act—thereby moving the partners to the right-hand column of interdependent response options—Partner B's direct, self-interested impulse to some degree favors reacting destructively rather than constructively (compare preferences for the upper and lower rows of the right-hand column of the given matrix): Partner A's destructive act may make Partner B feel angry, diminished, put upon, or otherwise distressed, and under these circumstances, reacting constructively is likely to seem more humiliating and less satisfying (upper row of the given matrix, – – – –) than is "getting it out of one's system" by reacting destructively in kind (lower row of the given matrix, −). Note that this is a no-win situation for Partner B: Although retaliation (−) may seem preferable to humiliation (−), the resultant consequences are by no means attractive in an absolute sense.

Of course it should be clear that the degree to which Partner B feels tempted to respond in kind will vary across interactions, and may be moderated by the severity of the destructive act, the importance of the problem situation, or the specific emotions and cognitive interpretations that are directly instigated by a given destructive act. But given the pervasiveness of tendencies toward reciprocity and the contingent nature of inclinations to cooperate (Axelrod, 1984; H. Kelley & Stahelski, 1970)—and given that a partner's destructive act often arouses intense negative emotions— we suggest that destructive acts on the part of one partner frequently engender impulses to react destructively in turn.

Transformation of Motivation and Effective Matrix
Interaction Preferences

However, self-interested, given matrix preferences do not directly guide behavior. In deciding how to deal with a specific interaction problem, partners explicitly or implicitly "take account of broader considerations" such as long-term goals, social norms, or knowledge of and concern for a partner's well-being. This process is termed *transformation of motivation*. A variety of motives may shape the transformation process, including desire to maximize the partner's outcomes (Max Other), desire to maximize joint outcomes (Max Joint), desire to achieve equity by minimizing the difference between partners' outcomes (Min Diff), or desire to "defeat" the partner by maximizing the relative difference between partners' outcomes (Max Rel; H. Kelley & Thibaut, 1978; McClintock, 1972).

The reconceptualized preferences resulting from transformation of motivation are termed the *effective matrix*, which represents interacting partners' feelings about joint outcomes at the time they actually react to a particular interaction situation— preferences that guide actual behavior (see matrix on the right in Fig. 3.2). Transformation of motivation typically leads individuals to relinquish preferences based on immediate self-interest, and instead act on the basis of broader interaction goals. In the Fig. 3.2 example Partner B decides that for any of a number of reasons— to avoid exacerbating the problem, promote healthy functioning, or show concern for A's outcomes even though A has behaved poorly— reacting constructively (upper row of the effective matrix, −) seems preferable to reacting destructively (lower row of the effective matrix, − − − −). Partner B's resultant behavior— accommodation—is produced by pro-relationship transformation (in this example, Max Joint transformation).

Empirical Demonstrations of Transformation
of Motivation

Does transformation of motivation actually occur during the course of interaction? Research on nonclose interactions supports the distinction between the given and effective matrices, providing evidence that is consistent with the transformation concept. For example, research on social value orientations has demonstrated that individuals behaving in accord with the given matrix exhibit shorter response latencies than do those who transform the given matrix. Specifically, individualists (whose choices presumably are based on self-interested, given matrix preferences) exhibit shorter response latencies when allocating funds to themselves and others than do competitors (who engage in Max Rel transformation) or cooperators (who engage in Max Joint or Min Diff transformation; Dehue, McClintock, & Liebrand, 1993). Also, individuals have been shown to assign different meaning to identical situations, depending on the specific transformation they have applied to that situation (e.g., McClintock & Liebrand, 1988; Van Lange & Liebrand, 1991). Moreover, in games research it has been demonstrated that prosocial choices are more probable when individuals are interdependent for longer periods of time, either due to extended interaction (i.e., more choice situations), or because they anticipate later face-to-face interaction (cf. Pruitt & Kimmel, 1977).

But in the context of ongoing close relationships, is transformation of motivation necessary to yield pro-relationship behavior? It might be argued that close partners automatically take one another's interests into account, or that in intimate relationships, self-interest and partner-interest are inextricably merged. However, research on behavior in close relationships provides evidence that is inconsistent with these arguments. For example, in descriptions of previously experienced accommodative dilemmas, the responses individuals actually enact (i.e., effective matrix preferences) are considerably more constructive than are the responses they considered enacting (i.e., given matrix preferences; Yovetich & Rusbult, 1994). That is, in ongoing relationships, overt pro-relationship behavior frequently represents a deviation from underlying, self-interested inclinations. In addition, when individuals are induced to set aside the concerns that normally influence social behavior—concern for the partner's feelings, the future of the relationship, and their public image or self-concept—and to indicate how they "earnestly wish to behave" (given matrix preferences), their response preferences are substantially less constructive than are those of individuals operating under conditions of normal social concern (Rusbult, Verette, Whitney, Slovik, & Lipkus, 1991). Also, individuals exhibit greater willingness to accommodate to the degree that level of interdependence is greater; when interdependence is weak, the underlying, self-interested desire to retaliate is especially evident

(Rusbult et al., 1991). Finally, in responding to a partner's destructive acts, the mean constructiveness of reactions is greater when individuals are given plentiful response time (i.e., ample time for transformation of motivation) than when they are given only limited response time. That is, when time to engage in transformation-relevant thinking is limited, lower levels of accommodation are evident (Yovetich & Rusbult, 1994).

Thus, self-interest and partner-interest are not inextricably merged: Consistent with our characterization of accommodation as the product of transformation of motivation, individuals do recognize disparities between self-interest and the broader welfare of a relationship (e.g., Rusbult et al., 1991). Also, individuals frequently are tempted to engage in behaviors that promote direct self-interest, even at the expense of a partner's well-being: Partners' direct, impulsive preferences are often self-interested rather than pro-relationship (e.g., Surra & Longstreth, 1990; Yovetich & Rusbult, 1994). And finally, transformation of motivation appears to underlie many aspects of accommodation: Congruent with the claim that it is often costly to take the partner's interests into account and "behave well," the individual's gut level response frequently is to not behave well (e.g., Yovetich & Rusbult, 1994).

We have suggested that transformed motivation underlies accommodation, proposing that such deviations from self-interest are not "automatic." However, this is not to imply that transformation necessarily operates as a function of conscious calculation. Individuals sometimes consciously decide to forego self-interest, but just as often, such "decisions" are the automatic product of established habits. Moreover, departures from self-interest are not necessarily experienced as costs. Individuals may sometimes feel remorseful or resentful when they forego self-interest, but just as often, such acts (a) become habit-driven, such that they are no longer experienced as costs, (b) are regarded as the "obviously desirable" or "sensible" thing to do so as to maintain a relationship, and (c) may even be experienced as pleasurable or self-reinforcing. Once a pro-relationship transformational tendency is established, the individual may accommodate in a fairly routine manner, only occasionally (if ever) doing so in a state of conscious awareness, and only occasionally (if ever) experiencing such behavior as antithetical to self-interest. In describing accommodation as "not automatic," we wish to suggest that such behavior stands as a departure from the individual's direct, gut level impulses, whether or not it results from conscious calculation, whether or not it is actively experienced as costly. Self-oriented, given matrix preferences "come first," even when such preferences are rapidly or habitually replaced by effective matrix preferences.

The fact that self-interest underlies interaction preferences should not be taken as a black mark on the human race. Logically, there is no good reason why concerns with self-interest and self-preservation should be less understandable—or more repellent—among humans than among other species. The self-oriented, given matrix impulse to "fight fire with fire" in the accommodative dilemma yields direct and indirect benefits. For example, the individual is directly protected by warding off the immediate interpersonal "attack." Moreover, indirect protection derives from signaling the "attacker" that the individual will not endure exploitation in the future. Rather than finding reason to criticize humans for their selfish impulses, we regard it as praiseworthy that although humans are impulsively inclined to retaliate rather than accommodate, this tendency is frequently curbed as a consequence of transformation of motivation. After all, isn't cooperative behavior more praiseworthy when it is personally costly to the cooperator than when it is "easy"?

Why is the Distinction Between the Given Versus Effective Matrix a Useful One?

What does the distinction between the given matrix and the effective matrix "buy" us scientifically? First, the empirical literature demonstrates that there are differences between that which individuals impulsively wish to do and that which they determine is the "smart thing" or the "right thing" to do based on the broader considerations underlying transformed motivation. To understand what transpires in ongoing relationships, it is important to take account of such differences. For example, although numerous clinical studies have uncovered evidence of accommodative behavior, by focusing on negative interaction behaviors or inadequate social skills, researchers have failed to fully understand (a) why accommodative dilemmas are meaningful for couples, and (b) why accommodation is linked with healthy functioning. An interdependence analysis makes it evident that this interaction phenomenon is especially meaningful because accommodative behavior entails setting aside one's self-interested impulses.

Second, the distinction between the given and effective matrices is important in that the disparity between such preferences stands as the "material" for self-presentation and attributional interpretation. When behavior departs from what which would be expected on the basis of the given matrix, we learn something about the individual's dispositions, intentions, goals, and values. Because the given matrix depicts self-interested preferences, it represents features of interaction that are "to be expected"— features that are operative among most individuals and in most relationships. In contrast, because preferences in the effective matrix are colored by transformation of motivation, the effective matrix represents the uniqueness of specific individuals in the context of specific relationships. For example, Holmes and Rempel (1989) suggested that noncorrespondent given matrix structures are "diagnostic," in that behavior in such situations reveals the individual's motives and goals. The accommodating individual has proven him or herself to be trustworthy by foregoing self-interest for the good of the relationship.

DISTAL DETERMINANTS OF TRANSFORMATION TENDENCIES: INDIVIDUAL DISPOSITIONS, RELATIONSHIP MACROMOTIVES, AND SOCIAL NORMS

What accounts for the pro-relationship shift in motivation that underlies accommodative behavior? Figure 3.3 schematically represents our model of the proximal and distal determinants of this phenomenon. Distal determinants are embodied in stable interpersonal orientations, including individual dispositions, relationship macromotives, and social norms. These classes of variable are assumed to shape motivation through their effects on the proximal events accompanying a given interaction, including event-specific cognitive interpretations and emotional reactions. (These proximal determinants are reviewed in a later section of the chapter.)

When an individual initially encounters a specific pattern of interdependence with a partner—a pattern such as the accommodative dilemma, for example—the pattern may be experienced as a unique interaction event, or a set of "problems and opportunities" to which the individual must react. In reacting to the problems and opportunities inherent in an interaction,

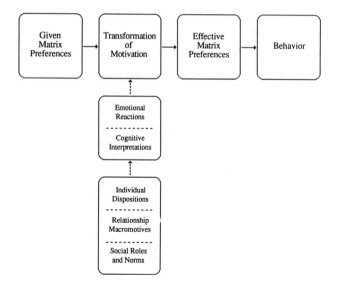

FIG. 3.3.The proximal and distal determinants of transformation of motivation.

individuals may respond deliberately or automatically. For example, the individual may consider the available options in light of surrounding circumstances, review feelings for a partner and goals for a relationship, and quite consciously and deliberately decide how to behave. Alternatively, the individual may react in a relatively more automatic and impulsive manner, being guided by the predominant emotional tone accompanying the interaction. In either event, experience has been acquired, and such experience may give rise to an habitual response pattern, or an "interpersonal orientation" toward a given pattern of interdependence.

If the individual's response to a specific pattern of interdependence yields undesirable outcomes, the individual is likely to behave differently in future experiences with similar patterns; if the reaction yields desirable outcomes, the individual is likely to react similarly in future situations with parallel patterns (win–stay, lose–change). Over time, certain patterns will be encountered with regularity, and a relatively stable orientation may emerge—for example, tendencies to cooperate in mixed-motive situations, or tendencies to behave loyally in accommodative dilemmas. *Interpersonal orientations* can be construed as pattern-contingent "solutions" to repeatedly encountered situations—solutions that on average yield desirable outcomes. As suggested earlier, stable orientations do not necessarily operate as a function of conscious awareness. Although individuals sometimes studiously calculate how they wish to behave, behavior is often an unconscious product of established habits (see Fletcher & Thomas, this volume). Interpersonal orientations exert their effects by (a) coloring perceptual processes, cognitive activities, and emotional experiences; and (b) giving rise to relatively stable, pattern-contingent transformational tendencies.

Interpersonal orientations are manifested in at least three forms: (a) interpersonal dispositions, or person-specific inclinations to respond to particular patterns of interdependence in a specific manner across numerous interaction partners; (b) macromotives, or relationship-specific inclinations to respond to particular patterns in a specific manner within the context of a given relationship; and (c) social norms, or rule-based inclinations to respond to particular patterns of interdependence in a specific manner, either across numerous interaction partners (e.g., never be the first to "defect") or within the context of a given relationship (e.g., never betray your spouse). We address each of these phenomena in turn in the following section of the chapter.

Interpersonal Dispositions

Through the course of development, individuals acquire a variety of interpersonal orientations (e.g., cooperating vs. competing; seeking vs. avoiding intimacy; cf. H. Kelley, 1983; Messick & McClintock, 1968). Different individuals experience different histories of interdependence—for example, they undergo different experiences with parents and siblings, and confront different opportunities and constraints in peer interactions. As a consequence of their unique histories, individuals acquire *interpersonal dispositions*, reflected in the probability of approaching certain classes of interdependent situations in predictable ways, and to apply particular transformations to those patterns with greater or lesser probability.

In light of the prevalence of work on attachment processes (cf. Ainsworth, Blehar, Waters, & Wall, 1978; Bowlby, 1969/1982; Hazan & Shaver, 1987; see also Shaver, Collins, & Clark, this volume), it is instructive to illustrate the development of interpersonal orientations in this domain. From the outset, it is important to note that high dependence on another human being is a dangerous proposition, in that dependence implies the ability of an interaction partner to move the individual through a wide range of out-comes—exceptionally good outcomes (e.g., affirmation, affection) as well as exceptionally poor outcomes (e.g., rejection, betrayal). Thus, interaction in the context of a highly interdependent relationship entails risk—in seeking intimacy, the individual risks the possibility of rejection or betrayal. Individuals develop avoidant attachment styles as a consequence of seeking intimacy and repeatedly experiencing rejection or betrayal as a consequence. Accordingly, avoidant individuals come to perceive intimacy situations as dangerous, and "solve" such dilemmas either by exploiting their partners or by avoiding intimacy situations altogether. Just as competitors elicit competitive behavior from others and create a distrustful and tough world for themselves (H. Kelley & Stahelski, 1970), avoidant persons elicit avoidance, and thus create a cold and barren world for themselves. In contrast, secure individuals have experienced interdependence histories in which attempts at intimacy have yielded good consequences. Accordingly, secure individuals perceive intimacy situations as safe and "easy," readily behave in a trusting manner, and create opportunities for partners to safely seek intimacy in return.

We have identified two dispositions that are especially relevant to under-standing pro-relationship transformation. First, since perspective-taking max-imizes the odds of gaining insight into interaction partners' preferences and motives (Davis, 1983)—and because knowledge of this sort is a prerequisite for informed transformation—individuals should enjoy greater interpersonal success to the degree that they approach interaction situations by putting themselves in their partners' shoes. Indeed, previous research has demon-strated that individuals scoring high in self-reported empathy and perspective-taking exhibit more benign attributions and emotions in accommodative dilemmas, are more inclined toward pro-relationship transformation, and enjoy relationships with superior adjustment (e.g., Davis & Oathout, 1987; Rusbult et al., 1991; Verette et al., 1995). Second, because psychologically feminine individuals are concerned with the quality of social interaction

(Bem, 1974), femininity should be associated with more positive, pro-relationship perceptual processes, cognitions, and motives. Consistent with this prediction, prior research has demonstrated that greater femininity is associated with greater tendencies toward pro-relationship transformation as well as superior adjustment (e.g., Antill, 1983; Lin & Rusbult, 1995; Rusbult et al., 1991).

Relationship-Specific Macromotives

A second type of interpersonal orientation exists at the level of the dyad. *Macromotives* are relationship-specific solutions that regulate behavior across a wide range of specific interdependence problems (cf. Holmes, 1981). For example, commitment and trust can be construed as long-term orientations that lead individuals to engage in Max Joint transformation of motivation in situations of moderate to low correspondence. In highly committed relationships with strong trust, individuals may fairly automatically accommodate rather than retaliate when their partners engage in potentially destructive acts, or may fairly unthinkingly exhibit willingness to sacrifice desirable outcomes for the good of a partner or relationship. Here, we illustrate the functioning of macromotives using a construct that has played a central role in our work on accommodation—commitment level.

Commitment level is the internal representation of dependence on a relationship, including long-term orientation and the sense of being linked to a relationship (Rusbult, 1983). Commitment subjectively summarizes the net influence of three key features of interdependent relationships (see Fig. 3.4): Commitment is stronger when satisfaction level is high (i.e., an individual loves a partner and has positive feelings about a relationship), when quality of alternatives is perceived to be poor (i.e., when specific alternative partners, the field of eligibles, or the option of noninvolvement are relatively less attractive), and when investment size is large (i.e., when many important resources are linked to a relationship and would be lost on termination). Strong commitment should promote pro-relationship behavior in that (a) long-term orientation enhances desire to maintain the integrity of a relationship; (b) in ongoing relationships, pro-relationship acts may yield direct personal benefit on later occasions, when a partner feels inclined to recipro-cate; and (c) pro-relationship behavior may send a message to the partner, communicating the committed individual's cooperative, long-term orienta-tion (cf. Axelrod, 1984; Holmes, 1981; H. Kelley, 1979).

Existing research provides good support for these assertions: Commitment level is not only the strongest predictor of voluntary decisions to remain in a relationship (Rusbult, 1983), but also promotes pro-relationship mainte-nance mechanisms such as derogation of tempting alternatives (Johnson &

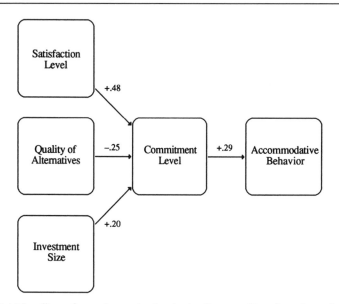

FIG. 3.4.The effects of commitment level and other features of interdependent relationships on accommodative behavior (from Rusbult, Bissonnette, Arriaga, & Cox, in press).

Rusbult, 1989), willingness to sacrifice (Van Lange, Rusbult, Drigotas, & Arriaga, 1995), and perceived relationship superiority (Rusbult, Van Lange, Verette, & Yovetich, 1995). Of particular relevance to this chapter, previous studies have demonstrated that commitment level strongly predicts willingness to accommodate, and that commitment largely or wholly mediates the impact on accommodation of satisfaction level, perceived quality of alternatives, and investment size (see Fig. 3.4; Rusbult, Bissonnette, Arriaga, & Cox, in press).

Social Norms

A third type of interpersonal orientation exists at a more global group or societal level (cf. Campbell, 1975). *Social norms* are broad rules for dealing with specific interdependence problems and opportunities. Interdependence theory identifies three manifestations of the existence of norms: (a) observed regularity of behavior, (b) in situations where such regularity is interrupted, the injured partly frequently attempts to regain control by appealing to the norm, and (c) the norm-breaker often feels guilty about having broken the norm (Thibaut & Kelley, 1959). For example, most societies develop rules regarding acceptable expressions of anger, presumably as a means of avoiding the chaos that might ensue if individuals were to freely given rein to hostile and violent emotions.

Likewise, everyday rules of civility and decency regulate interpersonal behavior so as to yield more harmonious interaction. As noted in the introduction to *Amy Vanderbilt's Everyday Etiquette,* manners govern behavior in situations that make people feel most uncomfortable—"the small and large problems confronting people in their everyday lives form the basis for [the rules of etiquette]. If we think we're 'doing the right thing,' we walk with more ease, we feel better about ourselves, and we interact far more humanely with our fellow men and women. Good manners are, after all, nothing more than a combination of kindness and efficiency" (Baldrige, 1978, p. vii). For example, in the absence of normative prescriptions, a wife might feel irritated when her husband offers his mother the front seat of the car when driving to a restaurant. But in light of the existence of salient norms regarding suitable behavior toward one's elders, such situations are rendered conflict-free.

Couples may also develop idiosyncratic, relationship-specific rules to solve their unique problems of interdependence. For example, although the temptation to become emotionally or sexually involved with alternative partners can sometimes be acute, the costs of doing so can be equally acute (e.g., insecurity, shame, conflict, relationship dissolution; Buunk, 1980). As a consequence, most couples either comply with existing cultural and religious norms regarding extra-relationship involvement, or develop their own norms as a means of governing such behavior and minimizing the negative impact of extra-relationship involvements. Typically, such rules specify the precise circumstances under which such involvements are acceptable (e.g., marriage primacy), as well as the conditions under which such behavior is unacceptable (e.g., high visibility). In a longitudinal study of extrarelationship involvement, couples who adhered to the ground rules of their marriage were found to exhibit lower levels of jealousy regarding their spouse's infidelity (Buunk, 1987).

PROXIMAL DETERMINANTS OF TRANSFORMATION TENDENCIES: EMOTIONAL REACTIONS AND COGNITIVE INTERPRETATIONS

Interaction involves some degree of ambiguity and uncertainty, even in the context of a long-term, ongoing relationship. For example, when a husband interrupts his wife's attempts at end-of-the-day conversation with a terse "Just be quiet for a moment!", she is likely to feel unsure what motivated his rudeness: "Did he have a bad day?" "Has the conversation touched on a sore issue?" "Is he dispositionally rude and inconsiderate?" The wife's behavioral response to her husband's potentially destructive act rests on her answers to such questions. To the extent that the wife's answers constitute a benevolent interpretation of her husband's act, accommodation should be more probable than retaliation. As illustrated in Fig. 3.3, our analysis of interaction phenomena assumes that the individual's internal construal of a given interaction event directly shapes transformation of motivation, and that these proximal, internal events are colored by the interpersonal orientations embodied in individual dispositions, relationship macromotives, and social norms. The following section of the chapter reviews these processes.

The implicit and explicit interpretations of another's behavior can be construed as *meaning analysis*—the process by which individuals deliberately or automatically discern the reasons for an event (cf. Berscheid, 1983; Frijda, 1988; Mandler, 1975). Meaning analysis is comprised of at least two related classes of internal experience—cognitive interpretations and emotional responses. It is useful to conceptualize internal experiences such as cognitions and emotions as part of the process of adaptation to specific patterns of interaction (H. Kelley, 1979, 1984)—meaning analysis is oriented toward rendering the social world predictable, and therefore controllable. As Fiske (1992) suggested, "thinking is for doing" (cf. Heider, 1958; H. Kelley, 1972); we extend this theoretical truism, proposing that "feeling is for doing" as well. That is, emotions are internal experiences that frequently prompt and direct action so as to adapt to the specific pattern of interdependence with which the individual is confronted, or to adapt to patterns of interdependence that will be encountered in the near or more distant future.

"One major feature of the structure of the causal environment is that it is unitized into interest-relevant 'situations.' Each situation can be characterized by the question, 'What interests are affected in what ways by what causes?' " (H. Kelley, 1984, p. 90). Although no two interdependence situations are precisely the same, situations possess sufficient regularity in their key features so that classifications can be made. Thus, although meaning analysis may involve quite deliberate, logical interpretation of the unique features of a given situation, such analysis may also (a) involve unconscious or automatic processing, and (b) take the form of category-based judgments rather than detailed cognitive representations. Moreover, the resulting interpretation may (c) be summarized in the form of an emotional reaction: "For each relatively homogeneous class of concrete situations, [individuals] have psychological systems that enable quick recognition of their relevance to the person's interests and that stimulate action promoting those interests" (H. Kelley, 1984, p. 91).

Cognitive interpretations and emotional reactions occupy a central position in guiding interaction via their role in (a) interpreting the direct significance of a specific event (e.g., "Was my partner rude because he suffered a bad day at work?"); (b) understanding the broader implications of the event (e.g., "Is he indifferent to my well-being?"); (c) apprehending the implications of this knowledge in light of one's own needs and preferences, thus summarizing the pattern of interdependence inherent in a specific interaction (e.g., "Taking into account this information along with knowledge of my own needs and preferences, what's this situation all about?''); and (d) directing behavioral reactions to that pattern (e.g., "Accordingly, should I indulge my impulse to say something nasty in return, or should I control this impulse and let it roll off my back?''). Retrospectively, internal experiences denote a change in the individual's welfare and serve as "summaries" of the causal factors that are relevant to that event. Prospectively, internal experiences prompt and direct behavior with respect to the particular causal structure inherent in a given event.

Cognitive Interpretations

Behaving in an effective manner—and maintaining gratifying long-term relationships—depends in part on interacting partners' abilities to read one another's preferences and intentions. Individuals engage in *cognitive interpretations* in the course of their attempts to uncover the direct meaning and broader implications of a partner's actions. Attributional analysis resides at the heart of interaction in at least two respects. First—and as noted earlier— the essential information for attributional activity lies in the disparity between given matrix and effective matrix preferences. "If the choice of a particular behavior departs from what would best suit one's personal, self-serving interests, then [the individual] will be providing evidence of [his or her] feelings and attitudes toward [a] partner" (Holmes, 1981, p. 262). Second, individuals can engage in informed transformation of motivation to the extent that they can predict interaction partners' preferences, motives, and probable behavior—prediction that rests in part on attributional activity. Thus, meaning analysis frequently involves interpreting the partner's given matrix and effective matrix preferences, and inferring the implications of these data for understanding the partner's intentions and motives.

Extant attribution theories suggest that attributional analysis is comprised of interpretations along three dimensions (e.g., Bradbury & Finchman, 1987, 1990; Weiner, 1986). The *stability dimension* refers to whether the cause of an observed behavior is inferred to be permanent versus temporary. When a partner is perceived to continually behave in an unpleasant manner—that is, when a partner's unpleasant behavior is judged to be stable—the individual expects such behavior to recur (or judges that it has in fact recurred). In an accommodative dilemma, the perception of greater stability should be associated with expectations of long-term frustration and distress, and accordingly should lead to decreased odds of accommodation. The *controllability dimension* refers to whether a partner is perceived to have had control over his or her actions. The concept of intent is inherent in this dimension, and as a consequence, this dimension has important implications for perceived responsibility. The perception of high controllability should be associated with the belief that a partner is responsible for the offending behavior, and therefore should be accompanied by decreased odds of accommodation. The *locus dimension* identifies the cause of an observed behavior as internal or external to the actor. When a partner's behavior is attributed to something external (e.g., "He's had a bad day at work"), there are minimal implications for the partner's longstanding intentions and dispositions (or for one's own self-esteem), and accommodating rather than retaliating should become more likely. In contrast, the perception of internal cause (e.g., "He's selfish, and doesn't care about our relationship") should be associated with broader, more negative implications regarding intentions and dispositions, and should elicit decreased accommodation.

Models of attributional activity tend to imply relatively conscious, deliberate attempts to understand the reasons underlying a partner's behavior. Indeed, this type of causal analysis is likely to be operative in many cases—for example, when the individual is highly dependent on a partner for achieving good outcomes, in unexpected or novel situations, or in situations that are exceptionally important to the individual (Berscheid, Graziano, Monson, & Dermer, 1976; Erber & Fiske, 1984; Neuberg & Fiske, 1987). However, it is reasonable to expect that other types of situation may elicit relatively more automatic or shallow processing (e.g., Chaiken, Liberman, & Eagly, 1989; Petty & Cacioppo, 1986; Sherman, Judd, & Park, 1989; Shiffrin & Schneider, 1977; Uleman & Bargh, 1989). For example, repeated experience with a particular pattern of interdependence may lead to relatively automatic cognitive interpretations of the causal factors underlying a given event. Moreover, such processes are importantly shaped by the interpersonal orientations embodied in dispositions (e.g., psychologically feminine individuals assume more benign reasons for objectionable partner behavior), relationship macromotives (e.g., committed individuals are motivated to disparage tempting alternatives), and social norms (e.g., individuals who obey the injunction to "count to 10" before reacting in a conflict situation are more likely to respond in a calm and accommodative manner).

Emotional Reactions

When challenged to define *emotion,* Frijda (cited in Shaver, Wu, & Schwartz, 1992) offered the following: "Emotions are changes in action readiness which have control precedence (which interrupt or compete with alternative mental and behavioral activities), changes caused by appraising events as relevant to concerns (hence giving rise to positive or negative feelings)" (p. 178). Thus, *emotional reactions* are "organized or patterned action tendencies." A prototype model of emotions (e.g., Shaver, Schwartz, Kirson, & O'Connor, 1987; see also Fehr & Baldwin, this volume; Fitness, this volume) is particularly well-suited for understanding the relevance of emotions to interaction.

Prototypes are formed as a consequence of repeated experience with particular patterns of interaction; a few basic types are assumed to underlie the structure of all emotional experiences. Of the basic emotion prototypes, two are most relevant to the accommodative dilemma: *loving emotions,* which flag concern with the long-term well-being of a relationship, should be associated with greater tendencies to accommodate; and *angry emotions,* which flag frustration and a concern with one's own well-being and self-protection, should be associated with lesser tendencies to accommodate.

As prototypes, specific emotional reactions (a) apply to a broad class of situations, (b) stand as abstract summaries of the meaning inherent in a given situation, and (c) have implications for the type of causal issues that are relevant to a given situation. In addition, we suggest that the emotional reactions accompanying specific situations influence effective matrix preferences through their impact on the transformation process. Just as repeated experience with particular patterns of interdependence may lead to specific attributions that are applied more or less automatically, emotions may also flag specific patterns of interdependence, serving as markers for the meaning of a given pattern and directing behavioral reactions to that pattern. For example, an individual may experience a sense of anxiety immediately preceding a familiar interdependence pattern in which the potential for conflict is great. These feelings may serve as a signal that the interdependence pattern is one of noncorrespondence, and cue the actor to respond appropriately (e.g., negotiate a solution that is acceptable to both parties).

More generally, emotional reactions to specific interaction problems may be shaped by dispositions, macromotives, and social norms. For example, experiencing attraction to an individual other than one's partner may be more likely to arouse feelings of guilt among highly committed individuals or among individuals who strongly adhere to the normative prescription that adultery is wrong. In turn, feelings of guilt may induce the individual to respond to temptation in an effective manner, either by behaving in a cool manner so as to drive away the alternative or by cognitively derogating the alternative so as to drive away the temptation. Emotions thus mediate the effects of interpersonal orientations on behavior, standing as a key component of the process by which individuals adapt to varying patterns of interdependence.

Empirical Demonstrations of the Role of Cognitions and Emotions in Directing Interaction

We propose that both cognitive interpretations and emotional reactions summarize the gist of a given interaction, embodying the meaning of a partner's actions (e.g., anger, blame, righteous indignation), encapsulating preferences for one's own and a partner's outcomes (e.g., desire for retaliation), shaping motivation (e.g., MaxRel motivation), and directing actual behavior (e.g., retaliating rather than accommodating). Moreover, we suggest that broader interpersonal orientations such as commitment partially shape the cognitions and emotions accompanying a given interpersonal event (see Fig. 3.5). Previous studies of couple attribution processes have provided indirect evidence that is congruent with this model, demonstrating that the tendency to form internal attributions for a partner's negative behavior is associated with reduced couple functioning (e.g., Fincham, Beach, & Baucom, 1987; Fincham & Bradbury, 1993; Jacobson, McDonald, Follette, & Berley, 1985).

Relatively more direct support for this model was revealed in two studies of attributions, emotions, and accommodative behavior in marriage and dating relationships (Verette et al., 1995). Both dating partners (Study 1) and spouses (Study 2) provided descriptions of recent accommodative dilemmas, reporting on their attributional interpretations of the event, their emotional reactions, and their actual behavior. In both studies, emotions and attributions accounted for substantial portions of the variance in tendencies to accommodate (see Fig. 3.5). In interactions instigated by their partners' destructive acts, individuals were more likely to react constructively (with voice and loyalty) and less likely to react destructively (with exit and neglect) to the degree that they experienced: (a) more positive emotions—more loving emotions, less angry emotions; and (b) more benign attributional interpretations—attributions to external/situational causes or bad luck rather than to the partner's unpleasant disposition or to lack of effort. Moreover, the

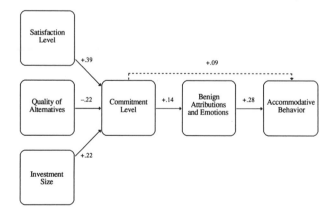

FIG. 3.5.The effects of cognitive interpretations, emotional reactions, and other features of interdependent relationships on accommodative behavior (from Studies 1 and 2, Verette et al., 1995).

emotions and attributions accompanying accommodative dilemmas partially (but not wholly) mediated the effects on accommodation of more distal determinants of accommodation (e.g., commitment level).

DIRECTIONS FOR FUTURE WORK

Several directions for future research seem promising. First, to fully understand the process by which emotions and cognitions influence transformation of motivation, it would be useful to conduct experimental studies of interaction in non-close relationships. For example, using mood-induction techniques, researchers could determine whether positive mood indeed causes pro-relationship transformation of motivation and accommodative behavior in response to a partner's destructive behavior. In parallel fashion, priming techniques could be used to induce benign interpretations of an interaction partner's destructive act, so as to examine the direct causal impact of cognitive interpretations on transformation of motivation and accommodative reactions to a partner's destructive behavior.

It would also be illuminating to examine the prevalence and consequences of attributional conflict, or "disagreement between a person and the partner about the cause of the person's behavior" (H. Kelley, 1979, pp. 99–100). Asymmetries in perceptions are likely to bear importantly on broader issues of couple adjustment. The existing evidence suggests that disparities in partners' perceptions of an event may be particularly evident in situations where one partner has engaged in a potentially destructive act (Passer, Kelley, & Michela, 1978). Although both partners utilize a dimension of explanation reflecting attitudes toward the partner (positive or negative), intentionality is the second central dimension among actors (similar to the controllability dimension discussed earlier), whereas partners tend to employ a second dimension that reflects attributions to the actors' traits as opposed to states or circumstances (akin to the stability and locus dimensions discussed earlier). Similarly, studies of everyday interaction demonstrate that individuals are more likely to perceive their own rather than their partners' acts of loyalty (Drigotas, Whitney, & Rusbult, 1995). Such asymmetries may have broader implications for key processes such as the emergence and maintenance of trust (cf. Holmes & Rempel, 1989) or distressed interaction patterns (cf. Bradbury & Fincham, 1990). For example, if trust rests on recognition of a partner's deviations from self-interest, asymmetries of this sort are likely to stand as a fundamental deterrent to the emergence and maintenance of trust.

In addition, although we have made some progress toward understanding the causes and consequences of transformation of motivation in accommodative dilemmas, much remains to be learned about the role of motivational shifts in promoting other relationship maintenance mechanisms, including:

derogation of alternatives—the tendency to cognitively disparage tempting alternative partners; *willingness to sacrifice*—the inclination to forego self-centered behavioral preferences, instead enacting behaviors that promote couple well-being; and *perceived superiority*—the tendency to perceive that one's relationship possesses a greater number of positive qualities and fewer negative qualities than other relationships. Are these processes, too, promoted by transformation of motivation? Given that willingness to sacrifice is a reaction to situations of noncorrespondence, it seems plausible that the model presented in this chapter is applicable to this phenomenon. However, given that derogation of alternatives and perceived superiority are essentially cognitive phenomena, it is less clear whether the transformation process applies to these maintenance mechanisms. Certainly, these cognitive phenomena are "motivated" processes—processes that are enhanced to the degree that threat to a relationship is greater (Johnson & Rusbult, 1989; Rusbult et al., 1995; see also Murray & Holmes, this volume). However, rather than resting on transformation of motivation per se, these phenomena may stand as independent "cognitive maneuvers" that support the decision to persist with a chosen line of behavior.

Finally, and most importantly, we hope it is clear that although this chapter has applied the concepts of interdependence theory to the task of understanding accommodation processes, the explanatory potential of the theory is much greater than this relatively focused application might suggest. Interdependence theory has clear potential to enrich our analysis of the entire domain of interdependence phenomena: from internal psychological processes such as the character and origins of self-knowledge to broad, cultural phenomena such as religious prescriptions regarding divorce; from exceptionally positive events such as selfless behavior to exceptionally negative events such as betrayal; from relatively basic research questions involving automatic cognitive processing to more applied questions centering on social policy regarding spousal violence. We hope that some of this potential has become evident through the course of developing our relatively focused analysis of accommodation processes.

SUMMARY AND CONCLUSIONS

The theoretical model and empirical evidence reviewed in this chapter concern accommodative behavior, a pattern of response that is initiated by an interaction partner's destructive act. To understand how couples sustain long-term, healthy functioning in the face of such threats, it is important to explain why individuals are sometimes willing to depart from their direct, self-interested behavioral preferences, instead placing greater value on pro-relationship behavior. We have suggested that the psychological process by which individuals come to forego self-interested behavior involves transformation of motivation. Moreover, we have proposed that the transformation process is directly shaped by the emotional reactions and cognitive interpretations that accompany a given interaction problem, arguing that this process is indirectly shaped by more distal determinants, including interpersonal dispositions, relationship-specific macromotives, and social norms. Although our program of research on accommodative behavior is still in its infancy, we hope that this work suggests the utility of employing interdependence theory as a formal model for understanding key interaction phenomena in ongoing relationships.

ACKNOWLEDGMENTS

Preparation of this chapter was supported in part by grants to the first author from the NIMH (No. BSR-1-R01-MH-45417) and NSF (No. BNS- 9023817).

REFERENCES

Ainsworth, M., Blehar, M. C., Waters, E., & Wall, S. (1978). *Patterns of attachment: A psychological study of the strange situation.* Hillsdale, NJ: Lawrence Erlbaum Associates.

Antill, J. K. (1983). Sex role complementarity versus similarity in married couples. *Journal of Personality and Social Psychology, 45,* 145–155.

Argyle, M., & Furnham, A. (1983). Sources of satisfaction and conflict in long-term relationships. *Journal of Marriage and the Family, 45,* 481–493.

Axelrod, R. (1984). *The evolution of cooperation.* New York: Basic Books.

Baldrige, L. (1978). *Amy Vanderbilt's everyday etiquette.* New York: Bantam Books.

Bem, S. L. (1974). The measurement of psychological androgyny. *Journal of Consulting and Clinical Psychology, 47,* 155–162.

Berscheid, E. (1983). Emotion. In H. H. Kelley, E. Berscheid, A. Christensen, J. H. Harvey, T. L. Huston, G. Levinger, E. McClintock, L. A. Peplau, & D. R. Peterson (Eds.), *Close relationships* (pp. 110–168). New York: Freeman.

Berscheid, E., Graziano, W., Monson, T., & Dermer, M. (1976). Outcome dependency: Attention, attribution, and attraction. *Journal of Personality and Social Psychology, 34,* 978–989.

Billings, A. (1979). Conflict resolution in distressed and nondistressed married couples. *Journal of Consulting and Clinical Psychology, 47,* 368–376.

Bowlby, J. (1982). *Attachment and loss: Vol. 1. Attachment* (2nd ed.). New York: Basic Books. (Original work published 1969)

Bradbury, T. N., & Fincham, F. D. (1987). Affect and cognition in close relationships: Towards an integrative model. *Cognition and Emotion, 1,* 59–88.

Bradbury, T. N., & Fincham, F. D. (1990). Attributions in marriage: Review and critique. *Psychological Bulletin, 107,* 3–33.

Buunk, B. (1980). Extramarital sex in the Netherlands: Motivations in social and marital context. *Alternative Lifestyles, 3,* 11–39.

Buunk, B. (1987). Conditions that promote breakups as a consequence of extradyadic involvements. *Journal of Social and Clinical Psychology, 5,* 271–284.

Campbell, D. T. (1975). On the conflicts between biological and social evolution and between psychology and moral tradition. *American Psychologist, 30,* 1103–1126.

Chaiken, S., Liberman, A., & Eagly, A. H. (1989). Heuristic and systematic information processing within and beyond the persuasion context. In J. S. Uleman & J. A. Bargh (Eds.), *Unintended thought* (pp. 221–252). New York: Guilford.

Davis, M. H. (1983). Measuring individual differences in empathy: Evidence for a multidimensional approach. *Journal of Personality and Social Psychology, 44,* 113–126.

Davis, M. H., & Oathout, H. A. (1987). Maintenance of satisfaction in romantic relationships: Empathy and relational competence. *Journal of Personality and Social Psychology, 53,* 397–410.

Dehue, F. M. J., McClintock, C. G., & Liebrand, W. B. G. (1993). Social value related response latencies: Unobtrusive evidence for individual differences in information processes. *European Journal of Social Psychology, 23,* 273–294.

Drigotas, S. M., Whitney, G. A., & Rusbult, C. E. (1995). On the pecularities of loyalty: A diary study of responses to dissatisfaction in everyday life. *Personality and Social Psychology Bulletin, 21,* 596–609.

Erber, R., & Fiske, S. T. (1984). Outcome dependency and attention to inconsistent information. *Journal of Personality and Social Psychology, 47,* 709–726.

Fincham, F. D., Beach, S. R. H., & Baucom, D. H. (1987). Attribution processes in distressed and nondistressed couples: 4. Self-partner attribution differences. *Journal of Personality and Social Psychology, 52,* 739–748.

Fincham, F. D. G., & Bradbury, T. N. (1993). Marital satisfaction, depression, and attributions: A longitudinal analysis. *Journal of Personality and Social Psychology, 64,* 442–452.

Fiske, S. T. (1992). Thinking is for doing: Portraits of social cognition from daguerreotype to laserphoto. *Journal of Personality and Social Psychology, 63,* 877–889.

Frijda, N. H. (1988). The laws of emotion. *American Psychologist, 43,* 349–358.

Geiss, S. K., & O'Leary, K. D. (1981). Therapist ratings of frequency and severity of marital problems: Implications for future research. *Journal of Marriage and Family Therapy, 7,* 515–520.

Gottman, J. M., & Krokoff, L. J. (1989). Marital interaction and satisfaction: A longitudinal view. *Journal of Consulting and Clinical Psychology, 57,* 47–52.

Gottman, J. G., Markman, H. J., & Notarius, C. I. (1977). The topography of marital conflict: A sequential analysis of verbal and nonverbal behavior. *Journal of Marriage and the Family, 39,* 461–478.

Greenshaft, J. L. (1980). Perceptual and defensive style variables in marital discord. *Social Behavior and Personality, 8,* 81–84.

Haynes, S. N., Chavez, R. E., & Samuel, V. (1984). Assessment of marital communication and distress. *Behavioral Assessment, 6,* 315–321.

Hazan, C., & Shaver, P. (1987). Romantic love conceptualized as an attachment process. *Journal of Personality and Social Psychology, 52,* 511–524.

Heider, F. (1958). *The psychology of interpersonal relations.* New York: Wiley.

Holmes, J. G. (1981). The exchange process in close relationships: Microbehavior and macromotives. In M. J. Lerner & S. C. Lerner (Eds.), *The justice motive in social behavior* (pp. 261–284). New York: Plenum.

Holmes, J. G., & Rempel, J. K. (1989). Trust in close relationships. In C. Hendrick (Ed.), *Review of personality and social psychology* (Vol. 10, pp. 187–220). London: Sage.

Jacobson, N. S., Follette, W. C., & McDonald, D. W. (1982). Reactivity to positive and negative behavior in distressed and nondistressed married couples. *Journal of Consulting and Clinical Psychology, 50,* 706–714.

Jacobson, N. S., McDonald, D. W., Follette, W. C., & Berley, R. A. (1985). Attributional processes in distressed and nondistressed married couples. *Cognitive Therapy and Research, 9,* 35–59.

Johnson, D. J., & Rusbult, C. E. (1989). Resisting temptation: Devaluation of alternative partners as a means of maintaining commitment in close relationships. *Journal of Personality and*

Social Psychology, 57, 967–980.

Kelley, E. L., & Conley, J. J. (1987). Personality and compatibility: A prospective analysis of marital stability and marital satisfaction. *Journal of Personality and Social Psychology, 52,* 27–40.

Kelley, H. H. (1972). Attribution in social interaction. In E. Jones, D. Kanouse, H. Kelley, R. Nisbett, S. Valins, & B. Weiner (Eds.), *Attribution: Perceiving the causes of behavior* (pp. 1–26). Morristown, NJ: General Learning Press.

Kelley, H. H. (1979). *Personal relationships: Their structures and processes.* Hillsdale, NJ: Lawrence Erlbaum Associates.

Kelley, H. H. (1983). The situational origins of human tendencies: A further reason for the formal analysis of structures. *Personality and Social Psychology Bulletin, 9,* 8–30.

Kelley, H. H. (1984). Affect in interpersonal relations. In P. Shaver (Ed.), *Review of personality and social psychology* (Vol. 5, pp. 89–115). Newbury Park, CA: Sage.

Kelley, H. H., & Stahelski, A. J. (1970). Social interaction basis of cooperators' and competitors' beliefs about others. *Journal of Personality and Social Psychology, 16,* 66–91.

Kelley, H. H., & Thibaut, J. W. (1978). *Interpersonal relations: A theory of interdependence.* New York: Wiley.

Koren, P., Carlton, K., & Shaw, D. (1980). Marital conflict: Relations among behaviors, outcomes, and distress. *Journal of Consulting and Clinical Psychology, 48,* 460–468.

Kurdek, L. A. (1993). Predicting marital dissolution: A five year prospective longitudinal study of newlywed couples. *Journal of Personality and Social Psychology, 64,* 221–242.

Lin, Y. H. W., & Rusbult, C. E. (1995). Commitment to dating relationships and cross-sex friendships in America and China: The impact of centrality of relationship, normative support, and investment model variables. *Journal of Social and Personal Relationships, 12,* 7–26.

Mandler, G. (1975). *Mind and emotion.* New York: Wiley.

Margolin, G., & Wampold, B. E. (1981). Sequential analysis of conflict and accord in distressed and nondistressed marital partners. *Journal of Counseling and Clinical Psychology, 49,* 554–567.

Markman, H. J. (1981). Prediction of marital distress: A five-year follow-up. *Journal of Consulting and Clinical Psychology, 49,* 760–762.

McClintock, C. G. (1972). Social motivation—a set of propositions. *Behavioral Science, 17,* 438–454.

McClintock, C. G., & Liebrand, W. B. G. (1988). The role of interdependence structure, individual value orientation and other's strategy in social decision making: A transformational analysis. *Journal of Personality and Social Psychology, 55,* 396–409.

Messick, D. M., & McClintock, C. G. (1968). Motivational bases of choice in experimental games. *Journal of Experimental Social Psychology, 4,* 1–25.

Neuberg, S. L., & Fiske, S. T. (1987). Motivational influences on impression formation: Outcome dependency, accuracy-driven attention, and individuating processes. *Journal of Personality and Social Psychology, 53,* 431–444.

Noller, P. (1980). Misunderstandings in marital communication: A study of couples' nonverbal communications. *Journal of Personality and Social Psychology, 39,* 1135–1148.

Passer, M. W., Kelley, H. H., & Michela, J. L. (1978). Multidimensional scaling of the causes for negative interpersonal behavior. *Journal of Personality and Social Psychology, 36,* 951–962.

Petty, R. E., & Cacioppo, J. T. (1986). The elaboration likelihood model of persuasion. In L. Berkowitz (Ed.), *Advances in experimental social psychology* (Vol. 19, pp. 123–205). New York: Academic Press.

Pruitt, D. G., & Kimmel, M. J. (1977). Twenty years of experimental gaming: Critique, synthesis, and suggestions for the future. *Annual Review of Psychology, 28,* 363–392.

Rusbult, C. E. (1983). A longitudinal test of the investment model: The development (and deterioration) of satisfaction and commitment in heterosexual involvements. *Journal of Personality and Social Psychology, 45,* 101–117.

Rusbult, C. E. (1987). Responses to dissatisfaction in close relationships: The exit-voice-loyalty-neglect model. In D. Perlman & S. Duck (Eds.), *Intimate relationships: Develop-*

ment, dynamics, and deterioration (pp. 209–237). Newbury Park, CA: Sage.

Rusbult, C. E. (1993). Understanding responses to dissatisfaction in close relationships: The exit-voice-loyalty-neglect model. In S. Worchel & J. A. Simpson (Eds.), *Conflict between people and groups: Causes, processes, and resolutions* (pp. 30–59). Chicago: Nelson-Hall.

Rusbult, C. E., Bissonnette, V. I., Arriaga, X. B., & Cox, C. L. (in press). Accommodation processes across the early years of marriage. In T. N. Bradbury (Ed.), *The developmental course of marital dysfunction.* New York: Cambridge.

Rusbult, C. E., Johnson, D. J., & Morrow, G. D. (1986a). Determinants and consequences of exit, voice, loyalty, and neglect: Responses to dissatisfaction in adult romantic involvements. *Human Relations, 39,* 45–63.

Rusbult, C. E., Johnson, D. J., & Morrow, G. D. (1986b). Impact of couple patterns of problem solving on distress and nondistress in dating relationships. *Journal of Personality and Social Psychology, 50,* 744–753.

Rusbult, C. E., Morrow, G. D., & Johnson, D. J. (1987). Self-esteem and problem solving behavior in close relationships. *British Journal of Social Psychology, 26,* 293–303.

Rusbult, C. E., Van Lange, P. A. M., Verette, J., & Yovetich, N. A. (1995). *Perceive superiority as a relationship maintenance mechanism.* Unpublished manuscript, Univeristy of North Carolina, Chapel Hill.

Rusbult, C. E., Verette, J., Whitney, G. A. Slovik. L. F., & Lipkus, I. (1991). Accommodation processes in close relationships: Theory and preliminary empirical evidence. *Journal of Personality and Social Psychology, 60,* 53–78.

Rusbult, C. E., & Zembrodt, I. M. (1983). Responses to dissatisfaction in romantic involvements: A multidimensional scaling analysis. *Journal of Experimental Social Psychology, 19,* 274–293.

Rusbult, C. E., Zembrodt, I. M., & Gunn, L. K. (1982). Exit, voice, loyalty, and neglect: Responses to dissatisfaction in romantic involvements. *Journal of Personality and Social Psychology, 43,* 1230–1242.

Rusbult, C. E., Zembrodt, I. M., & Iwaniszek, J. (1986). The impact of gender and sex-role orientation on responses to dissatisfaction in close relationships. *Sex Roles, 15,* 1–20.

Schaap, C. (1984). A comparison of the interaction of distressed and nondistressed married couples in a laboratory situation: Literature, survey, methodological issues, and an empirical investigation. In K. Hahlweg & N. S. Jacobson (Eds.), *Marital interaction: Analysis and modification* (pp. 133–158). New York: Guilford Press.

Shaver, P., Schwartz, J., Kirson, D., & O'Connor, C. (1987). Emotion knowledge: Further exploration of a prototype approach. *Journal of Personality and Social Psychology, 52,* 1061–1086.

Shaver, P. R., Wu, S., & Schwartz, J. C. (1992). Cross-cultural similarities and differences in emotion and its representation: A prototype approach. In M. S. Clark (Ed.), *Review of personality and social psychology* (Vol. 13, pp. 175–212). Newbury Park, CA: Sage.

Sherman, S. J., Judd, C. M., & Park, B. (1989). Social cognition. *Annual Review of Psychology, 40,* 281–336.

Shiffrin, R. M., & Schneider, W. (1977). Controlled and automatic processing II: Perceptual learning and automatic attending. *Psychological Review, 84,* 127–190.

Sullaway, M., & Christensen, A. (1983). Assessment of dysfunctional interaction patterns in couples. *Journal of Marriage and the Family, 45,* 653–660.

Surra, C. A., & Longstreth, M. (1990). Similarity of outcomes, interdependence, and conflict in dating relationships. *Journal of Personality and Social Psychology, 59,* 501–516.

Thibaut, J. W., & Kelley, H. H. (1959). *The social psychology of groups.* New York: Wiley.

Uleman, J. S., & Bargh, J. A. (Eds.). (1989). *Unintended thought.* New York: Guilford.

Van Lange, P. A. M., & Liebrand, W. B. G. (1991). Social value orientation and intelligence: A test of the Goal-Prescribes-Rationality Principle. *European Journal of Social Psychology, 21,* 273–292.

Van Lange, P. A. M., Rusbult, C. E., Drigotas, S. M., & Arriaga, B. A. (1995). *Willingness to sacrifice in close relationships.* Unpublished manuscript, University of North Carolina, Chapel Hill.

Verette, J., Rusbult, C. E., Arriaga, X. B., Peterson, S., Bissonnette, V. L., & Schmidt, G. W. (1995). *Proximal mediators of accommodation: Perspective-taking, emotional reactions, and cognitive interpretations.* Unpublished manuscript, University of North Carolina, Chapel Hill.

Weiner, B. (1986). *An attributional theory of motivation and emotion.* New York: Springer-Verlag.

Wills, T. A., Weiss, R. L., & Patterson, G. R. (1974). A behavioral analysis of the determinants of marital satisfaction. *Journal of Consulting and Clinical Psychology, 42,* 802–811.

Yovetich, N. A., & Rusbult, C. E. (1994). Accommodative behavior in close relationships: Exploring transformation of motivation. *Journal of Experimental Social Psychology, 30,* 138–164.

4

The Construction of Relationship Realities

Sandra L. Murray
John G. Holmes
University of Waterloo

Love to faults is always blind,
Always is to joy inclined,
Lawless, winged and unconfined,
And breaks all chains from every mind.

—Blake (1791)

In many ways, Blake's musings depict the platonic ideal of the romantic experience. Swept up in the experience of love, trusting, satisfied intimates see the best in their partners' virtues while being charitably, perhaps sensibly, immune to their faults. But, many psychologists would dispute this depiction—arguing instead that individuals' realistic understanding and acceptance of their partners' actual attributes represents the true ideal (e.g., Brickman, 1987; Swann, Hixon, & De La Ronde, 1992). However, our sympathies lie with Blake.

In this chapter, we argue that particular types of misunderstandings—in the form of positive illusions—characterize satisfying close relationships. In contrast, accurate understandings of a partner's true qualities may only engender doubt, precisely because reality so often falls short of a person's hopes. Consequently, individuals may need to construct idealized images of their partners to sustain feelings of confidence and commitment in the face of disappointing realities (Murray & Holmes, 1993, 1994; Murray, Holmes, & Griffin, in press).

In exploring these hypotheses, we first describe the dialectic of hope and doubt underlying individuals' desires to see their partners in idealized ways. We then turn to the specific construal processes that allow intimates to see one another's virtues and faults in the best possible light. We conclude by exploring how the cognitive structure of individuals' representations of their partners may instill greater or lesser degrees of confidence in the face of the continued risks posed by interdependence.

THE DIALECTIC: HOPE AND DOUBT

Early on in romantic relationships, intimates' absorption in their partners' virtues fuels their hopes for their relationship's success (Holmes & Boon, 1990; Weiss, 1980). Self-presentation, interaction across restricted, positive domains, and the desire not to perceive negativity (e.g., Brehm, 1988; Brickman, 1987) are all likely to strengthen the perception that one's partner really is the "right" person. Intimates' models of ideal relationships may also help them "fill in the gaps" in their limited knowledge about their partners, a process of wish fulfillment where realities become reflections of desires. In such ways, the projection of hopes and fantasies onto the limited evidence available creates perceptions that mirror intimates' hopes. Thus, the allure of a partner's apparent virtues may draw intimates into relationships (e.g., Brickman, 1987), creating feelings of confidence and hope that belie the lack of more representative experiences.

But, as interdependence increases, individuals begin interacting across broader, more conflictual domains, and the potential for partners to exhibit negative behaviors increases (e.g., Braiker & Kelley, 1979; Levinger, 1983). As time passes, negative behaviors that intimates once explained away as anomalies may show patterns of consistency that undercut such situational attributions (Kelley, 1972). Even in marriage, intimates may continue to uncover new sources of conflict in their relationships as new demands surface, such as balancing children and career (e.g., Hackel & Ruble, 1992). In fact, the potential for recurrent negativity and conflict may be greatest in marriage because of the strength and diversity of the bonds connecting husbands and wives. Discovering such harsh realities may then threaten feelings of confidence by raising the disturbing possibility that one's partner really isn't the right person after all.

We believe that such doubts are intolerable, precisely because negativity typically surfaces when individuals' hopes are already invested in their relationships. To add a further irony, intimates may discover their partners' more negative qualities only when the barriers to dissolution have also increased (e.g., perceived lack of alternative partners, children). In the face of this "romantic trap," individuals may need to reach some sort of cognitive resolution between their hopes and doubts to justify their continuing commitments (e.g., Abelson, 1959; Epstein, 1982; Festinger, 1957). Moreover, attachment theorists contend that individuals are strongly motivated to seek feelings of safety and security in their close relationships (e.g., Bowlby, 1977). The specter of doubt and negativity may frustrate such attachment concerns, heightening individuals' perceptions of the risks posed by depending on a less than perfect partner (e.g., Holmes & Rempel, 1989).

Masking Doubts and Constructing Convictions

Such competing hopes and fears are likely to intensify individuals' need to reach confident, unequivocal conclusions about their partners (e.g., Brehm, 1988; Brickman, 1987; Holmes & Rempel, 1989; Murray & Holmes, 1993). For individuals who are anxious-ambivalent in attachment style or dispositionally high on the need for certainty, this need for closure may be particularly pressing (e.g., Feeney & Noller, 1991; Sorrentino, Holmes, Hanna, & Sharp, 1995). We believe that intimates quell doubt and uncertainty by weaving idealized representations or stories that depict their partners' virtues and faults in the best possible light (Brickman, 1987; Murray & Holmes, 1993). Such defensive story telling bolsters confidence, essentially allowing individuals to commit to their partners without anxiety or reservations.

As we later explore, the potential for considerable flexibility in the construal of apparent negativity may play an integral role in this idealization process (Murray & Holmes, 1993). Behavior must be interpreted and given meaning, motives for that behavior must be inferred, and most indirectly of all, impressions of a partner's personal characteristics must be constructed (e.g., Gergen, Hepburn, & Fisher, 1986; Griffin & Ross, 1991). As a result, intimates are not bound by only one possible interpretation of one another's virtues and faults as dictated by some stern objective reality. Instead, they possess considerable license in constructing impressions of the partners they most want or need to see.

For instance, an individual might reconcile the threat posed by her partner's stubbornness during conflicts by interpreting it as a sign of integrity, rather than egocentrism. Alternatively, she might try to excuse this fault by embellishing her partner's generally tolerant nature. Finally, constructing "Yes, but . . ." refutations or excuses that link stubbornness to greater virtues might also lessen the threat posed by these misbehaviors. As these examples illustrate, confidence in an intimate partner may not allow for any significant nagging doubts or "loose ends" in one's story, as evidenced in less than positive, charitable construals of a partner's attributes (Murray & Holmes, 1993). A partner's positive and negative qualities may need to fit together into a unified whole or "gestalt" where the meaning of faults is interpreted in light of surrounding virtues (e.g., Asch, 1946; Asch & Zukier, 1984). This need to tell a coherent story should be strongest in the face of faults that pose the greatest threat to intimates' confidence in their partners. That is, individuals may be most likely to idealize attributes that are instrumental for promoting closeness and intimacy (e.g., Levinger & Breedlove, 1966). For instance, a person may feel little need to idealize or excuse her partner's inept dancing skills. However, the same partner's inexpressiveness may elicit storytelling simply because it instills greater doubt. Paradoxically, rather than weakening intimates' resolve, dealing with such doubts may actually strengthen convictions by motivating individuals to embellish their partners' virtues and minimize their faults.

CRYSTALLIZING HOPES: THE CONSTRUCTION OF POSITIVE ILLUSIONS

Happiness depends, as Nature shows, Less on exterior things than most suppose. (Cowper, 1782)

If our reasoning is correct, dating and even married individuals should see their partners in quite idealized ways—perceptions that may be quite different from those dictated by sterner realities (e.g., Johnson & Rusbult, 1989; Murray & Holmes, 1993; Murray et al., in press; Rusbult, Van Lange, & Verette, 1992). Furthermore, such hope-driven misunderstandings or "positive illusions" should promote feelings of confidence and satisfaction, whereas accurate understandings of a partner's less than perfect nature may actually dampen satisfaction.

Testing this "positive illusions" hypothesis leaves us on the brink of a perilous intellectual debate—finding an adequate definition for reality. After all, how can we index individuals' illusions without a benchmark for tapping their partners' "real" qualities? In the absence of a gold standard for measuring "truth," we turned to partners' own perspectives on their virtues and faults. Investigators typically use self-ratings as indices of individuals' personality traits, despite the necessary caveats associated with using self-reports to estimate reality. Using this subjective reality baseline allows us to index both the "illusory" and "reality-based" aspects of individuals' perceptions of their partners, as Fig. 4.1 illustrates.

Within this model, we apportion part of the variance in actors' perceptions to "illusion" and part to "reality" (i.e., Actor's Perception = Actor's Illusion + Partner's Reality). Even most social constructionist perspectives admit that "reality" constrains and structures an individual's interpretation of the social world. Therefore, actors' representations should at least partially

Partner's Self-Perceptions   Actor's Perception of Partner

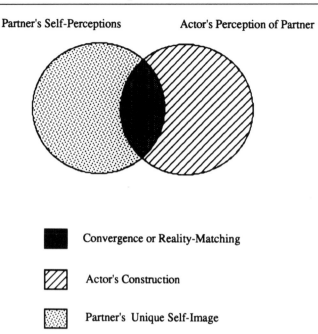

■   Convergence or Reality-Matching

▨   Actor's Construction

▨   Partner's Unique Self-Image

FIG. 4.1.   Isolating the "illusory" and "reality-based" components of actors' representations of their partners.

reflect the actual nature of their partners' virtues and faults (e.g., Kenny & DePaulo, 1993). Such reality-matching or convergence is reflected in the shaded area of Fig. 4.1. Actors' illusions, on the other hand, refer to the qualities that they see in their partners that their partners do not see in themselves. These constructions are reflected in the hatched area of Fig. 4.1.

   In contemplating our index of partners' realities, it is critical to note that we are not arguing that individuals possess true insight into the actual nature of their own attributes. In fact, there is every reason to believe that individuals' self-perceptions are in part constructions. For instance, individuals typically see themselves in much more positive, idealized ways than their actual attributes appear to warrant (e.g., Alicke, 1985; Brown, 1986; Greenwald, 1980; Taylor & Brown, 1988). But, given the considerable evidence that self-perceptions are already colored by positive illusions, individuals' self-perceptions should provide quite a conservative benchmark for indexing the idealized nature of their partners' perceptions.[1]

---

[1]The opposite argument is that actors actually know their partners better than their partners know themselves. If this is the case, calling Mary's idiosyncratic perception of John an "illusion" may be a misnomer. However, if actors' own self-impressions and ideals shape these idiosyncratic

Having settled on our conceptual model, the next challenge centers around finding statistical translations of the "reality" and "illusion" components of intimates' representations. Following a difference score approach, we could subtract the partner's reality from the actor's perception to obtain an index of construction or illusion. Unfortunately, creating these difference scores confounds, rather than separates, these perceptions (Humphreys, 1990). However, we can unconfound these perceptions by using path analysis to model the unique or independent effects of actors' perceptions and partners' realities (Cohen & Cohen, 1983).

Within a path analytic framework, we can isolate the constructed aspects of an individual's impression (the hatched area in Fig. 4.1) by partialling the effects of the partner's reality (i.e., partner's self-perceptions) out of the actor's perceptions. In other words, actors' illusions refer to their unique or idiosyncratic perceptions of their partners—essentially, what they see in their partners that their partners do not see in themselves (Murray et al., in press).

Constructing Perceptions: The Projection of Self and Ideals

In our thinking, intimates' desire to see their partners in the best possible light biases the nature of their illusions. More specifically, self- and relationship schemas may structure perceptions in such ways that imperfect partners become reflections of actors' wishes.

In terms of self-schemas (e.g., Markus & Zajonc, 1985), intimates might project their own positive qualities onto their partners, essentially including their partners in their own positive illusions (e.g., Aron, Aron, Tudor, & Nelson, 1991; Taylor & Brown, 1988). As an even more direct path to wish fulfillment, intimates may see their partners' attributes through the rosy filters provided by their images of the ideal partner. Such ideals may represent working models of the attributes individuals hope or need to find in an intimate partner in order to feel secure in their commitment (Bowlby, 1977). Like other schemas, individuals' self-perceptions and ideals may provide the template that shapes the nature of the illusions they construct (e.g., Baldwin, 1992).

Fig. 4.2 presents our model of "positive illusions" in romantic relationships. Turning first to the source of ideals, Paths a and d tap whether intimates' ideals reflect their own rosy self-perceptions. Paths b and c assess whether ideals are also attuned to the reality of their partners' self-perceptions. In the next level of our model, we break actors' perceptions of their partners into "illusion" and "reality" components. Our "reality"

---

perceptions, as we expect, such evidence of wish-fulfillment should undercut the actor's status as an unbiased arbiter of the truth.

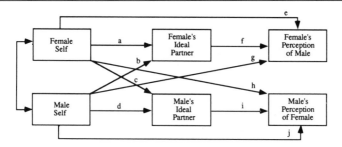

FIG. 4.2. "Positive illusions" in close relationships: The projection of self and ideals.

Paths g and h index the extent to which people's representations of their partners mirror their partners' self-perceptions. Turning to our "illusion" paths, Paths e and j index intimates' tendency to project their own rosy self-images onto their partners. Paths f and i index intimates' tendency to see their partners through the filters provided by their ideals, seeing them, not as they are, but as they wish to see them.

Each path in this model reflects a partial or unique effect. For example, Path e indexes one possible source of the female's "illusion"—how much she tends to see herself in her partner, holding the reality of her partner's actual or self-perceived attributes constant. Path f indexes another possible source of this construction—how much her ideals structure the nature of her impressions, again holding the reality of her partner's actual attributes constant.

To test this model, we asked both members of dating and married couples to rate themselves, their partners, their ideal partner and the typical partner on a variety of positive and negative, largely interpersonal attributes (e.g., kind and affectionate, demanding, responsive, critical). Participants' overall mean ratings of themselves and their partners on these attributes then provided our indices of the overall positivity of actors' impressions and partners' realities, respectively. By using these indices, we implicitly define the type of "reality matching" we can use as baselines within our path models. Actors accurately judge their partners' self-perceptions if they correctly estimate their partners' self-rated positivity across the different traits. On the other hand, actors' tendency to either exaggerate or underestimate the positivity of their partners' self-ratings provides an index of construction.

Our analyses yielded results consistent with our expectations: Actors' impressions of their partners appeared to reflect a mixture of "illusion" and "reality" (Murray et al., in press). First, married and dating couples' ideals were strongly related to their own self-perceptions (Paths a and d). The better, or more positively, individuals felt about themselves, the higher were their standards or expectations for the ideal partner. In contrast, the reality of their partners' qualities (Paths b and c) had little bearing on the ideal standards actors set. Also, the social reality paths (g and h) were significant for both samples, indicating that individuals' impressions were in part a reflection of their partners' "real" or self-perceived attributes.

Turning to our "illusion" paths, married and dating couples also projected their ideals onto their partners, apparently seeing them through the filter provided by these working models (Paths f and i). Higher hopes and ideals predicted rosier, more idealized impressions of an intimate partner. Among dating couples, individuals who saw themselves in a positive light projected their rosy self-images onto their partners, whereas individuals with more negative self-images were less generous in their depictions (Paths e and j). Married actors' self-perceptions had no significant, direct effect on their impressions. Thus, dating actors' self-perceptions structured their impressions of their partners both directly (e and j) as well as indirectly, through the projection of their ideals (f and i). In contrast, ideals completely mediated the link between self-perceptions and impressions for married couples.

Importantly, our evidence for positive illusions was not simply a result of individuals' tendency to see most everything in idealized ways—a Pollyanna effect. Individuals with more positive perceptions of their partners, for example, might see most people in a more positive light than seems warranted. However, when we included individuals' perceptions of the typical partner as a control variable within our model, the projection paths remained strong and significant. Therefore, the tendency for actors to see their partners through the filters provided by their self-perceptions and ideals reflects something more than just global positivity. Idealized constructions appear to be specific to actors' perceptions of their own romantic partners.

Bias or Positive Distortion. Intimates' "illusions"—what they see in their partners that their partners do not see in themselves—reflected the actors' tendencies to see their partners as they wished to see them, through the filters provided by their ideals and rosy self-images. However, these correlational analyses cannot address whether actors' impressions were in fact systematically more positive on average than their partners' self-perceptions, as we would expect. Finding evidence of such distortions would certainly strengthen our contention that actors' perceptions are idealized constructions. When we compared actors' and partners' perceptions within an ANOVA framework, the results supported our "positive illusions" hypothesis. Dating and married individuals evaluated their partners more positively than their partners saw themselves. Individuals also depicted their own partners more positively than the typical partner. Indeed, individuals may construct their impressions of the typical partner in ways that emphasize their partners' special virtues and minimize their faults (e.g., Johnson & Rusbult, 1989; Rusbult et al., 1992).

Individuals' representations do appear to be "positive illusions" when they are considered in light of their partners' own realities. This apparent distortion is particularly striking considering that our participants already seemed to idealize their own attributes; both dating and married individuals rated their own attributes much more favorably than the typical partner's attributes. In summary, married individuals appeared just as susceptible to the lure of seeing what they wanted to see in their partners, contradicting the common depiction of idealization as a malady confined to dating (e.g., Brehm, 1992).

Projected Illusions and Satisfaction

But do the idealized images actors construct leave them feeling happy and secure in their relationships, as we would expect? After all, understanding is often touted as the key to continued relationship satisfaction (e.g., Kobak & Hazan, 1991; Swann et al., 1992). According to this perspective, recognizing truths, even harsh truths, provides the foundation for satisfying close relationships by facilitating interpersonal adjustment and accommodation.

To explore the benefits of relationship illusions, we included actors' satisfaction as the criterion variable within our "positive illusions" path model. In path-analytic terms, actors' illusions should predict their satisfaction, above and beyond the influence of the partner's self-perceived reality. Consistent with our expectations, both dating and married individuals were more satisfied in their relationships to the extent that they held "positive illusions" about their partners. The more positive, the more idealized their constructions—controlling for the partner's actual attributes—the greater the satisfaction. Conversely, the more realistic or the less idealistic the perceptions, the less the satisfaction. Thus, the idealized realities intimates construct appear to be critical for satisfying dating and even marital relationships.[2]

These findings follow on the heels of a large literature arguing that idealism or optimism is critical for mental health (e.g., Greenwald, 1980; Janoff-Bulman, 1989; Taylor & Brown, 1988; Weinstein, 1980). Positive illusions, including idealized self-perceptions, exaggerated perceptions of control and

---

[2]We also examined the benefits of "positive illusions" at the level of specific traits. Such trait-specific illusions may predict satisfaction in the same way that idealizing the global nature of a partner's attributes appears to promote feelings of satisfaction. To explore this hypothesis, we calculated two idealization correlations per couple—that between the man's ideal for each trait and his perception of his partner on each trait and between the woman's ideal and her perception of her partner. These correlations index the degree to which intimates' ideals structure their perceptions of the relative descriptiveness of their partners' traits, although they are independent of the overall positivity of these ratings. When we correlated these indices with satisfaction, we found results consistent with the analyses on overall perceptions: Intimates were happier in their relationships when their impressions of their partners' attributes mirrored their hopes for the ideal partner.

unrealistic optimism, appear to function as buffers, protecting individuals' self-esteem in the face of the threats posed by negative information about the self (Taylor & Brown, 1988). Also, the perhaps illusory assumption that the world is in fact benevolent and meaningful may provide a sense of security in the face of uncertainty (Janoff-Bulman, 1989). From this perspective, happiness and contentment depend, not on people's acceptance of a stern reality, but on their ability to see themselves and their world in the best possible light.

FENDING OFF DOUBTS: STORYTELLING AND CONSTRUAL

It is the expectations of seeing [one's beloved] that has produced this unpleasant effect. It is this kind of thing that makes matter-of-fact people say that love is madness. What happens is that the imagination, violently wrenched out of delicious reveries in which every step brings happiness, is dragged back to stern reality. (Stendhal, 1927, p. 63)

Are positive illusions delicious reveries that instill only a transient sense of confidence, as Stendhal seems to suggest? Shouldn't discovering a partner's faults inevitably drag individuals back to harsher realities? Yet, despite the greater opportunity for married individuals to discover how their partners fall short of their ideals, they appear to be just as susceptible as dating couples to the lure of seeing what they want to see in their partners. Thus, the rigors of increased time and interdependence need not inevitably tarnish idealized perceptions. How then do intimates keep the reality of a partner's faults from intruding on their illusions?

We propose that individuals protect convictions—or positive illusions—by weaving cogent stories that depict potential faults or imperfections in their partners in the best possible light. In other words, intimates ward off doubts by constructing positive stories about seeming faults. In such confidence-instilling representations, negative attributes must be refuted or transformed, not left dangling as loose ends within the story (e.g., Brickman, 1987; Murray & Holmes, 1993; Taylor, 1991). Paradoxically, negativity may actually shape individuals' construction of idealized stories about their partners by motivating them to minimize their partners' faults and embellish their virtues (Brickman, 1987; Murray & Holmes, 1993).

Our emphasis on negativity as a trigger for storytelling parallels recent theorizing and research that links negativity and feelings of uncertainty to intimates' search for meaning or causal understanding, as reflected in increased relationship reflection and attributional activity (Acitelli & Holmberg, in press; Berscheid, 1983; Burnett, 1987; Fletcher, Fincham, Cramer,

& Heron, 1987; Harvey, Agostinelli, & Weber, 1989; Surra & Bohman, 1991). For example, Cate (1991) argued that relationship thinking often serves to quell feelings of uncertainty and thus bolsters satisfaction. Similarly, we believe that the process of integrating negativity within one's stories results in idealized perceptions that typically dispel doubt and solidify confidence in an intimate partner.

Maintaining Convictions: Fending Off Doubts

In exploring exactly how individuals ward off doubts, we draw from our own experiments on the idealization process as well as the broader relationships literature. Such defensive storytelling entails constructing excuses for misdeeds, turning faults into virtues, refuting the importance of faults, and embellishing the importance of virtues. As will become evident, intimates' ability to protect their illusions in the face of apparent negativity appears to rest on the vagaries inherent in the construal process.

Negativity and Situational Tagging: What Fault? As the first, most directly affirming response to negativity, individuals may simply deny that their partners' seemingly negative behavior reflects an underlying disposition or attribute. For example, if the individual attributes a partner's stubborn behavior to a bad day at work, such behavior need not elicit any concerns about an intimate's ultimate flexibility and generosity. Thus, intimates may create illusion-sustaining excuses for their partners' misbehaviors. Such excuses pre-empt dispositional inferences by minimizing the perceived stability and globality of negative behaviors (e.g., Kelley, 1972). Happily married couples, for example, typically attribute their spouses' negative behaviors to specific, unstable features of the situation (Bradbury & Fincham, 1990; Holtzworth-Munroe & Jacobson, 1985). By linking behaviors suggestive of negative traits to specific features of the situation, individuals avoid attributing threatening attributes in their partners and preserve idealized perceptions (e.g., Hall & Taylor, 1976).

Accommodation: You Didn't Mean It, Did You? Intimates' own, behavioral responses to specific transgressions might also reduce the threat posed by occasional misbehaviors. For instance, if an individual responds to a partner's stubbornness with patience and understanding, such tolerance or loyalty might then mollify the partner's obstinacy. In contrast, responding with equal stubbornness might only harden the partner's stance. Satisfied couples do tend to respond to their partners' transgressions constructively—by making a limited complaint or selflessly tolerating the offense (Rusbult, Johnson, & Morrow, 1986; Rusbult, Verette, Whitney, Slovik, & Lipkus, 1991). Giving a partner the benefit of the doubt might then afford this person the opportunity to "take it all back" and make amends, thereby reducing the threat posed by the initial misbehavior.

When Reality Beckons: Turning Faults Into Virtues. Situational tagging and accommodation may preserve illusions in the face of isolated misdeeds. But as interdependence increases, negativity is likely to recur (Levinger, 1983). Imagine, for example, that an intimate continues to act stubbornly—not only after bad days at work but even after good days. In the face of such accumulated evidence, partners may experience increasing difficulty avoiding dispositional or trait inferences (e.g., Kelley, 1972).

Nonetheless, intimates may still perceive positive attributes in behavioral evidence that at face value points to more negative, less charitable interpretations. Intimates' illusions may function as interpretive filters that color the meaning of potentially negative evidence. Poetic or interpretive license may be especially evident in this process of inferring attributes from behavior (Trope, 1986). If this is so, the meaning of a behavior or attribute may then be defined more by what a person desires to see than by any quality inherent in the attribute. As a result, intimates may come to see virtues in their partners' faults.

Challenging Convictions: A Threat Induction Paradigm

In a recent set of studies, we developed an experimental paradigm to examine precisely how individuals preserve idealized stories in the face of their partners' more chronic faults (Murray & Holmes, 1993, 1994). In designing these studies, we followed McGuire and Papageorgis' (1961) sage advice on the utility of challenging attitudes that are essentially cultural truisms (e.g., brushing one's teeth is good). We created negative attributes in the laboratory by threatening what we felt were relationship truisms for dating individuals. The truisms were "conflict in relationships is bad" in our first study and "differences are bad" in our second study. By arguing in favor of the opposite propositions (e.g., conflict is good), we turned apparent virtues (e.g., low conflict) into potential faults. Comparing the perceptions of threatened individuals to the "reality" baseline provided by controls then allowed us to directly observe the idealization process.

Experiment 1: Seeing Conflict Engagement in Avoidance. In the first study, we threatened dating individuals' positive illusions by depicting their partners' reluctance to initiate conflicts over joint interests as a significant fault. First, experimental and control participants completed a scaled measure tapping their dating partners' tendency to initiate such disagreements (e.g., "When I suggest an activity I enjoy but my partner does not enjoy, he or she is never reluctant to express his or her objection to this activity"). We then gave them 2 minutes to list instances of their partners' initiating disagreements over joint activities. As we anticipated, our dating subjects typically had considerable difficulty thinking of instances of their partners' initiating such disagreements. As a result, they readily depicted their partners as rarely initiating disagreements over joint interests. We then turned this conflict avoidance into a fault by exposing experimental subjects to a bogus *Psychology Today* article arguing for the intimacy-promoting nature of conflict engagement. Control subjects read this article at the end of the study.

By depicting conflict engagement as a fault, we expected to threaten experimental subjects' positive convictions about the level of intimacy in their relationships. Participants' responses to a scaled perceived intimacy index suggested that the article did indeed threaten their convictions, as they felt less secure and close to their partners than control subjects. We expected experimental subjects to dispel such doubts by transforming their partners' reluctance to initiate conflicts over joint interests—making it appear less negative or even positive. For example, these threatened individuals might embellish their partners' willingness to initiate conflicts across a broad variety of relationship domains exclusive of joint interests. To test whether threatened individuals saw such virtues in apparent faults, we then had all subjects describe their partners' general willingness to initiate conflicts on a scaled conflict index (e.g., "My partner expresses his or her needs even when he or she knows that these needs conflict with mine").

Next, we asked participants to write open-ended narratives describing the important ways in which their partners impeded or facilitated the development of intimacy in their relationships. (We made the conflict dimension equally salient for control and experimental participants by reminding controls of the focus of the forthcoming article.) Two independent raters coded these stories for indications of how individuals wove their partners' apparent faults around conflict into confidence-instilling representations. Our coding dimensions tapped individuals' depictions of their partners' virtues and faults around conflict engagement and conflict avoidance as well as their interpretation of the meaning or importance of these attributes.

Experiment 2: Seeing Differences in Similarities. We created negativity in the second study by depicting partners' inattention to their differences as an impediment to intimacy. To establish this threat, we first asked participants to provide concrete examples of similarities and differences between themselves and their dating partners. As we anticipated, these examples consisted primarily of similarities. As a result, our participants readily acknowledged that they were aware of very few differences. Experimental subjects then read a bogus *Psychology Today* article that argued that partners' awareness of their differences fosters relationship intimacy. Control participants read an article on an unrelated topic.

To explore the role of motivated construal processes in shaping the meaning of specific pieces of evidence, we then gave all participants the opportunity to provide any additional details they wished to their original pool of examples. As a primary response to the threat, we expected threatened individuals to provide details that turned this evidence of their similarities (a newly created fault) into evidence of their many differences (a newly found virtue). Two independent raters coded these open-ended accounts on dimensions tapping subjects' reinterpretation or reconstrual of these examples. These coding dimensions indexed subjects' reinterpretation of the meaning of specific pieces of evidence (e.g., turning a similarity into a difference) as well as their reinterpretation of the importance of these attributes (e.g., embellishing a difference or de-emphasizing a similarity).

All participants then completed a scaled measure tapping their perceptions of the degree to which they differed from their partners in a variety of domains (e.g., "I am aware of a variety of ways in which my partner's preferred ways of dealing with conflict differ greatly from my own"). Finally, we again asked participants to write open-ended stories describing the development of intimacy in their relationships. We coded these stories on dimensions tapping individuals' spontaneous exaggeration and embellishment of their many differences.

Defusing Doubts: Seeing Virtues in Faults. The results of both story telling experiments provided considerable support for intimates' ability to see virtues in apparent faults. Consider the results on the scaled measure of perceived conflict in our first experiment (see Fig. 4.3). In response to the threat, experimental subjects who scored low on the pretest index of conflicts over

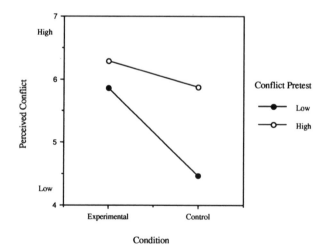

FIG. 4.3.   Mean perceived conflict as a function of condition and pretest conflict. From Murray and Holmes (1994). Reprinted with permission of Sage Publications, Inc., copyright © 1994.

joint interests constructed images of conflict-engaging partners (when compared to low-conflict controls). In contrast, threatened individuals who scored high on the pretest conflict index did not change their impressions of their partners' willingness to initiate conflicts (when compared to high conflict controls). In fact, low- and high-conflict experimental participants did not differ on this scaled conflict measure even though their original self-reports suggested that their conflict histories differed dramatically.

Such restructuring was also evident in participants' open-ended stories. In weaving these revised stories, low-conflict threatened subjects were most likely to focus on their partners' many virtues around engaging conflicts (e.g., "I feel he is facilitating our growth by increasingly being able to tell me when he disagrees with my opinions in all areas"). On both scaled and open-ended measures then, low-conflict threatened individuals reached conclusions attesting to their partners' many virtues in engaging conflicts from evidence pointing toward their partners' faults.

Threatened individuals in Study 2 also constructed virtues in apparent faults—finding evidence of their strengths around recognizing differences in the face of their overwhelming similarities. On the scaled differences index, threatened individuals reached conclusions attesting to their many, virtuous differences even though the reports of control participants strongly pointed to their similarities (see Table 4.1). Threatened individuals, in comparison to controls, were also significantly more likely to emphasize their awareness of their differences in their own, spontaneously structured stories. Most criti-

TABLE 4.1
Transforming Meaning: Seeing Virtues in Faults

Restructuring Indices[a]	High Threat Condition	Control Condition	F
Study 1: Seeing Conflict-Engagement in Conflict Avoidance[b]			
Perceived conflict scale (9 point)	5.86	4.47	4.02*
Open-ended stories: Constructing a conflict-engaging partner	3.00	0.50	4.73*
Study 2: Seeing Differences in Similarities[c]			
Perceived differences scale (9 point)	5.10	4.25	10.13**
Open-ended stories: Emphasizing awareness of differences	2.03	0.61	10.06**
Additional details: Recasting similarities as differences	1.00	0.23	12.49**

[a]The values for the open-ended indices refer to the mean number of occurrences of the designated category (e.g., mean number of statements depicting conflict-engagement as a virtue).
[b]The high threat condition refers to the low conflict experimental subjects while the control condition refers to the low conflict control subjects. The reported F reflects the pretest conflict by condition interaction, *$p < .05$. [c]The high threat condition refers to the experimental subjects. The reported F reflects the main effect for condition, **$p < .01$.
Note. From Murray and Holmes (1994). Reprinted with permission of Sage Publications, Inc., copyright © 1994.

cally, they even transformed the meaning of specific pieces of evidence. For example, in providing additional details to their original similarities, threatened individuals, in comparison to controls, were significantly more likely to recast their similarities as reflecting their differences (see Table 4.1). These examples illustrate this reconstrual of perceived faults:

> We are of similar intellectual ability (original) . . . *however, when it comes to using this ability I like to spend more time on my schoolwork than she does or than she would have me do* (detailed).

> We both feel insecure about starting a relationship because of past experiences (original) . . . both my partner and I feel compelled to make our relationship work because of past negative experiences; *although we differ in that her fear is loneliness while mine is rejection* (detailed).

Both experiments speak to the integral role poetic license plays in story telling. For example, the reports of low-conflict control participants (which provide an index of low-conflict individuals' "original" impressions of their intimates) depicted partners who rarely initiated conflicts. However, an apparent paucity of consistent data from their interpersonal histories did not constrain low-conflict threatened individuals in their construction of images of conflict-engaging partners. Similarly, threatened individuals in Study 2 constructed evidence of their many differences despite the overwhelming evidence of their similarities. Like revisionist historians, threatened individuals conveniently white-washed the past for the exigencies of the present.

Seeing virtues in faults may be a primary means for maintaining idealized perceptions of intimate partners. Such transformations may protect intimates' illusions from at least some of the challenges posed by negativity. But as evidence of their partners' faults continues to mount and crystallize, individuals may not always be able to reconstrue the meaning of negativity in this way. Eventually, intimates face seemingly incontrovertible evidence of their partners' negative qualities.

Re-Fencing Faults: "Yes, But . . ." Refutations. Acknowledging faults need not undermine intimates' positive illusions if they somehow re-fence or re-structure their narratives in ways that defuse the meaning of these imperfections. This re-fencing process (Allport, 1954) may depend partly on individuals' construction of specific, idiosyncratic theories that relegate their partners' virtues and faults to positions of more or less importance in their stories. Such relationship-affirming theories may be revealed through intimates' construction of refutational or "Yes, but . . . " arguments that acknowledge their partners' faults, yet simultaneously minimize their significance.

For instance, intimates might keep negativity from intruding on their illusions simply by denying the significance of their partners' weaknesses (e.g., "I know he isn't that expressive, but it really doesn't matter. I love him just the way he is"). Similarly, "Yes, buts . . . " that link faults to virtues in related domains may also contain the threat posed by negativity (e.g., "He's a rather closed type of man, but that's not so important. He shows he cares in other ways"; Holmes, 1991). If individuals integrate negativity but refute its implications in their storytelling, acknowledging their partners' faults need not pose any threat to their positive illusions. Affectively consistent attitudes may even depend on the presence of such refutational "Yes, but . . . " structures (e.g., Chaiken & Yates, 1985; Holmes & Rempel, 1989).

We found considerable evidence for the importance of such "Yes, buts . . . " in our first study. In response to the specter of conflict-avoidant partners, low-conflict threatened individuals were the most likely to embellish their partners' many virtues around engaging in conflicts, as we discussed. But despite this embellishment, they still grappled with their partners' weaknesses around conflict. Such residual feelings of ambivalence were revealed in their intimacy narratives, which contained the most frequent references to their partners' conflict-avoidance impeding intimacy (see Table 4.2). Even though such references were less frequent than references to their partners' conflict-related strengths, these individuals did not leave such threatening "loose ends" in their stories. Instead, they constructed refutational or "Yes, but . . . " arguments around these weaknesses (see Table 4.2). Such refutations minimized the importance of instances of a partner's conflict-avoidance, as these examples illustrate:

On many occasions, I could tell that a problem existed, but she refused to talk about it, almost afraid of an argument . . . *on the other hand, she is very receptive to my needs, and willing to adapt if necessary. This is beneficial to our relationship.*

I do not think that he realizes that not arguing impedes the development of intimacy because when I do things that bother him, he simply ignores them or adjusts to them. *However, this is changing and we are becoming closer all the time.* My partner is beginning to realize that ignoring problems only makes them build and occasionally he will initiate disagreements.

Intriguingly, this process may operate quite independently of apparent social reality constraints. In other words, considerable interpretive license may underlie theory construction. For example, intimates often construct refutations downplaying the importance of inexpressiveness—even though this requires contradicting widely endorsed cultural theories that identify expressiveness as a critical ingredient of relationship success (e.g., Fletcher & Fitness, 1993). As this example illustrates, satisfied intimates may reach

TABLE 4.2
Transforming Importance: Re-fencing Faults and Embellishing Virtues

Restructuring Indices[a]	High Threat Condition	Control Condition	F
Re-fencing or Refuting Faults			
Open-ended stories: Partner's faults around conflict avoidance[b]	1.27	0.14	6.49***
"Yes, but. . . " refutations: Explaining away conflict avoidance[c]	2.36	0.33	6.45**
Additional details: Explaining away differences[d]	0.12	0.48	3.81*
Embellishing Virtues			
Open-ended stories: Embellishing conflict engagement[c]	0.64	0.07	4.07**
Additional details: Embellishing differences[d]	0.32	0.06	4.52**
Open-ended stories: Embellishing differences[d]	0.79	0.03	11.61***
Additional details: Embellishing similarities[d]	0.74	0.16	5.84**

[a]The values for the open-ended indices refer to the mean number of occurrences of the designated category (e.g., mean number of Yes, but. . . " refutations). [b]The high-threat condition refers to the low-conflict experimental subjects while the control condition refers to the low-conflict control subjects. The reported F reflects the pretest conflict by condition interaction, **p < .05. [c]The high-threat condition refers to the low-conflict experimental subjects while the control condition refers to the low-conflict control subjects. The reported F reflects the main effect for condition, **p < .05. [d]The high-threat condition refers to the experimental subjects. The reported F reflects the main effect for condition, *p < .06, **p < .05, ***p < .01.

Note. From Murray and Holmes (1994). Reprinted with permission of Sage Publications, Inc., copyright © 1994.

conclusions about the importance of various traits or attributes that are tailored specifically to their partners' faults.

In other words, individuals' theories of the importance of various attributes may be dictated more by the attributes their partners possess than by any inherent significance attached to these traits. For example, Kunda (1987) showed that individuals construct self-serving theories that bolster their optimistic perceptions that they will not divorce (in the face of a 50% divorce rate) by linking their own attributes to marital success, at the expense of others' opposite attributes. Similarly, threatened individuals in Study 1 preserved their positive illusions by linking their partners' conflict engagement to greater closeness while steadfastly denying that instances of their partners' conflict avoidance had any bearing on intimacy.

Such flexibility in intimates' construal of the attributes most important in their relationships was also evident in Study 2. In providing additional details to their original examples of differences, threatened individuals were more likely to embellish or mushroom the significance of their differences by linking them to enhanced feelings of closeness, security and warmth. Such embellishment of differences also surfaced in their open-ended narratives. In contrast, control subjects tended to downplay the significance of such differences, as these contrasting examples illustrate:

Threatened participant: His views on important issues are the same as mine but he seems more firm in his beliefs (original) . . . I can see that he is very consistent with his feelings and attitudes and therefore *this makes it much easier for me to understand him and the reasons for his feelings and attitudes: It also helps me assess and understand myself* (detailed).

Control participant: I like talking a lot about us . . . he is quiet a lot (original) . . . *Actually, in general I talk a lot about anything so that is probably why he is more quiet* (detailed).

As these results attest, the desire to maintain idealized perceptions appears to guide the nature of the personal theories that intimates construct. When confronted by a potentially negative trait, individuals restructure their theories in ways that allow them to relegate their partners' faults to a tangential status in their stories. Through such transformations, individuals may prevent the reality of their partners' faults from intruding on their idealized perceptions.

Compensation: Masking Faults by Embellishing Virtues. Perhaps when individuals encounter clear evidence of their partners' faults, they sometimes protect their illusions simply by construing their partners' virtues in an even more positive light. For instance, threatened individuals in Study 2 appeared to compensate for the threat posed by their inattention to their differences by embellishing the significance of their similarities in promoting intimacy (see Table 4.2). If accentuating a partner's virtues can obscure his or her faults and quell doubts, an individual might not then need to directly reconstrue or refute negativity. Consistent with this theme, traditional "bank account" models assume that positivity might simply overshadow or mask negativity in satisfactory relationships (e.g., Gottman & Levenson, 1992).

Brickman (1987) focused on the role of compensation in masking feelings of uncertainty associated with a partner's faults. In his thinking, the strength of intimates' convictions rests on positive elements overshadowing and thus neutralizing negative elements. In this way, love and idealization are actually enhanced by perceptions of imperfections in romantic partners because awareness of faults motivates individuals to focus on and enhance their partners' positive qualities.

Existing research on compensation and self-interpretation also suggests that individuals might embellish their personal virtues to make up for perceived faults (Baumeister & Jones, 1978; Greenberg & Pyszczynski, 1985). In these studies, individuals were confronted with the knowledge that another person knew of a serious fault in their characters. These threatened individuals then emphasized their many virtues in domains unrelated to this fault, presumably in an attempt to reaffirm themselves in this critical other's eyes, and buffer self-esteem.

Steele (1988) also argued that allowing individuals to affirm valued, positive aspects of their identities can reduce feelings of dissonance associated with negative, identity-inconsistent elements. For example, individuals who chose to write counter attitudinal essays did not alter their attitudes if they were able first to reduce dissonance by affirming a valued aspect of their self-concepts (Steele & Liu, 1983). Apparently, affirming self-integrity in this way quells dissonance and allows individuals to tolerate or ignore potential threats to self, such as attitude-behavior inconsistencies. Similarly, affirming convictions by accentuating a partner's positive qualities might allow individuals to tolerate or ignore faults.

Other equally compelling lines of research, however, suggest that embellishing positivity may not really be as effective as defusing negativity in maintaining confidence. Rusbult and her colleagues argue that avoiding destructive behavior may be far more important for relationship satisfaction than attempting to maximize positive behaviors (Rusbult et al., 1986; Rusbult et al., 1991). Similarly, negativity in socioemotional behavior may be a particularly strong predictor of declines in satisfaction among newly married couples (Huston & Vangelisti, 1991). In these studies, positivity does not appear to overshadow negativity. Within this perspective, adding further positive elements to existing, idealized stories may have limited "marginal utility" for bolstering confidence as relationships progress.

We designed a recent study to explore whether positivity can compensate for negativity within individuals' narratives (Murray & Holmes, 1994). In this study, we modified the paradigm we used in our first experiment. Again, participants first depicted their partners as rarely initiating disagreements over joint interests. Participants in the two experimental conditions then read the *Psychology Today* article describing the intimacy-promoting aspects of engaging conflicts. Participants in the baseline experimental condition then completed the perceived conflict measure and intimacy narratives, as in Study 1. Participants in the compensation condition followed exactly the same procedure—but with one exception. After reading the article, they completed a "talk-aloud" exercise where they reflected on how important their partners' dependable nature was in promoting intimacy in their relationships. Thus, they were not left to their own devices in compensating for the fault (conflict avoidance), but were induced to focus on an important virtue. To provide an index of threatened individuals' compensatory ascription of increased value to their partners' virtues (such as dependability), all participants then indicated which of a variety of positive traits made their partners truly special and unique. Control subjects completed the dependability talk-aloud exercise and the dependent measures before they read the article on conflict.

Can juxtaposing positive and negative attributes in the compensation condition reduce individuals' need to directly reconstrue negativity? If focusing on their partners' dependability is sufficient to compensate for their partners' conflict avoidance, threatened individuals should not need to construct images of conflict-engaging partners (i.e., they should resemble individuals in the control condition). Further still, dependability might even become more important for these threatened participants, speaking to the possibility that individuals might embellish their partners' virtues in order to mask concerns about their faults. But, if individuals in the compensation condition still accentuate their partners' conflict-related virtues when compared to controls, this suggests that focusing on positivity is not sufficient to make up for faults.

We did not find any support for a simple buffering effect of compensation. On the perceived conflict measure, threatened individuals in both the compensation and baseline experimental conditions exaggerated their partners' willingness to initiate disagreements across a variety of domains. This restructuring occurred even though individuals in the compensation condition did in fact spontaneously embellish their partners' dependability relative to individuals in the control condition. Despite this evidence of threatened individuals' efforts to reaffirm the quality of their relationships, enhancing this important virtue was not sufficient to make up for their partners' weaknesses around initiating conflicts (as "bank account" models might suggest).

But, in simply asking whether or not individuals can obscure their partners' faults by embellishing virtues, we may have overlooked a potentially integral feature of good stories. Perhaps focusing on virtues only compensates for faults if individuals are able to forge direct cognitive links between their partners' positive and negative attributes. In constructing such "Yes, but. . . " arguments, individuals might be motivated to draw the positive attribute into the perceived domain of the negative attribute. For example, an individual might excuse his partner's general reluctance to pursue conflicts by countering with her dependability—which he construes as evidence of her willingness to be sensitive to his needs in problem-solving situations and pursue issues when it really counts. Similarly, a wife might excuse her husband's inattention to more mundane domestic chores (e.g., cooking, cleaning) by emphasizing his willingness to take responsibility for their children's leisure activities. Essentially, individuals may come to understand specific faults in the light of greater, *related* virtues that take the sting away from these imperfections (e.g., Holmes & Rempel, 1989).

To test whether threatened individuals did forge compensatory links between their partners' weaknesses around conflict and selected virtues, we had them rate how strongly each of a number of positive qualities (e.g., trustworthy, dependable, accepting, responsive) were related to their partners' tendency to engage or avoid conflicts. As we surmised, individuals in both the baseline experimental and compensation conditions drew more positive qualities into the realm of their partners' conflict behavior than controls. Threatened individuals appeared to account for or perhaps even excuse their partners' periodic reluctance to initiate conflicts by integrating this fault within the domain of related, perhaps greater virtues.

Suggestive support for the importance of such compensatory links was also evident in our first two studies. Low-conflict individuals threatened on the ground that they seldom fought over joint interests interpreted this fault within the broader context of their partners' (newly recognized) virtues around engaging conflicts in other important domains. Perhaps then, individuals can tolerate specific, limited imperfections if their partners' virtues within a potentially troublesome domain overshadow or in some way mute the significance of their faults.

Storytelling and the Construction of Illusions

Apart from protecting existing perceptions, defensive transformations of the meaning and significance of apparent faults may even strengthen intimates' illusions. Individuals may discover new, previously unrecognized virtues as they struggle to deal with one another's imperfections. For instance, low-conflict individuals discovered their partners' many important virtues around conflict engagement precisely because of their concerns about their partners' conflict avoidance. Similarly, as a counterpoint to the threat that they were simply idealizing their partners, threatened individuals in Study 2 discovered significant new virtues in recognizing differences between themselves and their partners (Murray & Holmes, 1993).

Individuals' struggle to deal with their own weaknesses may even lead them to see greater virtues in their partners if these weaknesses create doubts about their relationships. For example, people seem to defuse doubts posed by their own attraction to desirable others by disparaging the attractiveness of these potential mates (Johnson & Rusbult, 1989). Individuals' own partners appear especially attractive and desirable in light of such unattractive alternatives. Paradoxically then, positive representations of a partner may prosper—not in spite of a partner's negative qualities—but precisely because of these imperfections (e.g., Brickman, 1987).

THE TRANSMISSION OF ILLUSIONS

Weaving such idealized stories may sustain actors' satisfaction, but does being the target of such idealized perceptions also promote bliss? Shouldn't it be disconcerting for individuals to believe their partners only love an illusion—not their true selves? In fact, the fear that one's partner doesn't really understand or accept the "real me" might leave partners feeling vulnerable and uncertain. In this light, being idealized may detract from feelings of satisfaction, particularly if individuals really want their partners to see them as they see themselves (e.g., Kobak & Hazan, 1991; Swann et al., 1992). For example, Swann and his colleagues found that married individuals were more committed to their relationships when their partners verified their self-perceptions, even if this involved confirming a negative self-concept.

Despite these arguments, we found no evidence that individuals were happier in their relationships when their partners accurately understood their less than perfect natures. Instead, intimates actually appeared to be happier in their relationships when their partners idealized them (Murray et al., in press). In terms of the path model presented in Fig. 4.2, dating and married intimates were more satisfied in their relationship when their partners saw positive qualities in them that they did not see in themselves. Even in the critical case of individuals relatively low in self-regard, intimates still were most satisfied if their partners saw the best in them despite their own self-doubts.[3]

Idealized intimates may be happier in their relationships because their partners treat them as special, unique individuals, thereby encouraging intimates to live up to these pristine images (e.g., Snyder & Swann, 1978; Snyder, Tanke, & Berscheid, 1977). Also, if actors interpret their partners' behaviors through the rosy filters provided by their own ideals, their inclination toward "attributional charity" might also minimize the potential for overt conflict (e.g., Rusbult et al., 1991). Finally, individuals might contradict their partners' self-criticisms on valued but ambiguous traits, thereby bolstering their sense of self-worth. In these ways, unconditional

---

[3]To explore the link between self-verification and satisfaction, we conducted a series of regression analyses. In these analyses, the partner's self-perceptions and the actor's perception of the partner were first entered as main effects. The cross-product interaction term was entered in the next step. If self-verification promotes satisfaction, this analysis should yield a significant interaction term. Matches (i.e., seeing what your partner sees) should promote satisfaction, while mismatches should detract from satisfaction. However, we did not find any evidence that being idealized (i.e., mismatches) detracts from satisfaction.

The qualities examined by Swann and his colleagues, however, were more objective (e.g., physically attractive, athletic) than our more abstract, interpersonal traits. Maybe, self-verification is more important for such public, objective traits. To explore this possibility, we conducted the above analyses using Swann et al.'s actual attribute measure. However, we still found no evidence for the benefits of self-verification. Perhaps, self-verification is most important when the traits in dispute are central to the partner's self-concept and subject to ready verification by observers. In such cases, partners who fail to see such obvious weaknesses might be perceived as defensively denying an unpleasant "reality" that individuals themselves have been struggling to accept.

admiration—a sense of being valued and accepted in spite of one's faults and imperfections—may provide a foundation for relationship satisfaction and intimacy, assuring intimates that their partners truly care for them (Reis & Shaver, 1988).

CONFIDENCE OR CATASTROPHE?

In this chapter, we painted a portrait of satisfying relationships that differs dramatically from most current conceptions (e.g., Brickman, 1987; Swann et al., 1992). Rather than truly understanding one another, intimates seem to conspire in constructing idealized realities that both obscure one another's faults and embellish virtues. The more idealized the construction, the greater the satisfaction. In fact, the self-perceived reality of a partner's less than perfect nature appears to have a surprisingly small bearing on happiness. Yet, as relationships evolve, many intimates obviously experience great difficulty keeping such realities at bay: The high rate of relationship dissolution speaks to the inevitable disappointments many people ultimately face. Ironically, the positive illusions that initially ensure happiness may later serve to accentuate how a partner falls short of one's hopes.

We are currently following a longitudinal sample of dating couples to explore the long-term benefits of positive illusions. We believe that the resiliency of illusions—whether they provide the basis for continued satisfaction or eventual disillusionment—depends on the content and structure of the stories that intimates tell in the face of negativity. This hypothesized relation between confidence and cognitive structure has strong parallels to McGuire and Papageorgis' (1961) inoculation theory of attitude stability. Just as cultural truisms are vulnerable to threat, stories that focus only on virtues may be quite fragile, whereas stories that acknowledge but counter-argue faults may prove more resilient. In other words, the strategies individuals use in fending off doubts may result in narratives that are more or less likely to instill confidence over time.

If illusions rest on intimates' denial of disappointing realities, the stories woven around negative attributes may unravel as evidence inconsistent with the individual's construction intrudes again and again. For instance, if individuals deal with their doubts by turning faults into virtues, such blatant denial may leave them quite vulnerable to recurring evidence of negativity. Alternatively, intimates might compartmentalize faults and diminish their relevance by constructing personal theories that simply deny the significance of their partners' weaknesses. However, in stories with categories restricted to grievances, current doubts may prime past concerns without also being cushioned by a partner's virtues. As a result, individuals' illusions may be left quite vulnerable to disquieting resurgences of ambivalence (Holmes & Rempel, 1989).

Intimates may be more likely to reach a lasting sense of confidence if they weave idealized stories in such ways that their partners' faults actually remind them of greater virtues. Through this process of constructive linkage, the partner's many virtues can buffer or defuse the threats posed by a partner's apparent frailties. For instance, a wife might be less disturbed by her husband's laziness around household chores if she thinks his devotion to their children more than makes up for it. Continued confidence in an intimate partner may rest on this type of *structural integrity* within individuals' stories. For instance, high trust individuals actually evaluated their partners' behavior and motives in a laboratory interaction most positively when they had just been induced to recall a threatening situation where their partners disappointed them (Holmes & Rempel, 1989). Cushioning faults within virtues may protect intimates' positive illusions from the inevitable threats posed by renewed evidence of negativity. Therefore, intimates who see the best in one another—while still acknowledging their partners' faults—may possess the types of integrated representations most likely to be resilient over time.

If individuals interpret somewhat disappointing realities in the best possible light—without denying negativity—such positive illusions may ensure later satisfaction (e.g., Taylor, Collins, Skokan, & Aspinwall, 1989). Seeing their partners' faults in the best possible light may provide intimates with the security and optimism necessary to confront difficulties in their relationships. As well as providing constructive motivation, illusions may create resources of goodwill and generosity that prevent everyday hassles from turning into significant trivia (Holmes & Murray, in press). Intimates might even create elements of the idealized reality they perceive by treating their partners as special, unique individuals (e.g., Snyder & Swann, 1978; Snyder et al., 1977). In these ways, illusions may provide an effective buffer against the inevitable vicissitudes of time.

However, intimates may set themselves up for catastrophe if they fail to deal directly with troublesome issues that reflect latent incompatibilities in their goals and needs for the relationship (Holmes & Murray, in press). For example, many individuals ignore the implications of negativity and make decisions to marry largely on the basis of their positive feelings about their partners, as the present chapter would lead us to expect. In fact, apparent negativity, such as premarital conflict, is virtually independent of feelings of love and satisfaction at the point of marriage (Braiker & Kelley, 1979; Kelly, Huston, & Cate, 1985; Markman, 1979). But, such blatant compartmentalization in the service of idealization is not without its costs: Conflict and negativity prior to marriage, although initially divorced from satisfaction, predict later declines in satisfaction (e.g., Kelly et al., 1985; Markman, 1981).

Such "hidden realities" may have an insidious effect over time, eventually tarnishing relationship illusions and eroding confidence (e.g., Huston & Vangelisti, 1991; Rusbult et al., 1991). As the research just cited attests (e.g., Kelly et al., 1985; Markman, 1981), intimates' positive convictions may begin to waver if negativity is recurrent and exceeds their capacity to assimilate it into positive stories. Once this equilibrium is disturbed and confidence begins to erode, individuals may begin to actively test whether the partner really is "right" for them (Holmes & Boon, 1990). Framed in terms of Kruglanski's (1989) lay epistemic theory, intimates' primary motivation may shift from the need for specific closure, the focus of the present research, to a fear of invalidity. In effect, they may become more cautious and less charitable in their story-telling to protect themselves from the further dashing of their hopes.

Paradoxically, the interpretive license that sustained illusions may then provide the potential for catastrophe—a crisis of confidence. For instance, an individual might begin to entertain the hypothesis that her partner's stub-bornness really is a sign of unresponsiveness, rather than integrity, when her positive convictions begin to waver. Indeed, the very fragility of relationships may rest on the flexibility inherent in the construal process itself. Brickman (1987), for example, couched his description of romantic love in terms of catastrophe theory (e.g., Flay, 1978). He argued that passionate love is created out of intense ambivalence through intimates' commitment to idealized depictions of their partners. However, as ambivalence is only masked, recurring negativity may trigger a dramatic decrease in love. Inter-pretive license may provide the basis for such "shattered illusions." Ironi-cally, when doubt begins to erode hope, the same storytelling and construal processes that once sustained intimates' illusions may then support more jaded perceptions.

ACKNOWLEDGMENTS

We thank Dale Griffin for his invaluable contributions to our research and thinking. We also thank Julie Fitness, Garth Fletcher, and George Levinger for their thoughtful comments on an earlier version of this chapter. We are also indebted to Mary Dooley, Alisa Lenox, Julie Perks, Teresa Pizzamiglio, Renata Snidr, and Stephen Taylor for their assistance in conducting our research. This chapter was prepared with the support of a Social Sciences and Humanities Research Council of Canada (SSHRC) Doctoral Fellowship to the first author and a SSHRC research grant to the second author.

REFERENCES

Abelson, R. P. (1959). Modes of resolution of belief dilemmas. *Journal of Conflict Resolution, 3*, 343–352.

Acitelli, L. K., & Holmberg, D. (in press). Reflecting on relationships: The role of thoughts and memories. In W. Jones & D. Perlman (Eds.), *Advances in personal relationships* (Vol. 4). London: Jessica Kingsley Publishers.

Alicke, M. D. (1985). Global self-evaluation as determined by the desirability and controllability of trait adjectives. *Journal of Personality and Social Psychology, 49*, 1621–1630.

Allport, G. W. (1954). *The nature of prejudice.* Reading, MA: Addison-Wesley.

Aron, A., Aron, E. N., Tudor, M., & Nelson, G. (1991). Close relationships as including other in the self. *Journal of Personality and Social Psychology, 60*, 241–253.

Asch, S. E. (1946). Forming impressions of personality. *Journal of Abnormal and Social Psychology, 41*, 258–290.

Asch, S. E., & Zukier, H. (1984). Thinking about persons. *Journal of Personality and Social Psychology, 46*, 1230–1240.

Baldwin, M. W. (1992). Relational schemas and the processing of social information. *Psychological Bulletin, 112*, 461–484.

Baumeister, R. F., & Jones, E. E. (1978). When self-presentation is constrained by the target's knowledge: Consistency and compensation. *Journal of Personality and Social Psychology, 36*, 608–618.

Berscheid, E. (1983). Emotion. In H. H. Kelley, E. Berscheid, A. Christensen, J. H. Harvey, T. L. Huston, G. Levinger, E. McClintock, L. A. Peplau & D. R. Peterson (Eds.), *Close relationships* (pp. 110–168). New York: Freeman.

Bowlby, J. (1977). The making and breaking of affectional bonds. *British Journal of Psychiatry, 130*, 201–210.

Bradbury, T. N., & Fincham, F. D. (1990). Attributions in marriage: Review and critique. *Psychological Bulletin, 107*, 3–33.

Braiker, H. B., & Kelley, H. H. (1979). Conflict in the development of close relationships. In R. L. Burgess & T. L. Huston (Eds.), *Social exchange in developing relationships* (pp. 135–168). New York: Academic Press.

Brehm, S. S. (1988). Passionate love. In R. J. Sternberg & M. L. Barnes (Eds.), *The psychology of love* (pp. 232–263). New Haven, CT: Yale University Press.

Brehm, S. S. (1992). *Intimate relationships.* New York: McGraw-Hill.

Brickman, P. (1987). *Commitment, conflict, and caring.* Englewood Cliffs, NJ: Prentice-Hall.

Brown, J. D. (1986). Evaluations of self and others: Self-enhancement biases in social judgment. *Social Cognition, 4*, 353–376.

Burnett, R. (1987). Reflection in personal relationships. In R. Burnett, P. McGhee, & D. Clarke (Eds.), *Accounting for relationships: Explanation, representation and knowledge* (pp. 74–91). London: Methuen.

Cate, R. M. (1991, May). *Relationship thinking: A measure and some initial studies.* Paper presented at the third International Network Conference on Personal Relationships, Normal, IL.

Chaiken, S., & Yates, S. (1985). Affective-cognitive consistency and thought-induced polarization. *Journal of Personality and Social Psychology, 49*, 1470–1481.

Cohen, J., & Cohen, P. (1983). *Applied multiple regression/correlation analysis for the behavioral sciences.* Hillsdale, NJ: Lawrence Erlbaum Associates.

Epstein, S. (1982). Conflict and stress. In L. Goldberger & S. Breznitz (Eds.), *Handbook of stress* (pp. 49–68). New York: The Free Press.

Feeney, J. A., & Noller, P. (1991). Attachment style and verbal descriptions of romantic partners. *Journal of Social and Personal Relationships, 8*, 187–215.

Festinger, L. (1957). *A theory of cognitive dissonance.* Evanston, IL: Row, Peterson.

Flay, B. R. (1978). Catastrophe theory in social psychology: Some applications to attitudes and social behavior. *Behavioral Science, 23*, 335–350.

Fletcher, G. J. O., Fincham, F. D., Cramer, L., & Heron, N. (1987). The role of attributions in the development of dating relationships. *Journal of Personality and Social Psychology, 53*, 481–489.

Fletcher, G. J. O., & Fitness, J. (1993). Knowledge structures and explanations in intimate relationships. In S. Duck (Ed.), *Individuals in relationships* (Vol. 1, pp. 121–143). Newbury Park, CA: Sage.

Gergen, K. J., Hepburn, A., & Fisher, D. C. (1986). Hermeneutics of personality description. *Journal of Personality and Social Psychology, 50,* 1261–1270.

Gottman, J. M., & Levenson, R. W. (1992). Marital processes predictive of later dissolution: Behavior, physiology, and health. *Journal of Personality and Social Psychology, 63,* 221–233.

Greenberg, J., & Pyszczynski, T. (1985). Compensatory self-inflation: A response to the threat to self-regard of public failure. *Journal of Personality and Social Psychology, 49,* 273–280.

Greenwald, A. G. (1980). The totalitarian ego: Fabrication and revision of personal history. *American Psychologist, 35,* 603–618.

Griffin, D. W., & Ross, L. (1991). Subjective construal, social inference and human misunderstanding. In M. P. Zanna (Ed.), *Advances in experimental social psychology* (Vol. 24, pp. 319–359). New York: Academic Press.

Hackel, L. S., & Ruble, D. N. (1992). Changes in the marital relationship after the first baby is born: Predicting the impact of expectancy disconfirmation. *Journal of Personality and Social Psychology, 62,* 944–957.

Hall, J. A., & Taylor, S. E. (1976). When love is blind: Maintaining idealized images of one's spouse. *Human Relations, 29,* 751–761.

Harvey, J. H., Agostinelli, G., & Weber, A. L. (1989). Account-making and the formation of expectations about close relationships. In C. Hendrick (Ed.), *Review of personality and social psychology: Close relationships* (Vol. 10, pp. 39–62). Newbury Park, CA: Sage.

Holmes, J. G. (1991). Trust and the appraisal process in close relationships. In W. H. Jones & D. Perlman (Eds.), *Advances in personal relationships,* (Vol. 2, pp. 57–104). Greenwich, C.T: JAI Press.

Holmes, J. G., & Boon, S. D. (1990). Developments in the field of close relationships: Creating foundations for intervention strategies. *Personality and Social Psychology Bulletin, 16,* 23–41.

Holmes, J. G., & Murray, S. L. (in press). Interpersonal conflict. In E.T. Higgins & A. Kruglanski (Eds.), *Social psychology: Handbook of basic mechanisms and processes.* New York: Guilford.

Holmes, J. G., & Rempel, J. K. (1989). Trust in close relationships. In C. Hendrick (Ed.), *Review of personality and social psychology: Close relationships* (Vol. 10, pp. 187–219). Newbury Park, CA: Sage.

Holtzworth-Munroe, A., & Jacobson, N. S. (1985). Causal attributions of married couples: When do they search for causes? What do they conclude when they do? *Journal of Personality and Social Psychology, 48,* 1398–1412.

Humphreys, L. G. (1990). Erroneous interpretation of difference scores: Application to a recent example. *Intelligence, 14,* 231–233.

Huston, T. L., & Vangelisti, A. L. (1991). Socioemotional behavior and satisfaction in marital relationships: A longitudinal study. *Journal of Personality and Social Psychology, 61,* 721–733.

Janoff-Bulman, R. (1989). Assumptive worlds and the stress of traumatic events: Applications of the schema construct. *Social Cognition, 7,* 113–136.

Johnson, D. J., & Rusbult, C. E. (1989). Resisting temptation: Devaluation of alternative partners as a means of maintaining commitment in close relationships. *Journal of Personality and Social Psychology, 57,* 967–980.

Kelley, H. H. (1972). Attribution in social interaction. In E. E. Jones, D. E. Kanouse, H. H. Kelley, R. E. Nisbett, S. Valins, & B. Weiner (Eds.), *Attribution: Perceiving the causes of behavior* (pp. 1–26). Morristown, NJ: General Learning Press.

Kelly, C., Huston, T. L., & Cate, R. M. (1985). Premarital relationship correlates of the erosion of satisfaction in marriage. *Journal of Social and Personal Relationships, 2,* 167–178.

Kenny, D. A., & DePaulo, B. M. (1993). Do people know how others view them? An empirical and theoretical account. *Psychological Bulletin, 114,* 145–161.

Kobak, R. R., & Hazan, C. (1991). Attachment in marriage: Effects of security and accuracy of working models. *Journal of Personality and Social Psychology, 60*, 861–869.

Kruglanski, A. W. (1989). *Lay epistemics and human knowledge: Cognitive and motivational bases.* New York: Plenum Press.

Kunda, Z. (1987). Motivated inference: Self-serving generation and evaluation of causal theories. *Journal of Personality and Social Psychology, 53*, 636–647.

Levinger, G. (1983). Development and change. In H. H. Kelley, E. Berscheid, A. Christensen, J. H. Harvey, T. L. Huston, G. Levinger, E. McClintock, L. A. Peplau, & D. R. Peterson (Eds.), *Close relationships* (pp. 315–359). New York: Freeman.

Levinger, G., & Breedlove, J. (1966). Interpersonal attraction and agreement: A study of marriage partners. *Journal of Personality and Social Psychology, 3*, 367–372.

Markman, H. J. (1979). Application of a behavioral model of marriage in predicting relationship satisfaction of couples planning marriage. *Journal of Consulting and Clinical Psychology, 47*, 743–749.

Markman, H. J. (1981). Prediction of marital distress: A five-year follow-up. *Journal of Consulting and Clinical Psychology, 49*, 760–762.

Markus, H., & Zajonc, R. B. (1985). The cognitive perspective in social psychology. In G. Lindzey & E. Aronson (Eds.), *Handbook of social psychology* (3rd ed., Vol. 1, pp. 137–230). New York: Random House.

McGuire, W. J., & Papageorgis, D. (1961). The relative efficacy of various types of prior belief-defense in producing immunity against persuasion. *Journal of Abnormal and Social Psychology, 62*, 327–337.

Murray, S. L., & Holmes, J. G. (1993). Seeing virtues in faults: Negativity and the transformation of interpersonal narratives in close relationships. *Journal of Personality and Social Psychology, 65*, 707–722.

Murray, S. L., & Holmes, J. G. (1994). Story-telling in close relationships: The construction of confidence. *Personality and Social Psychology Bulletin, 20*, 650–663

Murray, S. L., Holmes, J. G., & Griffin, D. W. (in press). The benefits of positive illusions: Idealization and the construction of satisfaction in close relationships. *Journal of Personality and Social Psychology.*

Reis, H. T., & Shaver, P. (1988). Intimacy as an interpersonal process. In S. W. Duck (Ed.), *Handbook of personal relationships* (pp. 367–389). London: Wiley.

Rusbult, C. E., Johnson, D. J., & Morrow, G. D. (1986). Impact of couple patterns of problem solving on distress and nondistress in dating relationships. *Journal of Personality and Social Psychology, 50*, 744–753.

Rusbult, C. E., Van Lange, P. A. M., & Verette, J. (1992). *Perceived superiority in close relationships.* Paper presented at the sixth International Conference on Personal Relationships, Orono, ME.

Rusbult, C. E., Verette, J., Whitney, G. A., Slovik, L. F., & Lipkus, I. (1991). Accommodation processes in close relationships: Theory and preliminary research evidence. *Journal of Personality and Social Psychology, 60*, 53–78.

Snyder, M., & Swann, W. B. (1978). Behavioral confirmation in social interaction: From social perception to social reality. *Journal of Experimental Social Psychology, 14*, 148–162.

Snyder, M., Tanke, E. D., & Berscheid, E. (1977). Social perception and interpersonal behavior: On the self-fulfilling nature of social stereotypes. *Journal of Personality and Social Psychology, 35*, 656–666.

Sorrentino, R. M., Holmes, J. G., Hanna, S. E., & Sharp, A. (1995). Uncertainty orientation and trust in close relationships: Individual differences in cognitive styles. *Journal of Personality and Social Psychology, 68*, 314–327.

Steele, C. M. (1988). The psychology of self-affirmation: Sustaining the integrity of the self. In L. Berkowitz (Ed.), *Advances in experimental social psychology* (Vol. 21, pp. 261–302). New York: Academic Press.

Steele, C. M., & Liu, T. J. (1983). Dissonance processes as self-affirmation. *Journal of Personality*

120Murray and Holmes

and Social Psychology, 45, 5–19.

Stendhal (Beyle) M. (1927). *On love* (H. B. V., Trans.). New York: Boni & Liveright.

Surra, C. A., & Bohman, T. (1991). The development of close relationships: A cognitive perspective. In G. J. O. Fletcher & F. D. Fincham (Eds.), *Cognition in close relationships* (pp. 281–305). Hillsdale, NJ: Lawrence Erlbaum Associates.

Swann, W. B., Hixon, J. G., & De La Ronde, C. (1992). Embracing the bitter "truth": Negative self-concepts and marital commitment. *Psychological Science, 3,* 118–121.

Taylor, S. E. (1991). Asymmetrical effects of positive and negative events: The mobilization-minimization hypothesis. *Psychological Bulletin, 110,* 67–85.

Taylor, S. E., & Brown, J. D. (1988). Illusion and well-being: A social psychological perspective on mental health. *Psychological Bulletin, 103,* 193–210.

Taylor, S. E., Collins, R. L., Skokan, L. A., & Aspinwall, L. G. (1989). Maintaining positive illusions in the face of negative information: Getting the facts without letting them get to you. *Journal of Social and Clinical Psychology, 8,* 114–129.

Trope, Y. (1986). Identification and inferential processes in dispositional attribution. *Psychological Review, 93,* 239–257.

Weinstein, N. D. (1980). Unrealistic optimism about future life events. *Journal of Personality and Social Psychology, 39,* 806–820.

Weiss, R. L. (1980). Strategic behavioral marital therapy: Toward a model for assessment and intervention. In J. P. Vincent (Ed.), *Advances in family intervention, assessment and theory* (Vol. 1). Greenwich, CT: JAI Press.

5

Sociosexuality and Relationship Initiation: An Ethological Perspective of Nonverbal Behavior

Jeffrey A. Simpson
Texas A&M University

Steven W. Gangestad
University of New Mexico

Christi Nations
Texas A&M University

> *We respond to gestures with an extreme alertness and, one might also say, in accordance with an elaborate and secret code that is written nowhere, known to none, and understood by all.*
>
> —Sapir (1949, pp. 556)

Over a century ago, Charles Darwin (1872) observed that certain expressions tend to be elicited by specific kinds of events and social stimuli in different species. Although Darwin's primary claim to fame lies in his theory of evolution, his ground-breaking research on the expression of emotions in humans and animals suggested that nonverbal behavior may play a major role in structuring and regulating certain types of social interaction. Indeed, Darwin conjectured that some nonverbal expressions may have evolved so that individuals could more accurately express and decipher reactions and intentions in social encounters, thereby avoiding potentially debilitating and dangerous physical confrontations.

More recently, human ethologists claimed that nonverbal behaviors that are elicited in specific social contexts and that trigger complementary responses from other people function as *social signals* (see, e.g., Eibl-Eibesfeldt, 1989). These signals are believed to form a covert, species-wide communication system that regulates and governs social interaction in specific kinds of social situations (e.g., heterosexual relationship initiation, adversarial

121

play between children, social greetings). Aside from cross-cultural field observations (Eibl-Eibesfeldt, 1989) and a handful of laboratory studies (e.g., Grammer, 1990), relatively little is known about how frequently various nonverbal cues are displayed during different kinds of social interactions and what meaning they convey. This is unfortunate because much of the information that is communicated in dyadic interactions is exchanged through nonverbal channels (Birdwhistell, 1970), and this may be particularly true of initial interactions between strangers.

In recent years, attention has turned toward elucidating the "hidden language" that, as Sapir noted, seems to underlie nonverbal behavior. Historically, psychological theories that have sought to decipher the "meaning" of verbal and nonverbal behaviors have fallen into two camps. Some theorists have adopted a *structuralist* perspective toward meaning. The structuralist approach attempts to understand the meaning of complex concepts in terms of their simpler components, focusing on how these components are related to each other and to other similar concepts. Much of contemporary cognitive psychology, which emphasizes mental representational systems (i.e., associative networks) and how the meaning of concepts can be inferred from the semantic networks in which they are embedded, currently adheres to a structuralist perspective. Both Rosch's (1973, 1978) prototype theory of concepts and Anderson's (1983) notions about knowledge structures and associative networks are exemplars of this tradition. Understanding nonverbal communication from a structuralist perspective, therefore, entails trying to decipher the meaning of various behavioral cues from their associations with other elements in associative networks.

The *functionalist* perspective represents a second approach to understanding meaning. According to the functionalist perspective, the psychological meaning of a behavior can be inferred from the social context in which it occurs (e.g., the social context in which the behavior is routinely emitted) and the consequences or responses it elicits in others, including their perceptions, thoughts, emotions, and behaviors. Within philosophy, the functionalist perspective has been most clearly articulated by Wittgenstein (1953). In psychology, it has been advocated by educators (e.g., Dewey, 1896), radical behaviorists (e.g., Skinner, 1957), and ethologists (e.g., Eibl-Eibesfeldt, 1989). Thus, identifying the meaning of nonverbal communication from a functionalist perspective involves discerning the social context in which a behavior is evoked and what effects it has on the thoughts, feelings, and actions of others.

We have conducted a program of research that has sought to clarify the meaning of various nonverbal behaviors that men and women display in heterosexual relationship initiation settings using a functionalist approach. Guided by the dispositional strategy (Snyder & Ickes, 1985) and the sociosexuality construct (Gangestad & Simpson, 1990; Simpson & Gangestad, 1991b), we have studied how certain nonverbal behaviors may foster the development of relationships in which sexual intimacy occurs relatively quickly and without closeness and commitment. More specifically, we have developed a laboratory paradigm that has allowed us to simulate "live" interactions between subjects and videotaped confederates and, thereby, to document the frequency with which different kinds of nonverbal behaviors are displayed during relationship initiation. We have also examined how other individuals respond to different cues affectively by asking persons to rate their attraction to interactants who emit different nonverbal behaviors. In doing so, we have clarified the meaning of different nonverbal behaviors from a functional perspective by examining how frequently they are displayed in a relationship initiation *context* and what *consequences* they have in terms of attracting others. Furthermore, by examining the ways in which frequency of emission and affective consequences are moderated by the sociosexual orientation of interactants and perceivers, we have been able to extend our understanding of various nonverbal cues.

Knowledge structures can be classified into two broad categories (Baldwin, 1992): those that reflect *declarative* knowledge, and those that concern *procedural* knowledge. Declarative knowledge involves descriptive information about people and objects. Declarative knowledge structures are thought to operate as interconnected nodes in associative networks (Anderson, 1983). Procedural knowledge, in contrast, embodies the decision rules and skills that people use to pursue personal goals and achieve desired objectives (e.g., attracting a romantic partner). Procedural knowledge tends to be automatically activated by relevant eliciting stimuli in specific contexts, and it often operates at subconscious levels of awareness (Kihlstrom, 1987). Eibl-Eibesfeldt (1989) conjectured that both the expression and recognition of certain types of nonverbal cues emitted in relationship initiation settings may be governed by procedural knowledge structures that have evolved to foster clearer and more direct communication between interactants.

In what follows, we first describe a two-dimensional model into which most of the nonverbal behaviors that are typically emitted during relationship initiation can be placed. We then explain why human ethologists and evolutionary theorists have been particularly interested in discerning what kinds of nonverbal cues facilitate relationship initiation, and why it makes sense to focus initially on cues that convey immediate sexual interest without strong affection. We then discuss the dispositional strategy and describe the individual difference construct and measure that guided the present research: the construct (Gangestad & Simpson, 1990; Simpson & Gangestad, 1991b) and measure (Simpson & Gangestad, 1991a) of individual differences in sociosexuality. Next, we present the results of two laboratory investigations. The first investigation was conducted to discern the frequency with which individuals with a restricted versus an unrestricted sociosexual orientation spontaneously emit various nonverbal behaviors during heterosexual relationship initiation. The second investigation was designed to determine the affective responses that different kinds of nonverbal displays elicit in others. The findings of both investigations are discussed from an ethological perspective.

NONVERBAL BEHAVIOR AND RELATIONSHIP INITIATION: AN OVERVIEW

As Darwin observed, one central function of nonverbal behavior is to communicate "intent"—either accurately or deceptively—during interpersonal interactions. Burgoon and Hale (1984) proposed that certain nonverbal behaviors may serve relational communication functions that indicate how one person regards his or her relationship with another individual. Relational message content has two primary dimensions: an agonic dimension of *differential status/dominance* and an affiliative dimension of *equal status/intimacy*.[1] In general, dominance tends to be communicated by exerting control over conversational distance and patterns of touch, less frequent but more direct eye contact (e.g., staring), less smiling, and greater postural relaxation, whereas nondominance is expressed by more smiling, more laughing, and shoulder shrugging (see Burgoon, 1985). Intimacy, on the other hand, tends to be conveyed by close physical proximity, forward body lean, open body posture, frequent eye contact, and gesturing, whereas lack of intimacy is revealed by gaze aversion, increased distance, backward lean, and absence of smiling (see Andersen, 1985; Mehrabian, 1972). Dominance and intimacy, in fact, form the major axes of most circumplex models of interpersonal behavior (Wiggins, 1980).

Because dominance cues communicate that one person regards the other as lower in status, expressions of dominance usually undermine expressions of intimacy (Bateson, Jackson, Haley, & Weakland, 1956). Cues of nondominance, therefore, should co-occur with affiliative cues in most non-hostile relationship initiation settings (Eibl-Eibesfeldt, 1988; Givens, 1978). More specifically, nonverbal cues indicative of submission, appeasement, or nondominance such as head cants (Darwin, 1872; Key, 1975), laughing (Burgoon, 1985), and smiling (Eibl-Eibesfeldt, 1989) should be displayed in combination with cues conveying affiliation such as extended eye contact, open body posture, frequent gesturing, and forward lean (Andersen, 1985;

---

[1]A third major nonrelational dimension is emotional arousal, reflected by signals that indicate the amount of anxiety experienced during interaction (Burgoon & Hale, 1984).

Eibl-Eibesfeldt, 1989; Ekman, 1973). The former cues ostensibly communicate that the forthcoming interaction will be a friendly and nonthreatening one, paving the way for affiliative overtures to be made.

Human ethologists have speculated extensively about how various nonverbal behavioral cues regulate heterosexual relationship initiation (see Eibl-Eibesfeldt, 1989). The reason for this interest is clear: Selection pressures should have shaped both the expression of, and responses to, certain nonverbal behaviors in ways that specifically regulate initial heterosexual interactions that might lead to mating (Buss, 1985, 1991). Relational nonverbal cues that convey emotional closeness and commitment are not likely to govern relationship initiation because these attributes usually require extended periods of time to develop in relationships. Other nonverbal cues, however, might regulate the "sexualization" of initial heterosexual encounters.

In principle, two classes of cues should govern the initiation of relationships in which intimacy develops rapidly and without strong emotional ties. First, behavioral displays conveying both affiliation (e.g., eye contact, open/attentive body posture, forward lean) and nondominance (e.g., laughing, smiling) might communicate "contact readiness," thereby expediting the development of sexual intimacy (Eibl-Eibesfeldt, 1989). Second, specialized cues such as head cants (head tilts: Halberstadt & Saitta, 1987; Henley, 1977) and flirtatious glances (specialized sidelong glances coupled briefly with weak smiles: Eibl-Eibesfeldt, 1980) may have unique, context-specific meaning during these interactions. Both of these specialized cues have been conjectured to signal coy sexual interest without affection (Kendon & Ferber, 1973; Key, 1975; Morris, 1977).

THE DISPOSITIONAL STRATEGY AND SOCIOSEXUALITY

To investigate the functional meaning of different nonverbal cues displayed during relationship initiation, we adopted the *dispositional strategy* (Snyder & Ickes, 1985). This strategy proposes that people who are most likely to exhibit the behaviors or psychological processes of interest should be studied in order to better understand these behaviors and processes. According to this view, some of the regularity and consistency that is observed in social behavior stems from the relatively stable and enduring dispositions that people possess. By studying people who are most likely to display certain kinds of social behaviors more frequently and perhaps more prototypically (e.g., nonverbal cues conveying flirtation in initial interactions), one can achieve a better understanding of the meaning and nature of the social behaviors under investigation.

What individual difference construct identifies people who tend to be involved in relationships in which sex occurs quickly and without strong commitment, closeness, and emotional bonding? The sociosexuality construct (Gangestad & Simpson, 1990; Simpson & Gangestad, 1991a, 1991b) explicitly focuses on the extent to which individuals require closeness, commitment, and strong emotional bonds prior to having sex. People who have an *unrestricted sociosexual orientation* do not require much closeness and commitment before engaging in sex and, therefore, they have relationships in which sex and intimacy occur rapidly. Those who have a *restricted sociosexual orientation* expect more commitment and closeness prior to sex. As a result, they establish relationships in which intimacy evolves gradually and sex occurs only after emotional bonds have been formed. Recent research has found that unrestricted individuals, relative to restricted ones, engage in sex earlier in their relationships, are more likely to have concurrent sexual affairs, and are involved in relationships characterized by less commitment, investment, love, and emotional dependency (Simpson & Gangestad, 1991a). Restricted and unrestricted individuals also desire, choose, and actually acquire romantic partners who possess different kinds of personal attributes. Unrestricted people prefer and date partners who are more physically attractive and who have greater social visibility, whereas restricted people prefer and actually acquire partners who are more affectionate, responsible, and loyal to the relationship (Simpson & Gangestad, 1992). Evidence for discriminant validity has revealed that sociosexual orientation is not associated with general sex drive or measures assessing guilt, sexual satisfaction, and sexual anxiety (Simpson & Gangestad, 1991a).

Individual differences in sociosexuality are measured by the Sociosexual Orientation Inventory (Simpson & Gangestad, 1991a), which assesses components of an individual's past sexual behavior, their future (anticipated) sexual behavior, and their attitudes toward engaging in casual sex. Specifically, the Sociosexual Orientation Inventory contains five self-report indexes: (a) number of different sexual partners in the past year; (b) number of different sexual partners foreseen in the next 5 years; (c) number of times having engaged in sex with someone on one and only one occasion; (d) frequency of sexual fantasy involving partners other than the current partner (responded to on an 8-point Likert-type scale); and (e) three aggregated items assessing attitudes about engaging in casual, uncommitted sex (e.g., ''I can imagine myself being comfortable and enjoying casual sex with different partners''), which are answered on 9-point Likert-type scales. The five indexes are weighted and then aggregated to form the full measure (see Simpson & Gangestad, 1991a, for scoring instructions). Higher scores on the Sociosexual Orientation Inventory indicate an unrestricted sociosexual orientation, and lower scores reflect a restricted orientation.

THE FREQUENCY AND MEANING OF NONVERBAL
BEHAVIORS DISPLAYED IN A RELATIONSHIP
INITIATION CONTEXT

The relevance of the dispositional strategy for examining the functional meaning of nonverbal cues should be clear. We know that one consequence of how restricted and unrestricted individuals initiate relationships is how quickly sexual intimacy develops in their relationships. Although we cannot unequivocally demonstrate that systematic differences in unrestricted and restricted individuals' nonverbal displays cause differences in the rate at which sexual intimacy develops in their respective relationships, we can explore the regulatory function of nonverbal cues by correlating sociosexual orientation and the frequency with which different nonverbal cues are emitted during relationship initiation.

Thus, in our first study (Simpson, Gangestad, & Biek, 1993), individuals were interviewed by an attractive, opposite-sex person for a potential date over a two-way camera system. Unbeknownst to participants, the "interviewer" actually was a videotaped confederate and participants were unobtrusively videotaped during the interview. After the interview, raters assessed the frequency or duration with which 11 objective nonverbal behaviors believed to signal either contact readiness or coy sexual interest were displayed during the interview. To assess multichannel nonverbal cues, a second group of raters then evaluated each participant on 34 attributes designed to assess several major dimensions of nonverbal communication. Both sets of ratings were factor analyzed to identify the major dimensions underlying raters' evaluations.

Procedure

Two hundred and ten heterosexual college students who were *not* dating anyone at the time of the study participated in the first investigation. It had two phases.

In Phase 1, participants arrived at the lab (individually) and were led to a room containing a table, a chair, a color TV monitor (attached to a wall outlet), and a video camera (unobtrusively suspended in one corner of the room). The experimenter then read the following instructions:

> We're interested in observing how people choose dating partners. In one of the other rooms we've got an interviewer who is going to choose either you or one of two other people (also located in different rooms) for a lunch date paid for by the researchers. We're interested in what kinds of questions he/she asks people and how he/she decides whom to go out with.

The interviewer will appear on your monitor and introduce himself/herself. Then the screen will go blank while you introduce yourself. The interviewer will be able to see you through that camera (which was pointed out) and hear you through the microphone in the ceiling (which also was pointed out), just as you will be able to see and hear him/her. When you answer his/her questions, please look at the camera.

After you've introduced yourself, the interviewer will come back on and ask you six (self-generated) questions. The screen will go blank between each question so you can answer without distraction. His/her instructions are to choose one person for the lunch date based on your introductions and the answers each of you give to the six questions. For this portion of the study, the interviewer has been told *not* to answer any questions from you. He/she also has been told that he/she can only ask each question one time, so please pay careful attention.

You're going to be the second person he/she talks to, so it will be a few minutes until it's your turn. Do you have any questions before we get started? OK, when the interviewer appears on the monitor, please answer his/her questions as best you can. Just relax and be yourself.

Approximately 5 minutes later, the interviewer (one of two videotaped male confederates for women and one of two videotaped female confederates for men) appeared on the monitor and introduced him or herself.[2] The introduction depicted the interviewer as a warm, outgoing, interesting, friendly, and flexible person who enjoyed engaging in many different activities. Following the introduction, the interviewer asked the participant the first question: (a) "Please tell me about yourself, including who you are, what you like to do, and what you don't like to do." The monitor then went blank while the participant responded to the question for as long as he or she liked. When the participant had finished, the interviewer reappeared on the screen to ask the remaining five questions in a similar question–answer format. The five remaining questions, each of which was followed by a response from the participant, were: (b) "Think about an interesting, humorous, or fun experience that you've had in the past year, something that would give me a better idea what you are really like as a person. Describe this experience and tell me why it reveals something interesting or unique about you"; (c) "Imagine that you're in a bar or restaurant and you see someone whom you find very attractive. Show me what you'd do to get his/her attention"; (d) "Imagine that you've just met a guy/girl whom you find very attractive and whom you want to get to know better. How would you go

---

[2]Participants were interviewed by one of two different interviewers to ensure that effects were not specific to the style, appearance, or mannerisms of a single interviewer.

about striking up a conversation with him/her? Show me exactly what you would say and how you would say it"; (e) "Imagine that you and two or three other people are all interested in dating the same person. What would you say and do to persuade him/her that he/she should date you rather than the others?"; and (f) "Why should I choose you for this lunch date?"

Participants' answers to the interviewer's questions were videotaped. After completing the interview, participants indicated on Likert-type scales how interested they were in dating the interviewer. They then were led to another room to take part in an ostensibly different project while the interviewer decided whom to date.

During Phase 2, participants completed several self-report measures, including sociosexuality, extraversion (Eysenck & Eysenck, 1975), self-monitoring (Gangestad & Snyder, 1985), social self-esteem (the Texas Social Behavior Inventory: Helmreich, Stapp, & Ervin, 1974), shyness (Cheek & Buss, 1981), stress reaction (Tellegen, 1982), and social closeness (Tellegen, 1982). The measures other than sociosexuality were collected for discriminant validation purposes.

After the study was over, two groups of raters evaluated each interview. The first group rated participants' nonverbal behavior on 11 objective (i.e., explicit) behaviors. Using a stop watch, each rater recorded the amount of time during the interview each participant spent smiling, having direct eye contact (with the camera/interviewer), adopting an open body posture, leaning toward the camera/interviewer, looking downward, and canting (tilting) his or her head. Raters then counted the number of times each participant laughed, made demonstrative hand gestures, looked downward, displayed eyebrow flashes, and glanced flirtatiously at the camera/interviewer. These behaviors were assessed because they communicate intimacy or nondominance in most social contexts (Burgoon, 1985) and, either independently or in various combinations, they are thought to express "contact readiness" (Eibl-Eibesfeldt, 1989). We then aggregated the ratings for each behavior. To control for differences in the length of each interview, raters' aggregated scores on each behavior were divided by the amount of time each participant spent in the interview.

A second group of raters then evaluated participants' subjective nonverbal behavior. Specifically, they viewed each interview with the sound off and rated each participant on 34 attributes using Likert-type scales: animated, enjoyed the interview, self-confident, charming, engaging/interesting, poised, witty, competent, relaxed, anxious, flirtatious, seductive, social presence, phony/ingenuine, self-conscious, dull/boring, stimulating, concern with making a good impression, restrained/inhibited, arrogant, inviting, nice, self-disclosing, socially dominant, good at drawing attention, good at conveying interest (in the interviewer), humorous, ingratiating, forward/bold, shy/timid, sexually provocative, captivating, socially skilled, and sex appeal. Raters also evaluated how physically attractive each participant was. Ratings for each adjective were then aggregated.

We made ratings on these adjectives for three reasons. First, they tap three major dimensions known to underlie nonverbal communication: intimacy, dominance, and emotional arousal. Second, they assess several other nonverbal domains that should affect relationship initiation (e.g., self-confidence, phoniness, seductiveness). Third, they may identify important patterns or configurations of nonverbal cues that were not captured by the explicit cues.

Results

Sex Differences. Corroborating past research (see Hall, 1984), women behaved in a warmer and more intimate manner than did men. Relative to men, women smiled more during the interview, established more eye contact, leaned forward more, gazed down less often, laughed more frequently, displayed more flirtatious glances, and were rated as more sexually provocative.

Construction of Nonverbal Dimensions. To identify a smaller set of nonverbal dimensions, we factor analyzed the 11 objective nonverbal behaviors. Five factors emerged for each sex. For men, the five factors (along with the behaviors that defined each factor) were: Eyebrow Flashes/Expressive Gestures/Open Body Posture (number of eyebrow flashes, number of hand gestures, time spent in open body position); Smiling/Flirtatious Glances/Head Cants (time spent smiling, number of flirtatious glances, time spent in head cants); Downward Gazing (time spent in downward gaze, number of downward gazes, time spent having eye contact); Laughing (number of laughs); and Forward Body Lean (time spent leaning forward).

For women, the five factors included: Smiling/Eye Contact/Flirtatious Glances/Eyebrow Flashes (number of flirtatious glances, number of eyebrow flashes, time spent in eye contact, time spent smiling); Downward Gazing (time spent in downward gaze, number of downward gazes); Open Body Position/Head Cants/Expressive Gestures (time spent in head cants, time spent in open body position, number of gestures); Smiling/Laughing (number of laughs, time spent smiling, time in open body position); and Forward Body Lean (time spent leaning forward). Factor scores were computed on each factor for both men and women.

Next, we factor analyzed the 34 nonverbal adjectives. Five identical factors emerged for men and women: Social Engagement/Dominance (good at drawing attention, social presence, not dull, engaging, socially dominant, animated, captivating, self-disclosing, stimulating, competent, not shy, not inhibited, enjoyed the interview, humorous, witty, self-confident, charming, socially skilled, and desire to make a good impression); Interest/Invitation (inviting, ingratiating, bold, good at conveying interest, and flirtatious); Comfort (not anxious, relaxed, not self-conscious, self-confident, and not shy); Provocativeness (sex appeal, provocative, and seductive); and Pretentiousness (phony, arrogant, and not nice). We then computed factor scores for each participant on each factor.

Correlations Between Objective Behaviors and Subjective Factors. To explore the relations between our explicitly coded and implicitly coded nonverbal behaviors, we correlated the objective nonverbal factors (constructed from the 11 discrete behaviors) and the subjective nonverbal factors (constructed from the 34 adjectives).

The results for men, which are presented in Table 5.1, revealed that greater perceived Social Engagement/Dominance was associated with higher scores on the Eyebrow Flashes/Expressive Gestures/Open Body Position factor (i.e., more frequent eyebrow flashes, more frequent gestures, and more time spent in an open body position) and the Smiling/Flirtatious Glances/Head Cants factor (i.e., more time spent smiling, more frequent flirtatious glances, and more time spent canting the head). Greater perceived Interest/Invitation was associated with lower scores on both the Eyebrow Flashes/Expressive Gestures/ Open Body Position factor and the Downward Gaze factor (i.e., less looking downward). More Provocativeness was associated with higher scores on the Smiling/Flirtatious Glances/Head Cants factor, and more Pretentiousness was associated with lower scores on the Forward Body Lean factor (i.e., less time spent leaning forward).

TABLE 5.1
Correlations Between Objective and Subjective Factors for Men

	Subjective Factors				
Objective Factors	Engagement/ Dominance	Interest/ Invitation	Comfort	Provocative	Pretentiousness
Eyebrow flashes/ expressive gestures/ open body	.29**	−.32***	.16	−.16	−.13
Smiling/ flirtatious glances/ head cants	.22*	.07	.19+	.21*	.06
Downward gaze	−.11	−.59***	−.17+	−.01	−.17+
Laughing	.18+	−.05	−.17+	−.06	.10
Forward lean	.07	−.08	−.18+	−.03	−.21*

Note. All correlations are two-tailed.
+*p* < .10. **p* < .05. ***p* < .01. ****p* < .001.

The results for women, which are presented in Table 5.2, indicated that Social Engagement/Dominance was associated with higher scores on the Smiling/Eye Contact/Flirtatious Glances/Eyebrow Flashes factor (i.e., more time spent smiling and having eye contact with the interviewer, and more frequent flirtatious glances and eyebrow flashes), the Open Body Position/ Head Cants/Expressive Gestures factor (i.e., more time spent in an open body position and canting the head, and more frequent gestures), and the Smiling/Laughing factor (i.e., more time spent smiling, and more frequent laughing). Greater perceived Interest/Invitation was associated with higher scores on the Smiling/Eye Contact/Flirtatious Glances/Eyebrow Flashes factor, and with lower scores on the Downward Gaze factor (i.e., less looking downward). Finally, more Provocativeness was associated with higher scores on the Smiling/Eye Contact/Flirtatious Glances/Eyebrow Flashes factor.

Sociosexuality and Interview Ratings. We next examined relations between sociosexuality and the objective nonverbal factors. For men, regression analyses in which all five objective factors were entered as predictors and sociosexuality was treated as the criterion indicated that sociosexuality was associated with three nonverbal behavioral factors. Unrestricted men smiled and displayed flirtatious glances (Smiling/Flirtatious Glances/Head Cant factor) and laughed (Laughing factor) significantly more often during the interview than did restricted men. They also were less inclined to gaze downward (Downward Gaze factor). When parallel analyses were conducted for women, sociosexuality was significantly associated with only one factor.

TABLE 5.2
Correlations Between Objective and Subjective Factors for Women

	Subjective Factors				
Objective Factors	Engagement/ Dominance	Interest/ Invitation	Comfort	Provocative	Pretentiousness
Smiling/ eye contact/ flirtatious glances/ eyebrow flashes	.42***	.19*	.15	.24*	.13
Downward gaze	.09	− .44***	− .13	.04	.06
Open body/ head cants/ expressive gestures	.33***	− .05	.11	− .06	.09
Smiling/laughing	.29**	− .05	.04	− .15	− .08
Forward lean	.06	− .07	− .03	− .01	− .03

Note. All correlations are two-tailed.
*$p < .05$. **$p < .01$. ***$p < .001$.

Unrestricted women were more likely to lean forward (Forward Body Lean factor) compared to restricted women.

To clarify the size of these effects, we identified men and women who were highly unrestricted (persons who scored in the top one third of the Sociosexual Orientation Inventory distribution within their gender) and those who were clearly restricted (persons who scored in the lower one third). Highly unrestricted men, compared to restricted men, spent a significantly larger percentage of time smiling (12.47% vs. 6.32%) and a smaller percentage of time gazing downward (24.28% vs. 30.31%) during the interview. Highly unrestricted men also displayed considerably more laughs per minute (.55 vs..34) and more flirtatious glances per minute (.10 vs. .05). Highly unrestricted women, relative to their restricted counterparts, spent a significantly larger percentage of time leaning forward (22.91% vs. 10.66%) and canting their heads (4.46% vs. 2.98%). Thus, highly unrestricted people displayed some of these nonverbal behaviors nearly twice as often as did highly restricted people.

Regression analyses in which all five impression factors were entered as predictors and sociosexuality was treated as the dependent variable indicated that unrestricted men were rated higher than restricted men on two dimensions: Pretentiousness and Social Engagement/Dominance. Specifically, unrestricted men were perceived as more pretentious and more socially engaging/dominant. No effects were found for women on the impression factors.

Discriminant Analyses. These effects, of course, could be attributable to other variables that are correlated with sociosexuality or certain nonverbal displays. For example, people with an unrestricted sociosexual orientation tend to be higher in self-monitoring and more extraverted than people with a restricted orientation (Simpson & Gangestad, 1991b), and both extraverts (Eysenck, 1976) and high self-monitors (Snyder & Simpson, 1984) are known to establish romantic relationships often and easily. Unrestricted individuals also may be less shy, have greater social self-esteem, display less anxiety in social situations, and have a stronger need to socialize than restricted individuals. Furthermore, unrestricted men tend to be more physically attractive than restricted men (Simpson et al., 1993). Each of these attributes might hasten the development of sexual intimacy in initial hetero-sexual encounters. To discount these potential confounds, we conducted additional analyses in which measures representing each of these variables were statistically controlled. These analyses revealed that the effects for sociosexuality just reported were not attributable to individual differences in self-monitoring, extraversion, physical attractiveness, shyness, social self-confidence, stress reaction, or social closeness. Furthermore, because restricted and unrestricted individuals did not differ in how much they wanted to date the interviewer, these effects probably do *not* stem from differential motivation to "perform well" on the part of restricted and unrestricted people.

Objective Nonverbal Cues and Subjective Nonverbal Impressions: An Ethological Perspective

Confirming past research on sex differences in nonverbal behavior, the first investigation revealed that women behaved in a warmer and more intimate manner than did men. Moreover, men with an unrestricted sociosexual orientation smiled more, laughed more, gazed downward less often, and displayed flirtatious glances more frequently during relationship initiation than did restricted men. Unrestricted men also were rated as more socially engaging/dominant and more pretentious. Unrestricted women were more likely to lean forward and cant their heads compared to restricted women. These results indicate that unrestricted individuals are more likely to display certain nonverbal behaviors believed to signal contact readiness. Yet only a subset of the behaviors thought to convey contact readiness were associated with sociosexuality. What might account for this?

Contact readiness can be expressed through behaviors that reflect different forms of relational communication, including submissiveness, warmth, lack of anxiety, and flirtation (Burgoon, 1985). Different forms of relational communication, therefore, should involve different kinds of nonverbal cues. Flirtation is unique among different forms of relational communication in that it usually is witnessed only in romantic interactions. If flirtation takes place early on during interactions between strangers, it may sexualize initial encounters by communicating a person's view of the relationship as primarily a sexual one (Eibl-Eibesfeldt, 1988; Givens, 1978). Even though sociosexuality was associated with different nonverbal behaviors for men and women, most of the behaviors with which it did correlate are flirtatious gestures.

Unrestricted women were more inclined to lean forward and cant their heads during the interview. Forward body lean usually connotes interest in and attentiveness to others during friendly interactions (Coker & Burgoon, 1987; Knapp, 1983; Mehrabian, 1972). By drawing interactants closer together, forward leans also accentuate the impact of other nonverbal cues that emanate from the head and face. Previous researchers have claimed that head canting may serve as a flirtatious gesture designed to signal coy sexual interest without affection in heterosexual interactions (Kendon & Ferber, 1973; Key, 1975; Morris, 1977). In accord with these speculations, women who spent more time canting their heads were seen as more interested in the interviewer and more sexually provocative. Head canting also has been conjectured to communicate submissiveness (Key, 1975; Morris, 1977), ingratiation (Goffman, 1976), or appeasement (Goffman, 1979), attributes that reflect the less powerful position that women have traditionally held in society (Henley, 1973, 1977). However, head canting was not associated with perceptions of less social engagement or less dominance in women. This suggests that head cants do not always imply submissiveness, at least during initial heterosexual encounters.

Unrestricted men displayed more flirtatious glances, smiled more, and laughed more during the interview. Givens (1978) proposed that flirtatious glances signal strong sexual interest in heterosexual interactions. Supporting this claim, men who displayed more flirtatious glances were perceived as more interested in the interviewer and more sexually provocative.

Cross-cultural field research by Eibl-Eibesfeldt (1989) showed that frequent smiling and laughing tend to co-occur with flirtatious glances because such looks are usually set up by weak smiles and playful laughs. Smiling, in fact, is one of the best predictors of perceived interpersonal warmth (Bayes, 1970) and intimacy (Argyle, 1972). Smiling was strongly associated with greater perceived social engagement/dominance and with greater interest in the interviewer. When coupled with flirtatious glances, however, frequent smiling appears to convey a specialized kind of intimacy, namely sexual intimacy, even in the absence of strong emotional ties.

Despite smiling and laughing more frequently, unrestricted men were seen as more engaging and socially dominant. The Social Engagement/Dominance dimension probably reflects the global level of immediacy and dominance displayed during the interview. Immediacy is a multidimensional construct that consists of nonverbal behaviors indicating warmth/closeness, inclusion of the other, and direct involvement in the interaction (Andersen, 1985). It typically is communicated by several multichannel nonverbal cues, including open body position, forward body lean, smiling, laughing, eye contact, and gesturing (Andersen, 1985). Many of these cues also convey nonaggressive social dominance during friendly encounters, especially when one is trying to make a good impression (Mehrabian, 1969). The Social Engagement/ Dominance dimension correlated positively with several nonverbal behaviors known to convey immediacy (Mehrabian, 1972) and dominance (Mehrabian, 1969). Sadalla, Kenrick, and Vershure (1987) found that perceived social dominance enhances the attractiveness of men and their desirability as dating partners. Thus, unrestricted men may be more successful at initiating sexual relationships quickly because their nonverbal actions express greater immediacy and social dominance without suggesting that they will be dominating in the relationship.

Little is known about what kinds of nonverbal cues foster the impression of pretentiousness in relationship initiation contexts. For men, greater perceived pretentiousness was associated with less time leaning forward in the interview. Backward leans during initial encounters often communicate less immediacy (Burgoon, Buller, Hale, & DeTurck, 1984), and they may be interpreted as deliberate attempts to appear overrelaxed and overconfident. For women, greater pretentiousness was associated with more frequent hand gestures and flirtatious glances. Women who gesture more during nonromantic interactions are perceived as more persuasive and competent (Mehrabian & Williams, 1969). When frequent gesturing occurs during initial heterosexual interactions, however, higher levels of competence may be interpreted as excessive boastfulness, confidence, or arrogance.

Besides smiling more and displaying more flirtatious glances, unrestricted men also were perceived as more pretentious. Smiles reflecting genuine, spontaneous enjoyment and interest (Duchenne smiles) can be distinguished from false smiles used to deceive others and simulate enjoyment or interest (Ekman, Davidson, & Friesen, 1990; Ekman, Friesen, & O'Sullivan, 1988). Thus, people who appeared more pretentious may have been rated this way because they displayed more false smiles and feigned laughs during the interview.

AFFECTIVE REACTIONS ELICITED BY
NONVERBAL BEHAVIORS

The first investigation revealed what restricted and unrestricted men and women spontaneously do nonverbally in initial heterosexual interactions. The second investigation was conducted to identify the affective reactions associated with different kinds of nonverbal cues (Gangestad, Simpson, & DiGeronimo, 1994). More specifically, it sought to determine the degree to which men and women—particularly unrestricted and restricted men and women—are differentially attracted to different kinds of nonverbal displays during initial heterosexual interactions. Relatively few studies have investigated how individual differences of perceivers interact with target characteristics to influence initial attraction (for an exception, see Cunningham, Barbee, & Pike, 1990). Instead, most past research has used several raters to assess physical attractiveness, typically averaging attractiveness ratings across all raters to obtain an aggregated measure. Such measures can be fairly reliable if many raters are used. By averaging across raters, however, the unique variance contained in a single rater's (or subgroup of raters') perceptions is canceled out.

People, of course, do not present others with a list of their relevant attributes and personal qualities in everyday encounters. Rather, their behavioral styles and attributes must be inferred from their self-presentations in social interactions. If individuals evaluate other people's initial self-presentations on different criteria, they may be "turned on" or "turned off" depending on whether the presentation conveys the qualities they are looking for in a romantic partner. Recent research has indicated that two major dimensions underlie mate choice criteria: a potential partner's Personal/ Investment Qualities and their Physical Attractiveness/Social Status (Simpson & Gangestad, 1992). This research also has found that unrestricted men and women place more importance on the physical attractiveness and social status of a potential partner, whereas restricted men and women emphasize a potential partner's personal characteristics and their willingness to invest in the relationship.

This finding suggests that unrestricted and restricted individuals should respond differently to certain nonverbal signals. Given their interest in allowing intimacy to develop more slowly, restricted individuals and those who value a romantic partner's personal/investment qualities should be less attracted to persons who display signals that facilitate the rapid development of intimacy between strangers (e.g., flirtatious glances and head cants). By contrast, unrestricted individuals and those who stress a potential partner's physical attractiveness/social status should be more attracted to persons who display these signals. Moreover, physically attractive persons should be especially appealing to unrestricted individuals.

The interviews of persons who had been videotaped in the first investigation (i.e., targets) were viewed by opposite-sex perceivers as part of the second investigation. After viewing each target, perceivers answered questions about their global attraction to the target.

Procedure

Targets and Perceivers.   Eighty students who were interviewed in the first investigation served as targets, and 150 students from a different university were perceivers.

Overview.   Prior to the study, a set of raters evaluated each target in terms of his or her physical attractiveness and sex appeal. To obtain physical attractiveness ratings uncontaminated by behavioral displays, raters evaluated targets before they started interacting with the interviewer. Ratings were summed to form a physical attractiveness index for each target.

Perceivers then viewed 20 one-minute videotaped segments of targets being interviewed. Specifically, they saw the first minute of each interview when interviewees were answering the question "Tell me about yourself, including who you are, what you like to do, and what you don't like to do." Each segment depicted a different target. Perceivers viewed the tapes with the sound off. After viewing each target, they answered four questions about the target's global attractiveness: "How attracted are you to this person's style?"; "If you were available and you knew it would be on a short term basis, how willing would you be to date this person?"'; "To what extent do you think it would be possible to have a successful long-term relationship with this person?"'; and "To what extent do you feel you could really 'hit it off' with this person?" Responses to these questions, which were made on Likert-type scales, were aggregated to form a measure of global attractiveness of the target to the perceiver. Perceivers also inferred other qualities that might be relevant to each target's suitability as a romantic partner (e.g., faithful and loyal, kind and understanding, respected, responsible, financially successful, and good parent). These attributes, which also were rated on Likert-type scales, were summed across all perceivers for each target.

After rating the videotapes, perceivers completed the Sociosexual Orientation Inventory, they indicated how long they had dated their last sexual partner before having sex with him or her, and they responded to the Mate Preference Questionnaire (Simpson & Gangestad, 1992). This questionnaire asked perceivers to rate how important each of 15 attributes was in their choice of a romantic partner. On the basis of previous research (Simpson & Gangestad, 1992), responses to this questionnaire were aggregated into two composite measures: Physical Attractiveness/Social Status (comprised of the attributes physical attractiveness, sex appeal, social status, and financial resources); and Personal Attributes/Investment Qualities (comprised of the attributes faithfulness and loyalty, similarity of values and beliefs, good parenting qualities, responsibility, kindness and understanding, and stability of personality). Because these composite measures correlate with sociosexuality in opposite directions (Simpson & Gangestad, 1992), a single Physical Attractiveness/Social Status versus Personal Attributes/Investment Qualities measure was computed by taking the difference between the two components.

To create a composite measure of Unrestricted versus Restricted Sociosexual Orientation/Mate Preference, we identified the first factor running through the three measures previously listed. We then standardized each variable within each sex and aggregated them.

Results

Aggregated Perceptions. To determine which nonverbal displays appeal to opposite-sex persons in general, we aggregated all perceivers' global attractiveness ratings to form a global attractiveness index for each target. We then correlated targets' scores on these global attractiveness indexes with their physical attractiveness, their displays of the 11 nonverbal behaviors, their scores on the 5 nonverbal objective factors (constructed in the first investigation from the 11 behaviors), and their scores on the 5 nonverbal impression factors (constructed in the first investigation from the 34 adjectives).

Female perceivers rated men who gazed downward less often and maintained more open body posture as more attractive. Attractive men also conveyed the impression of being more provocative, more pretentious, and more relaxed. Male perceivers rated women who were more provocative, more pretentious, and who avoided an open body posture as more attractive. On average, downward gazes displayed by men produced less attraction than downward gazes exhibited by women, whereas open body posture displayed by women resulted in less attraction than open body posture exhibited by men. Not surprisingly, physical attractiveness was strongly related to global attractiveness ratings for both male and female targets.

Many behavioral cues were correlated with physical attractiveness. To determine what impact these cues had on global attractiveness independent of physical attractiveness, we examined relations between these cues and global attractiveness with physical attractiveness partialed out. Higher scores on the Eyebrow Flashes/Open Body Posture/Expressiveness factor and lower scores on the Downward Gaze factor were associated with higher global attractiveness ratings for men. Higher scores on the Comfort factor also were associated with more global attractiveness in men. Higher attraction ratings for women were associated with less open body posture and greater provocativeness.

When targets' physical attractiveness was partialed out, some sex differences emerged. Greater perceived Social Engagement/Dominance and higher scores on the Eyebrow Flashes/Open Body Posture/Expressiveness factor were associated with higher attractiveness ratings when these nonverbal behaviors were displayed by men. More downward gazing, on the other hand, was associated with lower attractiveness ratings for men. Greater provocativeness predicted higher attractiveness ratings when displayed by women, while more open body posture on the part of women was associated with lower attractiveness ratings.

Effects of Perceiver Sociosexuality/Partner Choice on Target Attractiveness. To examine the moderating influence of perceiver sociosexual orientation/partner preference on target attractiveness, we first divided female and male perceivers at the median into two subsamples: those with an unrestricted orientation/partner preference and those with a restricted orientation/partner preference. For each male target, we then calculated the mean global attractiveness ratings made by restricted and unrestricted women. Similarly, for each female target, we calculated the mean global attractiveness ratings made by restricted and unrestricted men.

As indicated in Table 5.3, ratings of global attractiveness made by unrestricted individuals correlated more highly with targets' physical attractiveness than did ratings made by restricted individuals. Furthermore, targets rated highly by unrestricted perceivers were judged to be more sexually provocative. These targets also displayed more flirtatious glances and scored higher on the Smiling/Flirting/Head Cants factor.

TABLE 5.3
Correlations Between Targets' Global Attractiveness and Nonverbal Behaviors as a Function
of Perceivers' Sociosexual Mate Preference

	Male Targets		Female Targets		UNR v RES		
	UNR	RES	UNR	RES	Overall	Men	Women
Nonverbal Behaviors							
Smiling	.22	.21	.22	.16			
Eye contact	.30	.32	.11	.18			
Open body posture	.31	.35	−.28	−.38			
Body lean	−.04	−.06	.00	−.02			
Downward gaze (time)	−.57	−.54	.02	−.02			
Gestures	.02	−.01	−.11	−.16			
Downward gazes (#)	.03	−.09	.05	.01			
Eyebrow flashes	−.06	−.03	.19	.10			
Laughs	.06	.16	.15	.13			
Flirtatious glances	.05	−.10	.18	.06	**	+	+
Head cants	.23	.08	.03	.01		+	
Gaze aversion intermit.	.48	.27	−.05	.01	**		
Behavioral Factors							
Open body/expressive	.17	.18	−.07	−.08			
Smiling/flirting	.30	.18	.18	.11	*		
Downward gaze	−.39	−.44	.06	−.02			
Laughing	.07	.21	.16	.17		+	
Forward body lean	−.05	−.06	.00	.01			
Impression Factors							
Engagement/dominance	.16	.15	.06	−.04			
Interest/invitation	.04	.03	.10	.08			
Comfort	.34	.37	.25	.25			
Provocativeness	.67	.46	.54	.50	**	**	
Pretentiousness	.35	.28	.32	.31			
Physical Attractiveness	.88	.79	.83	.77	*	*	

Note. Behavioral factors were calculated separately for men and women.
UNR = Unrestricted perceivers; RES = Restricted perceivers.
+ *p* < .10. **p* < .05. ***p* < .01.

When we examined male and female targets separately, male targets who
were preferred by unrestricted women were rated as more physically attractive
and provocative. Their gaze aversions also were more intermittent, and they
displayed slightly more head cants and more flirtatious glances. Men who
were preferred by restricted women also scored higher on the laughing factor.
Female targets who were more appealing to unrestricted men displayed more
flirtatious glances. The same pattern of findings emerged when targets'
physical attractiveness was partialed out.

Once targets' physical attractiveness was held constant, targets preferred by
unrestricted perceivers were judged to be more unrestricted in their sociosexual orientation, less faithful and loyal in relationships, and less kind and

understanding. Unrestricted male perceivers were more attracted to female targets who were inferred to be more unrestricted in sociosexuality, less faithful, less kind and understanding, and more socially influential. Furthermore, unrestricted male perceivers' attraction to targets correlated positively with targets' actual sociosexual orientation, indicating that unrestricted male perceivers were more attracted to female targets with higher scores on the Sociosexual Orientation Inventory.

Nonverbal Behavior and Affective Reactions: An Ethological Perspective

The second investigation revealed that nonverbal displays substantially affect global attraction during relationship initiation. As a rule, the nonverbal displays that enhance the attractiveness of men appear to differ somewhat from those that enhance the attractiveness of women. Independent of their physical attractiveness, more attractive men maintain eye contact, avoid downward gazes, and adopt an open, expressive behavioral style of nonverbal interaction. By contrast, more attractive women avoid an open body posture and appear sexually provocative. Compared to attractive men, more attractive women also behave in a less open, expressive, and engaged manner.

For men, frequent downward gazing had a stronger and more negative effect on their attractiveness ratings than any other nonverbal display. This finding is understandable when one recognizes that downward gazes signal submissiveness in most interaction settings (Burgoon & Hale, 1984). For women, open body posture was more strongly related to reduced attractiveness than any other display. Unless coupled with threatening displays (e.g., staring), open body posture generally conveys a willingness to interact freely (Burgoon & Hale, 1984). These sex differences appear to be consistent with previous research which indicates that women devalue a mate's submissiveness (Buss, 1989; Kenrick, Sadalla, Groth, & Trost, 1990; Sadalla et al., 1987) and that men are most attracted to women who appear coy (Key, 1975) or hard to get (Walster, Walster, Piliavin, & Schmidt, 1973).

Although they did not affect global attraction for all perceivers, specialized displays believed to convey flirtation influenced attraction as a function of perceivers' sociosexual orientation and mate preferences. Specifically, individuals with an unrestricted sociosexual orientation and a preference for romantic partners who are more attractive and higher in social status were more attracted to persons who engaged in flirtatious glances, canted their heads, and displayed intermittent gaze aversions. Individuals with a restricted sociosexual orientation and a preference for romantic partners who have compatible personal qualities and are willing to invest in relationships were more attracted to persons whom they inferred to be loyal and faithful, kind and understanding, and restricted in sociosexuality. Finally, unrestricted women were more attracted to men who were more physically attractive, more sexually provocative, and tended to have an unrestricted sociosexual orientation.

The second investigation provides additional support for the link between head canting and flirtatiousness. Head canting enhanced targets' attractiveness among precisely those perceivers (unrestricted individuals) who were most attracted to other displays believed to be flirtatious in nature: flirtatious glances and intermittent gaze aversions. Head canting and flirtatious displays, therefore, seem to function similarly in heterosexual relationship initiation contexts. Eibl-Eibesfeldt (1980) offered an interpretation of head canting that is congruent with these results. He argues that head canting reduces the threat associated with prolonged eye contact. Eyespots arouse perceivers most strongly when they are presented along a horizontal plane. Vertically tilted eye contact decreases arousal (Coss, 1972). Thus, head canting should serve the same functions as intermittent gaze aversions and sidelong looks characteristic of flirtatious glances because each operates as an agonistic buffer that reduces the threat of sustained eye contact. As alluded to earlier, displays conveying non-threat may be essential for the rapid development of sexual intimacy (Givens, 1978).

The impact of frequent head cants, flirtatious glances, and intermittent gaze aversions on global attractiveness was strongest when these cues were displayed by men. This suggests that these signals might function more effectively as agonistic buffers when they are emitted by men. Women usually pose little physical threat to men compared to the threat men can pose to women. Consequently, agonistic buffers should play a more important role in reducing male threat than in reducing female threat. The second investigation, however, reveals that consistent gaze aversion is not a good way for men to reduce threat because it detracts from their global attractiveness. More effective male agonistic buffers seem to be those that reduce eye contact minimally, such as head cants, sidelong looks, and intermittent gaze aversions. Interestingly, unrestricted men were more attracted to women who did not maintain eye contact. This suggests that consistent gaze aversion may be a relatively effective agonistic buffer for women.

GENERAL CONCLUSIONS

In this chapter, we have attempted to elucidate some of the "hidden language" underlying nonverbal behavior in a specific social context—heterosexual relationship initiation. To do so, we adopted a functionalist perspective, seeking to understand the "meaning" of signals that regulate interaction in terms of the consequences they have in this context. Because one cannot observe the entire course of an individual's relationship history in a laboratory setting, we melded the functionalist approach with the dispositional strategy. Specifically, we identified individuals who varied in sociosexual orientation and tried to discern how the nonverbal behavior of restricted and unrestricted people might differentially regulate and channel the way in which they initiate relationships. Two components should be involved in regulating social interaction: the emission of a nonverbal signal, and the perceptual effect it evokes in the perceiver. We examined both of these components in two investigations. By documenting the kinds of nonverbal behaviors that restricted and unrestricted individuals spontaneously display during relationship initiation as well as which behaviors they find attractive in others, we were able to identify some potential regulatory functions of certain nonverbal cues.

Consider one example of what this approach has yielded. In the first investigation, men with a history of unrestricted sociosexual behavior were more likely to emit a cluster of nonverbal behaviors when interviewed by an attractive woman, including flirtatious glances and hand cants (i.e., the Smiling/Flirtatious Glances/Head Cants factor). This suggests that flirtatious glances and head cants that are displayed by men might facilitate the development of sexual intimacy without closeness and commitment during initial heterosexual encounters. Moreover, the second investigation revealed that one consequence of more flirtatious glances and head canting by men is greater interest on the part of women with a history of unrestricted sociosexual behavior. Although unrestricted women were not necessarily more attracted to men who displayed these cues, they were not turned off by them, as was true of restricted women. Thus, the development of sexual intimacy without closeness and commitment is associated with both the emission of more flirtatious glances and head cants on the part of men and greater attraction to these cues on the part of women.

The ways in which specific cues displayed by women might govern the nature and development of their relationships is less clear. The first investigation indicated that women with a history of unrestricted sociosexual behavior leaned forward more during the interview, but the second investigation found that unrestricted men did not perceive women who leaned forward as more attractive relative to restricted men. Certain aspects of women's displays and nonverbal demeanor, however, did differentially affect how attractive they were to restricted and unrestricted men. Unrestricted men perceived women who were inferred to be more unrestricted in sociosexuality as less faithful and loyal, as less kind and understanding, and as more attractive than did restricted men. Moreover, women who actually were more unrestricted were more attractive to unrestricted men than to restricted men. We do not know the precise nature of the nonverbal cues that mediate these effects, but they will be explored in future research.

During the past three decades, a voluminous amount of research has been devoted to heterosexual relationship initiation, nonverbal behavior, and perceptions of attractiveness. The bulk of research within each area, however, has been relatively static and noninterpersonal in nature. Instead of studying what people spontaneously do to facilitate relationship initiation during dyadic interactions, past research has all-too-often side-stepped the complicated yet necessary task of studying the dynamic flow of ongoing interpersonal interactions. As a consequence, we still know relatively little about how people convey romantic interest in others through nonverbal channels during initial heterosexual encounters; we know little about the meaning that different nonverbal behaviors have in relationship initiation settings; we know little about how an individual's nonverbal behavioral style affects evaluations of his or her global attractiveness; and we know little about what kinds of people find what kinds of nonverbal displays most appealing. Couched within an ethological perspective of nonverbal behavior, the present research provides some preliminary answers to these important issues.

REFERENCES

Andersen, P. A. (1985). Nonverbal immediacy in interpersonal communication. In A.W. Siegman & S. Feldstein (Eds.), *Multichannel integrations of nonverbal behavior* (pp. 1–36). Hillsdale, NJ: Lawrence Erlbaum Associates.

Anderson, J. R. (1983). *The architecture of cognition*. Cambridge, MA: Harvard University Press.

Argyle, M. (1972). *The psychology of interpersonal behavior* (2nd ed.). London: Penguin Books.

Baldwin, M. (1992). Relational schemas and the processing of social information. *Psychological Bulletin, 112*, 461–484.

Bateson, G., Jackson, D. D., Haley, J., & Weakland, J. (1956). Toward a theory of schizophrenia. *Behavioral Science, 1*, 251–264.

Bayes, M. A. (1970). An investigation of the behavioral cues of interpersonal warmth. *Dissertation Abstracts International, 31*, 2272B.

Birdwhistell, R. (1970). *Kinesics and context*. Philadelphia: University of Pennsylvania Press.

Burgoon, J. K. (1985). Nonverbal signals. In M. L. Knapp & G. R. Miller (Eds.), *Handbook of interpersonal communication* (pp. 344–390). Beverly Hills, CA: Sage.

Burgoon, J. K., Buller, D. B., Hale, J. L., & DeTurck, J. L. (1984). Relational messages associated with immediacy behaviors. *Human Communication Research, 10*, 351–378.

Burgoon, J. K., & Hale, J. L. (1984). The fundamental topoi of relational communication. *Communications Monographs, 51*, 193–214.

Buss, D. M. (1985). Human mate selection. *American Scientist, 73*, 47–51.

Buss, D. M. (1989). Sex differences in human mate preferences: Evolutionary hypotheses tested in 37 cultures. *Behavioral and Brain Sciences, 12*, 1–49.

Buss, D. M. (1991). Evolutionary personality psychology. *Annual Review of Psychology, 42*, 459–491.

Cheek, J. M., & Buss, A. H. (1981). Shyness and sociability. *Journal of Personality and Social Psychology, 41*, 330–339.

Coker, D. A., & Burgoon, J. K. (1987). The nature of conversational involvement and nonverbal encoding patterns. *Human Communication Record, 13*, 463–494.

Coss, R. G. (1972). *Eye-like schemata: Their effect on behavior*. Unpublished master's thesis, Department of Psychology, University of Reading, Reading, MA.

Cunningham, M. R., Barbee, A. P., & Pike, C. L. (1990). What do women want? Facialmetric assessment of multiple motives in the perception of male facial physical attractiveness. *Journal of Personality and Social Psychology, 59,* 61–71.

Darwin, C. (1872). *The expression of the emotions in man and animals.* London: Appleton.

Dewey, J. (1896). The reflex arc concept in psychology. *Psychological Review, 3,* 357–370.

Eibl-Eibesfeldt, I. (1980). Strategies of social interaction. In W. Von Raffler-Engel (Ed.), *Aspects of nonverbal communication* (pp. 45–65). Bath, England: Pitman.

Eibl-Eibesfeldt, I. (1988). Social interactions in an ethological, cross-cultural perspective. In F. Poyatos (Ed.), *Cross-cultural perspectives in nonverbal communication* (pp. 107-130). Toronto: C. J. Hogrefe.

Eibl-Eibesfeldt, I. (1989). *Human ethology.* New York: Aldine de Gruyter.

Ekman, P. (1973). *Darwin and facial expression: A century of research in review.* New York: Academic Press.

Ekman, P., Davidson, R. J., & Friesen, W. V. (1990). The Duchenne Smile: Emotional expression and brain physiology II. *Journal of Personality and Social Psychology, 58,* 342–353.

Ekman, P., Friesen, W. V., & O'Sullivan, M. (1988). Smiles when lying. *Journal of Personality and Social Psychology, 54,* 414–420.

Eysenck, H. J. (1976). *Sex and personality.* London: Open Books.

Eysenck, H. J., & Eysenck, S. B. G. (1975). *Manual of the E.P.Q. (Eysenck Personality Questionnaire).* London: University of London Press.

Gangestad, S. W., & Simpson, J. A. (1990). Toward an evolutionary history of female sociosexual variation. *Journal of Personality, 58,* 69–96.

Gangestad, S. W., Simpson, J. A., & DiGeronimo, K. (1994). *"Good looking, but not my type": Heterosexual attraction as a function of nonverbal displays and perceiver sociosexuality.* Unpublished manuscript, University of New Mexico, Albuquerque.

Gangestad, S., & Snyder, M. (1985). "To carve nature at its joints": On the existence of discrete classes in personality. *Psychological Review, 92,* 317–349.

Givens, D. B. (1978). The nonverbal basis of attraction: Flirtation, courtship, and seduction. *Psychiatry, 41,* 346–359.

Goffman, E. (1976). Gender advertisements. *Studies in the Anthropology of Visual Communication, 3,* 69-154.

Goffman, E. (1979). *Gender advertisements.* New York: Harper & Row.

Grammer, K. (1990). Strangers meet: Laughter and nonverbal signs of interest in opposite-sex encounters. *Journal of Nonverbal Behavior, 14,* 209–236.

Halberstadt, A. G., & Saitta, M. B. (1987). Gender, nonverbal behavior, and perceived dominance: A test of the theory. *Journal of Personality and Social Psychology, 53,* 257–272.

Hall, J. A. (1984). *Nonverbal sex differences: Communication accuracy and expressive style.* Baltimore, MD: Johns Hopkins University Press.

Helmreich, R., Stapp, J., & Ervin, C. (1974). The Texas Social Behavior Inventory (TSBI): An objective measure of self-esteem or social self-confidence. *Journal Supplement Abstract Service Catalog of Selected Documents in Psychology, 4,* 79.

Henley, N. M. (1973). Status and sex: Some touching observations. *Bulletin of the Psychonomic Society, 2,* 91–93.

Henley, N. M. (1977). *Body politics: Power, sex, and nonverbal communication.* Englewood Cliffs, NJ: Prentice-Hall.

Kendon, A., & Ferber, A. (1973). A description of some human greetings. In R. P. Michael & J. H. Crook (Eds.), *Comparative ecology and behaviour of primates: Proceedings of a conference held at the zoological society, London, November 1971.* New York: Academic Press.

Kenrick, D. T., Sadalla, E. K., Groth, G., & Trost, M. R. (1990). Evolution, traits, and the stages of human courtship: Qualifying the parental investment model. *Journal of Personality, 58,* 97–116.

Key, M. (1975). *Paralanguage and kinesics (nonverbal communication).* New York: Scarecrow.

Kihlstrom, J. F. (1987). The cognitive unconscious. *Science, 237*, 1445–1452.

Knapp, M. L. (1983). Dyadic relationship development. In J. M. Wiemann & R. P. Harrison (Eds.), *Nonverbal interaction* (pp. 179–207). Beverly Hills, CA: Sage.

Mehrabian, A. (1969). Methods and designs: Some referents and measures of nonverbal behavior. *Behavioral Research Methods and Instruments, 1*, 203–207.

Mehrabian, A. (1972). *Nonverbal communication*. Chicago: Aldine-Atherton.

Mehrabian, A., & Williams, M. (1969). Nonverbal concomitants of perceived and intended persuasiveness. *Journal of Personality and Social Psychology, 13*, 37–58.

Morris, D. (1977). *Manwatching: A field guide to human behavior*. New York: Abrams.

Rosch, E. (1973). On the internal structure of perceptual and semantic categories. In T. E. Moore (Ed.), *Cognitive development and the acquisition of language* (pp. 111–144). New York: Academic Press.

Rosch, E. (1978). Principles of categorization. In E. Rosch & B. B. Lloyd (Eds.), *Cognition and categorization* (pp. 27–48). Hillsdale, NJ: Lawrence Erlbaum Associates.

Sadalla, E. K., Kenrick, D. T., & Vershure, B. (1987). Dominance and heterosexual attraction. *Journal of Personality and Social Psychology, 52*, 730–738.

Sapir, E. (1949). The unconscious patterning of behavior in society. In D. Mandelbaum (Ed.)., *Selected writings of Edward Sapir in language, culture and personality* (pp. 544–559). Berkeley: University of California Press.

Simpson, J. A., & Gangestad, S. W. (1991a). Individual differences in sociosexuality: Evidence for convergent and discriminant validity. *Journal of Personality and Social Psychology, 60*, 870–883.

Simpson, J. A., & Gangestad, S. W. (1991b). Personality and sexuality: Empirical relations and an integrative theoretical model. In K. McKinney & S. Sprecher (Eds.), *Sexuality in close relationships* (pp. 71–92). Hillsdale, NJ: Lawrence Erlbaum Associates.

Simpson, J. A., & Gangestad, S. W. (1992). Sociosexuality and romantic partner choice. *Journal of Personality, 60*, 31–51.

Simpson, J. A., Gangestad, S. W., & Biek, M. (1993). Personality and nonverbal social behavior: An ethological perspective of relationship initiation. *Journal of Experimental Social Psychology, 29*, 434–461.

Skinner, B. F. (1957). *Verbal behavior*. New York: Appleton-Century-Crofts.

Snyder, M., & Ickes, W. (1985). Personality and social behavior. In G. Lindzey & E. Aronson (Eds.), *Handbook of social psychology* (3rd ed., pp. 883–947). New York: Random House.

Snyder, M., & Simpson, J. A. (1984). Self-monitoring and dating relationships. *Journal of Personality and Social Psychology, 47*, 1281–1291.

Tellegen, A. (1982). *A brief manual for the Differential Personality Questionnaire*. Unpublished manuscript, University of Minnesota, Minneapolis.

Walster, E., Walster, G. W., Piliavin, J., & Schmidt, L. (1973). "Playing hard-to-get": Understanding an elusive phenomenon. *Journal of Personality and Social Psychology, 26*, 113–121.

Wiggins, J. S. (1980). Circumplex models of interpersonal behavior. In L. Wheeler (Ed.), *Review of personality and social psychology* (Vol. 1, pp. 265–294). Beverly Hills, CA: Sage.

Wittgenstein, L. (1953). *Philosophical investigations*. New York: MacMillan.

6

Gender and Thought in Relationships

Linda K. Acitelli
Amy M. Young
University of Michigan

"It came out of the blue," said John. On the contrary, Mary argued, "It had been building up for years." "It" is the event of their marital separation. How could John and Mary have such differing views of the same (and such an important) relationship event? Mary can point out several conversations that provide evidence that the relationship started on its descent long ago. John recalled the gist of these conversations but disagrees on their import, "Yes, there were some financial difficulties; sometimes we disagreed about how to discipline the kids; and sometimes she didn't like it when I worked late, but I didn't think we had problems with our marriage." Mary, on the other hand, saw each of these issues as stemming from the main problem in their marriage—an inability to communicate. John, who focuses on the issues discussed rather than on the way they were communicated, did not understand why Mary was so unhappy. Mary, who sees communication as the glue that holds relationships together, could not understand how John missed the point.

This scenario is an illustration of how partners can have different views of the same relationship. Moreover, as the reader may have noted, we have deliberately chosen descriptions that reflect stereotypical gender differences as often depicted in the media and academic sources. One partner (Mary) has been socialized to see interactions with her partner as having implications for the quality of their relationship. The other partner (John) has been socialized to think about the marital relationship only when there is a problem that needs to be solved. These differences in socialization could presumably lead partners to have different mental models of their relationships and to behave differently in close relationships as well. Convergent evidence of such links between gender, knowledge structures, and behavior within close relationship settings can be found in the literature in the close relationships arena, and in other psychological domains, and are examined in this chapter.

The purpose of this chapter, therefore, is to explore the different ways that men and women think about relationships, and to posit a connection between the ways men and women view relationships and the ways they view themselves. This link between relationship cognition and self-cognition may be one of the underlying mechanisms that explains some of the gender differences in behavior that have been revealed in the research on close relationships.

After briefly addressing the value of examining gender differences, this chapter consists of three main sections. The first section begins with a discussion of thinking about relationships and then presents evidence that men and women think differently about relationships. For example, women tend to think more frequently and in a more complex fashion about relationships than men do. Here, we develop the hypothesis that such gender differences stem from the different ways that men and women think about themselves. The second section presents evidence for the development of the relational self in women and the development of the separate self in men. That is, self-concepts (schemas, images, etc.) of women are more likely than men to include other people or relationships. In the third section, the work and theorizing on gender differences in cognition are linked to gender differences in close relationship behavior. Finally, a concluding section summarizes the body of the chapter and presents implications for future research.

RESEARCHING SEX AND GENDER DIFFERENCES

In recent years, there has been considerable debate among scholars about the value of studying sex or gender differences (e.g., Baumeister, 1988; Canary & Hause, 1993; Eagly, 1990). Some critics argue that such research invites discrimination against women. These critics believe that people will automatically assign differing values to characteristics based on difference alone. However, gender differences *ipso facto* do not invite discrimination. How a researcher chooses to report or interpret gender differences can influence whether or not there will be negative ramifications. Eagly pointed out that a great deal of the gender-difference research actually portrays women in a positive light. This positive view of women is especially true with respect to research on close relationships that casts women as the relationship "experts."

Some psychologists have maintained that gender differences are small and therefore unimportant. Eagly and Wood (1991) conducted meta-analytic aggregations of sex-difference findings, leading Eagly (1990) to conclude that "the magnitude of these findings is fairly typical of social psychological research more generally" (p. 560). Thus, psychologists who wish to dismiss the sex-difference findings as inconsequential, must do the same for many other social psychological findings.

On the other hand, the significance of a mean difference is sometimes exaggerated. For example, if researchers find that women are more verbal than men, it does not mean that all women are more verbal than all men in all situations. Thus, three points need to be kept in mind: One point is that means show tendencies of populations, not individuals. Therefore, mean differences do not entail that all individuals in a given population are different from all individuals in another. Second, gender differences are contextually specific. That is, we would expect to see the most marked gender differences in situations that affect men and women differently. Maccoby (1990), who has studied gender differences in child development, argued that behavioral differences between the sexes are minimal when children are tested individually. When gender differences do emerge, they emerge primarily in social situations. Moreover, Eagly and Wood (1991) demonstrated that in contexts where sex-role expectations are salient, consistent gender differences in behavior are, in part, the result of normative beliefs about appropriate actions for men and women. Within the context of close heterosexual relationships, for example, sex-role expectations can sometimes prescribe how men and women relate to each other. Thus, it is more than appropriate to study gender differences in the relationship context, it is essential to gaining a full understanding of close relationships (e.g., see Peplau & Gordon, 1985).

The third point is that means are not the only important statistical indices in an examination of gender differences. For example, variances and correlations are equally important. Men may be quite different from women in terms of the variability of a particular characteristic, while the means may turn out to be identical. Furthermore, even if the means are the same, the associations between variables may be different. Hence, instead of asking only whether women think more about relationships than men do, we also question how thinking about relationships affects men and women differently. For example, do the correlates between thinking about relationships and other variables like satisfaction vary according to gender?

Much has been written about cognition within the context of a close relationship (e.g., Fletcher & Fincham, 1991). Although many studies have examined attributions or perceptions of individual partners, often these attributions or perceptions do not focus explicitly on the relationship between two people. Only recently have researchers begun to examine how people think about their relationships rather than about self and partner as individuals. The following section highlights the research that reveals gender differences in thinking about relationships rather than individuals.

THINKING ABOUT RELATIONSHIPS

An important distinction guiding the focus of this section is that between the work on cognition within the context of a relationship and the work on cognition about a relationship. Cognition (e.g., attributions) may occur within the context of a relationship and yet not focus on the relationship per se. Instead, it might focus on the self, partner, or a particular situation.

Distinguishing between thinking about persons and thinking about relationships is important because the consequences of such lay thinking can be different depending on the focus of the cognition. For example, in their study of attributions in relationships, Fletcher, Fincham, Cramer, and Heron (1987) demonstrated that cognitive attention focused on the relationship and interaction between partners (as opposed to just the self or the partner), was generally associated with higher levels of happiness, commitment, and love. Furthermore, spouses who think of themselves as a couple are happier than those who see themselves as two separate people (Acitelli & Antonucci, 1991; Scott, Fuhrman, & Wyer, 1991). Perhaps people who see themselves as a couple face everyday marital tasks in terms of "we," rather than "I" alone. The "we're in this together" attitude may help couples through conflicts by placing them on the same side, rather than as two adversaries pitted against one another.

Burnett (1984, 1987) investigated the content and incidence of thinking about relationships in order to determine whether such thinking is common or rare, superficial or deep. In various studies (Burnett, 1984, 1987), people were asked to write about relationships in response to open-ended questions. They also filled out questionnaires on attitudes toward thinking and talking about relationships. Burnett's work revealed gender differences in the content and frequency of relationship thought.

Burnett's (1984) findings depict "men in general as less interested, thoughtful and communicative about relationships, placing less value on analysis and discussion about relationships . . ." (p. 9), regardless of what kind of relationship they were thinking or talking about. Burnett (1987) concluded that men are primarily concerned with forming, keeping, and maintaining relationships "regardless of what goes on within them," whereas women "care more about monitoring and evaluating the intrinsic relationship events and experiences" (p. 89). This conclusion is consistent with other research indicating that the status of being married is a more important predictor of men's well-being than the emotional quality of the marriage, whereas for women the emotional quality of the relationship is the more important predictor (Gove, Hughes, & Style, 1983; Hess & Soldo, 1985).

Performing factor analyses on a scale designed to assess relationship thinking in premarital relationships, Cate, Koval, Lloyd, and Wilson (1995) found two broad factors: partner thinking (e.g., "I wonder how my partner feels about our relationship") and positive affect (e.g., "I think about all the fun my partner and I have had together"). Consistent with Burnett's (1987) findings, Cate et al. found that females scored higher than males on both partner thinking and positive affect thinking. In his Relationship Awareness Scale, Snell (1988) found trends toward gender differences in three aspects of relationship thinking designated as relationship consciousness (the tendency to think about internal, dynamic features of a relationship), relationship monitoring (the tendency to think about the public impression created by one's intimate relationship), and relationship anxiety (the tendency to experience anxiety and shyness in an intimate relationship). Women scored higher on both relationship consciousness and relationship monitoring. On the other hand, men tended to score higher on relationship anxiety, indicating perhaps that men feel inadequate due to their awareness of the social norms that place women in the "relationship expert" role.

However, there are limitations to fixed response questions that ask respondents to report how often they think about relationships. Aside from the obvious questions of accuracy (did the respondent really think about the relationship three times last week?), there is also the question of validity. For example, the researcher does not really know if the respondent is thinking about the relationship or thinking about the partner as an individual. Indeed, Cate et al. (1995) define relationship thinking as "conscious thought processes that are focused on relationship patterns, *aspects of the partner,* and subjective conditions that are formed through interaction with a romantic partner" (italics added).

In order to counteract the limitation of fixed responses to a questionnaire, open-ended interviews were conducted with married couples in a study by Acitelli (1992). In this research, respondents were asked to talk about their lives, not their relationships, since they had been married, and their open-ended responses were coded for relationship talk. Although they were not asked about relationship thinking, the extent to which spouses talked about the relationship was used as a measure of how much attention respondents paid to relationships in general. Relationship talk was coded based on the definition of *relationship awareness* (Acitelli, 1988, 1992). Relationship awareness is defined as a person's thinking about or focusing attention on interaction patterns, comparisons, contrasts between partners in the relationship, and thoughts about the relationship as an entity. As predicted, wives tended to talk more about their marital relationships than did their husbands. Thus, we have evidence that women spontaneously focus more attention on relationships than men do.

Thus far, we have reported mean differences concerned with the frequency of thinking about relationships, but there are other important questions to be asked. Is the nature of relational thinking different between men and women? When men and women think about relationships, do they think in different terms, or at different levels of complexity? Furthermore, are there gender differences in the correlates of relationship cognition?

Antecedents and Content of Relationship Thinking. Burnett (1987) asked respondents to indicate what triggered relationship-oriented thoughts and to describe their content. When referring to what prompted the men to think about relationships, they mentioned problems and crises more often than women. With regard to both the contents of, and conclusions resulting from, the thoughts, assessments of the relationship were more common among women than men. Responses to the questionnaires revealed that men experienced more difficulty with the task of writing about relationships than women: Men had more difficulty explaining relationships, and they were less likely to enjoy analyzing personal relationships than were women.

In order to assess the complexity of relationship thinking, Martin (1991) developed a measure that assesses the complexity or degree of elaboration of relational thoughts. Modeled after Crockett's (1965) Role Category Questionnaire, which elicits descriptions of persons, the Relational Cognition Complexity Instrument (RCCI) requires respondents to write descriptions of three of their relationships. Responses are coded by counting the number of times that relational constructs (which are distinguished from personal constructs) occur in the descriptions. "Differentiation" or complexity scores are obtained by summing the number of different (or unique) relational constructs mentioned by the respondents. As predicted, females scored higher on this scale than males did.

Conclusion. A consistent finding among these researchers is that women think more, and with more complexity, about relationships than men do. One explanation for this finding is that in Western society, women are socialized to be the relationship experts, as more responsible, perhaps, for the outcomes of relationships. A consequence of this responsibility would be that women consciously think more about their relationships than men would. As Cate et al. (1995) found, some of this cognitive activity may take the form of reviewing past events, which may account for the finding that women have more vivid memories about past relationship events than do their male partners (Ross & Holmberg, 1992). This finding was revealed by Ross and Holmberg through respondents' ratings of their own recollections as well as researchers' ratings of the vividness of respondents' open-ended responses to questions about relationship events. Furthermore, when couples in the study by Ross and Holmberg were asked to recall events during a joint interview, husbands were more likely to ask their wives for help in remembering events.

Thus far, evidence has been presented that men and women think differently about relationships. We now turn to evidence that indicates that thinking about relationships has different outcomes for men and women.

CORRELATES OF RELATIONSHIP COGNITION WITH WELL-BEING AND RELATIONSHIP SATISFACTION

Few studies have examined the correlations between relationship thinking and other variables separately for men and women. Some may not have done so because it would have steered work in directions that were not part of the original purposes. Others have been unable to because of small sample sizes. Thus, we report the few studies that do provide such correlations according to gender. In addition, we also describe some relevant studies that did not specifically examine relationship thinking.

Studies of Relationship Cognition and Communication. In the interview study (Acitelli, 1992) previously reported in which couples were asked to talk about their lives, as opposed to their relationships, open-ended responses were coded for relationship awareness, based on the definition provided previously. Results show that, for wives, both marital and life satisfaction were related to the amount of time husbands spent talking about the marital relationship. It was also demonstrated that this finding was not merely due to the degree to which the husband spoke about the relationship in positive terms. Conversely, husbands' marital and life satisfaction were not related to the degree to which either spouse focused on the relationship during the interview. This study suggests that focusing attention on the marital relationship is important to wives, especially when husbands are doing the attending.

To date, there are no other studies (to our knowledge) that report correlations between relationship thinking and satisfaction separately for men and women. Another study, however, demonstrates that talking about the relationship is perceived by spouses differently in different situations. In this experimental study, Acitelli (1988) examined the effects of talking about the relationship on perceptions of spouses' feelings of contentment. Married couples read stories about couples where spouses either talk or do not talk about the relationship in pleasant or unpleasant situations. In a short questionnaire following each story, individual spouses rated the fictional spouses' feelings.

Results of this study showed that talking about the relationship was perceived as making partners feel better than not talking about the relationship regardless of the gender of the respondent or the affective tone of the story (pleasant or unpleasant). Yet affective tone was shown to interact with the fictional characters' gender such that relationship talk during good times was perceived to have more of a positive impact on wives in the stories than on husbands in the stories, especially if the husband was doing the talking. In this context, husbands' talk about the relationship was judged to have more of an impact on wives than wives' talk was perceived to have on husbands (which is consistent with the findings from the earlier interview study).

The interactions also revealed that the discrepancy between ratings of husbands' feelings for relational talk and nonrelational talk was greater in an unpleasant story than in a pleasant story. Hence, relationship talk was perceived as making more of a difference to husbands in unpleasant situations than in pleasant ones. This pattern was not found for ratings of wives' feelings. This gender difference may reflect the point that husbands view relationship talk as instrumental (used as a tool for fixing things, so it is especially valuable in a conflict situation), whereas wives are seen to feel equally as good about relationship talk in either setting. Scott et al. (1991) posited that women may be more likely to view conversations with their partners as relationship relevant and thus store the conversation as a relationship memory. Men, on the other hand, are postulated to store conversations exclusively in terms of the issue discussed. Thus, it is not surprising that men would see relationship talk as a means to an end, whereas women may see it as an end in itself or something to be valued for its own sake, with important consequences for relationship satisfaction (see Duck, Rutt, Hurst, & Strejc, 1991; Wheeler & Nezlek, 1977, for further elaboration of this point).

Studies of Perceptions of Conflict and Social Support in Marriage.   Other studies consistently demonstrate that relational variables, variables that emphasize the connection between partners, are more important to wives' well-being and relationship satisfaction than to husbands'. These relational variables include wives' understanding of husbands in conflict situations, wives seeing their husbands as similar to themselves, and wives giving to and receiving social support from their husbands. We now describe a few of these studies.

One study (Acitelli, Douvan, & Veroff, 1993) focused on newlywed spouses' perceptions of each other's behaviors during conflict. In this study, wives' marital well-being, compared to husbands', was more strongly linked to the relationship between spouses' perceptions. On the other hand, husbands' marital well-being, compared to wives', was more strongly associated with spouses' separate reports. Thus, in the context of conflict where gender differences are likely to be exposed, husbands and wives reveal their orientations to being separate and connected, respectively. How partners perceive one another during conflict can play a major role in shaping their own marital norms, exposing differences they may not have "seen" before, and can have consequences for marital well-being, especially in the early years of marriage.

As part of a larger project on the first years of marriage (Veroff, Douvan, & Hatchett, 1985), interviews were conducted with newlywed couples. Spouses were asked (separately) to think of the last time they had a disagreement (in the last month) and to report whether they or their spouses exhibited certain behaviors during this disagreement. Spouses rated themselves and their partners on similar items, so the investigators were able to derive measures of similarity, perceived similarity, and understanding of behaviors of self and spouse during conflict (see Acitelli et al., 1993, for a more detailed explanation of the method for calculating such measures). These perceptual congruence variables were then related to the marital well-being of husbands and wives separately.

In general, the findings indicated that for husbands, the more they reported demonstrating constructive behaviors, the happier they were with their marriages, and the less both husbands and wives reported using destructive tactics, the happier the husbands were with their marriages. For wives, with regard to the constructive behaviors, how partners' perceptions are related to one another is more important than each of their reports considered independently. For example, the degree to which wives understood their husbands and the degree to which they saw their husband as similar to themselves were related to their marital well being. Wives' marital well-being was also related to their reports of destructive behavior. As with the constructive behaviors, wives' understanding of their husbands' destructive behaviors was positively related to wives' marital well-being (Acitelli et al., 1993).

This study not only demonstrates that the distinction between constructive and destructive conflict behaviors is important but that different variables are important to the marital satisfaction of husbands and wives. Note that, compared to husbands, wives' marital well-being was more connected to how their perceptions related to their husbands', while, compared to wives, husbands' marital well-being was more strongly related to what each spouse perceived they were doing individually.

Another study (Acitelli & Antonucci, 1994) revealed a gender difference in the importance of social support in marriage. Giving to and receiving support from one's spouse in times of trouble may be one of the most important interactional connections between spouses in a marital relationship. Data for this study (Acitelli & Antonucci, 1994) were taken from the Social Supports of the Elderly project (Kahn & Antonucci, 1984). In this study the researchers examined how perceptions of social support within older marital dyads were linked to marital satisfaction, and general well-being. Like the study on perceptions of conflict by Acitelli et al. (1993), the investigators examined perceptual congruence variables, only this time the items being judged were degree of social support that spouses were giving and receiving. Thus, in this study, perceived similarity was equivalent to perceived reciprocity, and actual similarity was equivalent to actual reciprocity.

Respondents were married couples whose average age was 74 and mean length of marriage was 43 years. During interviews, spouses were asked to indicate who in their social network provided them with various kinds of social support and from whom in their network they received these same supports. Thus, respondents indicated whom they could confide in; who provided them with reassurance, respect, sick care; who they would talk to when upset, nervous or depressed; and who they would talk to about health. Respondents also indicated to whom they gave these same kinds of support. By summing the number of times respondents identified their spouses on these items, aggregate scores of both giving and receiving social support were derived. The researchers also calculated the level of reciprocity reported by one spouse (perceived reciprocity) and a reciprocity score based on both spouses' separate reports (actual reciprocity). The indices of well-being were responses to questions on positive and negative affect, health, marital, and life satisfaction.

Results showed that perceptions of giving, receiving, and reciprocity were more consistently related to wives' well-being than to husbands' well-being. These findings suggest that perceptions of social support within marriage are more important to the marital satisfaction of wives than to the marital satisfaction of husbands. Such a result can be interpreted both methodologically and theoretically. Perhaps the measures of social support assessed behaviors that were perceived as supportive to women but not to men. Note that most of the social support items were indicative of partners talking intimately to each other, a behavior that is often shown to vary by gender. Furthermore, the support received from wives may match husbands' expectations of marriage so well that it had no effect on their marital satisfaction. Other scholars (Hochschild, 1983; Thompson, 1993) suggest that when wives' actions confirm their husbands' sex-role expectations, there may be little recognition of those actions. Conversely, for women in this data set, reciprocity of emotional social support with husbands was more unusual (women are more likely to both give and receive from children and friends; Depner & Ingersoll-Dayton, 1985). Hence, variations in perceived reciprocity of support had relatively strong relations with wives' well-being.

Conclusion.   In summary, the evidence previously presented indicates that wives' well-being is tied to relationally oriented perceptions (relationship thinking and talking, wives' understanding of husbands, wives seeing their husbands as similar to themselves, wives giving to and receiving social support from their husbands), whereas such relationship perceptions are not related to husbands' well-being. These gender differences lead to questions about possible moderators and mediators of relationship awareness and satisfaction. Perhaps the different effects of relationship awareness on men and women is moderated by the way they see themselves. Some theorists (e.g., Jordan & Surrey, 1986; Markus & Oyserman, 1989) proposed that a woman's self-concept is more relational than a man's self-concept. That is, instead of consisting of personality descriptors relatively independent of others (e.g., decisive, enterprising), the self-concepts of women (compared to men) are more likely to implicate others with whom they have relationships (e.g., describing themselves as a mother or a partner). Individuals with a relational self-concept may have a clear sense of their distinctiveness as individuals; however, their uniqueness may well be based on particular configurations of relationships instead of individual attributes (Markus & Oyserman, 1989).

Furthermore, Markus and Oyserman argued that individuals with a relational (or interdependent) self-concept value relationships for different purposes than individuals with a separate (or independent) self-concept. Those with an independent self-concept view relationships as a means of defining their distinctiveness through contrast with others, as though others are foils for the self. On the other hand, individuals with an interdependent self-concept value relationships for the interaction and connection to others. Thus, it may be that men and women tend to enter into a relationship for different reasons, value the relationship for different purposes, and hope to obtain different outcomes from the relationship.

GENDER AND THE SELF

How and why women and men develop self-concepts that differ with regard to separateness and connectedness is an issue that many theorists have debated (Block, 1984; Chodorow, 1978; Miller, 1986). Chodorow provided the interesting argument that the societal organization of caregiving to infants and children fosters a relational self-concept in females and a separate self-concept in males. Males and females experience the process of self-formation differently because girls retain a longer attachment to their mothers than do boys. Being the opposite sex of their sons, mothers perceive their sons as "other," and thus push their sons toward independence much earlier than their daughters. Daughters, on the other hand, are perceived by their mothers as being similar to themselves so that they experience a longer period of attachment to their primary caregivers.

According to Chodorow, the period of gender-role identification also encourages males and females to develop the potential to relate to others differently. Because females are of the same sex as their primary caregiver, they are able to develop their gender-role identification within the context of their primary relationship. Males, on the other hand, do not have their primary relationship with a parent of the same sex, so that their gender-role identification cannot be with their primary caregiver. Proper gender identification for boys requires a disengagement from their relationship to their mothers. Furthermore, fathers often have less contact with their children than their mothers do, decreasing the accessibility of a male figure for boys to model themselves after. Thus, gender identification for boys is based on an abstract notion of what it means to be masculine rather than an identification with a parent. Chodorow asserted that because of their close and undisrupted bonds to their mothers, females are more likely than males to grow up with a strong sense of their ties to others, to value relationships more, and to establish relationships that are more interpersonal and emotionally intense. Because boys go through key developmental periods with a weaker attachment to their mothers than girls experience, males will eventually develop a self-concept that de-emphasizes emotional connection with others.

Research that examines differences in the self-concepts of males and females at different developmental periods supports the claim that a female's self is more relational than a male's self. McGuire and McGuire (1988) presented open-ended questions, such as "Tell us about yourself," to 560 children with mean ages of 7, 9, 13, and 17 (70 boys and 70 girls at each age level). The questions were presented orally to the children, and they were allowed 5 (uninterrupted) minutes to respond. The responses provided differed according to gender for all age groups. First, the girls were more likely than boys to mention other people in their responses to the questions about themselves, indicating that girls are more likely than boys to view themselves through their relationships with others. Second, the girls were less likely than the boys to describe the people in their responses in broad depersonalized categories. This finding suggests that girls think with more detail about relationships than boys do. Third, the children were more likely to mention the same-sex parent than the opposite-sex parent. For example, 67% of the girls' references to parents were mentions of their mother, whereas 40% of the boys' references to parents were mentions of their mothers. This finding is consistent with Chodorow's argument that girls are more likely to define themselves in terms of a relationship with someone that they are close to emotionally, whereas boys define themselves according to a relationship that does not involve such a strong emotional attachment.

Douvan and Adelson (1966) found similar results from their national sample of adolescent boys and girls, in which more than 3,000 boys and girls aged 12 to 18 were individually interviewed on issues relating to adolescent development. Respondents were asked various questions concerning educational plans, job aspirations, dating, friendships, and values. The investigators found that boys and girls focus on distinct issues during their identity development. For boys, identity rested on issues of achievement, autonomy, and the development of occupational plans. On the other hand, identity development for girls rested on the issues of friendship, dating, and popularity. It appeared to be mainly through their intimate relationships that girls developed a sense of their own individuality, whereas boys developed their sense of self through a realization of their distinctiveness from those around them. Counter to Erikson's (1950) model of identity development, the investigators concluded that "the girl is much more likely to gain a developed identity in consequence of intimacy rather than as a precursor of it" (p. 349). Douvan and Adelson's work demonstrates that relationships and connection to others are essential elements of the female adolescent's self-concept, more important, perhaps, than for adolescent males.

Research on the self-concepts of adults indicate that these gender differences continue into adulthood. Lang-Takac and Osterweil (1992) showed that men are more likely to define themselves according to a separateness orientation than women. The separateness orientation is comprised of (a) a separation of one's own emotions and the emotions of another in interpersonal interactions, and (b) an emphasis on independence and autonomy. Women compared to men were shown to be more likely to adopt a connectedness orientation, which was defined as (a) the ability to recognize another's feelings and to share those feelings, and (b) a desire for intimacy with others.

Research conducted by Markus, Crane, Bernstein, and Siladi (1982) also supports the claim that there are gender differences in the self-concept of adults. These investigators administered the Bem Sex-Role Inventory (BSRI; Bem, 1974) to 267 individuals to determine whether respondents have a masculine or feminine self schema. As usual, the respondents who scored high in masculinity on the BSRI were predominately men, whereas respondents who scored high in femininity on the scale were predominately women. The BSRI, which indicates whether an individual has a feminine, masculine, or androgynous sex-role identity, can also be interpreted as measuring a separate versus a relational view of the self. The masculine scale, which consists of items such as assertiveness, independent, and ambitious, can be seen as representative of a separate orientation. Furthermore, the feminine scale, which consists of items such as affectionate, understanding, and sensitive to needs of others, is indicative of a relational orientation.

In this study (Markus et al., 1982), respondents also rated a list of trait adjectives to the extent to which each adjective described themselves. After finishing the adjective checklist, the respondents wrote out as many adjectives from the scale as they could recall. It was found that individuals who scored high in masculinity on the BSRI were better able to recall masculine traits than those who scored low in masculinity. Similar results were found for individuals who scored high in femininity with the recollection of feminine traits.

The researchers also examined the length of time required for individuals who scored high or low in masculinity and femininity to determine whether masculine or feminine trait was descriptive of them. For this section of the study, 61 respondents completed three scales relevant to masculine behavior (aggressive, dominant, and acts as a leader) and three scales relevant to feminine behavior (gentle, emotional, and sensitive) to determine whether they had a masculine or feminine self schema. Next, respondents were presented with 60 adjectives from the BSRI, and researchers measured the time required for respondents to determine whether the adjectives were accurate self descriptions. As predicted, it took less time for those individuals who scored high in masculinity to respond to masculine traits (mainly men), and they were also more confident in their decisions than those individuals who scored low in masculinity. Similar results were found for those individuals who scored high in feminine traits (mainly women) with their responses to feminine adjectives.

The investigators concluded that individuals with masculine or feminine schemas have highly developed knowledge structures for their particular gender types but relatively undeveloped knowledge structures for the other types. Thus, individuals are more perceptive of stimuli that reflect their own self schemas, whether it be feminine or masculine. Given that the BSRI can be construed as measuring a relational versus separate orientation, this research further buttresses the argument that women's self concepts are more relational than men's.

Baucom and Voirin (unpublished raw data, cited in Baucom, Notarius, Burnett, & Haefner, 1990) found similar distinctions with regard to cognition in relationships. In this study, the investigators examined the relationship between sex-role identity and attributions in relationships, using a measure developed by Baucom (1976). In this scale, those high in masculinity are described as assuming control over their environments, and being goal-oriented, confident, and assertive. Those scoring high on femininity are described as interpersonally sensitive, attuned to the feelings of others, highly socialized, and open to expressing emotions. As in the previous study, the concept of separate and connected self concepts are clearly similar to what Baucom et al. meant by masculine and feminine sex-role identity.

In this study, sex-role identity was correlated with different ways of thinking about self, partner, and relationship. The researchers found that when attempting to search for causes for a spouse's negative behavior, "masculine" spouses focused on the individual, whereas "feminine" spouses adopted a more relationship focus. This finding was present regardless of the sex of the spouse, suggesting that it is not being male or female that predicts these differences in cognitive activity, but rather the view of oneself as primarily interpersonally or individually oriented.

We have postulated that differences in relationship cognition are linked to differences in self-concept. We now re-examine some established patterns of marital interaction that reveal gender differences in behavior. Perhaps the mechanisms underlying such behaviors are connected to gender differences in both self and relationship cognition.

GENDER AND BEHAVIOR IN CLOSE RELATIONSHIPS

This discussion of gender differences in behavior in marital relationships is not meant to provide an exhaustive literature review, but rather to highlight key findings. The following section illustrates how gender-based views of self may be associated with different views of relationships, which can then be linked to gender-differentiated behaviors in relationships.

Several studies have examined behavior patterns of distressed and nondistressed married couples during problem-solving situations. One pattern that has been established in the literature that reveals gender differences in behavior is the demand–withdraw pattern of marital interaction, especially in distressed marriages. This pattern has been described as one spouse (usually the wife) attempting to engage in problem solving, sometimes resorting to demands, and the other spouse (usually the husband) trying to avoid or withdraw from the conversation (Heavey, Layne, & Christensen, 1993). This pattern has been found in a number of naturalistic studies (Baucom et al., 1990; Christensen, 1988; Christensen & Heavey, 1990; Gottman & Krokoff, 1989). Heavey, Layne, and Christensen (1993) stated that this pattern "appears truly to be the result of the additive effects of gender differences and the nature of larger social structures in which these marriages exist" (p. 25). Specifically, women are socialized to place greater importance on relationships and have a greater desire for closeness than men do. Thus, when men, who value independence and status, withdraw from engaging in a problem-solving discussion, women try to draw men closer by assuming the more demanding role.

There is some evidence that the demand–withdraw pattern may be tied to gender differences in self-concepts. Sayers and Baucom (1991) studied the role of sex-role identity in the communication patterns of distressed couples by videotaping spouses engaged in problem-solving interactions. Results indicated that femininity in distressed wives was associated with more frequent and longer negative interaction sequences, and both feminine wives and husbands were less likely to terminate the negative sequences than were their partners. Moreover, masculinity in wives was related to shorter negative sequences. These findings parallel those of the demand–withdrawn pattern where wives, who are less likely to inhibit negative responses, interact with husbands who try to control the emotional tone of the situation by terminating negative sequences or withdrawing. However, Sayers and Baucom noted that wives, in general, were not more negative than husbands, nor was the degree of negative reciprocity greater for wives than husbands. The authors reported that sex-role identity (or differential views of the self) determined these negative interaction patterns rather than sex per se.

Another well-established finding is that when marital separation or divorce occurs, wives are more likely than their husbands to be the initiators of the breakup (e.g., Levinger, 1979; Pettit & Bloom, 1984). This finding may be related to the pattern of wives pursuing closeness, and their husbands withdrawing from the interaction. Wives, in turn, perceive that they are receiving less closeness than they desire, helping to create a vicious cycle. The demand–withdrawn pattern suggests that wives have higher expectations for closeness in their marriages than husbands do. We speculate that because wives' higher expectations for closeness are not met, they are more likely than their husbands to think that something is wrong with the relationship, and thus are more likely to be disappointed with it.

We postulate that different self-concepts underlie these differing expectations of relationships. The way that men and women define themselves may lay the groundwork for their different expectations about what constitutes a satisfying relationship. As stated earlier, women are more concerned with the emotional quality of the marriage, are more likely to see conversations as having implications for the relationship, and tend to value behaviors that foster a greater intimacy. Thus, wives may interpret many of the husbands' behaviors as having negative implications for the relationship, whereas the husband interprets his own behaviors quite differently. Behaviors that establish separate boundaries, behaviors that husbands may interpret in terms of "just being themselves" may be seen by wives as violations of what is important to establishing a good relationship, or even as an insult to wives' sense of self (Acitelli, 1992).

Evidence that men and women may attach different meanings to what could be construed as a relationship problem is provided by Sprecher's (1992) study of responses to inequity. In this study, respondents were asked to imagine a scenario where they were giving more in the relationship than they were receiving, and also a scenario where they were to imagine that they were the overbenefited partner. After reading each story, respondents were asked to indicate how they would expect to feel in this situation. Interestingly, the results showed that the amount of distress women expected to feel (in response to both types of inequity) was greater than the distress men expected to feel. Furthermore, women were also more likely than men to expect to do something in order to restore equity in the relationship. On the other hand, men were more likely than women to say that they would do nothing to restore equity.

The fact that women expect to be more distressed about inequity may again be a reflection of women perceiving the situation as having more relationship implications than men do. Perceiving the relationship as unequal may signal a much more fragile relationship for women than it does for men. For men, their more separate sense of self may make an inequitable relationship less distressing. Sprecher's results also indicate that "even when men and women become equally distressed about an underbenefiting inequity, women will be more likely to act to restore equity" (p. 67). This research supports Wood's (1993) idea that society's designation of women as relationship "experts" places an unequal share of responsibility on women to make relationships work.

Research by Levenson, Carstensen, and Gottman (1993) makes a similar point by demonstrating that wives' physical and psychological health are more closely tied to marital satisfaction than are husbands'. They link this finding to the demand–withdrawn pattern by explaining that when a marriage is in trouble, wives take on the emotional work of repairing it while husbands are more likely to withdraw. This withdrawal not only buffers husbands from the unhealthy consequences of marital disorder, but adds to the wives' emotional burden as well. When marriages are distressed, wives' health suffers more than husbands'. Interestingly, results from the aforementioned study of social support in older married couples (Acitelli & Antonucci, 1994), indicated that when wives perceived that their marriages were supportive, the negative association between wives' health problems and marital satisfaction was diminished. This result suggests that husbands may have the tools to prevent such negative consequences for wives, but that they do not often use them. Indeed, not relating in an intimate fashion has been demonstrated to be a male preference rather than an inability (Reis, Senchak, & Solomon, 1985).

This section has highlighted a few key findings that illustrate what can happen when two individuals with different views of the self get married and try to build a relationship. Wives with relational self-concepts may have different expectations for their marriages than husbands with independent self-concepts. Wives, being more relationally oriented than husbands, usually expect more in the way of connection and closeness than husbands do. When such closeness is not forthcoming, wives might express the desire for more closeness, whereas the independent or separate husbands are likely to withdraw. This interaction pattern may lead to wives' developing negative evaluations of their marriages. Indeed, if the relationship gets to the point of separation, it is usually wives who initiate the breakup.

The goal in this section was not to portray all male–female relationships in a negative light, but rather to suggest that behavior patterns in marriages may be linked to the views that men and women have of themselves. To reiterate a point made previously, the findings reported here do not mean that all heterosexual relationships exhibit these behavior patterns. What they do suggest, however, are statistical trends for men and women to have different expectations and cognitions about relationships that lead them to interact in characteristic ways.

SUMMARY AND IMPLICATIONS
FOR FUTURE RESEARCH

After briefly outlining some reasons for examining gender differences in relationships, this chapter focused on gender differences in thinking about relationships. Although there are only a few studies with this specific research focus, the results consistently indicate that women think more about relationships and in a more complex fashion than men do. Furthermore, there is evidence that women are predisposed to consciously analyze a wide range of relationship events or attributes, whereas when men think about relationships, it is usually a specific response to some crisis or problem with the relationship. In addition, several studies point to the idea that relational variables (variables concerned with interpersonal ties, such as talking about the relationship or being supportive of one's spouse) are predictive of marital happiness for wives, but not for husbands.

Next, the idea that the gender differences just outlined stem from differences in the way that men and women view themselves was presented. This proposition was followed by theory and research indicating that the development of the self is different for boys and girls. In general, we argued, girls develop their sense of self primarily through relationships to others, whereas boys develop a sense of self through becoming independent from others. Not only is there empirical evidence that demonstrates how these different selves might develop, but there are also indications that these different types of self-concepts are related to different ways of thinking and behaving in relationships.

One clear direction for further research are studies that directly test these postulated associations between self-concept, relationship cognition, and interaction patterns in relationships. However, it should be noted that most of the research presented here focused on married couples. Given the work of Burnett (1987) and others indicating that men are more concerned with forming a relationship and less concerned with the dynamics of an already established relationship, it is possible that gender differences in the frequency of thinking about relationships would be less apparent in dating couples than it would be in married couples.

Furthermore, changing societal norms for relationships between men and women may be associated with changes in gender differences in relationship cognition, and these shifts, in turn, may be associated with age-cohort differences. For example, older women might be more relationship oriented than younger women, whereas older men might have a greater separateness orientation than younger men. Hence, gender differences in frequency of thinking about relationships may be more pronounced in older than younger married couples. Research is needed to answer such questions.

Theory and research support the idea that the self-concepts (or self-schemas) of men and women develop differently. We would also suspect that their relationship schemas (Baldwin, 1992; Planalp, 1985, 1987) or views of relationships develop differently. As already noted, there is good evidence that women develop more elaborate and complex relational schemas than men. However, we need research that examines both the development of schemas that represent a general type of relationship based on societal norms (e.g., the marital relationship) and the development of specific mental models of a particular relationship (see Surra & Bohman, 1991, for further elaboration of this point). These two types of schemas presumably interact with one another and continually adapt and change. The cultural model may be more similar between the sexes and less amenable to change than specific models of particular relationships. This line of questioning might also benefit from cross-cultural studies. Just as Markus and Kitayama (1991) showed that self-schemas vary across cultures, it is likely that relational schemas vary as well. Whether or not the gender differences in thinking about relationships we have described here are consistent across cultures is a question that remains to be answered.

Future research might also discover if and how relationship schemas come to be shared between relationship partners. Duck (1994) emphasized the importance of discovering how relationship partners come to share similar meanings of their relationships. Presumably as two relationship partners experience the same events and interact over long periods of time, they begin to form similar mental models about their own relationship. However, we also know that couples can build and retain remarkably disparate personal models of their relationships. Studying gender differences in relationships provides one way of furthering our understanding of both similarity and disparity in relationship thinking among couples. The possibilities for new research ideas seem endless. Not only may this research fulfill the goal of greater understanding between the sexes, it can enhance the science of personal relationships.

166 Acitelli and Young

REFERENCES

Acitelli, L. K. (1988). When spouses talk to each other about their relationship. *Journal of Social and Personal Relationships, 5,* 185–199.

Acitelli, L. K. (1992). Gender differences in relationship awareness and marital satisfaction among young married couples. *Personality and Social Psychology Bulletin, 18,* 102–110.

Acitelli, L. K., & Antonucci, T. C. (1991). *Using two national surveys to see how couples view their relationships in 1976 and 1986.* Paper presented at the third International Network Conference on Personal Relationships, Normal, IL.

Acitelli, L. K., & Antonucci, T. C. (1994). Gender differences in the link between marital support and satisfaction in older couples. *Journal of Personality and Social Psychology, 67,* 688–698.

Acitelli, L. K., Douvan, E., & Veroff, J. (1993). Perceptions of conflict in the first year of marriage: How important are similarity and understanding? *Journal of Social and Personal Relationships, 10,* 5–19.

Baldwin, M. W. (1992). Relational schemas and the processing of social information. *Psychological Bulletin, 112,* 461–484.

Baucom, D. H. (1976). Independent masculinity and femininity scales on the California Psychological Inventory. *Journal of Consulting and Clinical Psychology, 44,* 876.

Baucom, D. H., Notarius, C. I., Burnett, C. K., & Haefner, P. (1990). Gender differences and sex-role identity in marriage. In F. D. Finchman & T. N. Bradbury (Eds.), *The psychology of marriage: Basic issues and applications* (pp. 150–200). New York: Guilford Press.

Baumeister, R. F. (1988). Should we stop studying sex differences altogether? *American Psychologist, 43,* 1092–1095.

Bem, S. L. (1974). The measurement of psychological androgyny. *Journal of Consulting and Clinical Psychology, 42,* 155–162.

Block, J. H. (1984). *Sex role identity and ego development.* Washington, DC: Jossey-Bass.

Burnett, R. (Ed.). (1984). *Thinking and communicating about personal relationships: Some sex differences.* Paper presented at the second International Conference on Personal Relationships, Madison, WI.

Burnett, R. (1987). Reflection in personal relationships. In R. Burnett, P. McGhee, & D. C. Clarke (Eds.), *Accounting for relationships: Explanation, representation and knowledge* (pp. 74–93). London: Methuen.

Canary, D. J., & Hause, K. S. (1993). Is there any reason to research sex differences in communication? *Communication Quarterly, 41,* 129–144.

Cate, R. M., Koval, J. E., Lloyd, S. A., & Wilson, G. (1995). The assessment of relationship thinking in dating relationships. *Personal Relationships, 2,* 77–95.

Chodorow, N. (1978). *The reproduction of mothering: Psychoanalysis and the sociology of gender.* Berkeley: University of California Press.

Christensen, A. (1988). Dysfunctional interaction patterns in couples. In P. Noller & M. A. Fitzpatrick (Eds.), *Perspectives on marital interaction* (pp. 31–52). Clevedon, England: Multilingual Matters.

Christensen, A., & Heavey, C. L. (1990). Gender and social structure in the demand/withdraw pattern of marital interaction. *Journal of Personality and Social Psychology, 59,* 73–81.

Crockett, W. H. (1965). Cognitive complexity and impression formation. In B. A. Maher (Ed.), *Progress in experimental personality research* (2nd ed., pp. 47–90). New York: Academic Press.

Depner, C. E., & Ingersoll-Dayton, B. (1985). Conjugal social support: Patterns in later life. *Journal of Gerontology, 40,* 761–766.

Douvan, E., & Adelson, J. (1966). *The adolescent experience.* New York: Wiley.

Duck, S. W. (1994). *Meaningful relationships: Talking, sense, and relating.* Thousand Oaks, CA: Sage.

Duck, S. W., Rutt, D. J., Hurst, M. H., & Strejc, H. (1991). Some evident truths about conversation in everyday relationships: All communications are not created equal. *Human Communication Research, 18,* 228–267.

Eagly, A. H. (1990). On the advantages of reporting sex comparisons. *American Psychologist, 45,* 560–561.

Eagly, A. H., & Wood, W. (1991). Explaining sex differences in social behavior: A meta-analytic perspective. *Personality and Social Psychology Bulletin, 17,* 306–315.

Erikson, E. (1950). *Childhood and society.* New York: Norton.

Fletcher, G. J. O., & Fincham, F. (Eds.). (1991). *Cognition in close relationships.* Hillsdale, NJ: Lawrence Erlbaum Associates.

Fletcher, G., Fincham, F. D., Cramer, L., & Heron, N. (1987). The role of attributions in the development of dating relationships. *Journal of Personality and Social Psychology, 53,* 481–489.

Gottman, J. M., & Krokoff, L. J. (1989). Marital interaction and satisfaction: A longitudinal view. *Journal of Consulting and Clinical Psychology, 57,* 47–52.

Gove, W. R., Hughes, M., & Style, C. B. (1983). Does marriage have positive effects on the psychological well-being of the individual? *Journal of Health and Social Behavior, 24,* 122–131.

Heavey, C. L., Layne, C., & Christensen, A. (1993). Gender and conflict structure in marital interaction: A replication and extension. *Journal of Consulting and Clinical Psychology, 61,* 16–27.

Hess, B., & Soldo, B. (1985). Husband and wife networks. In W. J. Sauer & R. T. Coward (Eds.), *Social support networks and the care of the elderly: Theory, research and practice* (pp. 67–92). New York: Springer.

Hochschild, A. (1983). *The managed heart.* Berkeley: University of California Press.

Jordan, J. V., & Surrey, J. L. (1986). The self-in-relation: Empathy in the mother-daughter relationship. In T. Bernay & D. W. Cantor (Eds.), *The psychology of today's woman: New psychoanalytic visions* (pp. 81–104). Cambridge, MA: Harvard University Press.

Kahn, R. L., & Antonucci, T. C. (1984). *Supports of the elderly: Family/friends/professionals* (Final report to the National Institute on Aging). Washington, DC: U.S. Government Printing Office.

Lang-Takac, E., & Osterweil, Z. (1992). Separateness and connectedness: Differences between the genders. *Sex Roles, 27,* 277–289.

Levenson, R. W., Cartensen, L. L., & Gottman, J. M. (1993). Long- term marriage, age, gender, and satisfaction. *Psychology and Aging, 8,* 301–313.

Levinger, G. (1979). A social psychological perspective on marital dissolution. In G. Levinger & O. C. Moles (Eds.), *Divorce and separation: Context, causes, and consequences* (pp. 37–60). New York: Basic Books.

Maccoby, E. E. (1990). Gender and relationships: A developmental account. *American Psychologist, 45,* 513–520.

Markus, H., Crane, M., Bernstein, S., & Siladi, M. (1982). Self- schemas and gender. *Journal of Personality and Social Psychology, 42,* 38–50.

Markus, H., & Oyserman, D. (1989). Gender and thought: The role of the self concept. In M. Crawford & M. Hamilton (Eds.), *Gender and thought* (pp. 100–127). New York: Springer-Verlag.

Markus, H. R., & Kitayama, S. (1991). Culture and the self: Implications for cognition, emotion, and motivation. *Psychological Review, 98,* 224–253.

Martin, R. W. (1991). Examining personal relationship thinking: The relational cognition complexity instrument. *Journal of Social and Personal Relationships, 8,* 467–480.

McGuire, W. J., & McGuire, C. V. (1988). Content and process in the experience of the self. In L. Berkowitz (Ed.), *Advances in experimental social psychology* (pp. 97–144). New York: Academic Press.

Miller, J. B. (1986). *Toward a new psychology of women* (2nd ed.). Boston: Beacon Press.

Peplau, L. A., & Gordon, S. L. (1985). Women and men in love: Gender differences in close heterosexual relationships. In V. E. O'Leary, R. K. Unger, & B. S. Wallston (Eds.), *Women, gender, and social psychology* (pp. 257–291). Hillsdale, NJ: Lawrence Erlbaum Associates.

Pettit, E. J., & Bloom, B. L. (1984). Whose decision was it? The effects of initiator status on adjustment to marital disruption. *Journal of Marriage and the Family, 46,* 587–595.

Planalp, S. (1985). Relational schemata: A test of alternative forms of relational knowledge as guides to communication. *Human Communications Research, 12,* 3–29.

Planalp, S. (1987). Interplay between relational knowledge and events. In R. Burnett, P. McGhee, & D. D. Clarke (Eds.), *Accounting for relationships: Explanation, representation, and knowledge* (pp. 175–191). London: Methuen.

Reis, H. T., Senchak, M., & Solomon, B. (1985). Sex differences in the intimacy of social interaction: Further examination of potential explanations. *Journal of Personality and Social Psychology, 48,* 1204–1217.

Ross, M., & Holmberg, D. (1992). Are wives' memories for events in relationships more vivid than their husbands' memories?. *Journal of Social and Personal Relationships, 9,* 585–604.

Sayers, S. L., & Baucom, D. H. (1991). Role of femininity and masculinity in distressed couples' communication. *Journal of Personality and Social Psychology, 61,* 641–647.

Scott, C. K., Fuhrman, R. W., & Wyer, R. S. (1991). Information processing in close relationships. In G. J. O. Fletcher & F. D. Fincham (Eds.), *Cognition in close relationships* (pp. 37–67). Hillsdale, NJ: Lawrence Erlbaum Associates.

Snell, W. (1988). *The relationship awareness scale: Measuring relationship consciousness, relationship-monitoring, and relationship anxiety.* Paper presented at the 34th annual meeting of the Southwestern Psychological Association, Tulsa, OK.

Sprecher, S. (1992). How men and women expect to feel and behave in response to inequity in close relationships. *Social Psychology Quarterly, 55,* 57–59.

Surra, C., & Bohman, T. (1991). The development of close relationships: A cognitive perspective. In G. J. O. Fletcher & F. Fincham (Eds.), *Cognition in close relationships* (pp. 281–305). Hillsdale, NJ: Lawrence Erlbaum Associates.

Thompson, L. (1993). Conceptualizing gender in marriage: The case of marital care. *Journal of Marriage and the Family, 55,* 557–569.

Veroff, J., Douvan, E., & Hatchett, S. (1985). *The early stages of marriage* (NIMH Grant Proposal, MH 41253-01). Bethesda, MD: NIMH.

Wheeler, L., & Nezlek, J. (1977). Sex differences in social participation. *Journal of Personality and Social Psychology, 35,* 742–754.

Wood, J. T. (1993). Engendered relations: Interaction, caring, power, and responsibility. In S. W. Duck (Ed.), *Understanding relationship processes 4: Social context and relationships* (pp. 26–54). Newbury Park, CA: Sage.

What We Know, What We Don't Know, and What We Need to Know About Relationship Knowledge Structures

Harry T. Reis
C. Raymond Knee
University of Rochester

After receiving and reading the six chapters on which we were asked to comment, we felt daunted by the breadth and depth of ideas contained in them. Early one evening, as twilight set in after a long day of exploring different themes and approaches to no avail, we decided to continue our conversation while walking through a densely wooded section along the towpath to the Erie Canal. Many thoughts crossed our minds as we walked through the woods, wondering how we might extract some higher order meaning from the many concepts and studies presented to us in these chapters. Suddenly, as we reached a section of the woods neither of us had seen before, we came upon a small, wizened figure sitting on a log.

"Who are you?" we said.

"I am Sal, the Jedi Master who specializes in relationships," he (or so we assumed because gender was unclear) replied.

"Where did you come from?" we continued. We had not noticed him before, lost as we were in thoughts about these six chapters.

He smiled enigmatically, and chuckled for several moments before answering. "Where I come from does not matter. I can see that you are lost. Perhaps you are so concerned with the map that you cannot see where you are."

We pondered this pronouncement skeptically for a moment. After all, we had read Kahlil Gibran and M. Scott Peck in college. Nevertheless, we had to admit that Sal was right. We were indeed lost, at least intellectually, and could use whatever guidance he might be able to provide.

"Sal, can you help us understand the great truths about relationships?" we asked.

He chuckled again and replied, "Help you I can, hmmm? Perhaps. Relationships are one of the most potent forces in people's lives, but there is a great disturbance in the force. The Imperial Empire of Ignorance has kept many people in the dark about the nature and functioning of relationships, and this substantially hampers their well-being. You two are part of the rebel alliance of relationship researchers seeking to end the tyranny of ignorance, no? Perhaps I can help you see what you already have seen but cannot see."

This sounded tautological to us, and we pushed for specifics, but Sal resisted our entreaties, saying only "If you will return to this spot for the next 6 days, hmmm, each night I will teach you something about relationships." And then he vanished.

As we returned to the university, we decided to tell no one of our encounter, fearing that any papers in which we cited Sal (personal communication) as evidence for one or another proposition would be summarily rejected. Nevertheless, as genuinely inquisitive scholars (and still having a commentary to write), we could not resist seeking out Sal the following evening as suggested.

When we arrived, Sal was not there, and we began to wonder whether we had succumbed to false memory syndrome. But suddenly we heard his high-pitched chuckle beyond us. We turned around, and there he was. Without prompting, he spoke in clear, unambiguous terms. "The way in which two people reconcile their self-interests is the hallmark of a relationship." And then, as quickly as he had appeared, he was gone.

We pondered his assertion for a moment. We knew that Rusbult, Yovetich, and Verette (chap. 3) made a similar point in emphasizing the importance of accommodation in close relationships. Partners, no matter how compatible, inevitably face conflicting priorities, goals, schedules, and needs. These competing interests can be contended with in many ways, some of which are beneficial to a relationship, others of which are detrimental. Accommodation, which involves a constructive response to a partner's destructive behavior, seems a particularly compelling example of a relationship-enhancing transformation. That is because in the process of accommodation, a partner sends the implicit message that nurturing the relationship is paramount to the specific issues under contention.

Relationship cognition, which Acitelli and Young (chap. 6) describe as explicit thought about patterns of interaction within a relationship, seems a helpful part of this process. That is, accommodation would seem to require some degree of prior thought about the relationship, and about how conflicting interests should be addressed. (Incidentally, if it is the case, as Acitelli and Young argue, that women engage in relationship thinking more readily than men do, then it seems implied that women should accommodate to their partners more than men do, in both same-sex and opposite-sex relationships.) Of course, accommodation can result from either general beliefs about the nature of relationships, or from beliefs about a specific relationship, as Fletcher and Thomas (chap. 1) indicate. That is, one might accommodate because one believes that people should not make waves in a relationship, or because one is so much in love with a partner that any self-sacrifice seems trivial.

Accommodation, of course, is not limited to intentional decisions to forego destructive conflict; in many instances, the tendency to accommodate is enhanced by constructive re-interpretation of circumstances, in the manner that Murray and Holmes (chap. 4) describe. For example, "Yes, but . . ." refutations or masking a partner's faults by embellishing virtues would facilitate an accommodative response. These authors describe how relationship stories are often constructed so as to minimize perceptions of threat and maximize the personal sense of security. We therefore see Rusbult et al. and Murray and Holmes describing complementary, and sometimes concurrent, processes. Both chapters describe how partners contend with threats to a relationship. Murray and Holmes directly attribute these processes to the sense of personal security that positive relationships provide (which is also apparent in Shaver, Collins, and Clark, chap. 2); in Rusbult et al.'s model, the proximate cause is prosocial, relationship- maintaining motives. In both perspectives, however, self-interest is ultimately served by the maintenance and enhancement of ongoing relationships.

Our minds were so full of thoughts that the sun had already set by the time we emerged from the woods. We realized that Sal's first percept had lived up to his promise. Excitedly, we awaited the next evening's encounter. We got there early, but he was already waiting.

"Sal, your teaching last night was very helpful. But why is self-interest a problem for relationships? Aren't relationships inherently rewarding?" we asked.

Sal chortled and smugly shrugged what passed for his shoulders. "Tsk-tsk," he said, "you haven't listened to anything that I've said. Relationships may be rewarding, but how people cope with negativity and other threats to their relationships is more important than the positive features of those relationships." And then he stepped behind the log on which he had sat and disappeared again.

We were at first skeptical about this assertion. After all, nearly all theoretical models of human well-being propose that participation in satisfying close relationships is fundamental to human well-being (Baumeister & Leary, 1994; Reis, 1990). Furthermore, relationship satisfaction is a major determinant of happiness (Argyle, 1987; Myers, 1992) and good health (Cohen, 1988). (As the Beatles observed, "Love is all you need.") But then we began to reconsider some of the chapters in this volume. For example, we remembered that the attachment system is most likely to become activated when some threat is perceived to feelings of security. In that event, the impact of attachment on adult relationships might not be evident *except* under conditions of risk and threat.[1]

Murray and Holmes point out that relationship partners weave "cogent stories that depict potential faults or imperfections in their partners in the best possible light." Much as positive illusions about the self have been shown to augment individual well-being, these construals may also contribute to beneficial perceptions of one's relationships and oneself. From a functional perspective, doubts, threats, and faults might therefore be desirable, by providing partners with opportunities to actively construct positive, relationship-affirming views. (The attitude change literature demonstrates that messages subjects actively participate in constructing tend to be more persuasive than messages that are received passively; Eagly & Chaiken, 1993.)

There are limits to people's ability to reconstrue, of course. One limiting factor is the frequency of negativity. Gottman (1993) concluded that the ratio of positive to negative behaviors was about 5:1 in stable marriages, regardless of absolute levels. Notarius and Markman (1993) suggested that one "zinger" may erase 20 acts of kindness. Even in distressed marriages, then, positive acts and expressions may be more common than negative ones. Too much negativity and/or threat may exceed partners' ability or desire to reframe. It is unclear whether this process is gradual, as Murray and Holmes seem to imply, or cataclysmic, as Fletcher and Thomas note. The direction of causality is also unclear; that is, does the weight of recurrent negativity eventually overtax partners' capacity to reinterpret threats, or does subtle (and perhaps unconsciously noticed) disenchantment lessen their desire to do so?

Negative events and threats may also have greater impact on relationships because they tend to garner more attention and thought. Perhaps this is because negative acts tend to be more diagnostic than positive acts in dispositional inferences of this sort (Reeder & Brewer, 1979). Fletcher and Thomas suggest that negative events may generate more attributional activity because they are unexpected. All other things being equal, people tend to expect relationship partners to behave positively, so that negative behavior is more likely to violate expectations and therefore require explanation. This is what Holtzworth-Munroe and Jacobson (1985) found—greater attributional activity for negative than positive events. Of course, the impact of a given

---

[1] Interestingly enough, infant attachment researchers use a paradigm—the Strange Situation—in which a child's response to a threatening situation is assessed. Some adult attachment researchers have employed adult analogues of this situation (Kobak & Hazan, 1991; Simpson, Rholes, & Nelligan, 1992). Although questionnaire measures are generally not threatening, and may therefore not directly activate the attachment system, they nevertheless tend to ask subjects to recall or consider situations in which the attachment system was activated.

cognition on a relationship depends on its content—some attributions are relationship affirming ("She criticized the dinner I made tonight because she knows what a great cook I can be"), whereas other explanations are destructive ("She criticized the dinner I made tonight because nothing I do is good enough for her"). The key point here is that negative events provide a salient stimulus that induces partners to think about relationship events, one way or another; positive events, in contrast, because they are less noticeable, may be less likely to stimulate attributional activity.

Interestingly enough, Rusbult et al. drew a similar conclusion in suggesting that accommodation, or how one contends with a partner's negative behavior, may be more diagnostic and influential than reactions to positive relationship behaviors. After all, most persons find it easy to reciprocate positivity. Unpleasantness, bad manners, aggravation, and selfishness are inevitable in close relationships, and the manner in which partners respond to such behavior may matter more than the mere fact of their occurrence. For example, in a 3-year longitudinal study, Gottman and Krokoff (1989) showed that conflict, although harmful in the short-run, may actually predict long-term increases in marital satisfaction. This is presumably because conflict may instigate processes that lead to resolution. Constructive responses to conflict include validation, responsive listening, and problem solving, whereas destructive responses include defensiveness, stubbornness, and withdrawal.

A substantial literature demonstrates that negativity is the single best predictor of marital distress and dissolution (e.g., Gottman, 1984; Huston & Vangelisti, 1991). However, even that literature suggests that how negativity is dealt with ultimately matters the most. That is, negative affect reciprocity—cycles in which partners respond to each other's negative affect with heightened negative affect—are most destructive, whereas responses that involve validation, acknowledgment, and accommodation may be beneficial in the long run. Thus, conflict, far from being inevitably deleterious, may provide couples with unique opportunities that have far-reaching implications.

As we finished our wanderings and neared campus, we recognized that Sal was right after all—the Beatles may have had a point, but how partners contend with the inevitable negatives, threats, and risks that arise in a close relationship seems more consequential. We realized that Sal was a gold mine. If we could only extract more wisdom from him, we might generate enough hypotheses for a large research grant. Exhausted but eager, we left the woods and awaited the next evening's encounter.

The evening was cool, and twilight arrived early. The woods were misty and foggy, and we squinted myopically, looking for signs of Sal. As we sought him, we continued the previous evening's discussion. We began to design our next study.

"Why not ask subjects to describe the inner needs and beliefs that cause them to behave poorly towards their partners?" one of us suggested. Before the other could answer, a voice spoke out from behind us. Without turning, we knew instantly that it was Sal.

"I can see that your training will be more challenging than I thought," he said. "Do you not realize that knowledge structures can influence relationship behavior both with and without awareness?"

We spun around, and asked Sal what he meant.

He replied, "You want that I should do all the work, hmmm? Think about it." And then he ambled into the by now dimly lit brush.

We realized that Sal had pinpointed an important distinction with implications that the relationships literature has barely explored. Knowledge structures are usually studied, as Fletcher and Thomas note, by asking partners to describe their ideologies about relationships, or to characterize a specific relationship. However, several lines of evidence suggest that this approach, although useful, addresses only part of the impact of knowledge structures. As an example, we considered verbal and nonverbal behavior. Fletcher and Thomas propose that interactants typically monitor nonverbal behavior less closely than words. They therefore suggest that nonverbal behavior is more likely to reflect automatic processes of chronically accessible relationship beliefs and needs. Certainly, relationship talk is important, as Acitelli and Young, and others (e.g., Duck, Rutt, Hurst, & Strejc, 1991) have shown. But nonverbal behaviors can also inform us about knowledge structures, either through their direct meaning or in the way that they qualify spoken messages (Montgomery, 1981; Patterson, 1982). This is evident in Simpson, Gangestad, and Nation's chapter (chap. 5). Although one cannot be certain, it seems reasonable to presume that in their studies, targets' displays, and subjects' inferences, were often automatic; that is, that they did not require deliberate, thoughtful processing.

Nevertheless, we feel that it is unwise to link nonverbal behavior with automatic processing, and words with controlled processing. Zuckerman, DePaulo, and Rosenthal (1981) proposed a leakage hierarchy for deception, arguing that facial cues can be controlled better than bodily gestures, which in turn are more controllable than paralinguistic (i.e., vocal) cues. Similarly, some verbal content, like a spontaneous angry retort in a heated argument, is relatively automatic, especially when compared to a carefully reasoned reply. We believe that it will be more fruitful to consider how either channel of behavior can reflect varying degrees of automatic and controlled processing of relationship-relevant information.

Fletcher and Thomas describe an elegant experiment demonstrating that general relationship beliefs may influence processing of relationship information in an unconscious and unintentional fashion. We regard this study as important for several reasons. One reason is that it indicates just how widespread and deeply ingrained the influence of relationship thoughts and beliefs may be, often occurring automatically and outside of conscious awareness. (A rapidly expanding literature documents the pervasive operation of implicit attitudes, beliefs and stereotypes in social judgment; Greenwald & Banaji, in press.) Also, this study highlights the interface between the relationships and social cognition literatures, a conjunction that in our opinion receives inadequate attention. As several of these chapters show, relationship beliefs may function in a manner similar to beliefs about the self, which have been studied extensively under rubrics such as self-schemas (Markus, 1980) and self-prototypes (Rogers, 1982). Acitelli and Young exploit this link, in suggesting that relationship schemas may develop from self-schemas. (Later, we suggest that the obverse causal sequence is even more compelling.) Moreover, as with any well-learned or chronically accessible beliefs, relationship schemas may influence perception, affect, and cognition outside of awareness (Bargh, 1993; Bornstein & Pittman, 1992).

Social cognition and relationship researchers would both profit from integration of their literatures. We extend and develop this point later; for now, we note the need for researchers to consider more closely how relationship beliefs may affect relationship behavior outside of awareness. For example, it seems unlikely that Murray and Holmes's subjects realized that their interpretations of their partners' behaviors had been influenced by self-serving (and simultaneously relationship-serving) needs. Their findings dovetail nicely with existing studies of social motives. Needs, motives, and goals have been shown to profoundly affect diverse social judgments and actions, and subjects are often unaware of this influence (e.g., Kunda, 1990; Nisbett & Wilson, 1977). It seems likely that such processes are potent and influential in much relationship- relevant affect, cognition, and behavior, yet they have received little attention.

The need to consider processes that occur outside of conscious awareness applies throughout this volume. Shaver et al. note that existing studies of working models in adult attachment theory focus primarily on beliefs that people consciously articulate. However, given the literature cited here, and given the strong conceptual links between attachment theory and other psychodynamic approaches (e.g., object relations theory; Mitchell, 1988), it seems evident that internal working models of self and others, developed as they are out of early relational experiences, will have conscious and unconscious components. Both sorts of components are likely to exert considerable influence on adult social relations, and both may operate automatically or in a controlled fashion. We are not advocating that people are substantially or necessarily aware of the forces that guide their behavior; rather, we merely wish to highlight the importance of beliefs and processes that are not readily accessible to most persons.

In a somewhat different vein, this consideration also applies to Rusbult et

al.'s model of accommodation. They imply that the benefits of accommodation accrue mostly when partners are aware of the others' sacrifice. (To
paraphrase them, the meaning of a partner's accommodative behavior is
uncovered by inferring the intentions or motives that underlie disparities
between each other's given and effective matrices.) Accommodators and their
partners, however, may have different thresholds for recognizing accommodation. One reason is that recipients of an accommodative gesture are less
likely to be aware of the given matrix being renounced than are accommodators. Also, self-serving attributional biases suggest that whereas accommodators are likely to focus on the generosity of their sacrifice, recipients may
feel that the merits of their own position have won the day.

This logic suggests that accommodation may sometimes be "invisible"—
that is, that recipients may be unaware that their partners have set aside
self-interest for the good of the relationship. Interestingly, a study by Bolger,
Kessler, and Schilling (1991) suggests that spousal social support may be more
beneficial when it is invisible, presumably because visible support highlights
the recipient's need for help. (Under some circumstances, receiving aid from
others, especially close others, can threaten self-esteem; Nadler, 1991; Searcy
& Eisenberg, 1992.) Also, "visible" accommodations make salient inconsistencies in partners' given matrices, a realization that may conflict with
romantically idealized beliefs about compatibility and shared perspectives. Of
course, accommodators may also vary in the degree to which their acts are
deliberately accommodative—some accommodation emerges spontaneously
from dispositions like empathy and altruism, whereas other accommodation
is an explicit attempt to resolve a particular conflict. It would be interesting
to examine affective and behavioral implications of accommodative acts of
which partners are differentially aware.

We began to feel that our meetings with Sal were bearing fruit. Nonetheless, our secretary and significant others were beginning to look at us
strangely. Perhaps our nightly forays qualified as obsessional, but we were too
exhilarated by our mentor's breadth of insight to quit. (Who among us
would not leave work early if given the chance for personal lessons with
Leonardo da Vinci?)

The next day, we went looking for Sal in the usual place. By now the
routine was becoming familiar, and as we awaited his arrival, we sensed that
Sal would be pleased with our progress.

"Since so much of relationship behavior occurs without awareness,
perhaps we should only study tangible behavior from now on," one of us
remarked. "That way, we could be sure of our observations, as the old
behaviorists knew well."

"Good idea," the other replied.

All of a sudden, a voice behind us said, rather sarcastically, "Oh, really?"

We were surprised at this, and said, "But Sal, isn't that the natural
implication of what you have been teaching us?"

"My boys," Sal answered, "the fact that the study of relationships presents many thorny and perplexing puzzles hardly justifies limiting one's research to the most obvious data. You must respect the fact that, as my fellow Jedi Master Berscheid said in an inspiring 1982 lecture (published in 1986), if the complexity inherent in relationships makes them exceedingly difficult to understand, it is also what makes this enterprise so important *and* fascinating. Did you think it was going to be easy, hmmm?"

For once, we were speechless, and after a lengthy pause, Sal continued.

"Relationships are multifaceted and must be studied from multiple perspectives. You want to gain insight about relationship behavior. That sort of enlightenment requires understanding how people think about relationships, and not just how they act. You might consider expanding your understanding of relationship knowledge structures."

And then, as was his habit, Sal disappeared, leaving us to weigh the implications of his latest tidbit.

We knew, of course, that the knowledge structure approach had established its niche in the relationships literature. Too often, however, researchers fail to fully consider the subtle interplay between these knowledge structures and behavior. That is, relationship cognition can provide critical clues to understanding relationship behavior in the fullest possible light. For example, in their chapter, Acitelli and Young describe several important differences in how men and women think about relationships. They propose that women tend to think about relationships more frequently, and in a more complex fashion, than men do. Furthermore, they assert that relationship thinking, as an end to itself, may be more important to women's well-being than men's.

Not all researchers would agree with these claims. Although many sex differences along these lines have been reported, other studies suggest that sex similarities may be greater than sex differences. (For example, Reis, 1987, found that although women's same-sex relationships were more intimate than men's, intimacy was equally correlated with well-being in both sexes. Others, such as Duck & Wright, 1993, contend that sex differences are more a function of the researcher's operational definitions than actual differences.) Nevertheless, if Acitelli and Young's provocative hypothesis is correct, it may help explain some of the observed behavioral differences that have been reported (e.g., Buss, 1994; Dindia & Allen, 1992; Hall, 1984; Maccoby & Jacklin, 1974; Tannen, 1990). That is, sex differences in relationship thought may provide a proximal explanation for behavioral differences. It seems noteworthy to us that in accounting for sex differences, most researchers focus on distal explanations, such as genetics, physiology, and socialization practices. Including proximal and distal causes within a single conceptual model may be more informative.

Perhaps more importantly, at least in general terms, knowledge structures provide the necessary and critical link for understanding how past relationship experience comes to influence current behavior. For example, to account for the impact of early experiences with caregivers on adult behavior, Bowlby proposed the idea of "inner working models." (Most developmental theories offer comparable constructs to account for this connection; cf. Ricks, 1985.) As Shaver et al. discuss in great detail, these models organize relational experience into a dynamic network of beliefs, images and motives pertaining to the self in relation to others. Early in life, these models are relatively primitive and fluid. Gradually, infants incorporate innumerable specific instances, emotions, and thoughts into a reasonably coherent network of expectations, beliefs, and images, presumably as part of the fundamental developmental task of making sense of oneself and the environment. For example, infants whose caregivers are typically unresponsive and cold may come to expect such treatment from significant others, and may interpret this expectation to mean that they are unlovable. Over time, and with cognitive maturation, these models become better organized, more elaborate, and relatively fixed as the developing child seeks to create a coherent and stable representation of self in relation to others. Epstein's (1980) theorizing is similar. He proposed that the self-concept consists of a hierarchically organized series of postulates about the self inductively derived from emotionally significant experiences. Of course, relationship events are a major source of these experiences.

Because internal working models are presumed to be dynamic and motivating, once formed they play an important role in guiding subsequent behavior (see Shaver & Hazan, 1993, for a summary of relevant evidence). As such, these models provide a necessary mediating link between early and later experience. How else could one account for the impact of early life circumstances on the adult behavior of beings whose actions are choiceful, nonrandom, and motivated?

More generally, as Baldwin (1992) noted, some version of an internalized cognitive model that synthesizes ongoing relational experiences into a coherent mental representation seems essential in any account of the impact of prior activity on present social interaction. The comparison-level construct, for example, posits that standards based on past experience will influence how current relationships are evaluated (Thibaut & Kelley, 1959). The significance of experientially driven cognitive representations is not limited to individuals, but also applies to the development of relationships. Events that occur at one point in a relationship, especially early on, provide a context in which later events are interpreted. Thus, knowledge structures provide one mechanism by which relationship experiences are incorporated by the self, are stored and represented in autobiographical memory, and serve to guide future interaction. Any theory that seeks to account for present relationship behavior as a function of previous experiences requires such a construct.

Nevertheless, as presently portrayed, the notion of internal working models seems to us overly inclusive and undifferentiated. Shaver et al. remark that this concept has been "stretched almost to the breaking point," inasmuch as it incorporates an amorphous mixture of diverse and substantially varied constructs: autobiographical memories, beliefs, expectations, emotions, emotion regulation, goals, needs, motives, and behavioral styles, for example. We emphatically concur with their comment, as apparently did Hinde (1994). As we argue later, it is imperative for researchers to specify more precisely the nature and *modus operandi* of these models. One distinction that seems important to us is presented by Fletcher and Thomas, who note that relational beliefs are both general—one's ideology about typical relationships—and specific—how one feels about relationships with particular partners. Only a handful of relationship studies examine the interplay of these differing (and perhaps hierarchically nested) levels of analysis. It often seems implied that general and specific beliefs are largely consistent. This seems overly simplistic to us, in that it fails to account for the depth, complexity, and segmentation inherent in most knowledge structures. For example, Carnelly and Janoff-Bulman (1992) showed that adult children of divorce had pessimistic models of others in general and marriage as an institution, but still felt relatively optimistic about their own romantic relationships. More speculatively, we can easily envision someone who views close relationships as prototypically risky and dangerous, but who feels safe and secure in his own marriage. In fact, following the logic of Murray and Holmes, the former belief might actually bolster the latter.

We were beginning to feel more confident about our lessons. As we left the canal walking path shortly before sunrise, we were ready to take word processor in hand. But we still felt a bit unsure. Sal had taken our thinking to new levels before, and we wondered whether our growing sense of insight was only a self-serving illusion. We therefore approached Sal cautiously the next day.

"Sal, we think we're getting the hang of your teachings," one of us said, more hopefully than anything else. "Humans are innately and intrinsically social, but because they are also cerebral and reflective, much of their thought is bound to concern social bonds. Understanding these knowledge structures should therefore provide much enlightenment about relationships."

"Ah, you seem to be learning well, my young disciples. Perhaps there is hope for your careers after all. But I am still not sure you see all that is before you. You and your fellow scholars stress the importance of relationships in the development of individuals. But can you not also see, hmmm, how relationships helped mold your species into the kind of creatures that you are."

"But Sal," one of us retorted, "haven't you taught us that knowledge structures evolve out of an individual's social experiences?"

"Yes, my son, so indeed they do," Sal answered. "But you must also consider the functional question: Why do humans depend on relationships so extensively? Perhaps that is a good subject for you to ponder tonight, hmmm?" And with a grin and a chuckle, he sidled away.

It was apparent that Sal wanted us to consider the role of relationships in human well-being from the widest possible perspective. We suspected that this meant not merely describing behaviors, but also speculating about the adaptive functions of relationships. Sexual and natural selection are the cornerstones of evolutionary theory. As Simpson et al. show, because nonverbal cues may regulate access to reproductive (i.e., sexual) opportunities, accurate perceptions of the appropriate cues are adaptive. Their chapter demonstrates that men and women signal their willingness to engage in casual sex through particular nonverbal cues, and that these cues are used to form impressions about potential interaction partners. Thus, knowledge structures relevant to these nonverbal cues may be said to have significance in the evolutionary process of sexual selection.

Evolutionary principles are also fundamental to attachment theory. Bowlby's original theorizing grew out of the observation that infants who maintained proximity with a caregiver were more likely to survive. He therefore hypothesized that through natural selection, infants are born with an innate drive to seek proximity with caregivers, especially when threatened. This innate drive for attachment appears to underlie the motivational and emotional significance of affectionally close relationships throughout the life span (Ainsworth, 1989; Shaver & Hazan, 1993).

Knowledge structures interact with these evolutionarily based drives in at least two ways. First, as noted earlier, inner working models arise from repeated interactions with caregivers. Whereas the innate attachment drive may impel proximity seeking, as well as other core attachment behaviors, inner working models represent the closely related mental structures that arise as infants mature cognitively and begin to develop stable, organized understandings of their interactions with others. Thus, these two features might be seen as a motor that drives the system, and a computerized regulatory system that synthesizes past experience while preparing the organism for future circumstances. Second, many theorists have discussed the adaptive significance for the individual of participating in cooperative groups (e.g., Buck & Ginsburg, 1991; E. Wilson, 1975). Even in nonhuman species, successful functioning of such groups depends in large part on social knowledge, norms and rules, and effective communication systems. The information embodied in knowledge structures therefore has clear adaptive significance.

Our lessons with Sal had taken us far. Whereas we had begun by considering relationships in terms of the dilemmas they posed for self-interest, we now knew that relationships were essential not only for the well-being of the individual but also for the survival of the species. We felt ready at last to write our commentary, but we remembered that Sal had asked us to commit to 6 days. One final lesson remained.

Our anticipation of Sal's ultimate lesson was so great that neither of us slept that night. We arrived early, but Sal did not appear. We became uneasy. Had we offended our mentor, we wondered? We became more and more restless as we waited, and our thoughts jumped rapidly from one idea to another as we reflected on our lessons. Soon, in Sal's absence, we began to test these ideas on each other.

Several broad themes had emerged from our studies with Sal, and the authors of these chapters. We have been struck by the many interests shared by relationship and social cognition researchers. It seems evident to us that each literature has much to offer the other. Yet our impression is that to date this interaction is underexploited. Apparently, other commentators feel similarly. In recent reviews, S. Fiske (1992) and Schneider (1991) admonished social cognition researchers to consider more fully the impact of social and interpersonal variables on cognitive processes. Kenny (1994) and Baldwin (1992) called on social perception researchers to adapt their research paradigms and priorities to put these processes in their properly interactive and interpersonal context. Relationship variables are major components of this context. As Clark and Reis (1988), among others, noted, relationships may influence the operation of basic social psychological processes, and relationship research can do much to illuminate the boundary conditions and mechanisms intrinsic to them.

At the same time, major advances in social cognition research have only begun to percolate through the relationships literature. Berscheid (1994) highlighted several of these advances in her compelling discussion of relationship cognition. The chapters in this volume impressively demonstrate that understanding relationship knowledge structures is central to the broader endeavor of understanding relationships. Yet as long as relationship research fails to integrate state-of-the-art models of social cognition into its conceptualization of relationship cognition, we sell short one of our most fundamental scientific goals. In part, this may be because relationships research has focussed almost exclusively on "what" questions—what specific content differentiates one set of relationship beliefs from another—rather than "how" and "why" questions—how are mental representations of relationships structured? How do they operate? Why do relationships function as they do? Pursuit of these latter questions will surely be facilitated by closer consideration of current social cognitive models of person representation.

In a comprehensive review, Baldwin (1992) suggested that relational schemas have three components: a self-schema, an other-schema, and an interpersonal script (i.e., cognitive generalizations based on past experiences that specify how self and other will interact in given situations). Baldwin's first two components have received considerable attention in recent social cognition research. One current controversy contrasts prototype and exemplar models.[2] A long-standing view is that people form summary generalizations (also termed *prototypes, stereotypes,* and *schemas*) from past experience, and then use these abstractions in subsequent social perception and information processing (see Higgins & Bargh, 1987, for an overview of this research). The exemplar alternative (Smith & Zarate, 1992) posits that people also store in memory concrete representations of many specific individuals and occurrences, and that social judgment involves comparing new stimuli with known exemplars.

One demonstration of exemplar effects with special relevance for relationships research was provided by Andersen and Cole (1990). They demonstrated that particular significant others (e.g,. one's mother or best friend) are represented in memory as a discrete category, and that these exemplars influence social judgment more than stereotypes and specific traits do. That is, judges tended to inadvertently attribute traits possessed by a significant other to a hypothetical stimulus person who resembled that significant other on several other traits. As an aside, it is interesting to note that significant other representations exerted greater influence on social perception than representations of nonsignificant others. Expanding on this point, Aron, Aron, Tudor, and Nelson (1991) showed that social cognition about close partners incorporates many of the putatively special characteristics of self-perception. These and other studies (e.g., Prentice, 1990) suggest that other-representations may be quite similar in form and impact to self- representations when the other is familiar and close. Studies such as these substantiate the contention noted earlier that relational variables are likely to affect social cognition.

Substantial evidence supports both the prototype and exemplar approaches, and it now appears that each type of representation affects social judgment under certain circumstances. For example, Klein, Loftus, Trafton and Fuhrman (1992) found that specific exemplars and abstract generalizations both influenced trait judgments about the self and others, but that summary representations were favored when subjects had more experience with the person being judged. Trafimow and Wyer (1993) demonstrated that when people encounter events that resemble existing prototypes, they do not encode concrete exemplars; the latter tend to be used when prototype-inconsistent events occur. Although their research concerned relatively mundane everyday events, it seems reasonable to infer that similar principles apply to relationship-relevant events, and hence relationship schemas. These studies suggest that when sufficient information is available, as seems common with close relationship partners, prototypes are likely to emerge,

---

[2]These models have been applied to both self- and other-representation. For simplicity, we primarily discuss other-perception, although similar points can be made regarding self-perception.

and that social perception and judgment is likely to be influenced by these generalizations (see also von Hippel, Jonides, Hilton, & Narayan, 1993).

Other evidence, however, suggests that prototypic influence may be limited, and that, consistent with the exemplar view, people may rely on specific, contextually bound instances when making concrete, specific judgments. Srull and Wyer (1989) postulated that people often form situation-specific representations of others, and that social judgments are likely to be contextualized according to these contingent expectations. Interpersonal scripts, to use Baldwin's (1992) terminology, would seem to encompass such situation-specific expectations. Zuroff (1989) showed that prototypes affected global judgments, but not more specific judgments, presumably because the latter take more concrete instances into account. This distinction is reminiscent of Fishbein and Ajzen's (1975) postulate about predicting behavior from attitudes, which may have equal relevance to predicting relationship behavior: General attitudes predict behavior in general, and specific attitudes predict specific behaviors.

Other theoretical models of social judgment also have considerable implications for relationships research. For example, Pennington and Hastie (1991) proposed that people strive to create meaningful stories of events, and that these stories are constructed from available evidence. Consistent with their view, McGill (1993) showed that people construct causal scenarios out of the specifics of an episode, and use prototypic cases as background only to a limited extent. These stories, or causal accounts, then guide subsequent judgments. An intriguing feature of this approach, in contrast to models that emphasize preexisting knowledge structures, is that, given the availability of adequate cognitive resources, judgments are based on an epistemic analysis of the situation and relevant background information.

Finally, we note that person perception is organized not only around persons, but also around relationships. Relationships help structure encoding of information about persons. That is, perceivers spontaneously organize social information around close relationships, such that partners' characteristics are more likely to be confused with each other than random, nonassociated others (Sedikides, Olsen, & Reis, 1993). Similarly, A. Fiske and his colleagues (A. Fiske, Haslam, & Fiske, 1991; Haslam & Fiske, 1992) showed that person memory is organized along the lines of relationship type. These and other studies demonstrate that relationship variables play an important role in natural social cognition.

This smattering of social cognition research indicates that mental representations of self and others are considerably more complex, in both structure and operation, than is typically acknowledged and investigated in relationship research. (But see Collins & Read, 1993, for an exception.) For the knowledge-structure approach, as exemplified in this volume, to advance, it must begin to incorporate more complex notions, such as described previously, of how mental models of self, others, and relationships are structured and organized, and how these representations influence the feelings, thoughts, and behaviors that arise in relationships. Clearly, however, the existing social cognition literature is only a starting point in this endeavor (Berscheid, 1994). That is because the large majority of such studies utilize informationally restricted stimulus materials in noninteractive settings. In contrast, most relationship cognition occurs in the context of extensive information, strong motivational involvement, and lengthy, ongoing histories of interaction. Furthermore, purely cognitive models are likely to miss the mark, given that relationship cognition also reflects (as does most social cognition) personality-based drives and structures, such as motives, needs, defenses, and goals. Studies of relationship cognition should therefore help elucidate the roots of social cognition in social interaction and personality functioning, in addition to illuminating the fundamental role of mental models in relationships.

As noted earlier, the vast majority of relationship cognition research is based on studies of deliberate, conscious cognition— that is, participants in our studies are asked to think about and then describe their feelings and thoughts about relationships in general or some particular relationship. Epstein (1994) proposed two germane systems of cognitive processing, however, one rational and the other more experiential. The latter system is more typically affective, associationistic, and irrational, uses more simplifying heuristics and mental short-cuts, and is more likely to operate without awareness. This sort of relationship cognition is examined far less often in our research, yet compelling evidence suggests that it may be at least as influential, if not more so, than the fruits of the rational system. Bargh (1993) reported substantial evidence from the cognitive and social cognition literatures indicating that nonconscious[3] influences on social behavior may be common. Greenwald and Banaji (in press) showed the pervasive impact of attitudes, beliefs, and stereotypes through implicit or automatic processes. In fact, recent research by Wilson and his colleagues (T. Wilson, Dunne, Kraft, & Lisle, 1989) suggests that deliberate conscious thought (such as asking people to explain their affective preferences) may sometimes interfere with judgments that are typically made in a more automatic fashion. It behooves us to

---

[3]It may be helpful to note that the terms *conscious* and *nonconscious* are often used in this literature absent of their psychodynamic implications. That is, ever since Freud, unconscious cognition has referred to thoughts that are dynamically kept out of consciousness for ego-defensive reasons. In some current uses, nonconscious cognition refers to thoughts and processes of which people are unaware for reasons of speedy and efficient information processing, sheer difficulty in understanding or retrieving complex connections, or inattention. Some researchers prefer terms like *nonaware, implicit,* or *automatic cognition* to avoid confusion. We believe that both dynamic and nondynamic processes are relevant to understanding how knowledge structures affect relationships.

adapt methods used in studies of implicit, nonaware cognition to the relationships domain, and then to determine the relative impact of these differing forms of cognition on relationship phenomena.

The need for more sophisticated studies of relationship-relevant cognition seems particularly evident in attachment theory, if only because the working model construct is so central to the impact of attachment on relationship affect and behavior. (We do not mean to single out attachment theory for criticism; we cite it only as a salient example. In our minds, the general point applies throughout the relationships literature.) Shaver et al. demonstrate well how diverse and comprehensive these knowledge structures may be, and we share their suggestion that the working model construct may have been stretched too far. This may be because the overwhelming majority of studies examine the descriptive content of working models in attachment, whereas dynamic process-oriented questions are more rarely investigated. For example, to us, one of Bowlby's (1969) most interesting concepts is *defensive exclusion*: the notion that information or events that might threaten the security of the attachment system are blocked from conscious perception of recall. Crittenden (1990) showed that cognitive-defensive processes of this sort are at the heart of Bowlby's theorizing. Yet little research has directly examined specific mechanisms by which these processes operate in attachment-related phenomena and settings. (A recent paper by Baldwin, Fehr, Keedian, Seidel, & Thomson, 1993, provides a noteworthy step in the right direction.[4]) Of course, the nature of these processes may be inferred from others areas of research, such as social cognition, the self, cognitive psychology, and personality psychology (particularly psychodynamic approaches; see especially Hardaway, 1990; Westen, 1991), but generalization should serve as a source of hypotheses, not as a substitute for explicit empirical investigation. Several chapters in this volume highlight potentially fruitful directions in which such research might proceed.

RELATIONSHIPS AND THE SELF

Another general point that emerged in our studies concerns the link between the self, both as an object of perception and as a source of motivation, and relationship cognition. This link is made most clearly by Acitelli and Young, who suggest that gender differences in relationship thinking may derive from gender differences in the self-concept. The general notion that the self is somehow responsible for relationship thinking and behavior also appears

---

[4]Similarly, the Dorfman-Botens and Shaver study cited by Shaver, Collins, and Clark, and a recent dissertation by Green-Hennessy (1994) are also helpful, optimistic signs, but these studies are as yet unpublished.

elsewhere. For example, Rusbult et al. describe how individual dispositions, which certainly include self-conceptions, may serve as distal determinants of the transformation of motivation. And Simpson et al.'s research seems predicated on the notion that the self- concept, defined in terms of beliefs about sociosexuality, affects encoding and decoding of interpersonally relevant nonverbal cues.

These chapters show how self-cognition influences relationships cognition, an important step. Shaver et al.'s chapter, in contrast, calls attention to the obverse causal pathway, namely, that relationships cognition may influence self-cognition. We suggest that outside of the developmental realm, this latter course of affairs has not received sufficient attention by researchers interested in knowledge structures. That is, relationship variables have substantial impact on the self and self-perception. Although this link provides a cornerstone of social development research in childhood and adolescence, less well examined are the developmental and contemporaneous effects of adult relationships on the adult self-concept. To provide some indication of how relationships research might benefit from explicit investigation of this issue, we briefly review several lines of evidence.

Developmental theorists have long held that the sense of self emerges from early interpersonal relations. For example, object-relations theorists generally argue that the nature of interactions with objects (i.e., significant others) leads people to develop an organized set of beliefs about the self that facilitates or represents feelings of connectedness with the other (see Greenberg & Mitchell, 1983, for an excellent summary). These beliefs constitute personality, of course, and provide the content of self-schemas. Similarly, Mahler (1977) suggested that the process of differentiating between self and others, which she called *separation-individuation,* depends on the quality of interaction between infants and their caregivers. This process, through which infants begin to see themselves as unique individuals, underlies the development of self-identity. Bowlby's theorizing about attachment relied heavily on the notion of attachment as a relationship (and not as a characteristic of individuals), which he called a *goal-corrected partnership,* out of which complementary representations of self and others emerge. In short, there is substantial evidence within developmental research to indicate that early relationships play a critical role in shaping the self.

Such influence is not limited to the vulnerable period of early development. The self is a fundamentally social product, an observation of William James (1890) that many theorists have echoed. Research in the *symbolic interaction* tradition (Stryker & Statham, 1985), for example, provides empirical support for the often cited contention by Cooley (1902) and Mead (1934), among others, that the responses of others help shape the self. A recent set of studies by Jussim, Soffin, Brown, Ley, and Kohlhepp (1992) examined and supported the hypothesis that "reflected appraisals" may influence the self-concept indirectly, through subjects' perceptions of the evaluations of others. Even better evidence for the impact of relationships and relational variables on the self was provided by Baldwin, Carrell, and Lopez (1990). They found that self-evaluations were affected by relationship schemas primed without subjects' awareness. That is, subjects who were subliminally shown the disapproving facial image of a significant other evaluated their performance more negatively than subjects shown an approving face, or a disapproving face of an unfamiliar person. Finally, if people enter close relationships in order to "expand the self," as Aron et al. (1991) suggested, then the self should show substantial changes as a function of the nature of those relationships.

Moreover, in certain contexts, the self may assume a more intrinsically relational nature than is typically conceived. Research on individualism-collectivism indicates that in collective cultures, the self is evaluated less as an autonomous agent, and more as a member of significant social groups, usually the family (Markus & Kitiyama, 1991; Triandis, 1994). Thus, relatively speaking, situations are interpreted in terms of their implications for the group more than for the individual, and behavior is enacted to fulfill the group's needs, goals and plans, rather than the individual's. The self in this value system is subsumed within a representation of self-with-others (Berscheid, 1994), a notion that can readily incorporate both the subjective and objective aspects of the self.

We therefore believe that relationship researchers might profitably consider in greater depth the manner in which relationships and relationship experiences influence the adult self. Such research is prevalent in developmental psychology, and it would be useful to expand these efforts to examine how the organization and functioning of the adult self-concept is influenced by relational circumstances.

CONCLUSION

Dawn approached as we completed our peregrinations. We had been so absorbed in our discussions that we had not realized that Sal had not appeared for our final, promised lesson. Suppressing the urge to panic, we tried to reinterpret our foreboding in the most positive light.

"Perhaps he feels that we have learned all that we need to learn," one of us suggested (albeit more with hope than with conviction).

"No, I don't think so," said the other. "I suspect that Sal feels that the final lesson is not his to teach us, but rather ours to learn. We have much to understand about relationships. Sal's final lesson is that we must do our research and teaching well, with a spirit of openness to ideas, a commitment to rigorous thought and empirical study, and an appreciation of the joys and pains of relationships. I bet that is what Sal would say if he were here. Like all good mentors, he probably hopes that our lessons with him have advanced our thinking enough so that we could figure this out for ourselves. That is why he did not appear for our final session. That lesson is one we must teach ourselves, as we have already begun."

Suddenly a familiar high-pitched voice intoned from the dim light behind us. "You have learned your lessons well, my disciples. Much work awaits you, if you are to overcome the legions of ignorance. May the force be with you in your relationship research and theorizing."

ACKNOWLEDGMENTS

We gratefully acknowledge the helpful feedback of several colleagues who were kind enough to read and comment on prior versions of this chapter: Linda Acitelli, Art Aron, Peggy Clark, John Holmes, Caryl Rusbult, Phillip Shaver, Jeff Simpson, and of course Julie Fitness and Garth Fletcher.

REFERENCES

Ainsworth, M. D. S. (1989). Attachments beyond infancy. *American Psychologist, 44,* 709–716.
Andersen, S. N., & Cole, S. W. (1990). "Do I know you?": The role of significant others in general social perception. *Journal of Personality and Social Psychology, 59,* 384–399.
Argyle, M. (1987). *The psychology of happiness.* New York: Methuen.
Aron, A., Aron, E. N., Tudor, M., & Nelson, G. (1991). Close relationships as including other in the self. *Journal of Personality and Social Psychology, 60,* 241–253.
Baldwin, M. W. (1992). Relational schemas and the processing of social information. *Psychological Bulletin, 112,* 461–484.
Baldwin, M. W., Carrell, S., & Lopez, D. F. (1990). Priming relationships schemas: My advisor and the Pope are watching me from the back of my mind. *Journal of Experimental Social Psychology, 26,* 435–454.
Baldwin, M. W., Fehr, B., Keedian, E., Seidel, M., & Thomson, D. W. (1993). An exploration of the relational schemata underlying attachment styles: Self-report and lexical decision approaches. *Personality and Social Psychology Bulletin, 19,* 746–754.
Baumeister, R., & Leary, M. (1994). *The need to belong: Desire for interpersonal attachments as a fundamental human motivation.* Unpublished manuscript, Case Western University, Cleveland, OH.
Bargh, J. A. (1994). The four horsemen of automaticity: Awareness, intention, efficiency, and control in social cognition. In R. S. Wyer & T. K. Srull (Eds.), *Handbook of social cognition* (2nd ed., Vol. 1, pp. 1–40). Hillsdale, NJ: Lawrence Erlbaum Associates.
Berscheid, E. (1986). Mea culpas and lamentations: Sir Francis, Sir Isaac, and "the slow progress of soft psychology." In R. Gilmour & S. Duck (Eds.), *The emerging field of personal relationships* (pp. 267–286). Hillsdale, NJ: Lawrence Erlbaum Associates.
Berscheid, E. (1994). Interpersonal relationships. *Annual Review of Psychology, 45,* 79–129.
Bolger, N., Kessler, R. C., & Schilling, E. A. (1991). *Visible support, invisible support, and adjustment to daily stress.* Unpublished manuscript, New York University, New York.
Bornstein, R. F., & Pittman, T. S. (Eds.). (1992). *Perception without awareness.* New York: Guilford Press.

Bowlby, J. (1969). *Attachment and loss: Vol. 1: Attachment.* New York: Basic Books.

Buck, R., & Ginsburg, B. (1991). Spontaneous communication and altruism: The communicative gene hypothesis. *Review of Personality and Social Psychology, 12,* 149–175.

Buss, D. M. (1994). *The evolution of desire: Strategies of human mating.* New York: Basic Books.

Carnelly, K. B., & Janoff-Bulman, R. (1992). Optimism about love relationships: General vs. specific lessons from one's personal experiences. *Journal of Social and Personal Relationships, 9,* 5–20.

Clark, M. S., & Reis, H. T. (1988). Interpersonal processes in close relationships. *Annual Review of Psychology, 39,* 609–672.

Cohen, S. (1988). Psychosocial models of the role of social support in the etiology of physical disease. *Health Psychology, 7,* 269–297.

Collins, N. L., & Read, S. J. (1993). Cognitive representations of attachment: The structure and function of working models. *Advances in Personal Relationships, 5,* 53–90.

Cooley, C. H. (1902). *Human nature and the social order.* New York: Scribner's.

Crittenden, P. M. (1990). Internal representational models of attachment relationships. *Infant Mental Health Journal, 11,* 259–277.

Dindia, K., & Allen, M. (1992). Sex differences in self-disclosure: A meta-analysis. *Psychological Bulletin, 112,* 106–124.

Duck, S. W., Rutt, D. J., Hurst, M. H., & Strejc, H. (1991). Some evident truths about conversation in everyday relationships. All communications are not created equal. *Human Communication Research, 18,* 228–267.

Duck, S. W., & Wright, P. H. (1993). Reexamining gender differences in same-gender relationships: A close look at two kinds of data. *Sex Roles, 28,* 709–727.

Eagly, A. H., & Chaiken, S. (1993). *The psychology of attitudes.* Orlando, FL: Harcourt, Brace & Jovanovich.

Epstein, S. (1980). Self-concept: A review and the proposal of an integrated theory of personality. In E. Staub (Ed.), *Personality: Basic issues and current research* (pp. 82–132). Englewood Cliffs, NJ: Prentice-Hall.

Epstein, S. (1994). Integration of the cognitive and the psychodynamic unconscious. *American Psychologist, 49,* 709–724.

Fishbein, M., & Ajzen, I. (1975). *Belief, attitude, intention, and behavior: An introduction to theory and research.* Reading, MA: Addison-Wesley.

Fiske, A. P., Haslam, N., & Fiske, S. T. (1991). Confusing one person with another: What errors reveal about the elementary forms of social relations. *Journal of Personality and Social Psychology, 60,* 656–674.

Fiske, S. T. (1992). Thinking is for doing: Portraits of social cognition from daguerreotype to laserphoto. *Journal of Personality and Social Psychology, 63,* 877–889.

Gottman, J. M. (1993). The roles of conflict engagement, escalation, and avoidance in marital interaction: A longitudinal view of five types of couples. *Journal of Consulting and Clinical Psychology, 61,* 6–15.

Gottman, J. M. (1994). *What predicts divorce? The relationship between marital processes and marital outcomes.* Hillsdale, NJ: Lawrence Erlbaum Associates.

Gottman, J. M., & Krokoff, L. J. (1989). Marital interaction and satisfaction: A longitudinal view. *Journal of Consulting and Clinical Psychology, 57,* 47–52.

Green-Hennessy, S. J. (1994). *Differences in information processing and organization among Ainsworth's attachment types.* Unpublished doctoral dissertation, University of Rochester, New York.

Greenberg, J., & Mitchell, S. (1983). *Object relations in psychoanalytic theory.* Cambridge, MA: Harvard University Press.

Greenwald, A. G., & Banaji, M. R. (in press). Implicit social cognition: Attitudes, self-esteem, and stereotypes. *Psychological Review.*

Hall, J. A. (1984). *Nonverbal sex differences: Communication accuracy and expressive style*. Baltimore, MD: Johns Hopkins University Press.

Hardaway, R. A. (1990). Subliminally activated symbiotic fantasies: Facts and artifacts. *Psychological Bulletin, 107*, 177–195.

Haslam, N., & Fiske, A. P. (1992). Implicit relationship prototypes: Investigating five theories of the cognitive organization of social relationships. *Journal of Experimental Social Psychology, 28*, 441–474.

Higgins, E. T., & Bargh, J. A. (1987). Social cognition and social perception. *Annual Review of Psychology, 38*, 369–425.

Hinde, R. A. (1994). Early experience and relationships (Review of S. Duck's *Learning about relationships*). *Contemporary Psychology, 39*, 762–763.

Holtzworth-Munroe, A., & Jacobson, N. S. (1985). Causal attributions of married couples: When do they search for causes? What do they conclude when they do? *Journal of Personality and Social Psychology, 48*, 1398–1412.

Huston, T. L., & Vangelisti, A. L. (1991). Socioemotional behavior and satisfaction in marital relationships. *Journal of Personality and Social Psychology, 61*, 721–733.

James, W. (1890). *The principles of psychology*. Cambridge, MA: Harvard University Press.

Jussim, L., Soffin, S., Brown, R., Ley, J., & Kohlkepp, K. (1992). Understanding reactions to feedback by integrating ideas from symbolic interactionism and cognitive evaluation theory. *Journal of Personality and Social Psychology, 62*, 402–421.

Kenny, D. A. (1994). *Interpersonal perception: A social relations analysis*. New York: Guilford.

Klein, S. B., Loftus, J., Trafton, J. G., & Furhman, R. W. (1992). Use of exemplars and abstractions in trait judgments: A model of trait knowledge about the self and others. *Journal of Personality and Social Psychology, 63*, 739–753.

Kobak, R. R., & Hazan, C. (1991). Attachment in marriage: Effects of security and accuracy of working models. *Journal of Personality and Social Psychology, 60*, 861–869.

Kunda, Z. (1990). The case for motivated reasoning. *Psychological Bulletin, 108*, 480–498.

Maccoby, E. E., & Jacklin, C. N. (1974). *The psychology of sex differences*. Stanford, CA: Stanford University Press.

Mahler, M. (1977). *The psychological birth of the infant*. New York: Basic Books.

Markus, H. (1980). The self in thought and memory. In D. M. Wegner & R. R. Vallacher (Eds.), *The self in social psychology* (pp. 102–130). New York: Oxford University Press.

Markus, H. M., & Kitiyama, S. (1991). Culture and the self: Implications for cognition, emotion, and motivation. *Psychological Review, 98*, 224–253.

McGill, A. (1993). Selection of a causal background: Role of expectation versus feature mutability. *Journal of Personality and Social Psychology, 64*, 701–707.

Mead, G. H. (1934). *Mind, self, and society*. Chicago: University of Chicago.

Mitchell, S. A. (1988). *Relational concepts in psychoanalysis*. Cambridge, MA: Harvard University Press.

Montgomery, B. M. (1981). Verbal immediacy as a verbal indicator of open communication content. *Communication Quarterly, 30*, 28–34.

Myers, D. G. (1992). *The pursuit of happiness: Who is happy—and why*. New York: William Morrow.

Nadler, A. (1991). Help-seeking behavior: Psychological costs and instrumental beliefs. In M. S. Clark (Ed.), *Review of personality and social psychology: Vol. 12. Prosocial behavior* (pp. 290–311). Newbury Park, CA: Sage.

Nisbett, R. E., & Wilson, T. D. (1977). Telling more than we can know: Verbal reports on mental processes. *Psychological Review, 84*, 231–259.

Notarius, C., & Markman, H. (1993). *We can work it out: Making sense of marital conflict*. New York: Putnam.

Patterson, M. L. (1982). A sequential functional model of nonverbal exchange. *Psychological Review, 89*, 231–249.

Pennington, N., & Hastie, R. (1991). A theory of explanation-based decision making. In G. Klein, J. Orasanu, & R. Calderwood (Eds.), *Decision making in action: Models and methods*. Norwood, NJ: Ablex.

Prentice, D. (1990). Familiarity and differences in self- and other-representations. *Journal of Personality and Social Psychology, 59*, 369–383.

Reeder, G. D., & Brewer, M. B. (1979). A schematic model of dispositional attribution in interpersonal perception. *Psychological Review, 86*, 61–79.

Reis, H. T. (1987). *The impact of social interaction on health during the transition to adult life*. Unpublished final report to the National Science Foundation, University of Rochester, New York.

Reis, H. T. (1990). The role of intimacy in interpersonal relations. *Journal of Social and Clinical Psychology, 9*, 15–30.

Ricks, M. H. (1985). The social transmission of parental behavior: Attachment across generations. *Monographs of the Society for Research in Child Development, 50*, 221–227.

Rogers, T. B. (1981). A model of the self as an aspect of the human information processing system. In N. Cantor & J. F. Kihlstrom (Eds.), *Personality, cognition, and social interaction* (pp. 193–214). Hillsdale, NJ: Lawrence Erlbaum Associates.

Schneider, D. J. (1991). Social cognition. *Annual Review of Psychology, 42*, 527–561.

Searcy, E., & Eisenberg, N. (1992). Defensiveness in response to aid from a sibling. *Journal of Personality and Social Psychology, 62*, 422–433.

Sedikides, C., Olsen, N., & Reis, H. T. (1993). Relationships as natural categories. *Journal of Personality and Social Psychology, 64*, 71–82.

Shaver, P. R., & Hazan, C. (1993). Adult romantic attachment: Theory and evidence. In D. Perlman & W. H. Jones (Eds.), *Advances in personal relationships* (Vol. 4, pp. 29–70). London: Jessica Kingsley.

Simpson, J. A., Rholes, W. S., & Nelligan, J. (1992). Support- seeking and support-giving within couples in an anxiety provoking situation: The role of attachment styles. *Journal of Personality and Social Psychology, 62*, 434–446.

Smith, E. R., & Zarate, M. A. (1992). Exemplar-based model of social judgment. *Psychological Review, 99*, 3–21.

Srull, T. K., & Wyer, R. S. (1989). Person memory and judgment. *Psychological Review, 96*, 58–83.

Stryker, S., & Statham, A. (1985). Symbolic interaction and role theory. In G. Lindzey & E. Aronson (Eds.), *Handbook of social psychology* (3rd ed.). New York: Random House.

Tannen, D. (1990). *You just don't understand: Women and men in conversation*. New York: William Morrow.

Thibaut, J. W., & Kelley, H. H. (1959). *The social psychology of groups*. New York: Wiley.

Trafimow, D., & Wyer, R. S. (1993). Cognitive representation of mundane social events. *Journal of Personality and Social Psychology, 64*, 365–376.

Triandis, H. C. (1994). *Culture and social behavior*. New York: McGraw-Hill.

von Hippel, W., Jonides, J., Hilton, J. L., & Narayan, S. (1993). Inhibitory effect of schematic processing on perceptual encoding. *Journal of Personality and Social Psychology, 64*, 921–935.

Westen, D. (1991). Social cognition and object relations. *Psychological Bulletin, 109*, 429–455.

Wilson, E. O. (1975). *Sociobiology: The new synthesis*. Cambridge, MA: Harvard University Press.

Wilson, T. D., Dunn, D. S., Kraft, D., & Lisle, D. J. (1989). Introspection, attitude change, attitude-behavior consistency: The disruptive effects of explaining why we feel the way we do. *Advances in Experimental Social Psychology, 22*, 287–343.

Zuckerman, M., DePaulo, B. M., & Rosenthal, R. (1981). Verbal and nonverbal communication of deception. *Advances in Experimental Social Psychology, 14*, 1–59.

Zuroff, D. C. (1989). Judgments of frequency of social stimuli: How schematic is person memory? *Journal of Personality and Social Psychology, 56*, 890–898.

II

KNOWLEDGE STRUCTURES
AND EMOTIONS

7

Emotion Knowledge Structures in Close Relationships

Julie Fitness
Macquarie University

Several years ago, a number of theorists took social cognition to task for its neglect of the emotional and motivational nature of our social thinking. Wicklund and Frey (1981), for example, described the human being within the information-processing metaphor as being reduced to lonely cognizing about information inputs; Forgas (1983) called for a serious consideration of the crucial role that mood and emotions play in our thinking about, and memory of, social episodes and interactions; and Fiske and Taylor (1984) pleaded for some affective irrigation of the arid field of social cognition.

Within the field of close relationships, a small group of theorists and researchers have been assiduously applying insights and models derived from social cognition to a wide range of interpersonal processes (e.g., Baldwin, 1992; Fletcher & Fincham, 1991; Miller & Read, 1991; Planalp, 1987; Scott, Fuhrman, & Wyer, 1991), and our understanding of cognitive structures and processes in close relationships is, accordingly, becoming increasingly sophisticated. However, just as traditional social cognitive theorizing has paid insufficient attention to motivational and affective phenomena, so too has this tendency carried over into social-cognitive models of close relationship interaction; a lacuna even more pernicious, given the overtly affective nature of such interactions (Fletcher & Fitness, 1993).

It is encouraging to find, then, that recent attempts to incorporate affective phenomena into models of social cognition are beginning to filter through into the field of interpersonal relationships. For example, speculation is mounting about the effects of moods (broadly conceived as positive or negative) on cognitive processing in interpersonal interactions (Forgas, 1991). In addition, Bradbury and Fincham (1987, 1991) proposed a contextual model of marital interaction that incorporates both mood effects and attribution–emotion linkages in relational information processing.

A third approach that is gaining momentum in the close relationship area, and that is the focus of this chapter, derives from research on prototypes and knowledge structures (e.g., Fehr & Russell, 1984). The crux of this approach is that people share socially constructed knowledge about the nature and course of emotions like anger, hate, love, and jealousy in the context of close relationships, and that this emotion knowledge has considerable impact on perceptions, expectations, and memories of emotional events within close relationships.

In the first section of this chapter, I briefly review current thinking about the nature and function of emotion, with particular reference to evolutionary, cognitive appraisal, and prototype, or knowledge structure, approaches. I then describe research carried out by Fitness and Fletcher (1993) to investigate emotion knowledge structures in marriage, and discuss the role of such structures in social-cognitive models of relationship interaction. In the second section of the chapter, current theoretical understandings of mood effects on information processing are reviewed, with special reference to the close relationship context. In particular, I argue that it may be a useful theoretical approach and research strategy to conceive of moods as themselves comprising knowledge structures, which drive particular forms of appraisals, action tendencies, and behaviors. The chapter concludes with a call for more research into emotion knowledge structures, both within and beyond the close relationship context.

THE NATURE AND FUNCTION OF EMOTION: CURRENT MODELS

In every area of psychological enquiry, from the neurobiological to the social constructivist, theorists are now acknowledging the fundamental role of affective phenomena in human behavior (Davidson & Cacioppo, 1992). Of course, there are disagreements about how emotions might best be defined, what their parameters are, and how one might most usefully go about studying emotional phenomena. Despite these long-standing arguments, however, the current literature reveals a considerable degree of convergence amongst emotion theorists about a number of important issues, including an acceptance that emotions are real, that emotions share an intimate relationship with, but can be distinguished from, cognition, and that emotions can no longer be dismissed as the "froth on top of the real business of behavior" (Oatley, 1992, p. 133).

Evolutionary Accounts of Emotion

One particularly important area of convergence among current biological, cognitive, and social accounts of emotion derives from a growing interest in the "why" of affective phenomena; that is, the functional and motivational significance of emotions and moods. The strength of this approach is that the functional question can be asked and answered on a number of different levels, all of which provide complementary, rather than competing, accounts. At the evolutionary level, for example, there is considerable speculation about the adaptive significance of particular kinds of emotions, such as fear, anger, or sexual jealousy, in the lives of our ancestors (Panksepp, 1992; Plutchik, 1980; Tooby & Cosmides, 1990; see also Simpson, Gangestad, & Nations, chap. 5, this volume).

According to this approach, certain basic emotions, or emotion systems, comprise evolutionarily based configurations of perceptions, motives, appraisals, physiological processes, and expressive behaviors, including distinctive facial expressions (Ekman, 1992). Such emotion systems are biologically hard-wired (although culturally malleable) in order that humans, from birth, can respond adaptively to particular kinds of situations (e.g., threat, or obstruction), and can communicate their needs effectively. Positive emotions like interest, and joy, are also assumed to have functional significance, serving both to motivate and reinforce goal-directed behaviors, such as exploration, and attachment (Izard, 1993).

Cognitive Accounts of Emotion

Moving from the distal, evolutionary approach to a more proximal level of analysis, theorists are also interested in the functions that specific emotions currently serve in people's everyday lives (Frijda, 1986; Lazarus, 1993; Oatley, 1992; Scherer, 1993). According to this approach, and in line with the evolutionary view, emotions are intimately connected with people's cognitive evaluations and appraisals of environmental events, in relation to their current concerns, needs, motives, goals, and plans. For example, in the close relationship context, partner-initiated interference with goal-related behavior is typically believed to trigger physiological arousal (to prepare the individual for dealing with the interruption), and some kind of negative emotion (Berscheid, 1983). The specific kind of emotion elicited depends on how the event is further appraised along a number of dimensions, such as causal locus and controllability. In addition, each specific emotion is held to be characterized by its own form of action readiness, or urge, such as attacking in anger, or withdrawing in disgust (Frijda, Kuipers, & ter Schure, 1989). This approach, then, does not deny the role of biology in emotion, but typically, its focus has been on the role of cognitive appraisals in differentiating emotional states.

Over the last 15 years, researchers have proposed various sets of cognitive appraisal dimensions to account for different emotions (e.g., Frijda, 1986; Roseman, 1984, 1991; Scherer, 1988; Smith & Ellsworth, 1985; Weiner, 1985). However, this approach has some problematic aspects. For example, theories of emotion-appraisal relationships are still in flux, with no two theorists in complete agreement about the particular kinds of appraisals that generate particular kinds of emotions.

Also, despite the acknowledgment that emotions are intimately related to people's needs, goals, and concerns, researches have tended to treat such distal motivating structures in a global, perfunctory way (e.g., simply as "something I want or do not want") while focusing instead on the more proximal cognitive appraisal dimensions associated with emotion-eliciting events, such as their novelty and perceived causal locus. From a social cognitive perspective, however, underlying beliefs, needs, concerns, and goals, are crucially important influences on information processing in close relationship interactions (Fletcher & Fitness, 1993). Such distal knowledge structures are likely, therefore, to play a major role in driving more proximal cognitive appraisals, emotions, and behaviors.

This point was nicely illustrated by Laux and Weber (1991), who found that during angry marital encounters each partner's behavior depended on his or her goals and intentions. For example, if a spouse was concerned primarily with maintaining harmony and preserving the relationship, then anger-escalation behaviors like attacking, or being insulting, were avoided. However, if a spouse's primary goal was to repair wounded self-esteem, then anger-escalation behaviors were more likely to occur. These contrasting interaction patterns also tend to distinguish nondistressed from distressed couples, respectively (Gottman & Levenson, 1986). Clearly, emotion dynamics between close-relationship participants are complex, and sets of highly abstracted cognitive appraisal dimensions can take us only so far in the quest to fully understand such dynamics.

Emotion Prototypes and Knowledge Structures

Recently, a more explicitly social approach to the cognition–emotion relationship has been advanced by emotion prototype theorists (e.g., Fehr, 1988, 1993; Fehr & Baldwin, chap. 8, this volume; Fitness & Fletcher, 1993; Sharpsteen, 1993; Shaver, Schwartz, Kirson, & O'Connor, 1987). According to this approach, emotions like anger, anxiety, jealousy, or love, comprise socially constructed knowledge structures, or scripts (Abelson, 1981), each telling a different story about a person's encounter with the environment in relation to his or her needs, motives, goals, or plans. From this perspective, and in line with current thinking about relational schemas (see Baldwin, 1992), emotion interactions can be regarded as distinct kinds of psychological situations, for which people learn affective rules, or prototypes; these emotion prototypes, in turn, influence people's perceptions, interpretations, and memories of emotional encounters, and direct their expectations of future emotional interactions.

If emotion prototype theory is correct, then it is clearly inappropriate to relegate the role of emotion to some kind of "bit part" within more inclusive interpersonal or relational scripts. Rather, it appears that emotion scripts themselves comprise coherent narratives, providing detailed information about the needs, goals, intentions, and behaviors of two interacting parties. For example, each script is characterized by particular kinds of emotion-eliciting scenarios, or core relational themes, such as being insulted; being threatened; or losing a loved one (Lazarus, 1993). Thus, when we learn that Paul is angry with Susan, we can assume that Susan has offended Paul in some way, or has thwarted his plans or expectations, and that her behavior may or may not have been intentional, but that Paul apparently believes it was. In addition, and like all good stories, people's emotion scripts comprise details (some more prototypical, or central, than others) of characteristic physiological symptoms (e.g., Paul is probably feeling hot and bothered); action tendencies (e.g., Paul may want to punish Susan in order that she doesn't behave that way again); behavioral responses (e.g., Paul may yell at Susan); control strategies (e.g., Paul may also go for a walk to help cool down); and likely partner responses (e.g., Susan may apologize, or retaliate).

Of course, cognitive appraisal analysis can be readily assimilated within this broader, emotion-script approach, in that the associations between different kinds of cognitive appraisals and self-attributed emotions should derive from overarching emotion knowledge structures (Shaver et al., 1987). However, until recently, cognitive appraisal dimensions have not been systematically incorporated within emotion prototype studies. In addition, and despite its emphasis on the social aspects of emotion knowledge, emotion prototype analysis has usually (like cognitive appraisal analysis) allowed subjects the freedom to choose whatever contexts they liked when recalling or imagining emotion episodes. Thus, the results of emotion prototype research tell us in a general way what makes people angry, or jealous, and the kinds of thoughts, urges, and behaviors that are likely to occur when people are experiencing these emotions. However, we cannot be sure from such studies what makes married partners, in particular, angry with one another; or when a spouse might consider it appropriate to express feelings of jealousy (if at all) to the other; or what might lead one spouse to feel hatred for the other, and how he or she might think and behave.

Clearly, analysis of specific emotion knowledge structures, including cognitive appraisal elements, within the context of a close, personal relationship like marriage, has the potential to enrich our understanding of emotions both within, and beyond, the interpersonal setting (Clark & Reis, 1988; Fitness & Strongman, 1991). In order to illustrate the utility of this combined approach to emotion knowledge structures in close relationships, I now briefly describe some recent studies that undertook an analysis of cognitive appraisals and emotion prototypes within the marital context (see Fitness & Fletcher, 1993, for a full description of this research).

EMOTION KNOWLEDGE STRUCTURES IN MARRIAGE

As previously noted, despite the emotional nature of marital relationships, remarkably little research has been conducted on the experience and expression of various kinds of emotions that regularly occur within them. The purpose of this research, then, was to explore married individuals' scripts for the emotion of love, along with such ostensibly negative, destructive emotions as anger, hatred, and jealousy. These emotions were ranked within the top six best examples of emotion, from a total of 213, in Shaver et al.'s (1987) study of laypeople's emotion knowledge. In particular, it was hoped to identify the kinds of subtle cognitive appraisal and/or prototype feature distinctions that might lead spouses to decide they were feeling one negative emotion rather than another— an intriguing question, given the potentially confounded nature of these three negative emotions. For example, although the layperson is convinced that jealousy is both a good example of an emotion (Shaver et al., 1987), and a dangerous, destructive emotion at that (Sommers, 1984), most theorists have been less willing to conceptualize jealousy as a distinct emotion in its own right. Rather, it has been more widely assumed that jealousy is a secondary, or compound emotion (Hupka, 1984), comprising elements of fear, anger, sadness, and even hatred (Oatley, 1992; Plutchik, 1980; Sharpsteen, 1993).

Interestingly, theorists have also been disinclined to categorize hatred as a distinct emotion, despite its exemplary status as a "real emotion" with laypeople (Fehr & Russell, 1984; Shaver et al., 1987). For example, Oatley and Johnson-Laird (1987) proposed that hate derives from the basic emotion of disgust, whereas others believe that hate is a personalized version of anger (Frijda, 1986). However, Ben-Ze'ev (1992) considered hate can be distinguished from anger in a number of ways. For example, he speculated that people experiencing hate want to avoid, or even eliminate, the source of their emotion; but because they also believe that changing the other's basic faults is beyond their power, this desire is associated with perceived self-impotence, or feelings of powerlessness. These speculations are in accord with some early research by McKellar (1950), who found that subjects' earliest memories of hate involved being bullied at school, and Roseman's (1984, 1991) proposal that hate (or dislike) is distinguished from anger by an appraisal of low self-power, as opposed to high self-power.

Emotion Scripts: Recalled Accounts

To investigate these issues within the close relationship context, a love, hate, anger, or jealousy questionnaire was randomly assigned to 160 married men and women, and they were asked to try and remember the most recent time they had felt their assigned emotion in relation to their partners. Subjects then answered a series of open-ended questions about various aspects of the emotional experience, including their mood before the event, details of the actual eliciting event (including what they remembered thinking, feeling, and saying), whether or not they had felt any urges to do something, and what the urges were, and how they had actually behaved during the incident. They were also asked about their emotion control strategies, the duration of the emotion, mood after the event, and their partners' reactions. Finally, subjects completed a number of Likert scales measuring their remembered cognitive appraisals, or interpretations, of the eliciting event.

Overall, the results supported both the cognitive appraisal and the prototype approaches to emotion, in that four distinct emotion profiles were obtained from subjects' accounts, despite some overlapping prototypical features and appraisals in common. In addition, the results provided some interesting insights into people's socially constructed knowledge about the nature and course of specific emotions in marriage. For example, as expected, subjects' recalled love accounts had very few features in common with hate, anger, or jealousy accounts, except that both love and anger events, as opposed to hate or jealousy events, had occurred recently (within the previous month). Also, both anger and love scripts featured urges (usually expressed) to interact with the partner, as opposed to hate or jealousy scripts, which featured urges (again, usually expressed) to withdraw from the partner.

Core Relational Themes

With respect to eliciting events, each emotion featured distinct relational themes, or scenarios, which could be readily associated with underlying concerns, motives, and needs. For example, love-eliciting events were overwhelmingly appraised as pleasant, desirable for the relationship, involving little effort and few perceived obstacles, and the cause of love was perceived as being global (e.g., "He's such a wonderful person") rather than situationally specific. Indeed, a number of subjects recalling love events reported that merely thinking about their spouses, and reflecting upon their mutual happiness, was sufficient to elicit intense feelings of love and fulfillment. For other subjects, the emotion of love was associated with feelings of security and safety, reminiscent of Hazan and Shaver's (1987) caregiving aspect of adult romantic attachment. For example, a 22-year-old lab technician wrote this account:

> An experiment had gone wrong at work, and I didn't know what I was going to do next with my sample. I didn't want to confront my boss, and I worked myself up into a real state. I told my husband, who works in the same division, that I just didn't know what to do. He took control of the situation and made me feel a lot better about myself and my capabilities, and said he'd sort the problem out with my boss. I thought how special he was, that he understands me, knows what I am like, and is prepared to be there and help.

Predictably, perhaps, hate-eliciting events reflected themes almost diametrically opposed to those reported in the love accounts. For example, whereas a number of subjects feeling love recalled feeling supported and cared for by their partners, subjects feeling hate reported feeling unsupported, or neglected, by their partners. In addition, hate-eliciting events were appraised as unpleasant, undesirable for the relationship, effortful, and involving a high level of perceived obstacles. Subjects also felt less in control of the situation when feeling hate than anger (as hypothesized by Roseman, 1984, and Ben-Ze'ev, 1992). The following example comes from a 22-year-old married student, writing about an event that had occurred 18 months previously:

> I contracted a particularly nasty venereal infection from my partner. What made me feel hatred was the fact that my partner did not tell me there was any such danger, and if she had told me, then the whole incident could easily have been avoided. I felt she was only thinking of herself, and not also of me. I felt that I had been experimented on. She had put my health at risk without telling me.

Another potent hate elicitor involved being humiliated by the spouse in public. For women, this often involved the partner having had too much to drink at a social occasion, and becoming boorish or aggressive, whereas several men reported feeling humiliated and hating their wives when they made jealous or angry scenes in public. Interestingly, both situations involved perceptions of powerlessness and a feeling of being trapped; and, as previously mentioned, the most frequently reported urge was to escape the situation. For example, one man reported thinking "how convenient it would be if she just dropped dead," while a woman remembered wishing her husband would "go away and never come back—just drop off the face of the earth." However, along with these negative cognitions about the partner, subjects also reported a substantial number of self-related negative cognitions (e.g., "I despised myself for being so weak," and "I thought, here I go again—why do I let this happen to me?").

Anger, on the other hand, was an altogether less demeaning, less helpless experience for our married subjects, who appeared much less likely to think badly of themselves than did subjects feeling hate. As other researchers have found (e.g., Averill, 1982; Scherer, Wallbott, & Summerfield, 1986; Shaver et al., 1978), the most usual anger elicitor was the perception of having been treated unfairly, or unjustly (as opposed to having been neglected or humiliated, which tended to elicit hate). The following example comes from a 23-year-old woman, writing about an incident that had happened 1 week previously:

> We were at a party having a good time, and mingling with everyone. I was sitting talking with two male friends, cramped on a chair. My partner later accused me of leading them on, as one guy had his arm around me. Being falsely accused made me angry; as there was no room to move, the action was harmless, as the guy had nowhere else to put his arm. I thought his accusation was ridiculous. It made me feel as if I had done something wrong, but why would I purposely try to hurt my partner like that?

Other examples included subjects being blamed for accidents, being expected to do more than their fair share of chores or child-minding, and not having an equal say in decision making (particularly with respect to finance and major purchases). Interestingly, anger events were appraised as more predictable and controllable than hate or jealousy events; this may, in part, reflect the familiarity people have with anger scripts, given that it is a very commonly experienced emotion, both inside and outside close relationships (see Fehr & Baldwin, chap. 8, this volume).

With respect to jealousy, few of our married subjects had weathered actual partner infidelity; rather, the most usual jealousy- eliciting event involved the spouse paying attention to, or spending time with, a member of the opposite sex. Reflecting a theme of threatened loss, this situation tended to elicit the most intense jealousy when the third party was the partner's ex-spouse, as the following example from a 22-year-old woman in a de facto relationship illustrates:

> My partner's ex-wife arrived in town and asked him to meet her for a drink. She asked him to come back to her (as I suspected!) and he basically told her things were definitely over. This did not prevent me from feeling extremely upset and jealous. Firstly, because she thought she could contact him out of the blue. Secondly, she is attractive. Thirdly, because I will never know precisely what went through his mind when he talked to her. I felt he was disloyal. I knew she wanted him back, and I wondered what games she would play to attempt this. I felt very insecure.

As this example makes clear, married subjects' experiences of jealousy were characterized by much brooding, wondering, and worrying. Indeed, although hate, and to a much smaller degree, anger, involved some negative thinking about the self, jealousy took top honors for negative, self-related cognitions. The content of these cognitions primarily involved bitter self-recriminations for being paranoid and insecure (e.g., "I was thinking how stupid I was") along with invidious self-comparisons with the third party. Similarly, the key cognitive appraisals obtained for jealousy related to the difficulty of understanding the situation, and the self's perceived lack of power over what was happening, compared with the partner's level of power. This theme was elaborated in the protocols with remarks like "she was throwing herself all over him and he just sat there, lapping it up"; in other words, he was not responsible for the woman's behavior, but he could have chosen to do something about it. Overall, then, jealousy shared more features in common with the experience of hate, than of anger.

Clearly, the results of this study demonstrate the utility of the emotion-script approach for telling us something interesting and important about different kinds of emotional interactions in the lives of married couples. In addition, the results are intriguing because the scripts obtained were based on real, recalled incidents in married people's relationships. However, an important area of debate in the emotion literature has concerned whether or not (or to what extent) such recalled accounts might differ from imaginary, hypothetical emotion accounts (e.g., see Rimé, Philippot, & Cisamolo, 1990). According to prototype theory, subjects should draw upon the same emotion knowledge structures whether recalling an emotion experience, or imagining an emotion incident in the life of a hypothetical married couple. Thus, both kinds of accounts should be similar, even allowing for the kinds of idiosyncratic details associated with specific, recalled accounts.

Emotion Scripts: Hypothetical Accounts

This hypothesis was tested (Fitness & Fletcher, 1993, Study 2) by having a new sample of 80 married men and women write fictional accounts of stereotypical love, hate, anger, and jealousy incidents in marriage, and by comparing these accounts with those obtained from the first study. Overall, the results showed a high degree of similarity between the kinds of features mentioned in the recall and hypothetical accounts, confirming the hypothesis that, whether recalling or imagining an emotion incident, subjects draw upon their emotion knowledge structures to provide the relevant features. However, there were three areas of dissimilarity.

First (and as expected), the recall accounts tended to include highly idiosyncratic details like negative, self-related cognitions, which the hypothetical accounts missed. Second, a much higher proportion of subjects in the recall-account study claimed they tried to control the expression of their negative feelings (more than 73% in each case), than did subjects in the hypothetical account study (less than 40% in each case). Rather, subjects in the hypothetical condition reported that spouses experiencing negative emotions would not hesitate to express them both verbally and physically. Thus, it appears that the hypothetical-account subjects failed to make allowances for the kinds of emotion-management strategies and accommodation processes couples regularly use to defuse confrontations, and maintain harmony within their marriages (Laux & Weber, 1991; Rusbult, Verette, Whitney, Slovik, & Lipkus, 1991; Rusbult, Verette, & Yovetich, chap. 3, this volume).

In a related vein, the third major difference between the two types of account concerned the urges and behaviors held to be associated with the emotion of hate. Specifically, in the hypothetical hate accounts, more than 50% of the subjects claimed that spouses feeling hate would have an urge to physically abuse their partners, as opposed to only 12.5% of subjects in the recall accounts. In addition, 42.5% of subjects in the hypothetical accounts claimed spouses would actually physically abuse their partners, slapping or hitting them, as opposed to only 2.5% of subjects in the recall hate accounts.

Of course, these results could have been a function of recall-account subjects being reluctant to admit to such destructive urges and behaviors. However, the results of a third study, in which subjects were required to match emotions with vignettes comprising varying amounts of cognitive appraisal and prototype information from Studies 1 and 2 (Fitness & Fletcher, 1993, Study 3) suggested this was not the case. For example, when prototype features alone from recalled and hypothetical hate accounts were presented, subjects matched both the avoidant and the abusive urges and behaviors with anger, rather than hate, suggesting that these particular features can be subsumed within an inclusive anger script (as hypothesized by Shaver et al., 1987). Overall, hate was most readily distinguished from anger in vignettes that combined appropriate cognitive appraisal information (e.g., low self-power and high perceived obstacles) with avoidant urges and behaviors (in line with our recalled emotion accounts).

In summary, it appears that people share socially constructed scripts, or knowledge structures, about the nature and course of various emotions in the context of close relationships like marriage, and that such emotion knowledge structures operate at two distinct (but overlapping) levels. That is, people appear to share knowledge about emotions and emotional expression in relationships generally, along with holding more specific, idiosyncratic, knowledge structures about the course of specific emotions within their own close relationships. For example, despite holding a general belief that jealousy is a destructive emotion, and damaging to a close relationship (Sommers, 1984), a spouse may express jealous feelings to her partner because in this particular relationship, such expression has positive outcomes (e.g., loving reassurance from a partner who appraises the jealousy as flattering—a frequently mentioned partner reaction in Study 1). Clearly, these results underscore the value of exploring emotion scripts in specific contexts, in order to pick up the kinds of fine-grained details missed by higher order emotion knowledge structures.

COGNITION, EMOTION, AND BEHAVIOR IN MARITAL INTERACTION

Having established that people hold knowledge structures about specific emotions within marriage, the next important issue to consider is the role such knowledge structures might play within the close relationship context. First, I describe current models of information processing in marriage; then, I discuss the role of emotion scripts in the dynamic interplay of cognition, affect, and behavior in relationship interactions.

Bradbury and Fincham's Contextual Model

As previously noted, the role of emotion in social cognitive models of information processing, has, for the most part, been ignored or superficially treated. Thus, Bradbury and Fincham's (1987, 1991) contextual model of marital interaction represents one of the most thorough attempts to date to integrate affective and cognitive processing in the close relationship context (see also Fincham, Bradbury, & Grych, 1990, for an explicit application of the model to conflict in close relationships). Their model was derived from Weiner's (1985) attributional theory of motivation and emotion, which was, in turn, based on some relatively early models of the cognitive appraisal approach to emotion (e.g., Arnold, 1960; Lazarus, 1966; Scherer, 1982).

Briefly, Bradbury and Fincham proposed that during an interaction such as a problem-solving discussion, behavioral input by one spouse (e.g., a critical remark) triggers an initial response (positive, negative, or affectively neutral) in the other, based on an immediate, primary appraisal of the behavior's negativity, unexpectedness, and/or motivational significance. Then, in an attempt to ascertain the meaning of what has just occurred, the spouse undertakes a secondary, causal search along the dimensions of locus, stability, and controllability. The outcome is a specific kind of emotion. For example, if the spouse appraises her partner's critical remark as internally caused, stable, and controllable (e.g., a function of his bad temper that only ever finds expression at home, as opposed to work), then she is likely to feel angry. On the other hand, if she appraises his remark as externally caused, unstable, and uncontrollable (e.g., "He rarely behaves like this, so must have had a terrible day at work") then she might feel sympathy or pity. Her subsequent response then becomes behavioral input for her partner, who processes it in the manner described.

One study that has explored these hypothetical attribution–emotion links in the context of marital interaction was conducted by Bradbury (1989). Using a discrete emotion-coding scheme developed by Gottman and Levenson called the Specific Affect Coding System (SPAFF; 1986), Bradbury found that, as expected, different patterns of causal locus, stability, and globality attributions for spousal behaviors, were related to the expression of specific emotions, such as anger, sadness, and contempt. Despite the limitations of the SPAFF coding scheme (see Fitness & Strongman, 1991), Bradbury's study makes an encouraging start in the exploration of attribution–emotion links within marital settings.

More recently, marital attribution research has demonstrated that causal attributions for partner behaviors are not restricted to the dimensions of internality, stability, and globality; they may also reflect blame, responsibility, intentionality, and selfish motivation (Bradbury & Fincham, 1990). To date, little work has explicitly examined the links between these kinds of attributions and emotions; however, one recent study found that responsibility attributions were related to reported anger in response to stimulus behaviors, and to the amount of anger displayed by wives during a problem-solving interaction with their husbands (Fincham & Bradbury, 1992).

Taking a wider perspective again, cognitive appraisal studies (including the research reported here) suggest that a spouse's self-attributed emotion depends not only on the perceived causal dimensions related to a partner-initiated behavior, but also upon self-related appraisal dimensions, such as the perceived level of self-power in the situation, and the perceived amount of effort required by the self to deal with it. Clearly, widening the scope of attributional analyses to include detailed cognitive appraisals of the kind reported here, adds considerable strength to Bradbury and Fincham's model, and allows for more specific predictions about cognition–emotion–behavior linkages in relationship interactions.

However, as previously discussed, emotions are also intimately related to each partner's underlying needs, goals, beliefs, and concerns, such as the desire to feel loved and secure, or the need for a partner's esteem, or the belief that passion, or intimacy, is an essential component of a successful relationship (Fletcher, Rosanowski, & Fitness, 1994). Thus, in order to fully understand (and predict) emotion between partners, we need to know which concerns, or goals, are currently active in the situation, along with the degree to which, and in what ways, the partner-initiated event has facilitated or thwarted them.

This last point is acknowledged in Bradbury and Fincham's model, which distinguishes between the proximal and distal context of an event. The proximal context refers to such variables as the thoughts and feelings of a spouse immediately prior to processing his or her partner's behavior. For example, a bad mood may influence perception processes, resulting in selective attention being paid to the negative aspects of the situation. Thus, a remark that might have been shrugged off one day is perceived as being unfairly critical the next. The distal context refers to dispositional constructs stored in long-term memory, such as an individual's needs, goals, and characteristic way of viewing the world.

The contextual model was further developed by Fletcher and Fincham (1991), who included in the distal context such constructs as overall relationship satisfaction, and relationship beliefs. All such knowledge structures are held to influence the way in which close relationship partners perceive and interpret each other's behaviors in interactive settings. However, although the potential importance of affective states (e.g., moods) in priming attributional activity in the proximal context is acknowledged in both models, the role that emotion knowledge structures (which should be included in the distal context) might play has been ignored (Fletcher & Fitness, 1993). I now discuss some of the theoretical implications that may be derived from locating emotion knowledge structures in spouses' distal information-processing contexts.

Emotion Knowledge Structures
and Information Processing

As marital therapists and clinicians will testify, spouses often quite consciously and deliberately draw on their emotion knowledge structures in order to achieve various instrumental goals (Johnson & Greenberg, 1985). For example, spouses may deliberately access emotion knowledge in order to manipulate their partners; perhaps feigning anger in order to intimidate; or "turning on the tears" to elicit sympathy, or remorse. Figuratively speaking, then, spouses learn which buttons to push, to achieve their own ends (see Clark, Pataki, & Carver, chap. 9, this volume).

At a less machiavellian level, spouses also consciously draw on emotion knowledge when attempting to understand and predict each other's emotional reactions to relationship events. For example, a spouse may deduce from his partner's tone of voice on the phone that she is angry with him, and that it probably has something to do with his latest spending spree, as evidenced by the credit card statement that arrived the day before. Based on previous experience, he can also make an educated guess about how long his partner's anger is likely to last, and whether or not a gift of flowers or a shamefaced apology will best assuage her rancour when he gets home.

However, just as spouses deliberately access their emotion knowledge structures in order to understand and predict their partners' emotional behavior, so too may spouses' emotion knowledge structures drive, at an automatic, unconscious level, their perceptions of that behavior. Indeed, spouses may become adept, both at provoking expected emotional reactions, and also at misperceiving ambiguous or inconsistent reactions. For example, a spouse may interpret her partner's silence as sulking, or perceive a partner's smile as an attempt to disguise angry feelings (although of course, spouses may also be quite correct in these perceptions).

Emotion knowledge structures should also influence spouses' memories about the frequency and nature of past emotional interactions (as Holmes, 1991, commented, couples have memories like elephants for past hurts). In particular, the "gap-filling" function of scripts suggests that partners' recall of past emotional experiences may be fleshed out with script-consistent features that, in fact, may not have occurred. It may also be the case that spouses mis-remember (or do not remember at all) particular emotion incidents that are not congruent with their beliefs about the kinds of emotions that are appropriate in marriage. For example, if jealousy is considered to be an unacceptable marital emotion, then a wife may remember her feelings about her husband paying close attention to an attractive young woman as worry that he not be exploited or look foolish ("I just didn't want to see you get hurt!"). In a similar way, spouses' beliefs about inappropriate marital emotions may also guide their interpretations of what they are actually feeling during emotional interactions (Planalp, 1987).

Finally, it seems reasonable to assume that the more experience people have with particular kinds of emotions, the more chronically accessible they might become. For example, Isen and Diamond (1989) speculated that depressed people may have greater facility with sad thoughts than others, and that people who are especially "well-practised at feeling anger, may find anger an easily induced companion" (p. 145) (the "chip-on-the-shoulder effect"). This has important implications for emotional interactions in close relationships, during which couples jointly construct shared emotion scripts and understandings. Such emotion scripts may become overlearned and chronically accessible, taking on a seemingly irresistible life of their own.

To illustrate, Scott et al. (1991) suggested that couples acquire rules (or "if–then" productions) about emotional interactions, such as "If my partner communicates emotion X to me, then I should communicate emotion X to my partner" (see also Fehr & Baldwin, chap. 8, this volume). Such a rule might lead partners in distressed relationships to automatically reciprocate negative emotions, leading to the kinds of negative affect spirals documented in the clinical literature (e.g., Burman, Margolin, & John, 1993; Gottman & Levenson, 1986). Similarly, Retzinger (1991) described the rage–shame cycles that characterize the conflictual interactions of many unhappy couples. Often, the actual point at issue in such conflicts is the least important aspect of the interaction. Rather, the immediate problem merely serves as a context for the familiar, shared emotion script to emerge, with its core relational themes of unmet needs, injured self-esteem, fear of abandonment, and so on. Such shared emotion scripts may become overlearned and routinized, and run with minimal physiological arousal (Berscheid, 1983). Many have even been described in the clinical literature as games (e.g., "Uproar"; "See what you've done now!"; and "You got me into this"; Byrne, 1964).

Summary

Clearly, emotion knowledge structures play a major role in the everyday lives and interactions of couples in close relationships. Thus, emotion-script analysis strengthens current models of relational information processing by providing a more elaborate picture of the kinds of events that precipitate different emotions, along with their likely cognitive, experiential, and behavioral features. This, in turn, helps to fill in some of the missing pieces in the puzzle of what actually happens in relationship interactions, when one partner thwarts (or facilitates) the goals, desires, beliefs, or plans of the other.

Finally, it seems likely that emotion scripts, like other distal knowledge structures, powerfully shape the way partners perceive, process, and remember each other's behaviors. Further research in this area holds the promise of building a better understanding of the complex interplay between cognition, emotion, and behavior in close relationships.

THE ROLE OF MOOD
IN CLOSE RELATIONSHIP INTERACTION

Along with distal emotion knowledge structures, another important affective influence on relational information processing derives from partners' immediate, proximal context; in particular, their moods at the time of interaction (Bradbury & Fincham, 1987; Fletcher & Fitness, 1993). I now briefly review the literature on the role of mood in social information processing and close relationships, and suggest some avenues for future investigation, in light of the knowledge structure approach.

Positive and Negative Moods

Recently, there has been an upsurge of interest in the effects of positive and negative moods on various aspects of cognitive processing, such as social perception, memory, decision making, and problem solving (Cunningham, 1988; Forgas, 1991; Isen, 1987). To roughly summarize a rapidly growing body of research, it appears that people in good moods tend to engage in simple, heuristic processing strategies, along with socially expansive behaviors, whereas people in bad (usually sad) moods tend to engage in effortful, analytic, processing strategies, along with socially avoidant behaviors.

Two models have been proposed to account for mood effects on cognitive processing. The first, affect-priming model (Bower, 1981; Forgas & Bower, 1988) proposes that concepts, emotions, and experiences, are represented as nodes within a semantic, associative network; activation of any node spreads automatically to other nodes, as a function of the strength of connection between them. Bradbury and Fincham (1987) adopted this approach when they hypothesized that depression affects cognitive processing during marital interaction via mood congruent recall; that is, partner behavior encoded in a depressed mood activates depression-related concepts and experiences, making it easier to recall other, depressing, partner behaviors. The second, affect-as-information model (Schwarz & Clore, 1988) proposes that people use a "how-do- I-feel-about-it?" heuristic when making judgments. That is, moods function as informational cues, especially under conditions of time constraint, or target unfamiliarity.

Recently, Forgas (1994a) integrated both the affect-priming and affect-as-information approaches into a multiprocess model of mood effects called the affect infusion model (AIM). AIM identifies four distinct information-processing strategies available to individuals when making social judgments. The first, direct retrieval strategy, involves minimal affect infusion, because the individual is simply retrieving a familiar, crystallized judgment. The second, motivated processing strategy, also involves minimal affect infusion, because goal strength (e.g., to make a fair, or correct judgment) overrides transient mood effects. The third, heuristic processing strategy, invokes the affect-as-information model; used when a judgment is considered unimportant, time is short, or the target is unfamiliar, this high affect-infusion strategy has people consulting their current mood when making their "quick and dirty" social judgments (Epstein, Lipson, Holstein, & Huh, 1992). The fourth, substantive processing strategy, invokes the affect-priming model; used when people are required to interpret novel or complex information about another, this is also a high affect-infusion strategy, with mood effects becoming stronger as processing time increases (in line with Bower's, 1981, principle of spreading activation).

One of the strengths of this model is that a number of specific predictions can be derived concerning mood effects in close relationships. For example, at the mundane, everyday level in longstanding relationships, it may be that spouses' opinions, judgments, and attributions about each other are crystallized and directly accessible, and so relatively impermeable to transient mood effects (whether negative or positive). Similarly, if information processing about partner behaviors is strongly motivated (e.g., by the goal of maintaining a good relationship) then that motivation should outweigh transient mood effects. On the other hand, both heuristic processing (perhaps when time is short and partner behavior is unexpected, but not too important), and substantive processing (when a spouse behaves atypically, and the behavior is important and/or personally relevant) should be more strongly subject to mood effects.

Some of these hypotheses were examined in a series of recent studies on mood and interpersonal conflict (Forgas, 1994b). For example, in one study, subjects saw happy, sad, or neutral movies (the mood induction); they then made causal attributions for simple versus complex conflicts in their intimate relationships. Results indicated that sad subjects inferred more internal, stable, and global causes for conflict than happy subjects, and that these mood effects had a much greater influence on subjects' explanations for serious than for minor conflicts. In accord with the AIM, subjects appeared to engage in complex, substantive information processing to make sense of the complex conflicts, and the longer they took to think about the conflict, the stronger the mood effects.

Moods and Emotions: Fuzzy Boundaries

These results provide a tantalizing glimpse of the theoretical and empirical riches to be gleaned in this area. In particular, researchers have yet to tease apart the potentially confounded effects of transient moods (a proximal variable) with overall relationship happiness (a distal variable), in relation to information-processing tasks of varying complexity. For example, we do not know whether a distressed spouse in a temporary good mood behaves more like a nondistressed spouse, with respect to the way he interprets positive or negative partner behaviors; or similarly, whether a nondistressed spouse in a temporary bad mood behaves more like a distressed spouse in her behavioral perceptions and interpretations.

However, one confusing aspect of a good deal of mood research to date concerns the lack of conceptual clarity about the nature of moods, as distinct from emotions, particularly with respect to so- called "bad" moods. In many cases, a bad mood is treated as being equivalent to a sad mood; however, negative mood inductions could also conceivably elicit irritable or worried moods, along with (or instead of) "the blues." In recognition of this problem, researchers have begun to speculate about the effects of specific, rather than global, negative moods on various aspects of cognitive processing, and this, too, looks to be a promising research area. For example, recent clinical studies by Mineka and Sutton (1992) demonstrated that anxiety and depression have different effects on information processing, with anxiety directing people's attention toward potentially threatening stimuli, and depression being associated with mood-congruent memory effects.

More specifically again, researchers are starting to explore the ongoing effects of discrete emotions, like anger, on social perception and information processing. For example, Keltner, Ellsworth, and Edwards (1993) reasoned that if sadness and anger are elicited by different appraisals of responsibility for a situation, so might these ongoing emotions have different (but predictable) effects on judgments of subsequent events, rather than simply producing a global, pessimistic bias. As predicted, they found that sad subjects perceived situationally caused events as more likely, and situational forces (such as a factory problem) as more responsible for an ambiguous event (e.g., "Your new car is a lemon"), than angry subjects. Angry subjects, in contrast, perceived other (human) caused events as more likely, and perceived other people to be more responsible for the same event (e.g., a dishonest salesman) than sad subjects.

In line with my previous arguments about the way in which spouses' emotion knowledge structures shape and direct perceptions, inferences, and memories of one another's behaviors, these results suggest that the role of cognitive appraisal in the ongoing experience of emotions, as opposed merely to their elicitation, has been underrated (see also Parkinson & Manstead, 1992). Rather than serving simply to pull emotional triggers, such appraisals appear to comprise integral elements of emotion scripts, both serving to direct our attention toward, and shape our interpretations of, environmental events and ongoing emotion experience.

The research also suggests that the boundaries between specific emotion states and ongoing mood states are fuzzy at best, and that feeling irritable, depressed, or anxious, should affect spouses' perceptions, interpretations, and memories of one another's behaviors in different, but specifiable, ways. In view of this conceptual fuzziness, it might be a fruitful theoretical and research strategy to incorporate the study of discrete moods within the knowledge structure approach, both in order to better delineate emotion-mood boundaries as well as to more specifically investigate their effects on information processing and behavior.

Summary

This chapter began with a brief overview of some current models of emotion, with a particular emphasis on their functional, cognitive, and social aspects. Emotion prototype theory was discussed, and relevant research on people's socially shared knowledge about various kinds of emotions within marriage was described. Some hypotheses about the role of emotion knowledge structures on close relationship information processing were proposed, along with a review of mood effects on relationship participants' perceptions and inferences about each other's behaviors.

Overall, my aim in this chapter was to highlight the potential of the emotion knowledge structure approach for extending and enriching our understanding of the emotional lives of couples in close relationships. Hopefully, researchers will pursue the exploration of emotion scripts for any number of different emotions, and in different relational contexts. The mapping of this sparsely charted territory has a valuable contribution to make, both to the study of emotion in general, and to the study of personal relationships in particular.

REFERENCES

Abelson, R. P. (1981). Psychological status of the script concept. *American Psychologist, 36,* 715–729.

Arnold, M. B. (1960). Perennial problems in the field of emotion. In M. B. Arnold (Ed.), *Feelings and emotions* (pp. 169–203). New York: Academic Press.

Averill, J. R. (1982). *Anger and aggression: An essay on emotion.* New York: Springer-Verlag.

Baldwin, M. W. (1992). Relational schemas and the processing of social information. *Psychological Bulletin, 112,* 461–484.

Ben-Ze'ev, A. (1992). Anger and hate. *Journal of Social Philosophy, 23,* 85–110.

Berscheid, E. (1983). Emotion. In H. H. Kelley, E. Berscheid, A. Christensen, J. Harvey, T. Huston, G. Levinger, E. McClintock, A. Paplau, & D. Peterson (Eds.), *Close relationships* (pp. 110–168). San Francisco: Freeman.

Bower, G. H. (1981). Mood and memory. *American Psychologist, 36,* 129–148.

Bradbury, T. (1989). *Cognition, emotion, and interaction in distressed and nondistressed couples.* Unpublished doctoral dissertation, University of Illinois, Chicago.

Bradbury, T., & Fincham, F. (1987). Affect and cognition in close relationships: An integrative model. *Cognition and Emotion, 1,* 59–87.

Bradbury, T., & Fincham, F. D. (1990). Attributions in marriage: Review and critique. *Psychological Bulletin, 107,* 3–33.

Bradbury, T. N., & Fincham, F. D. (1991). A contextual model for advancing the study of marital interaction. In G. J. O. Fletcher & F. Fincham (Eds.), *Cognition in close relationships* (pp. 127–150). Hillsdale, NJ: Lawrence Erlbaum Associates.

Burman, B., Margolin, G., & John, R. (1993). America's angriest home videos: Behavioral contingencies observed in home reenactments of marital conflict. *Journal of Consulting and Clinical Psychology, 61,* 28–39.

Byrne, D. (1964). *Games people play: The psychology of human relationships.* Great Britain: Penguin Books.

Clark, M., & Reis, H. (1988). Interpersonal processes in close relationships. *Annual Review of Psychology, 39,* 609–72.

Cunningham, M. (1988). What do you do when you're happy or blue? Mood, expectancies, and behavioral interest. *Motivation and Emotion, 12,* 309–331.

Davidson, R. J., & Cacioppo, J. T. (1992). New developments in the scientific study of emotion. *Psychological Science, 3,* 21–22.

Ekman, P. (1992). Are there basic emotions? *Psychological Review, 99,* 550–553.

Epstein, S., Lipson, A., Holstein, C., & Huh, E. (1992). Irrational reactions to negative outcomes: Evidence for two conceptual systems. *Journal of Personality and Social Psychology, 62,* 328–339.

Fehr, B. (1988). Prototype analysis of the concepts of love and commitment. *Journal of Personality and Social Psychology, 55,* 557–579.

Fehr, B. (1993). How do I love thee? Let me consult my prototype. In S. Duck (Ed.), *Individuals in relationships* (pp. 87–120). Newbury Park, CA: Sage.

Fehr, B., & Russell, J. A. (1984). Concept of emotion viewed from a prototype perspective. *Journal of Experimental Psychology: General, 113,* 464–486.

Fincham, F. D., & Bradbury, T. N. (1992). Assessing attributions in marriage: The relationship attribution measure. *Journal of Personality and Social Psychology, 62,* 457–468.

Fincham, F. D., Bradbury, T. N., & Grych, J. H. (1990). Conflict in close relationships: The role of intrapersonal phenomena. In S. Graham & V. S. Folkes (Eds.), *Advances in applied social psychology* (Vol. 5, pp. 161–184). Hillsdale, NJ: Lawrence Erlbaum Associates.

Fiske, S. T., & Taylor, S. E. (1984). *Social cognition.* Reading, MA: Addison-Wesley.

Fitness, J., & Fletcher, G. J. O. (1993). Love, hate, anger and jealousy in close relationships: A prototype and cognitive appraisal analysis. *Journal of Personality and Social Psychology, 65,* 942–958.

Fitness, J., & Strongman, K. T. (1991). Affect in close relationships. In G. J. O. Fletcher & F. Fincham (Eds.), *Cognition in close relationships* (pp. 175–202). Hillsdale, NJ: Lawrence Erlbaum Associates.

Fletcher, G. J. O., & Fincham, F. (Eds.). (1991). *Cognition in close relationships.* Hillsdale, NJ: Lawrence Erlbaum Associates.

Fletcher, G. J. O., & Fitness, J. (1993). Knowledge structures and explanations in intimate relationships. In S. Duck (Ed.), *Individuals in relationships* (pp. 121–143). Newbury Park, CA: Sage.

Fletcher, G. J. O., Rosanowski, J., & Fitness, J. (1994). Automatic processing in intimate contexts: The role of close relationship beliefs. *Journal of Personality and Social Psychology, 67,* 888–897.

Forgas, J. P. (1983). What is social about social cognition? *British Journal of Social Psychology, 22,* 129–144.

Forgas, J. P. (Ed.). (1991). *Emotion and social judgments.* Oxford: Pergamon Press.

Forgas, J. P. (1994a). Emotion in social judgments: A review and a new Affect Infusion Model (AIM). *European Journal of Social Psychology, 24,* 1–24.

Forgas, J. P. (1994b). Sad and guilty? Affective influences on the explanation of conflict in close relationships. *Journal of Personality and Social Psychology, 66,* 56–68.

Forgas, J. P., & Bower, G. H. (1988). Affect in social and personal judgments. In K. Fiedler & J. P. Forgas (Eds.), *Affect, cognition, and social behavior* (pp. 183–208). Toronto: Hogrefe.

Frijda, N. N. (1986). *The emotions.* Cambridge: Cambridge University Press.

Frijda, N. H., Kuipers, P., & ter Schure, E. (1989). Relations among emotion, appraisal, and emotional action readiness. *Journal of Personality and Social Psychology, 57,* 212–228.

Gottman, J. M., & Levenson, R. (1986). Assessing the role of emotion in marriage. *Behavioral Assessment, 8,* 31–48.

Hazan, C., & Shaver, P. (1987). Romantic love conceptualized as an attachment process. *Journal of Personality and Social Psychology, 52,* 511–524.

Holmes, J. (1991). Trust and the appraisal process in close relationships. In W. H. Jones & D. Perlman (Eds.), *Advances in personal relationships* (Vol. 2, pp. 57–106). London: Jessica Kingsley.

Hupka, R. B. (1984). Jealousy: Compound emotion or label for a particular situation? *Motivation and Emotion, 8,* 151–155.

Isen, A. (1987). Positive affect, cognitive processes, and social behavior. In L. Berkowitz (Ed.), *Advances in experimental social psychology* (Vol. 20, pp. 203–253). New York: Academic Press.

Isen, A., & Diamond, G. A. (1989). Affect and automaticity. In J. Uleman & J. Bargh (Eds.), *Unintended thought* (pp. 124–154). New York: Guilford.

Izard, C. (1993). Basic emotions, relations among emotions, and emotion-cognition relations. *Psychological Review, 99,* 561–565.

Johnson, S., & Greenberg, L. (1985). Emotionally focused couples therapy: An outcome study. *Journal of Marital and Family Therapy, 11,* 313–317.

Keltner, D., Ellsworth, P., & Edwards, K. (1993). Beyond simple pessimism: Effects of sadness and anger on social perception. *Journal of Personality and Social Psychology, 64,* 740–752.

Laux, L., & Weber, H. (1991). Presentation of self in coping with anger and anxiety: An intentional approach. *Anxiety Research, 3,* 233–255.

Lazarus, R. (1966). *Psychological stress and the coping process.* New York: McGraw-Hill.

Lazarus, R. S. (1993). From psychological stress to the emotions: A history of changing outlooks. *Annual Review of Psychology, 44,* 1–21.

McKellar, P. (1950). Provocation to anger and the development of attitudes of hostility. *British Journal of Psychology, 40,* 104–114.

Miller, L. C., & Read, S. J. (1991). On the coherence of mental models of persons and relationships: A knowledge structure approach. In G. J. O. Fletcher & F. Fincham (Eds.), *Cognition in close relationships* (pp. 69–99). Hillsdale, NJ: Lawrence Erlbaum Associates.

Mineka, S., & Sutton, S. (1992). Cognitive biases and the emotional disorders. *Psychological Science, 3,* 65–69.

Oatley, K. (1992). *Best laid schemes.* Cambridge: Cambridge University Press.

Oatley, K., & Johnson-Laird, P. (1987). Towards a cognitive theory of emotions. *Cognition and Emotion, 1,* 29–50.

Panksepp, J. (1992). A critical role for "affective neuroscience" in resolving what is basic about basic emotions. *Psychological Review, 99,* 554–560.

Parkinson, B., & Manstead, A. S. R. (1992). Appraisal as a cause of emotion. In M. Clark (Ed.), *Review of personality and social psychology, Vol. 13: Emotion* (pp. 122–149). Newbury Park, CA: Sage.

Planalp, S. (1978). Interplay between relational knowledge and events. In R. Burnett, P. McGhee, & D. Clarke (Eds.), *Accounting for relationships: Explanation, representation, and knowledge* (pp. 175–191). New York: Methuen.

Plutchik, R. (1980). *Emotion: A psychoevolutionary synthesis.* New York: Harper & Row.

Retzinger, S. (1991). *Violent emotions: Shame and rage in marital quarrels.* Newbury Park, CA: Sage.

Rimé, B., Philippot, P., & Cisamolo, D. (1990). Social schemata of peripheral changes in emotion. *Journal of Personality and Social Psychology, 59,* 38–49.

Roseman, I. (1984). Cognitive determinants of emotion: A structural theory. In P. Shaver (Ed.), *Review of personality and social psychology, Vol. 5: Emotions, relationships and health* (pp. 11–36). Beverly Hills: Sage.

Roseman, I. (1991). Appraisal determinants of discrete emotions. *Cognition and Emotion, 5,* 161–200.

Rusbult, C., Verette, J., Whitney, G., Slovik, L., & Lipkus, I. (1991). Accommodation processes in close relationships: Theory and preliminary empirical evidence. *Journal of Personality and Social Psychology, 60,* 53–78.

Scherer, K. (1982). Emotion as process: Function, origin, and regulation. *Social Science Information, 21,* 555–570.

Scherer, K. (1988). Criteria for emotion-antecedent appraisal: A review. In V. Hamilton, G. H. Bower, & N. N. Frijda (Eds.), *Cognitive perspectives on emotion and motivation* (pp. 89–126). Norwell, MA: Kluwer Academic.

Scherer, K. (1993). Neuroscience projections to current debates in emotion psychology. *Cognition and Emotion, 7,* 9–41.

Scherer, K., Wallbott, H., & Summerfield, A. (Eds.). (1986). *Experiencing emotion: A cross cultural study.* New York: Plenum Press.

Schwarz, N., & Clore, G. L. (1988). How do I feel about it? The informative function of affective states. In K. Fiedler & J. P. Forgas (Eds.), *Affect, cognitions, and social behavior* (pp. 44–62). Federal Republic of Germany: Hogrefe.

Scott, C. K., Fuhrman, R. W., & Wyer, Jr., R. S. (1991). Information processing in close relationships. In G. J. O. Fletcher & F. Fincham (Eds.), *Cognition in close relationships* (pp. 37–68). Hillsdale, NJ: Lawrence Erlbaum Associates.

Sharpsteen, D. (1993). Romantic jealousy as an emotion concept: A prototype analysis. *Journal of Social and Personal Relationships, 10,* 69–82.

Shaver, P., Schwartz, J., Kirson, D., & O'Connor, C. (1987). Emotion knowledge: Further exploration of a prototype approach. *Journal of Personality and Social Psychology, 52,* 1061–1086.

Smith, C., & Ellsworth, P. (1985). Patterns of cognitive appraisal in emotion. *Journal of Personality and Social Psychology, 48,* 813–838.

Sommers, S. (1984). Adults evaluating their emotions: A cross-cultural perspective. In C. Malatesta & C. Izard (Eds.), *Emotion in adult development* (pp. 319–338). Beverly Hills: Sage.

Tooby, J., & Cosmides, L. (1990). The past explains the present: Emotional adaptations and the structure of ancestral environments. *Ethology and Sociobiology, 11,* 375–424.

Weiner, B. (1985). An attributional theory of achievement motivation and emotion. *Psychological Review, 92,* 548–573.

Wicklund, R., & Frey, D. (1981). Cognitive consistency: Motivational and information processing perspectives. In J. P. Forgas (Ed.), *Social cognition: The psychology of everyday understanding.* London: Academic Press.

8

Prototype and Script Analyses of Laypeople's Knowledge of Anger

Beverley Fehr
Mark Baldwin
University of Winnipeg

If we are to understand each other and ourselves, we must understand the emotions; for love, anger, hatred, sorrow, and joy are at the core of what it means to be human. The study of emotion has fascinated psychologists since the inception of the discipline (e.g., James, 1902/1929; Woodworth & Schlosberg, 1954). Nevertheless, the task has not been an easy one. The complexity of studying this topic is reflected, in part, by the diversity of perspectives from which it has been analyzed. Following the lead of Darwin (1872/1965), some psychologists have taken a biological view of emotion (e.g., Ekman, 1980); at the opposite pole are those who conceive of emotions primarily as social constructions (e.g., Averill, 1982). Interestingly, in pursuing their disparate and sometimes conflicting paths, these and other theorists frequently have focused on the same emotion, namely anger. Anger is a key emotion for psychologists to study for a number of reasons. For instance, it is closely linked to the behavior of aggression (e.g., Mandler, 1984; Rubin, 1986), which obviously gives it considerable social import. Moreover, anger is one of the emotions that is frequently experienced in our closest, most intimate, relationships with others (e.g., Buss, 1989; Perlman, 1990). This may account, in part, for why anger is one of the emotions that is most likely to come to mind when laypeople are asked to name emotions (e.g., Fehr & Russell, 1984).

Recently, some psychologists have approached the study of emotion by turning their attention to the ways in which ordinary people think about emotions such as anger. The development of social cognitive methodologies for studying laypeople's knowledge structures has provided a means for empirically exploring this interest. Research efforts were first aimed at discovering the content and structure of laypeople's conceptions of emotion and types of emotion (e.g., Fehr & Russell, 1984). Since then, impressive gains have been made in research and theorizing on the implications of these knowledge structures, particularly for information processing and behavior in close relationships (see Fletcher & Fincham, 1991, for an overview of this work). The purpose of this chapter is to present recent social-cognitive research on knowledge structures pertaining to an emotion with profound interpersonal implications—the emotion of anger.

How do laypeople think about and experience the emotion of anger? An 18-year-old student, when asked to describe a situation in which she felt anger, wrote the following:

> My boyfriend of 2 years wanted to break up with me after a period of arguing. I love this person a great deal and I could just not bring myself to let go. I wasn't going to let this happen. So he told me that it was over (he was pretty cruel in the way he went about things). A feeling of complete rage and hatred overtook me. I lost control and had no idea of what I was doing. I started crying, yelling, cursing. It felt like I had died inside. This then changed to contempt and violence. I was just so hurt. I slapped him across the face, I threw my purse on the ground and broke the mirror. I picked up the purse and threw it at him. I ran after him punching, kicking, and screaming when I caught him. Then I calmed down, sat down, and just cried. Then I told him to leave.

Another respondent, a 19-year-old student, wrote the following:

> The event which made me angry was during a basketball game in which my friend kept annoying me by pushing and even throwing the ball at me on purpose. At first, I told myself to relax but he continued to provoke me. Becoming fed up, I decided he was not going to get away with it. So, I confronted him by "trash" talking him right in his face. At this point, I was ready to fight but told myself it's not worth it. We continued but he did not seem to understand that I was really pissed off. So, he pushed me and I tripped, falling to the ground. I snapped, all of a sudden I was screaming and shouting at him and got up off the ground and I felt a tingling hot sensation throughout my body as I took a swing at him. We fought for awhile and I don't remember what I was thinking about, I was just reacting to the situation. My friends broke it up and I walked away, got in my car, blasted the music, and sped off.

As these anger narratives suggest, laypeople have a rich and complex representation of the concept of anger. These accounts reveal that there is knowledge of different varieties of anger (e.g., rage, contempt, hurt, becoming "fed up," "pissed off," and so on). There is also evidence of a temporal sequencing of events, or an anger script. Both respondents describe certain antecedents of anger as well as a number of different behavioral responses to anger. The author of the first account describes a progression of angry feelings, beginning with rage and hatred, which changed to feelings of contempt. In the second example, there were initial attempts to control the expression of anger, until some threshhold of provocation was finally surpassed. Both accounts refer to a loss of control, at which point physical and verbal aggression ensued. Finally, there is some sort of resolution or termination of the episode—in the first case, calming down, crying, and asking the other to leave. In the second case, the protagonist leaves the situation.

There are also clear indications in these stories that anger, especially intense anger, is an interpersonal event. People are usually angered by the actions of other people. The response of the provocateur is also featured, leading in the second scenario to an escalation of conflict. Importantly, these examples also suggest that there are both similarities and differences in women's and men's accounts of anger experiences. Even though verbal aggression, physical aggression, and loss of control are reported in each account, most readers would suspect that the first account was written by a woman (even if the gender information were removed) and that the second account was written by a man. Features in the first account such as crying and feeling hurt tend to be associated with women's experience of anger (e.g., Averill, 1983; Crawford, Kippax, Onyx, Gault, & Benton, 1992). In the second account, the depiction of the struggle between wanting to fight, exercising self-control, and finally succumbing to the urge to aggress physically brands this story as a man's experience.

These anger narratives introduce the themes that are explored more fully in this chapter. Our focus is on laypeople's cognitive representation of anger. A central question to be addressed is: What is the content and structure of laypeople's knowledge of emotions such as anger? In the first section, we describe research that has examined laypeople's cognitive representation of the concept of anger itself, as well as their knowledge of different varieties of anger. We begin with studies that have conducted prototype analyses of types of anger. Next, we present research in which features of anger have been extracted from laypeople's anger accounts. These studies introduce the question of whether laypeople's knowledge of anger is organized in the form of scripts. We take up this issue in the second major section, beginning with a description of the current literature on interpersonal scripts and relational schemas, and concluding with the results of a recent study on women's and men's interpersonal scripts for anger. In the final section, we attempt to integrate the prototype and script approaches to uncovering laypeople's knowledge of anger. We discuss findings from a study designed to establish preliminary links between these two ways of exploring knowledge structures for representing the ordinary experience of anger.

TYPES AND FEATURES OF ANGER: THE PROTOTYPE APPROACH

Experts' attempts at generating a clear, agreed-upon definition of anger have not been successful (see Russell & Fehr, 1994). In order to understand how people experience and enact emotional states, a more reasonable starting point might be to explore laypeople's cognitive representation of emotion knowledge, that is, what do *they* think anger is? One approach to discovering the content and structure of laypeople's representation of emotion is suggested by prototype theory. According to this theory (Rosch, 1973; see Mervis & Rosch, 1981, for a review), many natural language concepts are not classically defined in terms of necessary and sufficient criterial attributes. Instead, these concepts have an internal structure, meaning that they are organized around prototypes (clearest cases, best examples) of the concept. Members of a category can be ordered in terms of their degree of resemblance to the prototypical cases. Boundaries between categories are therefore blurry, with prototypes shading into nonprototypes, which shade into nonmembers. Rosch's (e.g., 1973, 1975) research focused on the cognitive representation of natural object categories (e.g., furniture, fruit). She found that although laypeople were unable to produce classical definitions for these concepts, their knowledge of them was highly organized. Types of fruit such as apples and oranges were considered prototypical of the concept, whereas figs and tomatoes were considered nonprototypical. This internal structure influenced information processing in a variety of ways. For example, subjects verified the category membership of prototypical cases more quickly than that of nontypical cases. Prototypical instances were also more accessible in memory, more likely to be falsely remembered if they had not been presented, and so on (see Mervis & Rosch, 1981).

Since the publication of Rosch's studies on natural object categories, many of the major concepts in psychology have been re-conceptualized from a prototype perspective (see Fehr & Russell, 1984, 1991, for examples). Fehr and Russell (1984) documented the controversies and disagreements surrounding attempts to define the concept of emotion. The repeated failures to find an agreed-upon definition suggested that this concept, too, might be more amenable to a prototype, than a classical, conceptualization. Consistent with prototype theory predictions, the concept of emotion was found to have an internal structure: Love, hate, anger, sadness, and happiness were considered prototypical of the concept, whereas awe, pride, calmness, boredom, and respect were considered nonprototypical. This internal structure predicted how readily an emotion came to mind, whether it sounded natural to substitute it for the word "emotion" in a sentence, its degree of family resemblance to other emotions, among other effects. In a reaction time study, it was demonstrated that the category membership of prototypical emotions was verified more quickly than that of nonprototypical emotions; Subjects responded "yes" more quickly to a statement such as "Anger is an emotion" than to a statement such as "Awe is an emotion" (Fehr, Russell, & Ward, 1982).

Since then, similar findings have been reported for the concepts of love (see Fehr, 1993a, for a review), commitment (Fehr, 1988, 1993b), jealousy (Sharpsteen, 1993), loneliness (L. M. Horowitz, de S. French, & Anderson, 1982), and depression (L. M. Horowitz et al., 1982), to name but a few. The success of this approach in these domains raises the possibility that prototype analysis might be fruitfully applied to the emotion of anger. This emotion was among the most frequently listed in Fehr and Russell's analysis and received one of the highest prototypicality ratings (third out of 20). In Shaver, Schwartz, Kirson, and O'Connor's (1987) study, anger received the second highest typicality rating of 213 emotion words, and the highest rating when 418 emotion terms were rated for prototypicality in Tiller and Harris' (1984) research. Thus, anger appears to be one of the central prototypes in the layperson's lexicon of emotion concepts. Recently, there have been several attempts to further uncover the content and structure of this important emotion. These investigations, conducted from a prototype perspective, have taken two different forms. One is to focus on laypeople's cognitive representation of types of anger. The other is to focus on the features of anger. We begin with the former.

Types of Anger

When people think or speak of anger, they often discriminate among various instances of this category, including rage, spite, irritation, indignation, and so on. Even theorists such as Ekman (1992), who viewed anger as a discrete, bounded, biologically driven emotion, have begun to describe anger as a "*family* of related states" (p. 172). However, until recently, the content and organization of the family of anger terms in cognitive representation had not been empirically explored. In order to remedy this situation, Russell and Fehr (1994) and Mascolo and Mancuso (1991a) conducted research to test whether anger is cognitively organized as a prototype concept, such that some types are considered more prototypical than others.

Russell and Fehr began their exploration of laypersons' knowledge of anger by asking subjects to list instances of the category. Subjects ($N = 317$) generated 635 responses (185 were listed by three or more subjects).

Consistent with a prototype perspective, these responses varied in how readily they came to mind. Terms such as *frustration, hate,* and *mad* were listed by at least one third of the sample, whereas other items (e.g., *exasperation, mild* [anger], *contempt*) were listed by only 1% or 2% of the sample. A subset of these instances was targeted for further investigation in the remaining studies. These items were selected from the full range of frequency-of-listing scores but with an emphasis on those that were frequently generated. First, prototypicality ratings of these target instances were solicited (Study 2). The highest ratings were assigned to terms such as *fury, rage,* and *aggravation.* Intermediate ratings were given to terms such as *spite, bitterness,* and *irritation,* and the lowest ratings were assigned to *depression, sorrow,* and *fear* (see Table 8.1).

As in other prototype studies, this internal structure was found to influence information processing in a variety of ways. For example, reaction times to verify category membership were faster for prototypical, than nontypical, instances of anger (Study 4). Prototypical instances also were more easily substituted for the word "anger" in a sentence (Study 5). For example, the sentence "The little boy felt angry when he wanted to stay up late and his mother wouldn't let him" sounded quite natural when a prototypical instance such as *furious* was substituted for the word *anger*, but less natural when a nonprototypical instance such as *humiliated* was inserted.

These studies demonstrated that subjects could reliably order instances of anger in terms of how representative they were of the concept and further showed that this internal structure had the predicted effects. However, an unanswered question was whether people could rate their own emotional state according to how representative it was of *anger*. Johnson-Laird and Oatley (1989), for example, who favored a classical conceptualization of emotion, maintained that prototype theory does not apply to emotion experience. Their argument was based on the notion of privileged access—one simply knows whether or not one is angry. Study 3 of Russell and Fehr (1994) was designed to test whether people could calibrate their anger experiences in terms of degree (consistent with a prototype conceptualization) or whether people would make clear-cut yes–no judgments about their own emotional states. First, subjects were asked to recall several actual experiences of anger. They were then assigned to one of five conditions in which they were instructed to describe either the instance that was the clearest case of anger, the best example in the last week, a poor case of anger, a borderline case, or their most recent experience of anger. Finally, they rated the experience in terms of intensity and prototypicality (how good it was as an example of anger). If subjects made yes–no decisions concerning their own internal state, they should have used only the endpoints of the rating scale. However, they did not. Consistent with prototype predictions, most assigned intermediate typicality ratings to their experience. The ratings ranged

TABLE 8.1
Prototypicality Ratings for 32 Anger Terms

Type of Anger	Mean
Fury	5.08
Rage	4.95
Mad	4.80
Anger-at-self	4.68
Violent	4.68
Aggravation	4.30
Temper tantrum	4.28
Hate	4.23
Hostility	4.23
Fighting	4.18
Frustration	4.10
Annoyance	4.00
Yelling	3.98
Spite	3.90
Bitterness	3.90
Jealousy	3.70
Impatience	3.53
Upset	3.50
Irritation	3.48
Resentment	3.35
Failure	3.33
Humilation	3.23
Disturbed	3.18
Indignant	2.95
Disappointed	2.93
Tension	2.90
Discontent	2.88
Envy	2.85
Disgust	2.78
Depression	2.25
Sorrow	2.20
Fear	1.48

Note. From Russell and Fehr (1994, Study 3). Ratings were made on a scale ranging from 1 *(extremely good example)* to 6 *(extremely poor example of anger)*.

from an average of 3.56 in the "borderline case" condition (on a scale where 0 = *not an example at all* and 6 = *excellent example of anger*) to 4.73 in the "best case" condition.

An ambitious program of research that addressed similar issues was conducted by Mascolo and Mancuso (1991a). They selected 12 anger terms for futher study. As in Russell and Fehr's research, the highest typicality ratings were assigned to types of anger such as *rage, fury,* and *hostility.* Instances such as *spite* and *upset* similarly received the lowest ratings. The effects of this internal structure were explored in a number of studies. For example, in Study 3, the category membership of typical instances was verified more quickly than that of nonprototypical instances. In Study 4, when asked to list types of anger, subjects mentioned the prototypical instances more frequently than the nontypical instances. In Study 5, subjects were asked to generate the name of the higher order category to which the instances belonged. Anger was listed more frequently for typical than nontypical members. Prototypical kinds of anger were also considered more similar to one another than nontypical kinds of anger (Study 7).

Thus, it appears that laypeople's knowledge of anger is organized around prototypes of the category. Instances such as fury, rage, and hostility are considered highly representative of the concept. Other instances can be ordered in terms of their degree of resemblance to these prototypical cases. Moreover, there is evidence that this internal structure influences information processing in a number of different domains. Given that prototypical instances are said to capture the core meaning of a concept, one would expect that the anger account with which we opened this chapter, which was peppered with terms such as *rage, hatred,* and *contempt,* would be considered an extremely good example of anger. In fact, when asked to provide this rating, the respondent in question chose 7 on our 7-point scale!

Features of Anger

Another approach to uncovering laypeople's knowledge of anger has been to extract features of anger from subjects' descriptions of anger experiences. There have been a number of attempts to specify a list of anger features using various open-ended and direct questions (e.g., Averill, 1982; Davitz, 1969). Our focus in this section is on research explicitly conducted using a prototype approach. Three sets of researchers have conducted studies to derive features of anger from this perspective (Fitness & Fletcher, 1993; Mascolo & Mancuso, 1991b; Shaver, et al., 1987; see also Camras & Allison, 1989; Fischer, 1991; Lakoff & Kövecses, 1983 for related analyses). The Mascolo and Mancuso and Shaver et al. prototypes were based on accounts generated by undergraduates at U.S. universities; Fitness and Fletcher solicited responses from married students and nonstudents in New Zealand. All three studies identified a set of antecedents or eliciting events. Mascolo and Mancuso developed eight categories of antecedent attributes. The most frequent category was "Violation of an expected social convention (e.g., being lied to, deceived, betrayed, having rights violated, other is selfish, inconsiderate, or negligent)." This was followed by "Undesirable outcome (e.g., getting what was not wanted; not getting what was wanted)" and then "Situation is unfair, wrong, not the way it is 'supposed' to be." The most frequent antecedent of anger in Shaver et al.'s prototype was "Judgment that the situation is illegitimate, wrong, unfair, contrary to what ought to be," followed by "Real or threatened physical or psychological pain" and then "Violation of an expectation; things not working out as planned." Similarly, the experiences of marital anger described by Fitness and Fletcher's subjects were most frequently triggered by "Feeling unfairly treated by partner," followed by "Feeling badly treated or unsupported by partner."

Thus, consistent with the writings of many anger theorists, the experience of anger is commonly elicited by a perception that self has been treated unjustly or unfairly by another person (e.g., Averill, 1982; de Rivera, 1977). Closely related are elicitors depicting the violation of an expectation or norm for what is considered appropriate or acceptable behavior. Betrayal appears in all of the feature-listing studies (although in only 2% of Fitness and Fletcher's accounts). In the experts' writings, this cause also is considered important, although generally it is subsumed by the broader categories of unfair, immoral behavior or as a violation of expectations. Many anger theorists regard thwarting of a goal or frustration as a key elicitor of anger (e.g., Heinrichs, 1986; Hunt, Cole, & Reis, 1958; Kliewer, 1986; Mandler, 1984). This antecedent appears in the Shaver et al. and Mascolo and Mancuso prototypes (the latter use the phrase "the interruption of a goal-directed event; having a goal blocked"), but not with great frequency.

There are certain thoughts associated with the experience of anger. When angered, people seem to find it difficult to focus on anything else. They report obsessive thinking about the cause of the event, formulating a plan for revenge, imagining attacking the cause of their anger, and so on. Features such as "brooding" or "dwelling on the event" appear in all three prototypes.

Certain physiological reactions associated with anger emerged across these studies: tight, knotted stomach, tense muscles, headaches, feeling hot or flushed, nervousness, increased heartrate, perspiration, and shaking (knees, hands). The anger prototypes also included behaviors such as yelling, cursing, attacking the cause of anger, attacking something other than the offender (e.g., throwing things, slamming doors), withdrawing (e.g., walking out), crying, and trying to resolve the situation. In addition, a self-control component in which the person tried to suppress the intensity of his or her feelings or attempted to inhibit the expression of anger was evident in all three studies. Fitness and Fletcher found that nearly three quarters of their respondents indicated that they tried to control their anger, although 27% did not. The reasons given for the latter category were: wanting the partner to know one was angry (54%), the emotion was too intense to control (36%), and believing that it was healthier to express anger (10%).

Overall, the consensus across these prototypes is remarkable, given that the data were gathered in different countries, using different subject groups, and subjected to different coding schemes. Elements of these prototypes are easily recognizable in the anger accounts presented at the beginning of this chapter.

SCRIPT APPROACHES

The prototype approach to analyzing emotion knowledge confirms that emotions can be seen as collections of features including, among other things, prototypical causes (e.g., being criticized or thwarted by another person), physiological responses (e.g., flushed skin, pounding heart), cognitions (e.g., brooding), and actions (e.g., being verbally or physically aggressive). Having established the contents of an emotion prototype, one question that arises is the temporal sequencing or organization of the elements. Increasingly, writers are turning to the concept of scripts (e.g., Abelson, 1981; Fischer, 1991; Forgas, 1991; Schank & Abelson, 1977; Tomkins, 1991), or standardized event sequences, in recognition that features typically are organized temporally, beginning with an instigating event, proceeding to an attribution of intent, and so on. As Abelson (1981) said, "A sizeable set of inferences can be made from the knowledge that, say, 'John is angry.' A negative thing has happened to John; he blames it on someone; he regards it as unjust; he is aroused, flushed, and prone to swear or lash out; he may seek revenge on the instigator, and so on" (p. 727).

Thus, emotions can be conceptualized as prototypical event sequences—to know that someone is experiencing a particular emotion is to know that they are engaged in a particular series of events. Fehr and Russell (1984), among others, called for careful empirical analyses of the types of emotion script that Abelson described. As mentioned earlier, an observation made in most analyses of emotion in general, and anger in particular, is that emotions are typically interpersonal phenomena. Therefore, the most critical elements of an emotion script may well be its interpersonal features. For example, subjects' open-ended descriptions of anger almost always involve another person as the target of anger (e.g., in 88% of accounts in Averill, 1982; 91% in Shaver et al., 1987). In fact, de Rivera (1984; de Rivera & Grinkis, 1986) goes so far as to define anger as a type of social relationship. In exploring people's emotion-relevant cognition, therefore, it is useful to place the analysis of emotion scripts in the context of a larger literature on interpersonal processes and relational cognition.

Relevant to this task, a recent review (Baldwin, 1992) showed that writers from a number of diverse perspectives have begun to study relational schemas, or cognitive structures representing regularities in patterns of interpersonal relatedness (e.g., Baldwin, Fehr, Keedian, Seidel, & Thomson, 1993; Bretherton, 1990; Forgas, 1991; M. J. Horowitz, 1989, 1991; Planalp, 1985; Safran, 1990; Stern, 1985). These writers usually focus on interpersonal scripts, which represent prototypical interaction patterns derived by aggregating memories of specific interpersonal episodes. Importantly, links between events in the script can be construed as if–then contingencies, such that if a certain event happens (e.g., a behavior by self), it tends to be followed by a certain other event (e.g., a response by the other person). Or, if the first event is an action by another person and the second event is a response by self, the if–then rule automatically leads to the production of the behavioral tendency under that instigating circumstance (Anderson, 1983; Langer, 1989; Wright & Mischel, 1987). For example, an adolescent's script for getting the keys to the family car could include "If I want the car, then ask Dad politely for the keys." Different if–then rules can be organized into different "tracks" of a more general script (Abelson, 1981). Continuing with our example, two such tracks might be: "If Dad responds negatively to the initial request then begin whining and making promises" as well as "If Dad responds positively to the initial request then take the keys and appear grateful."

Analyzing an emotion such as anger from an interpersonal-script perspective raises a number of questions, which we have only begun to address in our research. The issue most relevant to this chapter is: What is the nature of the interpersonal script(s) associated with anger? Based on past research, we should expect that in an anger script a transgression of some kind by another person leads to an image of self as "angry" and to a proclivity to act in certain ways. These behaviors, in turn, lead to certain expected responses from the other person. These are issues that have been addressed in anger research, although usually in isolation. As we have seen, researchers have identified a set of common instigators of anger, and a range of actions that people often take when angry, including physical or verbal aggression, withdrawal, and so on (e.g., Averill, 1982; Fitness & Fletcher, 1993; Mascolo & Mancuso, 1991b; Shaver et al., 1987). Some have extended the analysis to ask about expected responses from others, such as reciprocated aggression, apology, and so on (e.g., Averill, 1982; Gergen & Gergen, 1988; Miller, 1991).

Our goal was to look in detail at the different relational tracks that go together to make up the domain of anger. That is, rather than seeking to identify a global, unitary "anger script," we were interested in people's expectations about if–then contingencies between various actions by self (e.g., aggression, avoidance) and reactions from others (e.g., rejection, apology). To realize the importance of expected reactions, one need only consider the socialization of anger behavior. A child might learn, for example, that "If I yell and stomp my feet then my parents will get angry and send me to my room," but "if I cry and say they hurt my feelings then my parents will apologize." Thus, the child's self-presentational behavior, and in all likelihood emotional experience, will be shaped by expectations regarding the responses of others (e.g., Frijda, 1986). These responses may instantiate the display rules of the culture, but they also may represent more idiosyncratic scripts, based on patterns established in a particular relationship.

Indeed, we accept the assumption, common to many models, that scripts might vary across cultures, or even across groups or individuals within the same culture. Consequently, we chose to explore variation between the genders, examining the possibility that different anger scripts would be revealed for women and men. Our hope was that some of the conflicting findings concerning gender differences in the causes and expression of anger might be clarified by examining the interpersonal anger scripts held by men and women in different situations. Thus, our first study examined the if–then expectations people have about anger-related behavior. How do women and men say they behave when angry? What reactions do they anticipate from others if they act in various ways?

Women's and Men's Anger Scripts

We (Fehr & Baldwin, 1992) sought to examine women's and men's cognitive representation of anger scripts, specifically their representation of the unfolding of an anger event. Research efforts have been hampered by the lack of a standard methodology for uncovering such scripts. However, an important start has been made by Gergen and Gergen (1988). They described a study in which they asked undergraduates to imagine that their roommate had just told them "I am really angry at you." The subjects were asked how they would respond to this statement. All subjects reported that they would ask their roommate why he or she was angry. The researchers then provided the subjects with a reason—they had betrayed their roommate's confidence—and asked them how they would respond next. These responses were then shown to a new group of participants, who were asked how they expected the angry roommate would react to the subject. Consistent with the notion of different if–then contingencies, it was found that the roommate's anticipated reaction differed depending on how the subject had responded: If the subject expressed remorse, for example, for having betrayed the confidence, then compassion, caution, or anger were seen as probable roommate reactions. If, however, the subject responded with anger, then it was expected that the roommate would express anger in return, which would serve to continue the interaction.

Miller (1991) applied a similar method in analyzing women's and men's descriptions of hypothetical conflicts between friends. She provided a range of potential responses at each juncture of the conflict, and asked subjects to indicate the likelihood of each response. Miller expected that men and women might well hold different anger scripts, given that the literature on conflict strategies is replete with gender differences. However, when women's and men's ratings were compared, few gender differences were found. The lack of gender differences could be attributable to the fact that most subjects described a conflict between same-gender friends. (Similarly, in Gergen and Gergen's study, the target relationship probably was same-gender given that undergraduates were asked to imagine an anger interaction with their roommate.) The scarcity of gender differences in Miller's study is just one example of the many inconsistencies in the anger literature. In the research on elicitors of anger, many studies report both gender similarities and differences (e.g., Buss, 1989; Campbell & Muncer, 1987; Lohr, Hamberger, & Bonge, 1988), with little congruence across studies.

The literature on expression of anger is equally unclear. Many writers (e.g., Bernardez-Bonesatti, 1978; Halas, 1981; Lerner 1980, 1985) argue that women avoid the direct expression of anger because they are socialized to be "nice" and to anticipate negative consequences for expressing anger. There is at least indirect evidence for this view that women shy away from the expression of anger (e.g., Greenglass & Julkunen, 1989; Kopper & Epperson, 1991; Lohr et al., 1988). However, there also is evidence that men avoid expressing anger, especially anger toward women (e.g., Allen & Haccoun, 1976; Blier & Blier-Wilson, 1989; Canary, Cunningham & Cody, 1988; Josephson & Check, 1990). We hoped that an analysis of women's and men's anger scripts would shed light on this confusing, contradictory state of affairs.

Overview

The purpose of this study (Fehr & Baldwin, 1992) was to explore the interpersonal scripts for anger held by women and men. Our focus was on the experience of anger in close relationships. The study was conducted in three phases. Phase 1 dealt with elicitors of anger in close relationships. Women and men rated how angry they would feel if their partner performed a number of anger-provoking acts. In Phase 2, we solicited subjects' possible responses when feeling angry. Finally, in Phase 3, we asked subjects what reactions they would expect from their partner in response to their expressions of anger. In so doing, we were able to examine in some detail the if–then contingencies between the subject's behavior and the anticipated reaction from the partner. Our subjects were 124 (51 male, 73 female) undergraduate students whose average age was 20.73 years.

Phase 1: Causes of Anger. We consulted the anger and conflict literatures to derive a set of instigators of anger in close relationships. The intent was to select a manageable, but nevertheless representative, pool of possible anger elicitors. In his research on conflict events in marriage, Peterson (1983) identified four major categories of instigating events: criticism, rebuff (one person appeals to another for a desired reaction, and the other fails to respond as expected), cumulative annoyance (the other person repeatedly engages in an annoying act), and illegitimate demand. We chose three of Peterson's set of elicitors: criticism, rebuff, and annoyance, because they also appeared frequently in other research on the causes of anger. We included two additional instigators: betrayal of trust and lack of consideration or negligence. Gergen and Gergen (1988), for example, used betrayal of trust as the instigating factor in their study of anger narratives. Averill (1982, 1983) focused on the illegitimacy of, or lack of justification for, behaviors (e.g., unwarranted criticism, unfair treatment), and also on negative behaviors that could be avoided but were allowed to happen through negligence or lack of consideration. The elicitors are shown in the first column of Table 8.2.

For each elicitor, we selected one event (generated by a different sample) that exemplified it (see Table 8.2). Subjects were asked to rate how angry each of these events would make them. Betrayal of trust was rated the most anger-provoking, followed by cancellation of plans, criticism, forgetting of

TABLE 8.2
Elicitors, Potential Responses and Anticipated Reactions to Anger

Elicitors	Subject's Response	Partner's Reaction
Betrayal of Trust	Avoid	Avoid
You have trusted your partner by telling some very personal information; then she or he uses the information to take advantage of you.	Aggress directly Talk it over/compromise Aggress indirectly Conciliate Express hurt feelings	Aggress directly Talk it over/compromise Aggress indirectly Conciliate Express hurt feelings Deny responsibility Reject Mock, minimize
Rebuff		
You have suggested that your partner and you spend the evening together. At the last minute, he or she cancels in order to do something else.		
Negligence/lack of consideration		
Your partner forgets your birthday.		
Cumulative annoyance		
Your partner persists in an extremely annoying habit (e.g., talking to you during movies, clicking pens, cracking knuckles).		
Unwarranted criticism		
Your partner criticizes you for small mistakes you make, or for your clothing or appearance.		

birthday, and annoying habit. Except for annoyance, the instigators received average anger ratings that were higher than the midpoint of the scale. It appeared, therefore, that we had chosen satisfactory examples of anger-provoking situations.

With regard to gender, women reported greater degrees of anger, overall, in response to the instigators than did men. However, this effect was moderated by a gender × instigator interaction, reflecting gender differences in how anger-provoking the various instigators were perceived. Although women gave higher ratings than men for all scenarios, this difference was the largest for forgetting of birthday and criticism, followed by cancellation of plans and betrayal of trust. Women and men did not differ significantly on their ratings of the annoyance event.

Thus, both men and women expected to feel most angered by a betrayal-of-trust event. However, overall, women were more angered by this and the other events (with the exception of cumulative annoyance). The finding that the gap between women's and men's ratings was especially large for negligence/ lack of consideration (forgetting of birthday scenario) and personal criticism is generally consistent with Buss' (1989) program of research. He presented women and men with a large sample of possible elicitors of upset and similarly found that women rated the elicitors, overall, to be more upsetting than did men. As in our study, there was also a gender × elicitor interaction; women's ratings of upset were higher for behaviors depicted in 5 of his 15 categories (e.g., neglecting-rejecting-unreliable, inconsiderate, insulting of appearance). Men were more likely to report feeling angered by their partner's behaviors depicted in three categories (which were not included in our study): physically self-absorbed, moody, and sexually withholding. Thus, there is evidence that women and men differ in their self-reports of what makes them angry and in how angry they become.

Phase 2: Subjects' Responses When Angry. There are many possible ways of categorizing the responses a person may make when angry. Most models separate behaviors that involve engagement (e.g., talking it over) from those that do not (e.g., avoidance). Many contrast positive or productive behaviors (e.g., expressing hurt feelings) with negative or counterproductive behaviors (e.g., expressing direct aggression). Drawing again from sources such as Peterson (1983) and Averill (1982), as well as the conflict styles depicted in Rahim's (1983) Organizational Conflict Inventory (ROCI), we narrowed down the possible responses to six categories: direct aggression (try to hurt your partner in some way, either verbally or physically), indirect aggression (e.g., complain to someone else, get angry at someone or something else), avoidance (e.g., withdrawing, becoming silent), talking it over (negotiating, compromising), expression of hurt feelings, and conciliation (give in, accept responsibility). These responses are listed in the middle column of Table 8.2. Our goal was to devise a measure that would be sensitive enough to detect potentially subtle differences between men's and women's anger scripts.

Subjects were asked to rate the likelihood of performing the six responses for each of the eliciting events (from Phase 1). In other words, they were presented with an instigator such as betrayal of trust, and asked how likely it was that they would respond to that event by avoiding the issue, expressing aggression directly, talking it over, and so on. These ratings were analyzed in a 2 (gender) × 5 (anger event) × 6 (type of response) analysis of variance. Every main effect and interaction was significant at the level of $p < .01$ or better; thus we highlight some of the more interesting findings. In a sense, ratings on these items can be taken as revealing the prototypicality of different actions in an overall anger script. The most prototypical, likely, responses were talking and expressing hurt feelings, followed by indirect aggression, avoidance, giving in, with direct aggression the least likely response.

The prototypicality of responses differed between the sexes, however. Women reported a higher likelihood of expressing hurt feelings and of using both direct and indirect aggression.[1] The finding that women report a greater likelihood of aggression flies in the face of longstanding evidence that men are more likely to behave aggressively, particularly in physical ways, than are women (see Berkowitz, 1993, for a review). However, this finding is consistent with the results of studies in which women report greater aggressiveness (see Stets & Straus, 1990). The studies that obtain this finding have typically focused on aggressive behavior in the context of close relationships. Indeed, there is evidence that men's anger is more likely to be directed at strangers, whereas women are more likely to be angered by the behavior of their relationship partner (e.g., Campbell & Muncer, 1987). In a related vein, several studies have found that women are more comfortable expressing anger directly to their male partner, whereas men would rather express anger to another man (e.g., Allen & Haccoun, 1976; Blier & Blier-Wilson, 1989). Thus, clear generalizations are difficult to make—factors such as the nature of the relationship and the gender of the provocateur may determine whether women or men are more likely to report aggression. It should also be kept in mind that women may simply be more willing to admit aggressive tendencies; Stets and Straus documented that men are more likely than women to underreport incidents of aggressive behavior in close relationship contexts.

The finding that women are more likely than men to express hurt feelings when angered has several precedents in the literature. This theme is evident

---

[1]It should be pointed out that neither women nor men endorsed the direct aggression response with high frequency; for both genders, the mean rating fell below 3 on a 7-point scale (where 7 = very likely that the subject would respond in that way).

in Crawford et al.'s (1992) analysis of women's memories of anger experiences (see also Halas, 1981; Lerner, 1985). They found that expression of hurt feelings was frequently accompanied by crying. Interestingly, in his study of anger episodes, Averill (1983) reported that when analyzing causes and expression of anger, only one gender difference emerged; namely, that women were four times as likely as men to report crying when angry.

The responses that were seen as more or less likely varied with the situation, however. The main finding here was that, not surprisingly perhaps, in the context of a partner's annoying habit the response of talking about it was more likely than in other situations, and the response of expressing hurt feelings was less likely. There was also a three-way gender × event × action interaction. Univariate analyses revealed significant gender differences in response ratings in three out of five situations (betrayal of trust, forgetting of birthday, and personal criticism). In the context of betrayal of trust, women were more likely than men to express hurt feelings and to engage in indirect aggression (all $ps < .05$); following a forgotten birthday these same two differences obtained, plus women were more likely to engage in direct aggression; following unwarranted criticism the same gender differences were produced. In addition, men were more likely than women to report conciliating/giving in when responding to criticism from their partner. Overall, one can conclude that when angered, people report that they would act quite differently depending on the cause of the anger. Further, women and men anticipate performing different behaviors, again depending on the instigating event. Looking at the entire pattern of means, it seems that gender differences in actions were most likely in situations where there were gender differences in level of anger (although note that the action × gender interactions remain even if level of anger is partialed out).

Phase 3: Anticipated Partner Reactions. In the previous phase, we attempted to include a range of possible responses when angry. In this phase, we drew again on the anger literature to investigate expected partner reactions, which we hypothesized would reflect if–then contingencies. We assumed that the partner could respond with any of the actions that were included in the previous phase (e.g., avoid, withdraw, talk it over). An advantage to using the same actions was that we then could determine whether an actor's action of hostility, for example, was likely to be associated with an expectation that the partner would reciprocate with hostility. We also included three additional behaviors that one could expect as a reaction to anger, drawn from a number of sources: denial of responsibility, rejection, and minimizing or mocking (e.g., Averill, 1982; Gergen & Gergen, 1988). The full set of expected partner reactions is shown in the last column of Table 8.2.

As in Phase 2, our intent was to sample both likely and unlikely reactions.

To understand a person's behavior it is not only necessary to ask about the anticipated results of the chosen action, but also about the anticipated results of unchosen actions. If a person is choosing between yelling and avoiding a conflict situation, he or she may elect avoidance not because the anticipated payoff is particularly good, but because the anticipated fallout from yelling is so bad. Thus, in this phase, we asked our respondents what they would anticipate as their partner's reaction, given a range of possible actions on their part. We were especially interested in gender differences in expectations about contingencies of behavior.

A questionnaire was designed in which the statement "If you are angry, and you _____ " appeared at the top of each page. The sentence was completed by inserting one of the six possible actions by self from Phase 2 (e.g., talk it over). Subjects then were asked to rate how likely it was that their partner would react in each of the nine ways (see last column in Table 8.2). This procedure was followed until subjects had supplied expected partner reactions for all six possible self-actions when angry. The ratings were analyzed in a 2 (gender) $\times$ 6 (self's action) $\times$ 9 (type of expected partner reaction) analysis of variance. Once again, all main effects and interactions except one (the gender main effect) were significant at the $p < .02$ level or better. The main effect for reaction indicates that some reactions overall were seen as more likely from one's partner than others. This was moderated by a reaction $\times$ gender interaction, to the effect that men were more likely to expect their partners to express hurt feelings ($p < .01$) and to reject them ($p < .01$), and women were somewhat more likely to expect to be mocked ($p < .10$).[2]

People's scripts were more complex than this, however. The significant subjects' action $\times$ partner's reaction effect indicates that subjects had if–then expectations for which responses were most likely to lead to which reactions. Generally speaking, people expected more positive reactions to positive responses on their part (e.g., talking it over, expressing hurt feelings) and more negative reactions to negative responses (e.g., directly or indirectly expressing aggression). This expectation might well derive from a history of interactions in which the valence of affect is reciprocated. For example, in the clinical literature, observational studies have revealed that when discussing conflict situations, spouses tend to reciprocate one another's affect, especially negative affect (e.g., Burman, Margolin, & John, 1993; Gottman, 1979).

The importance of studying the contingencies between actions and partner reactions is most evident when one examines the gender difference findings. The significant three-way gender $\times$ action $\times$ reaction interaction indicated

---

[2]The greater expectation by men of being rejected is surprising, given that in current feminist writings (e.g., Bernardez-Bonesatti, 1978; Lerner, 1985) women are portrayed as especially afraid that they will be rejected if they express anger.

that gender differences in expectations were not constant, but rather varied according to the script that was being followed. Univariate analyses revealed that there were significant gender × reaction interactions only in the context of certain actions on the part of self. Specifically, this interaction was significant only when self aggressed directly ($p < .001$), or avoided the issue ($p < .05$), and was marginally significant for indirect aggression ($p = .053$). Comparing men and women on the various anticipated reactions showed that in response to avoidance/withdrawal, men were more likely than women to expect their partners to talk and to express hurt feelings (all $ps < .05$); in response to indirect aggression, men were more likely to expect their partners to reject them and to express hurt feelings. When self engaged in direct rather than indirect aggression, the gender differences proliferated: Men were more likely to expect their partner to react by avoiding them, rejecting them, and expressing hurt feelings; women were more likely to expect their partner to deny responsibility and to mock them. Most importantly, these findings were in stark contrast to the expectations if self were to talk without hostility, express hurt feelings, or conciliate—in response to all of these more positive actions both genders agreed that partner would react in a correspondingly positive manner.

Thus, gender differences in expectations only appeared when these reactions were considered vis-à-vis certain actions by self. Specifically, gender differences were not evident in expectations of reactions to reasonably positive behaviors, only those to negative, nonconstructive behaviors. This may provide one explanation why many other studies have not found sex differences—the precipitating events and preliminary actions may not have been sufficiently negative.

The findings also shed some light on the few gender differences that have proved robust across different studies, such as the greater tendency for women to cry or express hurt feelings when angry. A fairly simple script analysis might be that these are the display rules associated with gender roles in the culture. One of our reasons for examining if–then expectations, however, is the assumption that a person's choices among various behaviors should be guided by the outcomes anticipated for the different acts (e.g., Fischer, 1991; Frijda, 1986). That is, a woman may, at times, choose to express hurt feelings not only because that is the gender-appropriate behavior, but also because she believes that other behaviors will not be effective and may in fact produce negative outcomes such as being mocked. There is obviously some overlap between the two explanations, as a woman might well expect that violating role-appropriate behavior will lead to negative consequences. By specifying the if–then expectations, however, we were able to examine in detail the interpersonal scripts that presumably guide people's choices on how to behave.

INTEGRATION OF PROTOTYPE
AND INTERPERSONAL SCRIPT APPROACHES

In the first part of this chapter, we explored the semantic network through which people understand the emotion of anger. In the second part, we examined the interpersonal expectations people had about different types of anger interactions. The ultimate goal, naturally, will be to integrate these two aspects to map out more fully the network of knowledge and associations that shapes emotion experience and behavior. That is, we would like to know which instigating events tend to lead to which types of anger, which then lead to which actions, which then lead to which expected responses from others. Of course, one would want to investigate gender differences as well, leading to about a 2 × 5 × 20 × 6 × 9 design, give or take a few conditions. This seems slightly overwhelming to us, if only because of space limitations on our hard drive! Therefore, as a first step toward the integration between script and prototype approaches, we elected to direct our examination at links between specific instigating factors and specific types of anger.

The Relation Between Anger Scripts and Anger
Prototypes: A Preliminary Analysis

In this study, we (Baldwin & Fehr, 1993) explored the relation between anger scripts and the prototypicality of the associated emotional reaction. We focused on the elicitors of anger depicted in subjects' anger accounts and sought to establish links between the various instigating events and the types of anger reactions they produced. We began our investigation by asking 141 undergraduate students to describe an occasion when they felt angry (two examples are given at the beginning of this chapter). They were instructed to supply as much detail as possible, including what happened, what they thought and felt, and what they did. Next, they rated the experience in terms of intensity and prototypicality as an anger experience. Finally, subjects received a list of 30 anger-related emotion terms (most were taken from Russell & Fehr, 1994; see Table 8.1) and were asked to rate each term for how well it described their feelings at the time.

First, we wondered how closely the prototypicality ratings gathered in Russell and Fehr's research (Study 2) would correspond to the ratings in this study, where subjects indicated the extent to which they experienced these types of anger during an actual anger episode. These ratings paralleled the typicality ratings in Russell and Fehr's study quite closely, with correlations in the .60 range (depending on the instigator). The five terms that were rated most descriptive across eliciting situations were: *anger, frustration, irritation, annoyance,* and *hostility.* Thus, anger itself was considered the emotion term that best described the experience. It is noteworthy that the types of anger that received the highest ratings were all considered prototypical in Russell and Fehr's (1994) research. Thus, the notion that prototypical instances capture the core meaning of a concept appears to apply to ratings of actual emotion experiences as well.

Next, we were interested in categorizing the accounts according to the type of instigator in order to determine if the likelihood of specific anger emotions would vary with the situation. Guided in part by the literature on causes of anger cited earlier (e.g., Averill, 1982; Peterson, 1983), we read through the accounts and inductively generated seven categories of anger elicitors: personal criticism, betrayal, unfair treatment, harassment (being "bugged" repeatedly by another person), rudeness/lack of consideration, powerlessness, and rebuff/rejection. Two judges then independently coded the accounts for the presence of these anger elicitors. Satisfactory interjudge agreement was obtained for six of the seven categories; the instigator rebuff/rejection received too few nominations from either judge to be included in our analyses.

At present, these data have not been fully analyzed. However, preliminary analyses revealed a significant instigator X anger term interaction, such that, as expected, the ratings of individual terms differed across instigating situations. One way to depict these differences is to compare the ratings in each situation with the overall sample means, to identify which emotion terms were rated as particularly descriptive in a given instigating situation. As Table 8.3 indicates, the different instigators did arouse quite different shadings of anger. For example, subjects who described a betrayal (e.g., a woman who discovered that the man she was dating was married) reported that they felt hurt, jealous, and depressed, but not annoyed. Subjects who portrayed an experience of being harassed (e.g., a woman whose dating partner shot elastics at her while she prepared lunch) tended to experience feelings of aggravation, annoyance, and arousal, but not hurt.

Given the pervasive gender effects in our previous study, we expected that women and men might well differ in the emotions they endorsed. There were, in fact, gender differences in the ratings of the anger terms. Women reported experiencing higher levels of hurt, resentment, pain, depression, and disappointment. In contrast, men reported higher levels of aggravation,

TABLE 8.3
Emotion Terms Receiving Elevated Ratings in Each Instigating Situation

Criticism	Betrayal	Harassment	Unfair Treatment	Rudeness	Powerlessness
Arousal	Pain	Aggravation	Spite	Annoyance	Frustration
Anxiety	Depression	Powerfulness	Bitterness	Irritation	Sorrow
Powerfulness	Jealousy	Annoyance	Frustration	Disgust	Fear
Hurt	Hurt	Arousal	Arousal	Disappointment	Aggressiveness
Resentment	Sorrow	Destructiveness	Hate	Spite	Disgust

powerfulness, destructiveness, and aggressiveness. One could ascribe these differences simply to gender roles, and the gender-appropriateness of different affects. However, closer examination suggests the operation of more complex and interesting processes, once again revealing patterns of contingencies. The results of our study reported in the previous section revealed that women may show a greater likelihood than men to express hurt feelings only in certain identifiable contexts. Similarly, in this study, it appears that the gender differences may be attributable more to the type of situation described rather than to differences that apply across all situations. One reason why women may report higher levels of depression and hurt, for instance, may be that they are more likely than men to describe episodes in which hurt feelings are the most appropriate response. Along these lines, 15% of women reported episodes in which they were betrayed by another person, whereas only one man (3%) did. Conversely, men were more likely (39% vs. 13% of women) to describe episodes of harassment (e.g., someone persisting at trying to start an argument or fight), which is an instigator that might be expected to produce the feelings of aggravation and aggressiveness that they tended to report.

These results again support the value of studying emotion in its relational context: Rather than focusing only on people's overall dispositions to act in one way or another, this approach directs attention to interpersonal contingencies and their role in shaping the experience of anger. That is, these studies suggest that women may not be more likely to respond with crying and hurt feelings whenever angry, but rather that they are more likely to experience being angered in situations when hurt feelings are a key element of the anger experienced (e.g., the betrayal of trust). Gender differences in reports of these feelings, then, may represent differential sensitivity to various instigators, different amounts of experience with various instigators, or different tendencies to think of these situations when discussing "anger," in addition to the potential main effect of gender in the likelihood of various feelings and behaviors (see Deaux & Major, 1987, for a related analysis).

CONCLUSION

There are many benefits to taking a social cognitive approach in the study of emotions such as anger. The notion of prototypes allows one to explore laypeople's conceptions of types and features of anger. Integrating a prototype analysis with an examination of the interpersonal scripts of anger places the emotion in its proper context, as an interpersonal rather than purely intrapersonal event. In so doing, we echo Russell's (1991; see also Fehr & Russell, 1984; Fischer, 1991) observation that prototypes, and scripts as well, are likely to be knowledge structures by which people represent their own experience, as well as response programs that determine, to some extent, their affect and behavior in different situations.

Much work remains to be done on the question of how individual interpersonal experiences become generalized into representations of prototypical patterns, with different tracks for specific situations (e.g., Abelson, 1981; Honeycutt, 1993; Lalljee, Lamb, & Abelson, 1992; Tomkins, 1991). One critical question, as mentioned earlier, involves the temporal ordering of events. In part to address this issue, we have chosen to begin our work by focusing on the if–then contingencies that people learn in their relationships. One advantage of this approach is that it is consistent with current thinking on how information processing is proceduralized through overlearning (e.g., Kihlstrom, 1987; Smith, 1984), so that when the person perceives or contemplates the occurrence of the first event this will automatically lead to an expectation of the second event. That is, a person's expectation that "If I express aggression directly then my partner will mock me" may become so automatic that the person may never even considers acting in that manner, for fear of that interpersonal outcome.

As our last study suggests, we feel it is also important to examine carefully the links between interpersonal and intrapsychic events. This is a central goal of much of the relational schema research described earlier, which attempts to integrate previously disparate aspects of social cognition such as self-schemas, impression formation, and scripts. In a larger sense, this task involves integrating insights from social cognitive, social constructionist, and interpersonal approaches into a general model of how laypeople think about their emotion experiences. An advantage of studying the scripts involved in anger and other emotions is that many novel research questions can be derived. One possibility would be to study the ways in which priming certain instigators and interpersonal expectations activates specific related affects, or vice-versa. One should also expect that cognition about interpersonal aspects of anger would display many of the processing characteristics observed in other domains, including memory biases, accessibility effects, and so on (e.g., Fiske & Taylor, 1991; Markus & Zajonc, 1985). In addition, people should be able to make quicker, more accurate judgments about highly prototypical patterns of instigators, affects, actions, and responses as opposed to nonprototypical features. For example, Lalljee et al. (1992) examined the event sequences that characterized different types of theft (e.g., white-collar theft, theft involving violence) and found evidence of prototype-based processing in a number of classification and interpretation tasks. This methodology could be fruitfully applied to the study of anger scripts.

Our research program has examined societal scripts for anger and related gender differences. Others (e.g., Abelson, 1981; Forgas, 1991) have underscored the distinction between societal scripts and more personal, idiosyncratic scripts, and we anticipate studying the latter more in the future. What, for example, are the anger scripts held by authoritarians, avoidantly attached people, or depressed individuals? What kinds of instigators make them angry? What types of anger do they feel? What do they do when they feel angry? How do they think others would respond if they were to speak their mind, throw a tantrum, break down and cry, or avoid discussing the issue altogether?

Our ongoing research also involves studying links between people's anger scripts and their observable behavior when in conflict situations. Following the lead of Gottman (1979), Holmes and Rempel (1989), and others, we are currently comparing married people's interpersonal expectations, as assessed by our questionnaires, with observations of how they interact with their spouses when discussing a conflict issue. These are initial steps toward the larger goal of articulating the relational maps that shape the experience and expression of emotion.

REFERENCES

Abelson, R. P. (1981). The psychological status of the script concept. *American Psychologist, 36,* 715–729.

Allen, J. G., & Haccoun, D. M. (1976). Sex differences in emotionality: A multidimensional approach. *Human Relations, 29,* 711–722.

Anderson, J. R. (1983). *The architecture of cognition.* Cambridge, MA: Harvard University Press.

Averill, J. R. (1982). *Anger and aggression: An essay on emotion.* New York: Springer-Verlag.

Averill, J. R. (1983). Studies on anger and aggression: Implications for theories of emotion. *American Psychologist, 38,* 1145–1160.

Baldwin, M. W. (1992). Relational schemas and the processing of social information. *Psychological Bulletin, 112,* 461–484.

Baldwin, M. W., & Fehr, B. (1993). [Self-reports of anger experiences and ratings of associated emotional reactions.] Unpublished raw data, University of Winnipeg.

Baldwin, M. W., Fehr, B., Keedian, E., Seidel, M., & Thomson, D. W. (1993). An exploration of the relational schemas underlying attachment styles: Self-report and lexical decision approaches. *Personality and Social Psychology Bulletin, 19,* 746–754.

Berkowitz, L. (1993). *Aggression: Its causes, consequences, and control.* New York: McGraw-Hill.

Bernardez-Bonesatti, T. (1978). Women and anger: Conflicts with aggression in contemporary women. *Journal of the American Medical Women's Association, 33,* 215–219.

Blier, M. J., & Blier-Wilson, L. A. (1989). Gender differences in self-rated emotional expressiveness. *Sex Roles, 21,* 287–295.

Bretherton, I. (1990). Communication patterns, internal working models, and the intergenerational transmission of attachment relationships. *Infant Mental Health Journal, 11,* 237–252.

Burman, B., Margolin, G., & John, R. S. (1993). America's angriest home videos: Behavioral contingencies observed in home reenactments of marital conflict. *Journal of Consulting and Clinical Psychology, 61,* 28–39.

Buss, D. M. (1989). Conflict between the sexes: Strategic interference and the evocation of anger and upset. *Journal of Personality and Social Psychology, 56,* 735–747.

Campbell, A., & Muncer, S. (1987). Models of anger and aggression in the social talk of women and men. *Journal for the Theory of Social Behaviour, 17,* 489–511.

Camras, L. A., & Allison, K. (1989). Children's and adults' beliefs about emotion elicitation. *Motivation and Emotion, 13,* 53–70.

Canary, D. J., Cunningham, E. M., & Cody, M. J. (1988). Goal types, and locus of control in managing interpersonal conflict. *Communication Research, 15,* 426–446.

Crawford, J., Kippax, S., Onyx, J., Gault, U., & Benton, P. (1992). *Emotion and gender: Constructing meaning from memory.* London: Sage.

Darwin, C. (1965). *The expression of the emotions in man and animals.* Chicago: University of Chicago Press. (Original work published in 1872)

Davitz, J. R. (1969). *The language of emotion.* New York: Academic Press.

de Rivera, J. (1977). *A structural theory of the emotions.* New York: International Universities Press.

de Rivera, J. (1984). The structure of emotional relationships. In P. Shaver (Ed.) *Review of personality and social psychology* (Vol. 5, pp. 116–145). Beverly Hills, CA: Sage.

de Rivera, J., & Grinkis, C. (1986). Emotions as social relationships. *Motivation and Emotion, 10,* 351–369.

Deaux, K., & Major, B. (1987). Putting gender into context: An interactive model of gender-related behavior. *Psychological Review, 94,* 369–389.

Ekman, P. (1980). *The face of man: Expressions of universal emotions in a New Guinea village.* New York: Garland STPM Press.

Ekman, P. (1992). An argument for basic emotions. *Cognition and Emotion, 6,* 169–200.

Fehr, B. (1988). Prototype analysis of the concepts of love and commitment. *Journal of Personality and Social Psychology, 55,* 557–579.

Fehr, B. (1993a). How do I love thee? Let me consult my prototype. In S. Duck (Ed). *Understanding relationship processes. Vol.1: Individuals in relationships* (pp. 87–120). Newbury Park, CA: Sage.

Fehr, B. (1993b). *Laypeople's conceptions of commitment.* Under revision.

Fehr, B., & Baldwin, M. W. (1992, July). *Gender differences in anger scripts.* Paper presented at the International Society for the Study of Personal Relationships Conference, Orono, ME.

Fehr, B., & Russell, J. A. (1984). Concept of emotion viewed from a prototype perspective. *Journal of Experimental Psychology: General, 113,* 464–486.

Fehr, B., & Russell, J. A. (1991). The concept of love viewed from a prototype perspective. *Journal of Personality and Social Psychology, 60,* 425–438.

Fehr, B., Russell, J. A., & Ward, L. M. (1982). Prototypicality of emotions: A reaction time study. *Bulletin of the Psychonomic Society, 20,* 253–254.

Fischer, A. H. (1991). *Emotion scripts.* Leiden: DSWO Press, Leiden University.

Fiske, S. T., & Taylor, S. E. (1991). *Social cognition* (2nd ed.). New York: McGraw-Hill.

Fitness, J., & Fletcher, G. J. O. (1993). Love, hate, anger, and jealousy in close relationships: A prototype and cognitive appraisal analysis. *Journal of Personality and Social Psychology, 65,* 942–958.

Fletcher, G. J. O., & Fincham, F. D. (Eds.). (1991). *Cognition in close relationships.* Hillsdale, NJ: Lawrence Erlbaum Associates.

Forgas, J. P. (1991). Affect and cognition in close relationships. In G. J. O. Fletcher, & F. D. Fincham (Eds.), *Cognition in close relationships* (pp. 151–174). Hillsdale, NJ: Lawrence Erlbaum Associates.

Frijda, N. H. (1986). *The emotions.* Cambridge, England: Cambridge University Press.

Gergen, K. J., & Gergen, M. M. (1988). Narrative and the self as relationship. *Advances in Experimental Social Psychology, 21,* 17–56.

Gottman, J. M. (1979). *Marital interaction: Experimental investigations.* New York: Academic Press.

Greenglass, E. R., & Julkunen, J. (1989). Construct validity and sex differences in Cook-Medley hostility. *Personality and Individual Differences, 10,* 209–218.

Halas, C. (1981). *Why can't a woman be more like a man?* New York: Macmillan.

Heinrichs, D. J. (1986). A psychoanalytic approach to anger management training. *Journal of Psychology and Christianity, 5,* 12–24.

Holmes, J. G., & Rempel, J. K. (1989). Trust in close relationships. In C. Hendrick (Ed.), *Review of personality and social psychology* (Vol. 10, pp. 187–220). London: Sage.

Honeycutt, J. M. (1993). Memory structures for the rise and fall of personal relationships. In S. Duck (Ed.), *Understanding relationship processes. Vol.1: Individuals in relationships* (pp. 60–86). Newbury Park, CA: Sage.

Horowitz, L. M., de S. French, R., & Anderson, C. A. (1982). The prototype of a lonely person. In L. A. Peplau & D. Perlman (Eds.), *Loneliness: A sourcebook of current theory, research, and therapy* (pp. 183–205). New York: Wiley.

Horowitz, M. J. (1989). Relationship schema formulation: Role-relationship models and intrapsychic conflict. *Psychiatry*, 52, 260–274.

Horowitz, M. J. (Ed.). (1991). *Person schemas and maladaptive interpersonal patterns*. Chicago: University of Chicago Press.

Hunt, J. McV., Cole, M. W., & Reis, E. E. S. (1958). Situational cues distinguishing anger, fear, and sorrow. *American Journal of Psychology*, 71, 136–151.

James, W. (1929). *The varieties of religious experience: A study in human nature*. New York: Longmans, Green. (Original work published in 1902)

Johnson-Laird, P. N., & Oatley, K. (1989). The language of emotions: An analysis of a semantic field. *Cognition and Emotion*, 3, 81–123.

Josephson, W. L., & Check, J. V. P. (1990). Revision of the conflict tactics scale. *LaMarsh Research Program Report* No. 39.

Kihlstrom, J. F. (1987). The cognitive unconscious. *Science*, 237, 1145–1152.

Kliewer, D. (1986). A life-cycle approach to anger management training. *Journal of Psychology and Christianity*, 5, 30–39.

Kopper, B. A., & Epperson, D. L. (1991). Women and anger: Sex and sex role comparisons of the expression of anger. *Psychology of Women Quarterly*, 15, 7–14.

Lakoff, G., & Kövecses, Z. (1983). The cognitive model of anger inherent in American English. *Berkeley Cognitive Science Report* No. 10.

Lalljee, M., Lamb, R. & Abelson, R. P. (1992). The role of event prototypes in categorization and explanation. In W. Stroebe & M. Hewstone (Eds.), *European review of social psychology* (Vol. 3, pp. 153–182). England: Wiley.

Langer, E. J. (1989). *Mindfulness*. Reading, MA: Addison-Wesley.

Lerner, H. E. (1980). Internal prohibitions against female anger. *American Journal of Psychoanalysis*, 40, 137–148.

Lerner, H. E. (1985). *The dance of anger*. New York: Harper & Row.

Lohr, J. M., Hamberger, L. K., & Bonge, D. (1988). The relationship of factorially validated measures of anger-proneness and irrational beliefs. *Motivation and Emotion*, 12, 171–183.

Mandler, G. (1984). *Mind and body: Psychology of emotion and stress*. New York: W. W. Norton.

Markus, H., & Zajonc, R. B. (1985). The cognitive perspective in social psychology. In G. Lindzey & E. Aronson (Eds.), *Handbook of Social Psychology* (3rd. Ed., Vol. 1, pp. 137–230). New York: Random House.

Mascolo, M. F., & Mancuso, J. C. (1991a). *Object and emotion categories: A structural comparison*. Unpublished manuscript.

Mascolo, M. F., & Mancuso, J. C. (1991b). *Prototype representations of anger, sadness and joy concepts*. Unpublished manuscript.

Mervis, C.B., & Rosch, E. (1981). Categorization of natural objects. *Annual Review of Psychology*, 32, 89–115.

Miller, J. B. (1991). Women's and men's scripts for interpersonal conflict. *Psychology of Women Quarterly*, 15, 15–29.

Perlman, D. (1990, June). *You bug me: A preliminary report on hassles in three types of relationships*. Paper presented at the Canadian Psychological Association Conference, Ottawa, Ontario, Canada.

Peterson, D. R. (1983). Conflict. In H. H. Kelley, E. Berscheid, A. Christensen, J. H. Harvey, T. L. Huston, G. Levinger, E. McClintock, L. A. Peplau, & D. R. Peterson (Eds.), *Close relationships* (pp. 360–396). New York: Freeman.

Planalp, S. (1985). Relational schemata: A test of alternative forms of relational knowledge as guides to communication. *Human Communication Research, 12,* 3–29.

Rahim, M. A. (1983). A measure of styles of handling interpersonal conflict. *Academy Management Journal, 26,* 368–376.

Rosch, E. (1973). On the internal structure of perceptual and semantic categories. In T. E. Moore (Ed.), *Cognitive development and the acquisition of language* (pp. 111–144). New York: Academic Press.

Rosch, E. (1975). Cognitive representations of semantic categories. *Journal of Experimental Psychology: General, 104,* 192–233.

Rubin, J. (1986). The emotion of anger: Some conceptual and theoretical issues. *Professional Psychology: Research and Practice, 17,* 115–124.

Russell, J. (1991). In defense of a prototype approach to emotion concepts. *Journal of Personality and Social Psychology, 60,* 37–47.

Russell, J. A., & Fehr, B. (1994). Fuzzy concepts in a fuzzy hierarchy: The varieties of anger. *Journal of Personality and Social Psychology, 67,* 186–205.

Safran, J. D. (1990). Towards a refinement of cognitive therapy in light of interpersonal theory: I. Theory. *Clinical Psychology Review, 10,* 87–105.

Schank, R. C., & Abelson, R. P. (1977). *Scripts, plans, goals, and understanding: An inquiry into human knowledge structures.* Hillsdale, NJ: Lawrence Erlbaum Associates.

Sharpsteen, D. J. (1993). Romantic jealousy as an emotion concept: a prototype analysis. *Journal of Social and Personal Relationships, 10,* 69–82.

Shaver, P., Schwartz, J., Kirson, D., & O'Connor, C. (1987). Emotion knowledge: Further explorations of a prototype approach. *Journal of Personality and Social Psychology, 52,* 1061–1086.

Smith, E. R. (1984). Model of social inference processes. *Psychological Review, 91,* 392–413.

Stern, D. N. (1985). *The interpersonal world of the infant.* New York: Basic Books.

Stets, J. E., & Straus, M. (1990). Gender differences in reporting marital violence and its medical and psychological consequences. In M. A. Straus & R. J. Gelles (Eds.), *Physical violence in American families: Risk factors and adaptations to violence in 18,145 families* (pp. 151–165). New Brunswick, NJ: Transaction Books.

Tiller, D. K., & Harris, P. L. (1984). *Prototypicality of emotion concepts: A discussion of normative data.* Unpublished manuscript, Oxford University, Oxford, England.

Tomkins, S. S. (1991). *Affect, imagery, consciousness: Vol.III. The negative affects: Anger and fear.* New York: Springer.

Woodworth, R. S., & Schlosberg, H. (1954). *Experimental psychology.* New York: Holt, Rinehart & Winston.

Wright, J. C., & Mischel, W. (1987). A conditional approach to dispositional constructs: The local predictability of social behavior. *Journal of Personality and Social Psychology, 53,* 1159–1177.

9

Some Thoughts and Findings on Self-Presentation of Emotions in Relationships

Margaret S. Clark
Sherri P. Pataki
Valerie H. Carver*
Carnegie Mellon University

Much of the emotion we experience in everyday life arises in the context of our social relationships (Averill, 1982; de Rivera, 1984; Scherer, Wallbott, & Summerfield, 1986; Schwartz & Shaver, 1987; Trevarthen, 1984). Consider anger, for example. Averill (1982) surveyed community residents regarding their experiences of anger and found that more than three quarters of the instances of anger reported involved another person. Csikszentmihalyi and his colleagues came to a similar conclusion regarding the experience of happiness. They gave adolescents and adults electronic pagers and asked them, among other things, how they were feeling each time they were randomly beeped during the day. Both adolescents and adults were more likely to report feeling happy when with friends than when they were alone (Csikszentmihalyi & Larson, 1984; Larson, Csikszentmihalyi, & Graef, 1982). Finally, Babad and Wallbott (1986) found not only that anger and joy were more likely to occur in social than in nonsocial contexts, but they also found the same was true for sadness.

Why should the experience and expression of emotion be more common in social than in nonsocial settings? There are, of course, many possible reasons. Other people's actions may elicit emotions in ourselves and our actions may elicit them in other people. Emotions may serve to communicate

---

*Valerie H. Carver is currently in the graduate program in social psychology at the State University of New York at Buffalo.

needs to others, and such communication only makes sense in social settings. The expressions of emotions may help people to control each other's behavior. Whatever the reasons, given the frequency with which emotions occur in social settings it is surprising that social psychologists have paid scant attention to the *social functions* that expressions of emotions serve.[1]

In this chapter we address some questions about the functions certain specific emotions may play in relationships and, about how, given those functions, people may come to intentionally and strategically utilize the expressions of emotions in relationships to achieve various goals. We ask, "How do we interpret the social meaning of other people's expressions of emotion?" "How do we respond to others' expressions of specific emotions?" and "Is it likely that we strategically learn to suppress or to express our own emotions for social purposes?" We argue that people strategically presenting emotions may have important implications for the development and maintenance of social relationships.

We focus primarily on three particular emotions: happiness, sadness, and anger. We believe that each of these emotions conveys specifiable and widely known kinds of social information about those who express these emotions and that, as a result, people learn to present emotions to others to accomplish specifiable social goals. In thinking about strategic self-presentation of these emotions, we have adopted a framework or typology of self- presentational strategies outlined by Jones and Pittman (1982). That is, based on what we know about how happy, angry, and sad people are viewed by others, we propose that people, implicitly knowing this information, often strategically present specifiable patterns of emotions to others in order to *ingratiate* themselves to others, *intimidate* others, get help from others (i.e., *supplication*), or simply present themselves to others in a positive light (i.e., *self-promotion*). These possible social goals are four of the five self-presentation goals discussed by Jones and Pittman in their well-known 1982 chapter on strategic self-presentation.

More specifically, we set forth the following hypotheses regarding self-presentation of emotions for ingratiation, intimidation, supplication, and self-promotion purposes: First, expressing happiness increases others' liking for us and, as a consequence, people often will choose to strategically present happiness (and to suppress competing negative emotions) when they are motivated to get others to like them. In other words, we think expressing happiness (and suppressing anger) is often used as an ingratiation strategy.

---

[1]Although it is clearly the case that social psychologists have almost entirely neglected the functions that emotions serve in social interactions, it should be noted that some sociologists (e.g., Gordon, 1981; Hochschild, 1983; Kemper, 1978; Schott, 1979), anthropologists (e.g., Lutz, 1985; Rosaldo, 1984), and developmental psychologists (e.g., Lewis & Michalson, 1983; Saarni, 1989) have attended to the functions that emotions serve in social interaction.

Second, expressing anger increases others' perceptions that we are dominant and intimidating and, as a consequence, people often will choose to strategically present anger (and to suppress competing emotions such as happiness) when motivated to get another to go along with their preferences. In other words, we believe anger is often expressed for intimidation purposes. Third, expressing sadness increases others' perceptions that we are helpless and dependent. As a consequence, people often will choose to strategically present sadness (and suppress other competing emotions) to elicit help from another (i.e., for supplication purposes) or to avoid having to take on tasks they would rather avoid. Finally, expressions of happiness, sadness, and anger can also influence the positivity of others' judgments about us. However, the nature of this influence will depend on the exact situation. For instance in most situations, a person's expression of anger may produce less positive judgments from others, whereas expressing happiness probably will increase the positivity of such judgments. However, when someone has endured a serious injustice, another person's expressions of anger and suppression of happiness on his or her behalf might lead to more positive judgments about that person. In any case, in general, we suspect people often control their displays of emotion for self-promotion purposes.

Not only do we argue that strategic self-presentations of emotion occur, but toward the end of the chapter, we further argue that such strategic self-presentations of emotion are common and that use of such strategies has many implications for understanding the functioning of relationships.

INGRATIATION: HOW DO OTHERS' EMOTIONAL EXPRESSIONS INFLUENCE OUR LIKING FOR THEM? WILL WE STRATEGICALLY PRESENT EMOTION FOR INGRATIATION PURPOSES?

Happiness

Does Expressing Happiness/Suppressing Sadness and Anger Make One More Likeable? We start with happiness and our case that presenting happiness together with suppressing felt sadness and anger can (and often does) serve as an ingratiation strategy. The idea that people express happiness and suppress negative emotion for ingratiation purposes rests, of course, on the assumption that people do like others who are feeling happy more than they like those expressing no particular emotion or those expressing negative emotions. We are not alone in making this assumption. For instance, Duck (1986) noted that there exist relationship rules about the expression of emotion and its functions and, as an example, he cited people exaggerating positive feelings expressed toward their bosses in efforts to cause those bosses to feel more positively toward them. He also commented that "when someone stares and smiles, then we know he or she likes us" (p. 43). Van Hoof (1972) noted that smiling is an active display of tranquillity, one associated with a friendly attitude, and Schneider, Hastorf, and Ellsworth (1979) noted that when we wish to flatter another person we may smile at them.

In addition, there is some empirical evidence that happy people are likeable. Clark and Taraban (1991), for instance, had subjects sign up for an experiment involving working with another person on word games. When the subject arrived, he or she was seated in front of a monitor and could see another subject (who was to be his or her partner) sitting at a similar desk. In fact, the monitor showed a videotape of one of four moderately attractive undergraduates, two male and two female. At this point the experimenter turned off the monitor and told the subject that the study actually dealt with impression formation. The experimenter continued by explaining that the first person to arrive (i.e., the other person) was always designated as the stimulus person and that this person would continue to believe the study was about word games. However, the second person, the subject, was going to form an impression of the stimulus person—first on the basis of a background information sheet, supposedly filled out by the other.

A manipulation of desire for a communal or an exchange relationship was included on this form (Clark, 1986). (Friendships and romantic relationships are common examples of communal relationships. In these relationships, members benefit each other in response to needs. Acquaintanceships and business relationships are often exchange relationships. In these latter relationships, members benefit one another with the expectation of receiving comparable benefits in repayment.) In the communal condition, the other was described as being new at the university and as interested in meeting others. In the exchange condition, the other was described in such a way as to convey that she was married and busy. Most importantly for the present point, a manipulation of expressed emotion appeared on the bottom half of the form. There, the other person had indicated that he or she currently felt either happy, sad, or angry (the three emotion conditions) or that he or she was in no particular mood. Two emotion conditions, the happy and the no-emotion condition, are relevant here. In the happy condition, the subject received a version with 1s (*not at all*) circled for "irritable" and "sad" and a 7 (*very much so at the moment*) circled for "happy." In contrast, in a no-emotion (control) condition, 1s had been circled for all three emotions.

After reading this background information, the subject rated the other on a number of dimensions including agreeableness, understanding, pleasantness, sympathy, friendliness, and likeability. These ratings were summed to form a measure of overall likeability. The pattern of results, shown in Fig. 9.1, is straightforward. Comparison of the happy with the no-emotion

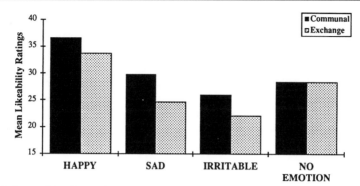

FIG. 9.1.   Liking for another (in communal and exchange relationships) as a function of the other expressing happiness, sadness, irritability, or not expressing any particular emotion.

conditions in that figure reveals that liking for the stimulus person was higher when that other person expressed happiness than when that other person expressed no particular emotion at all, and that this occurred both among subjects led to expect a communal relationship (e.g., a friendship, a romantic relationship) and among those led to expect an exchange relationship (e.g., an acquaintance or businesslike relationship) with the other person. Further evidence that expressions of happiness are associated with increased liking is provided by Shaver, Schwartz, Kirson, and O'Connor (1987), who found that subjects think happy or joyous people are also courteous and nice people.

What about suppressing sadness and anger? To make the case that suppressing sadness and anger are also potentially effective ways to ingratiate oneself to others we must make a case that expressing them decreases liking. There is good evidence for this. Shaver et al. (1987), for instance, found that irritability or anger is associated in people's minds with such things as cursing, yelling, screaming, complaining, being out of control, and stomping— behaviors that undoubtedly are not relished in any relationship and almost certainly are negatively associated with liking. Sommers (1984) found that among college students, target persons described as expressing predominantly negative moods were viewed as less likeable, social, and popular than others. Interestingly, her results revealed that females who expressed negative emotions were seen as even more unsociable and unpopular than males who expressed the same negative affect. Perhaps expressing negative emotions is seen as particularly out of character for a female and, therefore, as particularly informative. The Clark and Taraban (1991) study also provides some evidence of expressing irritability reducing liking. This study included not just a happy condition and a no- emotion condition, but also a condition in which the other expressed considerable irritability and no other emotion. As can be seen in Fig. 9.1, expressing irritability, on average, reduced liking for the irritable other. This occurred both among subjects led to expect an exchange relationship with the other and among those led to expect a communal relationship with the other, although the effect was only statistically significant in the communal conditions. Interestingly, however, expressing sadness only reduced liking among subjects led to desire an exchange relationship with the other. Perhaps expressing sadness, which would seem to call on the other to respond to one's needs—a point we emphasize later—seems appropriate in communal but not in exchange relationships. If so, it may only be suppressed for ingratiation purposes in the context of exchange relationships.

A later study revealed the same pattern of effects of anger on liking (Clark, 1993; Clark & Chrisman, 1991). In this study, students reported to a laboratory study on impression formation. They were told that a second person was present and that they would be forming impressions of one another. They expected to meet this other person shortly. First, however, they were told they were to exchange some background information with one another. The subject filled out a sheet indicating some simple information about him or herself and also rated his or her current mood. Then he or she received a similar sheet from the other person. This other person's information was identical in all cases, except for the mood indicated. The person either indicated he or she was feeling no particular mood at all, sadness, or anger. A simple question asked the subject to rate how much he or she liked the other on an 11-point scale ranging from 1 (*not at all likeable*) to 11 (*very likeable*). Results on this measure, as shown in Fig. 9.2, indicated that expressing anger tended to reduce liking. The fact that expressions of anger tended to decrease liking was also indicated by the fact that subjects exposed to the angry target also rated that target as being less agreeable, pleasant, understanding, sympathetic, and friendly than did subjects exposed to a target who expressed no particular emotion. Although there was a slight

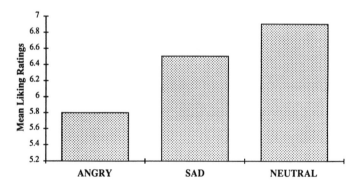

FIG. 9.2.   Liking for another as a function of the other expressing anger, sadness, or not expressing any particular emotion.

tendency for sadness also to be associated with less liking, this effect was not significant. Again, this may be due to sadness seeming appropriate to some subjects (who may have, on their own, desired a communal relationship with the other) but not to others (who may have preferred an exchange relationship).

Will People Strategically Present Happiness/Suppress Sadness and Anger to Others to Elicit Liking From Them? Taking evidence that happy people are more likeable to others than those in neutral or negative moods together with evidence that presenting negative emotions (at least anger) reduces likeability, a straightforward prediction is that people will often strategically present happiness and/or suppress expressions of negative emotions to ingratiate themselves to others. Is there any evidence that people, in fact, do so?

A recent study we conducted suggests the answer is yes (Clark, 1993). The study was simple. Subjects reported individually for an investigation of impression formation. After indicating his or her mood, the subject was told that another person was present who had also been recruited for the impression formation study. In fact, the experimenter went on to explain, the study was more complicated than had been explained at first, and the subject's job was to try to get the other person to like him or her as much as possible. In other words, the subject was given an ingratiation goal. Then the subject was asked to fill out a background form that would be given to the other person. Included in this form was another mood form. We were interested in whether, when given an ingratiation goal, subjects would inflate expressions of happiness and suppress expressions of anger and, perhaps, sadness.

The results are shown in Fig. 9.3. When given an ingratiation goal, expressions of happiness showed a significant increase and expressions of

Goal: Get Other to Like Me

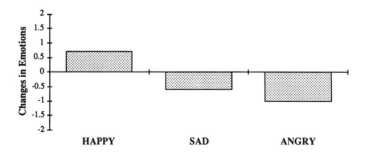

FIG. 9.3.   Self-presentations of happiness, sadness, and anger when given an ingratiation goal.

anger showed a significant decrease. Sadness also tended to drop.[2] It also is interesting to compare these results with what happened in a different condition, where we gave the subject the goal of simply allowing the other person to get to know him or her. When given this goal, expressions of happiness also increased (but anger was not suppressed). We interpret this finding as evidence that people to some extent spontaneously adopt an ingratiation goal in this context.

Other research also suggests people strategically present happiness and suppress anger in order to ingratiate themselves to others. Considering the evidence for strategically presenting happiness first, Godfrey, Jones, and Lord (1986) had subjects write down the ingratiation strategies they considered using, those that they had used, and those they thought were successful. Smiling was frequently mentioned. Rosenfeld (1966) conducted a study in which subjects were instructed to either make another person like them or to make another person not like them. Subjects smiled significantly more when trying to ingratiate themselves to the other than when trying to make the other not like them. Still other researchers (Purvis, Dabbs, & Hooper, 1984) found that those individuals who are high *openers* (i.e., people who are good at encouraging conversation) display more enjoyment when conversing with another than those individuals who are low openers. Turning to the evidence for people strategically suppressing anger to achieve or maintain liking, we note that Fitness and Fletcher (1993) showed that married couples frequently report controlling and inhibiting the display of strong negative emotions, and other research and theory on relationships highlights the importance of controlling displays of anger in the maintenance of relationships (e.g., Fehr & Baldwin, chap. 8, this volume; Fitness, chap. 7, this volume; Rusbult, Verette, Whitney, Slovik, & Lipkus, 1991).

SUPPLICATION: HOW DO OTHERS' EXPRESSION OF EMOTION INFLUENCE PERCEPTIONS OF NEEDINESS? WILL WE STRATEGICALLY PRESENT EMOTIONS FOR SUPPLICATION PURPOSES?

Sadness

Does Expressing Sadness/Suppressing Happiness and Anger Make One Appear More Needy? Is it plausible that people intentionally express sadness to get other people to help them or, in other words, use sadness as a supplication

---

[2]However, caution must be used in interpreting these results because it is *also* possible that merely giving our subjects the goal of getting the other to like them may have caused them actually to be happier and less irritated than they were at baseline. We are addressing this issue in current research.

strategy? Parents certainly comment that their children, even very young children, will display more tears following minor bumps and scratches when they have an audience than when they do not. This is illustrated in the following passage provided by Saarni (1989): "Four-year-old Joel turned the wheel of his tricycle too hard and tumbled onto the pavement. His hand smarted only a bit, but then he noticed his mother had looked up from her gardening. He screwed his face into a grimace, let out a moan, and peered with abject agony at his cupped hands. Mother dropped the shovel and ran over to comfort Joel" (p. 181). Moreover, a study by Hueber and Izard (1983, as cited in Izard, 1984), suggests it is adaptive for young infants to use distress expressions, as such expressions elicit nurturance from the caregiver.

But do adults do this as well? If we wish to claim that sadness may be used as an effective supplication strategy among adults, we must first establish that expressing sadness does cause one to appear more needy and dependent than normal.

The Clark and Taraban (1991) study, previously described, provides some evidence for this claim. In this study, not only did subjects indicate how much they liked the happy, sad, irritable, or neutral person whom they were about to meet, they also indicated how dependent (or needy) this person seemed to them to be. The results are shown in Fig. 9.4. Expressing sadness did increase the perceived neediness and dependency of the other, both among those led to desire a communal relationship with the other and among those led to desire an exchange relationship with the other.[3]

A second study offers further evidence consistent with the idea that expressing sadness makes us appear needy and dependent (Clark, 1993; Clark & Chrisman, 1991). This was the study previously described in which subjects were recruited for an impression formation study, and early on in that study received a background information sheet about the other including information about how that other was feeling—in particular, how happy, sad, and angry that other was feeling. In addition to rating liking for the other, subjects rated the perceived dependency, neediness, and self-reliance of the other. Ratings for these three adjectives were combined (after reversing the dependency ratings) and the results on this measure appear in Fig. 9.5. Again, the results were clear. Expressing sadness significantly increased perceived dependency.

---

[3]Interestingly, the other expressing any emotion when subjects had been led to expect an exchange relationship seems to have increased perceptions of that other's dependency. We interpret this as follows. Expressing emotions communicates information about one's needs (or lack thereof in the case of happiness). Although such communication clearly is called for in communal relationships, it is not called for in exchange relationships. Thus, a person who expresses much emotion in an exchange relationship may be seen as somewhat desperate for others' attention and, as a consequence, might be seen as needy or dependent.

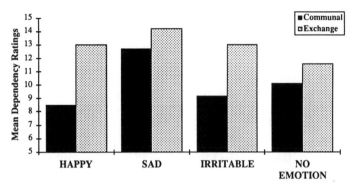

FIG. 9.4. Perceived dependency of another (in communal and exchange relationships) as a function of the other expressing happiness, sadness, irritability, or not expressing any particular emotion.

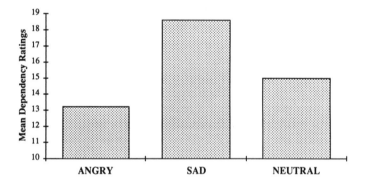

FIG. 9.5. Perceived dependency of another as a function of the other expressing anger, sadness, or not expressing any particular emotion.

Does Expressing Sadness Elicit Increased Help From Others? Still another study conducted by Clark (1994) suggests the answer to this question, at least sometimes, is yes. Subjects were recruited for a study supposedly aimed at answering the question of whether it was better (in terms of how many errors would be caught) for a person to proof his or her own work or better for someone else to proof it. Each subject believed there were three participants in each session and that he or she was the last to have arrived. The experimenter supposedly had started the other two subjects on their tasks—finding specified letter sequences in a large matrix of letters. The subject was told to wait until after the other two had finished their tasks. After they had finished, one of these subjects would proof his or her own work; the third subject would be free to leave and the subject would proof that other's work.

At this point, the experimenter explained that both of the others were really hoping that they would be able to leave the session early, and the subject was free to pick the particular packet he or she wished to proof. The two participants' packets of materials given to the subject included a rating of how that "subject" was feeling right then. The important condition to consider is the one in which the subjects were confronted with two subjects, one described as sad; the other described as feeling no particular emotion, respectively. The results showed that the sad person's packet was significantly more likely to be chosen than the packet of the person who expressed no emotion. (Of course, all information about these two people, other than their current mood, was appropriately counterbalanced. It also is noteworthy that expressions of happiness had no impact on receipt of help, whereas people who expressed anger received significantly less help than did control subjects.)

Another study also provides evidence that expressing sadness can elicit help from others—at least when a communal relationship is desired (Clark, Ouellette, Powell, & Milberg, 1987). In this study, subjects rated their current mood and were given materials with which to create a painting. Next, prior to starting their task, they discovered that another person would be working on a balloon sculpture in the same room. They were able to see the other's materials and found out that the other was either in no particular mood or was feeling sad. Moreover, they had been led to desire either a communal or an exchange relationship with this other person. Finally, they were casually presented with a choice by the experimenter (in the absence of that other) of helping the other out before beginning their own task by blowing up some balloons for her, or not helping her out. As expected, subjects desiring a communal relationship helped more than did those desiring an exchange relationship. More importantly for the present point, in the communal condition the other's sadness caused a significant jump in helping—evidence that expressing sadness can elicit increased help. However, it is important to note that in this study sadness did not increase helping when an exchange relationship was desired. We suspect that this is due to people feeling no special responsibility for each other's needs in exchange relationships.

Will People Strategically Present Sadness to Others to Elicit Help From Them? To this point, we have presented evidence that expressing sadness makes one seem needy and dependent and also elicits increased helping from another person (at least when a communal relationship is desired). But, will adults strategically present sadness to others to elicit helping? Parrott (1993) noted that bad moods, more generally, may serve this purpose saying that, "acting like one is in a bad mood can cause one to obtain desirable attention from others, as well as sympathy, aid, and exemption from normal duties" (p.

294). He also made the related point that displaying negative moods may serve as a test to see if the other person cares enough to respond. Talking about depression in particular, Hill, Weary, and Williams (1986) said that depressive symptoms may be used to "obtain sympathy and permit the avoidance of performance demands" (p. 214). We suspect ordinary sadness, in particular, is often utilized for such purposes.

We attempted to answer the empirical question of whether people might, indeed, intentionally express sadness to obtain help using the same kind of research already described. That is, we measured subjects' moods, then gave them the goal of getting another person to help them during an experimental session, and asked them to fill out a background information sheet, to be given to the other person, which included another assessment of their own moods (Clark, 1994).

In this study, we did not find evidence for strategic self- presentation of sadness to elicit helping. Instead, the obtained pattern of results looked more like the previous ingratiation results than our predicted supplication results, with expressions of happiness increasing and expressions of sadness and irritability decreasing. How do we interpret these results?

Apparently, our subjects' implicit strategies to get help involved getting people to like them, with perhaps the assumption that higher liking would lead to greater amounts of helping—an assumption that seems reasonable.[4] But why *not* choose expressions of sadness as a strategy? Our guess is that although people know that sadness can elicit perceptions of dependency and can elicit help especially in communal relationships, they also know that expressing sadness may be perceived as inappropriate in exchange relationships. Thus, given that, in our study, they did not know the other person at all and had no reason to suspect he or she wanted to develop a communal relationship, they may have been reluctant to express sadness strategically. Instead, they chose a safer (and potentially more effective) route toward eliciting help from a stranger—an ingratiation route.

Does this mean sadness is never strategically presented in order to elicit help? No. We still believe that sadness is likely to be strategically presented to elicit help. However we now suspect that such strategies may only be common (and frequently effective) within the context of communal relationships.

Certainly one type of relationship in which these criteria seem likely to be met is the relationship between parents and their very young children.

---

[4]Caution in interpreting these results is in order because merely assigning subjects the goal of getting help may have influenced their actual moods. However, in this case we think it is unlikely that being told to seek help would cause the particular pattern of emotional changes we observed.

Parents are very likely to feel a strong responsibility for the needs of their children,and both parents and children know that children are supposed to be dependent on their parents. So, this is one situation in which we think it is very likely that strategic self-presentations of sadness for supplication purposes occurs. Such strategies may also be common between spouses, close friends, and elderly parents and their adult children.

INTIMIDATION: HOW DO OTHERS' EMOTIONS INFLUENCE WHETHER WE ARE AFRAID OF THEM? WILL WE STRATEGICALLY PRESENT EMOTIONS FOR INTIMIDATION PURPOSES?

Anger

Does Expressing Anger Make One Appear Dominant and Intimidating? We already know (from evidence presented earlier) that expressing anger causes people to like one less, but do expressions of anger also carry with them any social advantages? In the Clark (1994; Clark & Chrisman, 1991) study already described, we assessed dominance judgments in reaction to neutral, sad, and angry people.

The results, presented in Fig. 9.6, were clear. Although expressions of sadness did not influence perceptions of how intimidating and dominant a person seemed, expressions of anger did. Angry people were seen as especially dominant—more dominant than people who expressed no particular emotion.

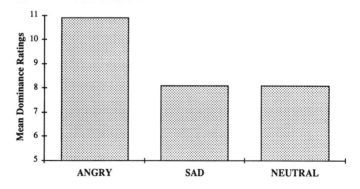

FIG. 9.6.   Perceived dominance of another as a function of the other expressing anger, sadness, or not expressing any particular emotion.

Will People Strategically Present Anger to Others to Intimidate Them or to Get Their Way? Given that anger causes people to appear dominant and intimidating, while simultaneously decreasing liking for the same individuals, the question of whether people will strategically express anger to get others to go along with their preferences becomes especially interesting. Such a strategy may work, but clearly it has costs. It is probably most often used when one person either cares little if the other likes him or her (e.g., in relationships with strangers), or when a person is so confident about the continuance of a relationship that he or she does not believe that such an emotional display will have negative ramifications for the relationship.

Most parents can recall situations in which they have intentionally displayed mild anger to get a dawdling child to brush his or her teeth, get dressed, or finish homework. Further, social psychologists also point out the possibility of using displays of irritability to accomplish desired goals. With regard to supervisors in a work setting, for instance, Parrott (1993) noted that "If one's workers have become complacent, a display of irritability may make them more anxious about their situations and induce more motivation and concentration" (p. 290).

Some empirical evidence that people will display anger to intimidate others has been reported by Averill (1982). He asked people to report on their own motives for expressing anger. Among other reasons, his subjects reported that they sometimes expressed anger to change another's behavior and sometimes to get another to do something for them.

We, too, have found evidence consistent with the idea of people strategically presenting anger for intimidation purposes. Using the same sort of paradigm already described, we tested the hypothesis that people would be willing to strategically present anger to a stranger in order to get that stranger to go along with one of their desires (Clark, 1993). In particular, upon arrival, subjects rated their current moods. Then subjects were led to expect they would be meeting with another person momentarily and that the two of them would be selecting a particular task on which to work. A variety of tasks were presumably available to the two participants. However, the subject was told his or her job was to get the other to agree to work on a set of math problems—a choice we believed would be relatively unpopular. Once subjects had been given this goal, they were allowed to fill out a background information sheet including scales on which they could rate their current moods. As can be seen in Fig. 9.7, subjects suppressed their happiness and increased the amount of anger they supposedly felt, just as one would expect if they strategically were using self-presentations of anger.

An examination of Fig. 9.7 shows that, against predictions, subjects also increased the amount of sadness they expressed. Interestingly, an examination of the data on a subject-by-subject basis revealed that the same subjects were responsible for both effects. Those who increased expressions of anger

Goal: Persuade Other

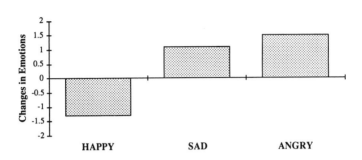

FIG. 9.7. Changes in self-presentations of happiness, sadness, and anger when given the goal of persuading another.

were usually the same people who expressed sadness. Our speculative interpretation is that this was a case in which one self-presentational strategy was serving as the backup for the other. That is, if people were not intimidated, perhaps they would go along with the request as a result of a supplication strategy or vice versa).[5]

SELF- PROMOTION: HOW MIGHT WE ALTER OUR EXPRESSIONS OF EMOTIONS TO APPEAR TO BE "GOOD" PEOPLE? MIGHT WE STRATEGICALLY PRESENT EMOTIONS FOR THIS PURPOSE?

To this point in this chapter, we have presented evidence that expressions of happiness, sadness, and anger carry with them particular potential interpretations about the person who expresses them and also evidence that people are well aware of these meanings and will strategically present their emotions to others in order to achieve particular goals. However, we believe that there is another, important reason why people may strategically suppress or inflate particular emotions, apart from those already considered. It might be called, in Jones and Pittman's (1982) terms, *self-promotion*. That is, people may suppress particular emotions or strategically present particular emotions to others to show that they are "good" people who adhere to important norms and values.

Consider, for example, the widely shared value that we should not hurt

---

[5]Again, caution in interpreting these results is in order because merely assigning the math problems and the task of getting the other to work on these problems may have caused our subjects to feel sad and/or angry. We address this issue in current work.

other people's feelings. It is our belief that this particular value leads to much strategic self-presentation of emotion. For instance, we suspect this sort of norm is what causes people to express joy and pleasure upon opening gifts (particularly gifts they do not like) in the presence of the gift giver; or to feign pleasure when attending a boring party (Schneider et al., 1979).

The norm that one should not hurt other people's feelings presumably not only causes us to express positive emotions when we "ought to," but also to suppress them should it be likely they would hurt another's feelings. For instance, people may suppress their pleasure upon hearing that they have been accepted at the graduate school they really want to attend when their good friend, who happens to be standing next to them as they open the acceptance letter, has recently been rejected from the same school. Parrott (1993) also provided some examples of suppressing positive moods for such purposes. He said, "When one wins an award coveted by another, or defeats an opponent in election or sport, or otherwise enjoys success in some area of life in which another is having difficulty, one's display of pleasure must be tempered because of one's desire to avoid humiliating the person, to avoid 'rubbing it in,' to avoid being perceived as arrogant or as flaunting one's advantage, or to honor obligations to provide consolation" (p. 289). We believe people also suppress positive emotions in situations in which to express them simply would seem disrespectful. Thus, as Parrott (1939) noted, there are occasions "in which one gets the giggles in church or feels cheerful and sociable when greeting one's rarely seen relatives at a funeral. The moods are pleasant, and it may seem a chore to stifle them, but that is what people do to be appropriate" (p. 289).

A second closely related reason for such strategic self- presentation of emotion (which does not involve self-promotion) is that many people presumably genuinely do not want to hurt others' feelings. We may express pleasure upon opening a gift we do not like, not only because we want to convey that we are nice people (perhaps to ourselves as well as to others), but probably also because we genuinely do care about others and wish not to hurt their feelings.

In connection with strategically presenting emotions for self- promotion purposes (or in order not to hurt another's feelings), we describe one final study in which we found some evidence for such strategic self-presentation of emotion (Pataki & Clark, 1993). In this study, we examined the possibility that people might strategically present more positive emotions than they actually feel to another person who is "marked" or "stigmatized" in some way—in the case of this study to a person who was considerably less physically attractive than average. Male subjects were recruited for a first impression study in which they were led to believe they would be interacting with a female subject. As in the previous studies, the subject was asked to fill out a background information sheet on which he indicated such things as his name, hometown, major, and hobbies, as well as why he had selected this particular study. The experimenter also took a photograph of the subject. The background information supposedly provided by the other person also included a photograph of either an attractive or unattractive female. The background sheet accompanying the attractive photograph indicated the other had signed up for the experiment because, as a new transfer student, she thought it might be interesting to meet new people. The background sheet accompanying the unattractive photograph indicated that the other student still felt she needed to meet some new people even though she had been at the university for more than a semester. These comments were included to strengthen the attractiveness manipulation—the idea being that perhaps the reason why the unattractive person still wished to meet new people is that her unattractiveness had made it difficult to form relationships during her first semester.

After receiving this background information, the subject was asked to complete a "confidential" form indicating his first impression of the other subject and was instructed to put it in a confidential folder after completion. Subjects were also asked to complete a form indicating their current mood. To examine whether moods would be strategically presented to the other, we created two "mood- expression" conditions—a *private* expression of moods condition (in which the mood form was marked confidential and the subject was instructed to put the completed form in the confidential folder) and a *public* expression of moods condition (in which the subject was instructed to put the completed form in a folder marked background information to be exchanged with the other subject).

Our intent was to compare expressions of mood in the private condition with those in the public condition—assuming that differences between conditions could be attributed to strategic self-presentation of mood in the public conditions. The results for expressed happiness are shown in Table 9.1. If one examines just the means for the private conditions, it is evident that our subjects were less happy regarding the prospect of meeting the unattractive female than regarding the prospect of meeting the attractive female. This is just what we expected. It also is consistent with the broader literature regarding people's reactions to the physical attractiveness of others

TABLE 9.1
Expressed Happiness in Private and in Public as a Function of a Potential Partner's Physical Attractiveness

	Other's Attractiveness	
	Low	High
Expression is public	2.2	2.4
Expression is private	0.1	2.8

(Crocker & Major, 1989; Eagly, Ashmore, Makhijani, & Long, 1991; Feingold, 1992; Hatfield & Sprecher, 1986).

However, the public conditions reveal a different story—there were no differences in expressions of happiness or of sadness to the attractive relative to the unattractive female. Or, looking at the results from a different perspective, note that when subjects were about to meet an unattractive female (but not when they were about to meet an attractive female) they expressed significantly more happiness in public than in private.

Our interpretation is straightforward. We assume that the subjects in the unattractive other/public expression condition intentionally expressed more happiness to the other than they felt. Our guess is that the norm "one should not judge a book by its cover" is widely shared and accepted (albeit a norm that's difficult to adhere to with regard to one's own private reactions). Hence, subjects may have strategically presented emotion in the unattractive other/public condition so as to feel good about themselves, and in order not to hurt the other's feelings.

SOME GENERAL COMMENTS ABOUT SELF-PRESENTATION OF EMOTION

Have We Covered All Varieties of Strategic Self-Presentations of Emotion That Exist for Social Purposes?

Although our own research, as well as the focus of this chapter, has centered on the self- presentations of happiness, sadness, and anger for purposes of ingratiation, supplication, intimidation, and self-promotion, we believe that other emotions may be strategically used to achieve similar goals. For example, nervousness is an emotion that we have not discussed, but one that may often be strategically inflated or concealed. That is, we would predict that people may sometimes present more nervousness than they really feel for supplication purposes (perhaps in situations in which the expression of sadness would seem less appropriate). For instance, a college student may play the role of a nervous computer phobic who is intimidated by new technology when he wants a quick solution from his computer whiz friend who happens to be sitting next to him. When his friend is unavailable, however, he may resort to pulling out a manual and helping himself, unaccompanied by any expression of nervousness. Or, to give another example, as a means of self-promotion, individuals may suppress nervousness when they want to appear to be competent and self assured. Certainly, most people who have gone through job interviews can recall making an effort to conceal any signs of nervousness.

In addition, the self-presentation goals discussed in this chapter represent only one set of the social goals that may be achieved through strategic presentation of emotion. We assume there are many other specific goals that often motivate or regulate emotional expression. For example, when feeling threatened, people may suppress nervousness as a means of self protection in questionable situations (e.g., walking alone at night). This type of strategic self-presentation is stressed in self defense courses with the admonition to walk "purposefully" to ward off potential pickpockets and other attackers. Also people may often control their emotions in order to adhere to the norms inherent in a social situation (and not necessarily to self-promote). Thus, people will express sadness at funerals and happiness at weddings without necessarily feeling those emotions. And, to give a final example, people may express or suppress emotions on occasion merely to live up to others' expectations and not cause social disruption. For example, Wortman and Silver (1989; Silver & Wortman, 1980) studied victims of major negative life events (e.g., death of very close others, rape) and they found much evidence indicating that feelings of distress and sadness may linger for years following such events. However, they noted that many people within these victims' social networks hold strong expectations or standards for faster recoveries (Coates, Wortman, & Abbey, 1979), and that awareness of such standards may motivate victims to conceal their ongoing feelings of distress.

Expressing Versus Feeling Emotions

Given our arguments to this point, the reader might interpret the self-presentation of emotion for social purposes as always involving the expression of a different emotion from that which one currently feels. However, we do not want to leave the reader with such an impression. First, strategic use of self- presentation need not involve replacing one mood with another. For example, one can move from feeling no particular emotion to expressing one for strategic purposes. Or, one can exaggerate or suppress the expression of a particular emotion one is actually feeling. Certainly, as Parrott (1993) noted, it is likely to be more difficult to present a mood to others that one does not feel, than to present a mood that one does feel. It is also more socially dangerous because one's true mood or feeling may "leak out" in ways that others can detect. Thus, we suspect that strategic self-presentation of emotion often involves subtle shifts, such as exaggerations or suppressions of already felt emotions, rather than wholesale shifts from feeling one strong emotion (e.g., anger) to expressing a completely different one (e.g., elation).

It is also worth pointing out that choosing to strategically present an emotion need not be taken to mean that the expressed emotion is not being "really" felt at the same time. After all, considerable social psychological research suggests that choosing to express an emotion may often cause people actually to come to experience that emotion (e.g., Laird, 1974).

SOME IMPLICATIONS OF STRATEGIC
SELF-PRESENTATION OF EMOTION

Although we have just started our research program on strategic self-presentation (and strategic suppression) of emotion, the results obtained thus far are encouraging. We are convinced, from our own work as well as from that of others, that adults do strategically present emotions in predictable ways and that it is worth pursuing some of the implications of such self-presentations for relationship formation and development. What are some of those implications?

Trust in Other's Expressions of Emotion

One major implication of this work, we believe, is that there will be certain people who will find it difficult to trust others' expressions of emotion, as well as certain situations in which most people will find it difficult to trust others' expressions of emotion. First, consider what sorts of groups might find it difficult to trust others' emotional displays.

We suspect that people who are frequent targets of strategic self- presentation of emotion will be less likely to trust others' emotional expressions than will those who are not frequent targets. The reason is that such people will often be in a position of attributional ambiguity (cf. Crocker, Cornwell, & Major, 1993; Crocker, Voelkl, Testa, & Major, 1991). That is, they will frequently be in positions of trying to answer the question, "Is the other person really feeling the particular emotion he or she is expressing, or might he or she be strategically presenting the emotion?" And, to the extent to which they face this ambiguity they are likely to discount the possibility that the other really is feeling the emotion. That is, trust in those emotions will drop.

Consider ingratiation strategies, for example. People who have power over others in the form of dispersing salient rewards or punishments are very likely to be targets of ingratiation. Powerful people, knowing this, should therefore be likely to mistrust others' expressions of warmth or satisfaction directed at themselves. In addition, they may lack confidence that the other is not feeling anger and sadness, given that such emotions may be suppressed for ingratiation purposes. This group of frequent targets would include bosses, interviewers, and such people as teachers and professors. At times it may also include the very wealthy (by virtue of the salience of their ability to reward others). There certainly are many anecdotal examples of wealthy people distrusting potential suitors' avowals of love or positive sentiment.

Or, consider supplication strategies. People who are in positions of low power are likely to use these, targeting people of higher power who have the ability and potential motivation to help them. Once again, people of high power may experience attributional ambiguity when faced with sadness expressed by those over whom they have power. Parents face this problem with their children. If the child comes to them with a sad face and asks to borrow some money to go to a movie with her friends, is she really sad? Or is she putting on the sad face to get the money?

Likely targets of intimidation may also find themselves discounting others' expressions of emotion. Thus, although a parent may have trouble figuring out if his or her child really is sad or is just putting on a show to get some help; one can easily imagine that a child may often find him or herself in the disquieting situation of having to figure out if the parent is really angry or merely putting on a show to get him or her to clean up his or her room.

Finally, consider strategic self-presentations designed not to hurt another's feelings and/or to make one feel good about oneself and to look good to others. A great number of people are likely to be the targets of such strategic self-presentations; namely, all those people who are visibly stigmatized or marked in some way. This group would include people of minority races, unattractive persons, and the physically handicapped. People are likely to convey more happiness to them and less sadness and anxiety than they really feel. Like others who are frequent targets of strategic self-presentation of emotion, they too may experience attributional ambiguity and should learn to discount emotional displays.

In fact, in a recent study we have obtained some evidence for at least one of these groups discounting others' expressions of emotion (Pataki & Clark, 1993, Study 2). Recall the study described earlier in which male subjects inflated their expressions of happiness when they were about to meet an unattractive female. We reasoned that if, indeed, people strategically present more positive emotions to unattractive people than they actually feel, then one consequence should be that unattractive people, compared to attractive folk, distrust positive emotional displays.

To test this idea, we made up a simple questionnaire that we sent to a group of university students (Pataki & Clark, 1993). Subjects were asked to imagine that they had been assigned to be a lab partner with a fairly attractive, opposite-sex other. Upon meeting each other for the first time, subjects were asked whether they thought the other accurately would express the amount of happiness that other was feeling, would inflate expressions of happiness a little (or a lot), or would suppress feelings of happiness a little (or a lot). Subsequently, we obtained photographs of the subjects from a freshman "picture book," had judges rate these pictures for physical attractiveness, and divided our sample of subjects into three groups of low-, medium-, and high-attractive subjects.

If people trust others' expressions of emotions they should report that the other would express his or her true feelings upon meeting them. However, as we had predicted, the group who was lowest in attractiveness deviated significantly from that expectation. Subjects in this group were significantly more likely to report that the other would inflate expressions of happiness than that the other would accurately report his or her true feelings of happiness. (Subjects average in attractiveness did seem to trust the other's emotions and, unexpectedly, those high in attractiveness actually tended to suspect others might suppress their positive feelings. Perhaps people do suppress their positive reactions to very attractive people lest their social interest not be reciprocated and perhaps attractive people are aware of this.)

Attending to the Other and Decreases in the Comfort of Social Interactions

The potential costs of strategic self- presentation of emotion do not end with decreases in trust. We strongly suspect there are other social implications as well. For instance, when one is in a state of attributional ambiguity about the causes of another person's emotional expressions, one may be far more motivated than normal to pay close attention to exactly what the other is saying, his or her facial expressions, and his or her "body language"—all in an effort to figure out how the other is really feeling. This process undoubtably is effortful and tension provoking. We suspect such a process would greatly reduce the comfort of such social interactions as well as lower the desire to maintain such social interactions.

A study conducted by Frable, Blackstone, and Scherbaum (1990) provides evidence that people who are deviant from normal (i.e., stigmatized or deviant in a positive direction) are, indeed, more aware of their social interactions than are others. Specifically, deviant subjects, when interacting with normal others, remembered more about the person with whom they were conversing, the setting in which they were conversing, and were also more likely to consider their conversation partner's point of view, than were normal subjects. We suspect these results were due, in part, to such people often being the targets of strategic self-presentations from others, in general, and of strategic self-presentations of emotions from others more specifically. To ascertain what the other really feels, these people may have felt compelled to attend very carefully to that other.

In summary, we suspect a combination of decreased trust in, and increased pressure to attend carefully to, others suspected of strategic self-presentations probably makes interactions stressful for those who believe they are the targets of such self-presentations. As a result, they may avoid such interactions. This argument is consistent with the results of a number of studies. For example, some research suggests that individuals who are stigmatized in some way (i.e., homosexual or mentally ill) are tense and uncomfortable when meeting others who are aware of their stigma (Farina, Allen, & Saul, 1968; Farina, Gliha, Boudreau, Allen, & Sherman, 1971). Our argument here, of course, is that some of this distress, tension, and desire to end interactions may be caused by strategic emotional presentations (or at least a suspicion of them), and consequent drops in trust and increases in effortful attention to one another's facial expressions, body language, and so on.

Interestingly, such interactions are likely to be stressful for the person who strategically presents emotion to a target as well because such persons must worry about whether their presentations will be successful. Some existing empirical work is consistent with this idea as well. For example, Kleck, Ono, and Hastorf (1966) found that when subjects interacted with a confederate sitting in a wheelchair (a likely target of strategic inflation of emotion in our opinion), they were more inhibited and controlled than they were when they interacted with the same individual but did not believe he was handicapped. They also sought to end the interaction sooner.

Strategic Self-Presentation of Emotion and the Relation Between Similarity and Attraction

Perhaps one of the most well-established effects in social psychology is that people seek out similar others with whom to interact (e.g., Berscheid, Dion, Walster, & Walster, 1971; Folkes, 1982; Stroebe, Insko, Thomson, & Layton, 1971; Warren, 1966). The typical explanation has been that similar others tend to validate our opinions and world views, thereby making them rewarding people with whom to spend time (Byrne, 1971; Byrne & Clore, 1970). But might there be another explanation for similar people ending up together—an explanation related to strategic self-presentation of emotion? We think so.

It should be evident from what we have argued thus far that it is differences between people that often lead them to strategically self-present emotions to others. For instance, differences in power may lead the person with higher power to use intimidation strategies, and the person with lower power to use supplication strategies. Differences in race may lead a person from the majority race to present positive emotions to the minority member, lest he or she appear biased, and differences in attractiveness may lead to the more attractive person presenting more positive emotion to the less attractive person than he or she feels. Moreover, the strategic self-presentation of emotion (or even the mere suspicion of such strategic self-presentation of emotion) will leave the target of the expression in a state of attributional ambiguity. This attributional ambiguity, in turn, may lead to decreased trust in the other and heightened motivation to carefully, effortfully attend to the other's actions in order to ascertain his or her true feelings. As we just noted, we assume that none of this is very pleasant for the person who is the target of the expression of emotion, nor, perhaps, for the person who is doing the strategic self-presentation. Indeed, empirical evidence backs this point up. As a result, people who believe or even suspect they may be targets of others' strategic self-presentations of emotions (because of power differences, racial differences or whatever) may seek out similar others specifically to avoid being the target of such presentations. In this regard, Jones et al. (1984) noted that, "One of the obvious options available to markable persons who wish to avoid strainful interactions is to seek out interactions with other markables. Because of the shared handicap or stigma, fellow markables can presumably interact with less awkwardness and strain" (pp. 200–201).

Although the awkwardness or stress associated with coping with strategic self-presentations of emotion alone may be sufficient to deter dissimilar people from making efforts to form intimate relationships with one another, there is another side to the argument that the existence of strategic self-presentation of emotion in social interactions is likely to deter the formation of intimate relationships with dissimilar others. In particular, recent research on interpersonal relationships clearly suggests that to develop an intimate relationship characterized by mutual caring (i.e., a communal relationship in Clark & Mills', 1979, terms), partners must be able and willing to (a) communicate their needs to each other (Clark & Mills, 1979, 1993), (b) reciprocate expressions of positive emotion (cf. Backman & Secord, 1959; Curtis & Miller, 1986), and (c) trust each other (Holmes, 1991; Holmes & Rempel, 1989). Yet, as our arguments to this point should make clear, suspicion of strategic self-presentation of emotion in relationships may interfere with all these things. If one suspects another of such self-presentations then one will not trust those emotional expressions nor consider them to be true indicators of the other's needs. Moreover, it seems likely that one will be very reluctant to reciprocate expressions of positive emotions. Thus, strategic self-presentation of emotions between dissimilar people may deter relationship formation not only because of the awkwardness and stress that may be inherent in coping with such strategies but also because such strategies may interfere with building trust, communicating needs, and reciprocating positive emotions.

CONCLUSION

We have tried to make a case that social psychologists should be examining the roles of emotional expression in adult social interaction. We have concentrated on discussing how people interpret and react to the expression of three emotions—happiness, sadness, and anger. We have argued that because there are predictable social reactions to expressions of these emotions, that people can use them for purposes of strategic self-presentation—that is for ingratiation, supplication, intimidation, and self-promotion purposes. Research on this topic is just beginning, and there is a great deal left to do. Nonetheless, we hope we have made a good case that such self- presentations do occur, that they may have substantial impacts on relationship formation and development (or lack thereof), and thus that they are worthy of further analysis and research.

ACKNOWLEDGMENT

Preparation of this chapter was supported by National Science Foundation Grant BNS- 9021603.

REFERENCES

Averill, J. R. (1982). *Anger and aggression: An essay on emotion*. New York: Springer-Verlag.
Babad, E. Y., & Wallbott, H. G. (1986). The effects of social factors on emotional relations. In K. R. Scherer, H. G. Wallbott, & A. B. Summerfield (Eds.), *Experiencing emotion: A cross-cultural study* (pp. 154–172). Cambridge, England: Cambridge University Press.
Backman, C. W., & Secord, P. F. (1959). The effect of perceived liking on interpersonal attraction. *Human Relations, 12,* 379–384.
Berscheid, E., Dion, K., Walster, E., & Walster, G. W. (1971). Physical attractiveness and dating choice: A test of the matching hypothesis. *Journal of Experimental Social Psychology, 7,* 173–189.
Byrne, D. (1971). *The attraction paradigm*. New York: Academic Press.
Byrne, D., & Clore, G. L. (1970). A reinforcement model of evaluative processes. *Personality: An International Journal, 1,* 103–128.
Clark, M. S. (1987). Evidence for the effectiveness of manipulations of communal and exchange relationships. *Personality and Social Psychology Bulletin, 12,* 414–425.
Clark, M. S. (1993, June). *Reactions to and strategic self- presentation of happiness, sadness and anger*. Paper presented at an invited symposium at the meetings of the American Psychological Society, Chicago, IL.
Clark, M. S. (1994). *Implications of self-presentations of happiness, sadness, and anger for receiving help*. Unpublished manuscript, Carnegie Mellon University, Pittsburgh, PA.
Clark, M. S., & Mills, J. (1979). Interpersonal attraction in exchange and communal relationships. *Journal of Personality and Social Psychology, 36,* 1–12.
Clark, M. S., & Chrisman, K. (1991). *Anger increases perceived dominance and decreases likeability; sadness increases perceived dependency*. Paper presented at the meetings of the American Psychological Association, Washington, DC.
Clark, M. S., & Mills, J. (1993). The difference between communal and exchange relationships: What it is and is not. *Personality and Social Psychology Bulletin, 19,* 684–691.
Clark, M. S., Ouellette, R., Powell, M., & Milberg, S. (1978). Recipient's mood, relationship

type, and helping. *Journal of Personality and Social Psychology, 53,* 94–103.

Clark, M. S., & Taraban, C. B. (1991). Reactions to and willingness to express emotion in two types of relationships. *Journal of Experimental Social Psychology, 27,* 324–336.

Coates, D., Wortman, C. B., & Abbey, A. (1979). Reactions to victims. In I. H. Frieze, D. D. Bar-Tal, & J. S. Carroll (Eds.), *New approaches to social problems* (pp. 21–52). San Francisco: Jossey-Bass.

Crocker, J., Cornwell, B., & Major, B. (1993). The stigma of overweight: Affective consequences of attributional ambiguity. *Journal of Personality and Social Psychology, 64,* 60–70.

Crocker, J., & Major, B. (1989). Social stigma and self-esteem: The self-protective properties of stigma. *Psychological Review, 96,* 608–630.

Crocker, J., Voelkl, K., Testa, M., & Major, B. (1991). Social stigma: The affective consequences of attributional ambiguity. *Journal of Personality and Social Psychology, 60,* 218–228.

Csikszentimihalyi, M., & Larson, R. (1984). *Being adolescent: Conflict and growth in teenage years.* New York: Basic Books.

Curtis, R. C., & Miller, K. (1986). Believing mother likes or dislikes you: Behaviors making the beliefs come true. *Journal of Personality and Social Psychology, 51,* 284–290.

de Rivera, J. (1984). The structure of emotional relationships. In P. Shaver (Ed.), *Review of personality and social psychology: Emotions, relationships, and health* (pp. 116–145). Beverly Hills: Sage.

Duck, S. (1986). *Human relationships.* London, England: Sage.

Eagly, A. H., Ashmore, R. D., Makhijani, M. G., & Long, L. C. (1991). What is beautiful is good, but . . .: A meta-analytic review of research on the physical attractiveness stereotype. *Psychological Bulletin, 110,* 107–128.

Farina, A., Allen, J., & Saul, B. (1968). The role of the stigmatized in affecting social relationships. *Journal of Personality, 36,* 169–182.

Farina, A., Gliha, D., Boudreau, L., Allen, A., & Sherman, A. (1971). Mental illness and the impact of believing others know about it. *Journal of Abnormal Psychology, 77,* 1–5.

Feingold, A. (1992). Good looking people are not what we think. *Psychological Bulletin, 111,* 304–341.

Folkes, V. S. (1982). Forming relationships and the matching hypothesis. *Personality and Social Psychology Bulletin, 8,* 631–636.

Fitness, J., & Fletcher, G. J. O. (1993). Love, anger, hate, and jealousy in close relationships: A prototype and cognitive appraisal analysis. *Journal of Personality and Social Psychology, 65,* 942–958.

Frable, D. E. S., Blackstone, T., & Scherbaum, C. (1990). Marginal and mindful: Deviants in social interactions. *Journal of Personality and Social Psychology, 59,* 140–149.

Godfrey, D. K., Jones, E. E., & Lord, C. G. (1986). Self-promotion is not ingratiating. *Journal of Personality and Social Psychology, 50,1* 106–115.

Gordon, S. (1981). The sociology of sentiments and emotions. In M. Rosenberg & R. Turner (Eds.), *Social psychology: Sociological perspectives* (pp. 161–185). New York: Plenum.

Hatfield, E., & Sprecher, S. (1986). *Mirror, mirror: The importance of looks in everyday life.* Albany: State University of New York Press.

Hill, M. G., Weary, G., & Williams, J. (1986). Depression: A self- presentation formulation. In R. Baumeister (Ed.), *Public self and private self.* New York: Springer-Verlag.

Hochschild, A. (1983). *The managed heart.* Berkeley: University of California Press.

Holmes, J. G. (1991). Trust and the appraisal process in close relationships. In W. H. Jones & D. Perlman (Eds.), *Advances in the appraisal process in personal relationships* (pp. 57–107). London: Jessica Kingsley.

Holmes, J. G., & Rempel, J. K. (1989). Trust in close relationships. In C. Hendrick (Ed.), *Review of personality and social psychology* (pp. 187–220). Beverly Hills: Sage.

Izard, C. E. (1984). Emotion-cognition relationships and human development. In C. E. Izard,

J. Kagan, & R. B. Zajonc (Eds.), *Emotions, cognition, and behavior* (pp. 17–37). Cambridge: Cambridge University Press.

Jones, E. E., Farina, A., Hastorf, A. H., Markus, H., Miller, D. T., & Scott, R. A. (1984). *Social stigma: The psychology of marked relationships.* New York: Freeman.

Jones, E. E., & Pittman, T. S. (1982). Toward a general theory of strategic self-presentation. In J. Suls (Ed.), *Psychological perspectives on the self* (pp. 00–00). Hillsdale, NJ: Lawrence Erlbaum Associates.

Kemper, T. (1978). *A social interactional theory of emotion.* New York: Wiley.

Kleck, R., Ono, H., & Hastorf, A. (1966). The effects of physical deviance upon face-to-face interaction. *Human Relations, 19,* 425–436.

Laird, J. (1974). Self-attribution of emotion: The effects of expressive behavior on the quality of emotional experience. *Journal of Personality and Social Psychology, 29,* 475–486.

Larson, R., Csikszentimihalyi, M., & Graef, R. (1982). Time alone in daily experience: Loneliness or renewal? In L. A. Peplau & D. Perlman (Eds.), *Loneliness: A sourcebook of current theory, research and therapy* (pp. 40–53). New York: Wiley-Interscience.

Lewis, M., & Michalson, L. (1983). *Children's emotions and moods.* New York: Plenum.

Lutz, C. (1985). Cultural patterns and individual differences in the child's emotional meaning system. In M. Lewis & C. Saarni (Eds.), *The socialization of emotion* (pp. 37–53). New York: Plenum.

Parott, W. G. (1993). Beyond hedonism: Motives for inhibiting good moods and for maintaining bad moods. In D. M. Wegner & J. W. Pennebaker (Eds.), *Handbook of mental control* (pp. 278–305). Englewood Cliffs, NJ: Prentice-Hall.

Pataki, S. P., & Clark, M. S. (1993). *Ambiguity in the self- presentation of positive emotion to others.* Paper presented at the American Psychological Society Meeting, Chicago, IL.

Purvis, J. A., Dabbs, J. M., Jr., & Hooper, C. H. (1984). The "opener": Skilled user of facial expression and speech pattern. *Personality and Social Psychology Bulletin, 10,* 61–66.

Rosaldo, M. Z. (1984). Toward an anthropology of self and feeling. In R. A. Schweder & S. R. LeVine (Eds.), *Culture theory: Essays on mind, self, and emotion* (pp. 137–157). Cambridge: Cambridge University Press.

Rosenfeld, H. M. (1966). Approval-seeking and approval inducing functions of verbal and nonverbal responses in the dyad. *Journal of Personality and Social Psychology, 6,* 597–605.

Rusbult, C. E., Verette, J., Whitney, G., Slovik, L., & Lipkus, I. (1991). Accommodation processes in close relationships: Theory and preliminary evidence. *Journal of Personality and Social Psychology, 60,* 53–78.

Saarni, C. (1989). Children's understanding of strategic control of emotional expression in social transactions. In C. Saarni & P. L. Harris (Eds.), *Children's understanding of emotion.* Cambridge, England: Cambridge University Press.

Scherer, K. R., Wallbott, H. G., & Summerfield, A. B. (1986). *Experiencing emotion: A cross-cultural study.* Cambridge: Cambridge University Press.

Schneider, D. J., Hastorf, A. H., & Ellsworth, P. C. (1979). *Person perception* (2nd ed.). Reading, MA: Addison-Wesley.

Schwartz, J. C., & Shaver, P. R. (1987). Emotions and emotion knowledge in interpersonal relationships. In W. Jones & D. Perlman (Eds.), *Advances in personal relationships* (pp. 197–241). Greenwich, CT: JAI Press.

Shaver, P., Schwartz, J., Kirson, D., & O'Connor, C. (1987). Emotion knowledge: Further exploration of a prototype approach. *Journal of Personality and Social Psychology, 52,* 1061–1086.

Schott, S. (1979). Emotion and social life: A symbolic interactionist analysis. *American Journal of Sociology, 84,* 1317–1334.

Silver, R. L., & Wortman, C. B. (1980). Coping with undesirable life events. In J. Garber & M. E. P. Seligman (Eds.), *Human helplessness* (pp. 279–375). New York: Academic Press.

Sommers, S. (1984). Reported emotions and conventions of emotionality among college students. *Journal of Personality and Social Psychology, 46,* 207–215.

Stroebe, W., Insko, C. A., Thomson, V. D., & Layton, B. D. (1971). Effects of physical attractiveness, attitude similarity, and sex on various aspects of interpersonal attraction. *Journal of Personality and Social Psychology, 18,* 79–91.

Trevarthen, C. (1984). Emotions in infancy: Regulators of contact and relationships with persons. In K. Scherer & P. Ekman (Eds.), *Approaches to emotion* (pp. 129–157). Hillsdale, NJ: Lawrence Erlbaum Associates.

van Hoof, J. A. R. A. M. (1972). A comparative approach to the phylogeny of laughter and smiling. In R. A. Hinde (Ed.), *Non- verbal communication.* Cambridge, England: Cambridge University Press.

Warren, B. L. (1966). A multiple variable approach to the assortive mating phenomenon. *Eugenics Quarterly, 13,* 285–298.

Wortman, C. B., & Silver, B. L. (1989). The myths of coping with loss. *Journal of Consulting and Clinical Psychology, 57,* 349–357.

The Role of Emotion Scripts and Transient Moods in Relationships: Structural and Functional Perspectives

Joseph P. Forgas
University of New South Wales

What is the role of affect in our personal relationships? Although this question has fascinated laymen, artists, and philosophers for centuries, scientific research on this issue is a surprisingly recent development. At present, our understanding of the mechanisms linking affect to cognition and behavior in relationships remains sketchy. The three chapters in this section by Fitness (chap. 7), Fehr and Baldwin (chap. 8), and Clark, Pataki, and Carver (chap. 9) present convergent evidence for the consensual, socially structured character of many prototypical emotional experiences and expressions in relationships. Clearly, the shared knowledge structures associated with different emotions play a critical role in the initiation, maintenance, and termination of personal relationships, as the chapters in this section illustrate. In addition, there is a complementary strategy addressing the functional consequences of affect for relationships that is also considered here.

This, by necessity, limited discussion has several objectives. The first part contains a brief historical introduction, and discusses three important conceptual issues relating to affect and cognition in relationships, concerning (a) the definition and distinction between affect, emotions, and moods; (b) the biological as against the cognitivist approaches to affect; and (c) the differences between research focusing on the *structural* components of emotions, as against the *functions* and consequences of affective states (cf. Forgas, 1995). The second part discusses the structural approach to emotion scripts eminently represented by the three chapters included here. The final section of this discussion takes a brief look at some complementary avenues for studying the functions of affect in relationships.

AFFECT AND COGNITION IN RELATIONSHIPS

The study of close relationships provides a vital domain for understanding the links between affect and cognition (Bradbury & Fincham, 1987, 1992; Forgas, 1991c). Affect is seen by some psychologists as the basic currency of all interpersonal behavior (Zajonc, 1980), and it certainly plays a decisive part in close relationships (Argyle & Henderson, 1985; Levinger, 1980, 1994). Schachter (1959) was among the first to show that aversive emotions can influence interpersonal preferences, as people apparently use a motivated affect-control strategy to guide their partner choices (Forgas, 1991b). Others, such as Feshbach and Singer (1957) found that fearful subjects perceived more anxiety in others, as if projecting their own feelings onto a target. Numerous studies also indicate that evaluations of others can be conditioned by the affective state of a person (Clore & Byrne, 1974; Griffitt, 1970), consistent with the view that "interpersonal attraction is a positive function of the subject's affective state" (Gouaux, 1971, p. 40). Affective reactions also play a critical role in structuring people's implicit cognitive representations about common relationship scripts (Forgas & Dobosz, 1980). Other research suggests that feelings also have a disproportionate influence on how people cognitively represent and structure their recurring social interaction episodes (Forgas, 1982).

There is thus strong cumulative evidence suggesting that affect is closely involved in both (a) the organization and representation of relationship information and knowledge (the *content* of relationship cognition), and (b) the processing of relationship judgments (the *process* of cognition). Recent affect-cognition theories in particular confirm that affect can significantly influence how we select, process, and remember relationship information (e.g., Bower, 1991; Buunk & Bringle, 1987; Clore, Schwarz, & Conway, 1994; Forgas, 1992a, 1995; Gottman, 1979; Noller & Ruzzene, 1991), with important consequences for our understanding of marital conflict and dysfunction (Fletcher, Fitness, & Blampied, 1990).

It is all the more suprising then that social psychologists were relatively late to pay serious attention to this topic. Although the emergence of the social cognition paradigm in the early 1980s provided a promising framework for investigating the links between thinking and feeling in relationships, this opportunity was left unrecognized until quite recently (Clore et al., 1994; Forgas, 1991c, 1995). Fortunately, during the past several years much has been done to fill the gaps in our knowledge about affect and cognition in relationships, a development to which this book in general, and the three chapters in this section in particular, make a significant contribution.

Much of the existing work on affect in relationships may be classified in terms of at least three fundamental conceptual differences in approach: (a) whether the investigation is concerned with specific *emotions* or nonspecific, diffuse *mood states*; (b) whether affect is conceptualized primarily as an evolutionary, biological phenomenon, or a cognitive phenomenon (the *biological* and *cognitivist* positions, respectively); and (c) whether the researchers are primarily interested in describing the features and knowledge structures comprising an affective state (the *structural* approach), or take the existence of an affective state for granted and are interested in its functions and consequences for thinking, judgments, and behavior in a relationship (the *functional* approach). I briefly consider these three fundamental dichotomies next.

EMOTION AND MOOD: STRUCTURAL AND FUNCTIONAL APPROACHES

Unfortunately, there continues to be little general agreement in the literature about how best to *define* such commonly used terms as affect, feelings, emotions, or mood (Fiedler & Forgas, 1988; Forgas, 1991a, 1991c; Frijda, 1986). The most general view seems to be that *affect* may be used as a broad, generic label to refer to both specific emotional states, and to broad, nonspecific moods. The concept of mood in turn may be defined as "low-intensity, diffuse and relatively enduring affective states without a salient antecedent cause and therefore little cognitive content (e.g., feeling good or feeling bad)" (Forgas, 1992a, p. 230). In contrast, specific emotions are typically seen as "more intense, short-lived and usually have a definite cause and clear cognitive content" (e.g., anger or fear; Forgas, 1992a, p. 230). Whereas emotional experiences such as love, hate, anger, or fear are characterized by a specific array of cognitive associations, moods often have few if any consciously available cognitive constructs associated with them.

It is not surprising, therefore, that emotion researchers typically explore the rich framework of cognitive knowledge structures within which emotions are embedded, an approach also illustrated by the three chapter presented here. In other words, much recent work on relationship emotions is structurally oriented. Such emotion scripts in relationships do have important consequences for the way partners think, feel, and behave toward each other, an issue clearly addressed in all three chapters. Even when the focus is on how emotional expressions may be strategically used in interpersonal situations, as is the case in the excellent chapter by Clark et al., it is again the consensually shared knowledge structures underlying an emotion that make such strategic use possible. It is worth noting that since emotional experiences (unlike moods) are rich in cognitive content as all three chapters included here emphasize, they often activate specific appraisal processes (Ellsworth & Smith, 1988; Ortony, Clore, & Collins, 1988), and can trigger directed, controlled processing strategies capable of selectively overriding their usual functional consequences. Thus, because of their elaborate cognitive content, the functional consequences of specific emotions can be complex, unpredictable, and highly context specific. There is now a growing number of studies showing that the functional consequences of even such a well-established emotion script as anger can be readily altered by subtle contextual factors eliciting controlled, motivated processing strategies (Berkowitz, 1993).

In contrast to emotions, moods often have no readily accessible antecedents and have little cognitive content and structure (Clore et al., 1994). Moods also tend to have few if any direct motivational effects, and most often serve as one source of "input to other processes that determine their motivational implications" (Martin, Ward, Achee, & Wyer, 1993, p. 317). Yet, precisely because of their low intensity and limited cognitive structure, moods may often have a more enduring, subtle, and insiduous functional influence on people's thinking, judgments, and behaviors than do emotions (Forgas, 1992a, 1993; Mayer, Gaschke, Braverman, & Evans, 1992; Sedikides, 1992, 1994). Perhaps not surprisingly then, most mood researchers tend to concentrate on the functional consequences of moods for cognition and behavior rather than on their antecedents or structural properties.

Much of contemporary research can in fact be classified as having either structural or functional orientation. Rarely do the same investigators look at both aspects of affect. Yet these two facets are likely to be intimately related: Certainly the cognitive structure of an emotion can have significant functional consequences, a point that is nicely illustrated in recent research by Keltner, Ellsworth, and Edwards (1993). In this study, sad subjects were more likely to identify situational causes for an ambiguous event, whereas angry subjects tended to identify internal, dispositional causes, consistent with the different knowledge structures of these affective states. In a somewhat similar vein, Mineka and Sutton (1992) found that anxiety and sadness also have different information-processing consequences: whereas anxiety cued attention toward threatening stimuli, sad mood tended to induce mood-congruent thinking. Thus, the structural properties of emotions can also shape the way people seek information and interpret events, a point also addressed in the chapters by Fitness, Clark et al., and Fehr and Baldwin presented here.

The Biological and the Cognitivist Perspectives

One further reason for the relatively late emergence of research on the role of emotions in personal relationships is due to enduring conceptual difficulties in the definition and classification of emotions. There are two competing conceptualizations in the literature, one emphasizing the biological and evolutionary roots of emotion (Ekman, 1992), and the other pointing to the cognitive, situational appraisal properties of emotions (Lazarus, 1984; Ortony et al., 1988). The biological/evolutionary account posits that emotions can be identified by distinct neural patterns, and have evolved because they have survival value in facilitating responses to various situations. For example, the anger/aggression "syndrome" refers to one such set of apparently hard-wired emotional associations that has received extensive attention in the literature (Berkowitz, 1993).

In contrast, cognitive theories imply a more flexible affective system, where actors need to appraise situations in terms of their current needs and goals as a necessary step for a selective affective response to occur (Frijda, 1986; Lazarus, 1984; Ortony et al., 1988). It is interesting that much of the recent affect literature is based on a cognitivist rather than a biological orientation. The three chapters included here also adopt a fundamentally cognitivist rather than a biological perspective. All three chapters also share another important feature: Instead of focusing on the a priori, theoretically derived appraisal characteristics of emotions, as many cognitively oriented emotion theorists have done (e.g., Ortony et al., 1988), the authors here approach emotions from the perspective of the layperson, as understood and experienced by people in their everyday relationships. It is perhaps unfortunate from the perspective of relationship research that there is relatively little interchange between the biological and the cognitivist paradigms of emotion research. After all, relationship emotions such as love, hate, or anger are not merely highly structured social and cognitive phenomena, but almost certainly have a profound biological and evolutionary significance about which we continue to know less than we should.

STRUCTURALIST APPROACHES

The structuralist approach to emotions suggests that specific affective reactions can be understood as composed of a set of prototypical features, incorporating both intrapsychic (e.g., plans, goals, ideas, facial expressions, and motives) and situational (e.g., actors, settings, props, etc.) characteristics. Cognitive principles of categorization (Rosch & Lloyd, 1978) play an important role in informing recent work on the structure of emotions in relationships, as illustrated by all three chapters included here. In particular, it is the principles of prototype analysis and of script analysis that both Fitness, and Fehr and Baldwin find most useful in elucidating how ordinary people deal with relationship emotions such as love, anger, or jealousy.

Lay Versus A Priori Models of Emotion

The chapter by Fitness summarizes the author's recent work on emotion prototypes for love, anger, hatred, and jealousy in married relationships. What are the structural elements that distinguish these four emotions? Fitness' data suggest that these emotion profiles differed in terms of such features as the pleasantness and degree of control in the eliciting situation, the perceived fairness of the partner's behavior, and a distinct set of cognitive, motivational, and affective reactions by the informant. The importance of these elements in defining the structure of relationship emotions was also confirmed by subjects reporting on hypothetical (rather than actual) affective experiences.

Fitness also points to the remarkable disjunction between what laypeople and what scientists consider prototypical emotions: Although there is little doubt in the minds of laypersons that jealousy and hatred are important "prototypical" emotions, theorists often characterize these feelings as derivative, and/or compound emotions (Frijda, 1986). Fitness' self-report questionnaire data established that contrary to some theory-driven models, her sample of 160 married men and women in New Zealand indeed saw these emotions as fundamentally distinct, prototypical affective experiences with relatively few overlapping features.

The difference between the structural features of emotions as seen by laypeople, and as predicted by theorists is also relevant to Fehr and Baldwin's work. These authors also take a prototype approach, but focus on one specific and very important emotion in relationships: anger. This work tells us a great deal about what anger is, how it arises, and what are its consequences. Unfair, unjust, or immoral behavior; violation of expectations; and the frustration of goal-directed action seem to be the major antecedent features of anger. Planning and fantasizing about revenge, obsessive thinking, and restricted attention are some of its cognitive features, whereas arousal, nervousness, and tension are its physiological components.

It is again interesting that although a priori structural theorists often emphasize the frustration of goal-directed action as a critical antecedent of anger (e.g., Berkowitz, 1993; Ortony et al., 1988), lay reports as discovered by Fehr and Baldwin more often point to being treated unjustly or unfairly, or the violation of social norms and expectations, as structural antecedents of anger. This is not a trivial difference. Unlike a priori emotion models, lay theories of emotion are deeply rooted within a moral, normative system of expectations (Harre, 1986). By taking lay representations seriously, these authors highlight an omission in emotion theories that take a priori logical and rational appraisal principles as their starting point.

Individual Differences in the Structure of Emotions

These analyses of laypeople's reports also point to the importance of individual differences in interpretations and perceptions. What is an anger-eliciting feature for one person may elicit little more than slight disappointment in someone else. Prototype theorists in the past have shown relatively little interest in exploring why one person's perfect emotion exemplar may be another person's poor exemplar. The unique goals, plans, and motivations that relationship partners tend to rely on when appraising affective situations (Gottman, 1979) have been insufficiently considered in structuralist analyses that tend to emphasize consensual rather than idiosyncratic emotion features. This can be particularly important in personal relationships, where shared and often idiosyncratic knowledge about the prototypical emotion patterns of a partner becomes part of the strategic knowledge in a relationship, influencing interaction strategies, memories, and judgments.

The Temporal Structure of Emotions: The Script Approach

What are the temporal links between various emotion features, and what are the antecedent conditions most likely to trigger a particular emotion script? Both Fitness, and Fehr and Baldwin emphasize the importance of understanding the temporal structure of events that constitute an emotional experience, and both chapters rely on the notion of emotion scripts to address this question. Prior work by researchers such as Bradbury and Fincham (1992) suggested that locating the partner's behavior along the causal dimensions of internality, stability, and globality should have a major influence on defining and triggering different emotional scripts. Despite the elegance of this model, it might suggest an excessively simplistic view of emotion appraisal in relationships, especially when contrasted with the more elaborate and finely grained analysis of other appraisal models (e.g., Ortony et al., 1988).

As both Fitness, and Fehr and Baldwin suggest, affective responses to relationship events are likely to be strongly influenced by a variety of other factors, such as how a partner appraises his or her own needs, plans, and goals, and the amount of control available. The revision of Bradbury and Fincham's (1987, 1992) contextual model by Fletcher and Fincham (1991) goes some way toward dealing with this problem. As is the case with other social schemata, emotion scripts are likely to influence what partners think, do, and remember in their relationships. These influences may be particularly marked when the information base is complex, ambiguous, or sketchy, as is often the case in real-life relationships. In such instances, emotion scripts may lead to an escalating spiral with affectively tinted constructions and interpretations (Gottman & Levenson, 1986). As Fitness observes, "the immediate problem merely serves as a context for the familiar, shared emotion script to emerge, with its core relational themes."

The script approach is also used by Fehr and Baldwin to examine the question: What are the "different relational tracks that go together to make up the domain of anger?" Instead of focusing on fixed anger scripts, this strategy seeks to uncover the pattern of transitional probabilities that link various anger features along a temporal continuum. This work uncovered interesting gender differences in the unfolding pattern of anger scripts in relationships, identifying three stages in the anger experience—elicitors, responses, and expectations of the partner's reactions. Several intriguing findings emerge; for example, women "reported a higher likelihood of expressing hurt feelings and using both direct and indirect aggression," and there was also a subtle interdependence between the quality of subjects' anger responses, and expectations of how their partners may react. Fehr and Baldwin's analysis also shows that differences between men and women's anger scripts in fact "may represent differential sensitivity to various instigators," rather than basic gender-based differences in the total anger syndrome. This work nicely complements the traditional social cognitive paradigm that habitually focuses on intrapsychic events without the much-needed interpersonal level of analysis (Forgas, 1981). Fehr and Baldwin also acknowledge, however, the need to pay more attention in the future to personal, idiosyncratic emotion scripts in relationships rather than the kind of social, consensual prototypes and scripts predominantly studied to date.

The Strategic Use of Emotion Scripts

In their insightful chapter Clark, Pataki, and Carver address a long-neglected issue in the study of affect in relationships: Given the widely shared consensual features of emotion scripts as shown by Fitness and by Fehr and Baldwin, can the communication of various emotional states also serve strategic purposes in the service of a person's interpersonal goals? Because people share assumptions about the structure, antecedents, and consequences of emotions such as happiness, anger, or sadness, Clark et al. argue that emotions are also frequently used to strategically trigger predictable scripts. In essence, this analysis recognizes that affect is not merely a private experience, but at the same time is a public event. Several strategic principles underlying emotional self-presentations are considered by Clark and her colleagues. Some are fairly straightforward, such as the suggestion that happiness enhances liking, whereas sadness, irritability, and other negative emotions reduce liking. Emotions such as sadness may also be used as part of a supplication strategy both by children and by adults, and may be effective in eliciting altruistic responses. Expressions of anger in turn may be employed to achieve intimidation and dominance, and as Clark et al. note, this strategy appears to be particularly effective when employed by females rather than males.

The experience of aching facial muscles due to too much forced smiling after a longish cocktail party provides convincing evidence that people indeed do habitually feign happiness to induce liking. Experimental research reviewed by Clark et al. (e.g., Clark & Taraban, 1991) is largely consistent with the suggested strategic use of happiness. Other work also confirms greater liking and more lenient treatment for others who display visible signs of happiness, such as smiling (Forgas, O'Connor, & Morris, 1983). However, there are some limits to the universality of this phenomenon. In circumstances when happiness appears situationally inappropriate (e.g., after committing a transgression), happy or smiling people may in fact be seen as more manipulative, suspicious, and overconfident, and are often judged as less likeable and are treated more unfavorably than are others who express less happiness (Forgas et al., 1983).

These strategic emotion communications are effective because "expressions of happiness, sadness and anger carry with them particular interpretations about the person . . . and also evidence that people are well aware of these meanings," suggest Clark et al. The role of social norms in the strategic communication of emotion is of course all-important, which may explain why expressions of anger may be more effective by females than by males. Indeed, strategic emotional messages are often dictated by social norms: People will be quite capable of expressing greater pleasure in the face of an unwelcome rather than a welcome encounter as long as this is what social desirability demands, suggest Clark et al. Moreover, these strategic self-presentations are often enacted automatically, without any need for conscious or effortful processing.

Are there individual differences in the strategic use of emotion scripts? Clark et al. consider some interesting possibilities here. For example, a person who habitually uses happiness to induce liking is probably limited in his or her use of anger to achieve dominance and intimidation. The pervasive need to appear consistent and predictable in our self-presentations imposes obvious constraints on how conflicting emotion scripts can be used. The ability to use emotion scripts skillfully may also be predicted by various established individual difference measures such as self-monitoring, machiavellism, extraversion, affect intensity, or need for cognition to mention but a few. This possibility deserves serious attention in future research. As with all strategic self-presentations, the success of the emotion script strategy also depends on the ability of the recipient of such messages to correctly discern underlying motives. Clark et al. suggest that people in positions of power who often receive such strategic communications tend to be more sceptical of emotional messages than is the case for the population at large. These analyses also highlight the very important role of different relationship types (communal vs. exchange) in cueing alternative responses. Whereas expressing sadness may be an effective means of eliciting help and support in a well-functioning communal relationship, happiness seems a more effective and less risky strategy for obtaining benefits in an exchange relationship.

Another interesting question raised by Clark et al.'s work is the extent to which the expression of an emotion for strategic purposes can remain unrelated to the actual experience of that emotion? There is in fact strong evidence suggesting that the expression and the experience of an emotion are intricately connected. Biological theories of emotion in particular suggest that there are close neural links between the expressive and the experiential aspects of affective states, indicating, for example, that the facial expression of an emotion alone may be capable of triggering the actual affective experience (Ekman, 1992). Several ingenuous experiments now confirm that even quite unremarkable changes in the configuration of facial muscles (to approximate "smile" or "frown" faces) do have demonstrable affective and cognitive consequences (Strack, Martin, & Stepper, 1988), confirming Clark et al.'s point that the expression of an emotion for strategic purposes usually also has experiential consequences.

SOME CAUTIONARY OBSERVATIONS

Despite the appeal and popularity of structuralist analyses of emotion scripts and prototypes, there are also some limitations to this approach. As Fitness points out, "with no two theorists in complete agreement about the particular kinds of appraisals that generate particular kinds of emotions," some of these theories seem to be based on essentially intuitive classifications. The careful analysis of layperson's reports about their emotional experiences is one way to achieve a greater degree of consensuality and reliability in such structural analyses, a method successfully employed here both by Fitness and by Fehr and Baldwin.

However, asking people to provide self-reports about their emotion scripts also presents some difficulties. For example, reconstructions of feelings by intimate partners may not always represent the true state of affairs, as people either may not know, or may not want to know the true reasons for, and features of, their emotional states. Reporting on intense affective experiences in a relationship is far from being a neutral social situation. Subjects will presumably seek not only to present a dispassionate analysis of what they have experienced, but almost certainly will also be motivated to justify and explain. Given that explanations of such events are usually made with reference to a normative, and even ethical context (Harre, 1986), what subjects report on is not necessarily the true features of their emotion scripts, but what they take to be acceptable and warrantable public explanations. As a consequence, their responses will partly reflect what occurred, but at least partly they will be molded by applicable social conventions. Thus, there is some danger in taking such verbal reports entirely at face value.

A related issue in relying on laypersons' comments about their emotion scripts is that the semantic and pragmatic features of the language they use necessarily intrudes on, and shapes the kind of prototype structure they report. What they produce may be as much a reflection of the emotion vocabulary provided by language as it is a true indication of their genuine affective experiences. And we do know that emotion vocabularies themselves, and even the meanings attached to particular emotion words over time, can and do fluctuate a great deal (Harre, 1986).

For example, can we really conclude that there are indeed two different underlying emotion experiences when two respondents variously describe their affective reactions to a partner as "angry" and "hateful"? Or to take another example, the study by Mascolo and Mancuso discussed by Fehr and Baldwin finds that certain types of anger (such as rage or fury) consistently receive higher typicality ratings than do other kinds, such as spite or disappointment. This certainly tells us something about the hierarchical semantic relationship between a basic-level emotional category such as "anger" and the way it is instantiated in different examplars such as "rage" (a good examplar) and "spite" (a less good examplar). But what does this tell us about about the actual emotional experiences these decontextualized labels describe? Is it not possible that some kinds of fury may be less good examplars of "anger" than are some kinds of spite? Such potentially confusing "travels in semantic space" are an inevitable consequence of relying on verbal reports of affective experiences.

In contrast to the quasi-linguistic methods predominantly used in many structural analyses of emotion scripts, much of the work reported by Clark et al. relies on controlled experiments to establish the strategic consequences of emotional displays. This methodology represents a powerful empirical approach to analyzing the features and consequences of emotion scripts. Perhaps a greater degree of methodological eclecticism, involving the combination of both linguistic, descriptive, and experimental, predictive methods within the same research program would offer the best approach for enhancing the reliability and validity of future structural investigations of emotion scripts.

The three chapters by Fitness, Fehr and Baldwin, and Clark et al. considered here offer convincing and convergent evidence for the importance of the structural approach to emotion scripts in understanding personal relationships. Other complementary approaches focus on the functions and consequences of transient affective states on thinking, judgments, and behavior in relationships. In the next section I briefly consider some of this work, in order to illustrate the broader context of recent affect–cognition research in relationships.

THE FUNCTIONALIST APPROACH:
THE CONSEQUENCES OF MOOD ON COGNITION
AND BEHAVIOR IN RELATIONSHIPS

Much recent evidence suggests that in addition to their structural features, transient affective states or moods also have important functional consequences for the way people think about, remember, interpret, and process social information (Bower, 1991; Clore et al., 1994; Forgas, 1992a; Sedikides, 1992, 1994). Intimate relationships provide us with an uncommonly rich and varied range of experiences that require a great deal of cognitive monitoring and evaluation (Bradbury & Fincham, 1992; Fletcher & Fitness, 1992; Noller & Ruzzene, 1991). Because social cognition and judgments are inherently constructive (Heider, 1958), moods may influence what we attend to, what we remember, and how we interpret information (Bower, 1991; Fiedler, 1991; Forgas, 1991c, 1994a). Despite the recent emphasis on cognitive and attributional processes in relationships (cf. Fletcher & Fincham, 1991; Forgas, 1991c; Ginsburg, 1987), surprisingly little is known about the functional role of moods in relationship cognition. It now seems that affective states may influence both what people think (the content of cognition), and how people think (the process of cognition). The multiple functional consequences of affect were recently clarified in an integrative multiprocess theory, the affect infusion model (AIM; Forgas, 1992a, 1995).

Mood Effects on Relationship Cognition: The Affect Infusion Model

For our purposes, *affect infusion* may be defined as "the process whereby affectively loaded information exerts an influence on, and becomes incorporated into the judgmental process, entering into the judge's deliberations and eventually coloring the judgmental outcome" (Forgas, 1994a, p. 2). The AIM suggests that affect infusion is most likely when a person is engaged in *constructive processing* that requires the substantial transformation rather than mere reproduction of information, the use of an open information search strategy, and a degree of generative elaboration of stimulus details. As Fiedler (1990) suggested, affect "will influence cognitive processes to the extent that the cognitive task involves the active generation of new information as opposed to the passive conservation of information given" (pp. 2–3).

The AIM identifies four judgmental strategies, each marked by different affect infusion potentials. Two of these, the *direct access* of a preexisting, stored evaluation, and *motivated processing* in the service of a preexisting goal, require highly directed information search patterns and involve little constructive processing, making affect infusion unlikely (Forgas, 1991b). Many judgments, however, do require a degree of constructive processing. In these conditions, judges may use either *heuristic*, simplified or a *substantive*, generative processing to compute an outcome. These two high-infusion strategies involve some degree of open information search, and an element of constructive thinking (Fiedler, 1990, 1991; Forgas, 1992a), allowing affect either indirectly, through primed associations (Forgas & Bower, 1987), or directly (Schwarz & Clore, 1988) to infuse the outcome. Thus, the AIM can account not only for instances when affect leads to congruent judgment (during heuristic or substantive processing), but can also deal with situations when cognition is uninfluenced by, or indeed, is incongruent with prevailing mood, due to the operation of direct access, or motivated processing strategies (Berkowitz, 1993; Erber & Erber, 1994; Sedikides, 1994).

The AIM also identifies two distinct affect infusion mechanisms. During heuristic processing, mood itself may be used as information according to the affect-as-information principle, when subjects rely on a "how do I feel about it?" heuristic to compute a judgment (Clore et al., 1994; Schwarz & Clore, 1988). This simple strategy is probably rarely used when judging intimate relationships (Forgas, 1994b). According to the second, affect-priming principle, affect may indirectly infuse judgments during substantive processing through its selective influence on attention, encoding, retrieval, and associative processes (Bower, 1991; Clark & Waddell, 1983; Forgas & Bower, 1987). Consistent with the affect-priming model, numerous studies have found that moods will influence how people judge themselves and others and make interpersonal decisions (Forgas, 1991b; Forgas & Bower, 1987; Mayer et al., 1992; Salovey, O'Leary, Stretton, Fishkin, & Drake, 1991; Sedikides, 1992). The AIM suggests that affect-priming and affect-as-information are complementary avenues of affect infusion, operating under different (substantive vs. heuristic) processing conditions, and distinguishable in terms of processing latency, judgmental latency, memory, and other cognitive variables (Forgas, 1992a, 1994a, 1995).

The full model (Fig. 1) clearly specifies how various features of the judge (e.g., personal relevance, motivation, cognitive capacity, and affect), the target (familiarity, complexity, typicality), and the situation (public vs. private) may recruit different processing strategies, and lead to the presence or the absence of affect infusion effects. Several intriguing and counterintuitive hypotheses about relationship judgments are also suggested by the AIM. For example, as the complexity and heterogeneity of information about a partner increases, more prolonged and extensive processing may be required, increasing rather than reducing the likelihood of affect infusion during substantive processing, as found in several recent studies (Fiedler, 1991; Forgas, 1992b, 1993, 1994a, 1994b; Forgas, Levinger, & Moylan, 1994). Although a complete description of the AIM is beyond the scope of this discussion, a brief look at some functional mood effects on relationship cognition may be relevant here.

The Functional Effects of Mood on Relationship Cognition: Some Recent Evidence

The common purpose of the experiments described was to show that affect will infuse the way partners think about their personal relationship under

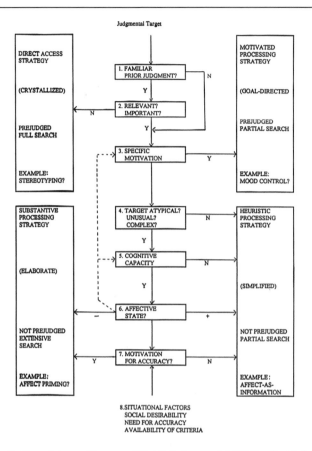

FIG. 1. Outline of the multiprocess Affect Infusion Model (AIM): affect infusion into social cognition and judgments depends on which of four alternative processing strategies is adopted in response to target, judge and situational features; direct access and motivated processing are low infusion strategies with little mood congruence in judgments, whereas heuristic and substantive processing are high infusion strategies with marked mood congruence in judgments. The flowchart also illustrates the hierarchical relationship between various factors determining processing choices, and the multiple informational and processing effects influence of affect on judgments (after Forgas, 1995).

conditions conducive to substantive, elaborate processing strategies. In one exploratory field study (Forgas et al., 1994, Exp. 1), subjects who have just seen a happy or a sad film (in fact, the unobtrusive mood induction) were asked to judge their romantic relationship. Based on recent work on relationship cognition (Fitness & Strongman, 1991; Fletcher & Kininmonth, 1991), and the AIM (Forgas, 1992a, 1994a), we predicted and found that temporary positive mood significantly enhanced relationship evaluations, whereas sad mood had the opposite effect. These effects were robust and uniform irrespective of the respondent's gender, or the longevity of their relationship. In a follow-up laboratory study (Forgas et al., 1994, Exp. 2), subjects first viewed happy and sad films (the mood induction), before making judgments about (a) their relationship, as well as (b) rating their partner on Rubin's (1973) "liking" and "loving" scales, and (c) rating conflict-resolution strategies on Levinger and Pietromonaco's (1989) Conflict Style Inventory. Again, happy subjects judged their relationship and their partners more positively, and these mood effects were undiminished even in long-term relationships, which, according to the AIM (Forgas, 1992a, 1994a, 1995), offer a more diverse informational base and thus continuing scope for affect infusion.

Mood and Explanations of Relationship Conflict. Affect may also influence how people explain their more or less serious relationship conflicts, with potentially important implications for social and personal adjustment, and ultimately, even for mental health (Fletcher et al., 1990; Weary, Marsh, & McCormick, 1994). Suggestive evidence for mood effects on causal attributions comes from several recent experiments (Forgas, Bower, & Moylan, 1990). In an exploratory field study (Forgas, 1994b, Exp. 1), people were approached in public places and asked to (a) read a brief literary passage designed to induce good or bad mood, and then (b) make causal attributions for previously recalled happy and sad events in their relationship. As predicted, happy subjects took greater credit for positive events and blamed more outside factors for negative events, whereas sad subjects credited their partners for happy episodes but blamed themselves for conflict events.

A major counterintuitive prediction of the AIM is that affect infusion might be greater in judgments about complex, serious rather than simple conflicts, because such events require more elaborate and constructive processing, providing greater scope for mood-primed material to influence the outcome (Bower, 1991; Fiedler, 1990, 1991; Forgas, 1992a). In a further field study, people who have just seen happy or sad movies were asked to attribute causes for their more or less serious relationship conflicts to three categories, internality, stability, and globality (Forgas, 1994b, Exp. 2). Sad mood led to more internal, stable and global attributions, whereas happy subjects identified more external, unstable, and specific causes. Remarkably, both positive and negative mood effects were significantly greater for judgments of serious rather than superficial conflicts, a counterintuitive finding consistent with the AIM predictions (Fig. 2). Finally, a laboratory experiment using a computer-controlled procedure confirmed that greater mood effects on serious conflicts were systematically linked to longer processing latencies, consistent with the more prolongued and substantive processing of these episodes (Forgas, 1994b, Exp. 3). Because simple and routine conflicts require less extensive processing, affect-infusion effects were limited. Complex and serious conflicts on the other hand require more

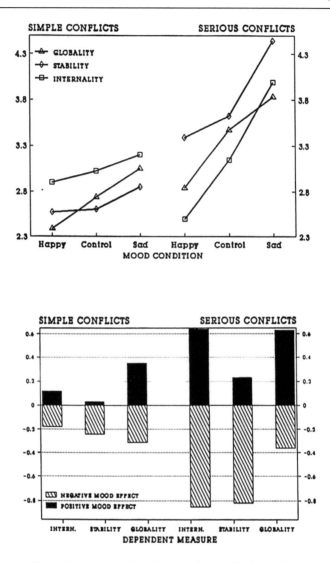

FIG. 2.   The effects of happy, control, and sad mood on attributions to internal, stable, and global causes for simple and serious relationship conflicts; both positive and negative mood effects are significantly greater for serious rather than simple conflicts (after Forgas, 1994b, Exp. 2).

elaborate and constructive thinking, that will paradoxically enhance rather than reduce the scope for affect infusion according to the AIM. These results establish that transient moods do indeed have a major functional influence on relationship cognition, with potentially important consequences for relationship maintenance and dysfunction (Fletcher et al., 1990; Noller & Ruzzene,

1991). Even temporary dysphoria in a marriage may give rise to an escalating spiral of mutual disapproval and negative attributions, leading to wholly pessimistic evaluations of the relationship and the partner. Of course, not all judgments or all relationships are equally susceptible to functional mood effects. In distressed marriages both partners may get caught up in each other's moods, whereas in nondistressed pairs one of the partners tends to remain more affectively neutral or accepting (Gottman, 1979). Trusting couples are also far more able to withstand each other's temporary affective oscillations than do nontrusting couples (Holmes, 1991).

Affective Influences on Judgments About Typical and Atypical Relationships. The role of affect on observer judgments about more or less typical relationships was also investigated in several studies, using pictures of more or less unusual, atypical and badly matched couples as stimuli (Forgas, 1993, in press). In addition to a clear pattern of mood-congruence in judgments, the size of mood effects once again was consistently greater when the target couple was odd and badly matched in terms of such features as physical attractiveness. In terms of the AIM, such atypical relationships should require longer and more constructive processing, allowing greater scope for affect-based associations to infuse the judgment. Indeed, mood effects on judgments were roughly proportional to the degree of visible mismatch between target couples (Forgas, in press, Exp.3; Fig. 3). A path model clearly supported the proposed mediational links between mood, relationship typicality, processing latencies, and mood congruence as implied by the AIM.

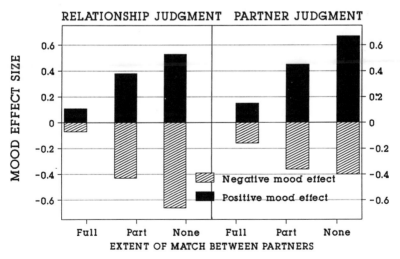

FIG. 3.   Mood effects on the perception of well-matched, partially matched, and badly matched couples: The size of the mood effect is proportional to the degree of mismatch (atypicality) between the couples (after Forgas, in press).

Affect and Motivated Processing in Relationship Cognition. According to the AIM however, mood-congruence is not a universal phenomenon, but is limited to instances when heuristic and substantive processing are employed. Affect will not infuse judgments when a highly targeted, motivated processing is adopted. People in bad moods may be particularly motivated to engage in targeted information search and retrieval strategies when a judgment is personally relevant (Clark & Isen, 1982; Erber & Erber, 1994), such as when selecting an interaction partner (Schachter, 1959). In some recent studies, we were able to document the step-by-step, targeted information search and processing strategies elicited by a combination of sad mood and a personally relevant interpersonal choice in people who were motivated to achieve a rewarding outcome in their affiliative choices (Forgas, 1991b). In some studies, descriptions about potential partners were provided on a series of information cards (Forgas, 1991b, Exp. 2), or on a computer screen, allowing the step-by-step tracing and recording of each subjects' decision path and reaction latencies (Forgas, 1991b, Exp. 3). Subjects in a bad mood and making a personal choice used a unique, motivated processing strategy, searching above all for a rewarding partner. As predicted by the AIM, there was no evidence for affect infusion in any of these motivated judgments. These results are also supported by other experiments, that find that depressed subjects selectively prefer others perceived as potentially most useful to them (Weary et al., 1994), and by reports that "when subjects were motivated to change their sad mood . . . they tended to recall mood incongruent, that is positively valenced material" (Erber & Erber, 1994, p. 86). In several intriguing experiments, Berkowitz (1993) also found that self-directed attention alone may be sufficient to induce motivated processing, and eliminate affect-infusion effects. Such motivated processing seems incompatible with affect infusion, and is probably an important and recurring feature of many relationship judgments.

SUMMARY AND CONCLUSION

Interest in the role of affect in relationships is clearly in the ascendancy in the contemporary literature. This chapter highlighted some of the enduring conceptual issues in the study of affect and cognition in relationships, and discussed two specific paradigms in greater detail: the structural analysis of emotion scripts as represented by the three chapters included here, and a complementary functionalist paradigm analysing mood effects on cognition. Convergent evidence from the three chapters by Fitness, Fehr and Baldwin, and by Clark et al. show that consensually shared emotion scripts have a significant influence on the way the antecedents and consequences of relationship emotions are perceived and interpreted by partners. Further, the highly structured character of these relationship emotions also makes it possible for people to use emotional displays strategically, as Clark et al. convincingly argued here. The study of how laypersons think about emotion scripts as illustrated by the work of Fitness and by Fehr and Baldwin also provides a useful counterbalance to the more conceptually driven, a priori appraisal theories common in the emotion literature.

A complementary perspective to the study of the structural features of affect in relationships is provided by research focusing on the functional consequences of moods on relationships, as briefly outlined in the final section of this chapter. The complex interplay between contextual variables, and the processing and informational consequences of affect itself was recently clarified in a multiprocess AIM (Forgas, 1992a, 1994a, 1995), which predicts that affect infusion into judgments depends on what kind of processing strategy is used by a judge. The AIM identified four alternative processing strategies available to judges in (direct access, motivated, heuristic, and substantive processing), and predicted that it is only during heuristic processing (due to the affect-as-information mechanism), and during substantive processing (due to affect priming) that affect infusion should occur, whereas direct access and motivated processing should produce no mood congruence. The choice between these four processing strategies is determined by a combination of judge, target, and situational features that can be specified in terms of a limited number of testable predictions (Fig. 1). A counterintuitive prediction of the AIM is that more extensive and substantive processing recruited by complex targets should paradoxically enhance, rather than inhibit affect infusion, as has been found in several recent studies of relationship judgments (Forgas, 1992b, 1993, 1994b, in press). Affect seems to play an important functional role in how people think about their relationships, their partners, and their conflicts, and may also have a major impact on real-life relationship satisfaction and adjustment.

As this brief overview of the complementary structural and functional perspectives on the role of affect in relationship cognition indicates, there has been an encouraging growth of interest in this fascinating research domain in recent years. Personal relationships provide one of the most relevant and ecologically valid domains for exploring the complex interdependence between affect and cognition. With the rapid accumulation of empirical findings, and the recent emergence of the first integrative theoretical models, investigations of the links between affect and cognition in relationships should continue to be of considerable importance in the future.

REFERENCES

Argyle, M., & Henderson, M. (1985). *The anatomy of relationships*. Harmondsworth: Penguin.
Berkowitz, L. (1993). Towards a general theory of anger and emotional aggression. In T. K. Srull

& R. S. Wyer (Eds.), *Advances in social cognition* (Vol. 5, pp. 1–46). Hillsdale, NJ: Lawrence Erlbaum Associates.

Bower, G. H. (1991). Mood congruity of social judgments. In J. P. Forgas (Ed.), *Emotion and social judgments* (pp. 31–55). Oxford: Pergamon Press.

Bradbury, T., & Fincham, F. (1987). Affect and cognition in close relationships: Towards an integrative model. *Cognition and Emotion, 1,* 59–87.

Bradbury, T., & Fincham, F. (1992). Attributions and behavior in marital interaction. *Journal of Personality and Social Psychology, 63,* 613–628.

Buunk, B., & Bringle, R. (1987). Jealousy in love relationships. In D. Perlman & S. Duck (Eds.), *Intimate relationships: Development, dynamics, and deterioration* (pp. 241–273). Beverly Hills: Sage.

Clark, M. S., & Isen, A. M. (1982). Towards understanding the relationship between feeling states and social behavior. In A. H. Hastorf & A. M. Isen (Eds.), *Cognitive social psychology* (pp. 73–108). New York: Elsevier-North Holland.

Clark, M. S., & Taraban, C. B. (1991). Reactions to, and willingness to express emotions in two types of relationships. *Journal of Experimental Social Psychology, 27,* 324–336.

Clark, M. S., & Waddell, B. A. (1983). Effects of moods on thoughts about helping, attraction and information acquisition. *Social Psychology Quarterly, 46,* 31–35.

Clore, G. L., & Byrne, D. (1974). The reinforcement model of attraction. In T. L. Huston (Ed.), *Foundations of interpersonal attraction* (pp. 143–170). New York: Academic Press.

Clore, G. L. Schwarz, N., & Conway, M.(1994). Affective causes and consequences of social information processing. In R. S. Wyer & T. K. Srull (Eds.). *Handbook of social cognition* (2nd ed., pp. 195–244). Hillsdale, NJ: Lawrence Erlbaum Associates.

Ekman, P. (1992). Are there basic emotions? *Psychological Review, 99,* 550–553.

Ellsworth, P. C., & Smith, C. A. (1988). Shades of joy: Patterns of appraisal differentiating pleasant emotions. *Cognition and Emotion, 2,* 301–331.

Erber, R., & Erber, M. W. (1994). Beyond mood and social judgment: Mood incongruent recall and mood regulation. *European Journal of Social Psychology, 24,* 79–88.

Feshbach, S., & Singer, R. D. (1957). The effects of fear arousal and suppression of fear upon social perception. *Journal of Abnormal and Social Psychology, 55,* 283–288.

Fiedler, K. (1990). Mood-dependent selectivity in social cognition. In W. Stroebe & M. Hewstone (Eds.), *European review of social psychology* (Vol. 1, pp. 1–32). Chichester: Wiley.

Fiedler, K. (1991). On the task, the measures, and the mood in research on affect and social cognition. In J. P. Forgas (Ed.), *Emotion and social judgments* (pp. 83–107). Oxford: Pergamon.

Fiedler, K., & Forgas, J. P. (Eds.). (1988). *Affect, cognition and social behavior.* Toronto: Hogrefe International.

Fitness, J., & Strongman, K. (1991). Affect in close relationships. In G. J. O. Fletcher & F. D. Fincham (Eds.), *Cognition in close relationships* (pp. 175–203). Hillsdale, NJ: Lawrence Erlbaum Associates.

Fletcher, G. J. O., & Fincham, F. (Eds.). (1991). *Cognition in close relationships.* Hillsdale, NJ: Lawrence Erlbaum Associates.

Fletcher, G. J. O., & Fitness, J. (1992). Knowledge structures and explanations in intimate relationships. In S. Duck (Ed.), *Understanding relationship processes* (pp. 269–302). Beverley Hills: Sage.

Fletcher, G. J. O., Fitness, J., & Blampied, N. M. (1990). The link between attribution and happiness in close relationships: The roles of depression and explanatory style. *Journal of Social and Clinical Psychology, 9,* 243–255.

Fletcher, G. J. O., & Kininmonth, L. (1991). Interaction in close relationships and social cognition. In G. J. O. Fletcher & F. D. Fincham (Eds.), *Cognition in close relationships* (pp. 235–257). Hillsdale, NJ: Lawrence Erlbaum Associates.

Forgas, J. P. (Ed.). (1981). *Social cognition: Perspectives on everyday understanding.* London: Academic Press.

Forgas, J. P. (1982). Episode cognition: Internal representations of interaction routines. In L.

Berkowitz (Ed.), *Advances in experimental social psychology* (pp. 59–104). New York: Academic Press.

Forgas, J. P. (1991a). Affect and cognition in close relationships. In G. Fletcher & F. Fincham (Eds.), *Cognition in close relationships*. Hillsdale, NJ: Lawrence Erlbaum Associates.

Forgas, J. P. (1991b). Affective influences on partner choice: The role of mood in social decisions. *Journal of Personality and Social Psychology, 61,* 208–220.

Forgas, J. P. (Ed.). (1991c). *Emotion in social judgments*. Oxford: Pergamon.

Forgas, J. P. (1992a). Affect in social judgments and decisions: A multiprocess model. In M. Zanna (Ed.), *Advances in experimental social psychology* (Vol. 25, pp. 227–275). New York: Academic Press.

Forgas, J. P. (1992b). On bad mood and peculiar people: Affect and person typicality in impression formation. *Journal of Personality and Social Psychology, 62,* 863–875.

Forgas, J. P. (1993). On making sense of odd couples: Mood effects on the perception of mismatched relationships. *Personality and Social Psychology Bulletin, 19,* 59–71.

Forgas, J. P. (1994a). The role of emotion in social judgments: The Affect Infusion Model (AIM). *European Journal of Social Psychology, 24,* 1–24.

Forgas, J. P. (1994b). Sad and guilty? Affective influences on the explanation of conflict episodes. *Journal of Personality and Social Psychology, 66,* 56–68.

Forgas, J. P. (1995). The Affect Infusion Model (AIM): Review and an integrative theory of mood effects on social judgments. *Psychological Bulletin, 117,* 1–28.

Forgas, J. P. (in press). Mood effects on judgments and memory about prototypical and atypical targets. *Personality and Social Psychology Bulletin.*

Forgas, J. P., & Bower, G. H. (1987). Mood effects on person perception judgements. *Journal of Personality and Social Psychology, 53,* 53–60.

Forgas, J. P., Bower, G. H., & Moylan, S. J. (1990). Praise or blame? Mood effects on attributions for success or failure. *Journal of Personality and Social Psychology, 59,* 809–819.

Forgas, J. P., & Dobosz, B. (1980). Dimensions of romantic involvement: towards a taxonomy of heterosexual relationships. *Social Psychology Quarterly, 43,* 290–300.

Forgas, J. P., Levinger, G., & Moylan, S. (1994). Feeling good and feeling close: Mood effects on the perception of intimate relationships. *Personal Relationships, 2,* 165–184.

Forgas, J. P., O'Connor, K., & Morris, S. L. (1983). Smile and punishment: The effects of facial expression on responsibility attribution by groups and individuals. *Personality and Social Psychology Bulletin, 9,* 587–596.

Frijda, N. H. (1986). *The emotions*. Cambridge: Cambridge University Press.

Ginsburg, G. P. (1987). Rules, scripts and prototypes in personal relationships. In S. Duck (Ed.), *Handbook of personal relationships* (pp. 23–41). Chichester: Wiley.

Gottman, J. M. (1979). *Marital interaction: Experimental investigations*. New York: Academic Press.

Gottman, J. M., & Levenson, R. (1986). Assessing the role of emotion in marriage. *Behavioral Assessment, 8,* 31–48.

Gouaux, C. (1971). Induced affective states and interpersonal attraction. *Journal of Personality and Social Psychology, 20,* 37–43.

Griffitt, W. (1970). Environmental effects on interpersonal behavior: Ambient effective temperature and attraction. *Journal of Personality and Social Psychology, 15,* 240–244.

Harre, R. (Ed.). (1986). The social construction of emotions. New York: Basil Blackwell.

Heider, F. (1958). *The psychology of interpersonal relations*. New York: Wiley.

Holmes, J. G. (1991). Trust and the appraisal process in close relationships. In W. H. Jones & D. Perlman (Eds.), *Advances in personal relationships* (Vol. 2, pp. 57–104). London: Jessica Kingsley.

Keltner, D., Ellsworth, P.C., & Edwards, K. (1993). Beyond simple pessimism: Effects of sadness and anger on social perception. *Journal of Personality and Social Psychology, 64,* 740–752.

Lazarus, R. S. (1984). On the primacy of cognition. *American Psychologist, 39,* 124–129.

Levinger, G. (1980). Towards the analysis of close relationships. *Journal of Experimental Social Psychology, 16,* 510–544.

Levinger, G. (1994). Figure versus ground: Micro and macro perspectives on the social psychology of personal relationships. In R. Erber & R. Gilmour (Eds.), *Theoretical frameworks for personal relationships* (pp. 95–139). Hillsdale, NJ: Lawrence Erlbaum Associates.

Levinger, G., & Pietromonaco, P. (1989). *A measure of perceived conflict resolution styles in relationships.* Unpublished manuscript, University of Massachusetts, Amherst.

Martin, L. L., Ward, D. W., Achee, J. W., & Wyer, R. S. (1993). Mood as input: People have to interpret the motivational implications of their moods. *Journal of Personality and Social Psychology, 64,* 317–326.

Mayer, J. D., Gaschke, Y. N., Braverman, D. L., & Evans, T. W. (1992). Mood congruent judgment is a general effect. *Journal of Personality and Social Psychology, 63,* 119–132.

Mineka, S., & Sutton, S. K. (1992). Cognitive biases and the emotional disorders. *Psychological Science, 3,* 65–69.

Noller, P., & Ruzzene, M. (1991). Communication in marriage: The influence of affect and cognition. In G. J. O. Fletcher & F. D. Fincham, (Eds.), *Cognition in close relationships* (pp. 175–203). Hillsdale, NJ: Lawrence Erlbaum Associates.

Ortony, A., Clore, G. L., & Collins, A. (1988). *The cognitive structure of emotion.* Cambridge: Cambridge University Press.

Rosch, E., & Lloyd, B. B. (Eds.). (1978). *Cognition and categorization.* Hillsdale, NJ: Lawrence Erlbaum Associates.

Rubin, Z. (1973). *Liking and loving: An invitation to social psychology.* New York: Holt, Rinehart & Winston.

Salovey, P., O'Leary, A., Stretton, M., Fishkin, S., & Drake, C. A. (1991). Influence of mood on judgments about health and illness. In J. P. Forgas (Ed.), *Emotion and social judgments* (pp. 241–263). Oxford: Pergamon.

Schachter, S. (1959). *The psychology of affiliation.* Stanford, CA: Stanford University Press.

Schwarz, N., & Clore, G. L. (1988). How do I feel about it? The informative function of affective states. In K. Fiedler & J. P. Forgas (Eds.), *Affect, cognition, and social behavior* (pp. 44–63). Toronto: Hogrefe.

Sedikides, C. (1992). Changes in the valence of self as a function of mood. In M. S. Clark (Ed.), *Review of personality and social psychology* (pp. 271–311). Beverly Hills: Sage.

Sedikides, C. (1994). Incongruent effects of sad mood on self-conception valence: Its a matter of time. *European Journal of Social Psychology, 24,* 161–172.

Strack, F., Martin, L. L., & Stepper, S. (1988). Inhibiting and facilitating conditions of the human smile: A nonobtrusive test of the facial feedback hypothesis. *Journal of Personality and Social Psychology, 54,* 768–777.

Weary, G., Marsh, K. L, & McCormick, L. (1994). Depression and social comparison motives. *European Journal of Scoial Psychology, 24*(1), 117–130.yL.

Zajonc, R. B. (1980). Feeling and thinking: Preferences need no inferences. *American Psychologist, 35,* 151–175.

III

KNOWLEDGE STRUCTURES AND RELATIONSHIP DEVELOPMENT

10

Changes in Knowledge of Personal Relationships

Sally Planalp
University of Colorado

Mary Rivers
Millikin University

Close relationships are no longer viewed as static states that two people are located "in" or a fixed possession that two people "have." Instead, we now view close relationships as ongoing processes that respond constantly to changes in both partners, their interactions, and their lives (Duck & Sants, 1983). Nevertheless, human beings are singularly ill-equipped to deal with constant change in their relationships; they strive for stable, trustworthy knowledge that can be used to predict and explain their partners' behavior and events that occur (Berger, 1988). How do people maintain stable beliefs in a constantly changing world? The answer to this question lies in studying the processes by which people modify, elaborate, and update their beliefs about their relationships.

In this chapter, we briefly review the research literature on how close relationships change and the literature on how knowledge changes (usually termed *schema change*). Then we turn to research reports of events that have challenged people's beliefs about their own relationships and partners. Based on these reports, we analyze how subjects sought explanations for the surprising events, drawing on existing theories of explanation and attribution. Finally, we relate our findings to schema change processes and we sketch out some implications for the metaphor of people as "intuitive scientists."

BRIEF REVIEW OF LITERATURE
ON RELATIONSHIP SCHEMA CHANGE

Relationships change in many ways—for better or for worse, gradually or suddenly, in understandable ways and in puzzling ways. Predictable changes are the stuff of which formal theories of relationship development and deterioration are made. Theorists are able to predict, for example, how self-disclosure and other interaction patterns are likely to change at different stages of relationships (Altman & Taylor, 1973; Knapp & Vangelisti, 1992). But theorists are not the only people who know about predictable changes in relationships; participants also have a sense of how their own relationships are likely to change (Honeycutt, Cantrill, & Allen, 1992; Honeycutt, Cantrill, & Greene, 1989).

Other changes may not be predictable in advance but are, nevertheless, understandable after the fact. This type of change also serves as the basis for formal theories, especially those that are grounded in participants' own understandings of changes. For example, studies of turning points in close relationships have revealed many different types of changes, both toward and away from intimacy and commitment (Baxter & Bullis, 1986; Bullis, Clark, & Sline, 1992; Surra, 1987; Surra, Arizzi, & Asmussen, 1988).

But there are also changes that are both unpredictable and difficult for both participants and theorists to understand, even after they have occurred. These, too, have their place in a complete account of relationship change because—quite simply—they happen. These are events that increase relational partners' uncertainty about each other or their relationship by challenging previously held beliefs and assumptions (Planalp & Honeycutt, 1985; Planalp & Rivers, 1988; Planalp, Rutherford, & Honeycutt, 1988).

Because relationships are beset by many different kinds of change, we must modify and update our knowledge of our relationships to accurately reflect their current status. If the changes are predictable, we have advance knowledge and can make adjustments in how we conceive of the relationship even before the actual changes occur. If the changes are understandable, we can alter the knowledge we have of the relationship, fit it into appropriate new categories and revise our beliefs. If the changes are unpredictable and difficult to understand, however, the process of changing the relevant knowledge structure is not so simple or so easy.

This type of change presents a serious challenge to formal theories as well, including theories of relationship development in particular and theories about changes in knowledge structures (or schemas) in general. As a starting point, we turn to the research literature on changes in knowledge structures (schemas) to find out what they tell us about how knowledge of relationships changes. Two general questions guide most of this research: What are the general types of changes and what processes underlie such changes in knowledge structures?

Models of Schema Change

Rothbart (1981) and Crocker, Fiske, and Taylor (1984) address the first question (What are the general types of changes?) by describing three models for schema change—bookkeeping, subtyping, and conversion. *Bookkeeping* involves making continuous, gradual adjustments in knowledge (such as updating levels of intimacy). *Subtyping* involves noting variations of the general schema (such as fair-weather friends, friends with romantic potential, and best friends). *Conversion* involves sudden, drastic changes in one's knowledge of a relationship (such as redefining a friendship as romantic or discovering an infidelity). Most types of relationship development and deterioration probably involve either bookkeeping or conversion. Some changes are gradual—spending more and more (or less and less) time together, increasing (or decreasing) levels of physical closeness, and increasing (or decreasing) feelings of love. Other changes are sudden, especially those tied to particular events, such as the first kiss, meeting the family, or discovering a betrayed confidence.

Changes made either by bookkeeping or by conversion are predictable if knowledge structures are already in place to handle them. To some extent, we can predict the behaviors of increasing intimacy or the outcomes of betraying a confidence because we have previous experience or culturally grounded knowledge about how these events often occur. Even if we cannot predict them, we can understand them after they have occurred if we are able to fit them into other available knowledge structures. We can understand what a relationship will be like when redefined by the participants as a romance instead of a friendship because we have a knowledge structure for romance available. We can also understand a gradually deteriorating marriage if we interpret it as resulting from the partner's characteristic selfishness or the stresses of chronic illness.

Predictable and understandable changes, however, are different from those that are neither predictable nor understandable in one crucial respect—in the first case, new information can be assimilated into existing knowledge but in the latter case, it cannot. Bookkeeping does not work here because the new information does not fit what is already on the books. Conversion does not work because there is no available plausible belief system to convert to. The dilemma, then, is to construct a new knowledge structure that can accommodate the new, surprising information.

Schema Change Processes

To explain how this happens, we turn to a second line of research that deals with the processes that underlie changes in knowledge structures. This work often comes under the heading of schema inconsistency or schema + tag (i.e., the schema is tagged with information that might modify it). Researchers have investigated how we pay attention to inconsistent information, match it to the appropriate schema, remember it, and tag the schema with it. A number of factors have been found to affect this process including amount of inconsistent information, ambiguity of the information, and processing load (see Planalp, 1987).

But how is inconsistent information processed when no existing knowledge structure presents itself as is an obvious candidate to tag and modify? Miller and Read (1991) and Read and Collins (1992), following Abelson and Lalljee (1988; Lalljee & Abelson, 1983) and Thagard (1989, 1992), provided a plausible account of how this process might work. First, the new information being processed activates related knowledge through spread of activation. Then, the most coherent set of modes is chosen as an explanation, based on criteria such as parsimony, breadth, contradiction, and analogy. That is, all other things being equal, the preferred explanation is the one that is simplest, most encompassing, has the fewest inconsistencies, and is most analogous to other explanations. For example, if you were trying to explain why your friend has not called for several days, you would prefer an explanation that is simple (her phone is broken), that explains the broadest range of events (it explains why Jane went over there last night and why you get that weird tone when you call), that has no inconsistencies (she didn't call Jane either), and that is analogous to other experiences (it's like that time your car broke down and people got really upset because you missed appointments).

It should be apparent from this example that explanatory coherence theories and attribution theories are closely related (attribution theories being one class of explanatory coherence theories). In fact, our original formulations of this work was framed in terms of attribution theory (Planalp & Rivers, 1988). But we have turned to explanatory coherence theory for several reasons. First, attribution logic is too specialized a system, confined to causal attributions but otherwise being relatively autonomous in terms of other cognitive structures and processes. Thagard's theory of explanatory coherence, on the other hand, operates within the by-now-standard social-cognitive framework of knowledge structures and cognitive processes. Second, Leddo and Abelson (1986) argued that the kinds of explanations people ordinarily give for events are more concrete than the abstract categories or dimensions central to the standard attributional account such as person and situation. Such concrete attributions often do not fit neatly into "person" or "situation" categories and fitting them along attributional dimensions may not fully capture their specific practical significance. We say that Laura didn't call because her phone was broken (not because of the situation) or that her phone was broken and she lives too far from her closest neighbor and she never really promised she'd call anyway. Third, Leddo and Abelson argued that we must use our knowledge to be able to separate useful and plausible explanations from useless or far-fetched alternatives. We don't usually consider possibilities such as Laura not calling because her hand didn't pick up the receiver (a useless explanation) or because her dog ate the phone (a far-fetched one, except, perhaps, for those of us who have listened to students' excuses for late term papers for some years). Attribution theory would be swamped by such choices but knowledge structures handle them easily.

There are also several advantages that the explanatory coherence model of knowledge change has over the schema + tag notion. First, picking a knowledge structure is not a multiple-choice test. One does not have to choose among several prepackaged but inadequate alternatives; instead a better one can be constructed. Second, one is not limited to considering preexisting, coherent knowledge structures. Activation can spread to various fragments and previously disconnected concepts that can then be brought together in unique ways. Third, one is in a position, not just to modify existing knowledge, but to come up with a completely different framework that explains the existing knowledge and the new, previously inconsistent information, in a coherent way. Because of these three properties, this model is able to deal with creative interpretations of puzzling data and change by conversion much better than the schema + tag model can.

Read and Collins (1992) suggested that we need to gather more open-ended data to better understand how people develop explanations for behavior. In line with their recommendation, we have turned to our earlier research on events that challenge people's beliefs about close relationships in order to examine more closely respondent's accounts of how they came to understand those events and how their beliefs had changed.

DESCRIPTIONS OF THE DATA

Our analysis is grounded in research on events that increased people's uncertainty about their close relationships or their partners. We asked respondents to report on "incidents in which you learn something about a person that makes you feel like you know the person or understand your relationship with him or her less well than you thought you did" (in other words, events that made them question the nature of their relationships). In order to avoid a negative bias, they were given one positive and one negative example of such events. Respondents filled out one seven-page questionnaire with some open- and some closed-ended questions and an additional two-page follow-up questionnaire. Quantitative analyses of two data sets have been reported earlier (Planalp & Honeycutt, 1985; Planalp et al., 1988) and detailed descriptions of respondents and methods can be found there. Here, we rely on qualitative analyses of the second data set (76 cases), which reveal issues and subtleties not revealed in the quantitative data. To illustrate the type of information gathered, we describe one case in depth. A brief description of all 76 cases is provided in the appendix.

Case 47

This was an opposite-sex friendship between people who had known each other for a year. The respondent (female) indicated that the relationship was not very important in her life (2 on 9-point scale) and that before the event occurred she was able to predict her friend's behavior moderately well (5 of 9) and his attitudes well (7 of 9).

She describes the event as follows: "George and I are friends and we have a lot of classes together. We have a lot of mutual friends, so we see each other a lot, especially on weekends. I always thought we got along good together, but after today I wonder if maybe he is only being my friend so he can copy homework assignments from me. Ordinarily, I'd gladly give a friend some help, but lately the only time he calls is to copy homework. Today it happened again, and I finally realized that maybe he's just using our friendship to get his homework."

In response to a question concerning whether anything led up to the event, she states, "Lately all we talk about is school and homework assignments, where before we'd usually talk about other things," and that she knew this was the case at the time. She thought her beliefs were challenged because she misinterpreted earlier information about her partner or their relationship (thought they were just friends) and that her partner would say that she made assumptions that turned out to be wrong, but would have been made by anyone.

Her emotional reaction was moderately strong (7 of 9) and negative (2 of 9). The event did not change her beliefs about herself (1 of 9) but changed her beliefs about her partner a great deal (9 of 9). After the event occurred, she was more confident than before about her ability to predict how her partner would behave ("I think this will happen again, unless I confront him") and indicated she could not answer the question about predicting attitudes ("Since I just realized today, I can't answer this"). A number of beliefs about the relationship were affected very strongly, including closeness (9 of 9), companionship (9), fairness (9), trust (9), honesty (8), and uniqueness (8; "I feel that he probably does this to other friends, who are also friends of mine"). Emotional involvement and duties/responsibilities were affected to a moderate degree (6). Other beliefs were affected very little, including beliefs about providing support (2 of 9), freedom/autonomy (2), and confiding (1; "never confided in him").

The respondent did not talk or argue over the issue with her partner, but avoided the issue, talked around it ("the last time he asked me for homework, I told him I didn't have it") and avoided the person ("I'm not sure how I'll act, but I'll probably avoid him until he proves to me that he is my friend without needing me only for my homework"). The respondent also talked to others a lot (9 of 9; "I told my roommates, who are also friend of his, they thought he is just a user and they were glad that I didn't give him the homework''). She thought that she and her friend became less close as a result of the event and she was much less confident that their relationship would continue (1 of 9) as a result.

After the event was over, she felt completely unable to predict her partner's behavior and attitudes (1 of 9). She states that "A lot of things have happened since I filled out the first form. After spring break this person did not come back to school. His parents, girlfriend, and best friend had no clue as to where he was. We found out about 2 weeks later that he moved to Hawaii. I guess he was doing poorly in school, if I would have known this I probably wouldn't have been so angry when he asked for my help. It seems that he was asking a lot of people and not many knew how serious his problems were." She states that if she had it to do over again "I would have gladly given him my homework and asked if there was any way I could have helped him out."

Events such as these provide an unusual and important (although limited) basis for theorizing about changing knowledge of relationships. The overwhelming majority of studies dealing with knowledge change have been done under tightly controlled conditions in the laboratory, using experimenter-generated information that is very simple and brief. By controlling exactly what the subjects know and report, this approach has the power to distinguish which factors are influential, to address factors that operate below the level of conscious awareness, and to address precise questions. Conversely, the approach we have taken here, which relies on respondents' own reports of real incidents, helps us learn more about the broad range of factors that influenced our respondents, what factors they considered without being prompted by an experimenter, and what information they had, were confronted with, and consciously sought out when trying to come to terms with their experiences.

To determine what factors were most important in producing changes in knowledge, we turned first to the existing literature and identified a number of factors that had been found to influence schema change. Then we discussed each case in depth and came to agreement on whether and how each factor was influential in these data. A discussion of each of those factors and our conclusions about its importance can be found in Planalp and Rivers (1988).

In general, we concluded that factors related to the schema + tag model were relatively inconsequential but that processes involved in seeking a satisfactory explanation for the surprising event dominated respondents' thinking. In other words, respondents did not seem to keep adding qualifications to their existing knowledge; instead they sought new explanations that could explain the surprising events in ways that were more satisfactory. Moreover, their explanation-seeking activities were more wide-ranging, sophisticated and complex than we had expected.

EXPLANATORY PROCESSES

Because our questions had not been developed initially to obtain data specifically about explanation-seeking, our findings were less tidy than we might have wished. Some respondents never revealed any cognitive activity at all, perhaps because none occurred or perhaps because they did not see it as part of the event. One type of event in particular seemed to produce little causal analysis—events that were bids for a different kind of relationship, such as a romantic partner telling the respondent he loved her (Case 21), an opposite-sex friend raising the issue of "fooling around" (Case 57), and one person's opportunity to go to Vienna leading her and her boyfriend to reflect on the nature of their relationship (Case 03). We can only speculate about why this type of event did not foster concerns for explanation. Perhaps they were not as unexpected as other types of events, not as negative, or perhaps bids for greater involvement in a relationship are simply taken at face value, and no ulterior motives are sought.

Other respondents indicated that explanation-seeking occurred but said little more about it. Some respondents were quite explicit regarding the nature of their musings as they pondered the locus of causality (the self, other, relationship, situation, discussed later), whereas others simply mentioned that they thought about the event and its meaning but revealed little about the nature of those thoughts. Finally, some respondents were entirely candid about the nature of their explanations, clearly assigned responsibility, and provided useful insights into the complex operations of their minds.

What Prompts Explanation-Seeking?

Violation of Expectations. Consistent with the literature reviewed earlier, explanation-seeking was typically instigated by the violation of expectations derived from knowledge structures, or schemas about people and relationships. For instance, in Case 5, the female respondent reported that her female roommate "couldn't talk with me about [her mother's cancer]," in spite of the importance of their friendship. This was clearly a violation of her expectation of deep self-disclosure in close friendships.

Expectations for appropriate behavior are also built into schemas created about a specific partner and one's relationship with him or her based on prior experience. A good example is Case 69. The female respondent reported that her friend was a fitness fanatic who did not smoke, and so when he suddenly smoked half a pack of cigarettes, she was compelled to seek an explanation for his behavior: He was seeking attention. Thus, when people we know behave in an uncharacteristic manner, explanatory processing is triggered.

One interesting type of triggering device was the absence of an expected event, such as when someone failed to call, failed to pay attention, failed to reveal information, or in some manner was guilty of the sin of omission. Lalljee and Abelson (1983) called these *contrastive* attributions, where the focus is on why someone did not do such-and-such. One general type of absence—sudden loss of contact or closeness—included about 10% of all events in our two studies (4%, Planalp & Honeycutt, 1985; 14%, Planalp et al., 1988).

Negative Events. Fletcher and Fitness (1993) stated that existing research indicates that attributions are most likely to be elicited when events are unexpected and negative. All the events we studied were unexpected (because that is what we asked for), most were negative, but some were positive. Almost all of the positive events involved a change from friendship to a romantic relationship. Usually these events were unambiguous and welcomed, and the resultant explanations were determined in a straightforward manner: Her kiss indicates sexual attraction, so this is a bid to redefine our relationship. This finding supports the conclusion that positive events do not elicit much attributional processing.

In at least two instances, however, the positive outcome was accompanied by more elaborate processing. In Case 40, the behaviors of the respondent's friend led her to believe that her partner wanted a romantic relationship, but her uncertainty is displayed in her confusion about his feelings for her. Similar confusion about how to interpret the other's actions was evident in our sole positive outcome case which didn't involve a romantic relationship (Case 32). In this instance, a shift from enemies to friends was initially met with some suspicion on the part of our respondent, who presumably entertained some negative attributions prior to deciding that O's behavior was motivated by a genuine desire for friendship.

Important Relationships. Important relationships were also more likely to induce explanation-seeking, although there were exceptions. Consistent with Weary, Stanley, and Harvey's (1989) conclusions, in relationships of little importance (e.g., Case 43), unexpected or undesirable events may have increased uncertainty about the relationship but they were often met with a "Who cares? Not me," approach. One plausible explanation is people do not need to predict future events in superficial or low priority relationships, because continued contact is unlikely.

Interestingly, there were many cases involving important relationships where speculation about the causality of an event was notably absent. For example, in Case 64, the respondent interpreted her roommate's negative behavior as "She's mad at me," and, even though this was an important relationship, she went no further in trying to understand the event. Similarly, the respondent in Case 59 speculated that "something more may be developing" as a response to his female friend's increased self-disclosure, but he did not appear to entertain additional explanations.

Nature of the Data

Amount and Patterning of Data. In our study, the sheer number of events that were inconsistent with previous knowledge seemed to have almost no direct bearing on the likelihood of triggering explanatory processing. While explanatory processes were provoked by recurring events (such as repeatedly asking for homework), many others were provoked by single events or moments of reflection (such as anticipating one person going overseas). Moreover, the distinction between single and multiple events was not always clear; often it was difficult to separate events from the stream of ongoing behavior. For instance, in Case 5, the respondent was unsettled by the fact that her friend and roommate failed to confide in her about the roommate's dying mother; rather, the roommate confided in another person with whom she was less close. It is unclear to us whether this is one event (roommate's unusual choice of confidante) or two events (failure to confide in the respondent coupled with opening up to another).

To further complicate matters, multiple events may not have been recognized until late in the sequence. Respondents noted that there were often hints that the event was coming but that they usually recognized them as such only in hindsight (see Planalp et al., 1988). For example, one respondent (Case 06) "ended up heavily kissing" his opposite-sex friend and noticed only afterward that the event had been preceded by "mutual gazes, feeling awkward afterward." This and other examples like it lie in the gray area between single and multiple events. In such cases, it is apparent that processing is activated by the single event, but processing quickly calls to mind and incorporates previously unacknowledged events (consistent with the findings of Read & Cesa, 1991).

When there were multiple events that provoked processing, this patterning of the data was often very clearly noted by respondents and seemed to have played an important role in explanation-seeking. This is consistent with Thagard's (1989, 1992) claim that explanations will be preferred if they account for a broad range of similar instances (criteria of explanatory breadth and analogy). Sometimes the event itself was an ongoing pattern, such as when two long-term friends had trouble finding things in common throughout a weekend visit (Case 58), when a respondent's opposite-sex friend hung up the phone several times (Case 27), and when an opposite-sex friend started "disclosing deeply and on a regular basis"(Case 59).

Another type of patterning was the co-occurrence of events, as would be predicted by attribution theory (Kelley, 1967). For example, Respondent 13 reported the following incident.

> My very good friend and roommate just became president of our sorority which she very much deserved. My group of friends was very happy for her. Since her election she has been snapping and telling everybody what to do. Since I am a slob and keep the room messy our room is not too clean. We got in an argument because she yelled at me to clean the room. Obviously, she thinks she can tell me what to do. She never cared before how the room looked and I think her new position has made her power-hungry which is something I would have never expected from her.

Respondent 68 also noted the co-occurrence between changes in her friend's morals and the degree of contact she had with her boyfriend, and attributed the change to the boyfriend's influence.

The most interesting examples of patterning involved more than one source of information, such as directly observed behavior combined with direct or indirect communication. For example, one woman heard through a mutual friend that her same-sex friend thought she was being insincere and hypocritical and also noticed that her friend "goes out of her way to do things without me then make sure I know what a good time she had" (Case 41). Another instance (Case 67) involved an opposite-sex friend who "has not been his 'usual' self—we don't talk, or when I call or see him, he is 'too busy studying, so be quiet.' We also have two classes together and always sat together, now he sits two rows away. Last night I asked him what was up— he replied that being 'friendly and communicative took too much energy.'" Patterns such as these may provide especially strong bases for drawing relational implications because they are based on naive triangulation across different sources of information.

Ambiguity and Deniability of Data. Some events provide more solid bases than other events for questioning expectations and for constructing alternative explanations, as pointed out in several of the commentaries on Thagard's (1989) model. Nonverbal cues, in particular, are often more ambiguous and easier to deny than are verbal cues (Burgoon & Saine, 1978; Leathers, 1976), making for shakier grounds for explanation. For example, someone can more easily deny that eye contact occurred at all or argue that it was friendly, not flirtatious, than she can deny or re-interpret verbal statements.

The events that led our respondents to question their beliefs about relationships varied in terms of how deniable or ambiguous they were. In some cases, a deniable act was committed which precipitated the questioning process. For example, the respondent in Case 14, recently reunited with his girlfriend, was confronted with explaining why she pulled away when he kissed her. She could have claimed that she did not pull away, was just getting more comfortable, was catching her breath, and so on. In other cases, events that were expected did not occur. These were especially untrustworthy because one cannot even be sure that the expected behavior didn't occur, much less what its absence means.

With the exception of omissions of behavior, the deniability and ambiguity of nonverbal behavior did not seem to influence explanatory processes in any major way. Some events were precipitated by observations that were denied directly by the partner. One such incident was Case 54, in which the respondent stated "I just was feeling that he [romantic partner] didn't want to make time for me. I felt he now had more important things to do and wanted more freedom." She indicated that her partner "would say nothing was wrong and that I let my imagination run away with me."

In some instances, however, the event was undeniable, and everyone involved agreed on what it meant for the relationship (e.g., kissing opposite-sex friend or romantic partner proposing; Cases 30 and 43). In the middle were cases in which the event itself could be verified easily, but the implications it had for the relationship were relatively open to interpretation. For example, in Case 40, the respondent stated the following:

> Recently Brent [opposite-sex friend] and I had been spending more time together and I got this vague impression that he wanted to be more than "just friends," but I'm still not sure. Last night (3/23) we went to a formal, and tonight we went dancing—our first "dates." Tonight he even ventured so far as to put his arm around me and (tentatively) hold my hand. Now, I am confused about how he feels about me.

Later she reported "I now feel that I may have misinterpreted his actions." Thus, it seemed that even though concrete confirmable events were often cited as the impetus for changes in beliefs, interpretations of those events as relevant to the relationship were often subject to challenge.

However, verbal messages can be subject to varying interpretations as well, and there were many instances where explanations were prompted by another's verbal communication. Some of these, such as Case 74 in which a relational partner hinted at a long-term relationship unwanted by the respondent, were as ambiguous as nonverbal behavior. However, even those verbal behaviors that were ostensibly direct and clear often prompted explanatory processing. Occasionally, these events precipitated a review of past events, seeking other forms of data to confirm the respondent's explanation. For instance, Respondent 24 indicated she was shocked when a male friend revealed he thought he was falling in love with her, but later reflection suggested that there were clues to his feelings that she had ignored.

Such events also often led to consultation with others, in an attempt to ratify the verbal message (as in Case 34 where the respondent consulted with another friend to confirm the first friend's revelation of illegal behavior) or to clarify one's own feelings about the event (Case 9).

Actively Gathering Data and Arriving at Explanations

As relationships increased in importance and/or as uncertainty increased, individuals seemed to assume a more and more active role in the entire interpretive process, from data gathering to hypothesis testing.

Extensive Gathering of Data. Respondents did not simply work with the information at hand; they often talked to their partners, conferred with their friends, or reflected on almost forgotten past events. We were surprised by the extent to which respondents engaged in detective work to augment the data they had already acquired. Passive strategies, dominated by a wait-and-see approach, occurred rarely, typically in less intense relationships. Active uncertainty-reducing strategies, involving the questioning of others, were common. Some respondents shared their dilemmas with others to verify their own perceptions, whereas others asked third parties about their experiences with the individual in question. Interactive strategies, such as direct confrontation of the partner, were also frequent, particularly when the nature of the relationship was at issue.

Hypothesis Testing. Consider the case of the young man in event Case 9. Reunited for the third time with his girlfriend, he finds her falling into old patterns of behavior, fault finding, and "trying to lay heavy guilt trips." Asked if there were other things he did to deal with the situation, he noted that "I would try to test my theory by rejecting her and letting her come back to me." Although Respondent 9 is the only one to report hypothesis testing explicitly, many of our respondents behaved in ways suggesting that their search for understanding was guided by presuppositions or hypotheses that they were investigating.

Types of Data Sought. Respondents sought out the kinds of data that both Kelley and Thagard would expect them to seek. Two of the dimensions from Kelley's (1971) covariation model seemed most salient: consistency and distinctiveness. Thagard's principles of acceptability (explanatory breadth) and contradiction would lead people to the same information.

Much of the respondents' retrospective examination of prior behavior indicated a search for *consistency*. The question, "Did anything lead up to this event?" was particularly revealing. Respondent 24 was surprised to discover that an opposite-sex friend had a crush on her; her own data were fairly sparse (upon reflection she recalled that they had been "running into each other more") but consultation with a friend revealed that her friend's behavior had been consistent with a romantic interpretation for some time. In addition to acquiring additional information, respondents frequently engaged in a re-evaluation of earlier events for clues that would illuminate the uncertain situation they were in. Not surprisingly, respondents often found clues they had previously ignored or they discovered that earlier behavior had interpretations they had not initially considered.

Respondents also sought *distinctiveness* information by conferring with friends. In Case 47 (described earlier), the respondent discovered that the friend who had been borrowing her homework for some time (high consistency) had been borrowing from others as well (low distinctiveness). Confirming whether the respondents' own experience was corroborated by others seemed to be one of the larger motivating forces behind talking with them.

There was less indication in our data of a search for consensus information (whether others engage in similar behavior). This was probably because our respondents knew very well that most people did not behave like the partner—that was why the event made them uncertain in the first place. In fact, rather than gathering data to determine whether others in similar situations behaved alike, the respondents were more likely to question their definition of the relationship. For example, in Case 26, the respondent and her boyfriend were out with another couple, she kissed the man and her boyfriend kissed the woman, but she never questioned whether others in similar circumstances did the same thing. For her there was no question that there was low consensus for their behavior. Thus, for a time, the respondent considered whether she actually liked the man she had been kissing (changing the nature of the relationship she had with him from friend to possible romantic partner), or whether their actions were the consequence of too much to drink.

Multiple Explanations and the Domino Effect. In some instances, one uncertainty-increasing event would provoke several explanations or attributions, often varying in their locus of causality (corroborating Leddo & Abelson's, 1986, argument). For instance, in Case 4 when the respondent's boyfriend was 5 hours late, she provided both an other-based explanation ("He is easy going, laid back") and a relationship-focused one (concern that the relationship was changing). Respondent 58 experienced a struggle to communicate and find things in common with an old friend. She entertained two explanations simultaneously—that the friend always had been superficial and that people grow apart and change. Respondent 41 first attributed her roommate's distance to their specific relationship, then later realized "she never lets herself get close to anyone."

A unique feature of this kind of explanatory process was what we have termed the *domino effect*. There were several instances in which a respondent would observe an event and choose an explanation; this explanation would then raise other questions, necessitating more explanation and/or data gathering, and thus a second and perhaps a third explanation would be made. For instance, in Case 9, the respondent explained his dating partner's behavior as "she's hurting me on purpose." This led him to believe that she was on a power trip, and that she wanted this relationship in order "to have someone whose emotions she could control."

Considering Alternative Explanations. Cognitive processing did not necessarily end once an explanation (or explanations) was selected. Although some of the continued processing focused on forming an explanation for the previous explanation (the domino effect), others simply portrayed the evolution of thought that occurred as the respondent's feelings altered, as new data came to light, or as discussion with others opened up new avenues for contemplation. For instance, Respondent 27's initial explanation for his romantic partner's avoidance was highly unflattering: "She doesn't like me." In a discussion with his brother, he entertained other explanations: "She came home drunk," "She spent the night with another man," "She's hiding something." These explanations then converged with his original one to become "She doesn't like me as much as I thought and she's inconsiderate." In another instance, Case 37, the respondent's same-sex friend broke a long-standing tradition of checking in when she came back to town. Initially, the respondent believed that her friend thought the relationship was one-sided, leading her to feel that her friend was petty. After additional reflection, however, she decided that her friend needed lots of reassurance in this relationship (her friendship with the respondent) because the rest of her life was such a problem.

Changes in Explanations Over Time. Miller and Porter (1980) found that as time passed, people were more likely to see both their own and others' behavior as more strongly guided by situational influences. In our data, explanations did change, but not necessarily toward more situational explanations. There were several cases in which the respondent later assumed responsibility for negative consequences, although tempered with face-saving qualifications (Case 12). Respondent 60 reported that "I've accepted he doesn't conform exactly to my expectations or knowledge of him" and, along the same lines, Respondent 55 reported that, "Our relationship is fitting to my attitudes and feelings now; at the time of the incident I was going through a diff. stage." More often, however, changes were in the direction of attributing more responsibility for the incident to the partner and less to the self. For instance, respondent 48 wrote, "I began to understand that it was just his style to be lax." Respondent 41 wrote "I realize she never lets herself get close to anyone. Likes people who look up to her for friends not a person on a mutual level," and Respondent 18 reported, "I feel that it wasn't such a big deal, however it changed my attitude now about him because I view his actions now as immature whereas before I thought his actions were because of me."

Miller and Porter thought that attributions shifted over time toward situations because people felt less need to be in control and were willing to believe that the situations rather than their own actions may have caused the event. Although we found little evidence that attributions became more situational, we did find suggestions that respondents may have felt less need to be in control because the event seemed less important than it had been originally. Respondents wrote, "I feel more relaxed about it" (70), "It was not a big deal—he was more hurt than I was" (63), and "I don't feel threatened so much anymore" (36). In other cases, the relationship became less important, making the incident less important as a result. Two examples are Respondent 11: "It's been a long time and I haven't talk to him in 3 mths. so I basically got on w/my life and tried not to think of him" and Respondent 49: "Because I don't interact that much with him anymore, I really don't think about it. Hence, I am not as disturbed when I do see him."

In several other cases, explanations changed because of intervening events, including discussions between partners, continued interactions, and other events that provided additional information. Examples of discussion are Respondent 73: "We've resolved a lot of the conflict. She feels I like her less, but I'm trying to minimize her uncertainty. I try to be more considerate. I listen to what she says," Respondent 54: "After the events were discussed, they were also agreed upon. We worked out the problems on both occasions," and Respondent 10: "Found out more about why we weren't getting together by finally talking to her about it. Now I understand more than I did before." Examples of continued interactions are Respondent 42: "Our relationship is fairly strong now & the event seems more irrelevant now than it did at the time & he has proven our friendship in several ways" and "Yes, because now that we have been through more in 3 months, I think I am better able to understand him." Finally, in Case 47 (described earlier), the respondent acquired further information about the partner that gave her a different perspective on the problem. She learned that the other person had moved to Hawaii and realized that his problems were more serious than she had thought.

It is also worth noting that many unexpected events did not lead to complex explanatory processes. Some of these events involved communication or behavior that was relatively closed to different interpretations, and hence the intricate data collecting, hypothesis testing, and speculation about alternative explanations, which is the focus of this section did not occur.

Content of the Explanations

In the preceding sections, we considered what prompted our respondents to seek explanations, what kinds of data they considered, and how they gathered data and searched for explanations. Next we consider the content of their explanations. For our respondents, two issues addressed in the attribution literature appeared to be particularly critical: locus and responsibility. In everyday language, they wanted to determine who or what was to blame for negative events. As noted earlier, they seemed to be less concerned with who or what deserved credit for positive events.

Locus. Locus refers to the location of the cause of an event: "The *devil* made me do it," "*I'm* just smart," "*He* hates *me*," and so forth. Kelley's (1967) original work suggested two possible loci for attributional causes: internal, referring to factors within the individual (either in a spatial sense or in the sense of what is controllable); and external, referring to factors residing outside the individual (or his or her control). However, subsequent work, especially by those studying close relationships, has noted the inherent problems with this approach and has elaborated upon these two factors (Fincham, 1985; Fletcher & Fincham, 1991). People involved in close relationships, for example, make attributions not only to the self ("I was in a bad mood") and the partner ("She has a lousy sense of humor"), but also to the relationship itself ("We've been seeing too much of each other") These are termed *interpersonal attributions* by Newman (1981).

Most of the attributions in our study fell into one of these four basic types: *self*, *other*, *interpersonal*, and *situational*. *Self* attributions assigned causality to the respondent. For instance, in Case 62, the respondent states "I distanced him," as an explanation for his fraternity brother assigning him a "bad little sister." Examples of attributions to the *other* person were attributing phone calls to "using our friendship to get his homework" (Case 47 cited earlier) and describing a romantic partner as "acting very immaturely, almost like a spoiled brat who cries when you take away a lollipop" (Case 23). Examples of *interpersonal* attributions were "I knew then that she didn't like me as much as I thought and was led to believe she did" (Case 56) and attributing the partner's smoking to "using this as an attention getter since I had been 'neglecting' him" (Case 69). Examples of *situational* attributions were attributing kissing opposite-sex friends to being very drunk and it being "just a crazy moment that got silly" (Case 26) or attributing a betrayal of confidence to another person who "twisted her arm to tell him" (Case 51).

The examples here are consistent with attribution theory but they also corroborate Leddo and Abelson's argument that the general categories of attribution theory are too abstract to capture the concrete explanations that people ordinarily give. Respondents said the event was caused by specific actions, attributes or motivations of the self or partner (my distancing behavior, her immaturity), specific situational influences (the alcohol), or specific aspects of the relationship (failure of liking, too much neglect). The problem with attribution theory is that it cannot predict or deal with these causes in terms of their specific content. Any theory that fails in this way must be regarded as limited in its explanatory power and depth.

Assigning an appropriate locus of attribution is a critical step in changing knowledge structures because it determines what structures must be changed. For example, one respondent entertained two interpretations for her difficulties with a long-term friend—that the two had never been similar (an interpersonal attribution) and that her friend had always been shallow (a partner attribution). Whether the attribution is made to specific qualities of the relationship, the friend, or both has important implications for future action and so must be encoded as a part of relationship or partner knowledge.

Responsibility. Determining the locus of causality, however, is not sufficient to assign responsibility. Saying that you, I, or we together caused something to happen does not imply in itself that you, I or we were responsible for it happening. The distinction between causality and responsibility is a critical one in the study of close relationships. Based on an extensive review, Fincham and Jaspars (1980) offered some "common sense" notions of the two, and we adopt these for our purposes here. For the naive actor, the essential ingredient for responsibility is accountability. Responsibility assumes the right to blame or praise the actor, to hold the actor accountable for the consequences of his or her actions.

The dilemma acknowledged with Fincham and Jaspars' frustration in delineating the distinction between causality and responsibility was encountered in our attempts to categorize our data. Although some events were clearly of one type or another, others were more elusive. It was necessary to rely on the language used by respondents to identify inferences about intentions, and respondents were not always straightforward. For example, In Case 20, the respondent's same-sex friend betrayed a confidence, and the attribution was "He's a jerk." It is not clear whether being a jerk is a description of the friend, the reason (or cause) for his betraying a confidence, or a trait for which the friend bears responsibility. In Case 26, our respondent speculated that drinking caused her and her boyfriend to engage in kissing the opposite-sex member of the couple they were with. It is not clear whether she thinks that they are responsible for the drinking, despite the drinking, or if "the beer made them do it."

In other cases, it is easier to infer that responsibility attributions were probably made. For example, the respondent in Case 29 concluded that his dating partner, who was great in person but uncommunicative on the phone, was "playing mind games." In Case 33, the respondent's same-sex friend obtained answers to a test and didn't share them with the respondent; his final attribution was "He was cut-throating." Respondents sometimes began with other kinds of attributions but often eventually moved to those that shifted some form of culpability, causality or blame, to the partner.

In any case, responsibility appeared to be salient to our respondents as a way of fully coming to terms with the event. Establishing responsibility (or lack thereof) serves several important social functions. First, people may save or lose face depending on whether they are held responsible for events. For example, it makes someone look better if you determine that events beyond his control made him ask for your homework than if you determine that he was trying to take advantage of you. Second, assigning responsibility may help people determine how much control they have in the situation For example, if I was responsible for leading you on, I should be able to prevent this happening in the future. Finally, rewards or punishment can be meted out accordingly (thus the importance of responsibility attributions in the law). If your partner was responsible for a negative event, he or she should make restitution; if you were, you should. Thus, determining responsibility makes it possible not only to settle events in one's own mind, but also to settle the score in the social world.

IMPLICATIONS FOR MODELS OF RELATIONSHIP SCHEMA CHANGE

Now we deal with what our reports of changes in relationships say about existing theories and models. The model we began with, schema + tag, was supported by our data only in that it predicts that inconsistencies with knowledge structures will be noticed, remembered, and processed in greater depth. Schema + tag says very little, however, about where you get the schema in the first place, or about the extensive cognitive processing involved in dealing with all the tagged information. Our data indicate that when expectations are violated and when no immediate alternative explanation is available, the tag may force you to look for a new schema altogether (a case of the tag wagging the dog). This finding goes well beyond the schema + tag model.

Attribution theory was useful for understanding what instigates searches for explanations (violations of expectations), what types of information will be used (consistency and distinctiveness), and the general loci to which causality or responsibility is assigned (self, other, relationship, situation). Although the types of explanations that our respondents gave fit into these general categories, their explanations were more concrete and grounded in more specific knowledge of the self, other, relationship or situation. Such knowledge falls outside the purview of current attribution theory.

The *explanatory coherence* model advanced by Miller and Read (1991), Read and Collins (1992), and Thagard (1989, 1992) seemed to capture our respondents' reports more completely and incorporates many of the attributes of the schema + tag model and attribution theory (albeit in a vague way). Like the schema + tag model, explanatory coherence is based on trying to get everything to fit into one schema or explanatory framework. Like attribution theory, explanatory coherence is a way of modeling the extensive cognitive work that goes into answering the "why" question.

Both attribution theory and explanatory coherence theory are able to explain the key process of assigning causality or responsibility to a certain locus, the most common loci being oneself, one's partner, the relationship or the situation. Unlike attribution theory, explanatory coherence theory is able to deal with the need to completely rethink what knowledge structure is relevant, to consider several alternative explanations, to be continually open to new incoming information, and to give the kinds of specific and multifaceted explanations that our respondents believed were warranted.

Explanatory coherence is not without its own limits, of course. If Thagard's computer model were a homunculus (or homuncula) it could not consciously control its thought processes, go back and reinterpret the data in light of a new explanation, trace the implications of one explanation for another, test hypotheses, go ask a friend whether an explanation sounds reasonable, or say "Who cares? Not me." To be complete, it must be capable of doing these things, because our respondents were.

One major advantage of Thagard's model is that it interfaces beautifully with existing theories of relationship knowledge structures, specifically *relational schemas*. Relational schemas are coherent subsets of knowledge about a particular domain—in this case about a specific relationship. Explanatory processes are triggered when a schema that has worked well in the past to understand events in a relationship no longer works easily. Then a much wider range of knowledge must be scanned to come up with a more adequate explanation. That explanation, then, can be used to update, modify or sometimes completely replace the original schema.

Because explanatory coherence must be used in combination with relationship knowledge (schemas) when dealing with close relationships, we must also ask what our findings say about theories of relational (or interpersonal) schemas in their various forms (for review, see Baldwin, 1992, but also Horowitz, 1991; Planalp, 1985; Safran, 1990a, 1990b, to name only some). Clearly, extensive knowledge about oneself, one's partner, and one's relationship with the partner is needed. What our data and interpretations call into question, however, is whether we need to separate knowledge of relationships (relational schemas) from all the other knowledge that might be needed to construct an explanation. We might be better served to posit a richly interwoven network of knowledge (including knowledge of self, other, the relationship, and situations) that is available for explaining events and can be used to construct new explanations when needed. Clearly, if relational schemas have any boundaries at all, they are extremely permeable and the connections between relational schemas and other knowledge structures are so dense that it may be difficult to draw any meaningful boundary. That is not to say that we should give up efforts to understand how people structure and use their knowledge of personal relationships, but rather that such efforts must ultimately be embedded within general theories of knowledge and cognitive processes.

Another important lesson we have learned from our data is that relational schemas are far from static. Because our data are biased toward change, we cannot draw any conclusions about the overall stability or fluidity of relational schemas, but what is clear is that they do change in response to inconsistent information. Schema theorists have always known that schemas must be capable of incorporating incoming information (assimilation) and of changing in response to incoming information (accommodation; Planalp, 1987), but the assimilation side of the coin has received much more research attention than has accommodation. Unless we are to be stuck with knowledge that makes us stupid because it is unresponsive to new information, we need to understand accommodation better. Again, to do this, we must develop processing models (such as Thagard's) which keep knowledge structures in touch with reality and draw on the vast explanatory resources that humans have.

What none of the models of relational schemas or knowledge structures deal with effectively is the role of consciousness. Clearly, most of our respondents were coming to terms with challenges to beliefs about their relationships by consciously thinking about them, at least some of the time. Yet none of the models of relational schemas or processes requires conscious thought at all. Schemas can be accessed, used to interpret interactions, tagged, updated, and reworked automatically, without conscious thinking. So why think in a self-conscious and explicit form? Our answer to that question is speculative, but a clue may lie in the active information seeking and hypothesis testing that we observed. Consciousness may coordinate cognitive processes that operate relatively automatically (although we may be aware of them to some extent) with processes that control action and will. For example, if Bill is aware that Sadie's infidelity may be because he has neglected her, he can choose to pay more attention to her. If that doesn't work, he can postulate a new explanation that she simply has a roving eye and leave her. Better yet, consciousness makes it possible for him to talk to Sadie or to his best friend to see if he can gather any new information or come up with even a more plausible explanation. This dramatically increases his power to come to terms with the event.

AFTERWORD: A NOTE ON THE INTUITIVE SCIENTIST

The metaphor that dominates most of the theories from which we have drawn (e.g., attribution theory and theories of cognition) is the "intuitive scientist." In many ways, our respondents did act like intuitive scientists. They observed events, were alerted to anomalies in their implicit theories, searched for plausible explanations, tested possibilities by gathering more evidence, and discussed their explanations with others. But their roles did not stop with those of the scientist; instead, they used their knowledge in ways that we would assign to other professions. They considered who was responsible for the events they observed and so functioned as intuitive lawyers. They considered the effects of the event on their relationships (whether good or bad), whether something could be done to make the relationship better, and, if not, whether to leave. So they acted like intuitive marriage counselors or therapists. They also put together a coherent account of the event for us (the researchers) and possibly for their friends as well, and so acted as intuitive storytellers. They were intuitive scientists, indeed, but they did not stay in the ivory tower. They also engaged the difficult practical problems of life.

APPENDIX: BRIEF DESCRIPTION OF CASES

Key: S = Self (person filling out questionnaire), P = Partner, SSF = Same-Sex Friend, OSF = Opposite-Sex Friend, RP = Romantic Partner, DP = Dating Partner.

01: OSF became RP.
02: SSF became extremely mad and rude when woken up early.
03: RP indicated desire for commitment to future together.
04: RP arrived 5 hours later than expected.
05: SSF did not talk about mother becoming gravely ill.
06: OSF wanted romantic relationship, then changed her mind.
07: RP of 1 month proposed engagement.
08: Dating relationship was terminated because P had reservations.
09: RP wanted to get back together after two previous breakups and makeups.
10: Old SSF from high school failed to contact S three times during visit home.
11: RP broke contact and starting seeing his former girlfriend.
12: OSF wanted romantic relationship but S did not.
13: SSF's position as president of sorority changed her behavior.
14: Dating relationship revived after termination, but DP rejected kiss.

15: Friendship deteriorated after S started to date OSF's roommate.
16: DP ignored S at a party.
17: RP was not home when called several times and blew up when asked about it.
18: RPs decided to take things as they come and not to be serious.
19: Fs became DPs.
20: SSF distorted something S said about third party.
21: P in nonserious, F-like relationship told S he loved her.
22: SSF broke up with her 2-year RP and is dating rich man 6 years older.
23: RP blamed S for small problem and acted immaturely.
24: OSF said he thought he was falling in love with S.
25: DP broke off relationship for reasons S couldn't understand.
26: RP and S kissed OSFs in moment of "reckless abandon."
27: OSF failed to respond to repeated messages, acted cold and evasive.
28: S discovered he had nothing in common with RP when she came to visit.
29: S gets along well with DP on dates, but she is distant on the phone.
30: OSF instigated romantic relationship suddenly.
31: SSF told him how important he was as a friend.
32: S became SSF with neighbor with whom she used to fight over noise.
33: SSF got answers to exam, but wouldn't share with them with S.
34: SSF told S about something illegal she was going to do.
35: SSF, whose main goal is to be married, broke up with her boyfriend.
36: S found out SSF is bisexual through sexual advance made toward him.
37: SSF implied friendship one-sided because S didn't call.
38: S broke up with RP, then messed around with other men in his presence.
39: SSF became totally disinterested in S and wrapped up in her own life.
40: S gets vague sense that OSF wants romantic relationship.
41: S found out that SSF thought she was being hypocritical.
42: OSF hung up on S several times on phone.
43: Former DP transferred schools without telling S, called 3 mos. later.
44: RP wouldn't tell S something about his brother.
45: DPs broke up after going out 2½ years.
46: OSF-ship changed after one person got engaged.
47: OSF called several times recently only to copy homework.
48: DP did not stop by when expected.
49: S overheard conversation which changed his view of OSF as "dating girls just for fun."
50: SSF-ship became less close after S spent semester overseas.
51: SSF betrayed confidence by telling roommate of DP that S was also dating someone else.
52: SSF dated guy S was interested in.
53: DP tried to make up, but S did not agree to it.
54: Conflict occurred over RP not having/making time for S.

55: Conflict occurred over S wanting to date other people.

56: Person S dated avoided him and seemed uncomfortable around him.

57: OSF who was dating S's other F said he wanted to fool around with S.

58: Long-distance SSFs had trouble communicating during visit.

59: OSF has been disclosing deeply; S suspects something more may be developing.

60: S found out RP had two abortions with previous girlfriends.

61: OSF agreed to date S, then changed her mind.

62: S criticized SSF's speech, then P gave S a bad fraternity "little sister."

63: DP told S he had to work, then went to dance with someone else.

64: SSF's behavior toward S was very negative, then changed quickly to positive.

65: S learned from third party that OSF had crush on her, but then avoided her.

66: OSF made remarks suggesting possible romantic relationship.

67: OSF has been uncommunicative lately.

68: SSF fell for RP that S hates and thinks is a bum.

69: RP, a fitness nut, smoked ½ pack of cigarettes.

70: Sudden breakdown in communication and distance from DP.

71: OSF of 7 years became RP, then avoided S, claiming he was too busy.

72: After summer apart, S approached OSF with hugs and received an "I'll see you later."

73: S moved in with SSF and found her to be self-centered, vain, insecure.

74: RP hinted at long-term commitment that he knew P didn't want.

75: SSF engaged in malicious behavior in conflict with roommate.

76: Things happened that usually don't between OSFs and ruined the close friendship.

77: Old boyfriend entered S's life.

78: S went to her dance with a F; exclusive DP then went to his dance with someone else.

REFERENCES

Abelson, R. P., & Lalljee, N. (1988). Knowledge structures and causal explanations. In D. Hilton (Ed.), *Contemporary science and natural explanation: Commonsense conceptions of causality* (pp. 175–203). London: Harvester Press.

Altman, I., & Taylor, D. A. (1973). *Social penetration*. New York: Holt, Rinehart & Winston.

Baldwin, M. W. (1992). Relational schemas and the processing of social information. *Psychological Bulletin, 112*, 461–484.

Baxter, L. A., & Bullis, C. (1986). Turning points in developing romantic relationships. *Human Communication Research, 12*, 469–493.

Berger, C. R. (1988). Uncertainty and information exchange in developing relationships. In S. W. Duck (Ed.), *Handbook of personal relationships* (pp. 239–255). New York: Wiley.

Bullis, C., Clark, C., & Sline, R. (1993). From passion to commitment: A comparison of college and adult romantic relationships using turning point analysis. In P. J. Kalbfleisch (Ed.), *Interpersonal communication: Evolving interpersonal relationships* (pp. 213–236). Hillsdale, NJ: Lawrence Erlbaum Associates.

Burgoon, J. K., & Saine, T. (1978). *The unspoken dialogue.* Boston: Houghton Mifflin.

Crocker, J., Fiske, S. T., & Taylor, S. E. (1984). Schematic bases of belief change. In J. R. Eiser (Ed.), *Attitudinal judgment* (pp. 197–225). New York: Springer-Verlag.

Duck, S., & Sants, H. (1983). On the origin of the specious: Are personal relationships really interpersonal states? *Journal of Social and Clinical Psychology, 1,* 27–41.

Fincham, F. (1985). Attributions in close relationships. In J. H. Harvey & G. Weary (Eds.), *Attribution: Basic issues and applications* (pp. 203–234). New York: Academic Press.

Fincham, F. D., & Jaspars, J. M. (1980). Attribution of responsibility: From man the scientist to man as lawyer. In L. Berkowitz (Ed.), *Advances in experimental social psychology* (Vol. 13, pp. 81–138). New York: Academic Press.

Fletcher, G. J. O., & Fincham, F. (1991). Attributional process in close relationships. In G. J. O. Fletcher & F. Fincham (Eds.), *Cognition in close relationships* (pp. 7–35). Hillsdale, NJ: Lawerence Erlbaum Associates.

Fletcher, G. J. O., & Fitness, J. (1993). Knowledge structures and explanations in intimate relationships. In S. Duck (Ed.), *Understanding relationship processes I: Individuals in relationships* (pp. 121–143). New York: Sage.

Honeycutt, J. M., Cantrill, J. G., & Allen, T. (1992). Memory structures for relational decay. *Human Communication Research, 18,* 528–562.

Honeycutt, J. M., Cantrill, J. G., & Greene, R. W. (1989). Memory structures for relational escalation. *Human Communication Research, 16,* 62–90.

Horowitz, M. (Ed.). (1991). *Person schemas and maladaptive interpersonal patterns.* Chicago: University of Chicago Press.

Kelley, H. H. (1967). Attribution theory in social psychology. In D. L. Vine (Ed.), *Nebraska symposium on motivation* (pp. 192–238). Lincoln, NE: Academic Press.

Kelley, H. H. (1971). *Attribution in social interaction.* Morristown, NJ: General Learning.

Knapp, M. L., & Vangelisti, A. L. (1992). *Interpersonal communication and human relationships* (2nd ed.). Boston, MA: Allyn & Bacon.

Lalljee, M., & Abelson, R. P. (1983). The organization of explanations. In M. Hewstone (Ed.), *Attribution theory: Social and functional extensions* (pp. 65–80). Cambridge, MA: Basil Blackwell.

Leathers, D. G. (1976). *Nonverbal communication systems.* New York: MacMillan.

Leddo, J., & Abelson, R. P. (1986). The nature of explanations. In J. A. Galambos, R. P. Abelson, & J. B. Black (Eds.), *Knowledge structures* (pp. 103–122). Hillsdale, NJ: Lawrence Erlbaum Associates.

Miller, D. T., & Porter, C. A. (1980). Effects of temporal perspective on the attribution process. *Journal of Personality and Social Psychology, 39,* 532–541.

Miller, L. C., & Read, S. J. (1991). On the coherence of mental models of persons and relationships: A knowledge structure approach. In G. S. O. Fletcher & F. D. Fincham (Eds.). *Cognition in close relationships* (pp. 69–99). Hillsdale, NJ: Lawrence Erlbaum Associates.

Newman, H. (1981). Communication within ongoing intimate relationships: An attribution perspective. *Personality and Social Psychology Bulletin, 7,* 59–70.

Planalp, S. (1985). Relational schemata: A test of alternative forms of relational knowledge as guides to communication. *Human Communication Research, 12,* 3–29.

Planalp, S. (1987). Interplay between relational knowledge and events. In R. Burnett, P. McGhee, & D. Clarke (Eds.), *Accounting for relationships: Explanation, representation and knowledge* (pp. 175–191). London: Methuen.

Planalp, S., & Honeycutt, J. M. (1985). Events that increase uncertainty in personal relationships. *Human Communication Research, 11,* 593–604.

Planalp, S., & Rivers, M. (1988). *Changes in knowledge of relationships.* Paper presented to the International Communication Association Convention, New Orleans.

Planalp, S., Rutherford, D. K., & Honeycutt, J. M. (1988). Events that increase uncertainty in personal relationships II: Replication and extension. *Human Communication Research, 14*, 516–547.

Read, S. J., & Cesa, I. L. (1991). This reminds me of the time when . . .: Expectation failures of reminding and explanation. *Journal of Experimental Social Psychology, 27*, 1–25.

Read, S. J., & Collins, N. L. (1992). Accounting for relationships: A knowledge structure approach. In J. H. Harvey, T. L. Orbuch, & A. L. Weber (Eds.), *Attributions, accounts, and close relationships* (pp. 116–143). New York: Springer-Verlag.

Rothbart, M. (1981). Memory processes and social beliefs. In D. Hamilton (Ed.), *Cognitive processes in stereotyping and inter-group behavior* (pp. 145–181). Hillsdale, NJ: Lawrence Erlbaum Associates.

Safran, J. D. (1990a). Towards a refinement of cognitive therapy in light of interpersonal theory: I. Theory. *Clinical Psychology Review, 10*, 87–105.

Safran, J. D. (1990b). Towards a refinement of cognitive therapy in light of interpersonal theory: II. Practice. *Clinical Psychology Review, 10*, 107–121.

Surra, C. A. (1987). Reasons for changes in commitment: Variations by courtship type. *Journal of Social and Personal Relationships, 4*, 17–33.

Surra, C. A., Arizzi, P., & Asmussen, L. A. (1988). The association between reasons for commitment and the development and outcome of marital relationships. *Journal of Social and Personal Relationships, 5*, 47–63.

Thagard, P. (1989). Explanatory coherence (and Commentaries). *Behavioral and Brain Sciences, 12*, 435–467.

Thagard, P. (1992). *Conceptual revolutions.* Princeton, NJ: Princeton University Press.

Weary, G., Stanley, M. A., & Harvey, J. H. (1989). *Attribution.* New York: Springer-Verlag.

11

Self and Self-Expansion
in Relationships

Arthur Aron
State University of New York at Stony Brook

Elaine N. Aron
Pacifica Graduate Institute

This chapter explores a way of looking at the role of the self in cognition and motivation in close relationships. The chapter has two main sections. In the first, we consider two hypotheses about self-relevant information processing in a close relationship. A major thread of social cognition research has concerned differences between cognitive processes relevant to self versus cognitive processes relevant to others. However, in most such studies "other" is a stranger or simply undefined. In this context, the first section of this chapter considers the following two hypotheses:

Hypothesis 1. Cognition about self versus other is on a continuum from self through close others to nonclose others.
Hypothesis 2. This continuum is produced by the extent to which close others are "included in the self."

Having offered some support for these two hypotheses, in the second main section of this chapter we explore three further hypotheses that relate this notion of including other in the self to relationship development:

Hypothesis 3. Developing a relationship expands the self by including other in the self.
Hypothesis 4. People are motivated to enter a relationship by the perceived opportunity to expand the self.

Hypothesis 5. Changes in relationship satisfaction over time are linked to changes in experiences of, and perceived opportunities for, self-expansion in the context of the relationship.

The overarching conceptual framework from which these five hypotheses-were generated has come to be known as the self-expansion model. It was originally put forward by Aron and Aron (1986) and has continued to be developed and refined in subsequent years. The self-expansion model is based on the postulate that a fundamental motivation is to expand the self and that one of the ways people seek to expand the self is by including others in the self in close relationships. We develop these themes in more detail in the context of considering the five hypotheses around which this chapter is organized.

THE SELF IN CLOSE RELATIONSHIPS

This section explores two hypotheses (already alluded to) that focus on the way people process information about self and others in close relationships. Initially we deal with the idea that cognition about self versus other is on a continuum.

Hypothesis 1. Cognition About Self Versus Other is on a Continuum From Self Through Close Others to Nonclose Others

Since the 1970s, a considerable body of social cognition research has demonstrated differences in processing information relevant to self versus information relevant to others. This work includes, for example, work on the uniqueness of self-representations, going back to the pioneering articles by Markus (1977) and Rogers, Kuiper, and Kirker (1977); it also includes the work focusing on differences in actor–observer perspectives in attributional processes going back to Jones and Nisbett (1971). More recently, a body of research has appeared that is converging toward a conclusion that self–other differences of these kinds are arranged along a continuum on which one extreme represents self, the other extreme represents a generalized other or a stranger of some kind, and in between are people with whom one has interactions and relationships.

For example, consider the issue of self-relevant information processing (the so-called "self-reference effect" that information processing and memory is enhanced for information related to the self). Bower and Gilligan (1979) found little difference in incidental memory for adjectives that subjects had earlier judged for their relevance to their own life or their mother's life, self and mother presumably being close on this continuum. Extending this continuum, Keenan and Baillet (1980) had subjects indicate whether trait adjectives were true of a particular person. The persons were self, best friend, parent, friend, teacher, favorite television character, and the U.S. president. They found a clear linear trend from self through president for time to make decision and number of adjectives recognized later. Similarly, Prentice (1990) showed that both the content and organization of self-descriptions and other-descriptions tended to follow a pattern in which familiar others were intermediate between self and unfamiliar others.

Similar findings have emerged regarding differences in attributional processes associated with actor versus observer perspectives (i.e.,elaborating on the original Jones and Nisbett, 1971, finding that people are more likely to make dispositional attributions about others but make situational attributions about self). Nisbett, Caputo, Legant, and Marecek (1973, Study 3) found that the longer people had been in a relationship with a close friend the less willing they were to make dispositional attributions about the friend.Similarly, Goldberg (1981) found that subjects made fewer dispositional attributions for people they had spent more time with, compared to people they had spent less time with.

Other research has followed this same theme of actor–observer differences in attribution using different approaches. Prentice (1990) had subjects describe various persons in specific situations and found least overlap between situations for descriptions of self, moderate overlap for a familiar other, and most overlap for an unfamiliar other. This suggests that people are making situational attributions for self and those close to self but are understanding those less familiar in terms that are not differentiated by situation. Using yet another approach, Sande, Goethals, and Radloff (1988) found that self, and then liked friends, and then disliked friend were progressively less likely to be attributed both poles of pairs of opposite traits (e.g., "serious–carefree"). The point here is that for self—and those liked by self—behaviors can vary, even to the extent of representing opposites, according to the situation. But for those distant from self, a single-sided trait description (i.e., a dispositional attribution) is quite adequate. Aron, Aron, Tudor, and Nelson (1991, introduction to Study 2) replicated Sande et al.'s procedure, but compared different degrees of closeness (as opposed to liking vs.disliking). They found choices of both traits were most frequent for self, next for best friend, and least for a friendly acquaintance.

In summary, these various studies, both those focusing on the self-reference effect and those focusing on actor–observer differences in attributions, suggest that there is a continuum from self to close others to less close others. That is, differences between self-cognition and other-cognition are reduced to the extent that the other is in a close relationship with self. (Most of the studies cited in the following section, on Hypothesis 2, also provide support for Hypothesis 1.)

Hypothesis 2. This Continuum is Produced by the Extent to Which Close Others Are "Included in the Self"

Now let us turn to Hypothesis 2—that this continuum is due to close others being included in the self. More precisely, we mean that elements of cognitive structures of close others overlap with elements of cognitive structures of self—the closer the relationship, the more the overlap. In Lewinian (1936) terms, the differentiated life-space region representing self is partially shared with that representing other.

The notion that in a relationship other is included in the self is consistent with a wide variety of current social psychological ideas on relationships. For example, Reis and Shaver (1988) identified intimacy as mainly a process of an escalating reciprocity of self-disclosure in which each individual feels his or her innermost self validated, understood, and cared for by the other. Wegner (1980) suggested that empathy may "stem in part from a basic confusion between ourselves and others" (p. 133), which he proposed may arise from an initial lack of differentiation between self and caregiver in infancy (Hoffman, 1976). Indeed, perhaps the most prominent idea in social psychology directly related to the present theme is the "unit relation," a fundamental concept in Heider's (1944, 1958) influential cognitive account of interpersonal relations. This idea is also related to Ickes, Tooke, Stinson, Baker, and Bissonette's (1988) idea of "intersubjectivity"—which Ickes and his colleagues made vivid by citing Merleau-Ponty's (1945) description of a close relationship as a "double being" and Schutz' (1970) reference to two people "living in each other's subjective contexts of meaning" (p. 167).

The notion of closeness as an overlap of selves has also been popular more generally among psychologists, starting with James (1890/1948). For example, Bakan (1966) wrote about "communion" in the context of his expansion on Buber's (1937) "I–Thou" relationship. Jung (1925/1959) emphasized the role of relationship partners as providing or developing unavailable aspects of the psyche, so leading to greater wholeness. Maslow (1967) took it for granted that "beloved people can be incorporated into the self" (p. 103). And from a symbolic interactionist perspective, McCall (1974) described "attachment" as "incorporation of . . . [the other's] actions and reactions . . . into the content of one's various conceptions of the self" (p. 219).

In a recent relevant study, Sedikides, Olsen, and Reis (1993) found that people spontaneously encode information about other people in terms of their relationships with each other, grouping them together by their relationships. This suggests that cognitive representations of other individuals are in a sense overlapped, or at least tied together as a function of these others being perceived as in close relationships with each other.

In our own research, we have conducted several studies that focus directly on the overlap of person identities when the relationship is of self and one other person. In one series of studies (Aron, Aron, & Smollan, 1992), we asked subjects to describe their closest relationship using an overlapping-circles measure, the Inclusion of Other in the Self (IOS) Scale. As shown in Fig. 11.1, the IOS Scale consists of a series of overlapping circles from which one is asked to select the pair that best describes a particular relationship. Respondents generally find this task very comfortable and the scale appears to have levels of reliability, as well as of discriminant, convergent, and predictive validity, that match or exceed other measures of closeness—measures which are typically more complex and lengthy. (For example, the correlation between a score on this test and whether people remained in a romantic relationship 3 months later was .46.)

Further, most measures of closeness seem to fall into one of two factors: They measure either feelings of closeness or behaviors associated with closeness. The IOS Scale, however, loads, to some extent, on both of these factors: Fig. 11.2 shows the results of a confirmatory factor analysis (replicating a similar result obtained in an exploratory analysis with a different sample). This suggests that the IOS Scale may be tapping the core meaning of closeness and not merely a particular aspect of it.

We interpret these various findings with the IOS Scale as suggesting that this symbolic description of overlapping selves may tap a readily accessible schema of relationship as self–other overlap. That is, it may be that people respond so effectively to this metaphor because it maps very directly on to the way a close relationship between self and other is actually represented cognitively.

Please circle the picture below which best describes your relationship

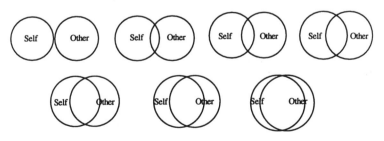

FIG. 11.1. IOS Scale (Aron et al., 1992). Respondents are instructed to select the picture that best describes their relationship.

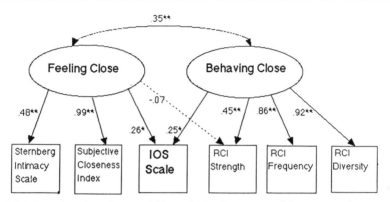

FIG. 11.2.   Covariance latent variable model for six measures of closeness (confirmatory factor analysis). Path coefficients are standardized parameter estimates. The dotted path was part of the predicted model, but was not significant. IOS = Inclusion of Other in the Self Scale. RCI = Relationship Closeness Inventory. *p < .05. **p < .01. From Aron et al. (1992, p. 605).

A further approach we have taken to explore the second hypothesis was based on an adaptation of a research paradigm developed by Lord (1980, 1987). Lord presented subjects with a series of 60 concrete nouns. Each noun was displayed for 10 seconds, during which time subjects were instructed to form as vivid and as interesting a mental image as possible of themselves (or a target person) interacting with whatever the noun referred to (e.g., a mule). In Lord's main study, the target person was sometimes self and sometimes Johnny Carson. After the series had been completed, and after the subjects had carried out a distraction task, they were asked to recall as many of the nouns as they could. Lord found *fewer* words were recalled in the self-image condition than in the other-image condition—a particularly interesting finding given that in most research paradigms self-reference facilitates memory.

Lord interpreted these results in terms of a figure–ground difference between one's experience of self and other when acting in the world. Self, being ground, is less vivid and thus imaging things interacting with the self is less enhancing to memory than imaging them interacting with someone other than self. We reasoned that if this figure–ground difference represented a different way of understanding and appreciating the world, then if other were included in one's inner world, other should become more like ground and less like figure—that is, more like the self. Therefore, we replicated Lord's procedures, again using as target persons self and a prominent entertainment personality (we used Cher). But we also added a third target, a close other, the subject's mother.

In our study (Aron et al., 1991, Experiment 2), as in the Lord study, recall was greatest for words imaged with the entertainment personality. But recall for words imaged with mother was similar to that for words imaged with self. (Mean number of words recalled were 6.80 for self, 7.15 for mother, and 8.95 for Cher.) We also replicated this study using self, mother, and friend of mother, substituting friend of mother for Cher in order to avoid the alternative interpretation that a media personality would be especially vivid. The pattern of results was again a clear continuum from self to close other to nonclose other.

In the follow-up study, we also asked subjects to rate their similarity, closeness, and familiarity with their mother. Using these data, we computed for each subject the difference between the recall for words imaged with mother's friend minus recall for words imaged with mother. This difference, hypothetically indicating the degree to which other is included in the self, correlated .56 with ratings of closeness to mother. At the same time, the correlations of this difference with similarity and with familiarity were both quite small (.13 and .16, respectively).

Our final study to date exploring this phenomenon (Aron et al., 1991, Experiment 3) focused on the idea that if being in a close relationship means other is included in the self, then to the extent one is in a close relationships with someone there should be a tendency to confuse traits of self with traits of the other. In this study, married subjects first rated a series of trait adjectives for their descriptiveness of themselves, their spouse, and an entertainment personality. After a distracting intermediate task they made a series of "me"–"not-me" reaction time choices to these trait words. The prediction was that there would be most confusion—and thus longer response latencies— for trait words that were different between self and spouse. (That is, the confusion is hypothesized to arise because one is asked here to rate these traits as true or false for self, but if other is part of self, when self and other differ on a trait, the difference is a discrepancy between two parts of "self.")

The results were as predicted—longer response times when the trait was different between self and spouse.[1] (Mean for traits that were the same was 1,059 ms; for traits that were different, the mean was 1,123 ms.) We also obtained the same pattern of results in a follow-up study in which other, instead of an entertainment personality, was a friend of the spouse.

---

[1]The study was actually a bit more complicated. We were concerned that traits on which self and spouse were rated similarly might be responded to more quickly as true (or false) of self because such traits might be true (or false) of everyone. Thus, it would be easy to make a quick decision about whether they are true (or false) of self. To avoid this, we included in the analysis of traits "true of self and spouse" only those traits that were also rated as false for the entertainment personality (or, in the follow-up, false of friend of spouse). Similarly, in the analysis for those traits that were rated "false of self and spouse," we included only those traits that were also rated as true for the entertainment personality (or friend of spouse). We took similar considerations into account in selecting which traits to consider as different between self and spouse.

In the follow-up study, we administered the IOS Scale (the overlapping-circles measure of closeness described earlier) and computed for each subject the difference between average response time to spouse-different words minus average response time to spouse-similar words. The IOS Scale and this difference correlated .59.

There are, of course, other possible explanations for some of these findings. For example, several researchers, including Prentice (1990) in her study described earlier, emphasized familiarity as the key factor underlying a self–other continuum. But in the Prentice study, and virtually all of the previous studies in which the continuum has been found, familiarity and closeness (as well as similarity, amount of interaction, etc.) have not been considered separately. In two of the studies just described—the memory and reaction-time studies—the effects were clearly correlated with degree of perceived closeness, and in one of them, we explicitly measured familiarity and similarity and the correlations between these variables and the effect were quite small.

To conclude this first section, we think there is a strong body of evidence in support of our first hypothesis—that there is a continuum in processing information about persons from self, to close others, to nonclose others. Although support for the second hypothesis is more preliminary, the principle of including other in the self does seem to explain the data supporting the first hypothesis in a parsimonious way, and the studies we have conducted so far which are directly relevant to the second hypothesis have been entirely consistent in its support.

SELF-EXPANSION IN DEVELOPING RELATIONSHIPS

Having discussed our basis for maintaining that other is included in the self in a close relationship, we now turn to the implications of this notion for understanding the role of the self in the development of relationships—both the direct application of this idea (in Hypothesis 3) and its application in conjunction with additional propositions associated with the self-expansion model (in Hypotheses 4 and 5).

Hypothesis 3. Developing a Relationship Expands the Self by Including Other in the Self

If in a close relationship other is included in the self, then when one enters a close relationship the self should be expanded to include aspects of the other. There have not been any studies that have tested this hypothesis directly. However, data from two relevant studies provide preliminary support.

In one study, conducted by Sedikides (personal communication, October

1992), self-descriptions of subjects who were currently in a close relationship, compared to self-descriptions of subjects not in a close relationship, included terms representing significantly more different domains of the self. We have also conducted a relevant study (Aron, Paris, & Aron, in press) that focused specifically on "falling in love." In this study, we tested 325 students five times, once every 2½ weeks over a 10-week period. At each testing, the subjects listed as many self-descriptive words or phrases as came to mind during a 3-minute period in response to the question, "Who are you today?" (This method was adapted from McGuire & McGuire's, 1988, work on the spontaneous self-concept.) At each testing subjects also answered a number of other questions that included items indicating whether the subject had fallen in love since the last testing. (This was the fall term and for most subjects it was their very first term at college; thus it was not surprising that 108 of the 325 fell in love.)

Following the general idea of Sedikides' approach, we analyzed the self-descriptions by content domains (words or phrases related to social statuses, to each of the major emotions, to family relationships, etc.). Consistent with the model, we found a significantly greater increase in the number of different content domains included in the self-descriptions from before to after falling in love than was found for average changes from before to after other testing sessions of the falling-in-love group, and when compared to typical testing-to-testing changes for subjects who did not fall in love. In a second study, with a new sample of 529 subjects (in which 138 fell in love), we administered scales measuring self-esteem and self-efficacy. As predicted, we found a significantly greater increase in these variables from before to after falling in love than was found for average changes from before to after other testing sessions of the falling-in-love group, and when compared to typical testing-to-testing changes for subjects who did not fall in love. (Furthermore, in both of these studies we also measured changes in mood and found that the patterns of change in self-concept domains and the increased self-esteem and self-efficacy remained even after controlling for mood change.)

Thus, these studies lend preliminary support to our third hypothesis that the formation of a close relationship expands the self by including, to some extent, the relationship partner in the self.

Hypothesis 4. People are Motivated to Enter a Relationship by the Perceived Opportunity to Expand the Self

Hypothesis 4 requires the additional assumption that expanding the self (by including other in the self through a relationship) is desirable. Elsewhere (Aron & Aron, 1986), we have argued at length that self-expansion is a fundamental human motivation. Self-expansion is the desire for enhanced potential efficacy—greater material, social, and informational resources. Such self-expansion leads both to the greater ability to achieve whatever else one desires (i.e., both to survival and to specific rewards), as well as to an enhanced sense of efficacy (Bandura, 1977; Deci, 1975; White, 1959).

Furthermore, we have argued that it is precisely the perceived potential for increased self-efficacy through a close relationship (by including other in the self) that is the basic motivator for people to seek such relationships. Extending this argument one step more, we have argued that self-expansion motivation directs selectivity in attraction. That is, among potential close relationship partners, one is most attracted to those others that offer the greatest potential for self-expansion via a relationship with them. Finally, following a kind of value-expectancy approach, we have reasoned that attraction to a particular other should be determined by two main factors:

1. The perceived degree of potential expansion of self that is possible through a close relationship with a particular other.
2. The perceived probability of actually obtaining that expansion with the other—that is, the probability that one could actually form and maintain a close relationship with this particular other.

The first factor can be summarized as "desirability" (or reward value); the second, as "probability" (or likelihood of achieving that reward value). As noted, this analysis is basically an application of classic value-expectancy analysis (e.g., Rotter, 1954) to our notion that relationships provide rewards by enhancing self through including other in self.

Implications for Initial Attraction.   The delineation of these two factors has been useful (Aron & Aron, 1986) in making sense of longstanding findings in the attraction literature that had previously seemed paradoxical. For example, based on the extensive work of Byrne (1971) and others (e.g., Newcomb, 1956), a basic tenet of the social psychology of attraction had been that similarity leads to attraction. However, Walster and Walster (1963) found that under conditions in which self is led to believe that other likes self, there is actually a preference for dissimilar partners. In the same vein, Jones, Bell, and Aronson (1972) found that when self is led to believe other likes self, the preference for those with similar attitudes is eliminated. Although this exception to the general rule that similars attract has been long known, no general explanation has been provided for it. Applying our two-factor model of attraction, these results makes sense. Perceived similarity serves as an indication that a relationship could develop and be maintained. That is, similarity serves to enhance the probability of self-expansion through our second motivational factor. But if, as in the studies just cited, probability of forming a relationship is made highly likely by knowing other likes self, then further probability information (provided by similarity information) adds no incremental benefit. Indeed, under these circumstances, our model would predict that dissimilarity could enhance attraction by increasing the potential for self-expansion—the more different a person is, the more new perspectives the person can add to the self.

Turning to our own research relevant to the two-factor perspective, let us first consider a series of studies we conducted on experiences of falling in love (Aron, Dutton, Aron & Iverson, 1989). In this research, we first summarized theory and research on falling in love and attraction as suggesting 11 main predictors—similarity, familiarity, and so forth. We then located 50 students who had fallen in love in the last 6 months and asked them to write, at some length, about what happened. A content analysis focused on which if any of these 11 predictors was mentioned in the account as preceding, or as a cause of, the falling in love. The two most commonly mentioned precursors were desirable characteristics of the other (such as good looks and personality), corresponding to our first motivational factor (desirability), and discovering other likes self, corresponding to our second motivational factor (probability). Desirable characteristics of other were mentioned in 78% and discovering other likes self in 90% of the accounts; the next highest two categories had 62% and 44%.

In a follow-up study we collected shorter, more retrospective accounts of falling in love from 100 postcollege-age subjects (people attending adult education seminars) and analyzed them in the same way, with essentially the same results: 56% mentioned desirable characteristics, 68%, discovering other likes self, and the next highest category had only 34% of mentions.

In yet another follow-up study, 277 subjects responded to specific questions about their most recent experience of falling in love. Again, desirability and discovering other likes self were rated as relevant far more frequently (75% and 90%, respectively) than any other category (the next highest was 40%).

We also found the same basic results looking at accounts of initiation of strong friendships, whether through content analysis of open-ended descriptions or using structured questionnaires. In other studies, this same basic pattern was found for experiences of falling in love among ChineseAmerican and Mexican American students in the United States (Aron & Rodriguez, 1992) and among students in Japan and Russia (Sprecher et al., 1994).

In summary, using a variety of methods and samples, we have consistently found the same two key precursors to falling in love—precursors that are directly consistent with the self-expansion model. However, because these predictions might well be made by other approaches as well, we wanted to examine the motivations for attraction in a context in which we made a somewhat more complex and specific set of predictions using the general model. This brings us to our work on the motivations for unreciprocated strong attractions or "unrequited love"—that is, loving someone who doesn't love you. This research program, which we summarize briefly here, is described in detail in Aron, Aron, and Allen (1995).

Implications for Unreciprocated Love.   Unrequited love is both practically important and interesting theoretically. It is of considerable practical importance because our data and others' have found it is quite widespread and also because it often generates substantial unhappiness, being a common cause of depression and suicide (e.g., Fiske & Peterson, 1991). This topic is theoretically interesting because unreciprocated attraction is a kind of motivational paradox—if the motivation for attraction to a particular person is the desire for a relationship with that person, why does the attraction occur and maintain itself when a relationship with that person is apparently not possible? In terms of the two-factor motivational view of attraction we have been examining, the probability of a relationship, indicated by other liking self, is clearly supposed to be very central. Yet it is precisely this factor that seems to be missing in unreciprocated attractions.

Thinking about unreciprocated attraction in the context of the self-expansion framework led us to postulate an expanded, three-factor motivational model for attraction. The first two factors are the same as before: desirability (perceived potential expansion of efficacy through a close relationship with this particular person) and probability (perceived probability of forming and maintaining a close relationship with this person). We thought unreciprocated attraction might arise three ways. Desirability might be the main element, in the sense that if a relationship with other is seen as extremely valuable, then one might be attracted even if the probability is low. It is a bit like betting on the lottery—small odds but big winnings. As for the second way unrequited love might arise, emphasizing probability, we reasoned that sometimes individuals may initially feel quite certain that their love is reciprocated but then later discover it is not. However, by then they are already in love with the other. The third, additional, path to this state is more specifically predicted by the self-expansion model, and involves wanting the expansion associated with enacting the culturally scripted role of lover, but not necessarily wanting a relationship. When this factor of desiring the state of being in love is foremost, unrequited love is highly rewarding, but only from the viewpoint of self-expansion, which recognizes this common element of seeking self-efficacy among seemingly contradictory rewards.

To test this three-factor motivational model, we first developed a psychometrically adequate questionnaire measure of our key variables, then administered this questionnaire to a new sample of 907 subjects. The first and most important prediction in this research was that each of these three motivational factors would significantly and independently predict intensity. This prediction was supported. Using a latent variable modeling technique, the overall fit of the model was good, and a variety of other models—for example a single-factor model—proved to have significantly worse fits. Most important, each of the three key paths in the causal model was significant. That is, in the context of this model and our measurement method, desirability of other, probability of a relationship developing, and desirability of the state of being in love each significantly and independently predicted intensity of the unreciprocated attraction. Standardized parameter estimates for these paths were .32, .09, and .16, respectively. The path from probability to intensity, however, although significant, was quite small. This is not surprising given the fundamental problem that self-identified unreciprocated attraction is, by the nature of the situation, a condition in which the probability of a relationship developing has come to seem low or nonexistent.

In addition to the main hypothesis, we also examined what we felt was an important set of subsidiary hypotheses having to do with individual differences. These hypotheses were developed by asking the following question: "If people differ in the relative emphasis of different motivational factors for seeking close relationships, what might explain these differences?"

One likely answer seemed to be that such differences would be due to crucial experiences in previous close relationships—perhaps most saliently, with one's earliest caregiver.

In this light, we reasoned that attachment style—especially as this concept has been developed by Hazan and Shaver (1987) into a three-part typology of adult relationship orientations—might play a central role in determining the means through which the individual seeks self-expansion. In the context of the self-expansion model we interpreted the attachment theory work as suggesting that early experiences shape one of the more important channels through which people seek to expand—through relationships. Those who were regularly successful in their early attempts to expand through interpersonal closeness become "securely attached," those who were regularly unsuccessful become "avoidants," and those who had inconsistent experiences become "anxious-ambivalents."

Specifically, we reasoned as follows: Secure individuals would have little experience with unreciprocated attraction. When they did they would be the group especially likely to do so by mistake—that is, the probability factor might be more important for them than for other groups. Avoidants might be unlikely to be attracted to anyone, but when they were, unreciprocated attraction would be ideal for them—they can experience being in love without the risk of a relationship. And for these individuals, it is precisely our third factor, desirability of the state, that should be especially salient for them compared to the other attachment types. Finally, anxious-ambivalents (also called anxious-preoccupieds) should have little trust in reciprocation yet have great expectations for the potential rewards of such a relationship. Such individuals would seem to be primed for experiencing unreciprocated love, and their experience of it should be especially driven by desirability of the other.

Our first prediction then was about which style would be correlated with the highest incidence of experiencing unreciprocated love. Specifically, based on the reasoning just given, we expected the greatest incidence among anxious/ambivalents, the next greatest among avoidants, and the least among secures. This is what we found. Of the 432 subjects in our study who completed questionnaires measuring their attachment style, 89% of anxious-ambivalents, 78% of avoidants, and 74% of secures reported having ever experienced unreciprocated love.

More interestingly, we also predicted that the relative importance of the different motivational factors would differ among the three attachment styles. That is, based on the reasoning just summarized, we expected that the path coefficient from desirability to intensity would be highest for anxious-ambivalents compared to the same path for the other attachment styles, that the path for probability to intensity would be highest for secures, and the path to intensity for desirability of the state itself would be highest for avoidants and lowest for anxious-ambivalents.

To test these hypotheses, we constructed a multiple group latentvariable model as shown in Fig. 11.3. In this model, each measurement model path is constrained to be equal across the three groups, but the paths in the causal model are free to vary across the three groups. As can be seen from the diagram, the paths for desirability and desirability of the state showed the predicted pattern: For desirability, the strongest link was for anxious ambivalents and the smallest for avoidants; for desirability of the state, exactly the reverse was found. Only on probability (which as noted earlier is problematic to measure in the context of self-identified unreciprocated attraction) did we not find the predicted pattern.

Also as part of this research program we conducted a number of additional analyses that showed that the basic three-factor motivational model is robust over (a) individual differences in love styles (Hendrick & Hendrick, 1986) and (b) different types of unreciprocated love (those that are secret, those in which the other was once in a love relationship with the self but no longer, and those in which other and self are in a relationship but not a love relationship).

In summary, we have explored the theoretical foundation and considered two lines of research—the precursors to falling in love and the motivations for unreciprocated love—yielding results that are consistent with Hypothesis 4; namely, that people are motivated to enter a relationship by the perceived opportunity to expand the self.

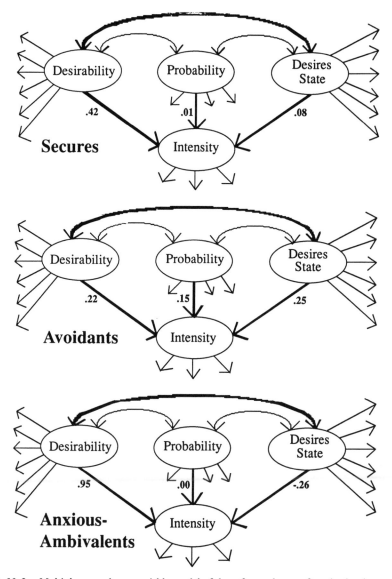

FIG. 11.3. Multiple group latent variable model of three-factor theory of motivation in unreciprocated love, divided into groups according to attachment style, fitted to data for 341 subjects who reported experiencing unreciprocated love. (All measurement model paths are constrained to be equal across groups.) Only the parameter estimates for the three key causal paths are shown for each group; for these paths, *$p < .05$, **$p < .01$. Constraining the three key causal paths to be equal across groups, yielded a significantly worse fit, $\chi^2(6) = 18.15$, $p < .01$. Constraining only the path for Desirability to Intensity to be equal across groups, the difference in fit was $\chi^2(2) = 15.75$, $p < .01$; for Probability, $\chi^2(2) = 1.15$, ns; and for Desirability of the State, $\chi^2(2) = 7.29$, $p < .05$. The key result was that, consistent with the hypotheses, Desirability had the highest parameter estimate for the anxious-ambivalents and Desirability of the State had the highest parameter estimate for the avoidants and the lowest for anxious-ambivalents. A prediction regarding Probability was not confirmed. From Aron, Aron, and Allen (1995).

Hypothesis 5. Changes in Relationship Satisfaction Over Time are Linked to Changes in Experiences of, and Perceived Opportunities for, Self-Expansion in the Context of the Relationship

The final hypothesis we consider in this chapter is that changes in relationship satisfaction over time are linked to changes in experiences of, and perceived opportunities for, self-expansion in the context of the relationship. This hypothesis rests on yet another assumption, in addition to the ones already considered. The two we have already considered were (a) in a relationship other is included in the self and thus expands the self, and (b) people are motivated to enter relationships in order to gain this self-expansion by including others in the self. The new, additional assumption is that the process of expanding the self is itself highly rewarding, as distinguished from the mere possession of the value of the expansion (the expand*ing* vs. being expand*ed*). This general principle that the process of acquiring rewards is highly satisfying, over and above the possession of the reward, follows from classic work on habituation and on assimilation and contrast, as well as on work specifically focusing on attraction and love (e.g., Aronson & Linder, 1965; Huesmann, 1980; Solomon, 1980). (Actually, the finding in the last section that avoidants appear to seek expansion by being in love—rather than by having a relationship—also supports this idea.)

A well-established finding in the literature on long-term relationships is that, on the average, romance and satisfaction decrease with time (e.g., Tucker & Aron, 1993)—"love fades." From the present point of view, what happens is that when people first fall in love there is often a rapid, exhilarating expansion of self. People stay up all night talking, sharing, just doing everything they can to merge selves. But eventually one gets to know the other fairly well, and this rapid expanding process inevitably slows down. In simpler language, one "gets used to the other." It would still be upsetting to lose the relationship, but it is not as exciting at it once was.

One line of reasoning that we have advanced based on this kind of notion is that if people need to associate self-expansion with a relationship to be attracted to the relationship, then for an ongoing relationship to be attractive, it must continue to be associated with self-expansion (Aron & Aron, 1986). To test this idea, Reissman, Aron, and Bergen (1993) conducted the following experiment: Fifty-three volunteer married couples were randomly assigned to one of three groups. Couples in the first group, the exciting-activities group, were instructed to spend 1½ hours each week doing one of a set of activities we listed for them. These were all activities that were selected because both had rated them as exciting on independently completed prestudy questionnaires. Couples in the second group, the pleasant-activities group, were assigned activities both had rated as pleasant. A third group of couples served as a waiting-list, no-activity control group.

All three groups were measured on relationship quality using Spanier's (1976) Dyadic Adjustment Scale at the start of the study and again 10 weeks later. (Subjects also completed Edmonds', 1967, Marital Conventionalization Scale at each testing, to permit statistical control for social desirability response set.)

The results were consistent with our model—and contrary to the way most other theorists had interpreted the importance of the time couples spend together (e.g., Orden & Bradburn, 1968). The exciting-activity group, compared to the pleasant-activity group, showed a significantly greater increase in relationship satisfaction over the 10 weeks. This difference was of moderate effect size (partial $r = .32$). At the same time, there was no significant difference for the other planned orthogonal contrast (partial $r = .04$), comparing the control group that spent no extra time together to the two experimental groups taken together. In other words, just spending time together did not increase satisfaction. But doing something exciting, and therefore presumably self-expanding, did increase satisfaction. We take these data as providing preliminary support for our Hypothesis 5, that changes in relationship satisfaction over time are linked to changes in experiences of, and perceived opportunities for, self expansion in the context of the relationship.

CONCLUSION

In this chapter, we considered the role of the self in close relationships by focusing first on theory and data relevant to the idea that closeness implies processing self-information as if other were "included in the self."Second, we explored three hypothesized implications (and preliminary supporting evidence) of thinking about relationships in terms of self-expansion: The impact on the self of forming a relationship, ways in which the desire for self-expansion directs motivations in attraction, and ways in which the process of expanding the self serves as a source of satisfaction in ongoing relationships.

Most of the theory and data we have presented was generated on the basis of the self-expansion model (Aron & Aron, 1986). We understand this model as a conceptual framework that sensitizes researchers to variables and relationships that might otherwise be missed. We believe that the various theoretical insights and research programs that have been generated by this model (much of which is summarized in this chapter) lends support to the utility of this conceptual framework as a heuristic of this kind. On the other hand, we do not present this conceptual framework as a precise theory, but rather as a source of precise theory, a platform for viewing relationships that opens up directions that otherwise might not be considered. Further, the developing body of research around this perspective both shapes the overall conceptual framework and provides a set of methods and concepts that we believe offer considerable promise for furthering our understanding of cognition and motivation in close relationships, including the central role the self may play in these processes.

REFERENCES

Aron, A., & Aron, E. N. (1986). *Love as the expansion of self: Understanding attraction and satisfaction*. New York: Hemisphere.

Aron, A., Aron, E. N., & Allen, J. (1995). *Motivations for unreciprocated love*. Manuscript submitted for review.

Aron, A., Aron, E. N., & Smollan, D. (1992). Inclusion of Other in the Self Scale and the structure of interpersonal closeness. *Journal of Personality and Social Psychology, 63*, 596–612.

Aron, A., Aron, E. N., Tudor, M., & Nelson, G. (1991). Close relationships as including other in the self. *Journal of Personality and Social Psychology, 60*, 241–253.

Aron, A., Dutton, D. G., Aron, E. N., & Iverson, A. (1989). Experiences of falling in love. *Journal of Social and Personal Relationships, 6*, 243–257.

Aron, A., Paris, M., & Aron, E. N. (in press). Falling in love: Prospective studies of self-concept change. *Journal of Personality and Social Psychology*.

Aron, A., & Rodriguez, G. (1992, July). Scenarios of falling in love among Mexican, Chinese, and Anglo-Americans. In A. Aron (chair), *Ethnic and cultural differences in love*. Symposium conducted at the Sixth International Conference on Personal Relationships, Orono, ME.

Aronson, E., & Linder, D. (1965). Gain and loss of esteem as determinants of interpersonal attraction. *Journal of Experimental Social Psychology, 1*, 156–171.

Bakan, D. (1966). *The duality of human existence: Isolation and commitment in Western man*. Boston: Beacon Press.

Bandura, A. (1977). Self-efficacy: Toward a unifying theory of behavioral change. *Psychological Review, 84*, 191–215.

Bower, G. H., & Gilligan, S. G. (1979). Remembering information related to one's self. *Journal of Research in Personality, 13*, 420–432.

Buber, M. (1937). *I and thou*. New York: Scribners.

Byrne, D. (1971). *The attraction paradigm*. New York: Academic Press.

Deci, E. L. (1975). *Intrinsic motivation*. New York: Plenum Press.

Edmonds, V. H. (1967). Marital conventionalization: Definition and measurement. *Journal of Marriage and the Family, 29*, 661-688.

Fiske, V., & Peterson, C. (1991). Love and depression: The nature of depressive romantic relationships. *Journal of Social and Clinical Psychology, 10*, 75–90.

Goldberg, L. R. (1981). Unconfounding situational attributions from uncertain, neutral, and ambiguous ones: A psychometric analysis of descriptions of oneself and various types of others. *Journal of Personality and Social Psychology, 41*, 517–552.

Hazan, C., & Shaver, P. (1987). Romantic love conceptualized as an attachment process. *Journal of Personality and Social Psychology, 52*, 511–524.

Heider, F. (1944). Social perception and phenomenological causality. *Psychological Review, 51,* 358–374.

Heider, F. (1958). *The psychology of interpersonal relations.* New York: Wiley.

Hendrick, C., & Hendrick, S. S. (1986). A theory and method of love. *Journal of Personality and Social Psychology, 50,* 392–402.

Hoffman, M. L. (1976). Empathy, role taking, guilt, and development of altruistic motives. In T. Lickona (Ed.), *Moral development and behavior* (pp. 134–143). New York: Holt.

Huesmann, L. R. (1980). Toward a predictive model of romantic behavior. In K. S. Pope (Ed.), *On love and loving* (pp. 152–171). San Francisco, CA: Jossey-Bass.

Ickes, W., Tooke, W., Stinson, L., Baker, V., & Bissonnette, V. (1988). Naturalistic social cognition: Intersubjectivity in same-sex dyads. *Journal of Nonverbal Behavior, 12,* 58–84.

James, W. (1948). *Psychology.* Cleveland: Fine Editions Press. (Original work published 1890)

Jones, E. E., Bell, L., & Aronson, E. (1972). The reciprocation of attraction from similar and dissimilar others: A study in person perception and evaluation. In C. G. McClintock (Ed.), *Experimental social psychology* (pp. 142–179). New York: Holt, Rinehart.

Jones, E. E., & Nisbett, R. (1971). The actor and the observer: Divergent perceptions of the causes of behavior. In E. E. Jones, D. Kanouse, H. Kelley, R. Nisbett, S. Valins, & B. Weiner (Eds.), *Attribution: Perceiving the causes of behavior* (pp. 79–94). Morristown, NJ: General Learning Press.

Jung, C. G. (1959). Marriage as a psychological relationship. In V. S. DeLaszlo (Ed.), *The basic writings of C. G. Jung* (R. F. C. Hull, Trans.; pp. 531–544). New York: Modern Library. (Original work published 1925)

Keenan, J. M., & Baillet, S. D. (1980). Memory for personally and socially significant events. In R. S. Nickerson (Ed.), *Attention and performance* (Vol. 8, pp. 652–669). Hillsdale, NJ: Lawrence Erlbaum Associates.

Lewin, K. (1936). *Principles of topological psychology* (F. Heider & G. M. Heider, Trans.). New York: McGraw-Hill.

Lord, C. G. (1980). Schemas and images as memory aids: Two modes of processing social information. *Journal of Personality and Social Psychology, 38,* 257–269.

Lord, C. G. (1987). Imagining self and others: Reply to Brown, Keenan, and Potts. *Journal of Personality and Social Psychology, 53,* 445–450.

Markus, H. (1977). Self-schemata and processing information about the self. *Journal of Personality and Social Psychology, 35,* 63–78.

Maslow, A. H. (1967). A theory of metamotivation: The biological rooting of the value-life. *Journal of Humanistic Psychology, 7,* 93–127.

McCall, G. J. (1974). A symbolic interactionist approach to attraction. In T. L. Huston (Ed.), *Foundations of interpersonal attraction* (pp. 217–231). New York: Academic Press.

McGuire, W., & McGuire, C. (1988). Content and process in the experience of self. In L. Berkowitz (Ed.), *Advances in experimental social psychology* (Vol. 21, pp. 97–114). San Diego: Academic Press.

Merleau-Ponty, M. (1945). *Phénoménologie de la perception* [Phenomenology of perception]. Paris: Gallimard.

Newcomb, T. M. (1956). The prediction of interpersonal attraction. *American Psychologist, 11,* 575–586.

Nisbett, R. E., Caputo, C., Legant, P., & Marecek, J. (1973). Behavior as seen by the actor and as seen by the observer. *Journal of Personality and Social Psychology, 27,* 154–164.

Orden, S. R., & Bradburn, N. M. (1968). Dimensions of marriage happiness. *American Journal of Sociology, 73,* 715–731.

Prentice, D. A. (1990). Familiarity and differences in self- and other-representations. *Journal of Personality and Social Psychology, 59,* 369–383.

Reis, H. T., & Shaver, P. (1988). Intimacy as interpersonal process. In S. Duck (Ed.), *Handbook of personal relationships: Theory, research and interventions* (pp. 367–389). Chichester, England: Wiley.

Reissman, C., Aron, A., & Bergen, M. R. (1993). Shared activities and marital satisfaction: Causal direction and self-expansion versus boredom. *Journal of Social and Personal Relationships, 10,* 243–254.

Rogers, T. B., Kuiper, N. A., & Kirker, W. S. (1977). Self-reference and the encoding of personal information. *Journal of Personality and Social Psychology, 35,* 677–688.

Rotter, J. B. (1954). *Social learning and clinical psychology.* Englewood Cliffs, NJ: Prentice-Hall.

Sande, G. N., Goethals, G. R., & Radloff, C. E. (1988). Perceiving one's own traits and others': The multifaceted self. *Journal of Personality and Social Psychology, 54,* 13–20.

Schutz, A. (1970). *On phenomenology and social relations.* Chicago: Chicago University Press.

Sedikides, C., Olsen, N., & Reis, H. T. (1993). Relationships as natural categories. *Journal of Personality and Social Psychology, 64,* 71–82.

Solomon, R. L. (1980). The opponent-process theory of acquired motivation: The costs of pleasure and the benefits of pain. *American Psychologist, 35,* 691–712.

Spanier, G. B. (1976). Measuring dyadic adjustment: New scales for assessing the quality of marriage and similar dyads. *Journal of Marriage and the Family, 38,* 15–28.

Sprecher, S., Aron, A., Hatfield, E., Cortese, A., Potapova, E., & Levitskaya, A. (1994). Love: American style, Russian style, and Japanese style. *Personal Relationships, 1,* 349–369.

Tucker, P., & Aron, A. (1993). Passionate love and marital satisfaction at key transition points in the family life cycle. *Journal of Social and Clinical Psychology, 12,* 135- 147.

Walster, E., & Walster, G. W. (1963). Effect of expecting to be liked on choice of associates. *Journal of Personality and Social Psychology, 67,* 402–404.

Wegner, D. M. (1980). The self in prosocial action. In D. M. Wegner & R. R. Vallacher (Eds.), *The self in social psychology* (pp. 131–157). New York: Oxford University Press.

White, R. W. (1959). Motivation reconsidered: The concept of confidence. *Psychological Review, 66,* 297–333.

12

Rewriting Relationship Memories: The Effects of Courtship and Wedding Scripts

Diane Holmberg
Joseph Veroff
The University of Michigan

In this section of the volume, authors examine the connections between knowledge structures and relationship development. However, in this chapter we propose that relationships do not simply unfold over time, quiet and unobserved. They are also *perceived* to have developed by the people in those relationships; they may seem to have developed, changed, or remained steady over time, depending on the perceptions and memories held by the individuals involved. Looking back from the present, people in close relationships can reexamine the high and low points, the ebbs and flows through which every relationship travels. Individuals may think about how the relationship has changed over time, or they may notice how the basic foundations of their current relationship were laid down in their earliest meetings. Such remembering may be public or private, formal or informal. A woman, seeing her younger sister's latest boyfriend, fleetingly recollects the shyness of her own boyfriend on their first few dates; at their golden wedding anniversary, a couple regales their children with a detailed story of how they first met.

Regardless of the circumstances under which they arise, such memories are vitally important to any relationship. Memories are important because they forge links between the past and the present, engendering a sense of permanence and stability. In a long-term marriage, for example, the couple may conclude that if the relationship has endured as long as it has, coping with many challenges and changes, it will endure whatever else may transpire.

Memories can also be important because they provide a useful framework for understanding and interpreting current behaviors or events in the relationship. For example, a husband who is upset that his wife has been neglecting him on account of her work may recall previous times he has felt this way. If he sees a pattern emerge (e.g., her work is especially demanding for a few days at the end of each month, but eases up again when the new month begins), he may learn that such behavior is natural and expected, and says nothing about her feelings toward him or the relationship. In this way, his memories act as an important variable affecting his attributions, his emotions, and other aspects of his relationship. His views of the past affect how he experiences the present.

On the other hand, some recent work on memory in relationships has turned this equation on its head, examining how views of the present state of a relationship can affect how one remembers the past. In this chapter, we investigate that link, looking at how current beliefs and knowledge structures about a relationship may lead people to reconstruct their memories for earlier stages of that relationship. The first section of the chapter provides an overview of previous work on memory reconstruction in relationships, including a theory by Ross (1989) on how people's beliefs about relationship change may affect their relationship memories. In the second section, we extend Ross' theories by proposing that individuals may hold well-developed scripts of how relationships develop over time. These scripts can then color people's perceptions of relationship development. We discuss where these relationship scripts might come from, what effects they have, and how they might be measured. Finally, in the third section of the chapter, we present some data from a study of memory for relationships in which we examine how scripts held at the cultural, subcultural, and individual levels affect couples' relationship memories.

MEMORY RECONSTRUCTION IN RELATIONSHIPS: PREVIOUS PERSPECTIVES

Relationship Memories are Malleable

Memories are not simply static entities, representing a faithful, uncritical, and unchanging view of how things "really were." Work by Loftus, Miller, and Burns (1978) showed that even memories for relatively circumscribed and objective events, such as a movie of a car crash, can be altered by information introduced after the fact. Relationship memories seem even more likely to be malleable. First, the sheer amount of information available for recall makes keeping precise mental records of every detail nearly impossible. In a relationship lasting months or years, the idiosyncratic details of each interaction quickly blur into the watercolor wash of habit. A wife may not recall exactly what she and her husband did together 10 weekends ago, but drawing on her current knowledge of their usual practices, she could probably offer a fair reconstruction of events (e.g., they probably rented a movie one night, had friends over another night, and cleaned the house on Sunday). Actual memories may fade over time, but if necessary they can be reconstructed quite serviceably by drawing on current knowledge and expectations. In this way, "what was" can, consciously or unconsciously, be replaced over time by "what must have been."

Even if events are recent enough or important enough to be remembered in some detail, current perspectives can still have a large influence. Relationship memories are social memories, and like most social stimuli, they tend to be complex and sometimes ambiguous. Essentially the same factual memories can seem very different, depending on which elements are emphasized and which ones are downplayed, and also depending on the particular meanings and interpretations assigned to any given behavior. For instance, imagine if the neglected husband mentioned previously came to the conclusion that his wife was having an affair with someone at work. Suddenly, in retrospect, every late night, every phone call to a colleague, and every moment of preoccupation would take on a new and sinister meaning.

Previous Research on Memory Reconstruction in Relationships

These examples suggest that current perspectives on our relationships can influence memories for those same relationships, by changing the memories themselves (through reconstruction), the interpretation of those memories, or both. Some recent research lends credence to these hypotheses. For example, McFarland and Ross (1987) asked members of dating couples to rate themselves and their partners on a number of dimensions. Three months later, the participants returned and again rated themselves and their partners on the same dimensions. They also recalled their previous ratings. Individuals who changed in their ratings of their partners over the 3-month period showed a corresponding change in their memories—those who became more positive in their current ratings recalled their previous ratings as having been more positive than they actually were; likewise, those who became more negative in their current ratings also became more negative in their recalled ratings. Thus, participants allowed their current feelings about their partners to affect their memories of what the relationship had been like in the past.

In a similar vein, Duck, Pond, and Leatham (1991) examined how current evaluations of the overall state of a friendship affected memories for a particular interaction with that friend. They asked pairs of friends to participate in a videotaped interaction, then complete a number of scales assessing the interaction in particular and their relationship in general. Six weeks later, friends returned to the lab and recalled their previous ratings, as well as completing current ratings of the relationship. The current overall levels of satisfaction and intimacy in the friendship predicted changes in recall of the specific interaction. Again, those with particularly intimate and satisfactory friendships recalled the specific interaction as having been even more satisfying than they had initially rated it.

Two recent studies (summarized in Holmberg & Holmes, 1993) demonstrate that the current outlook on the relationship can affect memories at a number of different levels, showing memory changes in very specific interactions over the short term, and memory changes in overall descriptions of the relationship over the long term. In the first study, married couples were asked to keep diaries of their daily interactions over a period of 3 weeks. Approximately 1 month later, the partners were asked to recall their open-ended descriptions and closed-ended ratings of two particular events, one positive and one negative. Couples' current overall views of the relationship (specifically, their trust in the relationship) were highly predictive of changes in their memories of the attributions for and feelings about the specific events.

In a longer term study, Holmberg and Veroff (see Holmberg & Holmes, 1993) looked at how the memories of couples who experienced a large drop in their marital well-being over a 2-year period compared to the memories of couples who had remained stable in marital well-being. Although stories of the early stages of the relationship (courtship, wedding, and honeymoon) collected shortly after the wedding looked very similar in the two groups, differences emerged over time. Those couples who had experienced a drop in well-being showed corresponding changes in their memories for the early stages of the relationship. Their stories (especially the males') showed an increase in negative affect, especially affect directed toward the partner, and also an increase in statements reflecting ambivalence toward the relationship. Thus, as couples became less satisfied with the current state of the relationship, their dissatisfaction seemed to creep out retrospectively, infecting memories of the formerly happy courtship and wedding periods with negative affect and increased ambivalence.[1]

Mechanisms of Memory Reconstruction: Ross' Views

We see, then, that the current state of a relationship can and does influence how earlier stages of the relationship are recalled. But how exactly are these effects achieved? What are the mechanisms through which present views affect the past?

---

[1]See Acitelli and Holmberg (1993) for a more complete review and discussion of research on close relationship memories.

One possible mechanism is suggested in theoretical work by Ross (see Ross, 1989, for a review). Ross suggested that when individuals are unable to recall what things were like in the past, they, consciously or unconsciously, fill in the gaps by reconstructing a likely scenario. First, individuals assess how things are now; next, they invoke their personal theories of how things might have changed over time to help them adjust their present position appropriately. Thus, according to Ross' position, if I am extremely happy in my relationship now, and I believe that happy relationships are stable relationships, I will recall my past as having been just as satisfying as the present. On the other hand, if I am happy now, and I believe that relationships grow steadily closer and more satisfying over time, I will not reconstruct my past as having been very similar to the present; instead, I will emphasize some of the more negative aspects of the earlier stages of the relationship. In this way, the data will come to fit my theory that the relationship has got better and better over time. Of course, if my theories of how the relationship has changed or stayed the same over time do in fact match reality, then my heuristic will have worked perfectly—I will have achieved an accurate picture of what the relationship was like in the past. In many cases, however, individuals' theories are not accurate; they either use the wrong theories of change over time, or they apply those theories too strongly. In these cases, researchers will be able to detect memory biases systematically related to the theories individuals hold.

In Ross' work to date, the theories that have been shown to affect people's memories are usually relatively simple notions of stability or change over time. However, the same idea of theory-based reconstruction could be extended to other, more complex types of theories. For example, some of Ross' theories of stability or change are widely shared cultural beliefs, such as beliefs in how people change as they get older. These cultural beliefs, whether true or false, are passed on to successive generations through such means as TV portrayals, newspaper and magazine articles, jokes, stories, and some (usually very limited) personal experience. Through similar methods, the culture can often pass on more complex beliefs, theories, or scripts.[2]

MEMORY RECONSTRUCTION IN RELATIONSHIPS: A RELATIONSHIP-SCRIPTS PERSPECTIVE

We propose that one type of script the culture passes on to individuals is a script for how relationships develop over time. People do not enter their first romantic relationships blindly, with no idea of how relationships should

---

[2]We use the term *script* simply to refer to a knowledge structure that contains information about how things develop over time.

proceed. Instead, they often have quite well-developed scripts that tell them how relationships develop, what signals are good and bad in a relationship, how to tell when a relationship is progressing versus stagnating, what the logical next step in their relationship is, and so forth. In this chapter, we concentrate in particular on people's scripts of how courtships and weddings should proceed, since courtship and wedding stories are the foci of our empirical research. These courtship and wedding scripts may be held at the cultural, subcultural, or individual level. We examine each of these levels in turn.

Cultural Scripts

Scripts or theories of how courtships and weddings should proceed can come from a variety of sources. Some of the knowledge is broadly shared across a culture, and is transmitted through the usual carriers of that culture—the mass media, the schools, the churches, myths, proverbs, folk heroes, and so on. For example, children in North American cultures are exposed at a young age to cultural ideas and ideals of romance in fairy tales. Their teaching continues through the assimilation of proverbs ("Love is blind," "Birds of a feather flock together"). At religious services, they learn how love should lead to a special lifelong commitment ("till death do us part," "love bears all things, believes all things, hopes all things, endures all things; love does not come to an end;" 1 Corinthians 13:7–8). At school, they study *Romeo and Juliet* or other classic love stories. As they get older, they learn about relationship development whenever they tune the television to a soap opera, watch one of the annual flock of romantic comedies in the movie theaters, listen to any of thousands of love songs on the radio or on CD, pick up a book in the well-labeled romance section of the bookstore, read a women's magazine, or turn to the lifestyles section of any newspaper.

The particulars may vary, but the basic elements remain relatively constant. A man and a woman meet.[3] They are attracted to each other. One of them (most often the man) asks the other one out. If they "hit it off," they spend more and more time together, coming to depend on the other more and more. Their initial feelings of interest and attraction deepen into caring and love. At some point in this period, the relationship becomes exclusive. They eventually realize they want to be a permanent part of each others' lives. One of them (again, usually the man) officially proposes. After a period of

---

[3]Relationships indeed comprise a man and a woman in our society. The carriers of mass culture systematically exclude information on homosexual relationships. Gay men and women, perhaps more than any other group, have few role models in the mass culture. They must turn to others within the gay community for role models and for information on how they can expect their relationships to develop.

engagement, they formally commit to one another in a special ceremony, usually with family and friends in attendance.

Subcultural Scripts

Of course, although courtship and wedding beliefs are relatively widely shared within a culture, they are by no means completely universal. Different groups or subcultures within the wider culture have slightly different ideas of how a courtship and wedding should proceed. Some of the basic elements may change from group to group; more often, however, the subculture can elaborate and add more detail as to exactly how the script should progress for members of that group. The skeletal outline may remain much the same, but the fleshing out of the specifics can vary according to gender, age, religion, ethnic background, socioeconomic standing, and so forth.

Some knowledge of these particulars may come from paying special attention to role models in the mass media who most closely match the individual's own situation. In addition, people may observe and model the behavior of their own family and friends who come from similar backgrounds. These same family and friends may also provide direct advice on how things should or should not proceed. For all of these reasons, we might expect the particular scripts that people hold to be influenced by their sociocultural standing. We therefore pay attention to differences emerging in different subcultures as we examine some of the data to be presented.

Individual Scripts

Finally, on top of the general culture- or subculture-wide beliefs about the courtship and wedding, individuals no doubt have more personal beliefs about how relationships should proceed. For instance, people who firmly believe in egalitarian principles in a relationship might try to run their own courtship and wedding in a more egalitarian, less traditionally gender-typed fashion than is the norm in our society. They might make sure that in their own relationships, the male is not always the initiator. The woman would share responsibility for arranging dates, and the proposal and wedding planning would be joint endeavors. One is not tied blindly to the usual subcultural scripts. People can make a conscious decision that for them, things will be different.

The Effects of Scripts on Relationships

Thus, from cultural, subcultural, and individual perspectives, people can form relatively detailed scripts of how a courtship and wedding should normally proceed. Certainly, these beliefs might shape the courtship and wedding process "on-line," by affecting when individuals choose to get engaged, how they plan the wedding, and so forth. What we are most interested in, however, is how these beliefs might shape the courtship and wedding process in retrospect. These scripts, like the current status of the relationship, can be used as a tool for memory definition and reconstruction. How might these effects take place?

First, if individuals' memories for the details of their own relationship development become hazy over time, they might fill in some of the gaps using their knowledge of how things probably went, based on their script of how such matters usually work. Second, if their own or their partners' actions could be interpreted in multiple ways, they will interpret them in a way that is consonant with a well-known script. Third, in telling and retelling the story of their courtship and wedding to others, individuals will play up the aspects that seem "right," both to them and to their audience (namely those elements that closely approximate the usual script) while downplaying those aspects that seem extraneous to the usual relationship story. Through these processes of reconstruction, reinterpretation, and recapitulation, the court-ship and wedding stories of a group of individuals should, over time, come to more closely approximate these internalized scripts. We examine this general hypothesis in our empirical research in due course. First, however, we consider some methods by which these hypothesized relationship scripts might be measured.

In assessing the nature of relationship scripts, we could turn to direct measures, in which the script is explicitly laid out, or we could use indirect measures, in which the script is inferred from other measures. We examine each of these possibilities in turn.

Assessing Scripts Using Direct Measures

Experts' Analyses of Relationship Script Behavior. One way of helping deter-mine relationship scripts is to examine what experts report to be the normative progression of courtships and weddings in various societies. This procedure is based on the plausible supposition that relationship scripts (cognitive entities) are related to actual behavior and practice.

Information of this sort is not readily available in the research literature; however, there are some clues. Cate and Lloyd (1992), for example, summarized the history of courtship in the United States. Twentieth-century norms for courtship are profoundly different from those of the 19th century. For example, the idea of dating outside the home only emerged in the 20th century. In the past two centuries, there have been widely varying concep-tions of proper sexual behavior in courtship, of the ideal level of separation of the sex roles, and of the proper age of the marriage commitment.

In recent years, particularly dramatic changes have taken place. Since the

1960s, there has been a liberalization of sexual standards and an increased emphasis on women following careers. All of these changes have undoubtedly had an enormous impact on courtship scripts. The most important impact has been on sanctioning cohabitation. Surra (1990) reported that 40%–50% of Americans under the age of 30 cohabit at some point, which may normalize cohabitation as a potential script in courtship. Courtship scripts today may be quite different from those of a century ago.

Of course, changes in courtship-script behavior are not always unidirectional. For example, Bailey (1988) noted an increase in certain traditional courtship activities during the Reagan years (e.g., a return to elaborate formal weddings). Courtship scripts may change in a cyclical fashion, going from more liberal to more conservative norms and back again.

Wedding-script behavior has also been the focus of study; for example, Malinowski (1956) tried to identify wedding scripts that occur in *all* cultures:

> The wedding rite itself has invariably a magical or religious character. In most ceremonies the symbolism expresses the traditional view that in marriage bride and bridegroom are firmly united by a sacred bond. The joining of hands or fingers, the tying of a garment, the exchange of rings and chain—so familiar to us from our own civilization—are practiced throughout the world. Usually not merely the two consorts, nor even only the families of bride and bridegroom, but the whole community are drawn in. (p. 65)

The research literature does provide clues as to the courtship and wedding scripts individuals in a given time and place may hold; however, some difficulties remain. In particular, experts may not focus on the same aspects of relationship behavior as laypeople, especially because the two groups often have very different questions in mind. Cate and Lloyd, for example, asked how courtship has changed over time. Malinowski asked how weddings are similar across cultures. By focusing on issues of historical and cultural comparison, these experts may be emphasizing very different aspects of script behavior than they would if they were simply asking "what are the common scripts today?" Thus, this information may not map very well onto current lay conceptions of relationship development.

Individuals' Own Assessments. A better strategy for assessing relationship scripts would be to ask individuals explicitly for their beliefs about how courtships and weddings should and do proceed. Some difficulties still remain, of course. First, people may not have very accurate conscious access to the scripts that they hold. Second, care must be taken to assess the scripts *after* assessing their relationship memories, to avoid problems of the conscious tailoring of stories to reported scripts, in subjects' efforts to appear consistent. Nonetheless, a strategy of explicitly assessing the relationship scripts that individuals hold would be a fruitful one that should be pursued in future research. Unfortunately, such data are not available for use in the empirical study to be described. Instead we relied on more indirect methods of assessing relationship scripts. We next present three methods for indirectly inferring relationship scripts, the latter two representing the methods used in our own research.

Assessing Scripts Using Indirect Assessments

The Media.   One method of indirectly assessing relationship scripts would be to conduct a thorough analysis of the messages delivered by the media, schools, and other cultural institutions, attempting to extract the key components. Such an effort, although worthwhile, would be extremely time consuming and filled with methodological difficulties.

First, which particular sources should an investigator select? Information about relationships is imparted through so many different channels that it is not clear which are the appropriate ones on which to focus.

Second, the messages conveyed through cultural carriers are often subtle, having their effects only through prolonged cumulative exposure. There is no guarantee that coders would be able to extract the appropriate themes and identify the same messages that people would pick up through casual exposure and incidental learning.

Third, presentations in the media are not specifically designed to convey cultural expectations. They do so indirectly; however, their primary goal is to inform, to entertain, or to sell advertisers' products. Additional features may be added to the scripts to help serve these other purposes. For example, conflict and uncertainty may not be helpful in the development of relationships in real life; however, they do add an element of drama to fictitious relationships. The course of love therefore seldom runs smoothly in books or songs or movies. Are individuals able to discount these elements added for drama, or are they incorporated into their relationship scripts? Again, direct assessment of individuals' scripts would be necessary to answer this question. Until such evidence is available, however, assessing media presentations may not give us the best available indirect measure of people's scripts.

We now turn to two other indirect measures of relationship scripts that were used in our own research: inferring the ideal relationship script from research on successful relationship development, and inferring the typical relationship script from respondents' modal descriptions of their own relationship development.

Inferences From Research Findings.   Perceptive readers will have noted that our discussion of courtship and wedding scripts glosses over the issue of the precise information that these scripts contain. Do scripts reflect people's notions of how relationships should ideally progress, or instead, do they contain information on how relationships usually progress? Relationship scripts may contain information about normative relationship development, but may be normative in the sense of what should be true, or normative in the sense of what is generally true. We suspect that courtship and wedding scripts contain both kinds of information; again, future research directly assessing individuals' scripts can and should attempt to separate these components. For the present, however, we look at both aspects.

In assessing ideal scripts of courtship and weddings, we assume that people are at some level aware of what works in relationships and what does not. Therefore, ideal relationship scripts should approximate the most successful courtship patterns, that is, those that are associated with higher relationship well-being. Accordingly, we turned to the research literature to see what aspects of courtship development are in fact successful, in the sense that they are associated with higher relationship well-being. If people's ideal scripts do accurately reflect what works and what does not in relationships, then examining the research literature's findings should give an indirect approximation to those ideal scripts.

Inferences From Modal Responses. Individuals' courtship and wedding scripts may also contain information about the elements most commonly present in these events. Scripts may encode how people think relationships typically develop, as opposed to how they think relationships ideally develop.

These typical scripts are relatively easy for us to assess in the empirical work presented below. In this study, we had a representative sample of newlywed couples describe their courtships and their weddings. By studying the issues or themes that emerged most frequently in these stories, we can develop some ideas as to the most typical elements of courtships and weddings in our society. If individuals have an accurate assessment of typical relationship development, then their internal scripts should closely map these common issues and themes.

Having outlined what relationship scripts are, where they might come from, and how they might be assessed, we now turn to an empirical investigation of the effects of scripts on relationship memories.

AN EMPIRICAL INVESTIGATION OF SCRIPTS AND RELATIONSHIP MEMORIES

Method

In the following study, we used the logic outlined previously to infer individuals' ideal relationship scripts from research findings, and to infer their typical relationship scripts from the modal courtship and wedding descriptions of a representative sample. We then investigated changes in newlywed couples' relationship stories over a 2-year period, to test if their memories of relationship development indeed came to approximate their relationship scripts more closely over time, as we would hypothesize.

Subjects

In this chapter, we present new analyses of data collected for the Early Years of Marriage study, a longitudinal investigation of marriage and marital well-being in newly married couples. The initial sample consisted of 373 newly married couples (199 Black and 174 White), comprising a representative sample of Detroit-area newlyweds who filed for marriage licenses in the spring of 1986.

To be eligible for participation, the marriage had to be the first for both partners, and the wife had to be less than 35 years old, to allow for the possibility of childbirth during the relationship (see Veroff, Douvan, & Hatchett, 1992, for details of the study and the sample).

Procedure

Couples were interviewed in their homes 4 to 7 months after they were married, and then again 2 years later, in the third year of their marriage. The current study contains data from the 262 couples who participated in the study both in Year 1 and in Year 3.

Each partner completed an individual, standardized interview. The couple was also interviewed together. The couple interview took place in the presence of a same-race female interviewer, and was tape-recorded. As part of the couple interview, partners were asked, together, to tell the story of their relationship, in a open-ended fashion, from the time the first met, up until the present, and on into the future. Thus, for the early events in the relationship, such as the courtship, wedding, and honeymoon, we had the couples' memories for the same events collected at two points in time, 2 years apart. These twice-told memories of courtships and weddings were the focus of our investigation, with the opportunity to test how stories about the same experiences change over time.

In analyzing changes in couples' stories, we used a coding system designed to capture broad stylistic and thematic dimensions of the narratives (see Veroff, Sutherland, Chadiha, & Ortega, 1993a; and Orbuch, Veroff, & Holmberg, 1993, for further descriptions of the coding scheme). Coders were initially trained to a level of at least 80% agreement for each coding category. A random 10% of all narratives were check-coded to maintain 80% reliability as coding progressed. Disagreements were settled by discussion between the coder and the check-coder.

In this chapter, then, we turn to the research literature and to people's stories in Year 1 to help us develop hypotheses concerning the nature of the cultural and subcultural scripts of relationship development held by our respondents (we used a different strategy to assess individual-level scripts, described in more detail in the appropriate section). We hypothesized that elements of couples' stories that conformed to these scripts would be emphasized or exaggerated in memory. By comparing the courtship and wedding stories as told in Year 1 to the same stories as told in Year 3, we were able to determine if the prevalence of these script-related features indeed increased over the 2-year period.

Cultural Scripts and Hypotheses

Ideal Scripts Inferred From Previous Research

What does the research literature tell us about cultural ideals of relationship development? To our knowledge, research directly assessing people's general courtship scripts has not yet been conducted. There is some systematic research on relationship development, however, which may provide us with clues. Surra and her associates, for example, examined turning points in relationship development. Her methodology is to allow people to recreate the major turning points prior to their marriages, and then to inquire about the nature of these turning points.

Surra, Arizzi, and Asmussen (1988) asked 41 newlywed couples to make graphs of their changes in commitment to each other and then to indicate reasons for these changes. Some reasons reflected changes in intrapersonal commitments, and these were associated with the most rapid changes in commitment. Some reasons related to accelerated demands from the couple's network, but couples who gave such reasons were not faring well 4 years later. Other reasons involved alternate dating partners, which also were associated with low marital satisfaction later.

From these results, we could piece together a potential ideal script that suggests that courtship should involve the development of an intrapersonal commitment to a partner that makes alternate dating partners irrelevant, and that does not reflect pressures put on the couple by friends or family to become committed.

Gergen and Gergen (1987) identified a number of plots that couples use in describing how their relationship developed. One of these plot lines—a positively accelerating plot—Veroff, Sutherland, Chadiha, and Ortega (1993b) found to be positively associated with marital well-being 2 years later. One could infer that another ideal script that this culture uses is that couples' courtship should follow a positive incremental development; a relationship with many ups and downs, partings and comings together, and overcoming intense conflicts is less than ideal for courtship. This hypothesis is supported by Kelly, Huston, and Cate's (1985) results showing that a description of courtship with conflict is associated with marital dissatisfaction 2½ years later. A courtship with conflict does not seem to be an ideal script. This inference is also confirmed by Orbuch et al.'s (1993) report that positively accelerated but nonromantic courtship themes, emphasizing a gradual development of love from friendship without intense conflicts, are positively and significantly associated with marital well-being.

Typical Scripts Inferred From Modal Responses in the Current Study

Turning to our own sample's responses, what further information can we gather about typical courtship and wedding scripts? With regard to the courtship, Orbuch et al. (1993) found that 50% of couples in Year 1 saw the male as the initiator of the courtship scenario. This response was far more common than any others, such as initiation by the wife, by both together, or by other people.

The husband was also the most likely to propose marriage. The most popular response in Year 1 for our sample (55%) was to say that the husband was the initiator, although 41% said that the couple did it together.

The most popular single theme about the wedding was that it was a social occasion for friends and family to get together to acknowledge the couple's commitment. Twenty-eight percent mentioned such as theme; otherwise couples spoke of a number of different themes.

From the research literature and from our own sample's responses, then, we can piece together a sketch of a courtship and wedding script. The male initiates the relationship. The couple then grow steadily closer, forming an intrapersonal commitment which comes from within, rather than being spurred on by outside forces. The relationship is harmonious, with little conflict and few serious reversals. The male then proposes, and the couple is wed in a ceremony that is an important social occasion, bringing together not only the couple themselves, but also their friends and families.

Results

Turning to the changes in our couples' stories from Year 1 to Year 3, there is evidence that our couples' stories more closely approximated the normative cultural script over time. Year 3 memories shifted away from thinking of the wife's involvement in initiating the courtship (20% to 13%) or proposing marriage (19% to 12%). The wife's involvement, when mentioned, was usually indirect, through hints to the husband or mutual friends. Even this indirect involvement tended to be lost from the story over time. The more traditional pattern of the male as initiator and the woman as passive became even stronger.

Over time, our couples seem to emphasize the close and friendly nature of their relationships, while de-emphasizing tensions or conflicts. Nonromantic positively accelerated courtship themes, the very ones that were associated-with marital well being in the Orbuch et al. (1993) study, were those that showed the most prominent increase in the stories told in Year 3 (from 26% to 39%). By contrast, the romantic positively accelerated themes decreased (from 36% to 26%).

These results are nonobvious. On the surface it would appear that a romantic theme would be the most sanctioned script in the culture, and in the first year such stories did predominate (36% have this theme as the most salient in Year 1). But as Orbuch et al. (1993) argued, such a construction may generate disappointment in the day-to-day living of a marriage. Thus, couples may have reconstructed their courtship in less romantic terms, so that their current situation would not reflect dashed expectations. Individuals may reshape their memories to undo the illusions and dreams they once had that are currently difficult to realize.

In addition to describing their relationships in more friendly and less romantic terms, couples also reported fewer tensions in their relationship. For example, in Year 1, the majority of couples (63%) reported experiencing some tensions or conflicts when planning the wedding. By Year 3, however, the report of tensions has shown a dramatic decrease (only 41% of couples now reported experiencing any tensions in wedding planning).

Instead of focusing on tensions in planning the wedding, the couples were now focusing more on the wedding as a social occasion, a time for people in the newlyweds' lives to get together to acknowledge their couplehood. As the most salient theme about the wedding, the construction of the wedding as a social event acknowledging the couple went from 28% in Year 1 to 42% in Year 3. As recall of the minutiae of the wedding waned, and details of the food or clothes or music that were so figural in memory in the first year faded, then the basic cultural script of the wedding as an important social occasion apparently became dominant in the way couples thought about the event.

By the third year, then, our couples' stories showed some changes in the direction of our hypothesized courtship and wedding script. They were less likely to recall the wife initiating the relationship or the marriage. They were more likely to think of their relationship as a smooth and steady progression out of friendship, and less likely to recall problems or tensions along the way. Finally, they were more likely to describe their wedding as a pleasurable and important social event where their friends and families joined together to celebrate their union. Their stories, over time, more closely approximated the proposed normative script for relationship development in North American culture.

Subcultural Scripts and Hypotheses

Ideal Scripts Inferred From Previous Research

Although the script we have pieced together here may represent the basic outline of relationship progression in North American society, there may still be different ideal scenarios for different groups. Most relationship research on married couples is conducted on volunteer samples who tend to be predominantly White and middle class. In our sample, we have a large group of Black married couples. Blacks in the United States often face very different economic and social circumstances than do Whites; these differences in life circumstances could lead to different cultural visions and ideals, which could influence their normative beliefs about what is best in a relationship.

For example, Veroff, Chadiha, Leber, and Sutherland (1993) suggested that Black couples take a more individualistic stance to their marriage, whereas White couples take a more couple-interdependent viewpoint. In so doing, White couples may, over the early years of marriage, increasingly value the collaborative aspects of marriage, so that memories about times when they were more separate in their relationship, such as in their courtship, may fade (compared to Black couples). Black couples' ideal relationship scripts may put more emphasis on two independent individuals forming a relationship together, while still maintaining some degree of autonomy. White couples' relationship scripts, in contrast, may put more emphasis on two individuals merging together to form one couple, a whole that is different from and greater than the sum of the two parts.

Kochman (1981) noted another important difference between Black and White couples. In examining Black and White styles of conflict in everyday conversations, Kochman noted that Blacks are more likely than Whites to use conflict and tension as part of their ordinary experience, a banter that makes interpersonal life zestful. This acceptance of conflict by Blacks would suggest that recall of tension and conflict might have different meanings in the two groups. At some level, one might expect Black couples to think of tension and conflict as part of the script for courtship and weddings, whereas Whites are more likely to see tension and conflict as something to be avoided in these scripts.

Typical Scripts Inferred From Modal Responses in the Current Research

Consistent with the previous suggestion, Orbuch et al. (1993) found that in the first year of marriage, Black couples were more likely than White couples to see their courtships as involving intense feelings coming out of tension, conflict, and overcoming obstacles to their relationship.

Also, compared to the White couples' wedding narratives in the first year, the Black couples' wedding narratives were more infused with tensions (82% of Black couples mentioned some kind of tension in their story, as opposed to 70% of White couples), and the tensions that were mentioned were stronger (on a scale of 1 to 3, where higher numbers equal more tension, Whites averaged 2.27; Blacks averaged 2.41). Furthermore, Black couples' stories of the wedding contained more mentions of conflict about wedding planning (60% of Black couples vs. 42% of White couples described some conflict in wedding planning). These results all suggest that in the scripts of Black couples, there are more normative expectations for tension and conflict, so that by the third year there might be less of a decrement in related memories for tensions and conflict among Blacks than Whites, if not an increase.

We anticipated, then, that Black couples' scripts would emphasize more autonomy for the individuals within the relationship than would White couples' scripts, and that Black couples would be more accepting of conflicts or tensions within the relationship than would White couples.

Results

To some extent, the changes in couples' stories from Year 1 to Year 3 did reflect these subcultural differences in scripts. For example, over the 2-year period, White couples showed a decrease in discussing their courtship as if it were a story of one person in pursuit of the other (from 17% in Year 1 to 6% in Year 3). Black couples, on the other hand, did not show this change in memory reconstruction (they remained stable at 21%). White couples showed indications of moving away from stories emphasizing the two partners as separate individuals rather than as an emerging couple; Black couples, more comfortable with autonomy within the relationship, showed no such memory changes.

There were also some differences between White and Black couples in memory changes for tension and conflict in their wedding stories. For both White and Black couples, there was an average decrease in tensions in the wedding narrative over the 2-year period, as noted in the last section. However, White couples showed a decrease in all subcategories of tension (i.e., tension between the couple, within either of the partners, between the couple and outsiders). Black couples, on the other hand, showed a significant increase in one type of tension—interpreting tensions in the wedding narrative as resulting from characteristics of the husband (e.g., the husband insisting on a certain style of wedding, or the husband being particularly anxious about getting married). In at least this one area, then, Black couples were willing to acknowledge, and continued to acknowledge, that the road to marriage was not always completely free from roadblocks and difficulties. White couples, in contrast, steadily moved their stories away from all types of tension or conflict.

Furthermore, White husbands who dropped in their reported marital well-being were members of couples who showed a remarkable increase in the strength of marital tensions in the wedding stories (ratings increase from 1.83 to 2.58 on a 3-point scale). Such was not the case for the Black husbands-(ratings stay stable, from 2.37 in Year 1 to 2.42 in Year 3). That is, increased reports of tension in the third year narratives were not associated with lowered marital well-being for the Black husbands. Mentions of tension in the wedding script did not seem to be a sign of larger problems in the relationship for Black couples, although such mentions did seem to signal problems in White couples. We thus have some evidence that the memory of tension in courtship and wedding stories may be affected differently in Black couples and in White couples, probably because of the greater acceptance of conflict and tension in the Black couples' relationship scripts.

Individuals' Relationship Scripts

We now turn from culture or subculture-wide scripts to more individualized beliefs of how relationships should progress. Not all people have the same ideas or philosophies about what things are important in a relationship. Individual variations in relationship beliefs, and changes in one's relationship beliefs over time, could lead one to emphasize or de-emphasize different aspects of the usual cultural or subcultural scripts, or to add new elements of one's own.

In this section, then, we turn to respondents' own beliefs about relationships, to determine what elements might be particularly emphasized or de-emphasized in these idiosyncratic scripts.

Assessment of Individuals' Relationship Scripts

In this section, we have direct measures of respondents' relationship beliefs. Respondents in both Year 1 and Year 3 were asked to rate the importance of 16 "Rules for Marriage." These rules asked about a variety of issues in relationships, such as the importance of equality between the spouses, how disagreements should be dealt with, and so forth. Partners were first asked to rate the importance each of the rules to them personally, then compare their responses and decide on a joint importance rating for each rule.

We focus on the individuals' responses to these questions at the two time periods. By examining how these responses change over time, we can get some idea of what aspects of the relationship were emphasized or de-emphasized; this emphasis may be reflected in changes in personal relationship scripts. The question then is whether those relationship beliefs which remained particularly central to individuals over time would play a particularly important role in influencing memory reconstruction. On the other hand, if individuals were to change their beliefs about what is important in a relationship over time, would they then come to see their new rules as having played a role in their relationship from the beginning? We focus on the effects of two particular relationship beliefs on memory reconstruction, namely, beliefs about the importance of egalitarianism, and beliefs about the importance of minimizing conflict.

Hypotheses

Egalitarianism. As Cate and Lloyd (1992) pointed out, there has been increasing emphasis in the last few decades on egalitarianism within relationships, with couples sharing all tasks on an equal basis, rather than relying on a division of labor along traditional gender role lines. However, egalitarianism is still a concept that enjoys varying degrees of support; some couples endorse egalitarian norms wholeheartedly, whereas others are content with more traditional roles. Such variations in beliefs could be associated with variations in courtship or wedding scripts, which in turn could lead to differential memory changes in narratives.

We chose to look at an example of the effects of beliefs in the importance of egalitarianism on memories for wedding planning. In general, our couples were relatively egalitarian in their wedding planning. A majority (53%) told relationship narratives indicating that they planned the wedding together, either by themselves or with the help of others. However, if only one partner carried out the bulk of the wedding planning, it was almost invariably the wife (34% single out the wife, or the wife with others).

We assume that people who have particularly egalitarian beliefs are likely to have planned the wedding jointly; on the other hand, those who were content with relatively traditional division of labor along gender lines were probably content to go along with the more traditional arrangement wherein the bride and her family complete the bulk of the planning.

But what about those who changed over time in their level of egalitarian beliefs? Such individuals might have felt free to endorse the equal division of labor and engage in their fair share of all tasks during the courtship phase, when there were few joint tasks to be negotiated. Over time in marriage, however, they might be likely to fall into more traditional patterns and beliefs. The day-to-day tasks of deciding who does what can be very wearing; over time, many couples may find themselves falling into more traditional division-of-labor patterns simply as a matter of convenience.

These changes in practice might then lead to changes in theory or beliefs over time, so that individuals come to believe that not only do they not behave in an egalitarian manner, but furthermore that it is not important to them to do so. Finally, these new beliefs might be applied retrospectively to past events, leading individuals to reconstruct these events as less egalitarian than they initially had. We therefore hypothesized that those individuals who saw egalitarianism in a relationship as less important in Year 3 than they had in Year 1 would show corresponding changes in memory, so that they would be less likely to speak of planning the wedding as a joint endeavor in their narratives.

Conflict Minimization. We also examined changes in individuals' beliefs in the importance of minimizing overt conflict in relationships. The section on culture-wide scripts suggested that, in general, respondents in our sample believed that overt conflicts and tensions were not healthy in a relationship; the section on subcultural scripts suggested that this norm may be more strongly held by White couples than by Black couples.

Of course, not all couples, nor even all couples of one racial group, hold this norm to the same extent. Some are more comfortable with conflict and disagreement, seeing it as a healthy way to clear the air; others believe it to be a sign of weakness in a relationship, and as something to be avoided at all costs. Such differences in acceptance of conflict may well affect individuals' beliefs about the acceptability of conflicts or tensions during the courtship and wedding process, with associated differences in memory changes for those events over time.

A number of the rules for marriage dealt with the importance of minimizing overt conflict in the relationship (e.g., "If you're fighting, try to cool off before you say too much"; "You should always settle a fight quickly"; "When you disagree, always take time to listen carefully to one another's point of view"; "Always be ready and willing to compromise in a disagreement"). We hypothesized that those who changed over time in their endorsement of such conflict-minimizing rules would show corresponding changes in their recollections about the wedding, an event that often contains some degree of conflict.

Specifically, we expected those individuals who reported weaker endorsement of the importance of minimizing conflict (i.e., they came to accept that conflict from time to time is inevitable in a relationship) would remember an increased level in the amount of tension described in the wedding narrative.

Results

Egalitarianism. Table 12.1 suggests that, as hypothesized, changes over time in beliefs of the importance of egalitarianism in relationship in general were related to changes in memories for the degree of egalitarianism in the wedding planning. Table 12.1 compares the percentage of husbands in the two groups who recalled in their narratives that their weddings were planned together, with both partners contributing. The first group, "stable highs," consists of those husbands who were consistently high in egalitarianism. Both in Year 1 and Year 3, these men said that it was "very important" that men

TABLE 12.1
Percent of Husbands Saying the Wedding was Jointly Planned as a Function of Time and
Changes in Egalitarianism

	Time	
Egalitarianism	*Year 1*	*Year 3*
Stable highs	46	47
Decreasers	57	35

Note. "Stable highs" are those who rate the rule "Men and women should share equally in household chores" as "very important" in both Year 1 and Year 3. "Decreasers" are those who rate the same rule as "very important" in Year 1 but "not very important" in Year 3.

and women share equally in household chores. As Table 12.1 shows, this group also remained stable over time in their recall of how their wedding was planned.

The second group, the "decreasers," are those husbands who showed a drop over the 2-year period in their endorsement of egalitarian values.[4] In Year 1 they agreed it was very important to share equally in household chores, but by Year 3 they believed it was "not very important" As hypothesized, they also showed a corresponding change in their description of earlier events. In Year 1, they were very likely to report having aided in wedding planning; by Year 3, they were less likely to report the wedding as jointly planned. As current views on what is important in relationship change, so apparently do memories of relevant activities in the past.

Conflict Minimization. Our hypothesis that those who came to believe less strongly in the importance of minimizing conflict would recall an increased level of conflict in the wedding received some support. However, our findings were complicated by differences between Whites and Blacks in their level of comfort in acknowledging a certain amount of conflict or tension in their interactions. In the analysis of these data, race × group × time interactions consistently emerged. Table 12.2 shows the general pattern of results.

Table 12.2 displays coders' ratings of the amount of tension in the wedding narratives in Year 1 and Year 3, broken down by race and by husbands' endorsement of the rule "Always be ready and willing to compromise in a disagreement"[5] Again, there are two groups of respondents: "stable highs,"

---

[4]Very few individuals in our sample were in either the "stable low" group (consistently said egalitarianism was not important) or in the "increase" group (increased their endorsement of egalitarian values over time). These individuals were deleted from our analysis.

[5]This same pattern of results appeared for both husbands and wives across a number of different conflict-minimizing rules; these means represent the general pattern. Collapsing across rules is complicated by the fact that individuals are not always in the same group; they may be "stable highs" for one rule but "decreasers" for another.

TABLE 12.2
Amount of Tension in the Wedding Narrative as a Function of Time, Race, and Changes in
Conflict Minimization

	Time	
Conflict Minimization	Year 1	Year 3
	Blacks	
Stable highs	2.33	2.39
Decreasers	2.28	2.72
	Whites	
Stable highs	2.07	2.62
Decreasers	2.18	2.39

Note. Higher numbers indicate more tension on a 3-point scale. "Stable highs" are those
who rate the rule "Spouses should be ready and willing to compromise when they face a
disagreement" as "very important" in both Year 1 and Year 3. "Decreasers" are those who rate
the same rule as "very important" in Year 1 but "not very important" in Year 3.

who steadily maintain their belief in the importance of minimizing conflict,
and "decreasers," who believe that minimizing conflict is very important in
Year 1, but believe it is less important by Year 3.

Black respondents show exactly the pattern of responses we predicted:
Those who remained stable over time in their endorsement of the conflict
rule (i.e., "stable highs") also remain stable in their memories, showing little
change in the amount of tension reported in the wedding narrative in Year 1
and Year 3. In contrast, those who saw the conflict-minimizing rule as less
important over time (i.e., "decreasers") showed a corresponding increase in
the amount of tension displayed in their wedding narratives.

White respondents, somewhat puzzlingly, consistently showed exactly the
opposite pattern of results. For them, it was the "stable highs" who show the
increase over time in the amount of tension displayed in their wedding
narrative. It is possible that here again we are seeing Black–White differences
related to the fact that Blacks are somewhat more comfortable acknowledging
the presence of a certain degree of conflict or tension in their relationship.

For many White couples, conflict in the marriage is a charged topic, a sign
that all is not as it should be. Such people may have unrealistically high
expectations that conflict should never intrude on marital bliss, expectations
that in most cases cannot be maintained over years of marriage. Those
individuals who consistently insist, at an overt level, that all conflict should be
minimized, may find those tensions spilling out in a more indirect, covert
manner, such as in their recall of wedding events. In contrast, those who are
willing to acknowledge that sometimes conflicts will occur (i.e., "decreasers") will not leak such tensions into their memories.

Such interpretations are, of course, speculative. More controlled studies, in which Black and White couples engage in a conflictful interaction, and overt and covert assessments of related tension are taken, would be valuable. However, interpretation of such work would still be complicated by the fact that a conflictful interaction may have different general meanings and implications for couples in the two subcultures.

CONCLUSIONS AND FUTURE DIRECTIONS

The fact that the meanings and implications of relationship events can change depending on one's culture is an important point. We have given some illustrative examples of how memories for relationship events can be affected by one's cultural scripts, whether that culture is understood at a very broad level (i.e., North American society), at a somewhat narrower level (one's ethnic group), or at a idiosyncratic level in which each couple forms their own culture over time. At whichever level we understand culture, then, it can have an influence on how a relationship's past is perceived and understood.

We believe that the influence of culture on relationships is not restricted to memories of the past, however. At a broader level, people's understandings of how relationships can and should work no doubt color every aspect of the understanding of relationships—how ongoing interactions are interpreted, emotions are experienced, and predictions made about the relationship.

To date, much relationship research has assumed that respondents share similar understandings of relationship events (e.g., conflict is negative, signs of commitment are positive). This assumption is not necessarily unwarranted, given that most research to date has been done on relatively homogeneous samples (dating college students or White middle-class married volunteers). However, as our understanding of the basic processes of relationship knowledge expands, we must also remember to contextualize that knowledge. As a first step, researchers should fully describe the samples in research reports. Second, work on representative samples of relationships, or on underrepresented groups, should be encouraged. Finally, work specifically designed to assess the nature and impact of cultural beliefs and scripts about relationships should be undertaken.

Many questions in this area of research and theorizing remain. However, we would argue that an increased understanding of scripts and other relationship beliefs will help us understand the role of memory in close relationships.

REFERENCES

Acitelli, L. K., & Holmberg, D. (1993). Reflecting on relationships: The role of thoughts and memories. In D. Perlman & W. H. Jones (Eds.), *Advances in personal relationships* (Vol. 4, pp. 71–100). London: Jessica Kingsley.

Bailey, B. L. (1988). *From front porch to backseat: Courtship in the twentieth century.* Baltimore, MD: The Johns Hopkins University Press.

Cate, R. M., & Lloyd, S. A. (1992). *Courtship.* Newbury Park, CA: Sage.

Duck, S., Pond, K., & Leatham, G. (1991, May). *Remembering as a context for being in relationships: Different perspectives on the same interaction.* Paper presented at the meeting of the International Network on Personal Relationships, Normal/Bloomington, IL.

Gergen, K. J., & Gergen, M. M. (1987). Narratives of relationships. In R. Burnett, P. McGhee, & D. Clarke (Eds.), *Accounting for relationships* (pp. 269–288). New York: Methuen.

Holmberg, D., & Holmes, J.G. (1993). Reconstruction of relationship memories: A mental models approach. In N. Schwarz & S. Sudman (Eds.), *Autobiographical memory and the validity of retrospective reports* (pp. 267–288). New York: Springer-Verlag.

Kelly, C., Huston, T. L., & Cate, R. M. (1985). Premarital relationship correlates of the erosion of satisfaction in marriage. *Journal of Social and Personal Relationships, 2,* 167–178.

Kochman, T. (1981). *Black and white styles in conflict.* Chicago: University of Chicago Press.

Loftus, E. F., Miller, D. G., & Burns, H. J. (1978). Semantic integration of verbal information into a visual memory. *Journal of Experimental Psychology: Human Learning and Memory, 4,* 19–31.

Malinowski, B. (1956). Marriage as a religious institution. In R. Briffault & B. Malinowski (Eds.), *Marriage: Past and present* (pp. 64–73). Boston: Porter Sargent.

McFarland, C., & Ross, M. (1987). The relation between current impressions and memories of self and dating partners. *Personality and Social Psychology Bulletin, 13,* 228–238.

Orbuch, T. L., Veroff, J., & Holmberg, D. (1993). Becoming a married couple: The emergence of meaning in the first years of marriage. *Journal of Marriage and the Family, 55,* 815–826.

Ross, M. A. (1989). The relation of implicit theories to the construction of personal histories. *Psychological Review, 96,* 341–357.

Surra, C. A. (1990). Research and theory on mate selection and premarital relationships in the 1980s. *Journal of Marriage and the Family, 52,* 844–865.

Surra, C.A., Arizzi, P., & Asmussen, L.A. (1988). The association between reasons for commitment and the development and outcome of marital relationships. *Journal of Social and Personal Relationships, 5,* 47–63.

Veroff, J., Chadiha, L., Leber, D., & Sutherland, L. (1993). Affects and interactions in newlyweds' narratives: Black and White couples compared. *Journal of Narrative and Life History, 3(4),* 361–390.

Veroff, J., Douvan, E., & Hatchett, S. (1992). Marital interaction and marital quality in the first year of marriage. In W. Jones & D. Perlman (Eds.), *Advances in personal relationships* (Vol. 4, pp. 103–137). London: Jessica Kingsley.

Veroff, J., Sutherland, L., Chadiha, L., & Ortega, R. (1993a). Newlyweds tell their stories. *Journal of Social and Personal Relationships, 10,* 437–457.

Veroff, J., Sutherland, L., Chadiha, L., & Ortega, R. (1993b). Predicting marital quality with narrative assessments of marital experience. *Journal of Marriage and the Family, 55,* 326–337.

13

The Pursuit of Knowledge in Close Relationships: An Informational Goals Analysis

Jacquie D. Vorauer
Princeton University

Michael Ross
University of Waterloo

Shakespeare's claim that "love is blind" is now a cultural truism, and this belief may well have abounded in his day. Although we hesitate to dispute Shakespeare, we are intrigued by how romantic partners sometimes exhibit remarkable sensitivity to negative as well as positive behaviors and emotions that occur in the context of their relationships. Moreover, starry-eyed as partners can be, romantic attraction is frequently associated with intensive information-seeking efforts and vigilance: Uncertainties about aspects of their partners and their relationships often seem to prompt people to undertake a variety of overt, surreptitious, and even underhanded actions. In this chapter, we examine the direct and indirect strategies individuals might adopt to obtain answers to their questions, and discuss the implications of their informational search for their self-evaluations and feelings about their relationships. We consider how individuals' concerns are likely to change as their relationships progress, and analyze factors that influence people's vigilance for information about their partners and themselves. We conclude that lovers may be blind, but not always in the traditional sense of being motivated to ignore each other's faults and construct utopian views of their relationships.

A key issue raised by our analysis is whether individuals who are in love try to discover the "truth" about their partners or their relationships. There is good reason to suppose that people sometimes ignore information that is inconsistent with their beliefs and hopes. Swann (1983) argued that people orchestrate their social environments to confirm or validate what they already believe to be true: They avoid information that is inconsistent with previous knowledge, and reject such information when it is thrust upon them. One implication of Swann's research is that romantic partners may conduct a biased search for social information. Theory and research on positive illusions also suggests that romantic partners may ignore or discount information that challenges their preferences (e.g., Kunda, 1990; Murray & Holmes, 1993, chap. 4, this volume; Taylor, 1989).

We acknowledge that intimates are motivated to judge their partners favorably, and to be optimistic about the future of their relationships. However, we also maintain that these same individuals often endeavor to obtain realistic assessments and prognoses. They are willing to question their existing knowledge, and to abandon beliefs that are potentially out of date. Further, they seek diagnostic tests of their partners' devotion and characteristic traits. They are willing to risk uncovering unsavory information and are responsive to such information when they do encounter it. In this chapter, we examine the circumstances that prompt individuals to attempt to discover the truth about aspects of their romantic relationships, and analyze some potential outcomes of their efforts. We use the term *informational goal* (Vorauer & Ross, 1993a) to refer to the specific type of knowledge an individual seeks at a particular point in time. Informational goals prompt people to divert their cognitive and behavioral resources from alternative endeavors to an active search for new information. When pursuing informational goals, individuals are concerned with obtaining answers to the questions that are important to them. Ironically, a desire to obtain accurate information may invoke a number of systematic cognitive biases. Even though—indeed, because—the motivation to learn something new leads people to devote considerable effort to the scrutiny and interpretation of events and behaviors, it might be associated with inferential pitfalls that can have implications for individuals' feelings about themselves and their partners.

Before presenting our analysis of informational goals, we offer the following caveat. Our characterization of romantic relationships may strike some readers as too calculating, too cerebral. We focus on people's passion for knowledge rather than on their more earthly desires. We don't claim that's all there is to love, but we do assert that the quest for information is an important feature of close relationships. Our purpose is to describe the information gathering that people undertake in the context of intimate relationships. Accordingly, we present a framework for thinking about partners' pursuit of relationship knowledge.

A TYPOLOGY OF RELATIONSHIP-RELEVANT INFORMATIONAL GOALS

People can ask themselves a multitude of questions about their romantic relationships. To bring some order to the array of concerns individuals might have, we limit our focus to goals involving people (as opposed to places or things) and categorize them along three main dimensions: target, focus, and globality.

Target

People may seek information about themselves, their partners, their relationships, or other individuals. People often seem to crave information about themselves (*self* informational goals); they will even pay strangers to tell them what they are like. People in different eras and places have sought personal knowledge from supposed experts such as fortune tellers, palm readers, astrologists, phrenologists, graphologists, psychiatrists, psychologists, and counselors of various sorts. More commonly, individuals look to their friends, families, and romantic partners to obtain information about their own traits and abilities, such as how attractive or intelligent they are. Individuals with *partner* informational goals are interested in learning about their romantic partners' qualities. They may wish to assess whether their partners are caring, trustworthy, or ambitious. Individuals with *relationship* informational goals are curious about properties of their relationships. For example, they may wonder whether they and their partners are right for each other, and about their future together. Finally, people with *external* informational goals wish to learn about other individuals who might have a bearing on their relationships. A man may be interested in the physical and psychological attributes of his partner's mother because he believes that his partner will resemble her 25 years from now. A woman may be interested in discerning attributes of her partner's boss (e.g., her generosity and trustworthiness), because of the implications for her partner's future economic well-being.

In previous work, researchers and theorists have typically examined goals that involve learning about self independently from those that center on learning about other people. Our perspective emphasizes the interpersonal context in which individuals usually pursue self- and other-relevant goals. Social exchanges provide the conversation and behaviors for analysis. These interactions afford people with simultaneous opportunities to learn about themselves and others. Thus, individuals' inclination to pursue either type of objective will be affected by the extent to which the other goal category competes for their attention. Although people sometimes seek to satisfy a number of different objectives concurrently, or oscillate among them, their cognitive and behavioral resources are limited. To pursue one informational goal, individuals may often have to forego alternative goals.

Focus

We divide informational goals into two general classes, *inherent* and *reflected*.[1] Individuals with inherent goals are interested in assessing the attributes of people or relationships; individuals with reflected goals investigate others' opinions of people or relationships. Consider this distinction in reference to self informational goals. People pursue *inherent-self* informational goals when they seek information about aspects of themselves that they perceive to exist independently of the eye of the beholder, such as their abilities and enduring, central traits. People's efforts to assess their feelings about their partners or their relationships can also be characterized as inherent-self goals. Individuals pursue *reflected-self* informational goals when they attempt to determine how another person perceives them. A man may want to know whether his (potential) partner considers him to be intelligent or caring, apart from any interest or concern regarding the extent to which he "truly" possesses these traits.

The inherent/reflected distinction extends to all informational goals. For example, people with *inherent-partner* goals wish to determine the attributes of their partners; those with *reflected-partner* goals wonder how others (e.g., their best friends) view their partners. Individuals with *inherent-relationship* goals are curious about qualities of their relationships, and those with *reflected-relationship* goals wonder how others view their relationships: Do my parents feel that we are right for each other? Do my friends think that we make a good couple?

Globality

The final dimension concerns the degree to which people's informational goals are specific or global. In most social psychological research, researchers assign subjects specific goals; for example, subjects are asked to infer another person's attitude or ability. In everyday life, people's goals vary in their globality. A woman who attempts to assess her date's economic prospects or attitudes toward children is pursuing a relatively narrow, well-defined goal. A woman who is interested in learning anything and everything she can about her date is pursuing a general goal.

OBSTACLES TO UNCERTAINTY REDUCTION

It is not immediately obvious that the pursuit of relationship-relevant information should be an enduring source of concern for individuals. Romantic partners could conceivably reduce uncertainty about the topics that interest them quickly and without difficulty by simply asking each other for

---

[1]We previously used the term *relational* to refer to this category of goals (Vorauer & Ross, 1993a).

answers to the questions that are on their mind. Partners' frequent opportunities to communicate with one another enable them to develop and share extensive knowledge about relationship-relevant issues (Schlenker & Weigold, 1992; Surra & Bohman, 1991). The exchange of social information is an intricate and often subtle process, however (Goffman, 1955). A variety of social and self-protective concerns—which may be particularly active in the context of romantic relationships—may render individuals reluctant to adopt seemingly efficient and straightforward approaches to knowledge acquisition. Social norms govern self-disclosure and the exchange of interpersonal appraisals (e.g., Atlman & Taylor, 1973; Blumberg, 1972; Cansler & Stiles, 1981; Stiles, 1978; Stiles, Waszak, & Barton, 1977). These norms may sometimes inhibit individuals from communicating or soliciting explicit evaluations. People may feel that it is inappropriate to ask their partners certain kinds of questions. In addition, questions transmit information. Questioners reveal their vulnerabilities and uncertainties. A woman may worry that by quizzing her partner about his feelings toward her, she would inadvertently convey information about her insecurity and level of investment in the relationship. She may fear that such questions would influence her partner's perceptions of the balance of power between them. Ironically, individuals' concerns about controlling the information they convey to their partners with their questions may be greatest at the beginning of relationships, when their interest in acquiring answers may be maximal, and their knowledge about their relationships least well-developed. Partners may feel more comfortable adopting direct, information-seeking strategies as trust develops and closeness increases. Presumably, relationship construals will then be less precarious.

Note that respondents can either facilitate or inhibit their partners' search for information, depending on their own motives and concerns. A woman might cooperate with her partner, answering his queries to the best of her ability. Alternatively, her fears about the potential implications of revealing her feelings may render her reluctant to divulge this information to her partner when asked. Thus, she may make it difficult for her partner to reduce his uncertainty with direct information-seeking strategies. One possibility is that she deliberately deceives or misdirects him. In this case, her partner may cease searching for information, at least temporarily, believing that his questions have been answered. Another possibility, however, is that the woman thwarts her partner's efforts to obtain new knowledge by failing to answer his queries. The questioner may then seek alternative ways of finding answers.

THE DIAGNOSTICITY BIAS

Individuals can adopt indirect and possibly surreptitious strategies in order to obtain the information they need. Rather than asking for direct answers to their questions, they may observe their own and their partners' feelings, remarks, and behaviors, and make inferences about dispositions and interpersonal attitudes. How might people's goals affect the inferences they make from the evidence that they consider? We argue that the process of trying to learn as much as possible results in a systematic inferential bias, whereby individuals exaggerate the degree to which the data address their concerns. According to our framework (Vorauer & Ross, 1993a), people's motivation to answer their "burning" questions leads them to believe that events, behaviors, and emotions—regardless of how ambiguous they might be—convey meaningful information. Furthermore, as people's motivation to reduce uncertainty is specific to particular topics, so will be the inferences that they are inclined to make. Partners' desire to reach conclusions regarding the issues that are of interest to them should heighten the number of significant events and behaviors they identify, and lead them to ascribe goal-relevant meaning to those events and behaviors. This diagnosticity bias should be apparent in their attributions, particularly when the evidence they consider is open to a variety of possible interpretations. Many, perhaps all, social behaviors fall into this category.

Consider, as an example, a woman who is anxious to determine her partner's current level of affection and esteem for her. Her goal will predispose her to perceive that his behaviors reflect his feelings toward her. If he does the laundry when it is her turn, she may consider a variety of explanations for his behavior. Did he do it to please me? Because he plans to ask a favor in return? Because he didn't like the way I did it last time? Because he realizes that I have a tremendous amount of work to do today? Although the hypotheses vary in their implications, they share the implicit assumption that the behavior reflects something about her partner's attitude toward her. The woman's desire to reduce uncertainty about her partner's devotion will lead her to perceive many of his actions as having evaluative implications.

There is research evidence that individuals are generally inclined to perceive themselves as the target of another person's behavior (Fenigstein, 1984; Vorauer & Ross, 1993a; Zuckerman, Kernis, Guarnera, Murphy, & Rappaport, 1983). For example, Zuckerman and his associates had pairs of participants engage in short discussions with a confederate; the discussions were interrupted by the experimenter when the confederate summarized his or her opinion on an issue. Participants tended to see themselves rather than the other participants as the cause and target of the confederate's last statement. In other studies, students estimated the probability that a test singled out by a professor was their own versus a classmate's, or rated the likelihood that they or another participant had been randomly selected totake part in an experimental demonstration (Fenigstein, 1984). In both of these cases, participants provided higher estimates for themselves than for the other people.

We suggest that people's tendency to exaggerate the degree to which they are the target of another's actions is a function of the interests and concerns elicited by their current social context (Vorauer & Ross, 1993a, 1993b). The apparent ubiquity of self-as-target bias may reflect the ubiquity of the goal of acquiring self-relevant information (i.e., self informational goals). By perceiving themselves as the target of other people's behavior, individuals can make needed inferences about how those people view them. Such effects can be obtained in the laboratory among strangers. Imagine how much stronger the tendency may be in settings in which the other person is an individual's romantic partner, the person whose feelings he or she cares most about. Individuals' needs to plan their behavior and control their future outcomes in the context of their close relationships (e.g., "Should I risk a romantic overture?" "Should I mention marriage?" "Is an apology in order?") may often prompt them to take their (potential) partners' behaviors personally.

Along with Newman and Langer (1988; Newman, 1981), we speculate that individuals' perceptions of being the target of their partners' behavior are likely to be enhanced by feelings of mutual interdependence: Interdependence should heighten individuals' concern with predicting and controlling their partners' actions and feelings toward themselves. We would also emphasize the importance of shifting uncertainties and priorities. Individuals' readiness to take their partners' behavior personally should ebb and flow over time, depending on the strength of self informational goals relative to other concerns that may be operative both within and outside their relationships. Early in a relationship, when the need for reflected-appraisal information is great, individuals may be particularly prone to exaggerate the extent to which their partners' behavior is targeted at them. Additionally, as we discuss later, these concerns may be easily reactivated by such factors as the arrival of attractive alternative partners.

Other Manifestations of the Diagnosticity Bias

Although the diagnosticity bias may often result in self-as-target inferences, there are a variety of other forms that it might take. Indeed, there are as many potential manifestations as there are types of informational goals. Individuals should perceive events, emotions, and behaviors as providing clues about the issues that are of greatest interest to them, whatever those issues may be. For example, an interest in learning about their partners' qualities should heighten individuals' readiness to draw dispositional inferences from their partners' actions and remarks. Thus, those with partner informational goals should be especially likely to exhibit the fundamental attribution error, or correspondence bias (Jones, 1979; Ross, 1977). As a result, individuals might also underestimate their own influence on their partners' behavior (i.e., making character attributions instead).

Consider, then, some of the inferences that a woman might draw from her companion's laughter. If she is primarily concerned with learning what he thinks of her, she should be inclined to view his laughing as a reflection of his attitude toward her ("He thinks I'm amusing"). If instead she is interested in learning about him, she should be more likely to interpret his laughter as reflective of his disposition ("He has a good sense of humor"), or current mood state ("He's nervous"). If she is interested in assessing their relationship potential, she should draw inferences about the dynamic between them ("We're hitting it off really well"). Note as well that when individuals' informational goals are specific to particular domains, they should tend to draw inferences relevant to those domains. If the woman is especially interested in whether her companion is intelligent, she should be inclined to form conclusions from his behavior about this particular aspect of her personality.

The Inherent-Reflected Distinction and the Diagnosticity Bias

Cooley (1902), Mead (1934), and others in the symbolic interactionist tradition suggest that individuals develop their self-concepts primarily on the basis of others' evaluations of them (i.e., that people use reflected appraisals to infer their own traits and abilities). Our perspective highlights the influence of individuals' current uncertainties and priorities on their readiness to draw conclusions about themselves from others' actions and remarks. When individuals pursue inherent-self goals, they should be inclined to draw conclusions about their true personal qualities ("I'm am amusing person"); in contrast, when they pursue reflected-self goals, they should tend to draw relatively circumscribed inferences about other people's opinions of themselves ("He thinks I'm amusing"). This analysis extends to other types of informational goals. For example, whether a woman takes her mother's treatment of her fiance as indicative of his enduring traits should depend, in part, on whether she has an inherent- or reflected-partner goal.

This process can also occur in the opposite direction: People may use their knowledge about inherent characteristics to infer reflected appraisals. A woman may deduce people's impressions of herself, her partner, or her relationship from her own assessments. With respect to self informational goals, this latter process corresponds to the self-perception mechanisms discussed by Kenny and DePaulo (1993), whereby people refer to their self-concepts and behavior to determine another person's likely impressions of them. Just as a desire to learn about their own inherent traits and abilities may increase individuals' readiness to take others' reactions to heart, then, a desire to know how others view them may lead individuals to overestimate the congruence between their self-concepts and others' opinions of them.

Note that a similar process may occur with respect to interpersonal evaluations. Lovers who are uncertain about their partners' love for them might sometimes turn to their own feelings toward their partners to deduce this information. Projecting their personal sentiments on partners who harbor quite different feelings, they may systematically misread their behavior, framing ambiguous social actions in ways that reflect their own feelings, rather than their partners'. People may assume that their attraction is reciprocated when it is not, or assume that their partners are experiencing disenchantment similar to their own.

Analyzing Minutiae

To information-hungry individuals, then, the behaviors of the objects of their affection seem full of personal meaning. They notice and interpret even behavioral minutiae in accordance with their informational goals. An anxious suitor is likely to perceive a fleeting frown on his beloved's face as a sign of her dissatisfaction with him, rather than as an indication that the tamales that she had for dinner are exacting their revenge; he may also draw self-relevant inferences from her friendliness toward the waiter. Thus, a strong desire for knowledge may lead individuals to pursue information in a rather indiscriminate fashion. They might seek and extract evaluations even from sources they would otherwise consider uninformative, such as horoscopes or fortune-tellers. People's tendency to imbue random events and chance happenings with diagnostic significance provides the strongest evidence for this claim. Consider, for example, the actions of the man who plucks the petals off of a flower in a desperate attempt to determine whether she loves him or loves him not, or how a woman, anxious to assess whether she and her partner are "meant" for each other, may read meaning into whether they are able to find jobs in the same city.

Obviously, people are not always wrong when they infer that another person's ambiguous social behavior is directed at them. Particularly in the early stages of a relationship, individuals may signal their interest (or lack thereof) indirectly through meaningful glances and additional forms of oblique communication (see Simpson, Gangestad, & Nations, chap. 5, this volume). Indirect communication allows partners to explore each other's intentions without overt confrontation, and to avoid the possible discomfort of directly rejecting or being rejected. Psychological research indicates that thin slices of expressive behavior can indeed convey considerable information (Ambady & Rosenthal, 1992). We maintain only that when individuals are pursuing informational goals, they will be biased toward drawing goal-relevant inferences from such behaviors. Furthermore, whether individuals draw inferences discrepant from those of their partners or outside observers should depend on whether their informational goals diverge. Suppose that a woman is interested in her partner's reactions to her at the same time that he is interested in her reactions to him. She may then take his behaviors personally, while he may perceive the identical actions as conveying impressions about his personality characteristics.

Detecting and Constructing Nonoccurrences

Informational goals may also heighten an individual's readiness to code the absence of particular behaviors as meaningful. People possess scripts for how romantic interludes should unfold. When a woman's date omits a behavior in her dating script, such as bringing her flowers, she may take the deviation personally rather than infer that his dating script differs from hers. As well, a desire to evaluate her date's feelings toward her may lead the woman to imagine, afterward, a wide array of behaviors that could have occurred, but did not. She might note that they failed to stop by the neighborhood pub, and wonder if perhaps he wanted to avoid his friends (Did he not want to be seen with her? Did he want to be alone with her?). Thus, the woman's informational goal might lead her to "construct" choices for her date that render whatever events did happen all the more significant.

Beyond Partners' Behavior: Diagnosticity Bias in Self-Inferences and in Inferences Outside the Relationship

The diagnosticity bias is not limited to the inferences that individuals draw from their partners' actions. They may also be too ready to attach significance to their own feelings and behavior. When people are anxious to assess their feelings toward their partners or their relationships, for example, they may be inclined to "jump to conclusions" from their mood states. Suppose that a woman who is uncertain of her love for partner has to decide whether to increase her commitment to their relationship. She may then monitor her emotions closely, drawing inferences from her affective states. She may be too ready to attribute her mood to her feelings about her partner, rather than to other plausible causes (e.g., her satisfaction with her job).

A related possibility is that informational goals lead individuals to exaggerate the amount of personal information their actions convey to their partner. A woman who is concerned about her (potential) partner's impressions of her might try to deduce his appraisal from her own actions. She may review how she behaved toward him during their last interaction, imagining his probable reactions to her remarks and behaviors. In attempting to perceive her actions from his perspective, the woman might ignore the possibility that he was not concerned about forming an impression of her at the time; her behavior might therefore have conveyed fewer "signals" than she supposes. Furthermore, her desire for appraisal information, coupled with accessible self-knowledge, may lead her to overestimate the congruence between his actual response to her and her view of herself. Recent research suggests that individuals' feelings of transparency are heightened when they are interested in deducing another person's opinion of themselves: They perceive that more of their personal qualities can be accurately discerned from their behavior if they have reflected-self informational goals, rather than other objectives such as task goals (Vorauer, 1993).

Individuals' perceptions of the visibility of their attributes might influence how they behave toward their partners, as well as the judgments they make about them. A woman's assumptions about the personal information her partner possesses about her may guide the amount of effort she devotes to communicating her feelings and goals to him. Her beliefs about how well he knows her personality and preferences may also affect her inferences regarding the intentions underlying his behavior. In particular, feelings of transparency may increase the likelihood that the woman will take her partner's behavior personally. If she believes that she has clearly communicated her needs to him, then she may be more apt to take his "insensitive" behavior as a personal affront, or as evidence of a lack of caring. At earlier stages, individuals' sense that their attraction or romantic interest is readily apparent may lead them to take a lack of "response" as rejection.

People's tendency to exaggerate the meaningfulness of behavior also extends to persons beyond their relationship. As we already noted, individuals are often interested in assessing other people's appraisals of their partners. While pursuing this goal, a man may be prone to exaggerate the degree to which others' behaviors are directed at his partner and reflect evaluations of her. This form of diagnosticity bias may help explain the apparently irrational jealousy that people sometimes experience. People's relationship-relevant informational goals may also influence their interpretation of outsiders' behavior toward themselves. On meeting her partner's parents for the first time, a woman may be intensely concerned about their impressions of her. She may interpret their formality and reserve as indications that they think she is not good enough for their son. The woman is perhaps less likely to make a different, but plausible, inference for the reticence of his parents: They are nervous about meeting her, and are as concerned as she is with making a good impression.

Vigilance and Volatility

Our analysis suggests that early in relationships, when the desire for information is high and knowledge is scant, people's feelings and inferences about their partners and relationships should be volatile. Ever ready to make inferences from their partners' behaviors, individuals may vacillate dramatically from one extreme interpretation to another (he loves me; he loves me not) in reaction to seemingly contradictory evidence. Individuals may also construe their own mood swings as indications of their feelings toward their partners. Such dramatic shifts in interpretation should decrease in frequency as individuals gain more information about each other's feelings. From our perspective, the decline occurs, in part, because people's informational goals change; as relationships mature, individuals are less inclined to search either their own or their partners' behavior for indications of their feelings toward each other. However, volatility should resurface whenever and wherever individuals' informational goals are activated; further, it should endure indefinitely in domains where uncertainty is chronic. Note that when the evidence contains some degree of mixed signals, informational goals may sometimes actually slow the process of uncertainty reduction. Greater attention to and analysis of isolated behaviors may heighten partners' awareness of inconsistencies in each other's actions and feelings.

Process

What is the mechanism by which the diagnosticity bias is produced? Researchers and theorists have argued that attributional processing is triggered by negative, unexpected, or script-inconsistent behaviors (Holtzworth-Monroe & Jacobson, 1985; Langer, 1978; see Weiner, 1985). Our approach emphasizes, in addition, how "top–down" factors may instigate the pursuit of information. The informational goals framework suggests that individuals may subject virtually any behavior, expected or not, positive or negative, to considerable scrutiny if they seek to acquire social knowledge.

We propose that the process by which informational goals lead people to exhibit a diagnosticity bias has two main components. First, informational goals heighten the accessibility of relevant knowledge structures. For example, depending on what they wish to learn about, people's self-concepts, personality theories, or relationship schemata may be activated. Bruner (1957) described the impact of category accessibility on thresholds for categorization of stimuli: "The greater the accessibility of a category, (a) the less the input necessary for categorization to occur in terms of this category, (b) the wider the range of input characteristics that will be accepted as fitting the category in question, and (c) the more likely that categories that provide a better or equally good fit will be masked" (p. 15). Bruner's analysis has received substantial empirical support. For example, information is likely to be categorized in terms of chronically accessible and recently primed constructs (see Higgins, 1989, for a review). Similarly, we propose that the effect of informational goals on assessments of the diagnosticity of social information reflects, in part, individuals' lowered thresholds for categorizing behaviors as goal-relevant.

Second, informational goals motivate people to devote cognitive resources to examining their own and others' behavior. When people are anxious for information, they scrutinize events and behavior closely, looking for clues that may provide answers to the questions that are currently important to them. They divert resources from alternative pursuits to search for "signals" that are relevant to their interests. In addition, inferential activity increases, reflecting individuals' eagerness to imbue potential evidence with meaning. People will subject their own and their partners' behavior (or, according to the nature of their goals, the way they interact together or the reactions of outside observers) to in-depth analysis. The increased effort individuals devote to scrutiny and analysis of the evidence, coupled with the enhanced accessibility of pertinent knowledge structures, results in a diagnosticity bias.

Note, then, that our perspective diverges from current approaches in social cognition theory and research, which emphasize cognitive laziness as a source of inferential errors and biases (Fiske & Taylor, 1991). We suggest that the diagnosticity bias occurs, in part, because of the great effort that individuals with informational goals devote to analyzing events and behaviors.

The Diagnosticity Bias as Reduced Skepticism

We now consider a final and rather different possible manifestation of the diagnosticity bias. To this point, we have focused on how individuals' informational goals may affect the meaning they attach to ambiguous behaviors and feelings. An intense desire to reduce uncertainty about particular topics may also reduce people's tendency to question the sincerity of explicit communications from their partners, such as direct evaluations or self-reports. Informational goals may render individuals more likely to accept their partners' statements at face value than they would otherwise be.

There are a variety of factors that might lead people to be skeptical of direct communications, in the absence of a strong need to obtain answers to "burning" questions. If individuals believe that their partners lack sufficient self-insight or understanding of the dynamics of their relationships to provide them with the information they need, they may doubt the validity of explicit feedback. They may also doubt that their partners will be completely honest with them. When individuals suspect that their partners are concerned with their well-being or wish to avoid conflict, they may be skeptical about favorable appraisals. Similarly, if individuals suppose that self-presentational motives are operative, they may wonder whether their partners are being untruthful, or withholding information.

Individuals' doubts about their partners' motives and knowledge may sometimes render them hesitant to accept direct communications at face value. However, they may be inclined to abandon their skepticism when they are anxious for information. People's desire for knowledge may reduce their tendency to consider alternative, goal-incongruent, accounts for their partners' remarks. Thus, when individuals pursue informational goals, they may exhibit a diagnosticity bias in their interpretations of direct feedback and self-reports, as well as in the meaning they attach to ambiguous events and behaviors.

BEHAVIORAL EFFORTS TO ACQUIRE INFORMATION

The influence of romantic partners' desire to learn about themselves and each other is not necessarily restricted to cognitive processes. Although people may be hesitant to ask questions directly, there are a variety of other actions that they might take to reduce uncertainty about the issues that are of concern to them: Individuals might seek out and engineer situations to maximize the information they can acquire from behavioral observation. For example, people may arrange to observe their (potential) partners' behavior across different social contexts. Individuals' desire to increase the information available to them may also lead them outside their relationships. They may observe other couples for social comparison, or solicit outsiders' opinions of their partners and relationships. Furthermore, people may sometimes endeavor to create events or situations that will yield information particularly relevant to their concerns. If a woman is uncertain about her feelings for her partner, she may want to see how she reacts to their spending time apart from one another. If she is interested in learning about his feelings, she may flirt with another man, or arrange for her partner to see the man flirting with her, anxious to observe her partner's reactions to the scenario.

In some cases, individuals might try to increase the diagnosticity of the evidence by removing their own behavior as a potential account for their partners' actions. Thus, a woman might refrain from directly expressing her needs to her partner, to examine how sensitive he will be on his own initiative. Or she may try to learn whether her partner is trustworthy by giving him an opportunity not to be (Boon & Holmes, 1991; Holmes, 1990). To see if her partner will keep his promise to call her, she might resist the impulse to phone him herself.

Partners' behavioral efforts to acquire information can be either overt or surreptitious. Furthermore, partners can invoke the search for information jointly as well as individually. To evaluate their relationships, couples may agree to try living together, to separate temporarily, or to go to a counselor. When couples take joint action to acquire information, their pursuit of knowledge will necessarily be overt, although each partner's true intentions and purposes may not be.

Do individuals' behavioral information-seeking efforts have ramifications for the diagnosticity bias? We suspect that the bias will not be eliminated by such endeavors: Information-seekers may sometimes not fully appreciate the limited value of the data yielded by their behavioral search. Consider cases where individuals solicit the opinions of outside observers. Information-seekers may not recognize the extent to which the assessments they receive from observers are affected by observers' motives (e.g., to provide reassurance). Moreover, in many circumstances, information-seekers provide outside observers with much of the knowledge on which observers base their judgments. Information-seekers may then fail to realize the extent to which they have influenced observers' opinions by providing selective reports. A similar analysis may apply to individuals' efforts to increase the diagnosticity of their partners' behaviors. People may not always appreciate how the tests of devotion or integrity they design are based on their private, idiosyncratic construals of a given situation. A woman who encourages other men to treat her in ways that could potentially make her partner jealous may assume that he will share her perception of events, when in fact he may see warm and friendly behavior rather than romantic overtures.

PEOPLE'S INFORMATIONAL GOALS CHANGE AS THEIR RELATIONSHIPS MATURE

People are not inclined to spend all of their waking hours pursuing self, partner, or relationship informational goals. People instigate an informational search primarily when they lack knowledge that is important to them. At the beginning of a relationship, a person's (potential) partner is often a virtual stranger; consequently, the partner introduces a great deal of uncertainty into the person's everyday life. Individuals want to know how their partners feel toward them, how others evaluate their partners, what their partners are like, and so forth. The order in which people pursue these various types of knowledge depends, in part, on their informational priorities (e.g., how much they care about what others think). In addition, whether a particular search is prolonged versus brief in duration will be influenced by external circumstances that affect the ease or difficulty of attaining, for instance, reflected appraisals as opposed to inherent partner information. After partners learn about the issues that are initially important to them, they may begin to pursue informational goals that center on new domains or situations that they encounter (e.g., How well will we get along during family gatherings? Will we enjoy traveling together?).

People's goals are therefore likely to shift from global to more specific as they get to know their romantic partners better. However, the informational goals of romantic partners seem likely to remain at a relatively global level in comparison to those pursued in other kinds of relationships. Laws, social norms, and specific interests constrain the types of information that people request from others in most relationships (e.g., employer–employee). In contrast, informational boundaries in romantic relationships are much more expansive. As couples discuss the day's happenings over dinner, for example, they solicit and are genuinely interested in a level of detail that would have little appeal to anyone else, except perhaps their parents.

Information can be important to romantic partners because it helps them to predict their future outcomes and plan their behavior. Choice points in relationships may activate such concerns, and thereby elicit especially intense information-seeking efforts. Early on, for example, individuals may wish to assess whether potential partners would welcome or reject romantic overtures. Alternatively, they may have to decide how to respond to romantic overtures. Romantic unions are characterized by an expectation of exclusivity that does not accompany most other types of close relationships. One partner will have to satisfy a wide variety of an individual's needs. Thus, people's latitudes of acceptance and rejection may be particularly well-defined in the realm of romance. Before deciding whether to increase their involvement in relationships, people might seek to evaluate their partners against an extensive set of criteria. Furthermore, individuals might wonder how their partners evaluate them along these same dimensions (Am I what this person is looking for?).

Stay–leave decisions are likely to arise periodically once individuals have become romantically involved. Whether the informational goals that people pursue at these points center on themselves or their partners will presumably depend on how power is distributed in their relationships. Power is associated with the level of satisfaction individuals receive from relationships, as well as the level they would obtain from alternative arrangements (Thibaut & Kelley, 1959). Individuals possess high power when their alternatives would provide almost as much satisfaction as their current relationships; they can opt out of the current relationships with little cost as they reach their "break even" point. People have low power within relationships when that association provides much greater satisfaction than alternative arrangements would provide; they are then highly dependent on both the relationships and their partners.

The informational goals of people with low power should be focused on their partners, as these individuals will want to predict and control their partners' stay–leave decisions. They should be attuned to—and vigilant for changes in—their partners' relationship satisfaction, their partners' feelings toward them, the quality of alternatives available to their partners, and how they themselves stack up against these alternatives (in their partners' eyes). In contrast, individuals who possess high power will be concerned with monitoring their own satisfaction with their relationships, their feelings toward their partners, the quality of alternatives available to them, and how their current partners compare to alternatives. The closer the person with higher power is to "breaking even," the greater the individuals' interest in obtaining these respective types of information should be.

Presumably, concerns about stay–leave decisions subside as partners' commitment to their relationships increases. As couples take steps to formalize and publicize their intentions to continue their relationships (e.g., by getting married), and as they deal with the costs of accommodating to one another's traits and preferences, they may grow less interested in assessing whether they or their partners would be more satisfied in relationships with others. The high divorce rate suggests, however, that for many couples concerns about stay–leave decisions are never fully reconciled, or are revived at later points in their relationships.

Partners' informational goals may also vary systematically with the level of trust that has evolved between them. Boon and Holmes (1991) associated the development of trust with three sequential relationship stages. The romantic love stage is distinguished by strong positive feelings, idealization of partner, and high feelings of trust that may have little basis. Romantic love is succeeded by the evaluative stage: Individuals submit their partner and relationship to a closer and more realistic examination. Finally, individuals enter the accommodation stage, where they make a "leap of faith" beyond that permitted by the evidence. Boon and Holmes argued that in the third stage, trust becomes "a necessary construction permitting an illusion of control, a resolution of the uncertainty continually promoting a sense of vulnerability" (p. 204). The Boon and Holmes model has a number of implications for individuals' search for information about themselves and their partners. People may pursue informational goals concerning trust-relevant attributes and interpersonal attitudes most fervently during the second stage in this sequence: In particular, individuals' concerns may focus on dimensions such as predictability and dependability, components of trust that have been identified as important by researchers (Rempel, Holmes, & Zanna, 1985).

Once trust is established, individuals enjoy the security of knowing that they can depend on their partners and that they are cared for. They will still seek new knowledge, but their informational goals during this maintenance phase may stem from a need to make practical decisions rather than from interpersonal evaluation. Couples may have to resolve such issues as how to pool resources, share household duties, decide where to live, and so forth. Over time, individuals' goals may also come to focus more on the relationship than on either individual in isolation: Concerns about "keeping love alive," not taking each other for granted, and general relationship improvement may become more prevalent.

Theorists have proposed a variety of other stage models of relationship development (e.g., Kerckhoff & Davis, 1962; Lewis, 1972; Murstein, 1976;

Reiss, 1960). According to these models, the best predictors of progress in a relationship change over time, and include factors such as physical attraction, value similarity, need complementarity, and successful role performance. If individuals are attuned to the qualities of their relationships that affect their satisfaction most powerfully at different stages, then their informational goals should shift over time in predictable ways as they pursue knowledge in the domains that are currently significant.

Some theorists have questioned the validity of stage models of relationship development, arguing that relationships follow their own individual course, rather than a preordained sequence of stages (Leigh, Homan, & Burr, 1987; Rubin & Levinger, 1974; Stephen, 1987). Our analysis does not depend on whether the pattern of relationship development is idiosyncratic or general. Nor does it require that individuals accurately identify the qualities of their relationship that affect their satisfaction. Rather, we suggest that people's information-seeking efforts are guided by their beliefs about the factors that are important to their satisfaction, regardless of the validity of these ideas (see also Fletcher & Fitness, 1992a; Fletcher & Thomas, chap. 1, this volume).

The Self–Other Dichotomy in the Context of Close Relationships

Over time, romantic partners may experience a "merging" of self and other. For example, theorists have argued that individuals' self- definitions may incorporate their important relationships (Aron & Aron, 1986, chap. 11, this volume; Aron, Aron, Tudor, & Nelson, 1991; Markus & Kitayama, 1991). The particularly close bond that emerges between romantic partners has implications for their pursuit of informational goals. Individuals are likely to be more curious about their partners' attributes and evaluations of themselves than they are about other people. Such curiosity may often stem from concerns about predicting and planning behavior. Another possible reason for people's interest in their partners is their desire for self-expansion. Aron et al. (1991) suggested that "people are motivated to enter and maintain close relationships to expand the self by including the resources, perspectives, and characteristics of the other in the self" (p. 243). These authors suggest that intimates act as though some or all of their partners' attributes are their own. Thus, individuals may want information about their partners in order to know how to think about their new, expanded selves. In the context of their close relationships, then, individuals' self- and other-centered goals might sometimes overlap rather than compete. Learning about other becomes equivalent to learning about self.

The merging of self and other that accompanies close relationships affects public perceptions as well as private conceptions of self. Individuals judge other people, in part, by the accomplishments and attributes of their associates (Sigall & Landry, 1973). This suggests another way in which close relationships might affect informational goals. A man may be interested in another person's opinion of his romantic partner because he believes that the person's opinion will have implications for how he himself is viewed. His partner is an extension of himself: Through her actions and qualities, she has the capacity to change others' views of him. Hence, even before getting involved, individuals may examine other people's reactions to their potential partners to learn how relationships would affect their public images. Once they have entered relationships, individuals might continue to be curious about the impressions their partners convey to others. People may also want to know (and possibly influence) their partners' judgments of other associates (e.g., friends, family). A woman may draw inferences about her partner's feelings toward her from his reactions to those individuals who are close to her. If the woman's partner disparages her best friend, she may perceive him as derogating a part of herself.

Conceivably, individuals grow more inclined to look to their partners for inherent-self information as their relationships mature. Over time, people may come to expect that their partners' evaluations of their own attributes will be particularly accurate. Long-term partners have observed each other's behavior across many different contexts, and have been audience to one another's innermost thoughts and feelings; consequently, they may have unique insights into each other's characters. Individuals might also attach special significance to their partners' opinions because they do not draw a clear distinction between their partners' reactions to them and how they feel about themselves, by virtue of their emotional bond.

In our analysis, we have tended to emphasize how partners' pursuit of knowledge might reflect the utility of various types of social information at different points in their relationships. Individuals' growing affective bond with their partners might also enhance their curiosity about their partners' personal qualities or opinions of themselves: They may value this information, apart from any practical purpose it might serve. For example, a woman may wish to learn about her partner's hopes, dreams, and fears not because she wants to predict some aspect of his behavior or decide whether to commit to a relationship with him, but because she finds these issues intrinsically interesting.

Romantic partners' susceptibility to the diagnosticity bias may depend on the extent to which their informational goals are need- versus curiosity-driven. Conceivably, people are most vulnerable to the bias when they need information to plan their behavior or predict their future outcomes—that is, when they are anxious to obtain answers quickly. When the search reflects more exploratory, curiosity-driven motives (see, e.g., Aron & Aron, 1986), individuals may be more discriminating with respect to the cues they consider to be relevant.

CHRONIC VIGILANCE: THE ROLE OF UNCERTAINTY

Despite regular, prolonged opportunities over many years to observe and interpret their partners' (and their own) behaviors and feelings, people may continue to devote considerable energy to making inferences about their relationships and analyzing relevant issues. How can we account for the chronic vigilance that individuals sometimes exhibit in the context of their romantic relationships? Researchers have linked the tendency to engage in attributional analysis to marital dissatisfaction (e.g., Holtzworth-Monroe & Jacobson, 1985) and periods of relative instability or uncertainty in a relationship (Newman & Langer, 1988; Surra & Bohman, 1991). In the present analysis, we attempt to delineate some of the factors that may enhance partners' subjective perceptions of instability and sustain their feelings of uncertainty about relationship-relevant issues. We propose that shifting circumstances and people's theories of change are important causes of continued monitoring.

Shifting Circumstances

People's life circumstances change; partners have opportunities to learn more about each other as they confront new situations. A couple conducting a long distance relationship because of jobs in different locations may find work in the same city and live together for the first time. They may then monitor each other's behaviors in their new, shared environment, discovering information that either enhances or diminishes their love for each other. Alternatively, external circumstances (e.g., jobs, wars) may force a couple to live apart. Separation may provide them with the potential to acquire additional information about their feelings for each other. Moreover, the shared experiences of births, deaths, illnesses and other vicissitudes of life offer opportunities for individuals to learn more about themselves, their partners, and their relationships. The additional information that people acquire from shifting circumstances sometimes serves to confirm prior beliefs (e.g., I knew that I could count on him), whereas at other times it adds new elements to their view of self or partner (e.g., he's no good in an emergency). Changes in external circumstances may sometimes revive uncertainty by leading partners to question beliefs and theories they currently possess. A woman may wonder how her partner's evaluation of her will change once they start living together. She may worry that his love will wane upon exposure to her annoying habits and morning personality, even though she was previously confident of his devotion. She may also wonder whether living together will affect her own satisfaction with the relationship.

More generally, a shift in circumstances might alter people's perceptions of how their present relationships compare to other possible relationships.

People choose to remain in a particular relationship when it is preferable to the alternatives (Thibaut & Kelley, 1959). Because the options available to individuals and their partner can frequently undergo change, uncertainty about these issues may be continually revived. The arrival of an alluring alternative partner may prompt an otherwise satisfied and secure woman to re-assess her own or her partner's satisfaction with their relationship. The attractiveness of an alternative partner is also to some extent uncertain. People can only guess about how satisfying they will ultimately find alternative relationships, and how they will feel being apart from their current partners.

Note that people are not simply passive recipients of changes stemming from their environment. They initiate change on their own. They sometimes undertake programs of action to alter themselves, their partners, and/or their relationships. Such projects will presumably influence informational goals. After engaging in these efforts, people should be interested in assessing the impact of their actions.

Theories of Change

Individuals may monitor feelings and behaviors even when external circumstances are stable: Their implicit theories about changes in themselves and their relationships can generate and prolong uncertainty about relationship-relevant issues. For example, people may worry (or hope) that their partners' current feelings toward them will "wear off" if nothing is done to sustain the feelings. Alternatively, their theories may predict that love will deepen with the passage of time. Thus, partners may sense the potential for change in their relationships even at times when their behavior patterns are highly routinized. Partners' beliefs about how long the impact of isolated behaviors will last may also affect monitoring. A woman who has betrayed her husband may wonder whether he will forgive her with the passage of time. A few weeks after giving his wife an extravagant anniversary gift, a man may wonder whether she still feels the appreciation and adoration she expressed when he made the gesture. Note that the direction of the hypothesized change should influence people's desire to obtain information. If the change is potentially negative, then partners may search for evidence of its onset to protect either themselves or the relationship from harm. If the theorized change is benign or even positive in terms of its implications for themselves or the relationship, however, then there is less need for vigilance (unless the starting point involves negative feelings or beliefs, such that improvement is crucial).

Individuals may also hold theories dictating that discrepancies between their own and their partners' evaluations of themselves or their relationships are inherently unstable. For example, if people sense that their partners' current evaluation of them is inconsistent with their self-concept, they may be likely to consider the opinion impermanent and look for evidence of change. They might believe that others—especially close others—ultimately discover, for better or worse, what they are truly like (i.e., their inherent self). Furthermore, depending on whether the move to agreement involves an improvement or decline in their partners' opinions, individuals may engage in behaviors designed to promote or prevent the change they anticipate. In either case, they may wish to monitor the success of their endeavors.

People's theories about the particular relationship dimensions that are likely to change should serve to focus their search for information, determining whether and in which domains they are vigilant. Conceivably, people believe that interpersonal evaluations are more ephemeral than personality dispositions. For example, they may consider a partner's level of love or commitment to be more transient than his or her traits. Theories that lead people to suspect that change will occur in domains of importance to them seem likely to engender chronic monitoring: Any knowledge they currently possess, no matter how sound that knowledge may be, has the potential for becoming out of date and inaccurate.

COORDINATING INFORMATIONAL GOALS

In our analysis of the impact of informational goals on people's behaviors and cognitive processes, we have tended to treat each individual in isolation. It is important to emphasize, however, that a relationship is a dynamic system. Both partners have informational objectives, and their goals may or may not be complementary. When partners pursue similar informational goals, such as evaluating their relationship, they may cooperate in their attempts to learn (e.g., by agreeing to live together or apart for a while) and thus be better able to acquire the information they seek. Partners may face more obstacles in finding answers to their questions when their goals are at odds, or when they misunderstand each other's goals. As people often fail to make their informational goals explicit to their partner, such misunderstandings may be quite common. We suggest that individuals' assumptions about their partner's motives will be influenced by their own informational objectives. A woman who enters an interaction with a reflected-self goal will tend to presume that her partner's behavior indicates his assessment of her. This assumption permits her to infer that his behavior is relevant to her goal. Indeed, she may well assume that he is currently evaluating her. In contrast, if she pursues an inherent-partner goal, she may be less concerned with her partner's evaluation of her. To extract goal-relevant information from his behavior, she will simply need to assume that her partner is motivated to act in accordance with his preferences and beliefs.

Perhaps most interesting for our analysis are situations in which both individuals in an interaction strive to assess the other's opinions of themselves. In such circumstances, their informational goals may lead them to misinterpret each other's behavior. They may be unaware that they both consider themselves to be the object of appraisal: They might mistakenly believe that their partner is evaluating them. We suspect that partners' interactions are often characterized by such dual egocentrism. The implications of this misunderstanding can be profound. Each partner may follow his or her own goals, failing to provide the type of direct feedback that the other would prefer. In the absence of explicit evaluations, they each must make do with the information that they can obtain. They sift through the evidence, trying to extract any details that seem even remotely revealing of the other's assessment.

Informational goals that encompass people beyond the dyad are sometimes less problematic than goals centered on the partners. Suppose partners share the objective of evaluating a third person (an inherent-external goal). The social norms that affect discourse would not normally prevent partners from discussing such a goal, and pooling their information. Moreover, they may feel less need to disguise their feelings when making judgments about outsiders. They can provide direct and unequivocal information to each other. The irony is that partners may possess more accurate knowledge of what they think about other people than how they feel about each other: Fewer things are left unsaid.

This analysis of the coordination of informational goals has an important theoretical implication: It is necessary to take account of the social context in which informational goals are operative. Within a romantic relationship, a person's informational search is affected by what his or her partner is thinking and doing, and how well the partners communicate their goals to each other. Moreover, partners' informational goals will often extend beyond their dyad to the outside world. They may frequently cooperate in this search for outside information; they may also attempt to impede or control each other's acquisition of knowledge.

WANTING NOT TO KNOW?

We have presented people as eagerly seeking information, as dedicated scholars of personal relationships. Anecdotally, at least, people occasionally seem to resist knowledge about other individuals.[2] Spouses are sometimes portrayed as the "last to know" that their husband or wife is unfaithful, and

---

[2]People may also avoid information about themselves, suppressing or repressing particular thoughts. A discussion of such issues is beyond the purview of the present chapter.

parents as "the last to know" that their children are drug addicts, gay, or terminally ill.

Before assuming that such apparent ignorance involves motivated avoidance or misrepresentation of evidence, we should first consider several other possibilities. Individuals may feign ignorance, while knowing the truth. The facts may be too distressing for them to discuss, or they may feel that there is little advantage to confronting the issues directly. Alternatively, individuals may not know. They may be slow to discover the truth, because others withhold relevant information. An unfaithful husband may be especially motivated to conceal his dalliances from his spouse. The wife's friends may be aware of his actions, but reluctance to initiate discussions of such a painful subject with her, or to make her deal with issues that she appears unwilling to confront. They may also suppose that she knows the truth, but prefers not to consult with them.

A related possibility is that the evidence available is ambiguous. Accordingly, spouses and parents may interpret the information in line with their beliefs and expectations. Although their conclusions may support their preferences, their judgments may also be perfectly plausible in light of the evidence they have available to them at the time (although, with hindsight, they may later consider themselves to have been extremely naive). Even base-rate statistics may be on their side. Most children are heterosexual and not terminally ill. In their responses to survey questions, the majority of spouses indicate that they are faithful (Adler, 1993).

Of course, we don't insist that people always interpret information in a completely rational fashion. People's inferences are often guided by their preferences (Kunda, 1990). If the information is ambiguous (as it so often is), people may choose to interpret it in a way that is consistent with their desires and wishes. They may then ignore equally or more cogent interpretations of the evidence.

A final and quite different prospect is that people willfully decide not to know. They ignore, avoid, or misrepresent seemingly *unequivocal* information. The implications of this hypothesis are psychologically intriguing. At some level of awareness, people would have to know what information they want to avoid. For their avoidance strategy to be effective, they would then have to evade the information without being aware that they were doing so, or at least without knowing their motivation for doing so. The psychological processes underlying such deliberate ignorance may parallel those involved in perceptual defense. Modern research suggests that consciousness is a multistage process. Individuals can recognize, at preconscious levels of awareness, that a stimulus contains information that they wish to avoid knowing and defend themselves against the unwanted information (Dixon, 1981; Erdelyi, 1974).

In summary, people sometimes appear surprisingly unaware of the actions of their close associates. Often, the information that they lack has negative social or personal implications. Moreover, such ignorance seems most common in domains where individuals feel little power to effect change, or where the costs of acting on the information are high (e.g., asking for a divorce). In such contexts, it is tempting to suppose that people's lack of awareness indicates a desire to avoid obtaining information. As there are several other plausible explanations for people's apparent ignorance, however, we cannot conclude that a lack of knowledge necessarily reflects a preference not to know.

IS LOVE BLIND?

A discussion of deliberate ignorance leads directly to our final topic. A belief that new lovers are blind to each other's failings can be traced at least as far back as Shakespeare's play, the Merchant of Venice. From our perspective, love is not blind in the sense that lovers are motivated to ignore each other's faults and construct utopian views of their relationships. Even new lovers are interested in truth; their primary inferential error is that they are oblivious to irrelevance rather than to negativity. They read meaning into every nuance. But people's tendency to invest social behavior with surplus meaning does not explain why romantic partners' inferences about each other tend to be so positive. A proclivity to endow behavior with meaning could presumably yield unfavorable as well as complimentary conclusions. How can we account for the fact that lovers hold strongly idealized views of each other, especially early in the course of romantic relationships (Brehm, 1988)?

One answer to this question is that people's idealized views are grounded in reality. Individuals who are mutually attracted to each other are likely to be on their best behavior, especially early in a relationship when they are uncertain whether their feelings are reciprocated. Trying to create a favorable impression on their partners, they are likely to be careful about what they do and say. They behave how they think their partners would like them to act. Consequently, the early behavioral information on which partners base their inferences may support their extremely positive views of each other. Romantic partners err, however, in failing to fully appreciate the limited diagnostic value of that information. People have concerns besides pleasing their partners: They also want to accommodate other individuals, including themselves, whose interests may compete with their partners'. Over time, these concerns may come to exert a greater influence over people's behavior.

In summary, we consider the idealizations that may characterize the early phases of relationships to be the result of individuals' tendency to overestimate the diagnosticity of their partners' behavior. People fail to fully appreciate that their partners' behavior will vary across contexts and change as their relationships mature. A prolonged failure to see flaws in one's partners and relationships is probably a rare phenomenon. To the extent that blindness does occur, it is likely to be a relatively brief malady.

CONCLUSION

Close relationships provide a milieu in which people can acquire new knowledge about themselves and others. The informational goals framework offers a basis for understanding the origins, nature, and social implications of this pursuit of knowledge. People's queries may change as they and their relationships mature, but they are unlikely to run out of questions about themselves, their partners, or their relationships. In the current chapter, we analyzed the interplay between informational goals on the one hand, and inference processes, behaviors, and social contexts on the other. The relations are reciprocal. For example, informational goals affect the social contexts that people select and social contexts influence the goals that people pursue. While stressing people's interest in obtaining accurate information and forming valid inferences, we noted how both cognitive and social factors sometimes lead people to misinterpret what they perceive. In particular, we described a diagnosticity bias that influences individuals' interpretations of their own and other people's behavior. People's motivation to satisfy their informational goals leads them to exaggerate the degree to which the available evidence addresses their concerns. Finally, we emphasized throughout the parallels between the pursuit of self knowledge and the pursuit of social knowledge within an informational goals framework.

ACKNOWLEDGMENTS

Preparation of this chapter was supported by a SSHRC postdoctoral fellowship to the first author.

We thank Dale Miller, Sandra Murray, and Rebecca Ratner, along with the editors, for their helpful comments on an earlier draft.

REFERENCES

Adler, J. (1993, April 26). Sex in the snoring 90s. *Newsweek*, pp. 55–57.
Altman, I., & Taylor, D. A. (1973). *Social penetration: The development of interpersonal relationships*. New York: Holt, Rinehart & Winston.
Ambady, N., & Rosenthal, R. (1992). Thin slices of expressive behavior as predictors of interpersonal consequences: A meta-analysis. *Psychological Bulletin, 111,* 256–274.
Aron, A., & Aron, E. N. (1986). *Love and the expansion of self: Understanding attraction and satisfaction*. New York: Hemisphere.

Aron, A., Aron, E. N., Tudor, M., & Nelson, G. (1991). Close relationships as including other in the self. *Journal of Personality and Social Psychology, 60,* 241–153.

Blumberg, H. H. (1972). Communication of interpersonal evaluations. *Journal of Personality and Social Psychology, 23,* 157–162.

Boon, S. D., & Holmes, J. G. (1991). The dynamics of interpersonal trust: Resolving uncertainty in the face of risk. In R. A. Hinde & J. Groebel (Eds.), *Cooperation and prosocial behavior, trust, and commitment* (pp. 190–211). Cambridge: Cambridge University Press.

Brehm, S. (1988). Passionate love. In R. J. Sternberg & M. L. Barnes (Eds.), *The psychology of love* (pp. 232–263). New Haven, CT: Yale University Press.

Bruner, J. (1957). On perceptual readiness. *Psychological Review, 64,* 123–152.

Cansler, D. C., & Stiles, W. B. (1981). Relative status and interpersonal presumptuousness. *Journal of Experimental Social Psychology, 17,* 459–471.

Cooley, C. H. (1902). *Human nature and the social order.* New York: Scribner's.

Dixon, N. F. (1981). *Preconscious processing.* Chichester, England: Wiley.

Erdelyi, M. H. (1974). A new look at the new look: Perceptual defense and vigilance. *Psychological Review, 81,* 1–25.

Fenigstein, A. (1984). Self-consciousness and the overperception of self as a target. *Journal of Personality and Social Psychology, 47,* 860–870.

Fiske, S. T., & Taylor, S. E. (1991). *Social cognition* (2nd ed.). New York: McGraw-Hill.

Fletcher, G. J. O., & Fitness, J. (1992). Knowledge structures and explanations in intimate relationships. In S. W. Duck (Ed.), *Understanding relationship processes 1: Individuals in relationships* (pp. 121–143). Newbury Park, CA: Sage.

Goffman, E. (1955). On face-work. *Psychiatry, 18,* 213–231.

Higgins, E. G. (1989). Knowledge accessibility and activation: Subjectivity and suffering from unconscious sources. In J. S. Uleman & J. A. Bargh (Eds.), *Unintended thought* (pp. 75–123). New York: Guilford.

Holmes, J. G. (1990). Trust and the appraisal process. In W. H. Jones & D. Perlman (Eds.), *Advances in personal relationships* (Vol. 2, pp. 57–104). Greenwich, CT: JAI Press.

Holtzworth-Monroe, A., & Jacobson, N. S. (1985). Causal attributions of married couples: When do they search for causes? What do they conclude when they do? *Journal of Personality and Social Psychology, 48,* 1398–1412.

Jones, E. E. (1979). The rocky road from acts to dispositions. *American Psychologist, 34,* 107–117.

Kenny, D. A., & DePaulo, B. M. (1962). Do people know how others view them? An empirical and theoretical account. *Psychological Bulletin, 114,* 145–161.

Kerckhoff, A. C., & Davis, K. E. (1962). Value consensus and need complementarity in mate selection. *American Sociological Review, 27,* 295–303.

Kunda, Z. (1990). The case for motivated reasoning. *Psychological Bulletin, 108,* 480–498.

Langer, E. J. (1978). Rethinking the role of thought in social interaction. In J. H. Harvey, W. Ickes, & R. F. Kidd (Eds.), *New directions in attribution research* (Vol. 2, pp. 35–58). Hillsdale, NJ: Lawrence Erlbaum Associates.

Leigh, G. K., Homan, T. B., & Burr, W. R. (1987). Some confusions and exclusions of the SVR theory of dyadic pairing: A response to Murstein. *Journal of Marriage and the Family, 49,* 933–937.

Markus, H. R., & Kitayama, S. (1991). Culture and the self: Implications for cognition, emotion, and motivation. *Psychological Review, 98,* 224–253.

Lewis, R. A. (1972). A developmental framework for the analysis of premarital dyadic formation. *Journal of Marriage and the Family, 35,* 16–25.

Mead, G. H. (1934). *Mind, self, and society.* Chicago: University of Chicago Press.

Murray, S. L., & Holmes, J. G. (1993). Seeing virtues in faults: Negativity and the transformation of interpersonal narratives in close relationships. *Journal of Personality and Social Psychology, 65,* 707–722.

Murstein, B. I. (1976). The stimulus-value-role theory of marital choice. In H. Grunebaum & J. Christ (Eds.), Contemporary marriage: Structures, dynamics, and therapy (pp. 165–168). Boston: Little, Brown.

Newman, H. M. (1981). Communication within ongoing intimate relationships: An attributional perspective. Personality and Social Psychology Bulletin, 7, 59–70.

Newman, H. M., & Langer, E. J. (1988). Investigating the development and courses of intimate relationships. In L. Y. Abramson (Ed.), Social cognition and clinical psychology (pp. 148–173). New York: Guilford Press.

Reiss, I. L. (1960). Toward a sociology of the heterosexual love relationship. Marriage and Family Living, 22, 139–145.

Rempel, J. K., Holmes, J. G., & Zanna, M. P. (1985). Trust in close relationships. Journal of Personality and Social Psychology, 49, 95–112.

Ross, L. (1977). The intuitive psychologist and his shortcomings: Distortions in the attribution process. In L. Berkowitz (Ed.), Advances in experimental social psychology (Vol. 10, pp. 173–220). New York: Academic Press.

Rubin, Z., & Levinger, G. (1974). Theory and data badly rated: A critique of Murstein's SVR and Lewis's PDF models of mate selection. Journal of Marriage and the Family, 36, 226–231.

Schlenker, B. R., & Weigold, M. F. (1992). Interpersonal processes involving impression regulation and management. Annual Review of Psychology, 43, 133–168.

Sigall, H., & Landry, D. (1973). Radiating beauty: Effects of having a physically attractive partner on person perception. Journal of Personality and Social Psychology, 28, 218–224.

Stephen, T. (1987). Taking communication seriously? A reply to Murstein. Journal of Marriage and the Family, 49, 937–938.

Stiles, W. B. (1978). Verbal response modes and dimensions of interpersonal roles. Journal of Personality and Social Psychology, 36, 693–703.

Stiles, W. B., Waszak, C. S., & Barton, L. R. (1977). Professional presumptuousness in verbal interactions with university students. Journal of Experimental Social Psychology, 15, 158–159.

Surra, C. A., & Bohman, T. (1991). The development of close relationships: A cognitive perspective. In G. J. O. Fletcher & F. D. Fincham (Eds.), Cognition in close relationships. Hillsdale, NJ: Lawrence Erlbaum Associates.

Swann, W. B., Jr. (1983). Self-verification: Bringing social reality into harmony with the self. In J. Suls & A. G. Greenwald (Eds.), Psychological perspectives on the self (Vol. 2, pp. 33–66). Hillsdale, NJ: Lawrence Erlbaum Associates.

Taylor, S. E. (1989). Positive illusions: Creative self-deception and the healthy mind. New York: Basic Books.

Thibaut, J. W., & Kelley, H. H. (1959). The social psychology of groups. New York: Wiley.

Vorauer, J. D. (1993). Judging the observability of self and other: When do people feel transparent? Unpublished doctoral dissertation, University of Waterloo, Waterloo, Ontario.

Vorauer, J. D., & Ross, M. (1993a). Making mountains out of molehills: An informational goals analysis of self- and social perception. Personality and Social Psychology Bulletin, 19, 620–632.

Vorauer, J. D., & Ross, M. (1993b). A reflection of you versus a reflection of me: When do individuals take another's behavior personally? Unpublished manuscript.

Weiner, B. (1985). "Spontaneous" causal thinking. Psychological Bulletin, 97, 74–84.

Zuckerman, M., Kernis, M. H., Guarnera, S. M., Murphy, J. F., & Rappoport, L. (1983). The egocentric bias: Seeing oneself as cause and target of others' behavior. Journal of Personality, 51, 621–630.

Knowledge Structures
in Developing Relationships:
Progress and Pitfalls

Catherine A. Surra
The University of Texas at Austin

Contributors to this volume were given the aim of juxtaposing two themes: close relationships and knowledge structures. Accomplishing this task, by itself, is no small feat. The whole idea of knowledge structures originated in cognitive psychology, where research and theory on social cognition has been extensive. Yet, from the perspective of those of us who do work on close relationships, with its emphasis on the ways that partners are interconnected both behaviorally and cognitively, the work coming out of cognitive psychology seems decidedly nonsocial. What do we really know about the role of knowledge structures in close relationships? Although answers to this question are accumulating rapidly, the sum total of information about this topic is meager.

The authors of the chapters in this section on "Knowledge Structures and Relationship Development" were handed an even greater challenge: Examine the connections between knowledge structures and changes in close relationships over time. As a person who has studied these connections, I was happy to be in the position of reacting to what others have to say, rather than in the position of author as alchemist. It is important to recognize, then, that all of the authors who contributed to this volume were asked to break new ground; indeed, they were asked to move mountains. I would like my observations to be viewed in this light—with the understanding that the task was large and difficult and that any attempt to tackle it is a contribution from the start.

The theme of the section requires attention both to knowledge structures and to developmental change in relationships. Knowledge structures are permanent, organized stores of information that arise from individuals' interpretations of interactions with their environment. Once they are in place, knowledge structures affect the way subsequent interactions are interpreted and stored. In the case of close relationships, as in other cases, the term *interactions* needs to be interpreted broadly, for interactions with the partner and with other people, physical objects, institutions, and events all provide information relevant to relational knowledge structures. Examples of knowledge structures that are especially relevant to close relationships include causal accounts of relationship occurrences, conceptions of relational attitudes or constructs (e.g., partners' understandings of the meaning of love); and relationship-specific schema, which are representations of traits, beliefs, behaviors, and actions sequences that are relevant to a close other and one's relationship with that other (Surra & Bohman, 1991).

In reading the chapters in this section, I was also seeking information about what knowledge structures have to do with relationship development. To some people, development means growth on some dimension(s) of relationship involvement (e.g., closeness, stage of involvement, intimacy, frequency of joint behaviors). Indeed, for some, relationship development is equated with the evolution of closeness. When applied to relationships, however, development is not unidirectional; development can mean growth or *deterioration* along the dimensions of interest. Moreover, different dimensions can change in different directions simultaneously. Partners, for instance, can be falling more deeply in love at the same time that they are spending less time together. Likewise, the same relationship can develop differently for the coupled partners, as in the case where one partner is withdrawing from the relationship at the same time the other's feelings of closeness are growing stronger. Finally, in order to explain development fully, periods of maintenance, during which the relationship changes little, must also be examined. Thus, relationship development requires examination of periods of instability (formation, growth, deterioration) and periods of stability (Surra & Bohman, 1991). The key question raised in this section is: How do knowledge structures change with and how do they affect periods of instability and stability in close relationships?

CHANGES IN RELATIONAL KNOWLEDGE: PLANALP AND RIVERS

Planalp and Rivers (chap. 10, this volume) tackle head on the problem of changes in knowledge structures during periods of relationship instability. They report the results of a qualitative analysis of accounts of events in close relationships that made the respondents feel they knew their partners less well than they thought they did. This open-ended question produced narratives of events that increased uncertainty in relationships, a condition associated with periods of relational change. The narratives themselves, and the answers to other open-ended questions that the researchers asked, yield rich insights into the complex interconnections among the contents and processes of social cognitions during times of change. Many of the results are directly relevant to questions raised by the other chapters in this section.

Planalp and Rivers' chapter is strongly grounded in solid theorizing about cognition. They used their accounts to examine how well three key cognitive theories explain alterations in knowledge structures when inconsistent information is encountered: theories of schema inconsistency (or what Planalp and Rivers call "schema + tag"), explanatory coherence theory, and attribution theory (see Planalp & Rivers, chap. 10, this volume, for a review).

The authors address how well schema-inconsistency theory compares with theories of explanatory coherence to explain their findings, and concluded that the latter does a better job of accounting for the results. Explanatory coherence is especially applicable to understanding what people do with surprising or incongruent information that is not easily tagged. The theory provides a parsimonious account of what people do with such information in that the theory does not require that a piece of inconsistent information be tagged to some preexisting schema. Instead, an entirely new knowledge structure may result that brings together previously unconnected information in new ways. The resulting new knowledge structure is a qualitative overhaul of prior information, not a simple incorporation of inconsistent information. The theory also explains the ways in which many different knowledge structures come into play in the construction of the new schema.

All of the characteristics of the explanatory coherence model were present to some degree in Planalp and River's data. The nature of the events were such that major overhauls of knowledge were required, and a variety of other schema were called upon to arrive at a new, cogent explanation (e.g., generalized schema for what a particular close relationship is or should be like; schema for other specific close relationships). The new knowledge was revolutionary, rather than a simple adjustment of what already existed.

Although explanatory coherence does do a good job of explaining the data, schema inconsistency also seems to me to do a good job of explaining some results. In several cases there is evidence of the event being tagged to two types of preexisting knowledge structures, relationship-specific schema and generalized schema for classes of close relationships. In some instances, the very inconsistency with prior knowledge about what the partner and the relationship were like triggered the uncertainty; for example, in Case 69 where a romantic partner who is a known "fitness nut" smoked half of a pack of cigarettes. The role of generalized schema is discussed by Planalp and Rivers in the section on violation of expectations, where they reported results showing that respondents sought explanations for events that were inconsistent with prior knowledge about what relationships should be like. Thus, preexisting schema were important sources of information about definitions of inconsistency at the outset.

The next question concerns what happens to information that is tagged as inconsistent. This may be where explanatory coherence theories take over and do a better job of explaining how tagged information results in changes in schema. The adequacy of explanatory coherence theory, however, may depend on what was being explained and on whether the respondent was reporting on events that had already long-since occurred, or were continuing to unfold in the present. Some events are so shockingly out of line with prior knowledge and expectations that, consistent with explanatory coherence, an immediate reformation was required. For other events, it appeared to be an accumulation of data that led to the change. In this latter process, events happen over time and produce changes in knowledge only after some threshold level is reached or more conscious deliberation of the data is undertaken. Interpretations of still other events reported in the chapter were in flux for the respondents, and their implications were not as yet understood. The events that were continuing to unfold were apparent in the case where an opposite-sex friend did several things in a series that led a still confused respondent to question whether their relationship was becoming romantic. The latter two situations, reinterpretation of a series of events that occurred over time and of events still unfolding, may be instances in which previously tagged behaviors are pulled together to make sense of them in new ways, a process that is explained well by schema-inconsistency theories.

Planalp and Rivers' integration of attribution theory with theories of schema change is especially enlightening. Most important is an implicit conclusion from their results. Despite the power of models of schema change and despite the fact that attribution theory does not explain the data perfectly, attribution theory does illuminate an identifiable subprocess of cognitive change: people's attempts to locate causes and to understand who or what was responsible for events. Attributional processes are linked to a separate, identifiable, pervasive goal of cognitive processing during periods of relationship change: to explain why. What satisfied me about the authors' analysis was not attribution theory's inability to explain uncertainty increase, but its ability to explain well the processes of causal inference.

People who are trying to make sense of inconsistent information are, in many respects, information-hungry. Consistent with Vorauer and Ross' arguments, these individuals devote considerable cognitive and other resources to make sense of their changing relationships. They frequently, though not always, reported engaging in extensive rumination and conscious, willful deliberation of events. (Even in the cases where such thinking is not reported, it could be because respondents were not directly asked about it and, as a result, simply did not write about it.) Contrary to some of Vorauer and Ross' views, they often sought information directly from their partners by asking questions or discussing it with them. Consistent with Vorauer and Ross' views, respondents frequently searched out other members of their networks for validating, disconfirming, or novel information; they actively formed hypotheses and set up situations to test them; and they sought information in order to resolve competing hypotheses. The research by Planalp and Rivers nicely illustrates the processes that Vorauer and Ross say are triggered when informational goals are activated. In addition, Planalp and River's data demonstrate the ways in which knowledge reconstruction involves the integration of relationship-specific schema with scripts (cf. Holmberg & Ross, this volume).

In their section on "Implications for Models of Relationship Schema Change," Planalp and Rivers made a number of insightful points about how knowledge structures change. In this section, they are more integrative in their discussion of the two models of schema change and of attribution theory. The authors concluded that respondents relied on "a richly inter-woven network of knowledge." They argued further that "if relational knowledge structures have any boundaries at all, they are extremely perme-able and the connections between relational schemas and other knowledge structures are so dense that it may be difficult to draw any meaningful boundary." The authors' questioning about whether there *are* identifiable knowledge structures may be especially applicable during periods of great change in knowledge like the ones they sampled. During such periods, people extensively draw on knowledge of self, others, the relationship itself, and general expectations for relationships (Surra & Bohman, 1991) so much so that cognitions are in flux, and may have little definable structure at all. These conditions, however, may be temporary, and it may be much easier to detect clear boundaries during periods of stability than it is during change. Careful time sampling of narrative accounts, combined with the laboratory methods now being used to study cognition in relationships (e.g., Aron & Aron, chap. 11, this volume; Fletcher, Rosanowski, & Fitness, 1994) should be very revealing about the close connections between structures and processes of relational cognitions.

SELF-EXPANSION IN DEVELOPING RELATIONSHIPS: ARON AND ARON

In chapter 11, Aron and Aron provide an overview of their theory and research on self-expansion in relationships. Self-expansion is, at the same time, a motivation for entering and maintaining relationships and a product of relationships. In their book on the theory, Aron and Aron (1986) emphasized that self-expansion in relationships occurs in several domains, including, for example, resources, knowledge, skills, attitudes, and cognitions. In this chapter, Aron and Aron examine the cognitive features of self-expansion by reviewing their research on five key hypotheses derived from self-expansiontheory. The studies reviewed rely on an impressive variety of methods that tap relationship cognitions, ranging from measures of reaction times gathered in laboratory settings to analysis of respondents' open-ended narratives of relationship events.

Aron and Aron's thoughtful theorizing and careful application of methods make a valuable contribution on several fronts. Self-expansion theory enriches our understanding of self-schema. It explicitly lays out the way in which conceptions of others are linked to and help shape cognitive representations of the self. With respect to the study of relationships, the idea that relationships are a means of self-expansion takes us beyond the analysis of behavioral interdependence, and enables us to understand better the cognitive bases of interconnections between partners. Most importantly, the cognitive features of self-expansion have great potential for explaining developmental change in relationships.

In my model of the cognitive processes associated with relationship development (Surra & Bohman, 1991), I proposed that self-schema are one of at least four knowledge structures that are especially operative during periods of relationship instability. (The remaining three are generalized schema for classes of relationships; relationship-specific schema for past or already established close relationships; and conceptions of relationship constructs.) During periods of instability, information about the self serves to facilitate the perception, interpretation, and evaluation of the other's behaviors and other events relevant to the relationship. In relationships that are just forming, conceptions of the self provide a well-known and well-established basis for understanding the unknown other.

Early in relationships, people make assessments of the self in relation to the other; for example, how the self behaves compared to the other, how the other affects one's own behavior, how similar the other is to the self, what each contributes to the relationship, and so on (see Surra & Bohman, 1991, for a review of research). Out of the interpretations and judgments that are guided by self-schema and other representations that exist prior to the relationship, relationship-specific schema are formed. Relationship-specific schema are stores of information about the self in relation to the other and about the nature of the relationship itself. Once relationship-specific schema are in place, self-conceptions still come into play. During periods of growth and deterioration, self-schema help to guide the interpretation of behaviors and events that are inconsistent with prior relational knowledge, and foster the transformation and restructuring of existing relational knowledge.

With respect to relationship development, Aron and Aron's chapter contributes most to demonstrating that, in close relationships, the self does become cognitively connected to the other. The chapter also offers some insights and hypotheses about how this might occur. According to the authors' first two hypotheses, cognitive processing of information about close others is more similar to cognitive processing about the self than it is to cognition about nonclose others. This continuum of cognition and closeness, they hypothesized, derives from the fact that close others are included in the self. They reviewed a series of studies in support of their hypotheses. The most convincing support comes from their studies of reaction times associated with "me–not me" choices of traits that are either similar to or different from spouse traits. Reaction times for self-choices are longer for traits in which the spouse is different from the self; this was true for cases in which the self and the spouse both possess the trait and both do not possess it. In addition, in discussing the hypothesis that developing a relationship expands the self by including the other in the self (Hypothesis 3), Aron and Aron review evidence that the contents of self-descriptions changed significantly in descriptions of "Who am I" for subjects who fell in love compared to those who did not.

Aron and Aron are careful to note that such findings are consistent with their hypotheses; that is, the findings suggest that beliefs about the other are cognitively connected to beliefs about the self. The methodologies they used, however, do not permit one to draw conclusions about the exact nature of cognitive overlap between self and other; that is, to what extent is information about a close other incorporated into representations of self and to what extent are self conceptions incorporated into representations of a close other? Alternately, to what degree is information about the two of us in relation to one another merged with beliefs about our relationship to form a unique relationship-specific schema?

When it comes to explaining relationship development, the distinctions among these questions are not trivial. As Aron and Aron argue so persuasively, part of the experience of closeness is the experience of cognitively incorporating the other with the self. Closeness also involves cognitively linking the self to the other and of forming impressions about *us*. Understanding relationship development requires examination of the way self-knowledge is similar to, incorporated within, and separate from other-knowledge and from relational knowledge. As Aron and Aron's research suggests, closeness is associated with the extent to which self is connected to other. Presumably, people for whom knowledge about the self in relation to other, and knowledge about us, is low also have relationships that grow more slowly, compared to those for whom the self is linked extensively to the other.

Neither are the distinctions among self, other, and relational knowledge trivial for self-expansion theory. Aron and Aron's theory is concerned with self-expansion in which the other is "taken in" or incorporated within the other. Pardon the pun, but the implications of the theory seem to me to be much more expansive than the authors have so far explored. A developmental view of relationships also raises questions about the extent to which self-expansion means incorporating knowledge about the self into knowledge about the other and about the ways in which self-knowledge changes as the result of such linkages to the other. Such questions could be addressed by adapting the methods Aron and Aron have already employed to study self-expansion. Their laboratory methods could be used to compare processing time and errors in choices of "other has/does not have" this trait, for traits that are similar to or different from the self. A similar design could be used longitudinally to study how the same dependent variables change as partners become more (or less) involved. In a study of this sort, it would be useful to compare the variables for self-choices with those for other choices. Narratives of falling in love or other instances of relationship formation obtained longitudinally could also be coded for the occurrence and content of self, other, self in relation to other, and relationship descriptors.

Another question of interest concerns the role of self-expansion in relationships that are winding down or the processes leading to breakups. (Some attention to self-expansion and relationship maintenance can be found in their book; Aron & Aron, 1986.) By and large, Aron and Arons's research on self-expansion has focused on relationship growth, such as how self-expansion might occur when people fall in love (Hypotheses 3 and 4) or how it might increase marital satisfaction (Hypothesis 5). Self-expansion theory, however, raises many interesting questions about how the self detaches from the other when relationships are ending. The process by which this occurs is not likely to be self-expansion in reverse. When relationships end, self-knowledge may need to be rewritten in a way that incorporates a new conception of the self, one in which the self exists separate from the other. At the same time, the reasons why the self must separate from other need to be explained and understood. Thus, self-knowledge is still connected to the other and to the relationship, albeit in different ways and with different content. The reconstructed, rewritten relationship-specific schema is retained in its new form. Such conceptions of known close relationships, those ended and those still active, are apt to be influential in the formation of new relationships (Surra & Bohman, 1991; Surra & Milardo, 1991).

Of course, it is too easy and perhaps a bit presumptuous of me to design Aron and Arons's research for them and to specify the questions I wish they would study. I only hope that they continue their fruitful efforts on self-expansion in relationships to include more studies of developmental change.

REWRITING RELATIONSHIP MEMORIES:
HOLMBERG AND VEROFF

Chapter 12 by Holmberg and Veroff is concerned with how knowledge structures already in place are altered with the passage of time. They use data gathered from a large sample of spouses married 4 to 7 months to examine changes in recollections of courtship over a 2-year period. Their ideas are compelling, and nicely derived from some of the recent theorizing regarding memories, particularly Ross' (1989) work on the role of personal theories of change in the reconstruction of memories. The data reported here were taken from a larger project conducted by Veroff. The sampling techniques and methods of the larger project possess characteristics that researchers should envy because they are rooted in textbook principles of scientific observation. Veroff's random sampling of newlyweds in Detroit has yielded a representative, diverse picture of changes in marital relationships over the early years of marriage, with special attention to the predictors of the deterioration of marital well-being. Although many researchers eschew the values of random sampling, saying that it is not worth the effort and we just get volunteers anyway, the published papers by Veroff and his coauthors are yielding valuable insights into racial and socioeconomic diversity in the functioning of marital relationships.

In their discussion of the processes by which memories change with time, Holmberg and Veroff draw heavily on Ross' (1989) work on how long-term memories are formed. Ross maintained that memories are shaped by (a) assessments of one's present status on the attribute in question and (b) implicit theories about how attributes change over time. Holmberg and Veroff acknowledged the impact of the first influence on memories; they discussed, for example, the way in which partners modify past knowledge to be in line with current conditions in the relationship, such as the level of trust or well-being (also cf. Holmberg & Holmes, 1993). The chapter focused, however, on the second influence; specifically, scripts for the way courtships develop. The authors hypothesized that newlyweds' memories of the evolution of their courtship are reconstructed over time to be more consistent with scripts of how courtships ideally and typically evolve. They argue that reconstruction occurs as the result of fading memories, and gaps in memories are filled in with scriptlike information.

The authors' also outline some of the processes involved in relationship maintenance, as well as deterioration. Reconstructed memories are one means by which partners maintain the status quo. The past is remade so that, if the relationship is well off now, its formation is reconstructed in terms of more growth and positivity than actually occurred; if the relationship is worse off, the past is redesigned more negatively, presumably so that it is easier for partners to understand how they ended up where they are (for reviews, see

Berscheid, 1994; Holmberg & Veroff, chap. 12, this volume). The specific content of the reconstruction is aided by scripts, or generalized beliefs about close relationships, and other knowledge structures (cf. Fletcher & Thomas, chap. 1, this volume; Surra & Bohman, 1991).

Scripts for close relationships also operate during periods of instability (Surra & Bohman, 1991). According to an information-processing perspective, periods of instability in relationships are characterized by incoming information that is novel or inconsistent with prior knowledge, as in the case where a reliable spouse who walked in the door every evening at 6 p.m. for the past 10 years begins to work late unpredictably. In such situations, the inconsistent behavior is associated in memory with related, but consistent, behaviors and must be reconciled with them. The interpretation of inconsistencies are believed to be guided, in part, by scripts for what close relationships should be or are usually like, or generalized relationship schema (Surra & Bohman, 1991).

According to this view, scripts for courtship development should come into play whenever the patterns of interaction that characterize the relationship are in flux and whenever those patterns bear upon existing knowledge that pertains to how we ended up married to one another. Scripts, however, are only one means by which memories are reconstructed. Other knowledge structures, such as knowledge about the current state of the relationship and knowledge about other close relationships, will interact with scripts and current events to reshape recollections. Findings reported by Holmberg and Veroff (chap. 12,this volume; e.g., for individuals' scripts) suggest that the current state of the relationship is indeed interacting with scripts to produce memory changes, although it impossible to separate out the various sources of change with the data that are reported here. In order to examine the sources of change more precisely, it would be useful to compare within couples how their narratives changed over time, rather than to look at proportional changes across the entire sample. The authors' hypothesis can be viewed as part of an overarching goal: to understand the how various knowledge structures operate in developing relationships.

As the authors note, courtship scripts per se were not studied as part of the larger project. As a result, the operationalization of courtship scripts was post hoc. In order to construct the content of courtship scripts, the authors identify ideal and typical features of scripts. Ideal scripts were taken from the results from some of the findings on the premarital predictors of marital satisfaction. Ideal courtships, for instance, are assumed to be conflict-free because some research (Kelly, Huston, & Cate, 1985) has shown that retrospective reports of premarital conflict are negatively associated with marital satisfaction 2 years later.

At least two assumptions underlie this approach: (a) the ideal features of courtship are those that are associated with better quality marriages, and (b) laypersons have the same information that researchers have about these qualities. As Holmberg and Veroff themselves recognize, laypersons' conceptions of relationships frequently differ from from those based on scientific theory and observation. Findings from current research underscore the differences between laypersons' and researchers' views of relationships (Fehr, 1993; Surra, Jacquet, & Batchelder, in press). In addition, the features that laypersons believe will make for an ideal courtship may include those that are correlated with marital outcomes, but are probably not limited to these correlates. Holmberg and Veroff, for instance, argue that in courtship and wedding scripts, relationships are seen as "harmonious, with little conflict and few serious reversals." Yet evidence from other studies of courtship development indicate that for a large percentage of people, drama, passion, conflict, and reversals are central to their accounts of the experience (Surra, Arizzi, & Asmussen, 1988; Surra, Batcheler, & Hughes, 1995).

The authors derive the typical features of courtship scripts from the narratives gathered in the larger project at the first time of measurement. Because the authors have a representative sample of narratives, they argue, the narratives represent what is typical. The logic and method here are circular, however. If courtship narratives change over time, then newlyweds at Time 1 are already providing reconstructed information that should be more consistent with scripts than what actually occurred. The Time 1 narrative was treated both as a measure of scripts and as a standard for accurate memories against which the Time 2 narratives were compared.

To what extent are the Time 1 narratives scripted? This question is important for theories of relationship development generally and for the methods used in the Holmberg and Veroff chapter specifically. Findings from other research, even some from the same data set (Orbuch, Veroff, & Holmberg, 1993), suggest that the themes apparent in narratives of "how my courtship evolved" are quite variable and that no one typical script characterizes accurately newlyweds' knowledge about why their courtship evolved as it did (Surra, 1987; Surra et al., 1995; Surra & Hughes, 1995). Theoretically, it is important to understand the degree to which individuals' causal accounts of their courtship are the joint product of scripts and of events and experiences unique to specific relationships.

The gathering of data on memories, especially the extent to which they are affected by scripts, is especially affected by the way questions are asked (see, e.g., Schwarz, 1990). The questions and methods used to gather narratives of relationship development will affect the product that is obtained. Different answers are likely to be obtained depending upon the scope of the question with respect to time, events, and relationship dimensions (e.g., "Tell me the story of your courtship" vs. "Tell me what happened during this month that made your commitment change"). Answers are also likely to vary with the nature of instructions that accompany the questions and the events that are asked about (Berscheid, 1994). In attempting to get people to access memories in studies of sexual or dating history, for example, it is important to instruct people to think back to what actually happened. Respondents' answers when instructed to tell me the *story* of your courtship are likely to be different from their answers to think back and accurately report what happened during a given period of time.

The way in which questions about memories are asked also has theoretical implications. In what ways would jointly constructed memories for courtship, like those reported by Holmberg and Veroff (chap. 12, this volume), differ from those gathered from individual partners? Presumably, when partners are asked to talk jointly about courtship, the interaction between them produces a narrative that is different from the story each individual would report. The jointly constructed account may be a good source of information about transactive memory (Wegner, Giuliano, & Hertel, 1984) and about the communication processes by which partners access and modify one another's memories to produce a joint construction. Any interactions that partners have about their courtship, whether between themselves or in the presence of others (including interviewers), is likely to alter individual memories in a way that is consistent with a shared view of how "our relationship" evolved.

INFORMATIONAL GOALS AND CLOSE RELATIONSHIPS: VORAUER AND ROSS

The chapter by Vorauer and Ross is a provocative analysis of the processes and products of people's goals to seek information about themselves, their partners, and their relationships. Although processing goals are a central component of models of social cognition (e.g., Scott, Fuhrman, & Wyer, 1991), their role in cognition in close relationships has been given short shrift. (The role of intrapersonal goals, in contrast, has been addressed extensively by Read & Miller, 1989.)

Vorauer and Ross take the position that partners in close relationships have as a primary goal the seeking of social information. Social information includes knowledge about the self, the partner, and others, and about the way others see the self and one another. Although this goal may operate more strongly in some stages of relationships than others (e.g., the formative period), the authors maintain that it is a pervasive goal: "The informational goals framework suggests that individuals may subject virtually any behavior, expected or not, positive or negative, to considerable scrutiny if they seek to acquire social knowledge." According to the authors, even in established relationships people may be chronically vigilant because circumstances change, requiring constant reinterpretation and reevaluation of the state of affairs and because personal theories of change (e.g., of marital breakdown) prompt people to monitor behaviors for evidence of change.

The most obvious conclusion from the idea that people are information-seekers would seem to be that people seek information because they want to draw accurate conclusions. Vorauer and Ross, however, maintain that the motivation to seek information leads to an interesting paradox: the diagnosticity bias. The diagnosticity bias means that, even though individuals want accurate information, their very desire for it will prompt them to exaggerate the extent to which data are relevant to them and to misinterpret data. The exaggeration affects all phases of cognitive processing. Individuals, for example, will detect partners' behaviors (or the lack thereof) and interpret them as "personal" or "interpersonal" regardless of whether they are. Ironically, the need to know may bias interpretations such that meaning that is goal consistent is derived from ambiguous behaviors and also from behaviors that actually contain no meaning relevant to the goal (e.g., the goal to ascertain what another thinks of my new haircut may lead to over-interpretation.) All of these tendencies, and others outlined in the chapter, are consequences of the diagnosticity bias.

The concept of the diagnosticity bias and its consequences are at odds with current thinking about close relationships that is based on interdependence theory (Kelley, 1979; Kelley & Thibaut, 1978). The most recent conceptualizations of the theory emphasize that the essence of a relationship is that the behaviors of one partner have (affective) consequences for the other. The idea of mutual consequences flies in the face of the diagnosticity bias, which says, instead, that people in close relationships may take the other's behavior too personally. In an example from the chapter, a woman has a goal to determine her partner's affection for her. When her partner does the laundry for her when it is her turn, the woman asks herself a series of questions about the meaning of his behavior for her goal. The authors conclude by saying, "The woman's desire to reduce uncertainty about her partner's devotion will lead her to perceive many of his actions as having evaluative implications."

According to interdependence theory, the fact is that his behavior does have evaluative implications, whether or not it is her turn to do the laundry, whether he means it to be relevant to her, and whether the behavior is joint or separate. The fundamental feature of close relationships is that behaviors are indeed personal. A partner's assumption that the self is a target of the other, to use Vorauer and Ross' term, may be incorrect because it implies intention on the part of the partner that may or may not exist. Partners' resolution of questions about intentionality and motives are, however, at the very heart of interdependence. Partners' attributions about why others behave toward them as they do arise out of interdependence problems to become the substance for their beliefs about the other's personality and attitudes.

This analysis does not mean that the diagnosticity bias does not exist, but it does mean that the conditions under which it operates may be narrower than the authors have maintained. The key seems to lie in the linkage between the diagnosticity bias and informational goals and how that linkage changes developmentally in relationships. The most fruitful analysis of this point is found in Vorauer and Ross' discussion of how informational goals change as relationships mature. In this section, they argued that "people instigate an informational search primarily when they lack knowledge that is important to them." As they point out, informational goals and by extension, the diagnosticity bias, are probably most influential during periods of instability in relationships, particularly during relationship formation, growth, and deterioration. The characterization of individuals as "information-hungry," "oblivious to" irrelevant behaviors, and "chronically vigilant" probably applies best to periods of instability when uncertainties abound—when the partner and the relationship are not well understood and when the status of the relationship is unclear.

Situations of high uncertainty over any length of time are likely to be be aversive and exhausting. People are motivated to reduce uncertainty about relationships by gathering information about them precisely because such states are costly (Berger, 1979; Surra & Milardo, 1991). One of the attractions of established, committed relationships is the escape from the state of constant questioning. Continual diagnosis of a partner's behaviors would consume cognitive resources in a way that would make it difficult to do or think about anything else. Indeed, these kinds of obsessive cognitive states do seem to characterize certain phases of relationships (e.g., falling passionately in love and ending a marital relationship; cf. Surra & Bohman, 1991, for a review).

In established relationships that are in maintenance mode, however, informational goals are likely to be minimal (Surra & Bohman, 1991), as is the diagnosticity bias that accompanies them. If informational goals exist, they are likely to be specific in scope (Vorauer & Ross, chap. 13, this volume). During relationship maintenance, most behavioral data are consistent with prior knowledge, and they are processed easily and simply, without much attention or cognitive resources, as is the case with automatic processing (Fletcher & Fitness, 1993). In these sorts of relationships, partners process even inconsistent behaviors to be consistent with prior knowledge (see Surra & Bohman, 1991, for further review of this process).

The paradox outlined by Vorauer and Ross, in which the desire for accurate information results in inaccuracy and bias, is consistent with the view taken by much of the recent social psychological research on cognition in relationships. This research emphasizes the cognitive tricks people use in order to maintain or reinforce current conceptions of relationships (e.g., Holmberg & Holmes, 1993; Murray, Holmes, & Griffin, 1994) and the construal processes that people employ to delude themselves about their relationships (e.g., Murray & Holmes, 1993). Although its roots are less firmly planted in research on relationships than the illustrations just cited, the diagnosticity bias is another example of the emphasis in social psychology on the ways that people go wrong with their cognitive processing. Even when they want to be informed and accurate, people often misinterpret information about relationships.

Clearly, the evidence supports the view that the tendencies to idealize, ignore, and overdetect operate in relationships. In some cases, however, individuals who are motivated to make accurate relational assessments are able to do so, as in the case where partners describe their relationship as compatible and enjoyable and it is, in fact, compatible and enjoyable according to some objective measures (Surra et al., in press; Surra & Hughes, 1995). The motives to make rational, accurate assessments of relationship qualities are more firmly rooted in sociological and economic theories than they are in social psychology. The filter theory (or stage models) cited by Vorauer and Ross, for instance, are based on the assumptions that people deliberately and thoughtfully weigh different characteristics of partners at different stages of involvement before they decide whether to become more involved with the partner. Economic models underscore individuals' need to forecast as accurately as they can the likely outcomes of their relationships (e.g., Becker, 1991). Because the costs of misdiagnosis are higher in relationships with potential for permanent commitments (e.g., premarital and marital involvements), it may be that accuracy motives are more apparent in such relationships (Surra et al., in press).

CONCLUSIONS

The chapters in this section foretell the questions that are likely to consume the attention of researchers who study cognition in close relationships for the next few years. Are there identifiable knowledge structures that are specific to relationships? What is the content of these structures? What are the processes by which different knowledge structures interact when relationships change (e.g., knowledge of the self and other)? How does relationship-relevant knowledge change with other features of relationships? One final question central to close relationships, but not addressed much here (for an exception see Vorauer & Ross, chap. 13, this volume), concerns the connections between the experience of closeness and the degree to which partners *share unique relational knowledge*. Our ability to answer this even more complex question depends, in part, on the quality of our answers to the other questions. Questions such as these capture the fundamental features of what is social about cognition.

REFERENCES

Aron, A., & Aron, E.N. (1986). *Love and the expansion of self: Understanding attraction and satisfaction*. New York: Hemisphere.

Becker, G. S. (1991). *A treatise on the family*. Cambridge, MA: Harvard University Press.

Berscheid, E. (1994). Interpersonal relationships. *Annual Review of Psychology*, 45, 79–129.

Berger, C. (1979). Beyond initial interaction: Uncertainty, understanding, and the development of interpersonal relationships. In H. Giles & R. St. Clair (Eds.), *Language and social psychology* (pp. 122–144). Baltimore, MD: University Park Press.

Fehr, B. (1993). *Laypeople's conceptions of commitment*. Manuscript submitted for review.

Fletcher, G. J. O., & Fitness, J. (1993). Knowledge structures and explanations in intimate relationships. In S. Duck (Ed.), *Individuals in relationships* (pp. 121–143). Newbury Park, CA: Sage.

Fletcher, G. J. O., Rosanowski, J., & Fitness, J. (1994). Automatic processing in intimate contexts: The role of relationship beliefs. *Journal of Personality and Social Psychology*, 67, 888–897.

Holmberg, D., & Holmes, J. (1993). Reconstruction of relationship memories: A mental models approach. In N. Schwarz & S. Sudman (Eds.), *Autobiographical memory and the validity of retrospective reports* (pp. 267–288). New York: Springer-Verlag.

Kelley, H. H., (1979). *Personal relationships: Their structures and processes*. Hillsdale, NJ: Lawrence Erlbaum Associates.

Kelley, H. H., & Thibaut, J. W. (1978). *Interpersonal relations: A theory of interdependence*. New York: Wiley.

Kelly, C., Huston, T. L., & Cate, R. M. (1985). Premarital relationship correlates of the erosion of satisfaction in marriage. *Journal of Social and Personal Relationships*, 2, 167–178.

Murray, S. L., & Holmes, J. G. (1993). Seeing virtues in faults: Negativity and the transformation of interpersonal narratives in close relationships. *Journal of Personality and Social Psychology*, 65, 707–722.

Murray, S. L., Holmes, J. G., & Griffin, D. W. (1994, July). *The benefits of positive illusions: Idealization and the construction of satisfaction in close relationships*. Paper presented at the 7th International Conference on Personal Relationships, Groningen, The Netherlands.

Orbuch, T. L., Veroff, J., & Holmberg, D. (1993). Becoming a married couple: The emergence of meaning in the first years of marriage. *Journal of Marriage and the Family*, 55, 815–826.

Read, S. J., & Miller, L. C. (1989). Inter-personalism: Toward a goal-based theory of persons in relationships. In L. Pervin (Ed.), *Goal concepts in personality and social psychology* (pp. 413–472). Hillsdale, NJ: Lawrence Erlbaum Associates.

Ross, M. (1989). Relation of implicit theories to the construction of personal histories. *Psychological Review*, 96, 341–357.

Schwarz, N. (1990). Assessing frequency reports of mundane behaviors: Contributions of cognitive psychology to questionnaire construction. In C. Hendrick & M. S. Clark (Eds.), *Research methods in personality and social psychology* (pp. 98–119). Newbury, CA: Sage.

Scott, C. K., Fuhrman, R. W., & Wyer, R. S., Jr. (1991). Information processing in close relationships. In G. J. O. Fletcher & F. D. Fincham (Eds.), *Cognition in close relationships* (pp. 37–67). Hillsdale, NJ: Lawrence Erlbaum Associates.

Surra, C.A. (1987). Reasons for changes in commitment: Variations by courtship type. *Journal of Social and Personal Relationships*, 4, 17–33.

Surra, C. A., Arizzi, P., & Asmussen, L. A. (1988). The association between reasons for commitment and the development and outcome of marital relationships. *Journal of Social and Personal Relationships*, 5, 47–63.

Surra, C. A., Batchelder, M. L., & Hughes, D. K. (1995). Accounts and the demystification of courtship. In M. A. Fitzpatrick & A. L. Vangelisti (Eds.), *Explaining family interactions* (pp. 112–141). Thousand Oaks, CA: Sage.

Surra, C. A., & Bohman, T. (1991). The development of close relationships: A cognitive perspective. In G. J. O. Fletcher & F. D. Fincham (Eds.), *Cognition in close relationships* (281–305). Hillsdale, NJ: Lawrence Erlbaum Associates.

Surra, C. A., & Hughes, D. K. (1995). *Commitment processes in the development of premarital relationships.* Manuscript submitted for review.

Surra, C. A., Jacquet, S. E., & Batchelder, M. L. (in press). Commitment to marriage: A phenomenological approach. In W. H. Jones & J. Adams (Eds.), *The handbook of interpersonal commitment and relationship stability.* New York: Plenum.

Surra, C. A., & Milardo, R. M. (1991). The social psychological context of developing relationships: Interactive and psychological networks. In W. H. Jones & D. Perlman (Eds.), *Advances in personal relationships* (Vol. 3, pp. 1–36). London: Jessica Kingsley.

Wegner, D. M., Giuliano, T., & Hertel, P. T. (1984). Cognitive interdependence in close relationships. In W. Ickes (Ed.), *Compatible and incompatible relationships* (pp. 253–276). New York: Springer-Verlag.

Author Index

A

Abbey, A., 265, *272*
Abelson, R. P., 93, *116,* 198, *214,* 228, 229, 241, *242, 244, 245,* 302, 307, 315, 322, *323*
Achee, J. W., 278, *296*
Acitelli, L. K., 100, *116,* 150, 151, 153, 154, 155, 156, 162, 163, *166,* 348, *367*
Adelson, J., 158, 159, *166*
Adler, J., 392, *394*
Agnostelli, G., 101, *118*
Ainsworth, M. D. S., 25, 26, 27, 33, 35, 38, *53, 54,* 75, *86,* 180, *188*
Ajzen, I., 183, *189*
Alexander, P. C., 37, *54*
Alicke, M. D., 95, *117*
Allen, A., 269, *272*
Allen, J. G., 231, 234, *242,* 269, *272,* 336, 339, *342*
Allen, M., 177, *189*
Allen, T., 300, *323*
Allison, K., 226, *242*
Allport, G. W., 106, *117*
Altman, I., 300, *322,* 373, *394*
Ambady, N., 377, *394*
Andersen, S. M., 40, *54*

Anderson, C. A., 223, 229, *244*
Anderson, J. R., 40, *54,* 122, 123, *144,* 229, *242*
Anderson, P. A., 124, 135, *144*
Anderson, S. N., 182, *188*
Antill, J. K., 76, *86*
Antonucci, T. C., 150, 155, 163, *166, 167*
Arend, R., 38, *54, 59*
Argyle, M., 64, *86,* 135, *144,* 171, *188,* 276, *293*
Arizzi, P., 300, *324,* 357, *368,* 407, *412*
Arnold, M. B., 206, *214*
Aron, A., 96, *117,* 182, *187, 188,* 326, 327, 329, 330, 331, 333, 334, 335, 336, 339, 340, 341, *342, 344,* 386, 387, *394, 395,* 401, 404, *412*
Aron, E. N., 96, *117,* 182, *187, 188,* 326, 327, 329, 330, 331, 333, 334, 335, 336, 339, 340, 341, *342,* 386, 387, *394, 395,* 401, 404, *412*
Aronson, E., 334, 340, *342, 343*
Arriaga, X. B., 75, 77, 83, *89, 90*
Asch, S. E., 94, *117*
Ashmore, R. D., 41, *60,* 264, *272*
Asmussen, L. A., 300, *324,* 357, *368,* 407, *412*
Aspinwall, L. G., 115, *120*

Averill, J. R., 203, *214*, 219, 221, 226, 227, 228, 229, 232, 233, 235, 239, *242*, 247, 260, *271*
Axelrod, R., 69, 76, *86*

B

Backman, C. W., 270, *271*
Badad, E. Y., 247, *271*
Bailey, B. L., 353, *368*
Baillet, S. D., 327, *343*
Bakan, D., 47, *54*, 328, *342*
Baker, V., 328, *343*
Baldridge, L., 78, *86*
Baldwin, M. W., 7, 11, *23*, 41, 51, 52, *54*, 96, *117*, 123, *144*, 165, *166*, 178, 181, 183, 185, 187, *188*, 195, 199, *214*, 228, 230, 231, 238, *242*, *243*, 318, *322*
Banaji, M. R., 175, 184, *189*
Bandura, A., 334, *342*
Barbee, A., 136, *145*
Bargh, J. A., 15, 17, *23*, *24*, 44, 46, 52, *54*, 81, *89*, 175, 182, 184, *188*, *190*
Barnett, D., 36, *55*
Bartholomew, K., 26, 29, 35, 37, 42, 45, 52, *54*, *56*
Barton, L. R., 373, *396*
Batchelder, M. L., 407, 411, *412*, *413*
Bateson, G., 124, *144*
Baucom, D. H., 83, *87*, 160, 161, 162, *166*, *168*
Baumeister, R. F., 109, *117*, 148, *166*, 171, *188*
Baxter, L. A., 47, *54*, 300, *322*
Bayes, M. A., 135, *144*
Beach, S. R. H., 83, *87*
Becker, G. S., 411, *412*
Bell, L., 334, *343*
Belsky, J., 26, 41, *54*, *55*
Bem, D. J., 28, *55*, 76, *86*
Bem, S. L., 159, *166*
Benton, P., 221, 235, *243*
Ben-Ze'ev, A., 200, 202, *214*
Bergen, M. R., 340, *344*
Berger, C., 410, *412*
Berger, R. C., 299, *322*
Bergman, A., 47, *59*
Berkowitz, L., 234, *242*, 278, 279, 280, 287, 292, *293*
Berley, R. A., 83, *87*
Berman, E. H., 26, *61*

Bernardez-Bonesatti, T., 231, 236, *242*
Bernstein, S., 159, *167*
Berscheid, E., 18, *23*, 79, 81, *86*, 100, 113, 115, *117*, *119*, 177, 181, 184, 187, *188*, 197, 210, *214*, 269, *271*, 406, 408, *412*
Biek, M., 127, 133, *146*
Billings, A., 64, 67, *86*
Birdwhistell, R., 122, *144*
Biringen, Z., 42, 51, *55*
Bissonnette, V. I., 75, 77, 83, *89*, *90*, 328, *343*
Blackstone, T., 268, *272*
Blampied, N., 276, 289, 290, *294*
Blatt, S. J., 38, *58*
Blehar, M. C., 26, 27, 35, 38, *54*, 75, *86*
Blier, M. J., 231, 234, *242*
Blier-Wilson, L. A., 231, 234, *242*
Block, J. H., 157, *166*
Bloom, B. L., 162, *168*
Blumberg, H. H., 373, *395*
Bohman, T., 101, *120*, 165, *168*, 373, 388, *395*, 404, 406, 410, *413*
Bolger, N., 176, *188*
Bonge, D., 231, *244*
Boon, S. D., 92, 116, *118*, 382, 385, *395*
Bornstein, R. F., 175, *188*
Boudreau, L., 269, *272*
Bower, G. H., 211, *214*, *215*, 276, 286, 287, 289, *294*, *295*, 326, *342*
Bowlby, J., 25, 26, 28, 29, 30, 31, 43, *54*, 75, *86*, 93, 96, *117*, 185, *189*
Bradburn, N. M., 341, *343*
Bradbury, T. N., 19, *23*, 80, 83, 84, *86*, *87*, 101, *117*, 196, 206, 207, 210, 211, *214*, *215*, 276, 281, 286, *294*
Bradshaw, D., 27, *60*
Braiker, H. B., 92, 115, *117*
Braunwald, D., 36, *55*
Braverman, D. L., 278, 287, *296*
Breedlove, J., 94, *119*
Brehm, S. S., 92, 93, 99, *117*, 393, *395*
Brennan, K. A., 34, 36, 37, *54*, *60*
Bretherton, I., 26, 27, 30, 31, 42, 51, *55*, 228, *242*
Brewer, M. B., 52, *55*, 172, *191*
Brickman, P., 91, 92, 93, 100, 109, 112, 114, 116, *117*
Bridges, L. J., 41, *55*
Bringle, R., 276, *294*
Brown, J. D., 95, 96, 99, 100, *117*, *120*
Brown, R., 186, *190*

Bruner, J., 380, *395*
Buber, M., 328, *342*
Buck, R., 180, *189*
Buller, D. B., 136, *144*
Bullis, C., 300, *322*
Burgoon, J. K., 124, 129, 134, 136, 141, *144*, 309, *323*
Burman, B., 209, *214*, 236, *242*
Burnett, R., 100, *117*, 150, 151, 152, 160, 161, 164, *166*
Burns, H. J., 346, *368*
Burr, W. R., 386, *395*
Buss, A. H., 129, *144*, 219, 231, 233, *242*
Buss, D., 125, 141, *144*, 177, *189*
Buunk, B., 78, *86*, 276, 294
Byrne, D., 269, *271*, 276, *294*, 334, *342*
Byrne, E., 210, *214*

C

Cacioppo, J. T., 81, *88*, 196, *214*
Calverley, R. M., 37, 53, *56*
Campbell, A., 231, 234, *242*
Campbell, D. T., 77, *86*
Campbell, J., 51, *55*
Camras, L. A., 226, *242*
Canary, D. J., 148, *166*, 231, *242*
Cansler, D. C., 373, *395*
Cantor, N., 40, 42, *55*, *58*
Cantrill, J. G., 300, *323*
Caputo, C., 327, *343*
Carlson, E., 28, 34, 36, 38, *61*
Carlson, V., 36, *55*
Carlton, K., 64, *88*
Carnelley, K. B., 34, 37, 48, 52, *55*, *60*, 179, *189*
Carnochan, P., 46, *57*
Carrell, S., 187, *188*
Carstensen, L. L., 163, *167*
Caspi, A., 28, *55*
Cassidy, J., 30, 32, 33, 36, 39, 45, 50, 52, *55*, *59*
Cate, R. M. 101, 115, 116, *117*, *118*, 151, 152, *166*, 352, 353, 357, 363, *368*, 406, *412*
Cesa, I.L., 308, *324*
Chadiha, L., 356, 357, 360, *368*
Chaiken, S., 52, *56*, 81, *87*, 107, *117*, 172, *189*
Charnov, E. L., 26, *58*
Chavez, R. E., 64, *87*

Check, J. V. P., 231, *244*
Cheek, J. M., 129, *144*
Chodorow, N., 157, 158, *166*
Chrisman, K., 252, 255, 259, *271*
Christensen, A., 64, *89*, 161, *166*, *167*
Cicchetti, D., 26, 36, *55*, *56*, *57*
Cisamolo, D., 204, *216*
Clark, C. L., 26, 37, 51, 53, *56*, *58*, *60*, 300, *322*
Clark, M., 181, *189*, 200, *214*, 250, 251, 252, 253, 255, 256, 257, 258, 259, 260, 262, 267, 270, *271*, *272*, *273*, 282, 287, 292, *294*
Claussen, A. H., 35, *56*
Clore, G. L., 211, *216*, 269, *271*, 276, 277, 278, 279, 280, 281, 286, 287, *294*, 296
Coates, D., 265, *272*
Cody, M. J., 231, *242*
Cohen, J., 96, *117*
Cohen, P., 96, *117*
Cohen, S., 171, *189*
Coker, D. A., 134, *144*
Cole, M. W., 227, *244*
Cole, S. W., 40, *54*, 182, *188*
Collins, A., 277, 278, 279, 280, 281, *296*
Collins, N. L., 25, 34, 38, 40, 42, 44, 45, 48, 51, 52, *56*, 183, *189*, 302, 303, 318, *324*
Collins, R. L., 115, *120*
Conley, J. J., 65, *88*
Connell, J. P., 41, *55*
Conway, M., 276, 278, 286, 287, *294*
Cooley, C. H., 186, *189*, 376, *395*
Cornwell, B., 266, *272*
Cortese, A., 335, *344*
Cosmides, L., 197, *217*
Coss, R. G., 142, *144*
Cox, C. L., 77, *89*
Craik, K. J. W., 29, *56*
Cramer, L., 6, 8, 16, *23*, 100, *117*, 150, *167*
Crane, M., 159, *167*
Crawford, J., 221, 235, *243*
Crits-Cristoph, 47, *59*
Crittenden, P.M., 35, 36, 40, 41, 42, 43, *56*, 185, *189*
Crocker, J., 264, 266, *272*, 301, *323*
Crockett, W. H., 152, *166*
Csikszentimihalyi, M., 247, *272*, *273*
Cummings, E. M., 26, 36, *55*, *56*, *57*
Cunningham, E. M., 231, *242*
Cunningham, M. R., 136, *145*, 210, *214*
Curtis, R. C., 270, *272*

D

Dabbs, J. M., 254, *273*
Daniels, T., 35, *56*
Darwin, C., 121, *145,* 219, *243*
Davidson, R. J., 136, *145,* 196, *214*
Davis, K. E., 36, 38, *58,* 385, *395*
Davis, M. H., 75, *87*
Davitz, J. R., 226, *243*
Deaux, K., 240, *243*
Deci, E. L., 334, *342*
De S. French, R., 223, *244*
Dehue, F. M. J., 70, *87*
Deichmann, A. K., 4, *24*
De La Ronde, C., 91, 99, 113, 114, *120*
De Paulo, B. M., 95, *118,* 174, *191,* 376, *395*
Depner, C. E., 156, *166*
de Rivera, J., 227, 228, *243,* 247, *272*
Dermer, M., 81, *86*
DeTurck, J. L., 136, *144*
Devine, P. G., 52, *56*
Dewey, J., 122, *145*
Diamond, D. J., 209, *215*
DiGeronimo, K., 136, *145*
Dindia, K., 177, *189*
Dion, K. K., 38, *58,* 269, *271*
Dion, K. L., 38, *58*
Dixon, N. F., 392, *395*
Dobosz, B., 276, *295*
Dorfman Botens, D., 52, *56*
Douvan, E., 154, 155, 156, 158, 159, *166,*
    168, 356, *368*
Dozier, M., 32, 36, 52, *56*
Drake, C. A., 287, *296*
Drigotas, S. M., 77, 84, *86, 89*
Duck, S. W., 154, 165, *166, 167,* 174, 177,
    189, 249, *272,* 299, *323,* 347, *368*
Dunn, D.S., 184, *191*
Dutton, D. G., 37, *56,* 335, *342*

E

Eagly, A. H., 52, *56,* 81, *87,* 148, 149, *167,*
    172, *189,* 264, *272*
Edelstein, W., 36, *58*
Edmonds, V. H., 341, *342*
Edwards, K., 212, *215,* 278, *295*
Egelund, B., 36, *56*
Eibl-Eibesfeldt, I., 121, 122, 123, 124, 125,
    129, 134, 135, 142, *145*
Eichberg, C., 33, *54*

Eidelson, R. J., 12, *23*
Eisenberg, N., 176, *191*
Ekman, P., 49, *56,* 125, 136, *145,* 197, *214,*
    219, 223, *243,* 278, 284, *294*
Elicker, J., 28, 34, 37, 38, *56*
Ellsworth, P., 198, 212, 215, *217,* 250,
    262, *273,* 277, *294, 295*
Emmons, R. A., 39, 51, *56, 60*
Englund, M., 28, 34, 37, 38, *56*
Epperson, D. L., 231, *244*
Epstein, N., 12, *23*
Epstein, S., 93, *117,* 178, 184, *189,* 211, *214*
Erber, M., 287, 292, *294*
Erber, R., 81, *87,* 287, 292, *294*
Erdelyi, M. H., 392, *395*
Erikson, E., 159, *167*
Ervin, C., 129, *145*
Evans, T. W., 278, 287, *296*
Eysenck, H. J., 129, 133, *145*
Eysenck, S. B. G., 129, *145*

F

Farina, A., 269, 270, *272, 273*
Fazio, R. H., 51, *56*
Feeney, J. A., 34, 38, 52, *56, 57,* 93, *117*
Fehr, B., 51, *54,* 185, *188,* 196, 198, 200,
    214, 219, 220, 222, 223, 224, 225, 228,
    230, 231, 238, 239, 240, *242, 243, 245,*
    407, *412*
Feingold, A., 264, *272*
Fenigstein, A., 374, *395*
Ferber, A., 125, 134, *145*
Feshbach, S., 276, *294*
Festinger, L., 93, *117*
Fiedler, K., 277, 286, 287, 289, *294*
Fincham, F. D., 5, 8, 14, 15, 16, 19, *23,*
    80, 83, 84, *86, 87,* 100, 101, *117,* 149,
    150, *167,* 195, 196, 206, 207, 208, 210,
    211, *214, 215,* 220, *243,* 276, 281, 286,
    294
Fischer, A. H., 226, 228, 237, 240, *243,*
    315, 316, *323*
Fischer, K. W., 46, *57*
Fishbein, M., 183, *189*
Fisher, D.C., 93, *118*
Fishkin, S., 287, *296*
Fiske, A. P., 183, *189, 190*
Fiske, S. T., 40, *57,* 79, 81, *87, 88,* 181,
    183, *189,* 195, *215,* 241, *243,* 301, *323,*
    381, *395*

Fiske, V., 336, *342*
Fitness, J., 12, 14, 16, 17, 20, 21, *23,* 52,
    57, 107, *117,* 195, 196, 198, 200, 204,
    205, 207, 208, 210, *215,* 226, 227, 229,
    243, 254, *272,* 276, 286, 288, 289, 290,
    294, 307, *323,* 386, *395,* 401, 410, *412*
Flay, B. R., 116, *117*
Fleeson, J., 38, *61*
Fletcher, G. J. O., 5, 6, 8, 9, 12, 14, 15,
    16, 17, 18, 19, 20, 21, 22, *23, 24,* 52,
    57, 100, 107, *117,* 149, 150, *167,* 195,
    196, 198, 200, 204, 205, 207, 208, 210,
    215, 220, 226, 227, 229, *243,* 254, *272,*
    276, 281, 286, 288, 289, 290, *294,* 307,
    315, *323,* 386, *395,* 401, 410, *412*
Florian, V., 34, 35, 37, 38, *59*
Folkes, V. S., 269, *272*
Folkman, S., 50, *57*
Follette, W. C., 64, 83, *87*
Fonagy, P., 32, *57*
Forgas, J., 195, 196, 210, 211, 212, *215,*
    228, 241, *243,* 275, 276, 277, 278, 282,
    283, 286, 287, 288, 289, 290, 291, 292,
    293, *294, 295*
Fox, N. A., 42, *57*
Frable, D. E., 268, *272*
Frey, D., 195, *217*
Friesen, W. V., 136, *145*
Frijda, N. H., 79, *87,* 197, 198, 200, *215,*
    229, 237, *243,* 277, 279, 280, *295*
Fuhrman, R. W., 12, *24,* 150, 154, *168,*
    182, *190,* 195, 209, *216,* 408, *412*
Furnham, A., 64, *86*
Fury, G. S., 34, 36, 38, 51, *57*

G

Gangestad, S. W., 8, *24,* 123, 126, 127,
    129, 133, 136, 137, 138, *145, 146*
Gardner, W., 26, *58*
Gaschke, Y. N., 278, 287, *296*
Gault, U., 221, 235, *243*
Geiss, S. K., 64, *87*
George, C., 42, 44, 45, *57*
Gergen, K. J., 93, *118,* 229, 230, 232, 235,
    243, 357, *368*
Gergen, M. M., 229, 230, 232, 235, *243,*
    357, *368*
Gilligan, S. G., 326, *342*
Ginsburg, B., 180, *189*
Ginsburg, G. P., 286, *295*

Giuliano, T., 408, *413*
Givens, D. B., 124, 134, 135, 142, *145*
Gliha, D., 269, *272*
Godfrey, D. K., 254, *272*
Goethals, G. R., 327, *344*
Goffman, E., 135, *145,* 373, *395*
Goldberg, L. R., 327, *342*
Gordon, S. L., 149, *167,* 248, *272*
Gottman, J. M., 20, 21, *23,* 64, 67, *87,*
    109, *118,* 161, 163, *167,* 172, 173, *189,*
    198, 207, 209, *215,* 236, 241, *243,* 276,
    281, 291, *295*
Gouaux, C., 276, *295*
Gove, F., 38, *54*
Gove, W. R., 151, *167*
Graef, R., 247, *273*
Grammar, K., 122, *145*
Graziano, W., 81, *86*
Greenberg, J., 26, *57,* 109, *118,* 186, *189*
Greenberg, M. T., 26, 36, *55, 57*
Greenberg, S., 208, *215*
Greene, R. W., 300, *323*
Greenglass, E. R., 231, *243*
Green-Hennessy, S. J., 185, *189*
Greenshaft, J. L., 67, *87*
Greenwald, A. G., 40, *57,* 95, 99, *118,* 175,
    184, *189*
Griffin, D. W., 91, 93, 94, 96, 97, 113,
    118, 119, 410, *412*
Griffitt, W., 276, *295*
Grinkis, C., 228, *243*
Grossman, K., 31, 50, *57, 59*
Grossman, K. E., 31, 50, *57, 59*
Groth, G., 141, *145*
Grych, J. H., 206, *215*
Guanera, S. M., 374, *396*
Gunn, L. K., 65, 66, *89*

H

Hackel, L. S., 92, *118*
Haccoun, D. M., 231, 234, *242*
Haefner, P., 160, 161, *166*
Halas, C., 231, 235, *243*
Halberstadt, A. G., 125, *145*
Hale, J. L., 124, 136, 141, *144*
Haley, J., 124, *144*
Hall, J. A., 101, *118,* 130, *145,* 177, *190*
Hamberger, L. K., 231, *244*
Hanna, S. E., 93, *119*
Hardaway, R. A., 185, *190*

Harre, R., 280, 284, 285, *295*
Harris, P. L., 223, *245*
Harvey, J. H., 101, *118,* 307, *324*
Haslam, N., 183, *189, 190*
Hastie, R., 183, *191*
Hastorf, A. H., 250, 262, 269, 270, *273*
Hatfield, E., 264, *272,* 335, *344*
Hatchett, S., 155, *168,* 356, *368*
Hause, K. S., 148, *166*
Hazan, C., 25, 26, 27, 34, 36, 37, 38, 45,
    48, 51, 52, *57, 58, 60,* 75, *87,* 99, 113,
    118, 172, 178, 180, *190, 191, 202, 215,*
    337, *342*
Haynes, S. N., 64, *87*
Heavey, C. L., 161, 166, *167*
Heider, F., 79, *87,* 286, *295,* 328, *343*
Heinrichs, D. J., 227, *243*
Helmreich, R., 129, *145*
Henderson, M., 276, *293*
Hendrick, C., 12, *23,* 338, *343*
Hendrick, S., 12, *23,* 338, *343*
Henley, N. M., 125, 135, *145*
Hepburn, A., 93, *118*
Heron, N., 6, 8, 16, *23,* 101, *117,* 150, *167*
Hertel, P. T., 408, *413*
Hess, B., 151, *167*
Hesse, E., 33, 36, *59*
Heyman, R., 20, *24*
Higgins, E. T., 44, 52, *57,* 182, *190,* 380,
    395
Hill, M. G., 258, *272*
Hilton, J. L., 183, *191*
Hinde, R. A., 179, *190*
Hixon, J. G., 91, 99, 113, 114, *120*
Hochschild, A., 49, *57,* 156, *167,* 248, *272*
Hoffman, F. L., 328, *343*
Hofmann, V., 36, *58*
Holland, J. H., 42, *58*
Holmberg, D., 100, *116,* 152, *168,* 348,
    356, 358, 359, 360, *367, 368,* 405, 407,
    410, *412*
Holmes, J. G., 5, 6, 19, *24,* 52, *58,* 72, 76,
    80, 84, *87,* 91, 92, 93, 94, 95, 96, 97,
    100, 102, 105, 107, 108, 110, 111, 112,
    113, 115, 116, *118, 119,* 209, *215,* 241,
    243, 270, *272,* 291, *295,* 348, *368,* 370,
    382, 385, *395, 396,* 405, 410, 411, *412*
Holstein, C., 211, *214*
Holtzworth-Munroe, A., 101, *118,* 172,
    190, 380, 388, *395*
Holyoak, K. J., 42, *58*

Homan, T. B., 386, *395*
Honeycutt, J. M., 241, *244,* 300, 303, 307,
    308, *323, 324*
Hooper, C. H., 254, *273*
Horowitz, L. M., 35, 37, 42, 45, 52, *54,*
    223, *244*
Horowitz, M. J., 228, *244,* 318, *323*
Huesmann, L., 340, *343*
Hughes, D. K., 407, 411, *412, 413*
Hughes, M., 151, *167*
Huh, E., 211, *214*
Humphreys, L. G., 96, *118*
Hunt, J. McV., 227, *244*
Hupka, R. B., 200, *215*
Hurst, M. H., 154, *167,* 174, *189*
Huston, T. L., 110, 115, 116, *118,* 173,
    190, 357, *368,* 406, *412*
Hutt, M., 34, 36, 37, 38, *57*

I

Ickes, W., 20, 22, *23,* 122, 125, *146,* 328,
    343
Ingersoll-Dayton, B., 156, *166*
Insko, C. A., 269, *274*
Isen, A., 209, 210, *215,* 292, *294*
Iverson, A., 335, *342*
Iwaniszek, J., 66, *89*
Izard, C.,197, *215,* 255, *272*

J

Jacklin, C. N., 177, *190*
Jackson, D. D., 124, *144*
Jacobson, N. S., 64, 83, *87,* 101, *118,* 172,
    190, 380, 388, *395*
Jacobsen, T., 36, *58*
Jacquet, S. E., 407, 411, *413*
Jaffe, K., 37, *55*
James, W., 186, *190,* 219, *244,* 328, *343*
Janoff-Bulman, R., 37, *55,* 99, 100, *118,*
    179, *189*
Jaspers, J. M., 316, *323*
John, R., 209, *214,* 236, *242*
Johnson, D. J., 66, 76, 85, *87, 89,* 94, 98,
    101, 110, 112, *118, 119*
Johnson, S., 208, *215*
Johnson-Laird, P., 200, *216,* 224, *244*
Jones, E. E., 39, *58,* 109, *117,* 248, 254,
    261, 270, *272, 273,* 326, 327, 334, *343,*
    375, *395*

Jonides, J., 183, *191*
Jordan, J. V., 157, *167*
Josephson, W. L., 231, *244*
Judd, C. M., 81, *89*
Julkunen, J., 231, *243*
Jung, C. G., 328, *343*
Jussim, L., 186, *190*

K

Kahn, R. L., 155, *167*
Kanazawa, S., 16, *24*
Kaplan, N., 30, 32, 33, 34, 36, 38, 39, 44, 45, 51, 52, *57, 58, 59*
Karen, R., 26, *58*
Keedian, E., 51, *54*, 185, *188*, 228, *242*
Keelan, J. P. R., 38, *58*
Keenan, J. M., 327, *343*
Kelly, C., 116, *118*, 357, *368*, 406, *412*
Kelley, E. L., 65, *88*
Kelley, H. H., 7, *24*, 63, 69, 74, 75, 76, 77, 79, 84, *88, 89*, 92, 101, 102, 115, *117, 118*, 178, *191*, 309, 311, 315, *323*, 384, 389, *396*, 409, *412*
Keltner, D., 212, *215*, 278, *295*
Kemper, T., 248, *273*
Kendon, A.,125, 134, *145*
Kenny, D. A., 95, *118*, 181, *190*, 376, *395*
Kenrick, D. T., 135, 141, *145, 146*
Kerckhoff, A. C., 385, *395*
Kernis, M. H., 374, *396*
Kerr, K. L., 51, *58*
Kessler, R. C., 176, *188*
Key, M., 125, 134, 135, 141, *145*
Kihlstrom, J. F., 40, *55, 58*, 123, *146*, 241, *244*
Kimmel, M. J., 70, *88*
Kimmerly, N. L., 42, *57*
King, G. A., 44, 52, *57*
Kininmonth, L., 9, 14, 17, 18, 20, *23*, 288, *294*
Kippax, S., 221, 235, *243*
Kirker, W. S., 326, *344*
Kirkpatrick, L. A., 34, 36, 38, 52, *56, 58*
Kirson, D., 49, *61*, 81, *89*, 198, 199, 200, 203, 205, *216*, 223, 226, 227, 228, 229, *245*, 251, *273*
Kitayama, S., 165, *167*, 187, *190*, 386, *395*
Kleck, R., 269, *273*
Klein, S. B., 12, *24*, 182, *190*
Kliewer, D., 227, *244*

Knapp, M. L., 134, *146*, 300, *323*
Kobak, R. R., 32, 36, 44, 45, 52, *56, 58*, 99, 113, *118*, 172, *190*
Kochman, T., 360, *368*
Kohlhepp, K., 186, *190*
Kopper, B. A., 231, *244*
Koren, P., 64, *88*
Koski, L. R., 51, *60*
Koval, J. E., 151, *166*
Kovecses, Z., 226, *244*
Kraft, D., 184, *191*
Krokoff, L. J., 67, *87*, 161, *167*, 173, *189*
Kruglanski, A., 116, *119*
Krull, D. S., 4, *24*
Kuiper, N. A., 326, *344*
Kuipers, P., 197, *215*
Kunce, L. J., 35, *58*
Kunda, Z., 108, *119*, 175, *190*, 370, 392, *395*
Kurdek, L. A., 65, *88*

L

LaFreniere, P., 38, *58*
Laird, J., 266, *273*
Lakoff, G., 226, *244*
Lalljee, M., 241, *244*, 302, 307, 322, *323*
Lamb, M. E., 26, 41, *58*
Lamb, R., 241, *244*
Landry, D., 387, *396*
Langer, E. J., 229, *244*, 375, 380, 388, *395, 396*
Lang-Takac, E., 159, *167*
Larson, R., 247, *272, 273*
Laux, L., 198, 205, *215*
Layne, C., 161, *167*
Layton, B. D., 269, *274*
Lazarus, R. S., 49, 50, *57, 58*, 197, 199, 206, *216*, 278, 279, *295*
Leary, M., 171, *188*
Leatham, G., 347, *368*
Leathers, D. G., 309, *323*
Leber, D., 360, *368*
Leddo, J., 302, 315, *323*
Legant, P., 327, *343*
Leigh, G. K., 386, *395*
Lerner, H. G., 231, 235, 236, *244*
Levenson, R. W., 20, *23*, 109, *118*, 163, *167*, 198, 207, 209, *215*, 281, *295*
Levinger, G., 92, 94, 102, *119*, 162, *167*, 276, 288, 289, *296*, 386, *396*

Levitskaya, A., 335, *344*
Levy, K. N., 38, *58*
Lewin, K., 328, *343*
Lewis, M., 248, *273*
Lewis, R. A., 385, *395*
Le-Xuan-Hy, G. M., 4, *24*
Ley, J., 186, *190*
Liberman, A., 81, *87*
Liebrand, W. B. G., 70, *87, 88, 89*
Lin, Y., 37, *61, 76, 88*
Linder, D., 340, *342*
Linville, P.W., 51, *58*
Lipkus, I., 8, 9, *24,* 70, 71, 75, 76, *89,*
    101, 110, 113, 116, *119,* 206, *216,* 254,
    273
Lipson, A., 211, *214*
Lisle, D. J., 184, *191*
Liu, T.J., 110, *119*
Lloyd, B. B., 279, *296*
Lloyd, S. A., 151, 152, *166,* 352, 353, 363,
    368
Loftus, E. F., 346, *368*
Loftus, J., 12, *24,* 182, *190*
Logan, G. D., 16, *24*
Lohr, J. M., 231, *244*
Long, L. C., 264, *272*
Longstreth, M., 71, *89*
Lopez, D. F., 187, *188*
Lord, C. G., 254, *272,* 330, *343*
Lott, C. L., 4, *24*
Luborski, L., 47, *59*
Lutkenhaus, P., 50, *59*
Lutz, C., 248, *273*

M

Maccoby, E. E., 149, *167,* 177, *190*
Mahler, M., 47, *59,* 186, *190*
Main, M., 30, 32, 33, 34, 35, 36, 38, 39,
    42, 44, 45, 51, 52, *57,* 58, *59*
Major, B., 240, *243,* 264, 266, *272*
Makhijani, M. G., 264, *272*
Malinowski, B., 353, *368*
Mancuso, J. C., 223, 225, 226, 227, 229,
    244
Mandler, G., 79, *88,* 219, 227, *244*
Manstead, A. S. R., 213, *216*
Maracek, J., 327, *343*
Margolin, G., 64, 67, *88,* 209, *214*
Markman, H. J., 64, 67, *87, 88,* 115, 116,
    119, 172, *190*

Markus, H., 39, 43, 51, 52, *59,* 96, *119,*
    157, 159, 165, *167,* 175, 187, *190,* 241,
    244, 270, *273,* 326, *343,* 386, *395*
Marris, P., 26, *60*
Marsh, K. L., 289, 292, *296*
Martin, L. L., 278, 284, *296*
Martin, R. W., 152, *167*
Marvin, R. S., 36, *55*
Mascolo, M. F., 223, 225, 226, 227, 229,
    244
Maslin, C., 42, 51, *55*
Maslow, A. H., 328, *343*
Matas, L., 38, *59*
Mavin, G. H., 44, 52, *57*
Mayer, J. D., 278, 287, *296*
McCall, G. J., 328, *343*
McClintock, C. G., 69, 70, 74, *87, 88*
McCormack, L., 289, 292, *296*
McDonald, D., 64, 83, *87*
McFarland, C., 347, *368*
McGill, A., 183, *190*
McGuire, C. V., 158, *167,* 333, *343*
McGuire, W. J., 102, 114, *119,* 158, *167,*
    333, *343*
McKellar, P., 200, *216*
Mead, G. H., 186, *190,* 376, *395*
Mehrabian, A., 124, 134, 135, 136, *146*
Merleau-Ponty, M., 328, *343*
Mervis, C. B., 222, *244*
Messick, D. M., 74, *88*
Michalson, L., 248, *273*
Michela, J. L., 84, *88*
Mikulincer, M., 34, 35, 37, 38, *59, 60*
Milardo, R., 404, 410, *413*
Milberg, S., 257, *271*
Miller, D. G., 346, *368*
Miller, D. T., 270, *273,* 313, 314, *323*
Miller, J. B., 157, *167,* 229, 230, *244*
Miller, K., 270, *272*
Miller, L. C., 40, *60,* 195, *216,* 302, 318,
    323, 408, *412*
Mills, J., 270, *271*
Mineka, S., 212, *216,* 278, *296*
Mischel, W., 42, *55,* 229, *245*
Mitchell, S., 26, *57,* 175, 186, 189, *190*
Mongrain, M., 51, *60*
Monson, T., 81, *86*
Montgomery, B. M., 174, *190*
Moran, G., 26, 27, *60*
Morris, D., 125, 134, 135, *146*
Morris, S. L., 283, *295*

Morrow, G. D., 66, *89,* 101, 110, *119*
Moylan, S., 288, 289, *295*
Muncer, S., 231, 234, *242*
Murphy, J. F., 374, *396*
Murray, S. L., 5, 19, *24,* 91, 93, 94, 95, 96, 97, 100, 102, 105, 108, 110, 112, 113, 115, *118, 119,* 370, *395,* 410, 411, *412*
Murstein, B. I., 385, *396*
Myers, D. G., 171, *190*

N

Nachshon, O., 34, 37, 38, *60*
Nadler, A., 176, *190*
Nalbone, D., 51, *60*
Narayan, S., 183, *191*
Nelligan, J. S., 36, 38, 52, *61,* 172, *191*
Nelson, G., 96, *117,* 182, 187, *188,* 327, 330, 331, *342,* 386, *395*
Neuberg, S. L., 81, *88*
Newcomb, T. M., 334, *343*
Newman, H., 315, *323,* 375, 388, *396*
Nezlek, J., 154, *168*
Nezworski, T., 26, *54*
Nisbett, R. E., 42, *58,* 175, *190,* 326, 327, *343*
Noller, P., 34, 38, *57,* 64, *88,* 93, *117,* 276, 286, 290, *296*
Notarius, C. I., 64, 67, *87,* 160, 161, *166,* 172, *190*

O

Oathout, H. A., 75, *87*
Oatley, K., 196, 197, 200, *216,* 224, *244*
O'Connor, C., 49, *61,* 81, *89,* 198, 199, 200, 203, 205, *216,* 223, 226, 227, 228, 229, *245,* 251, *273*
O'Connor, K., 283, *295*
Ogilvie, D. M., 41, *60*
O'Leary, A., 287, *296*
O'Leary, K. D., 64, *87*
Olsen, N., 183, *191,* 328, *344*
Onizuka, R. K., 8, 9, *24*
Ono, H., 269, *273*
Onyx, J., 221, 235, *243*
Orbuch, T. L., 356, 358, 359, 360, *368,* 407, *412*
Orden, S. R., 341, *343*
Orsterweil, Z., 159, *167*

Ortega, R., 356, 357, *368*
Ortony, A., 277, 278, 279, 280, 281, *296*
O'Sullivan, M., 136, *145*
Ouellette, R., 257, *271*
Oxenberg, J., 4, *24*
Oyserman, D., 157, *167*

P

Pancake, V. R., 36, 38, *60*
Panksepp, J., 49, *60,* 197, *216*
Papageorgis, D., 102, 114, *119*
Papalia, D., 51, *60*
Paris, M., 333, *342*
Park, B., 81, *89*
Parkinson, B., 213, *216*
Parkes, C. M., 26, *60*
Parrott, W. G., 257, 260, 262, 265, *273*
Partridge, M. F., 35, *56*
Passer, M. W., 84, *88*
Pataki, S. P., 262, 267, *273*
Paterson, P. J., 26, 27, *60*
Patterson, G. R., 64, *90*
Patterson, M. L., 174, *190*
Pavelchak, M. A., 40, *57*
Pelham, B. W., 4, *24*
Peplau, L. A., 149, *167*
Pennington, N., 183, *191*
Perlman, D., 26, *54,* 219, *244*
Pervin, L. A., 40, *60*
Peterson, C., 336, *342*
Peterson, D. R., 231, 233, 239, *244*
Peterson, S., 75, 83, *90*
Pettit, E. J., 162, *168*
Petty, R. E., 81, *88*
Philippot, P., 204, *216*
Pietromonaco, P. R., 34, 37, 48, 52, *55, 60,* 289, *296*
Pike, C. L., 136, *145*
Piliavin, J., 141, *146*
Pine, R., 47, *59*
Pistole, C., 38, *60*
Pittman, T. S., 175, *188,* 248, 261, *273*
Planalp, S., 52, *60,* 165, *168,* 195, 209, *216,* 228, *245,* 300, 302, 303, 305, 307, 308, 318, 319, *323, 324*
Plutchik, R., 197, 200, *216*
Pond K., 347, *368*
Porter, C. A., 313, 314, *323*
Potapova, E., 335, *344*
Pottharst, K., 26, *60*

Powell, M., 257, *271*
Pratkanis, A., 40, *57*
Prentice, D., 182, *191,* 327, 332, *343*
Pruitt, D. G., 70, *88*
Purvis, J. A., 254, *273*
Pyszczynski, T., 109, *118*

Q, R

Radloff, C. E., 327, *344*
Rahim, M. A., 233, *245*
Rappoport, L., 374, *396*
Read, S. J., 25, 34, 38, 40, 42, 44, 45, 51, *56, 60,* 183, *189,* 195, *216,* 302, 303, 308, 318, *323, 324,* 408, *412*
Reeder, G., 172, *191*
Reis, H. T., 37, *61,* 114, *119,* 163, *168,* 171, 177, 181, 183, *189, 191,* 200, *214,* 227, *244,* 328, *343, 344*
Reiss, I. L., 386, *396*
Reissman, C., 340, *344*
Rempel, J. K., 52, *58,* 72, 84, *87,* 93, 107, 111, 115, *118,* 241, *243,* 270, *272,* 385, *396*
Retzinger, S., 209, *216*
Rholes, W. S., 36, 38, 52, *61,* 172, *191*
Ricks, M. H., 178, *191*
Ridgeway, D., 42, 51, *55*
Rime, B., 204, *216*
Rivers, M., 300, 302, 305, *323*
Robertson, E., 20, *23*
Rodriguez, G., 335, *342*
Rogers, T. B., 175, *191,* 326, *344*
Rosaldo, M., 248, *273*
Rosanowski, J., 16, 17, *23,* 207, *215,* 401, *412*
Rosch, E., 122, *146,* 222, *244, 245,* 279, *296*
Roseman, I., 198, 200, 202, *216*
Rosenfeld, H. M., 254, *273*
Rosenthal, R., 174, *191,* 377, *394*
Ross, L., 93, *118,* 375, *396*
Ross, M., 152, *168,* 346, 347, 349, *368,* 370, 372, 374, 375, *396,* 405, *412*
Rothbard, J. C., 27, 28, 34, 36, 38, *60*
Rothbart, M., 301, *324*
Rotter, J. B., 334, *344*
Rubin, J., 219, *245*
Rubin, Z., 289, *296,* 386, *396*
Ruble, D. N., 92, *118*
Rusbult, C. E., 8, *24,* 65, 66, 70, 71, 75,

76, 77, 83, 84, 85, *87, 88, 89, 90,* 94, 98, 101, 110, 112, 116, *118, 119,* 205, *216,* 254, *273*
Russell, J. A., 196, 200, *214,* 219, 220, 222, 223, 224, 225, 228, 238, 239, 240, *243, 245*
Rutherford, D. K., 300, 303, 307,308, *324*
Rutt, D. J., 154, *167,* 174, *189*
Ruvolo, A., 39, *59*
Ruzzene, M., 276, 286, 290, *296*

S

Saarni, C., 248, 255, *273*
Sadalla, E. K., 135, 141, *145, 146*
Safran, J. D., 228, *245,* 318, *324*
Saine, T., 309, *323*
Saitta, M. B., 125, *145*
Salovey, P., 287, *296*
Samuel, V., 64, *87*
Sande, G. N., 327, *344*
Sants, H., 299, *323*
Sapir, E., 121, *146*
Saul, B., 269, *272*
Saunders, K., 37, *56*
Sayers, S. L., 161, 162, *168*
Sceery, A., 44, *58*
Schaap, C., 64, *89*
Schachter, S., 276, 292, *296*
Schafer, W. D., 42, *57*
Schank, R. C., 13, *24,* 228, *245*
Scherbaum, C., 268, *272*
Scherer, K., 197, 198, 203, 206, *216,* 247, *273*
Schilling, E. A., 176, *188*
Schlenker, B. R., 373, *396*
Schlosberg, H., 219, *245*
Schmidt, G. W., 75, 83, *90*
Schmidt, L., 141, *146*
Schneider, D. J., 181, *191,* 250, 262, *273*
Schneider, W., 81, *89*
Schott, S., 248, *273*
Schutz, A., 328, *344*
Schwan, A., 31, *57*
Schwartz, J., 49, *61,* 81, *89,* 198, 199, 200, 203, 205, *216,* 223, 226, 227, 228, 229, *245, 247, 251, 273*
Schwarz, N., 211, *216,* 276, 278, 286, 287, *294, 296,* 407, *412*
Scott, C. K., 150, 154, *168,* 195, 209, *216,* 408, *412*

Scott, R. A., 270, *273*
Searcy, E., 176, *191*
Secord, P. F., 270, *271*
Sedikides, C., 183, *191,* 278, 286, 287, *296,* 328, 332, *344*
Seidel, M., 51, *54,* 185, *188,* 228, *242*
Senchak, M., 163, *168*
Sentis, K. P., 52, *59*
Sharp, A., 93, *119*
Sharpsteen, D., 198, 200, *216,* 223, *245*
Shaver, P., 25, 26, 27, 28, 34, 35, 36, 37, 38, 45, 46, 48, 49, 51, 52, 53, *54, 56, 57, 58, 60, 61,* 75, 81, *87, 89,* 114, *119,* 178, 180, *191,* 198, 199, 200, 202, 203, 205, *215, 216,* 223, 226, 227, 228, 229, *245,* 247, 251, *273,* 328, 337, *342, 343*
Shaw, D., 64, *88*
Sherman, A., 269, *272*
Sherman, M., 42, 51, *55*
Sherman, S. J., 81, *89*
Shiffrin, R. M., 81, *89*
Showers, C., 51, *60*
Shulman, S., 28, 34, 36, 28, *61*
Sigal, H., 387, *396*
Siladi, M., 159, *167*
Silver, R. L., 265, *273, 274*
Simpson, J. A., 8, 20, *24,* 36, 38, 52, *61,* 123, 126, 127, 133, 136, 137, 138, *145, 146,* 172, *191*
Singer, R. D., 276, *294*
Skinner, B. F., 122, *146*
Skokan, L. A., 115, *120*
Slade, A., 52, *61*
Sline, R., 300, *322*
Slovik, L. F., 70, 71, 75, 76, *89,* 101, 110, 113, 116, *119,* 206, *216,* 254, *273*
Smith, C. A., 198, *217,* 277, *294*
Smith, E. R., 182, *191,* 241, *245*
Smollan, D., 329, *342*
Snell, W., 151, *168*
Snyder, M., 113, 115, *119,* 122, 125, 129, 133, *145, 146*
Soffin, S., 186, *190*
Soldo, B., 151, *167*
Solomon, B., 163, *168*
Solomon, J., 35, 42, *57, 59*
Solomon, R. L., 340, *344*
Sommers, S., 200, 205, *217,* 251, *273*
Sorrentino, R. M., 93, *119*
Spanier, G. B., 341, *344*
Sperling, M. B., 26, *61*

Sprecher, S., 162, 163, *168,* 264, *272,* 335, *344*
Sroufe, L. A., 28, 34, 35, 36, 37, 38, 46, *54, 56, 58, 59, 61*
Srull, T., 183, *191*
Stahelski, A. J., 69, 75, *88*
Stanley, M. A., 307, *324*
Stapp, J., 129, *145*
Starzomski, A., 37, *56*
Statham, A., 186, *191*
Steele, C. M., 110, *119*
Steele, H., 32, *57*
Steele, M., 32, *57*
Stendhal (Beyle), M., 100, *120*
Stephen, T., 386, *396*
Stepper, S., 284, *296*
Stern, D., 40, *61,* 228, *245*
Stets, J. E., 234, *245*
Stevenson-Hinde, J., 26, *60*
Stiles, W. B., 373, 395, *396*
Stinson, L., 328, *343*
Strack, F., 284, *296*
Straus, M., 234, *245*
Strejc, H., 154, *167,* 174, *189*
Stretton, M., 287, *296*
Stroebe, W., 269, *274*
Strongman, K. T., 200, 207, *215,* 288, *294*
Strube, M. J., 4, *24*
Stryker, S., 186, *191*
Style, C. B., 151, *167*
Sullaway, M., 64, *89*
Summerfield, A., 203, *216,* 247, *273*
Surra, C. A., 71, *89,* 101, *120,* 165, *168,* 300, *324,* 353, 357, *368,* 373, 388, *396,* 398, 401, 402, 404, 406, 407, 410, 411, *412, 413*
Surrey, J. L., 157, *167*
Sutherland, L., 356, 357, 360, *368*
Sutton, S., 212, *216,* 278, *296*
Swann, W. B. Jr., 4, *24,* 91, 99, 113, 114, 115, *119, 120,* 369, *396*

T

Tanke, E. D., 113, 115, *119*
Tannen, D., 177, *191*
Taraban, C. B., 250, 251, *272,* 282, *294*
Taylor, D. A., 300, *322,* 373, *394*
Taylor, S. E., 95, 96, 99, 100, 101, 115, *118, 120,* 195, *215,* 241, *243,* 301, *323,* 370, 381, *395, 396*

Tellegen, A., 129, *146*
Teng, G., 20, *23*
ter Schure, E., 197, *215*
Testa, M., 266, *272*
Thagard, P. R., 42, *58,* 302, 308, 309, 318, *324*
Thibaut, J. W., 7, *24,* 63, 69, 77, *88, 89,* 178, *191,* 384, 389, *396,* 409, *412*
Thomas, G., 21, 22, *24*
Thompson, L., 156, *168*
Thompson, R. A., 26, *58*
Thomson, D. W., 51, *54,* 185, *188,* 228, 242
Thomson, V.D., 269, *274*
Tidwell, M., 37, 51, *60, 61*
Tiller, D. K., 223, *245*
Tobey, A. E., 36, *54*
Tolmacz, E., 35, 37, 38, *59*
Tomkins, S. S., 228, 241, *245*
Tooby, J., 197, *215*
Tooke, W., 20, *23, 328, 343*
Tota, M. E., 17, *23*
Trafimow, D., 182, *191*
Trafton, J. G., 12, *24,* 182, *190*
Trevarthan, C., 247, *274*
Triandis, H., 187, *191*
Trope, Y., 102, *120*
Trost, M. R., 141, *145*
Troy, M., 34, *61*
Trzebinski, J., 40, *61*
Tucker, P., 340, *344*
Tudor, M., 96, *117,* 182, 187, 188, 327, 330, 331, *342,* 386, *395*
Tulving, E., 41, *61*

U

Uleman, J. S., 15, *24,* 81, *89*

V

Vangelisti, A. L., 110, 116, *118,* 173, *190,* 300, *323*
van Hoof, J. A., 250, *274*
Van Lange, P. A. M., 70, 77, 85, *89,* 94, 98, *119*
Verette, J., 70, 71, 75, 76, 77, 83, 85, *89, 90,* 94, 98, 101, 110, 113, 116, *119,* 205, *216,* 254, *273*
Veroff, J., 154, 155, 156, 166, *168,* 356, 357, 358, 359, 360, *368,* 407, *412*
Verschure, B., 135, 141, *146*
Voelkl, K., 266, *272*

von Hippel, W., 183, *191*
Vorauer, J. D., 370, 373, 374, 375, 379, *396*

W

Waddell, B. A., 287, *294*
Wall, S., 26, 27, 35, 38, *54,* 75, 86
Wallbott, H., 203, *216,* 247, 271, *273*
Walster, E., 141, *146,* 269, *271,* 334, *344*
Walster, G. W., 141, *146,* 269, *271,* 334, *344*
Wampold, B. E., 64, 67, *88*
Ward, D. W., 278, *296*
Ward, L. M., 223, *243*
Warren, B. L., 269, *274*
Waszak, C. S., 373, *396*
Waters, E., 26, 27, 35, 38, 46, *54, 55, 61,* 75, *86*
Weakland, J., 124, *144*
Weary, G., 258, *272,* 289, 292, *296,* 307, *324*
Weber, A. L., 101, *118*
Weber, H., 198, 205, *215*
Wegner, D. M., 328, *344,* 408, *413*
Weigold, M. F., 373, *396*
Weiner, B., 15, *24,* 80, *90,* 198, 206, *217,* 380, *396*
Weinstein, N. D., 99, *120*
Weiss, R., 20, *24,* 64, *90,* 92, 120
Weller, A., 34, 37, 38, *59*
Westen, D., 42, *59,* 185, *191*
Wheeler, L., 154, *168*
White, R. W., 334, *344*
Whitney, G. A., 70, 71, 75, 76, 84, *87, 89,* 101, 110, 113, 116, *119,* 206, *216,* 254, *273*
Wicklund, R., 195, *217*
Wiggins, J. S., 124, *146*
Williams, J., 258, *272*
Williams, M., 136, *146*
Wills, T. A., 64, *90*
Wilson, E. O., 180, *191*
Wilson, G., 151, 152, *166*
Wilson, T. D., 175, 184, *190, 191*
Wittgenstein, L., 122, *146*
Wood, J. T., 163, *168*
Wood, W., 149, *167*
Woodworth, R. S., 219, *245*
Wortman, C. B., 265, *272, 273, 274*
Wright, J. C., 229, *245*
Wright, P. H., 177, *189*
Wu, S., 49, *61,* 81, *89*

Wurf, E., 39, 43, *59*
Wyer, R. S., 150, 154, *168,* 182, 183, *191,*
195, 209, *216,* 278, *296,* 408, *412*

X, Y

Yates, S., 107, *117*
Young, J. Z., 29, *61*
Yovetich, N. A., 70, 71, 77, 85, *89, 90*

Z

Zajonc, R. B., 96, *119,* 241, *244,*
276, *296*
Zanna, M. P., 385, *396*
Zarate, M. A., 182, *191*
Zembrodt, I. M., 65, 66, *89*
Zukier, H., 94, *117*
Zuckerman, M., 174, *191,* 374, *396*
Zuroff, D. C., 183, *191*

Subject Index

A

Accommodation, 63–86, 101, 170–171, 173, 176
  exit-voice-loyalty-neglect typology and, 65–67
  interdependence theory and, 63–64, 79, 82, 85–86
  transformation of motivation and, 67–86
    directions for future research into, 84–86
    distal determinants of, 73–78
    empirical demonstrations of, 70–73
    given and effective matrices and, 67–70, 73, 176
    proximal determinants of, 78–84
    willingness to sacrifice and, 85, 176
Affect, *see also* Emotion, Mood effects,
  and cognition in close relationships, 275–277
  definition of, 276
  knowledge structures and, 13
Affect Infusion Model, 211–212, 286–293
Aggression, 205, 221, 234, 240, 279, *see also* Anger
Anger, 49, 247, *see also* Emotion
  attempts to control, 198, 204–205, 221, 227, 254
  gender differences in, 221, 230–237

prototype and script approaches to, 197–200, 202–209, 212–213, 219–242, 278–282, 285
  strategic presentation of, 248–271, 283
  intimidation and, 259–261, 283
Anxiety, 27, 151, 198, 212–213, 264–265, 276, 278
Attachment, 26–51, 172, 175, 178, 185–186, 202, 328
  communication and, 31–33
  emotion regulation and, 40, 45–51
  coping mechanisms and, 50–51
  evolution and, 180
  figures, loss of, 31
  four category typology of, 35
  internal working models of, 28–33, 38–45, 178–179
    activation of, 43–45, 172
    compared with other social cognitive structures, 39–41
    content and structure of, 38–43
    representational networks of, 41–45
    research strategies for studying, 45, 51–53
    social support and, 44
  Strange Situation and, 28, 31, 50, 53, 172
  styles, 25–38
    anxious-ambivalent/preoccupied, 28, 32–36, 47–48, 50, 52, 93, 337–339

avoidant, 28, 31–32, 34–37, 50, 74–75,
  242, 337–339
dismissing, 32, 35–37, 47–48, 52
disorganised/fearful, 35–37, 47–49
secure, 27–28, 31–32, 37–38, 47, 50,
  52–53, 75
unrequited love and, 337–339
Attachment theory, 11
overview of, 26–38
Attraction, see also Sociosexuality, 334–336
Attribution theory, 5, 8, 80–81, 302, 309
and actor-observer effect, 327
and explanatory coherence theories,
  302–303, 309, 315–319, 399–400
and relationship schema change, 317
Attributional conflict, 84
Attributions in close relationships, 8, 13–16,
  21, 78–84, 92, 101, 149–150,
  172–173, 314–317
emotional reactions to, 79–84, 207–208
mood effects on, 289–290

B

Bem Sex-Role Inventory, 159–160
Betrayal, 227, 230–235, 239–240

C

Closeness, 329–332
Cognition in close relationships, 181–185,
  see also Attributions, Knowledge
  structures,
gender differences in, 150–158, 161, 165,
  170–171, 177,
relationship satisfaction and, 153–157
mood effects on, 211–212, 286–293
Cognitive processing, see also Knowledge
  structures, Lay relationship theories
controlled vs. automatic, 14–18, 174–175
verbal vs. nonverbal behavior and, 174
Commitment, 76–77, 81–83, 125–126,
  150, 223, 357
Communal relationships, 250–253, 257,
  270, 284
vs. exchange, 251–252, 257, 284
Concurrent Memory Load Paradigm, 16
Conflict, see also Marital interaction, Negativity
causes of in marriage, 231
engagement, 102–103

minimization, 364–366
mood effects on, 212, 289–290
positive illusions and, 112, 115
relationship satisfaction and, 154–155,
  173, 209
strategies, gender differences in, 230
Conflict Style Inventory, 289
Courtship scripts, 350–367, 406–408
Crying, 221, 235, 237, 240

D

Deception, 174
Demand-withdraw pattern, see Marital inter-
  action
Depression, 209, 211, 212–213, 223,
  239–240, 242, see also Sadness
Diagnosticity bias, see Informational goals
Disgust, 197, 200
Divorce, children of, 179
Dominance, 124
nonverbal indicators of, 130–133, 135

E

Early Years of Marriage Study, 356
Edmonds (1967) Marital Conventionalization Scale, 341
Egalitarianism, 363–365
Emotion, see also Anger, Attributions, Mood
  effects, Nonverbal behavior
biological/evolutionary theories of, 197,
  279
cognitive theories of, 47–50, 197–199,
  207, 279
appraisals in, 48–50, 199, 201–205,
  207, 213, 278–279, 284
consensus theory of, 46–49
and attachment, 40
definitions of, 79, 81
expressing vs. feeling, 265–266, 284
knowledge structures, 198–214, 219, 242
and information processing, 208–210
prototypes and scripts, 81–82, 198–206,
  222–242, 277, 279–282, 284–286
regulation and attachment, 45–51
self-presentation of, 247–271, 277–278,
  282–284
structuralist approaches to, 277–286
limitations of, 284–285
vs. functionalist approaches to, 277–286

Emotional reactions,
  attempts to control, 198, 204–205, 227
  attributions and, 79, 82–84, 206–208
  to nonverbal behaviors, 136–144
Emotion work, 49–50
Empathy, 75, 176
Empathic accuracy, 21–22
Evolutionary theory,
  and attachment, 180
  and knowledge structures, 180
  of emotion, 197, 279
Exit-voice-loyalty-neglect typology, 64–67
Explanatory coherence theories, *see also*
      Knowledge structures,
  attribution theory and, 302–303, 309,
      315–319, 399–400
  relational schemas and, 318–319

F

Fear, 49, 197, 200
Feeling rules, *see* Emotion work
Femininity, 75–76, 81, 159–161
Flirtation, *see* Sociosexuality

G

Gender differences, *see also* Sex differences
  in aggression and anger, 230–237
  in conflict strategies, 230
  in marital interaction, 161–164
  in relationship cognition, 150–165, 177
  and relationship talk, 153–154
  in self-concept, 157–165, 185
  reasons for studying, 148–150
  relationship satisfaction and, 153–157
    conflict and, 154–155, 161–163
    social support and, 155–156
  socialization of, 147, 157–159, 164
Guilt, 82, 126

H

Happiness, 150, 171, 247
  strategic presentation of, 248–271
Hatred, 200–205, 221–222, 226, 279–280,
      285

I

Inclusion of Other in the Self (IOS) Scale,
      329
Inequity in marriage, 162–163
Infidelity, 78, 319
Information in close relationships, 369–394,
      408–409
  behavioral efforts to acquire, 382–383
Informational goals, 369–394, 408–411
  changes in, 383–386
  chronic vigilance and, 388–390
  coordination of, 390–391
  diagnosticity bias in, 373–382, 409–411
  ignorance and, 393–394
  interdependence theory and, 409
  obstacles to uncertainty reduction,
      372–373
  self–other dichotomy and, 386–387
  typology of, 370–372
Ingratiation, 135
  happiness and, 248–254, 266–267
Interdependence theory, 3, *see also* Accom-
      modation
  comparison levels, 7, 178, 384–385
  informational goals and, 409
Internal working models of self and others,
      see Attachment
Interpersonal orientations, 74–78, 81–83
Intimacy
  attachment and, 75
  nonverbal cues to, 124–125, 129
  partner idealization and, 94, 103
  relationship satisfaction and, 9–10
  sexual, 123–124, 127, 133
Intimidation, 249, 267
  anger and, 259–261

J

Jealousy, 48, 78, 197–198, 200–205, 209,
      223
Joy, 49, 197, 247

K

Knowledge structures, 174–185, *see also* Cog-
      nition in close relationships, Explana-
      tory coherence theories, Lay relation-
      ship theories
  availability vs. accessibility of, 14

changes in, 299–320, 398–401
  explanatory processes for, 306–317
  models of, 301
  processes of, 301–303
declarative vs. procedural, 123
emotion, 198–214, 219–242
exemplar/abstract structures, 12, 181–183
gender, 160–161
progress and pitfalls in studying, 397–412

L

Lay relationship theories, 3–22, *see also*
      Knowledge structures, Relationship
      beliefs
  affect, role of in, 13
  contents and structure of, 6–12
    exemplar vs. abstract, 12
    general vs. specific, 6–10, 171, 179, 205
    procedural vs. declarative memory,
      11–12
  functions of, 4–6
  measurement problems, 12
  of change, 389–390
  on-line processing and, 13–22
    behavior and, 19–22
    controlled vs. automatic, 14–18,
      174–175
Loneliness, 223
Love, 82, 109, 126, 150, 198, 200, 202,
      222, 279–280, 393–394
  catastrophe theory of, 116
  falling in, 333, 335
  unrequited, 336–338
Love Attitudes Scale, 12
Love styles, 338

M

Macromotives, relationship specific, 76–77,
      83
Marital interaction, *see also* Conflict, Nega-
      tivity
  anger and, 242
  attributions and emotions in, 78–84
  contextual model of, 79–84, 196,
      206–208
    proximal vs. distal context and, 207
  distressed vs. nondistressed couples and,
      64, 67, 161–164, 198, 209, 212
  demand-withdraw pattern in, 161–163

gender differences in, 161–163
  exit-voice-neglect-loyalty typology of,
      64–67
  verbal vs. nonverbal behavior and, 20–21
Marital separation, 162
  accounts of, 19, 147
Masculinity, 159–161
Mate Preference Questionnaire, 138
Memory, 11–12
Memory of relationship events, 152–153
Memory reconstruction in relationships,
      345–367, 405–408
  mechanisms of, 348–349
  relationship satisfaction and, 348
  relationship-scripts perspective to,
      349–367
    courtship and wedding scripts in,
      350–367, 406–408
    Black vs. White couples' scripts and,
      360–367
Mood effects, 195–196, 207–208, 210–213
  Affect Infusion Model of, 211–212,
      286–293
  motivated processing and, 291–292
  on explanations for relationship conflict,
      289–290
  on interpersonal conflict, 212
  on judgments about typical and atypical
      relationships, 290–291
  on relationship evaluations, 288
Moods, contrast with emotions, 212–213,
      278
Motivation, 4–6
  models of, 4–6
  transformation of, *see* Accommodation
Motives, 175, 196–198

N

Negative affect reciprocity, 64, 67, 162, 173,
      209
Negativity, *see also* Conflict, Marital interac-
      tion
  and explanation seeking, 307
  and relationship satisfaction, 115,
      172–173
  as trigger for positive illusions, 100–112
Nonverbal behavior, *see also* Emotion, Socio-
      sexuality
  affect and, 20–21, 136–144
  evolution and, 121, 180

functionalist perspective to the study of, 122–144
  relationship initiation and, 124–144
  knowledge structures and, 124, 174, 180
  physical attractiveness and, 138–144
  sex differences in, 130–136, 138–144
  social interactions and, 121–122
  structuralist perspective to the study of, 122

O

Object relations theory, 25–26, 29, 175, 186

P, Q

Partner idealization, 92–94
Passion, *see* Sex
Physical abuse, *see* Aggression
Physical attractiveness, *see* Sociosexuality
Positive illusions in romantic relationships, 19, 91–116
  construction of, 94–99, 171
    projection of self and ideals in, 96–99
    experimental studies on, 5–6, 97–99, 102–112
  long-term benefits of, 114–116, 172
  motivation to construct, 92–94
  negativity as trigger for, 100–112
  relationship satisfaction and, 99–100, 113–115
  storytelling and, 93, 100–116, 171–172
  transmission of, 112–114

R

Rage-shame cycles, 209
Rahim's Organizational Conflict Inventory (ROCI), 233
Relational Cognition Complexity Instrument, 152
Relational schemas, 41, 181, 199, 221, 228, 241
  explanatory coherence and, 318–219
Relationship awareness, 151, 153
Relationship Awareness Scale, 151
Relationship beliefs, *see also* Lay relationship theories, 9–10, 16–18, 174–175, 179
Relationship Beliefs Inventory, 12
Relationship Beliefs Scale, 9–10
Relationship change, schemas of, *see* Knowledge structures

Relationship cognition, *see* Cognition in close relationships
Relationship development,
  models of, 385–386
  self-expansion and, 332–341
Relationship initiation, ethological perspective to, 124–144
Relaionship rules, 78
Relationship satisfaction, 9, 19, 171
  conflict and, 92, 154–155, 161–164, 173
  gender differences in, 153–157
  negativity and, 92, 172–173
  positive illusions and, 99–100, 113–115
  relationship beliefs and, 9
  self-expansion and, 340–342
  social support and, 155–156
Rubin's Liking and Loving Scales, 289

S

Sadness, 49, 200, 212–213, 222, 247, 278, *see also* Depression
self-presentation of, 50, 248–271, 282
Self-concept, 39, 41, 43–44, 51, 110, 113, 376, 402
  gender differences in, 157–161
  individualism/collectivism and, 187
  origins of, 178, 186
  relational nature of, 175, 186–187
Self-esteem, 110, 113, 176
Self-expansion in close relationships, 187, 325–342, 401–405
  attachment styles and, 337–339
  Inclusion of Other in the Self (IOS) Scale and, 326–328
  relationship development and, 332–341
    falling in love and, 333, 335
    initial attraction and, 334–335
    relationship satisfaction and, 340–342
  self–other cognition differences and, 326–328, 386–387
  unrequited love and, 336–339
Self-interest, 71–72, *see also* Accommodation
Self-monitoring, 133
Self-perceptions, positive illusions and, 95–98
Self-presentation of emotions, 247–271, 282–284
  attending to the other and, 268
  expressing vs. feeling and, 265–266

ingratiation and, 248–254, 266–267
intimidation and, 259–261, 267
nervousness and, 264–265
relation between similarity and attraction
  and, 269–271
self promotion and, 261–266
supplication and, 254–259, 267
trust in others' expression of emotions
  and, 266–268
Sex, importance of, 13
Sex differences, *see also* Gender differences,
  in nonverbal behavior, 130–136, 180
  in sociosexuality, 130–143
Social motives, 175
Social norms, 77–78, 81, 261–262, 283
Social support, 155–156, 163, 176
Sociosexual Orientation Inventory, 126
Sociosexuality, 123–144
  dispositional strategy and, 125–127, 143
  physical attractiveness and, 126, 133,
    137–143
  relationship initiation and, 127–144
  flirtation and, 134–136, 140–143
  nonverbal cues and, 127–144
  self-monitoring and, 133

restricted vs. unrestricted, 126–127
sex differences in, 130–143
Spanier's Dyadic Adjustment Scale, 341
Specific Affect Coding Scheme (SPAFF), 207
Story telling, *see* Positive illusions
Supplication, 249, 267
  sadness and, 254–259, 282
Symbolic interactionism, 186, 376
  and attachment, 328

T

Transformation of motivation, *see* Accommodation
Trust in others' expressions of emotions,
  266–268

U, V

Videotape techniques, 20–22, 127–130

W, X

Wishes and concerns, 47
Wish fulfillment, 92

ADT 5421